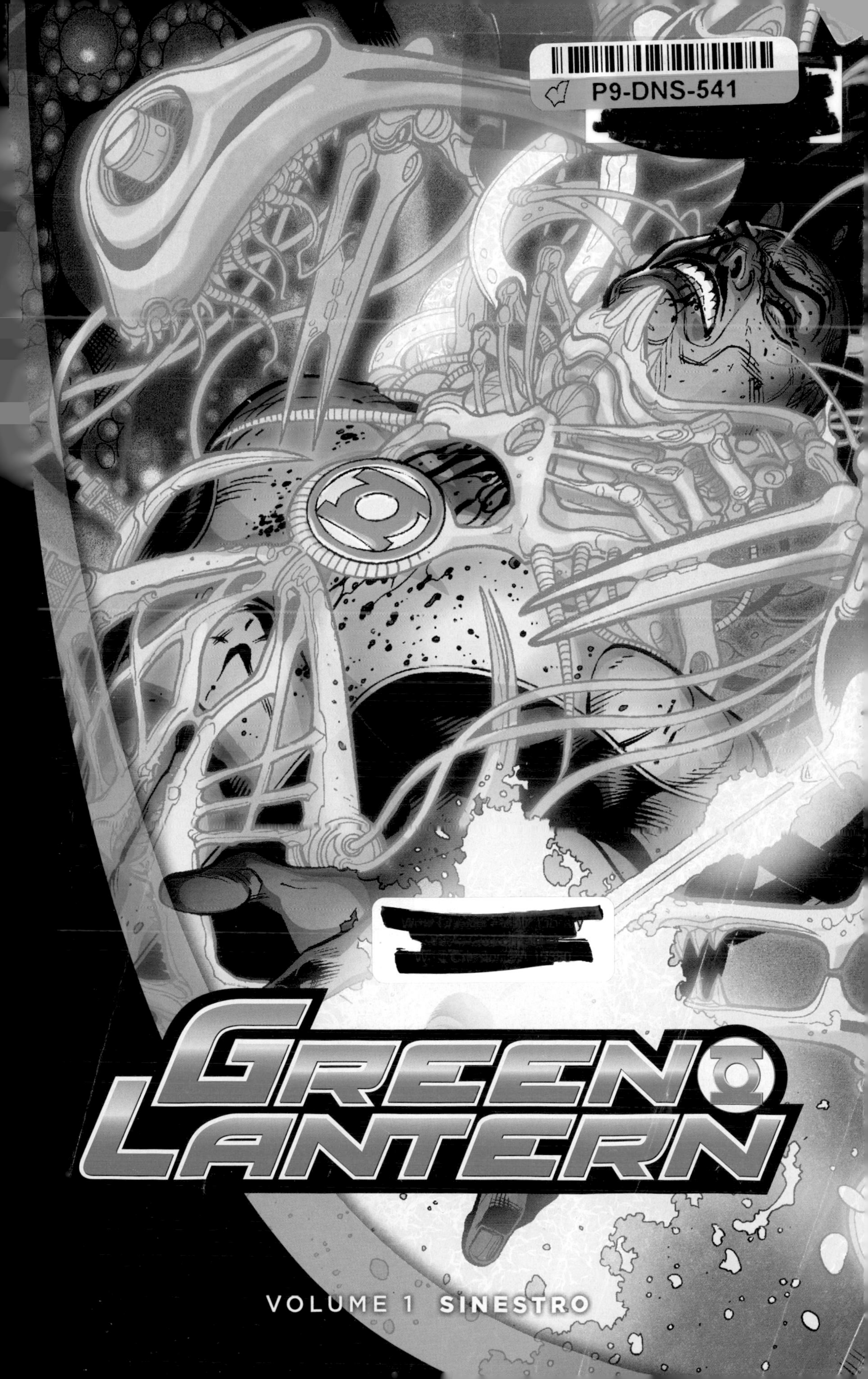
GREEN LANTERN
VOLUME 1 SINESTRO

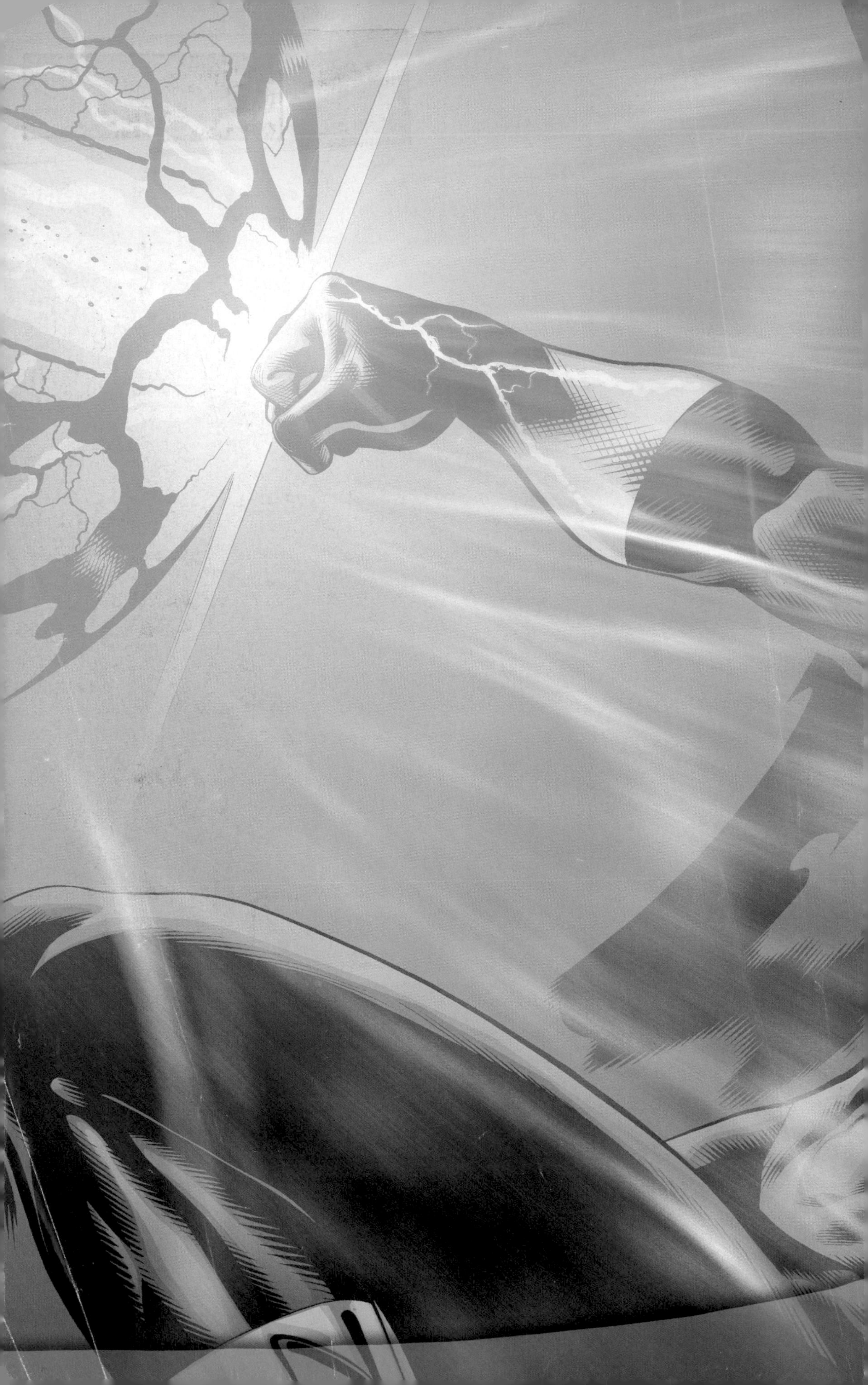

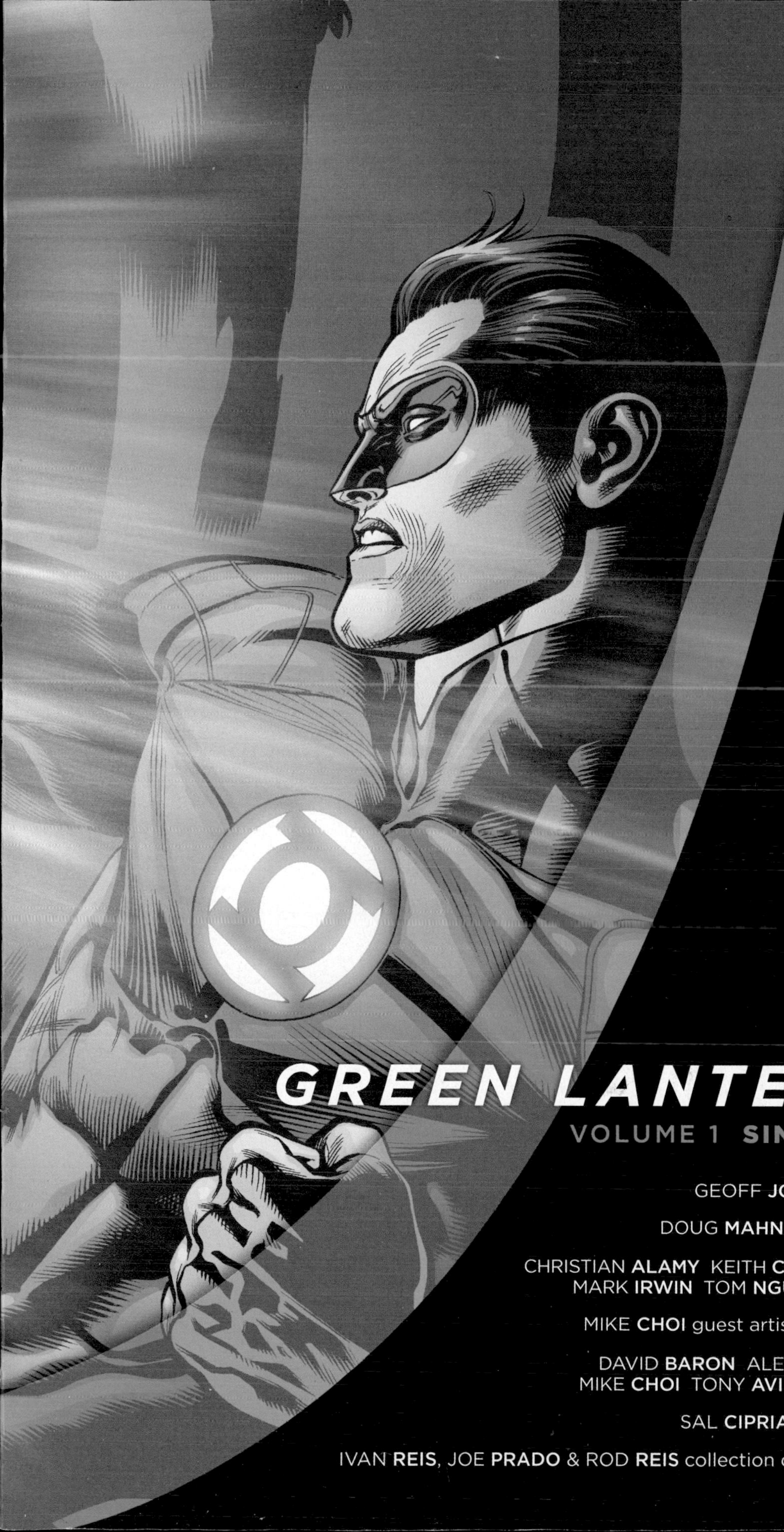

GREEN LANTERN

VOLUME 1 SINESTRO

GEOFF **JOHNS** writer

DOUG **MAHNKE** penciller

CHRISTIAN **ALAMY** KEITH **CHAMPAGNE**
MARK **IRWIN** TOM **NGUYEN** inkers

MIKE **CHOI** guest artist – issue six

DAVID **BARON** ALEX **SINCLAIR**
MIKE **CHOI** TONY **AVINA** colorists

SAL **CIPRIANO** letterer

IVAN **REIS**, JOE **PRADO** & ROD **REIS** collection cover artists

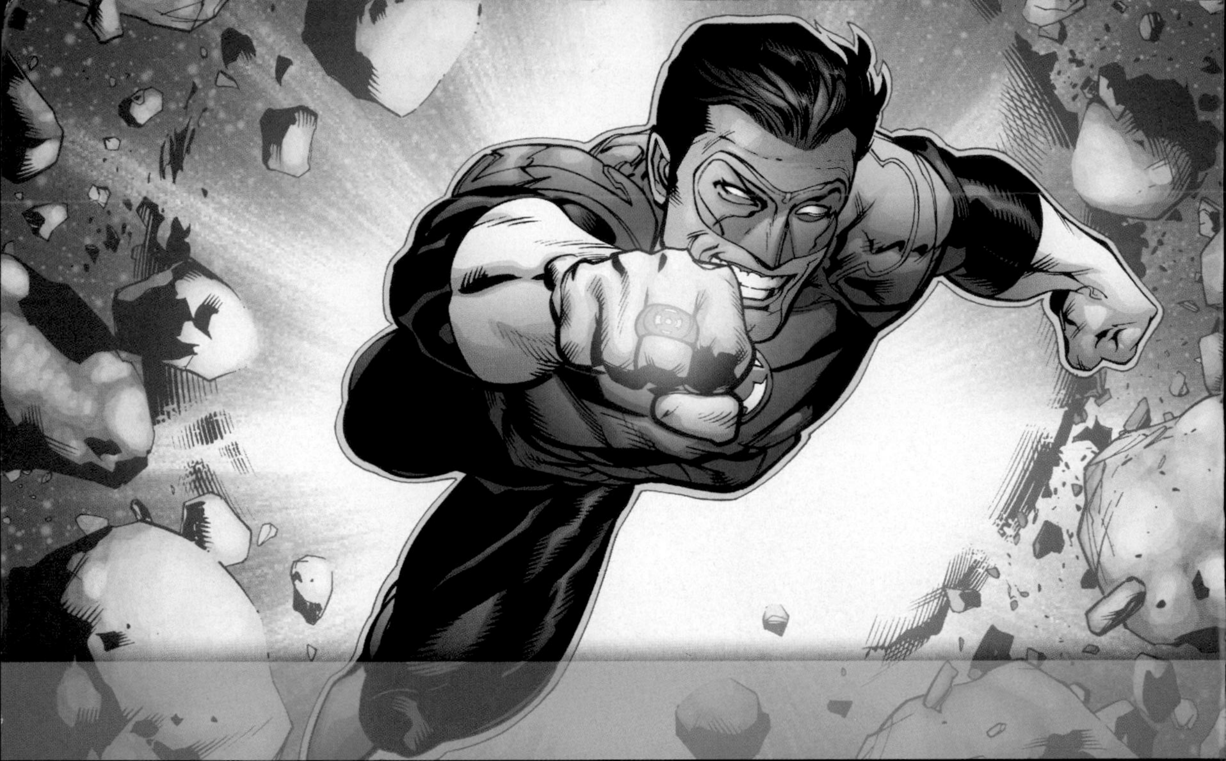

BRIAN CUNNINGHAM Editor – Original Series DARREN SHAN Assistant Editor – Original Series
PETER HAMBOUSSI Editor ROBBIN BROSTERMAN Design Director – Books
ROBBIE BIEDERMAN Publication Design

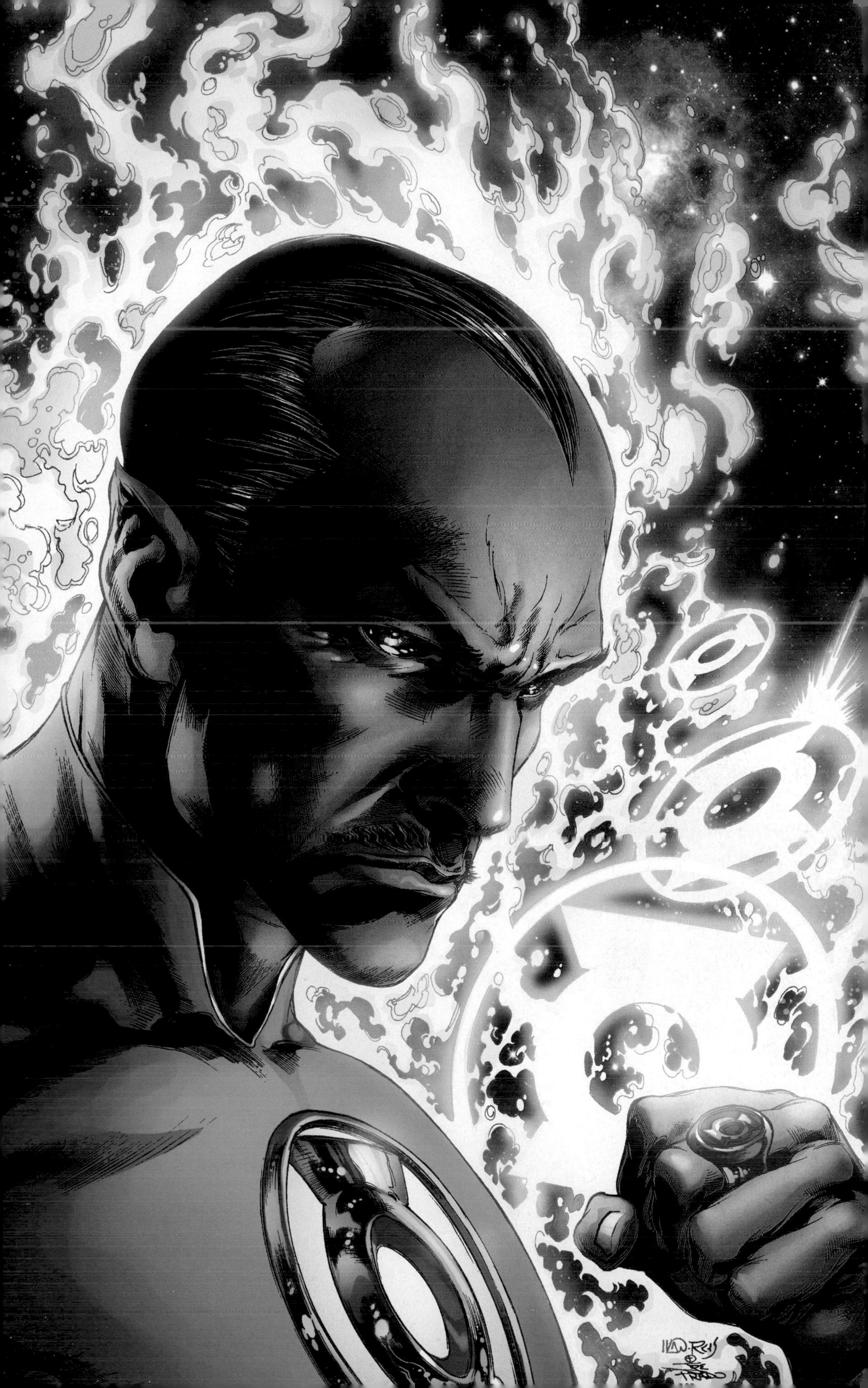

Ivan Reis, Joe Prado & Rod Reis

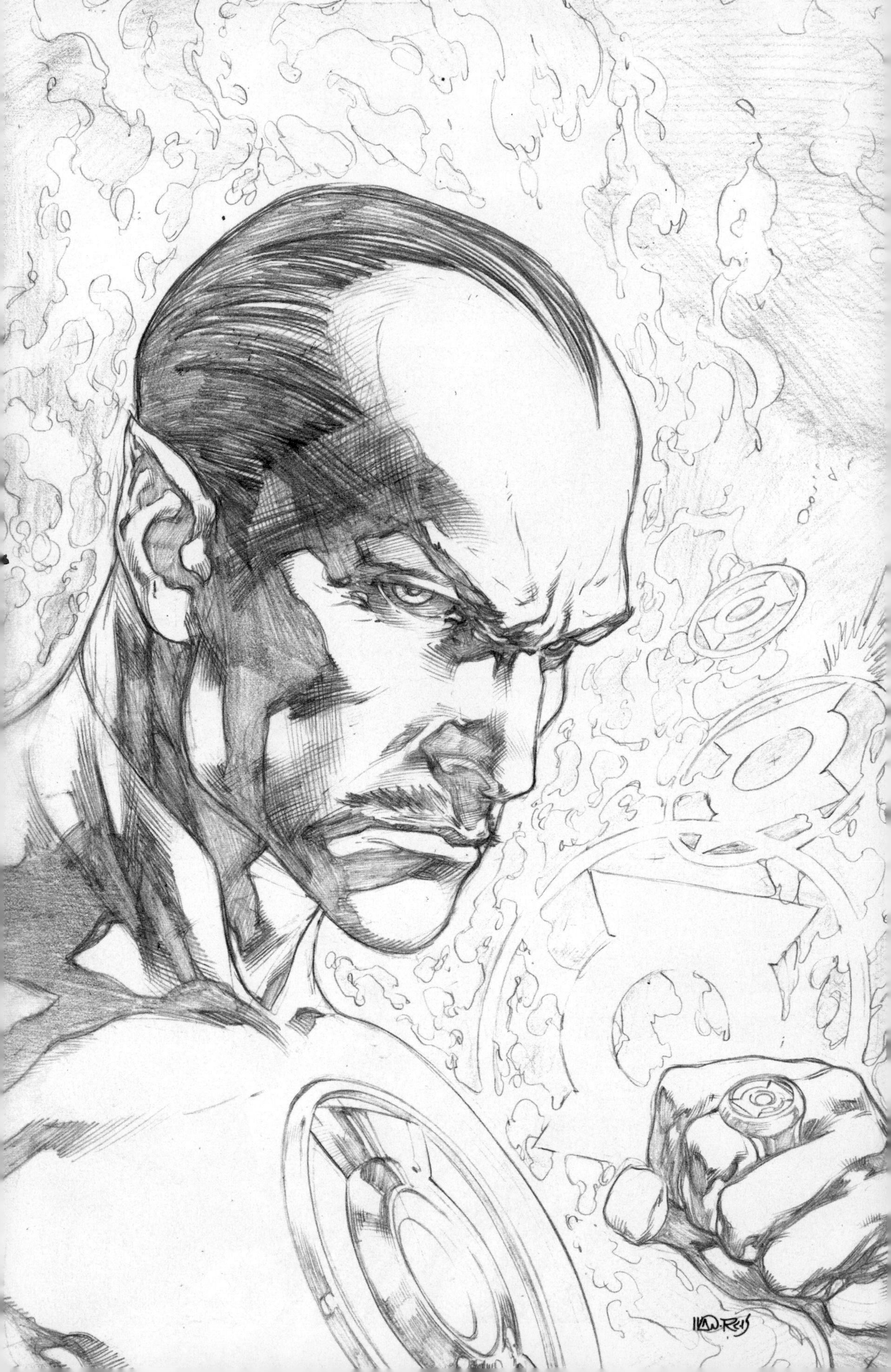

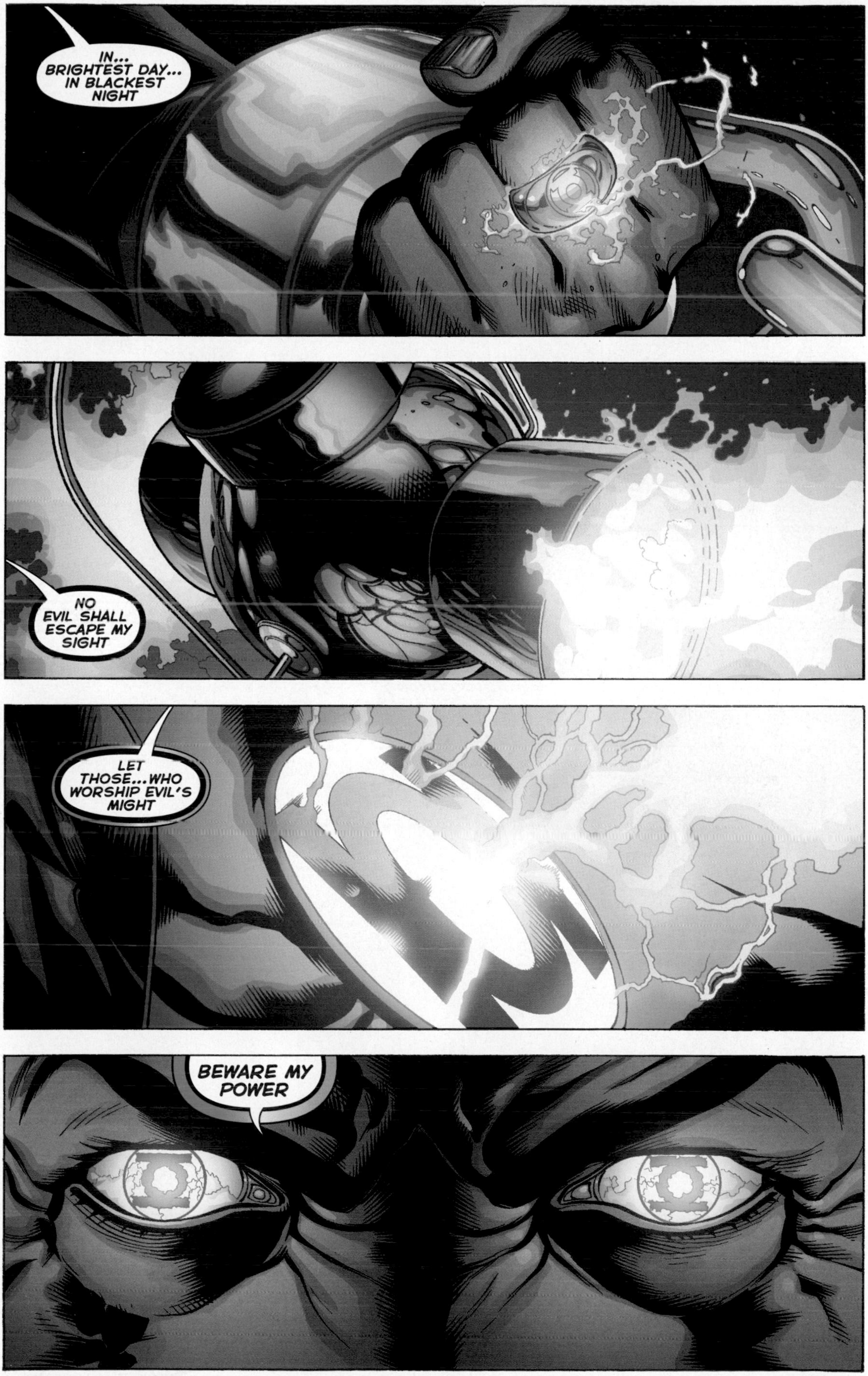
IN... BRIGHTEST DAY... IN BLACKEST NIGHT
NO EVIL SHALL ESCAPE MY SIGHT
LET THOSE...WHO WORSHIP EVIL'S MIGHT
BEWARE MY POWER

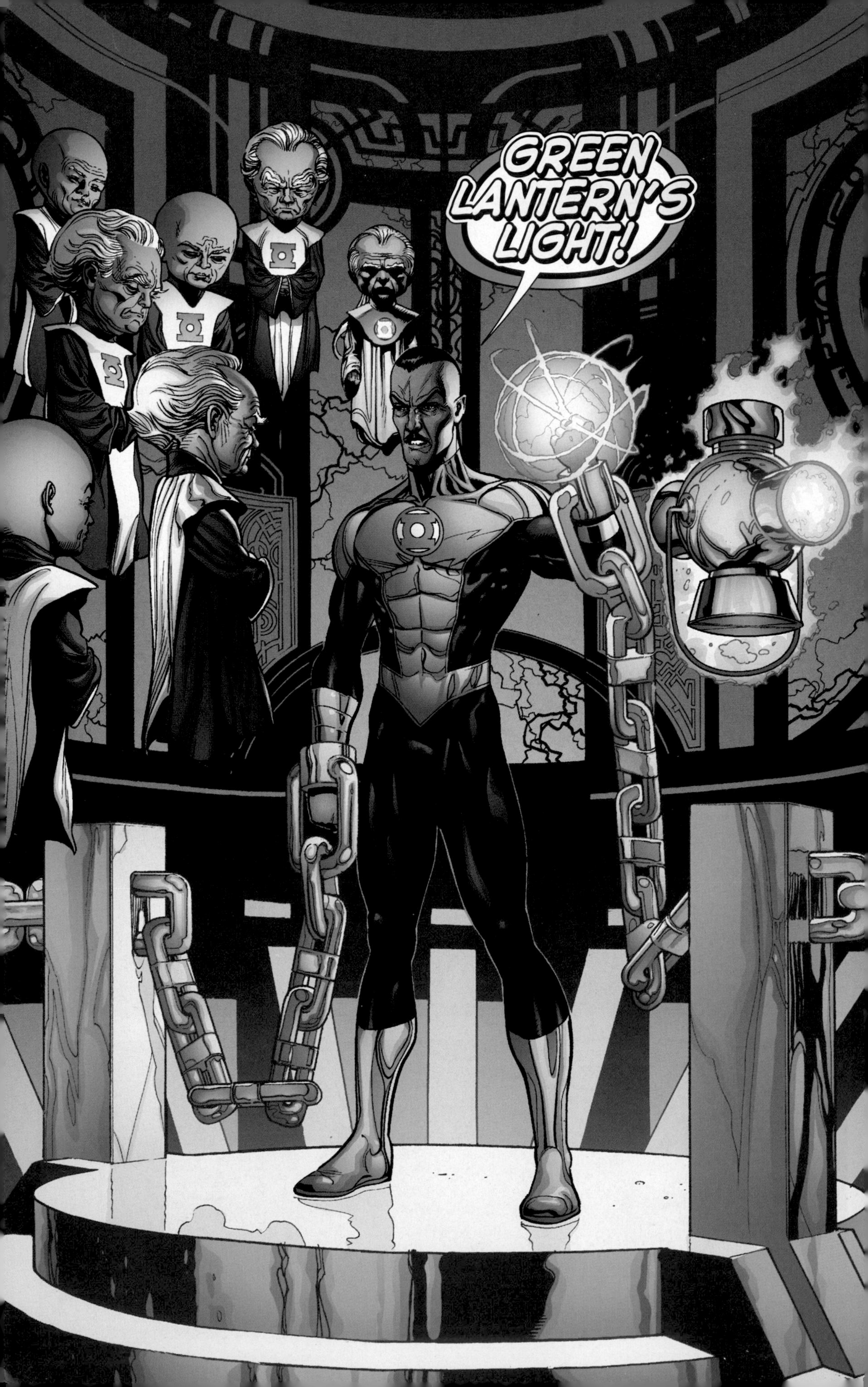
GREEN LANTERN'S LIGHT!

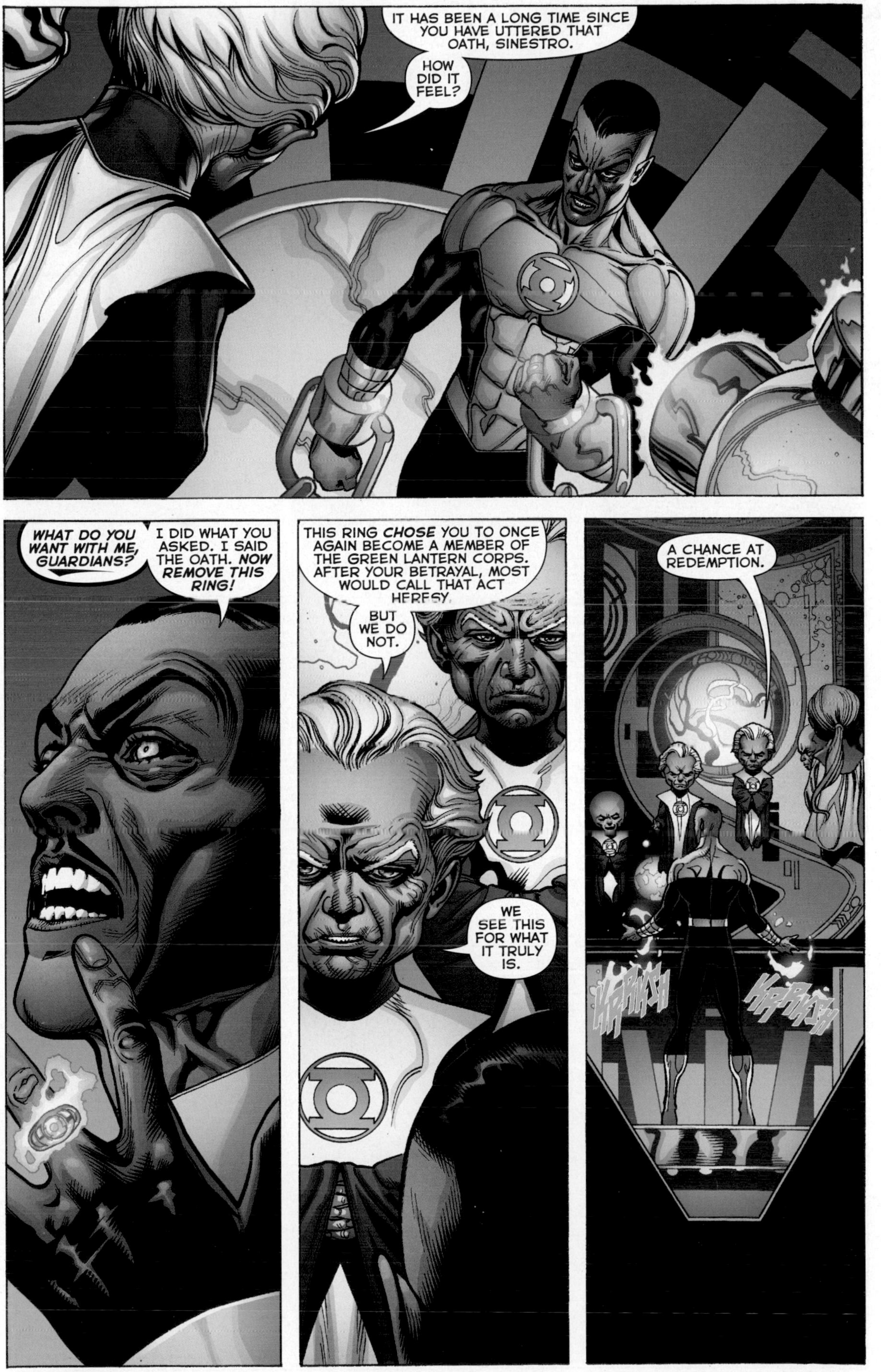
IT HAS BEEN A LONG TIME SINCE YOU HAVE UTTERED THAT OATH, SINESTRO.
HOW DID IT FEEL?
WHAT DO YOU WANT WITH ME, GUARDIANS?
I DID WHAT YOU ASKED. I SAID THE OATH. NOW REMOVE THIS RING!
THIS RING CHOSE YOU TO ONCE AGAIN BECOME A MEMBER OF THE GREEN LANTERN CORPS. AFTER YOUR BETRAYAL, MOST WOULD CALL THAT ACT HERESY.
BUT WE DO NOT.
WE SEE THIS FOR WHAT IT TRULY IS.
A CHANCE AT REDEMPTION.

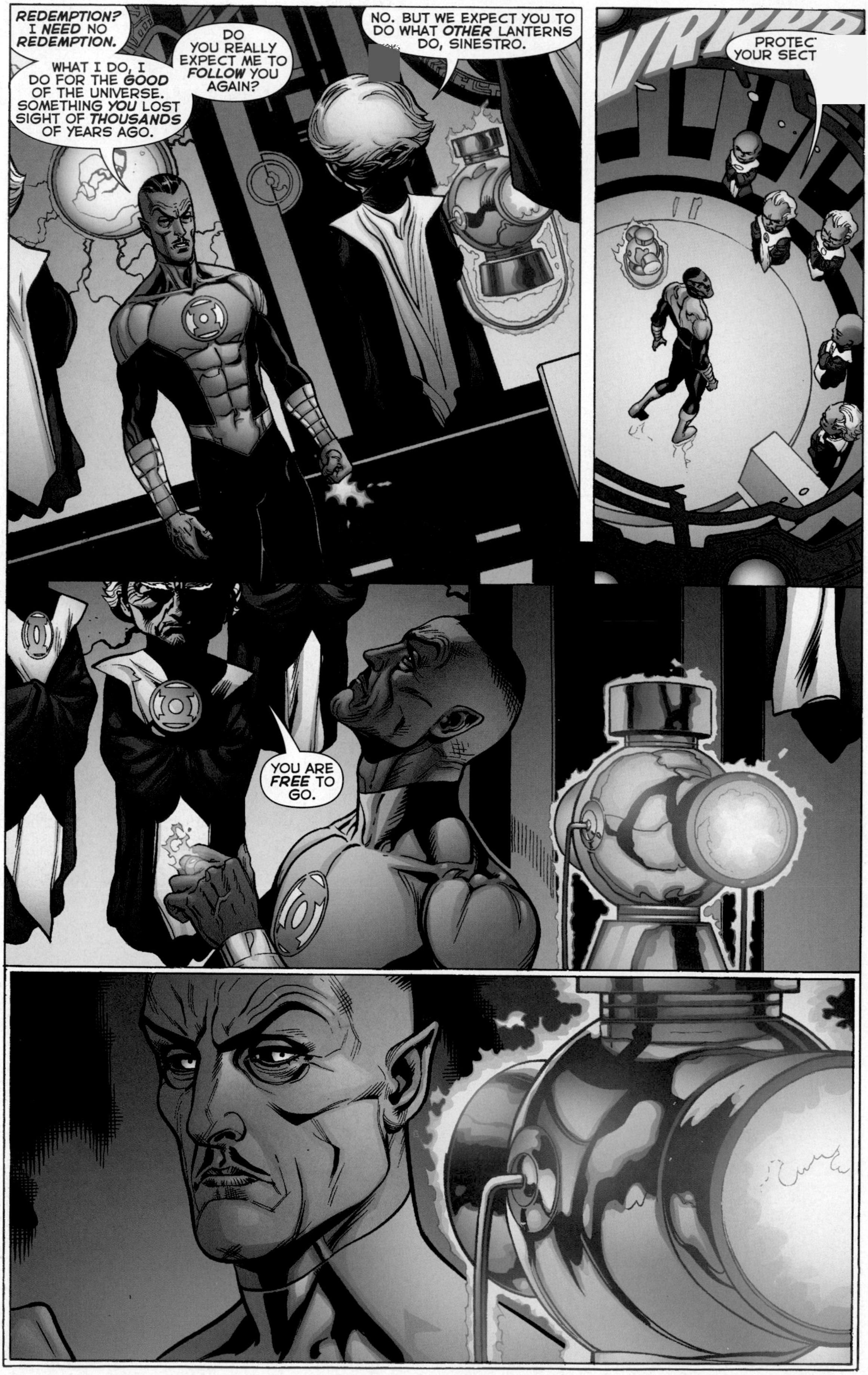
REDEMPTION? I NEED NO REDEMPTION.
WHAT I DO, I DO FOR THE GOOD OF THE UNIVERSE. SOMETHING YOU LOST SIGHT OF THOUSANDS OF YEARS AGO.
DO YOU REALLY EXPECT ME TO FOLLOW YOU AGAIN?
NO. BUT WE EXPECT YOU TO DO WHAT OTHER LANTERNS DO, SINESTRO.
PROTEC
YOUR SECT
YOU ARE FREE TO GO.

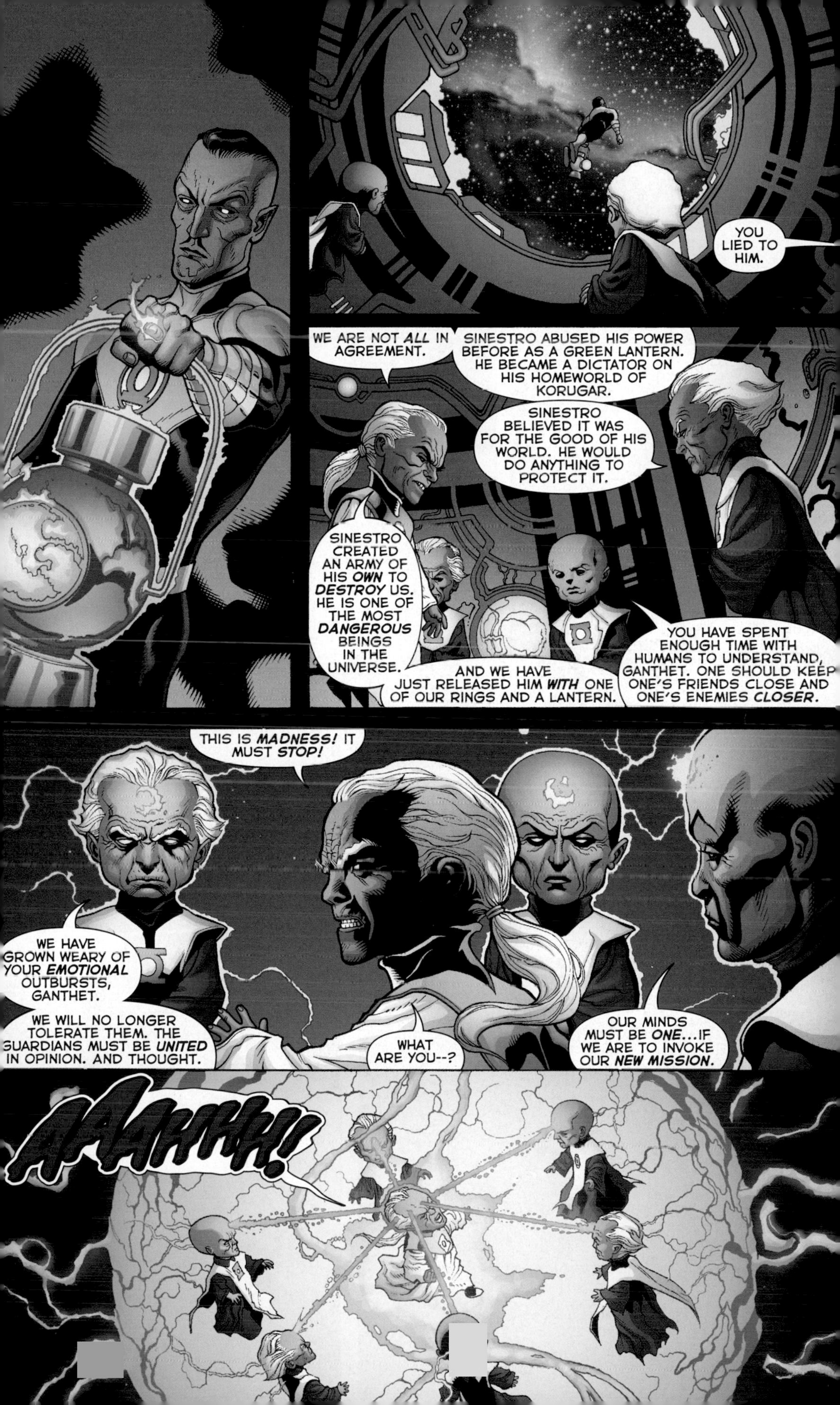
YOU LIED TO HIM.
WE ARE NOT ALL IN AGREEMENT.
SINESTRO ABUSED HIS POWER BEFORE AS A GREEN LANTERN. HE BECAME A DICTATOR ON HIS HOMEWORLD OF KORUGAR.
SINESTRO BELIEVED IT WAS FOR THE GOOD OF HIS WORLD. HE WOULD DO ANYTHING TO PROTECT IT.
SINESTRO CREATED AN ARMY OF HIS OWN TO DESTROY US. HE IS ONE OF THE MOST DANGEROUS BEINGS IN THE UNIVERSE.
AND WE HAVE JUST RELEASED HIM WITH ONE OF OUR RINGS AND A LANTERN.
YOU HAVE SPENT ENOUGH TIME WITH HUMANS TO UNDERSTAND, GANTHET. ONE SHOULD KEEP ONE'S FRIENDS CLOSE AND ONE'S ENEMIES CLOSER.
THIS IS MADNESS! IT MUST STOP!
WE HAVE GROWN WEARY OF YOUR EMOTIONAL OUTBURSTS, GANTHET.
WE WILL NO LONGER TOLERATE THEM. THE GUARDIANS MUST BE UNITED IN OPINION. AND THOUGHT.
WHAT ARE YOU--?
OUR MINDS MUST BE ONE...IF WE ARE TO INVOKE OUR NEW MISSION.
AAAHHHH!

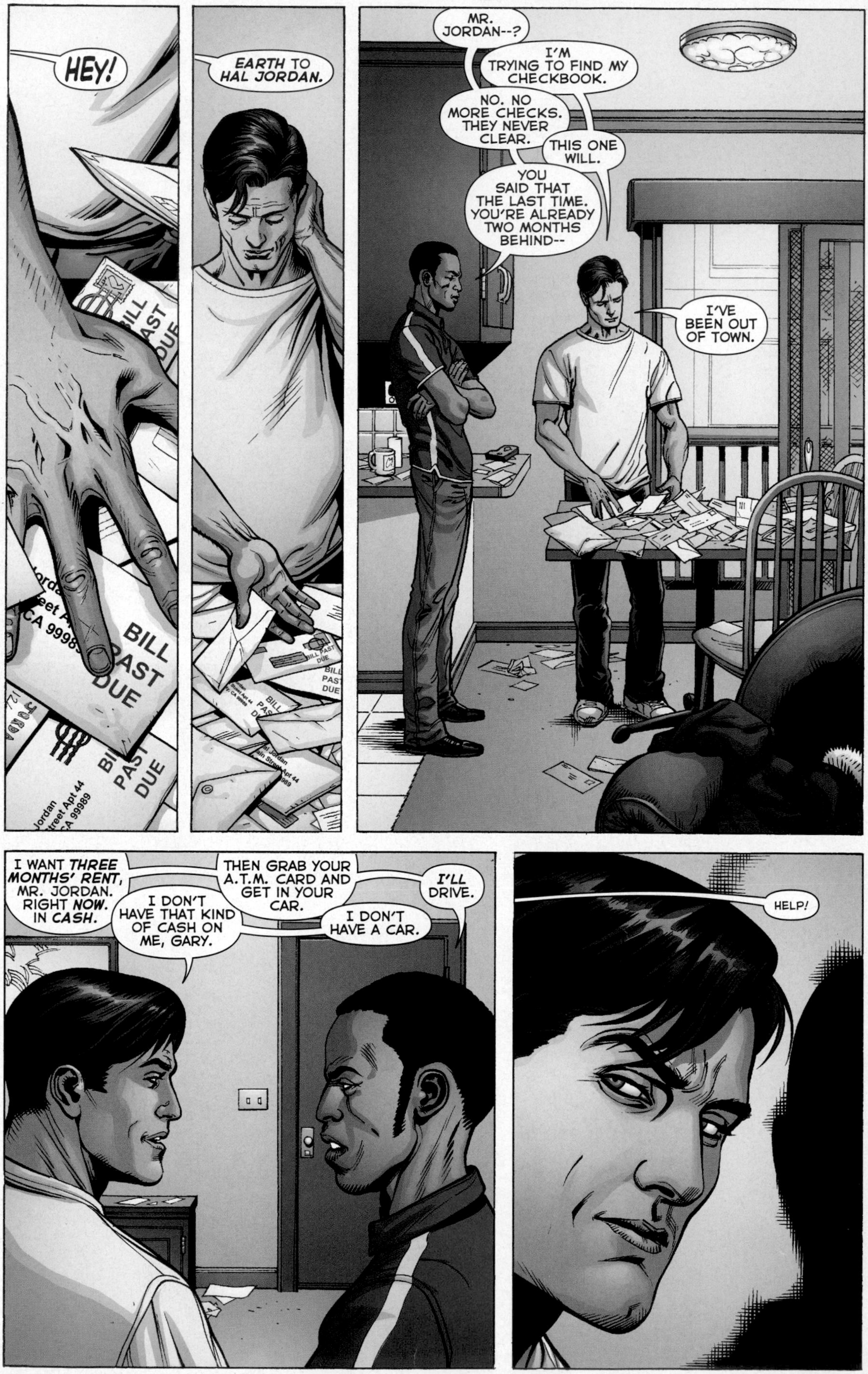
HEY!
EARTH TO HAL JORDAN.
MR. JORDAN--?
I'M TRYING TO FIND MY CHECKBOOK.
NO. NO MORE CHECKS. THEY NEVER CLEAR.
THIS ONE WILL.
YOU SAID THAT THE LAST TIME. YOU'RE ALREADY TWO MONTHS BEHIND--
I'VE BEEN OUT OF TOWN.
I WANT THREE MONTHS' RENT, MR. JORDAN. RIGHT NOW. IN CASH.
I DON'T HAVE THAT KIND OF CASH ON ME, GARY.
THEN GRAB YOUR A.T.M. CARD AND GET IN YOUR CAR.
I DON'T HAVE A CAR.
I'LL DRIVE.
HELP!

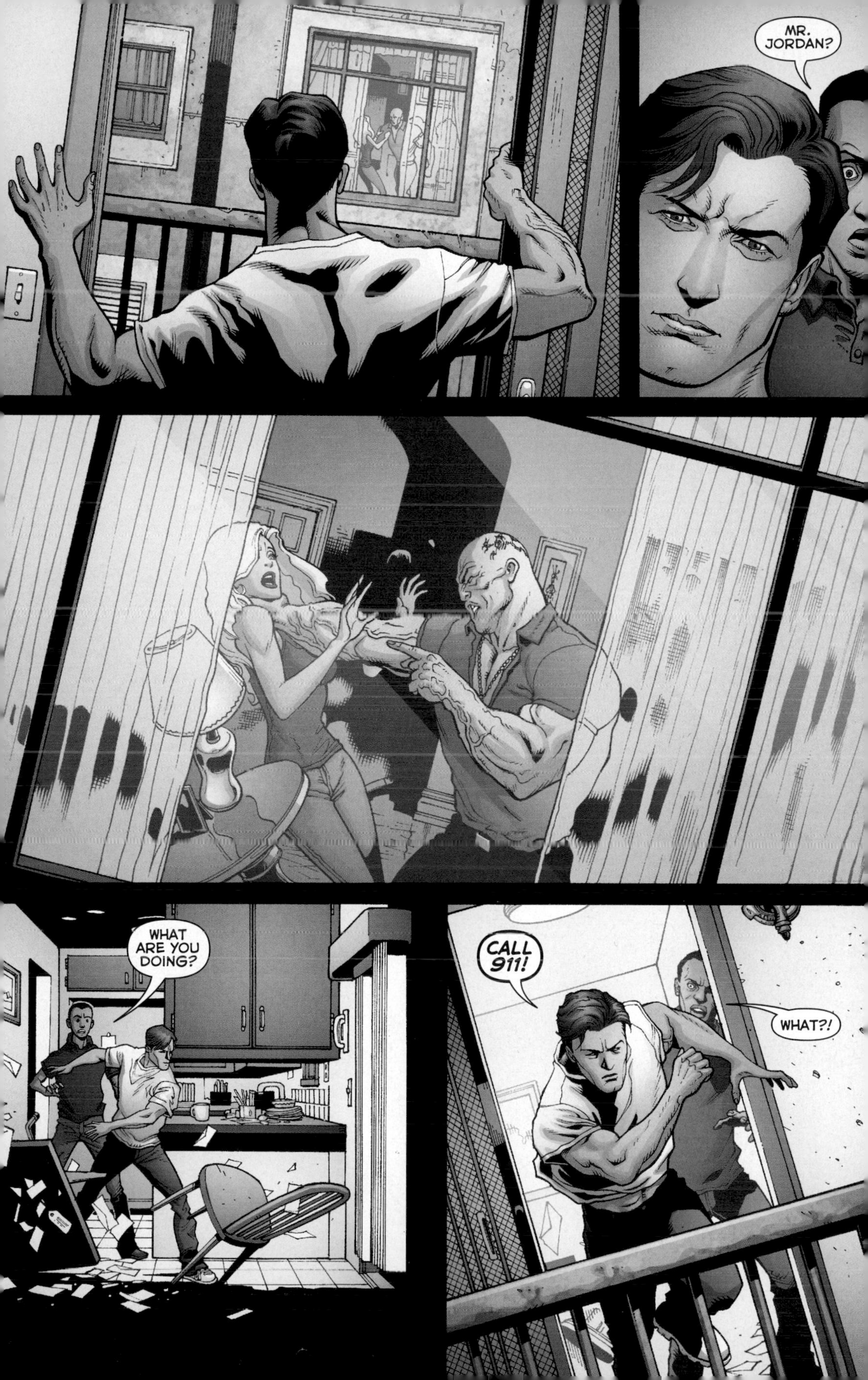
MR. JORDAN?
WHAT ARE YOU DOING?
CALL 911!
WHAT?!

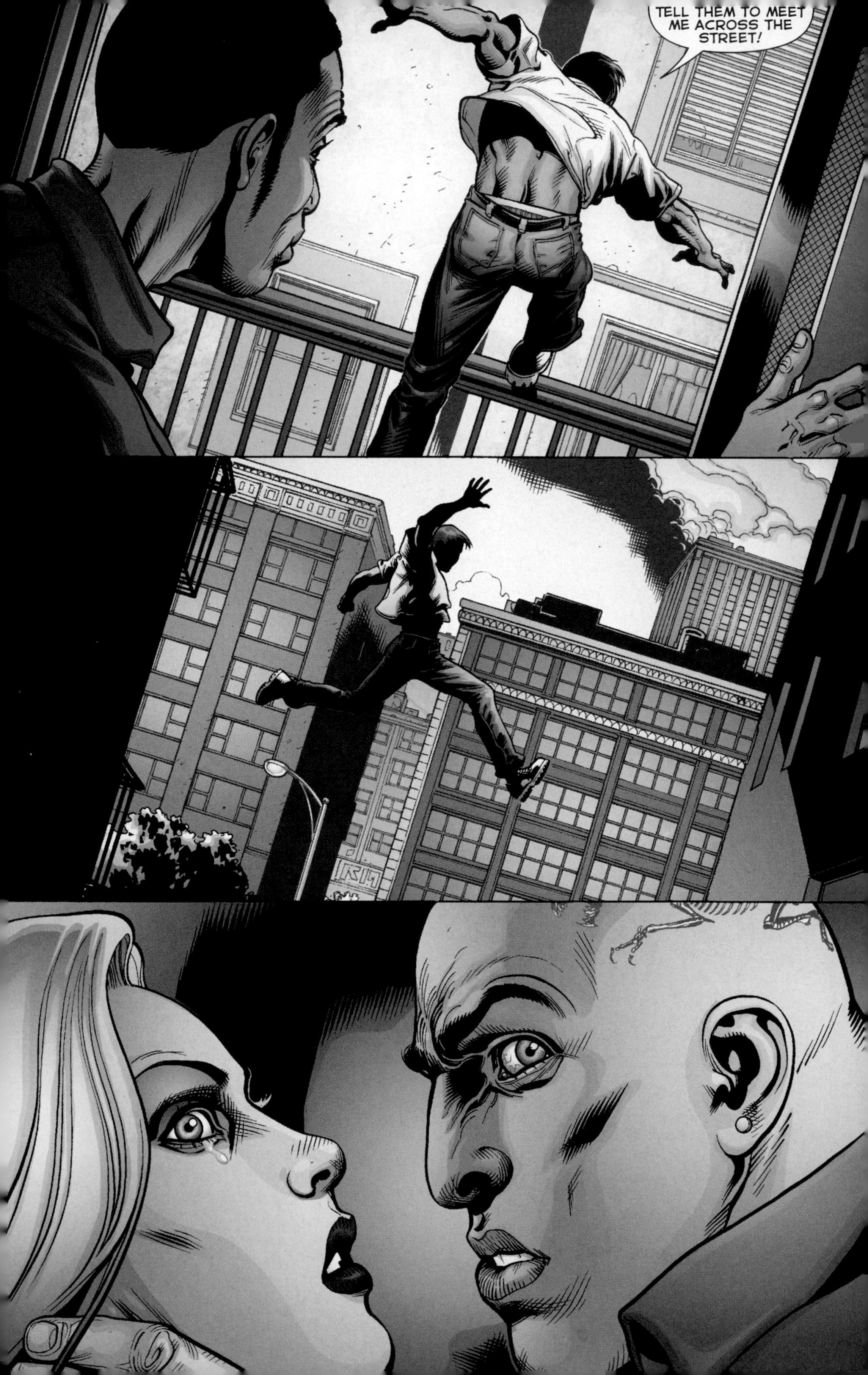
TELL THEM TO MEET ME ACROSS THE STREET!

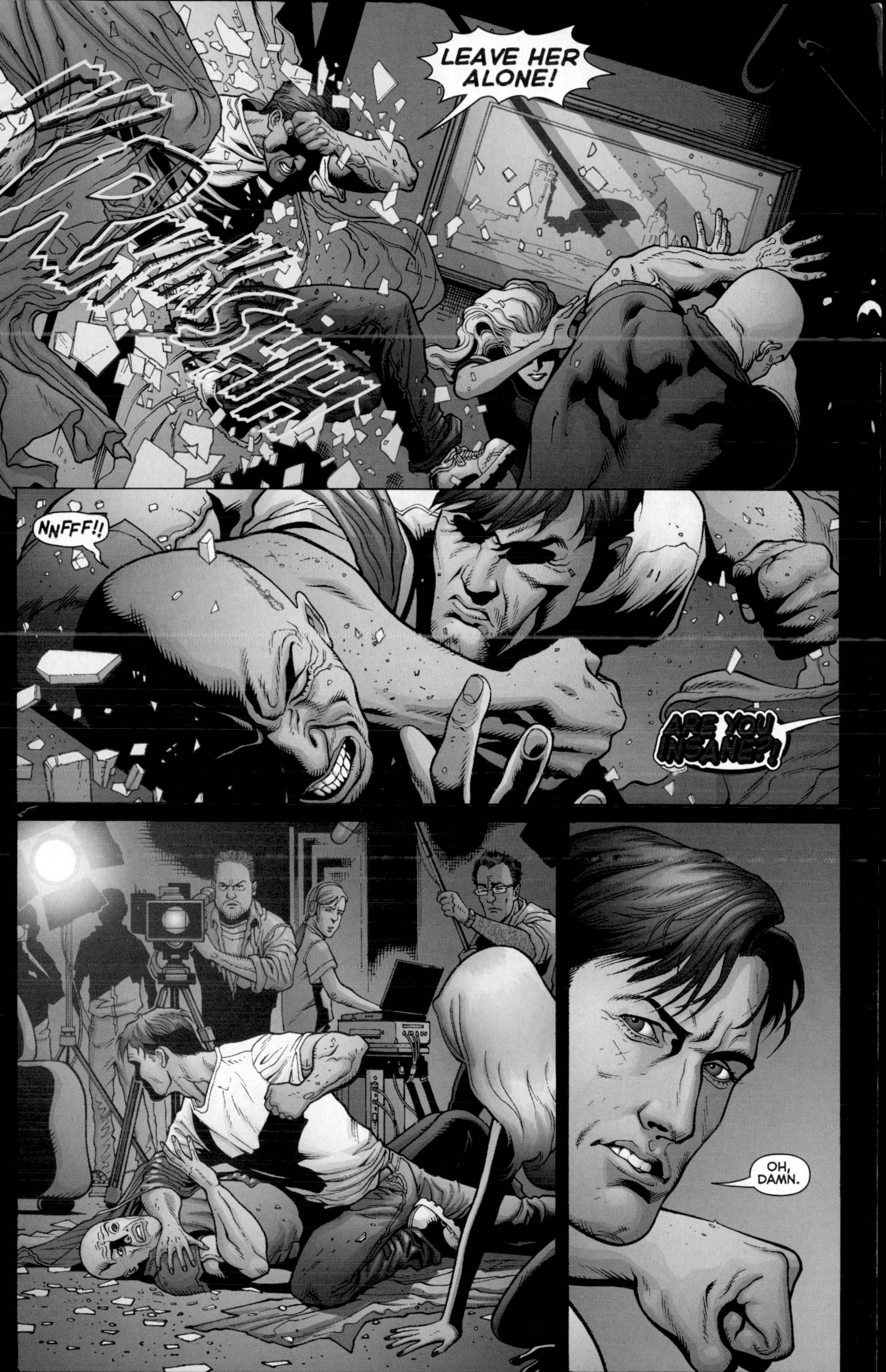
LEAVE HER ALONE!
NNFFF!!
ARE YOU INSANE?!
OH, DAMN.

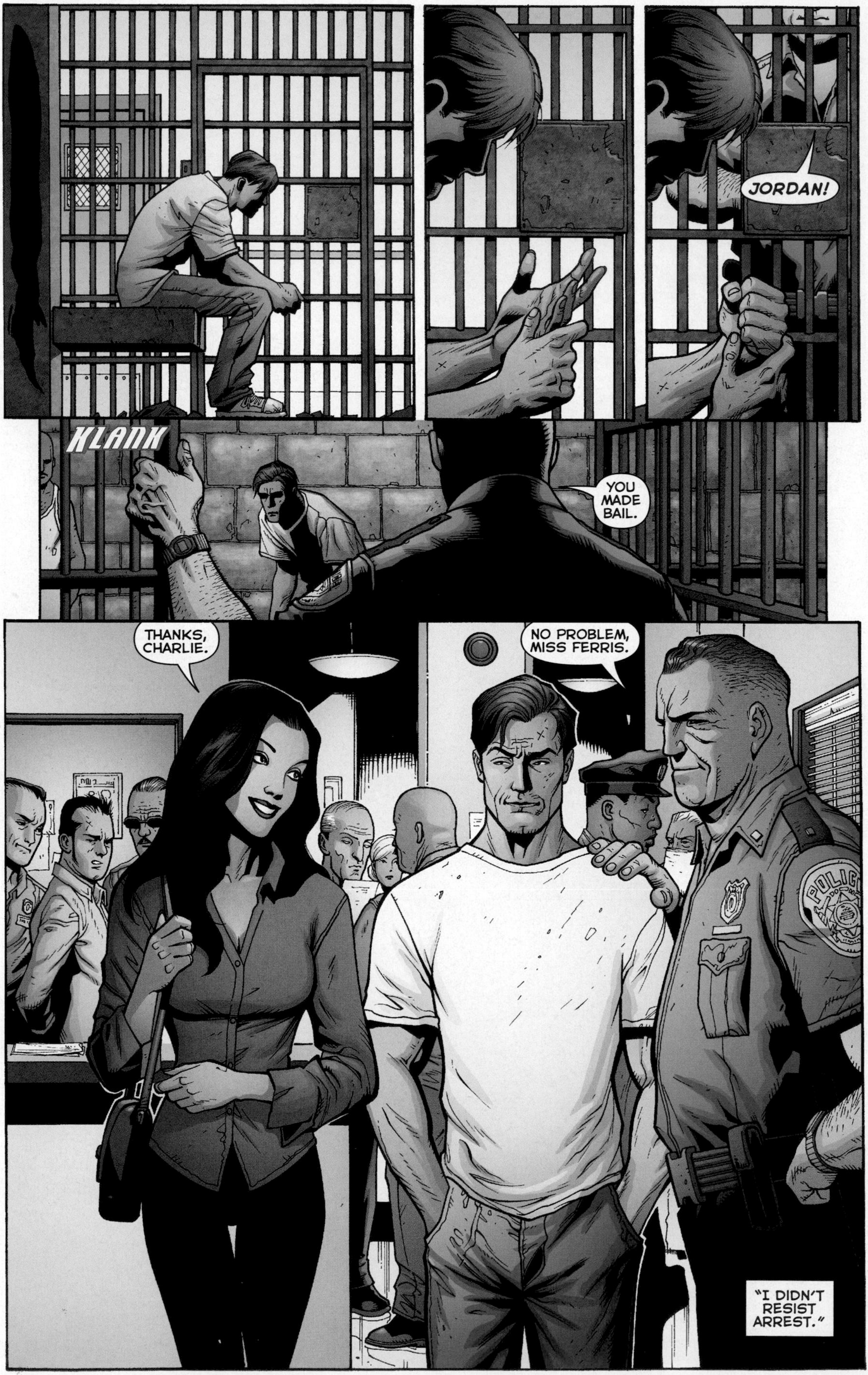
JORDAN!
KLANK
YOU MADE BAIL.
THANKS, CHARLIE.
NO PROBLEM, MISS FERRIS.
"I DIDN'T RESIST ARREST."

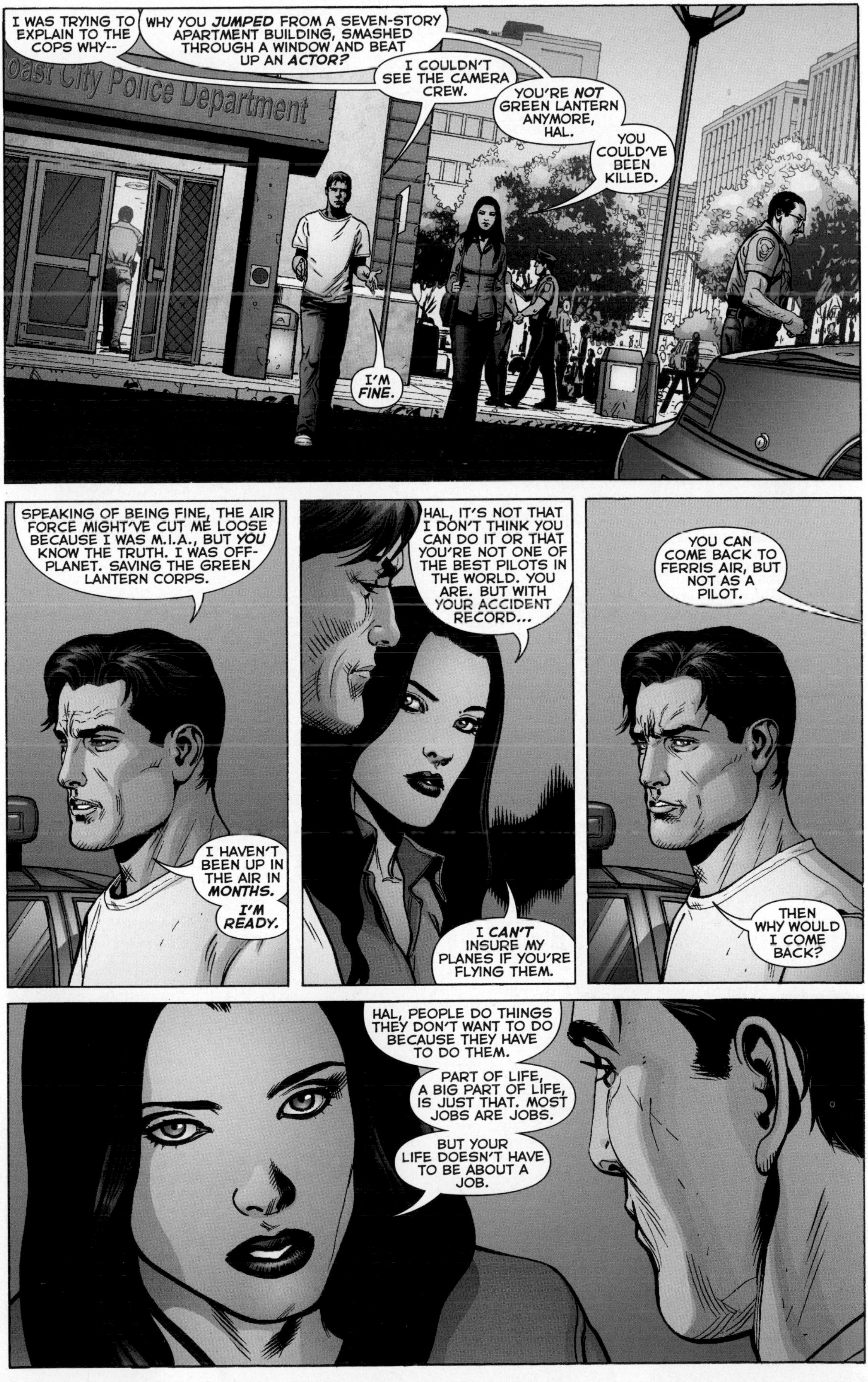

I WAS TRYING TO EXPLAIN TO THE COPS WHY--
WHY YOU *JUMPED* FROM A SEVEN-STORY APARTMENT BUILDING, SMASHED THROUGH A WINDOW AND BEAT UP AN *ACTOR?*
I COULDN'T SEE THE CAMERA CREW.
YOU'RE *NOT* GREEN LANTERN ANYMORE, HAL.
YOU COULD'VE BEEN KILLED.
Coast City Police Department
I'M *FINE.*
SPEAKING OF BEING FINE, THE AIR FORCE MIGHT'VE CUT ME LOOSE BECAUSE I WAS M.I.A., BUT *YOU* KNOW THE TRUTH. I WAS OFF-PLANET. SAVING THE GREEN LANTERN CORPS.
I HAVEN'T BEEN UP IN THE AIR IN *MONTHS.*
I'M READY.
HAL, IT'S NOT THAT I DON'T THINK YOU CAN DO IT OR THAT YOU'RE NOT ONE OF THE BEST PILOTS IN THE WORLD. YOU ARE. BUT WITH YOUR ACCIDENT RECORD...
I *CAN'T* INSURE MY PLANES IF YOU'RE FLYING THEM.
YOU CAN COME BACK TO FERRIS AIR, BUT NOT AS A PILOT.
THEN WHY WOULD I COME BACK?
HAL, PEOPLE DO THINGS THEY DON'T WANT TO DO BECAUSE THEY HAVE TO DO THEM.
PART OF LIFE, A BIG PART OF LIFE, IS JUST THAT. MOST JOBS ARE JOBS.
BUT YOUR LIFE DOESN'T HAVE TO BE ABOUT A JOB.

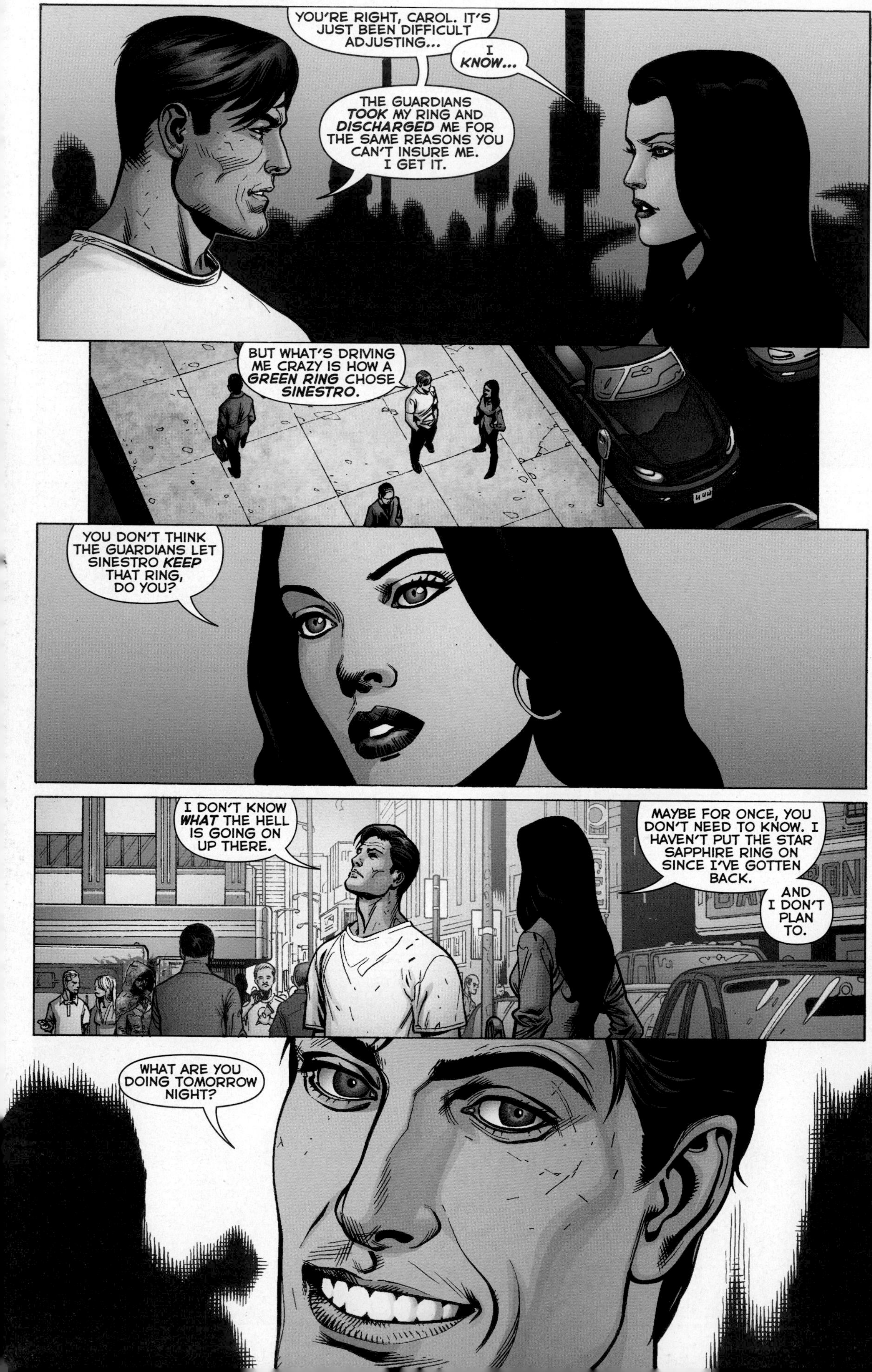
YOU'RE RIGHT, CAROL. IT'S JUST BEEN DIFFICULT ADJUSTING...
I KNOW...
THE GUARDIANS TOOK MY RING AND DISCHARGED ME FOR THE SAME REASONS YOU CAN'T INSURE ME. I GET IT.
BUT WHAT'S DRIVING ME CRAZY IS HOW A GREEN RING CHOSE SINESTRO.
YOU DON'T THINK THE GUARDIANS LET SINESTRO KEEP THAT RING, DO YOU?
I DON'T KNOW WHAT THE HELL IS GOING ON UP THERE.
MAYBE FOR ONCE, YOU DON'T NEED TO KNOW. I HAVEN'T PUT THE STAR SAPPHIRE RING ON SINCE I'VE GOTTEN BACK.
AND I DON'T PLAN TO.
WHAT ARE YOU DOING TOMORROW NIGHT?

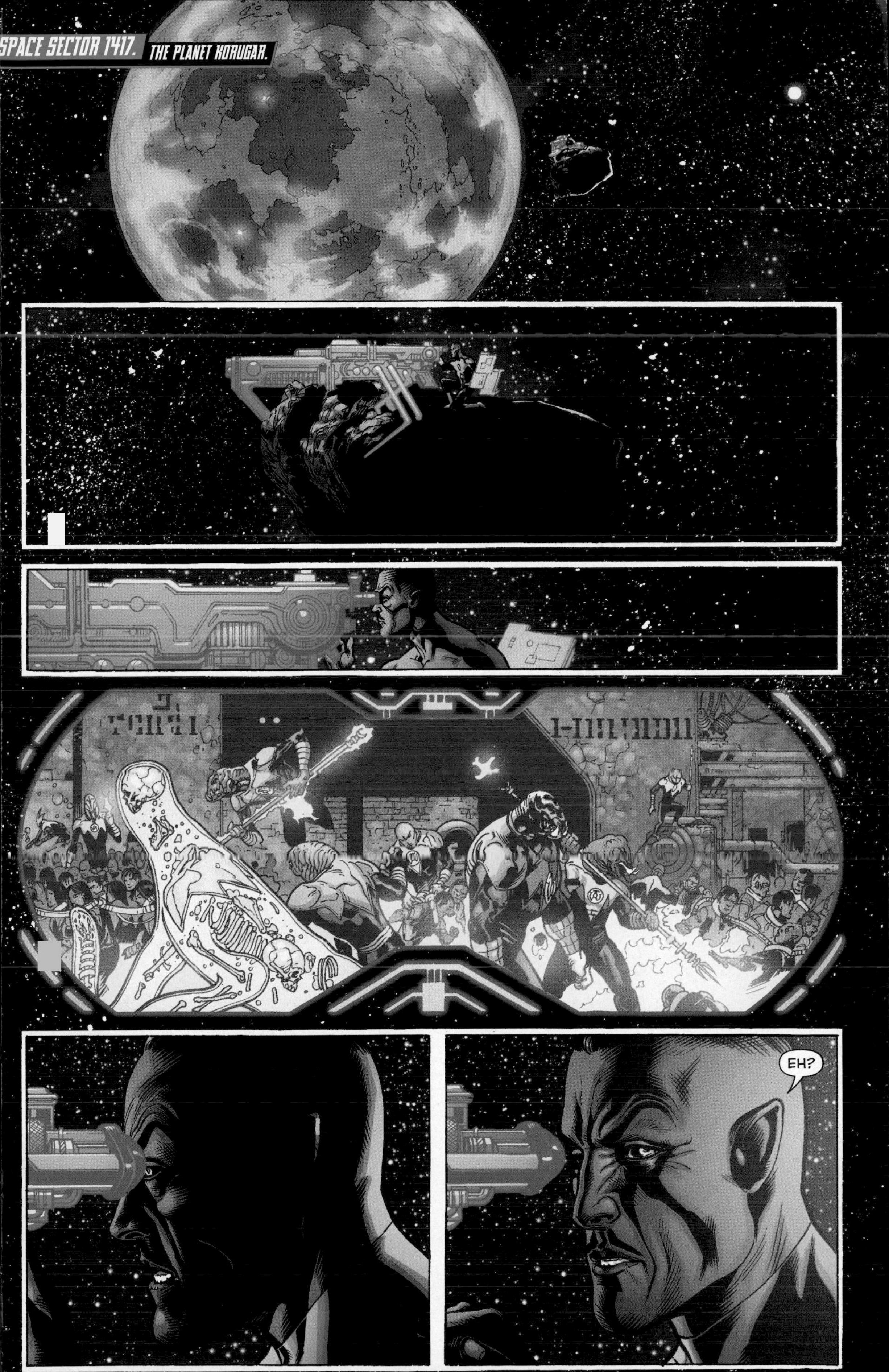
SPACE SECTOR 1417.
THE PLANET KORUGAR.
EH?

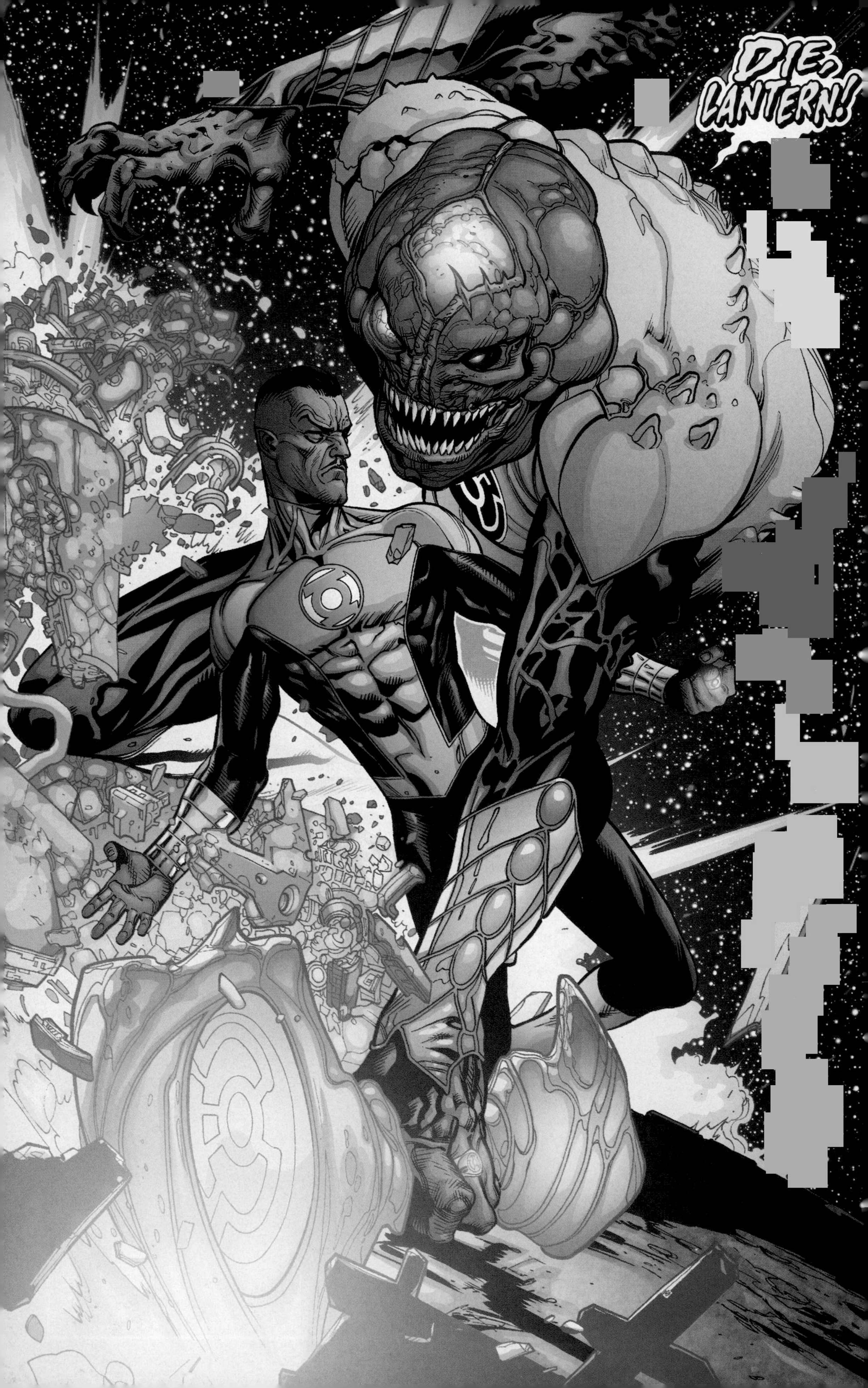
DIE, LANTERN!

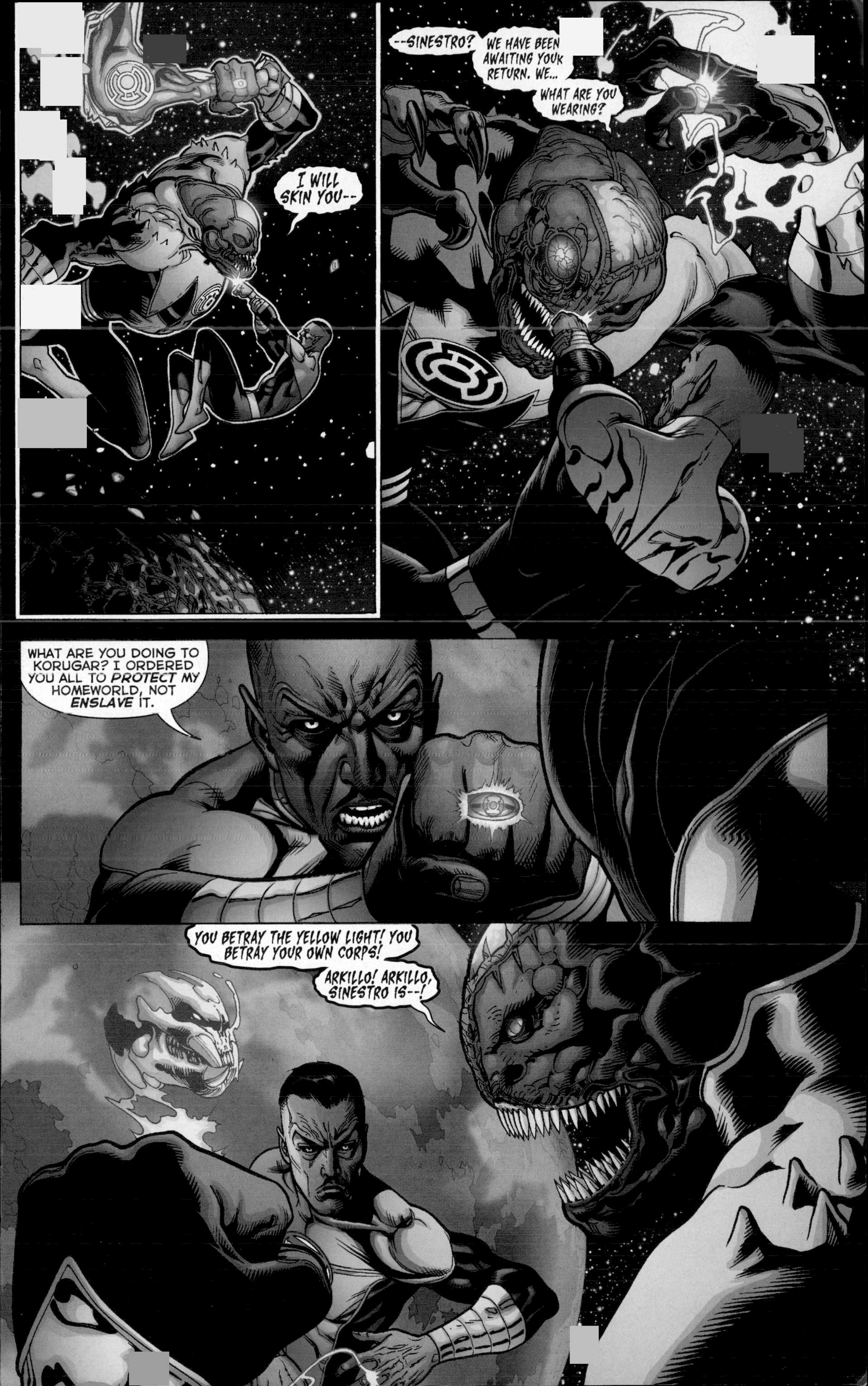
I WILL SKIN YOU--
--SINESTRO?
WE HAVE BEEN AWAITING YOUR RETURN. WE...
WHAT ARE YOU WEARING?
WHAT ARE YOU DOING TO KORUGAR? I ORDERED YOU ALL TO PROTECT MY HOMEWORLD, NOT ENSLAVE IT.
YOU BETRAY THE YELLOW LIGHT! YOU BETRAY YOUR OWN CORPS!
ARKILLO! ARKILLO, SINESTRO IS--!

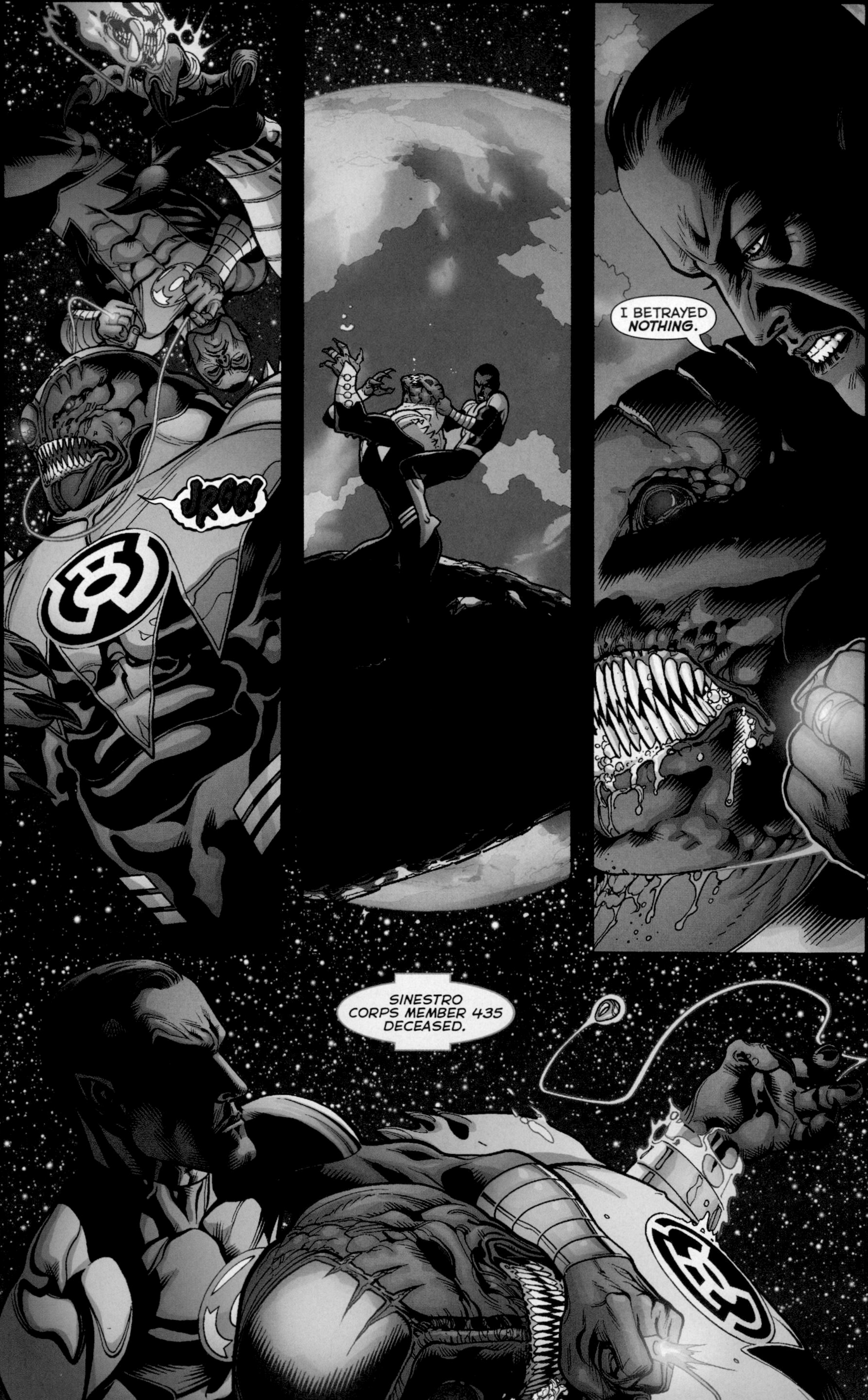
JROOM
I BETRAYED NOTHING.
SINESTRO CORPS MEMBER 435 DECEASED.

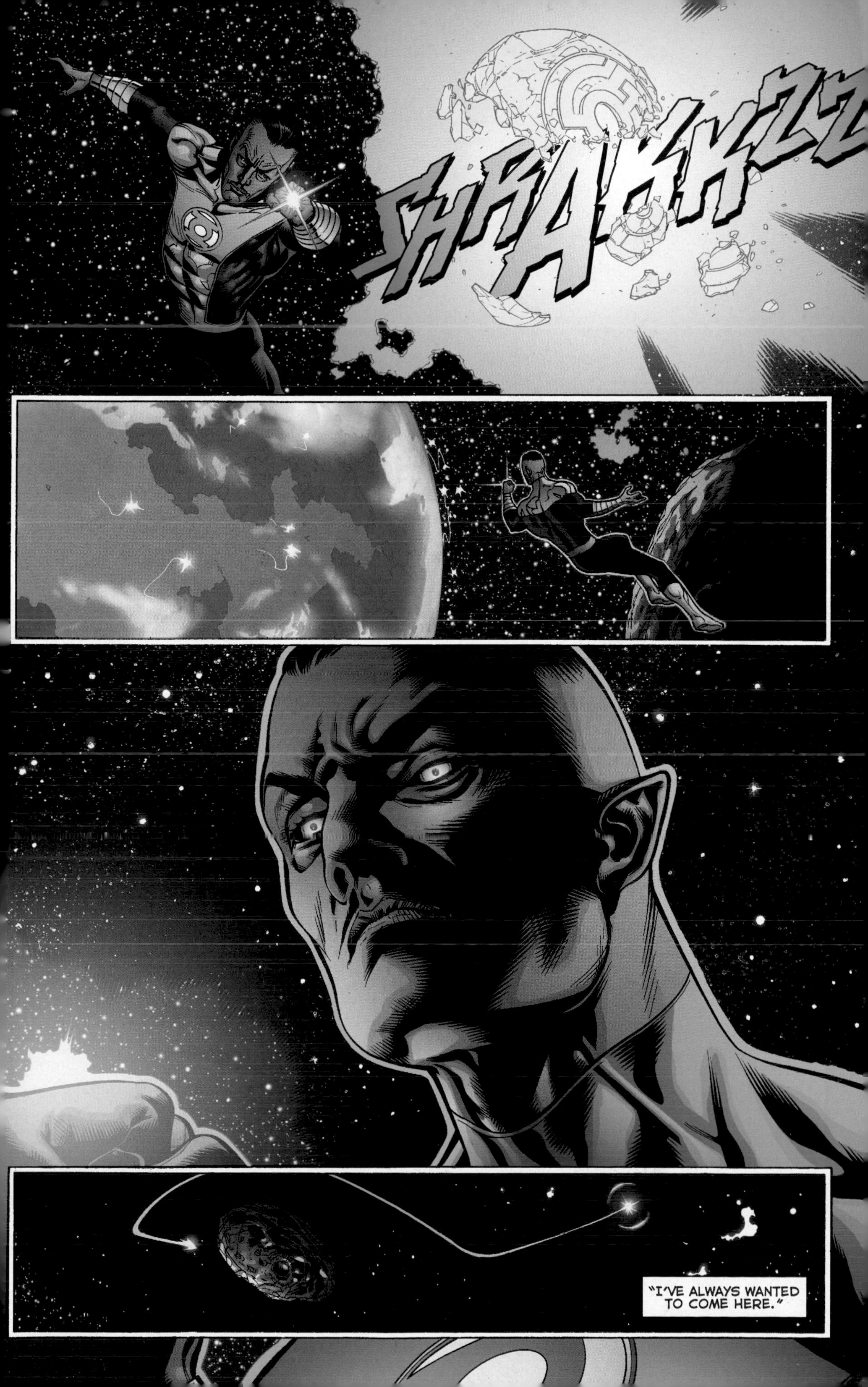
SHRAKKZZ
"I'VE ALWAYS WANTED TO COME HERE."

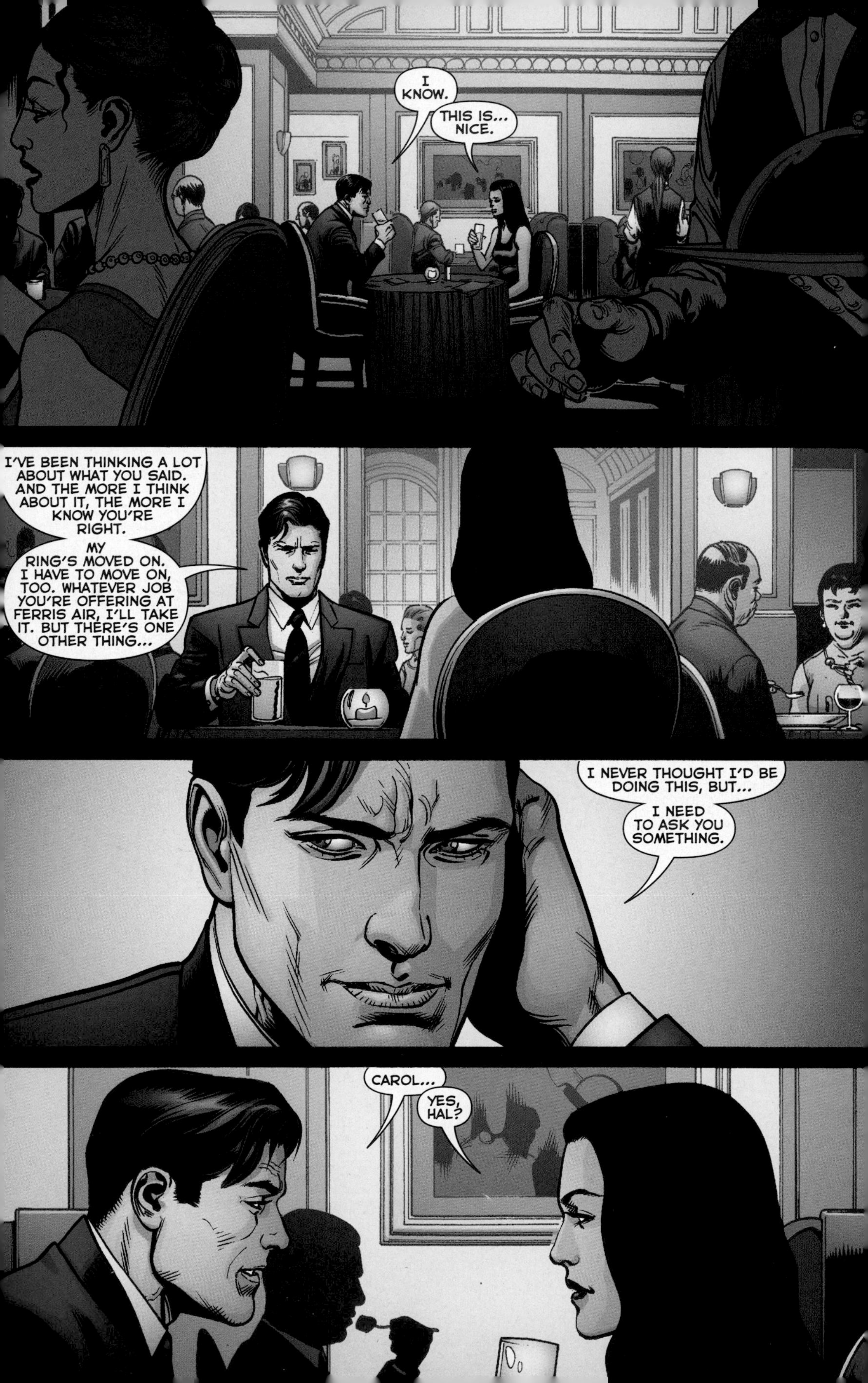
I KNOW.
THIS IS... NICE.
I'VE BEEN THINKING A LOT ABOUT WHAT YOU SAID. AND THE MORE I THINK ABOUT IT, THE MORE I KNOW YOU'RE RIGHT.
MY RING'S MOVED ON. I HAVE TO MOVE ON, TOO. WHATEVER JOB YOU'RE OFFERING AT FERRIS AIR, I'LL TAKE IT. BUT THERE'S ONE OTHER THING...
I NEVER THOUGHT I'D BE DOING THIS, BUT...
I NEED TO ASK YOU SOMETHING.
CAROL...
YES, HAL?

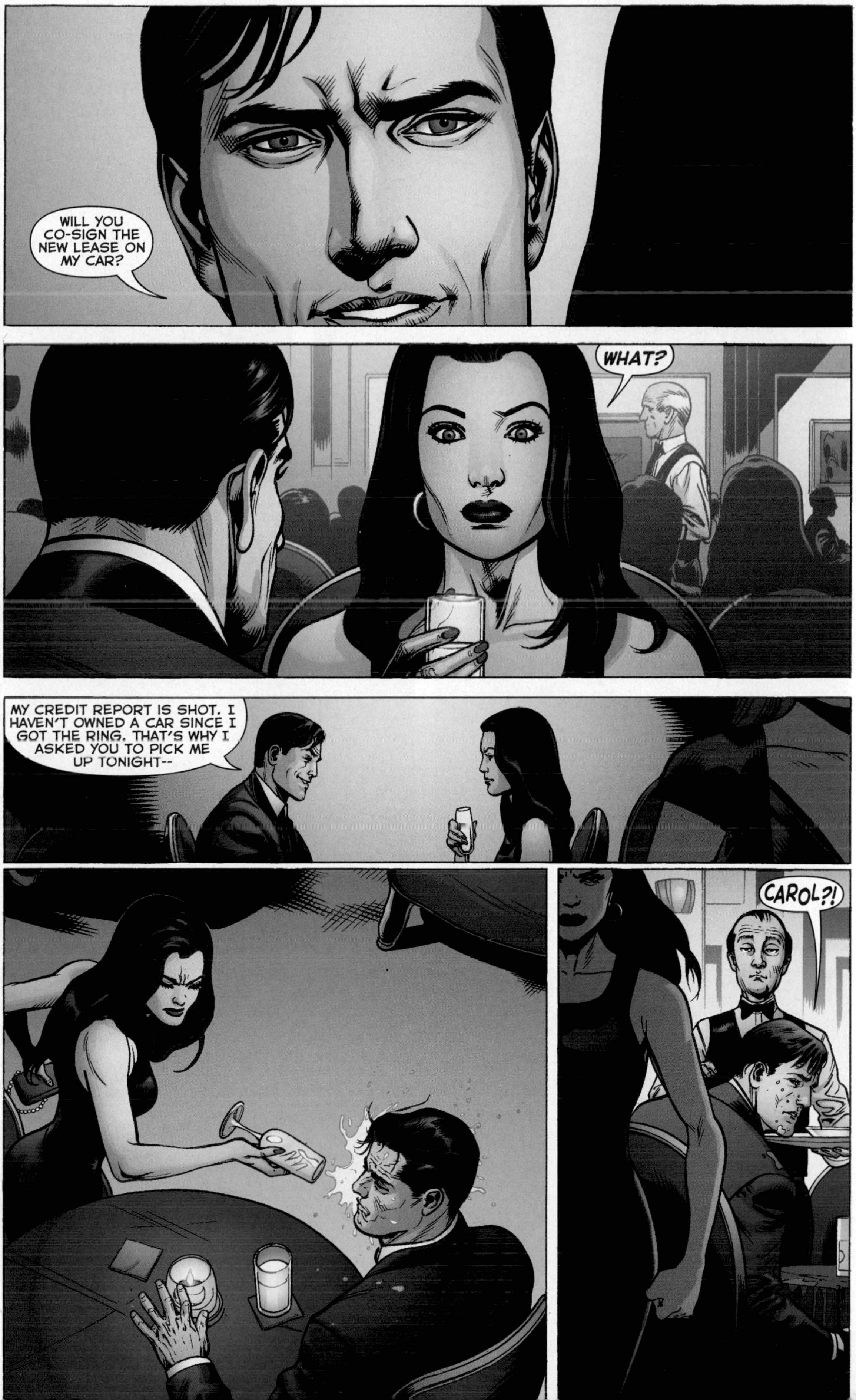
WILL YOU CO-SIGN THE NEW LEASE ON MY CAR?
WHAT?
MY CREDIT REPORT IS SHOT. I HAVEN'T OWNED A CAR SINCE I GOT THE RING. THAT'S WHY I ASKED YOU TO PICK ME UP TONIGHT--
CAROL?!

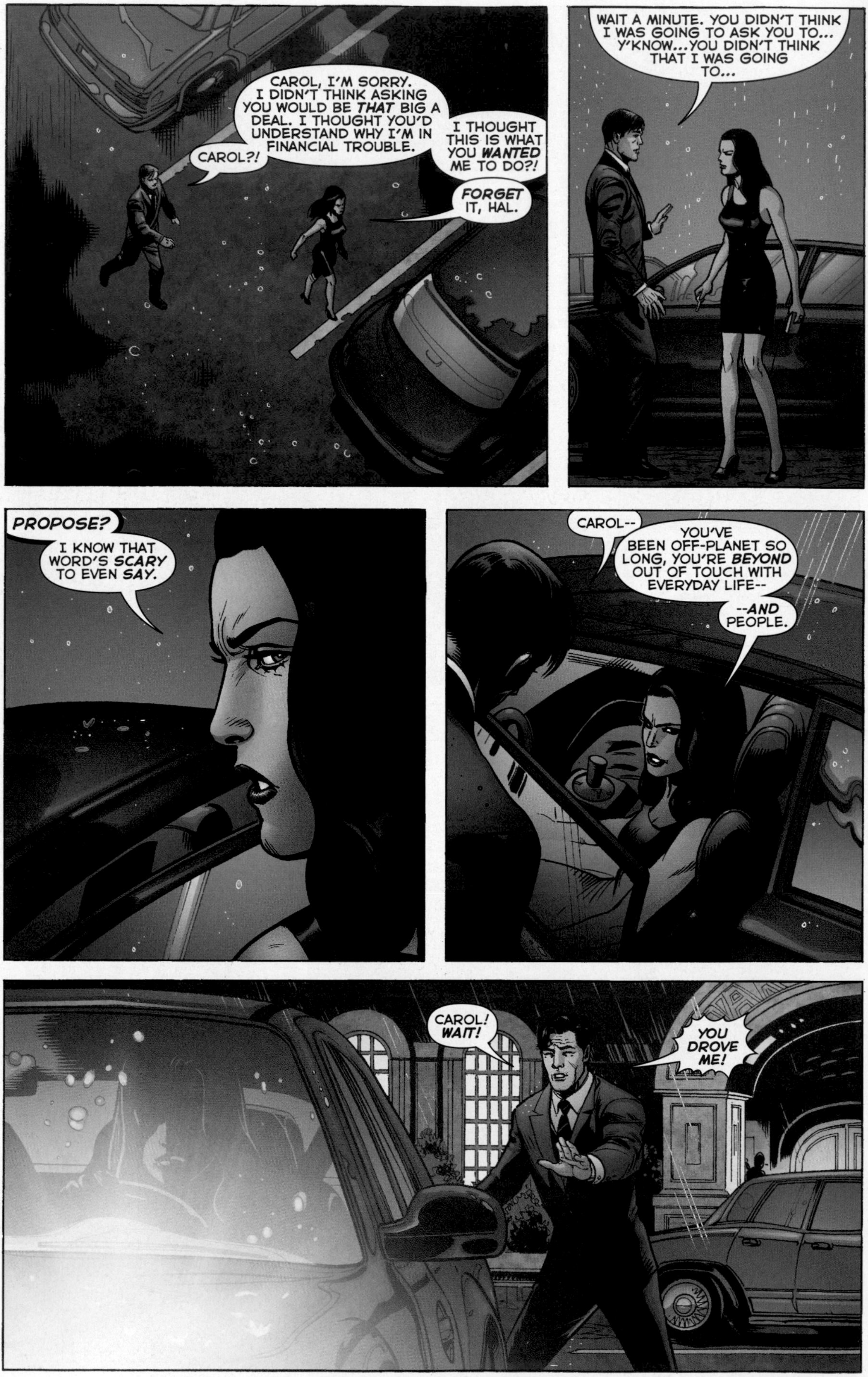
CAROL, I'M SORRY. I DIDN'T THINK ASKING YOU WOULD BE THAT BIG A DEAL. I THOUGHT YOU'D UNDERSTAND WHY I'M IN FINANCIAL TROUBLE.
CAROL?!
I THOUGHT THIS IS WHAT YOU WANTED ME TO DO?!
FORGET IT, HAL.
WAIT A MINUTE. YOU DIDN'T THINK I WAS GOING TO ASK YOU TO... Y'KNOW...YOU DIDN'T THINK THAT I WAS GOING TO...
PROPOSE?
I KNOW THAT WORD'S SCARY TO EVEN SAY.
CAROL--
YOU'VE BEEN OFF-PLANET SO LONG, YOU'RE BEYOND OUT OF TOUCH WITH EVERYDAY LIFE--
--AND PEOPLE.
CAROL! WAIT!
YOU DROVE ME!

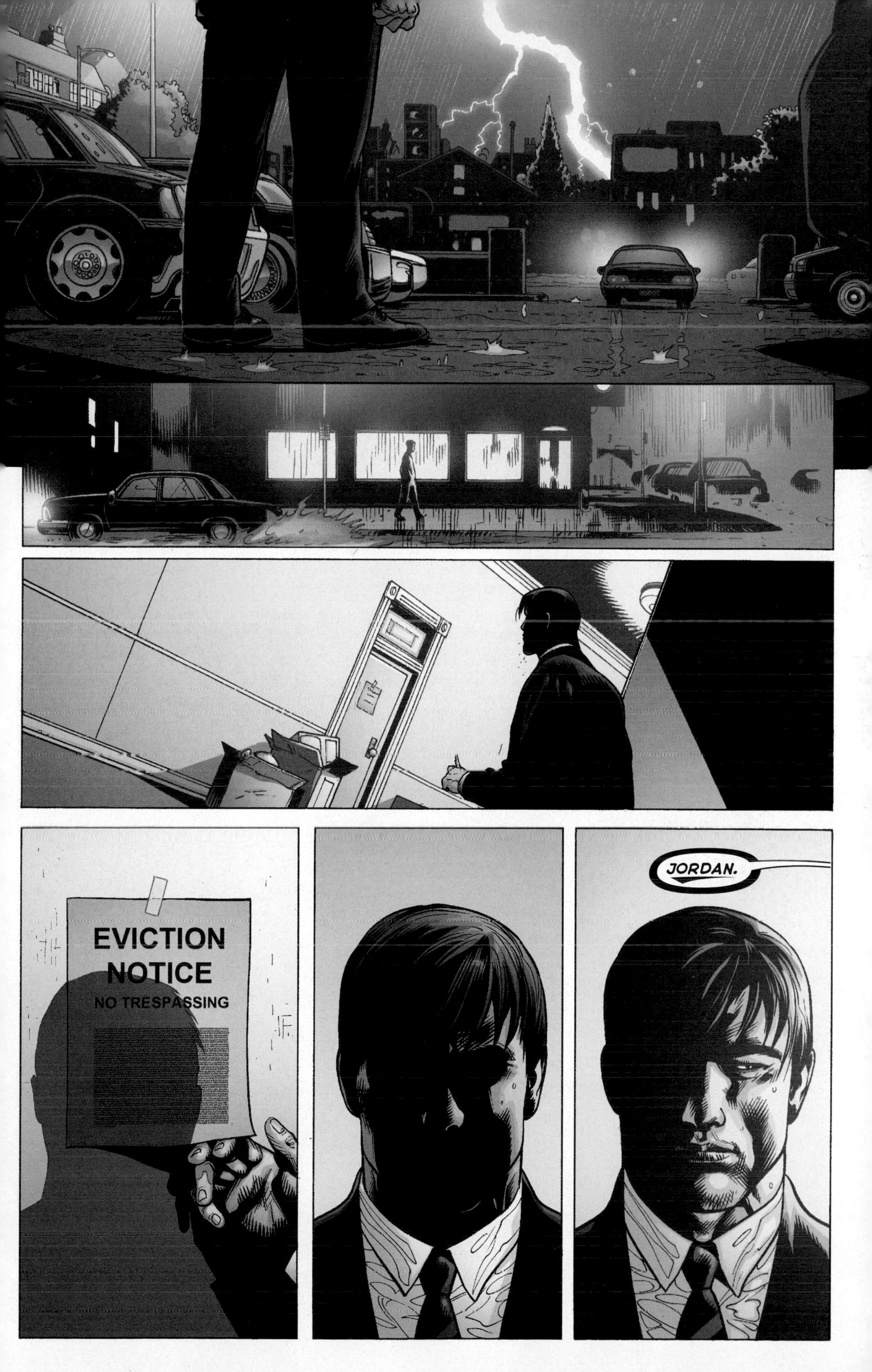
EVICTION NOTICE
NO TRESPASSING
JORDAN.

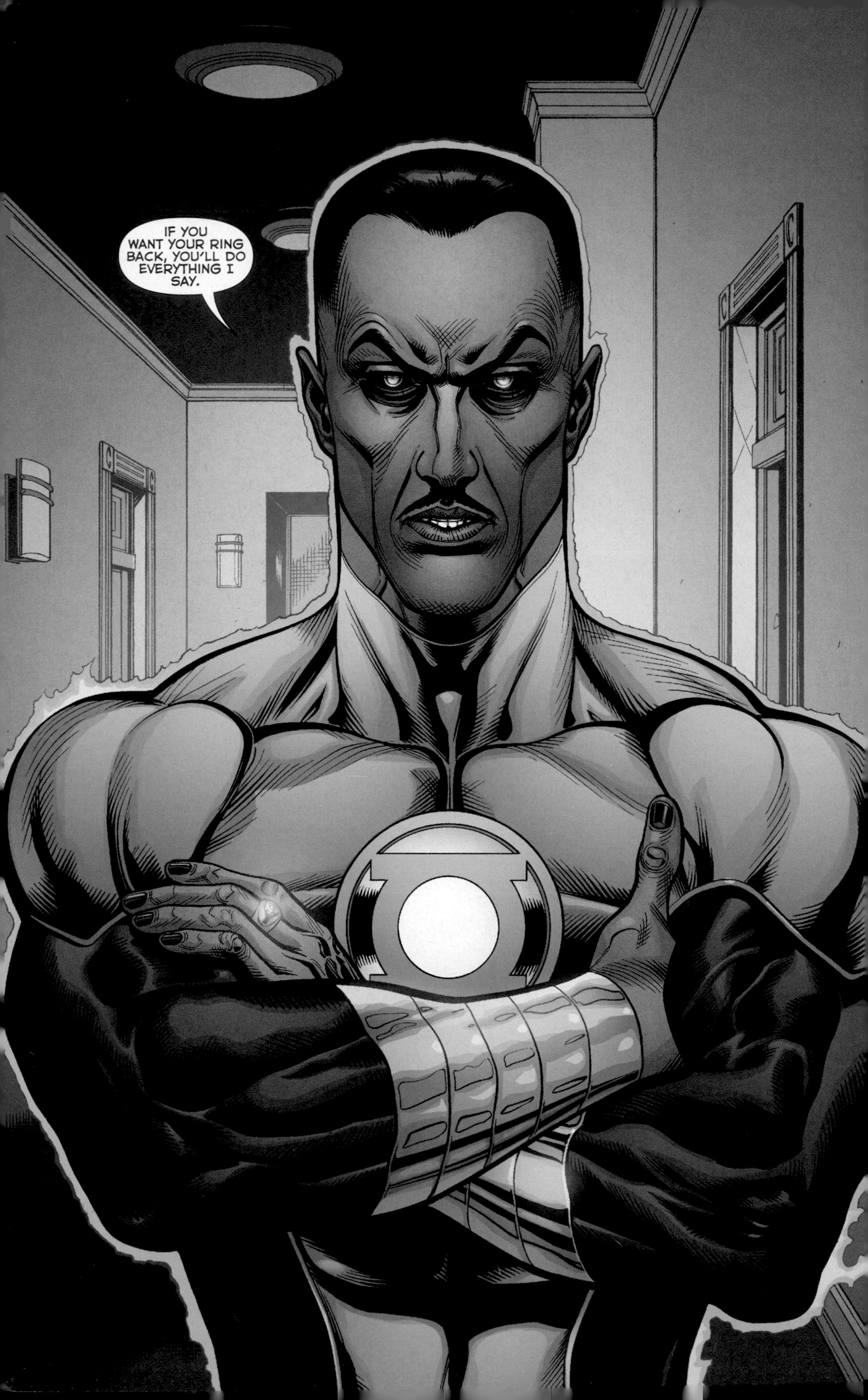
IF YOU WANT YOUR RING BACK, YOU'LL DO EVERYTHING I SAY.

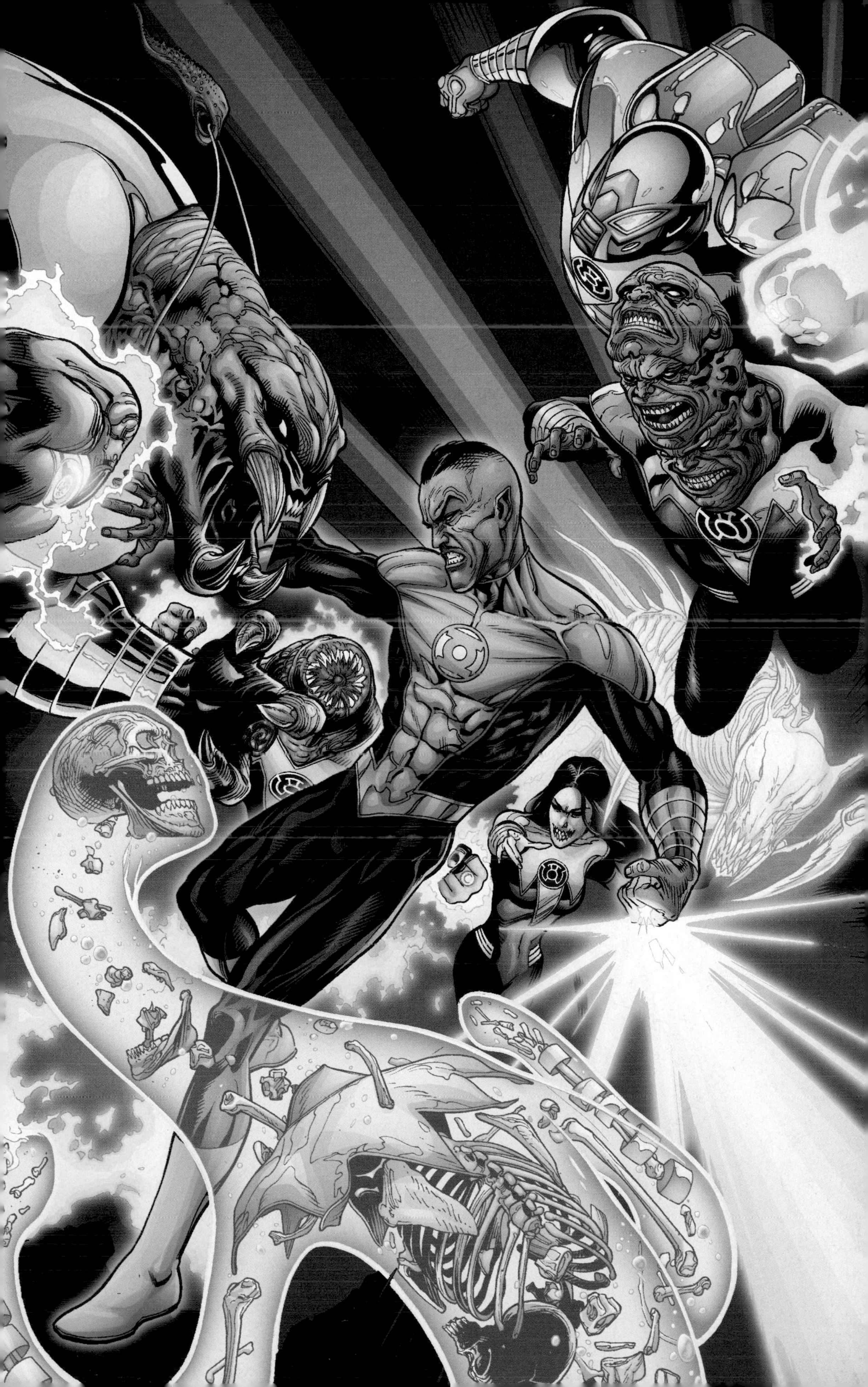

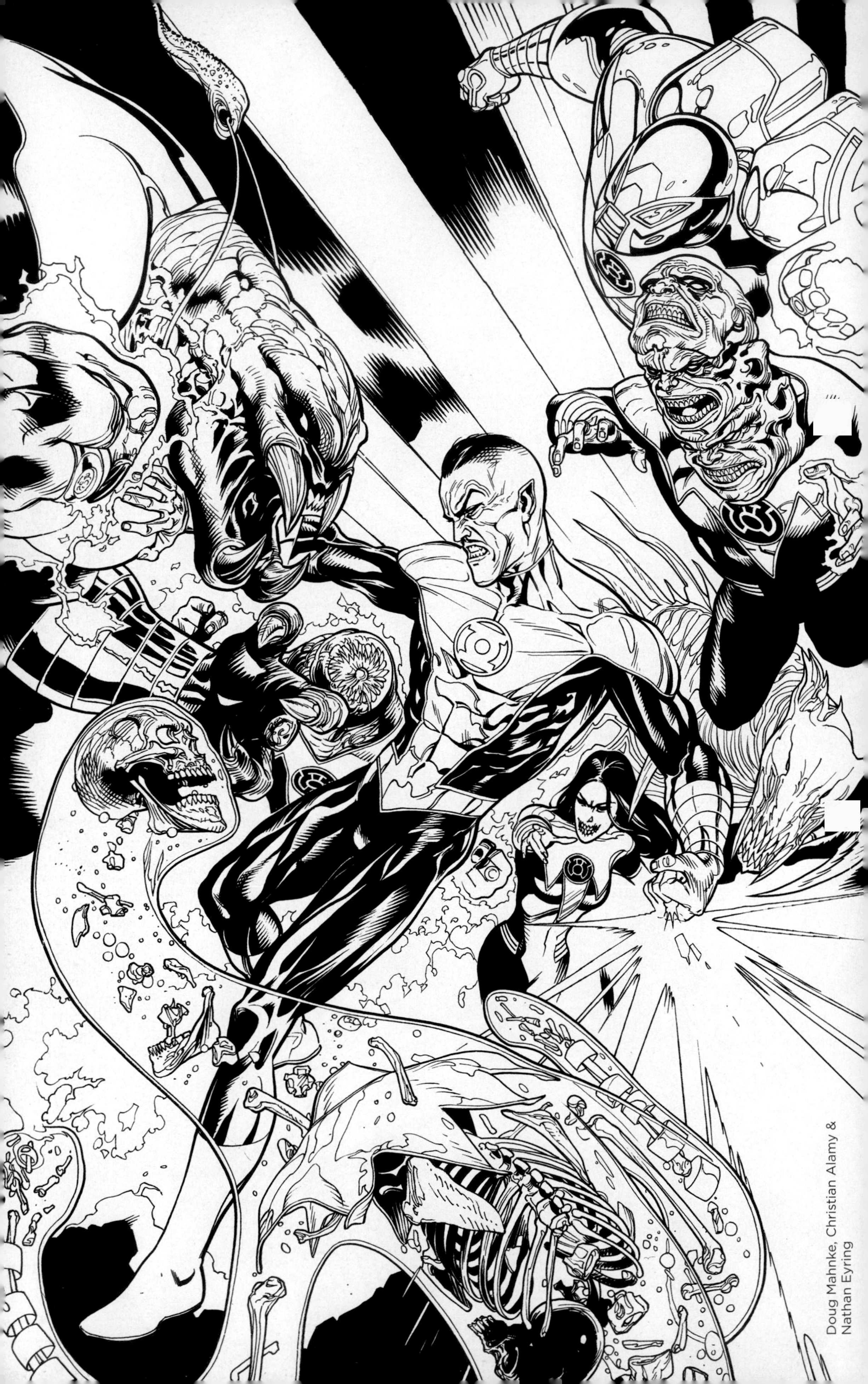

Doug Mahnke, Christian Alamy & Nathan Eyring

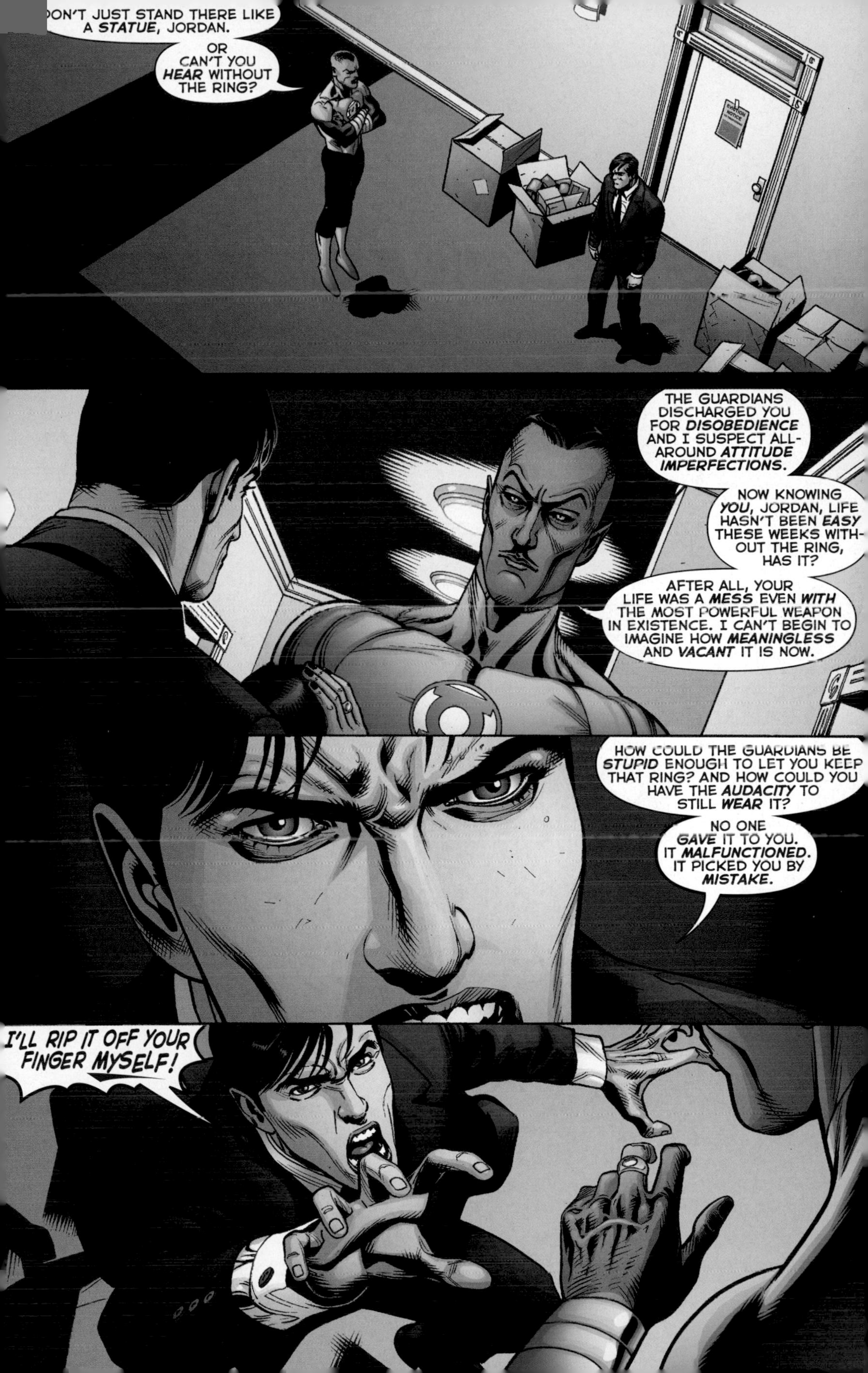
DON'T JUST STAND THERE LIKE A STATUE, JORDAN.
OR CAN'T YOU HEAR WITHOUT THE RING?
EVICTION NOTICE
THE GUARDIANS DISCHARGED YOU FOR DISOBEDIENCE AND I SUSPECT ALL-AROUND ATTITUDE IMPERFECTIONS.
NOW KNOWING YOU, JORDAN, LIFE HASN'T BEEN EASY THESE WEEKS WITH-OUT THE RING, HAS IT?
AFTER ALL, YOUR LIFE WAS A MESS EVEN WITH THE MOST POWERFUL WEAPON IN EXISTENCE. I CAN'T BEGIN TO IMAGINE HOW MEANINGLESS AND VACANT IT IS NOW.
HOW COULD THE GUARDIANS BE STUPID ENOUGH TO LET YOU KEEP THAT RING? AND HOW COULD YOU HAVE THE AUDACITY TO STILL WEAR IT?
NO ONE GAVE IT TO YOU. IT MALFUNCTIONED. IT PICKED YOU BY MISTAKE.
I'LL RIP IT OFF YOUR FINGER MYSELF!

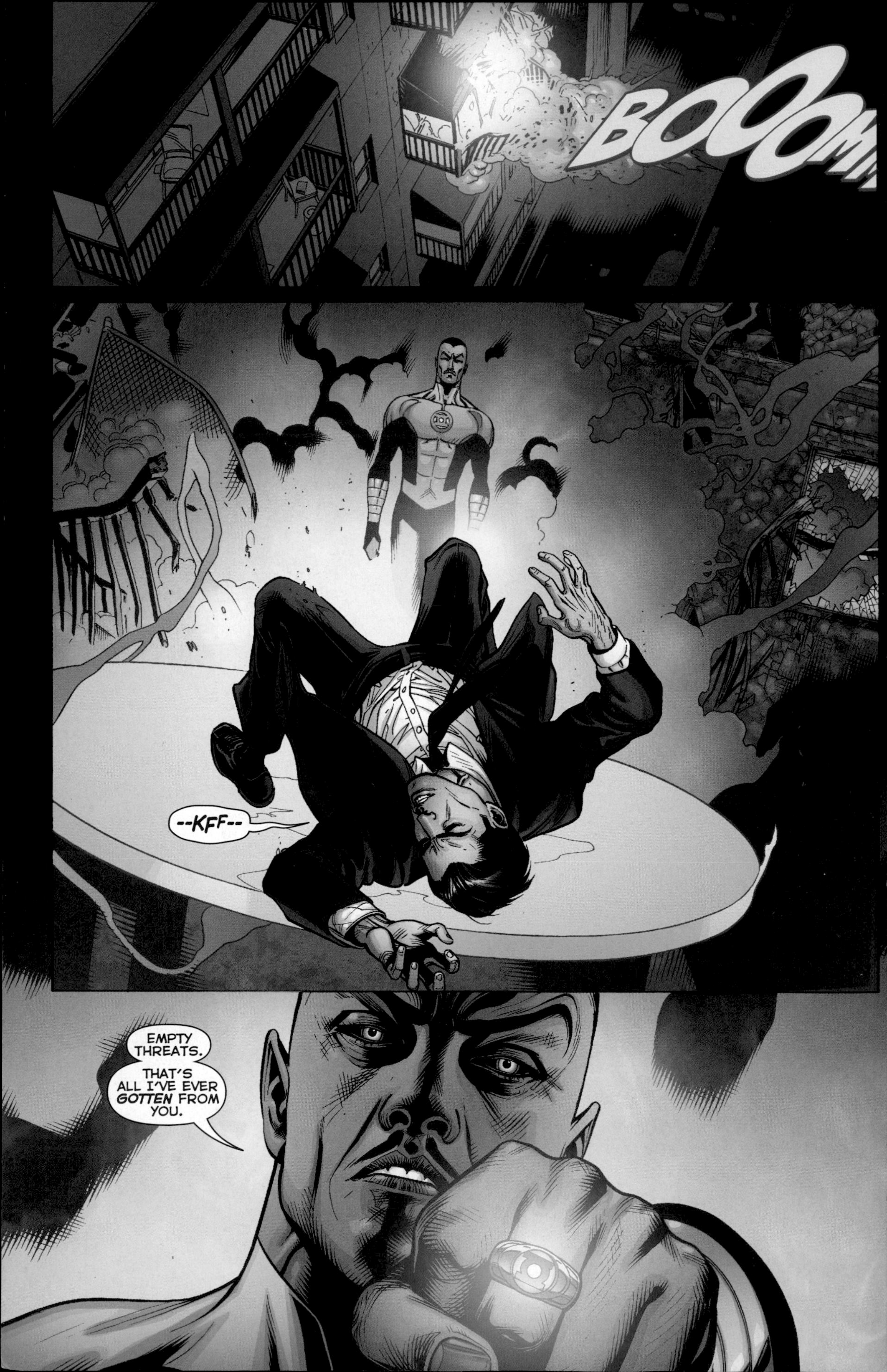
BOOOM
--KFF--
EMPTY THREATS.
THAT'S ALL I'VE EVER GOTTEN FROM YOU.

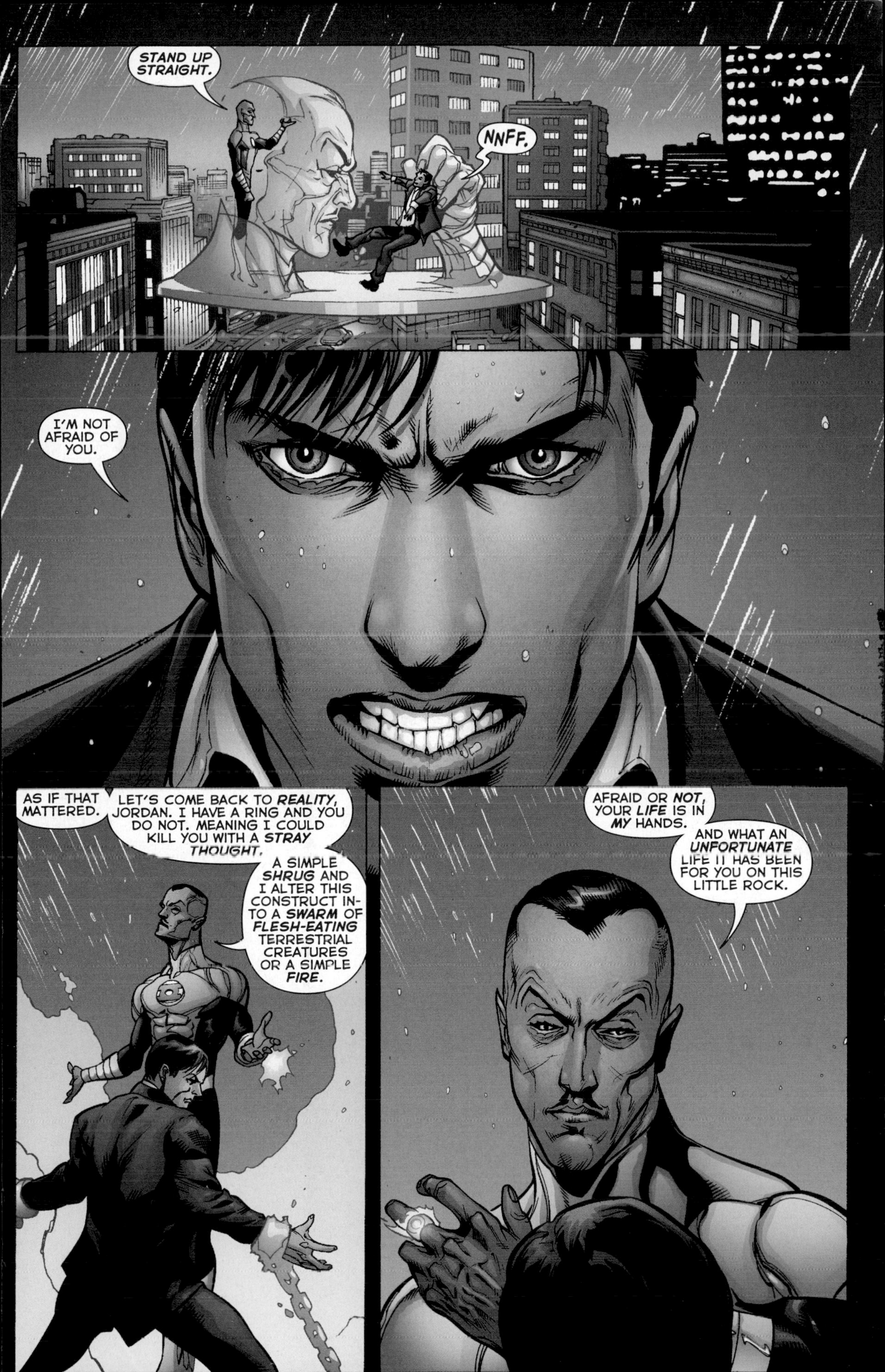
STAND UP STRAIGHT.
NNFF.
I'M NOT AFRAID OF YOU.
AS IF THAT MATTERED.
LET'S COME BACK TO REALITY, JORDAN. I HAVE A RING AND YOU DO NOT. MEANING I COULD KILL YOU WITH A STRAY THOUGHT.
A SIMPLE SHRUG AND I ALTER THIS CONSTRUCT INTO A SWARM OF FLESH-EATING TERRESTRIAL CREATURES OR A SIMPLE FIRE.
AFRAID OR NOT, YOUR LIFE IS IN MY HANDS.
AND WHAT AN UNFORTUNATE LIFE IT HAS BEEN FOR YOU ON THIS LITTLE ROCK.

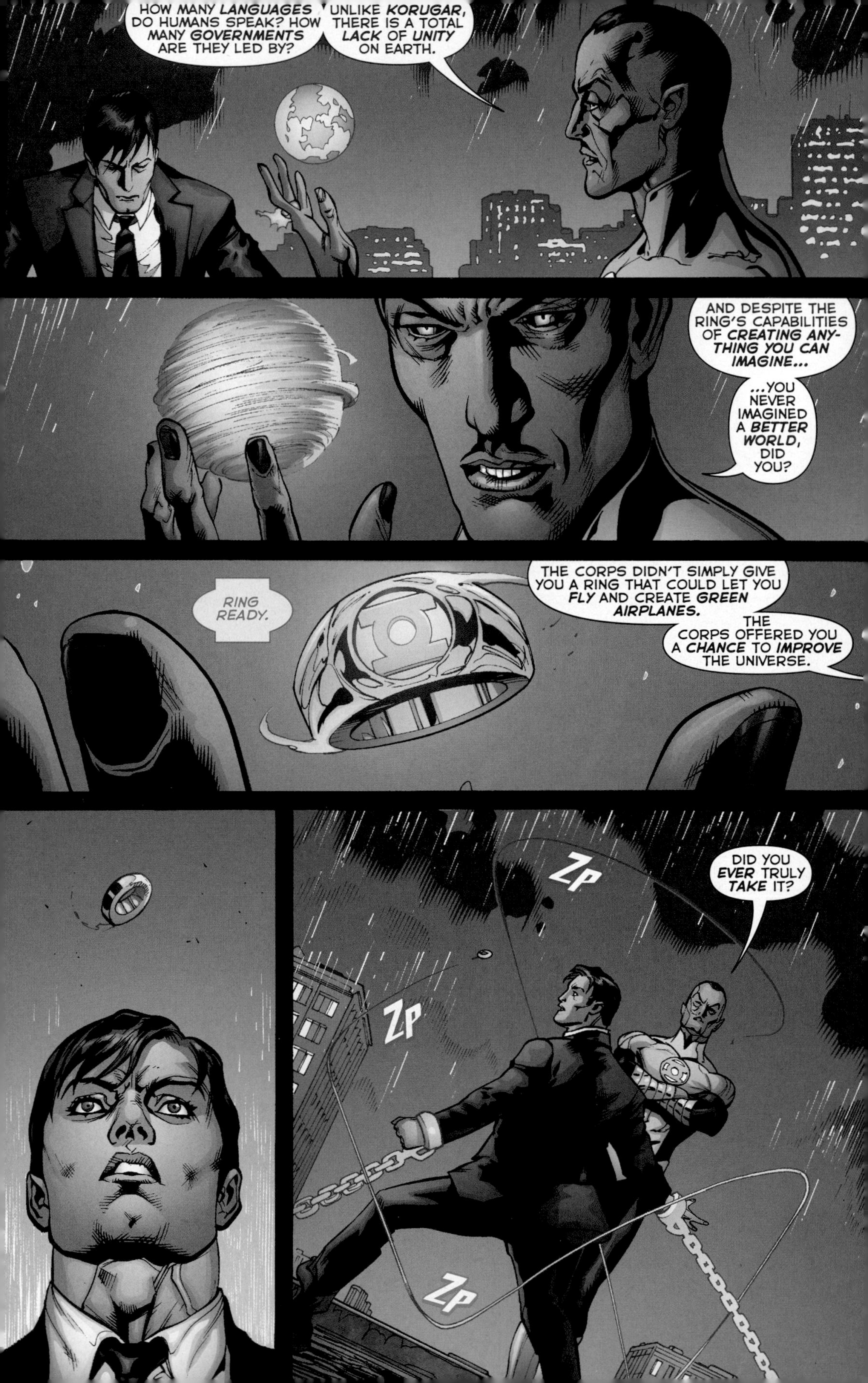
HOW MANY LANGUAGES DO HUMANS SPEAK? HOW MANY GOVERNMENTS ARE THEY LED BY?
UNLIKE KORUGAR, THERE IS A TOTAL LACK OF UNITY ON EARTH.
AND DESPITE THE RING'S CAPABILITIES OF CREATING ANYTHING YOU CAN IMAGINE...
...YOU NEVER IMAGINED A BETTER WORLD, DID YOU?
RING READY.
THE CORPS DIDN'T SIMPLY GIVE YOU A RING THAT COULD LET YOU FLY AND CREATE GREEN AIRPLANES.
THE CORPS OFFERED YOU A CHANCE TO IMPROVE THE UNIVERSE.
ZP
DID YOU EVER TRULY TAKE IT?
ZP
ZP

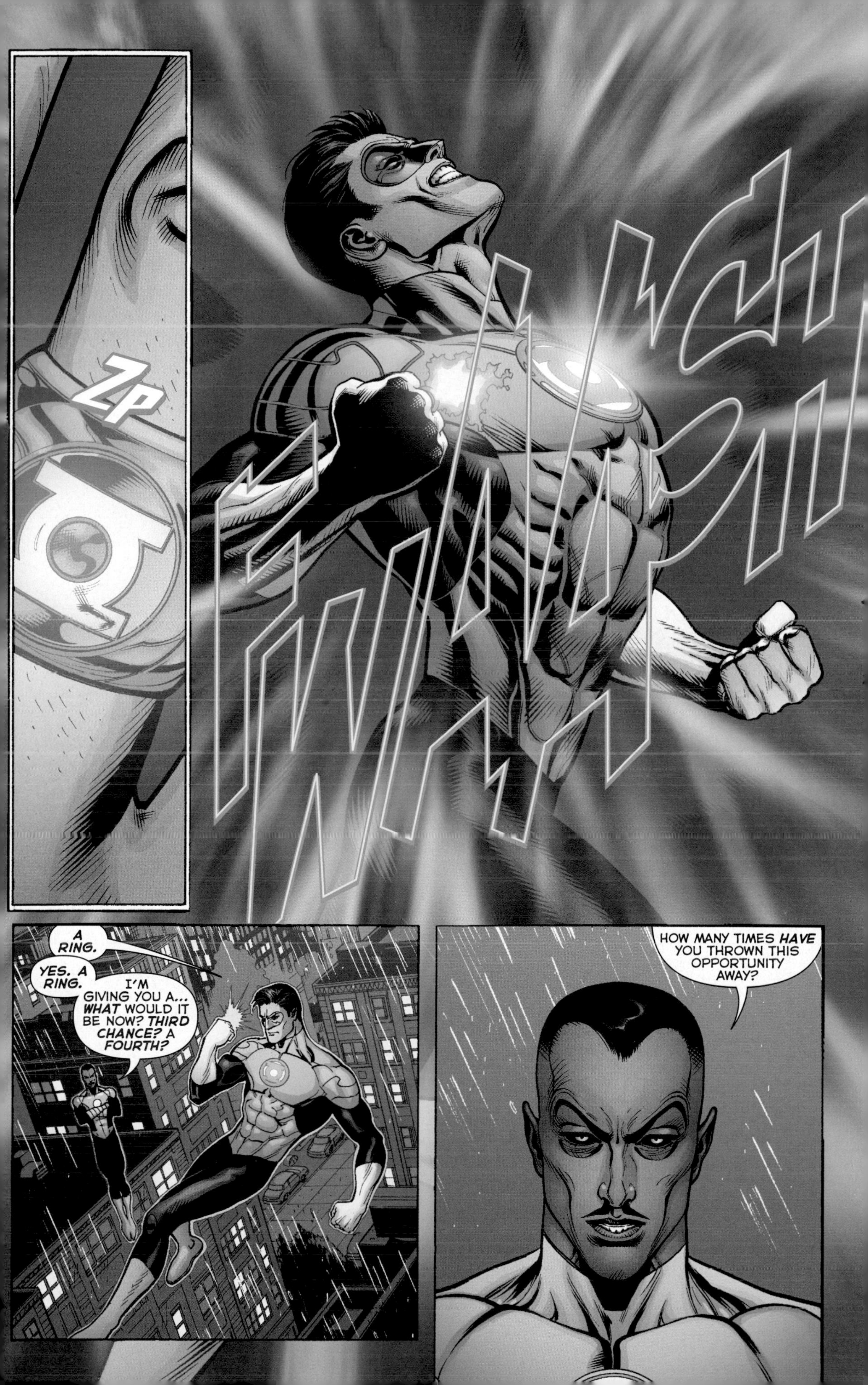

ZP
A RING.
YES. A RING.
I'M GIVING YOU A... WHAT WOULD IT BE NOW? THIRD CHANCE? A FOURTH?
HOW MANY TIMES HAVE YOU THROWN THIS OPPORTUNITY AWAY?

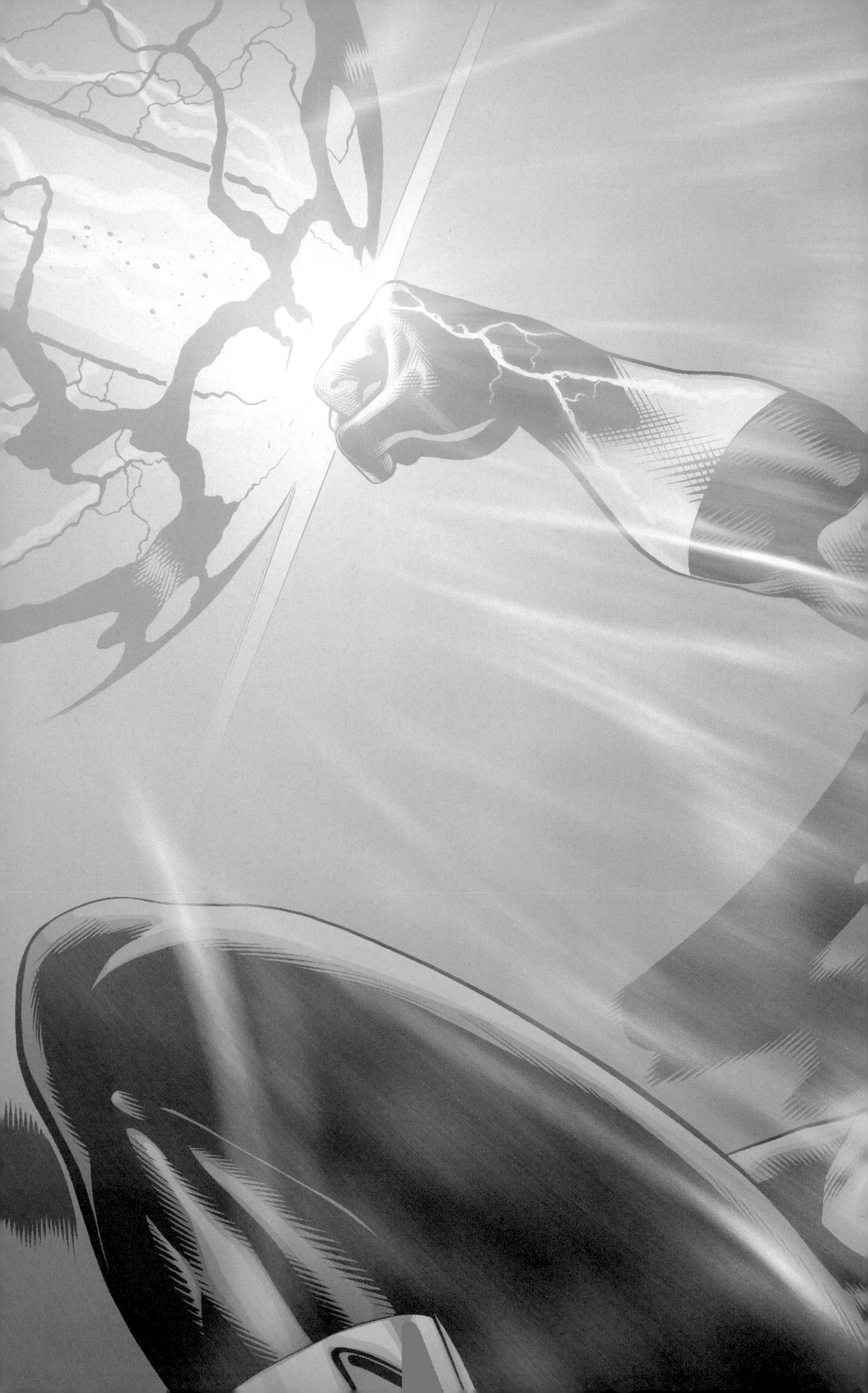

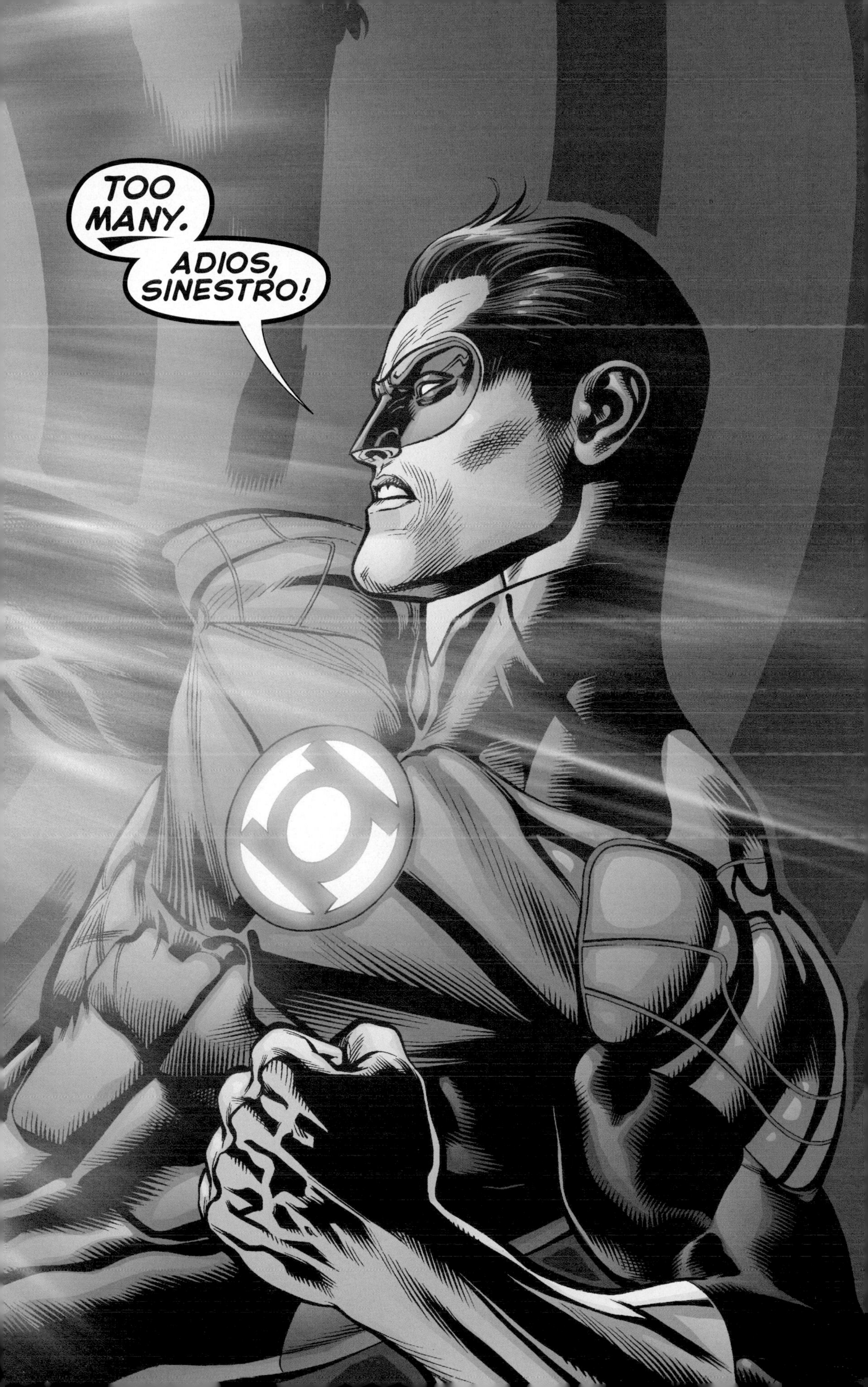
TOO MANY.
ADIOS, SINESTRO!

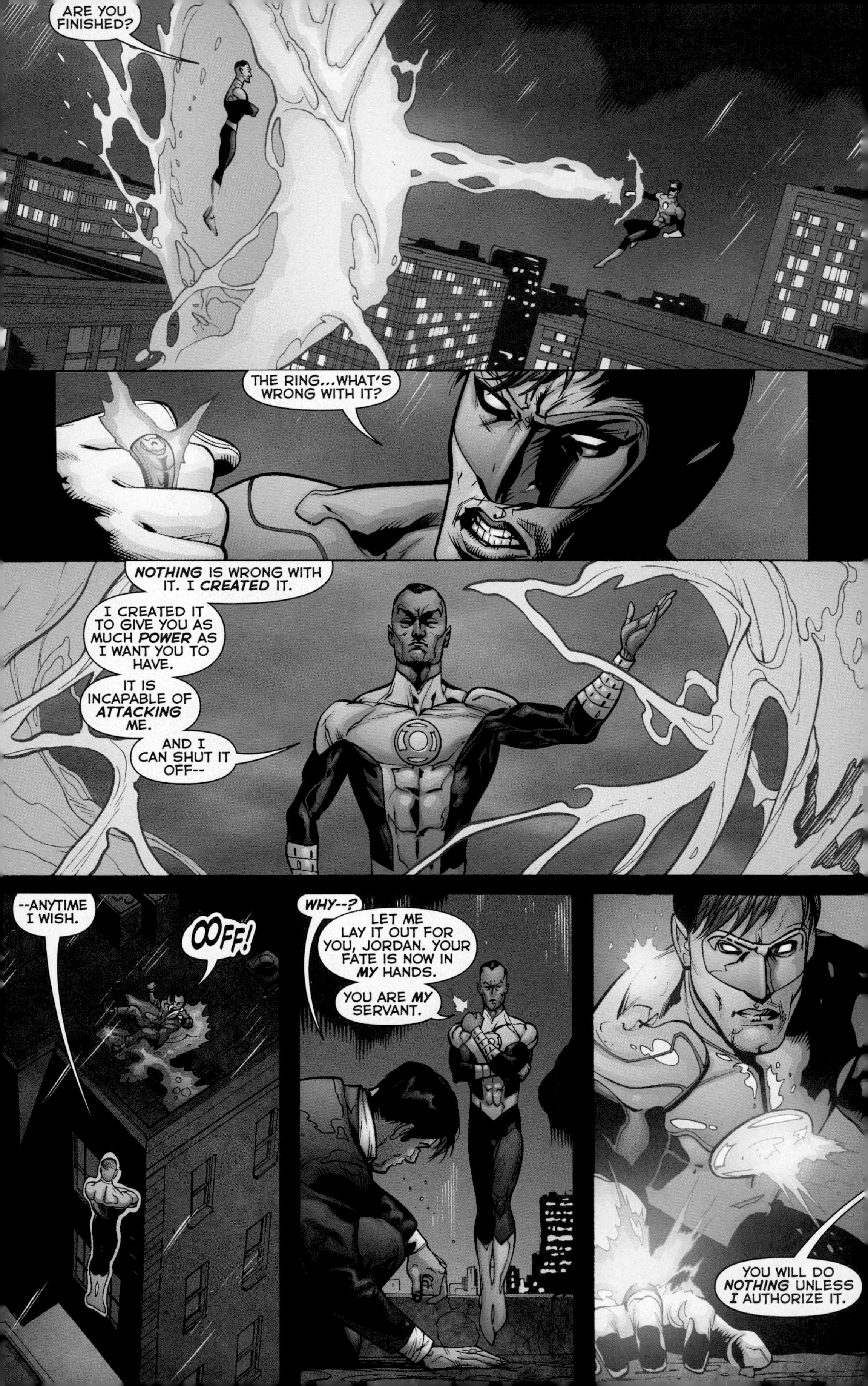
ARE YOU FINISHED?
THE RING...WHAT'S WRONG WITH IT?
NOTHING IS WRONG WITH IT. I *CREATED* IT.
I CREATED IT TO GIVE YOU AS MUCH *POWER* AS I WANT YOU TO HAVE.
IT IS INCAPABLE OF *ATTACKING* ME.
AND I CAN SHUT IT OFF--
--ANYTIME I WISH.
OOFF!
WHY--?
LET ME LAY IT OUT FOR YOU, JORDAN. YOUR FATE IS NOW IN *MY* HANDS.
YOU ARE *MY* SERVANT.
YOU WILL DO *NOTHING* UNLESS *I* AUTHORIZE IT.

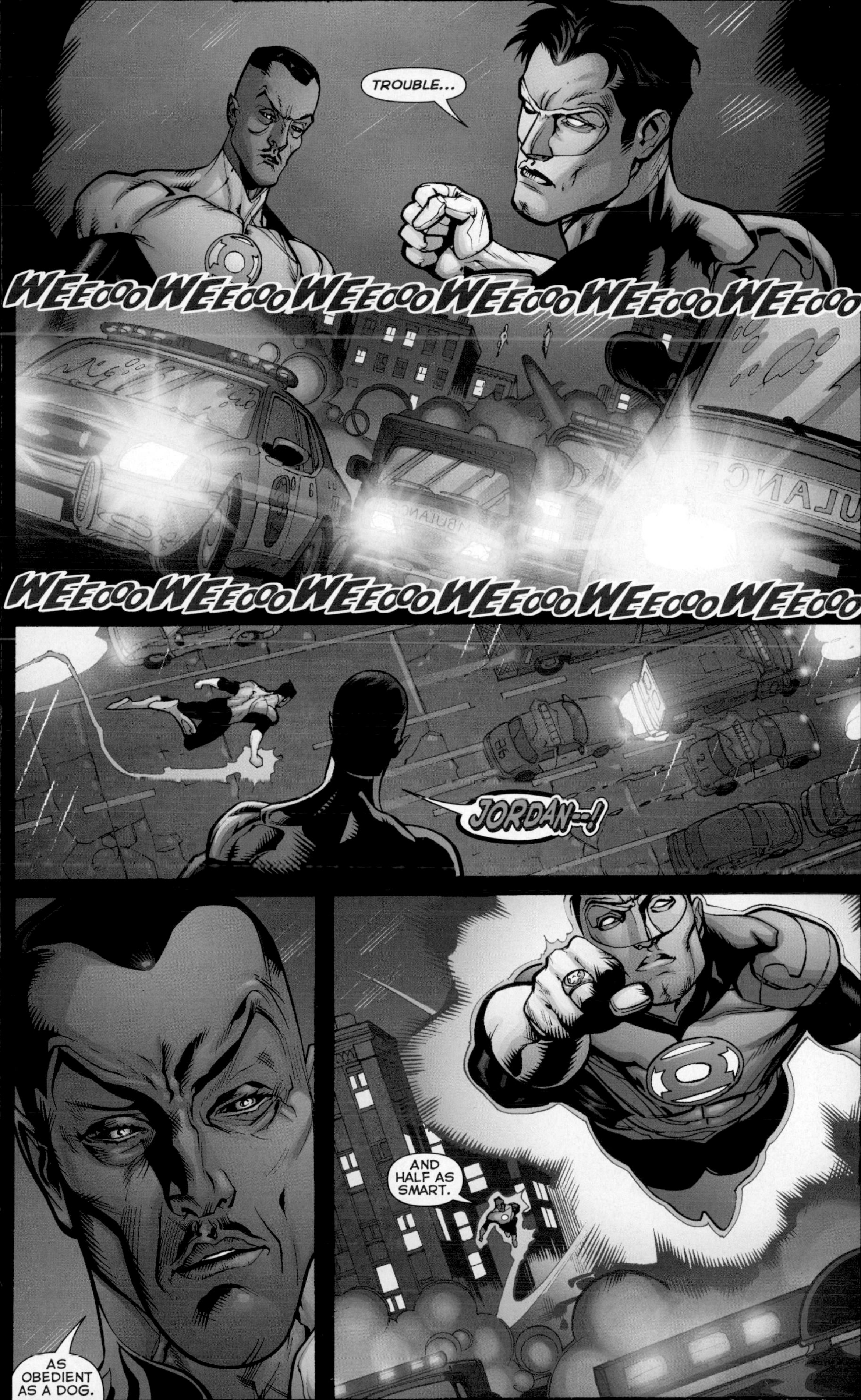
TROUBLE...
WEEOOO WEEOOO WEEOOO WEEOOO WEEOOO WEEOOO
WEEOOO WEEOOO WEEOOO WEEOOO WEEOOO WEEOOO
JORDAN--!
AS OBEDIENT AS A DOG.
AND HALF AS SMART.

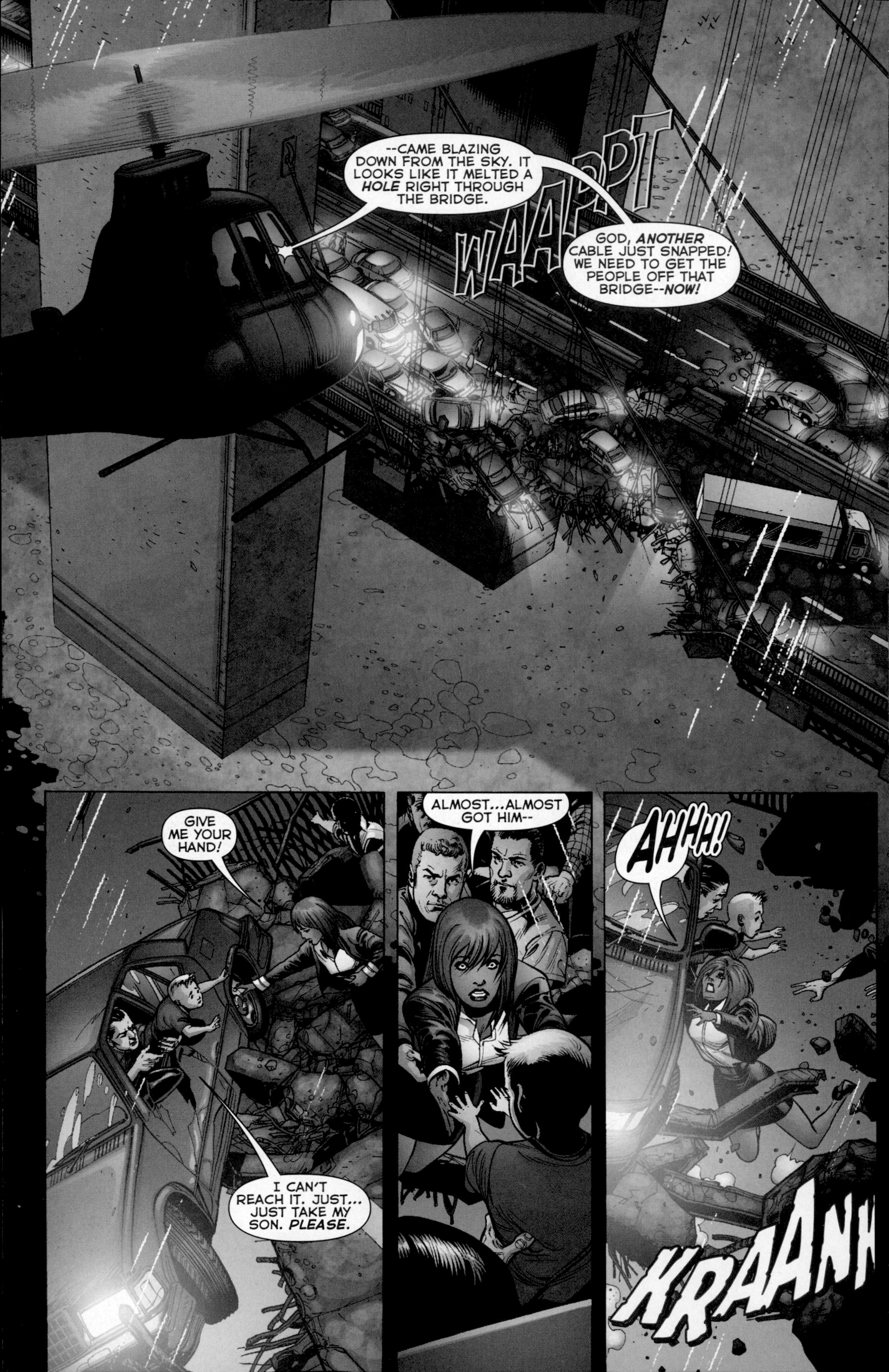
--CAME BLAZING DOWN FROM THE SKY. IT LOOKS LIKE IT MELTED A *HOLE* RIGHT THROUGH THE BRIDGE.
WAAAPT
GOD, ***ANOTHER*** CABLE JUST SNAPPED! WE NEED TO GET THE PEOPLE OFF THAT BRIDGE--***NOW!***
GIVE ME YOUR HAND!
I CAN'T REACH IT. JUST... JUST TAKE MY SON. ***PLEASE.***
ALMOST...ALMOST GOT HIM--
AHHH!
KRAANK

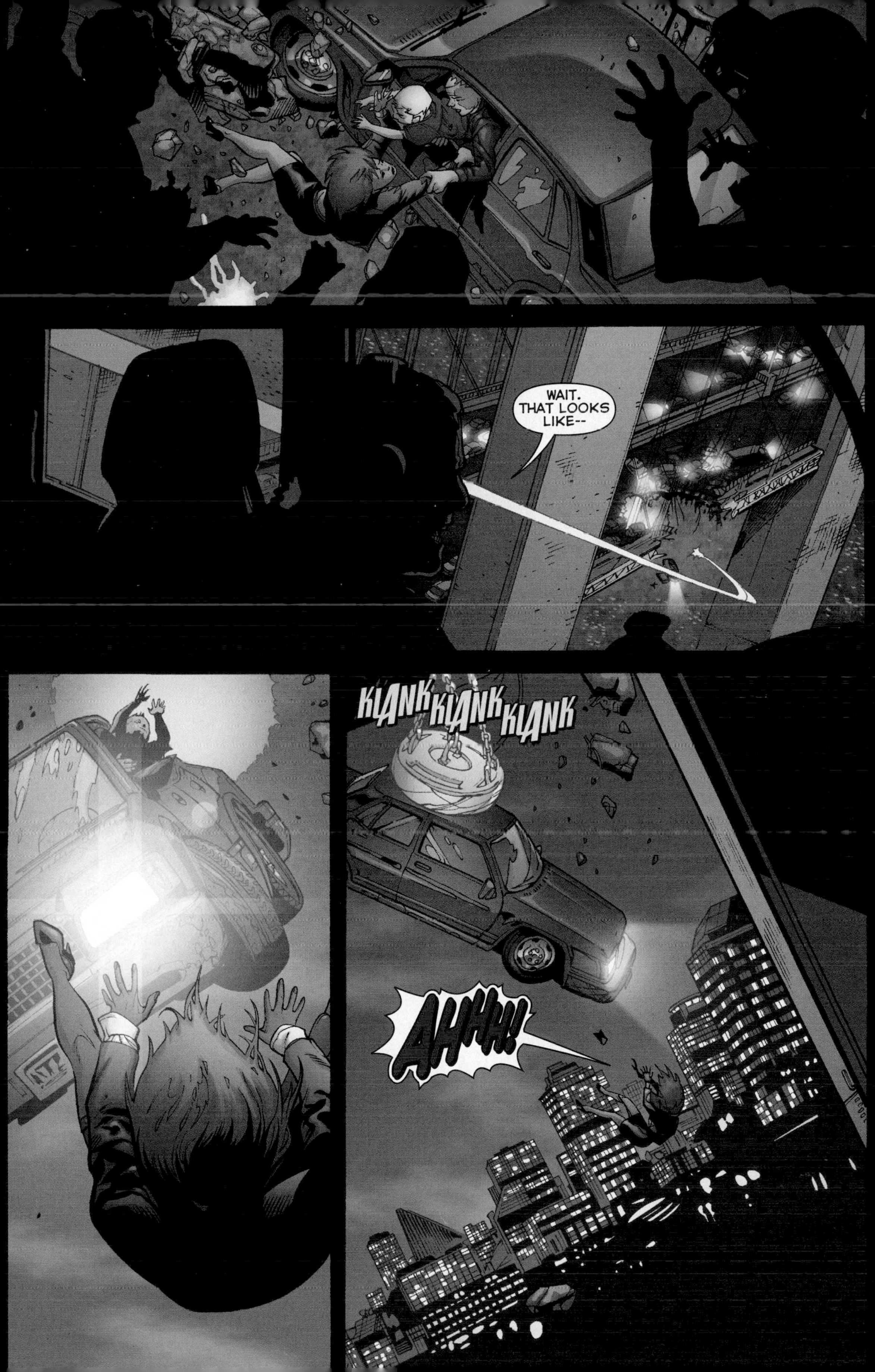
WAIT. THAT LOOKS LIKE--
KLANK KLANK KLANK
AHHH!

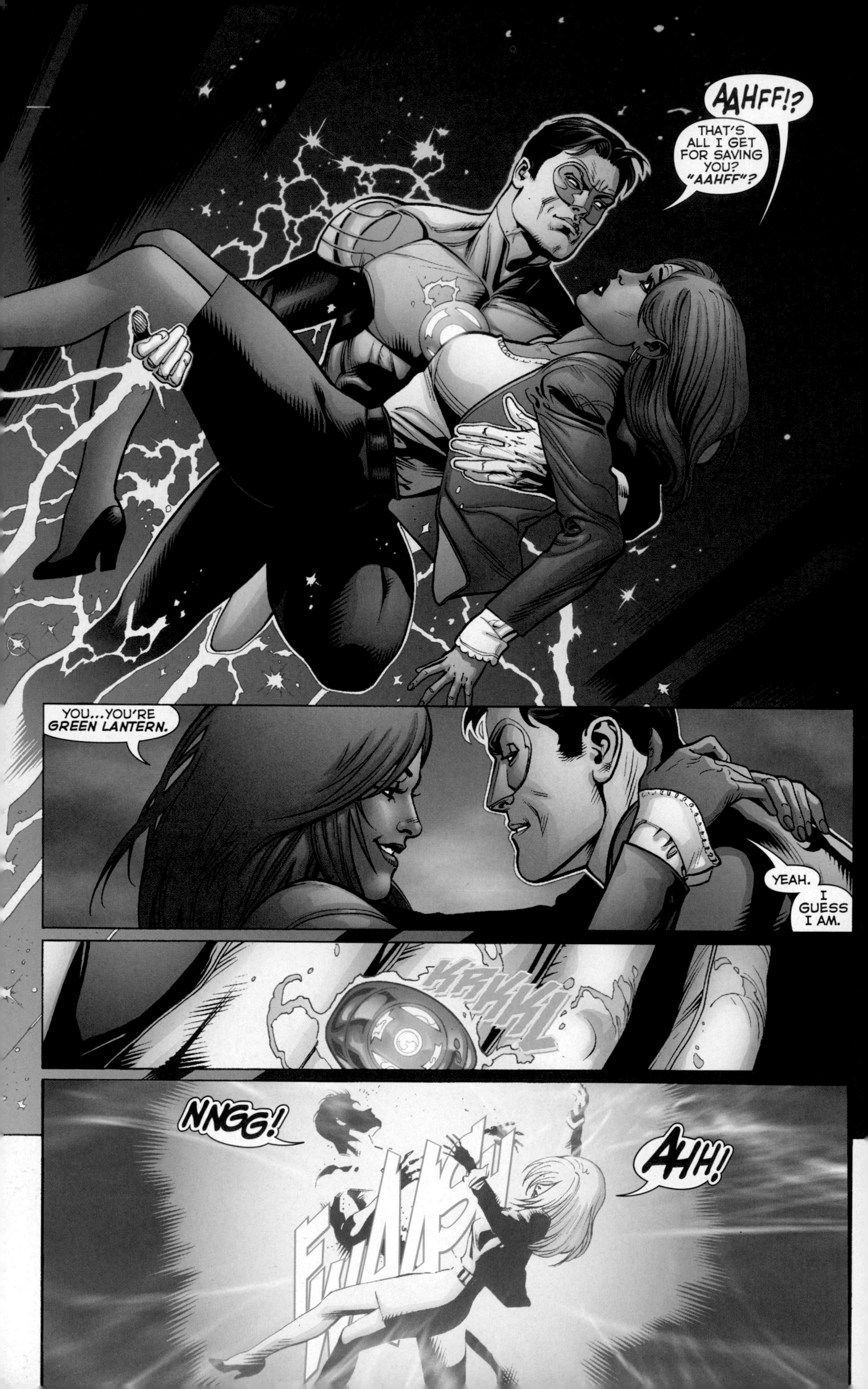
AAHFF!?
THAT'S ALL I GET FOR SAVING YOU? "AAHFF"?
YOU...YOU'RE GREEN LANTERN.
YEAH. I GUESS I AM.
KRKKL
NNGG!
AHH!
FZAAK

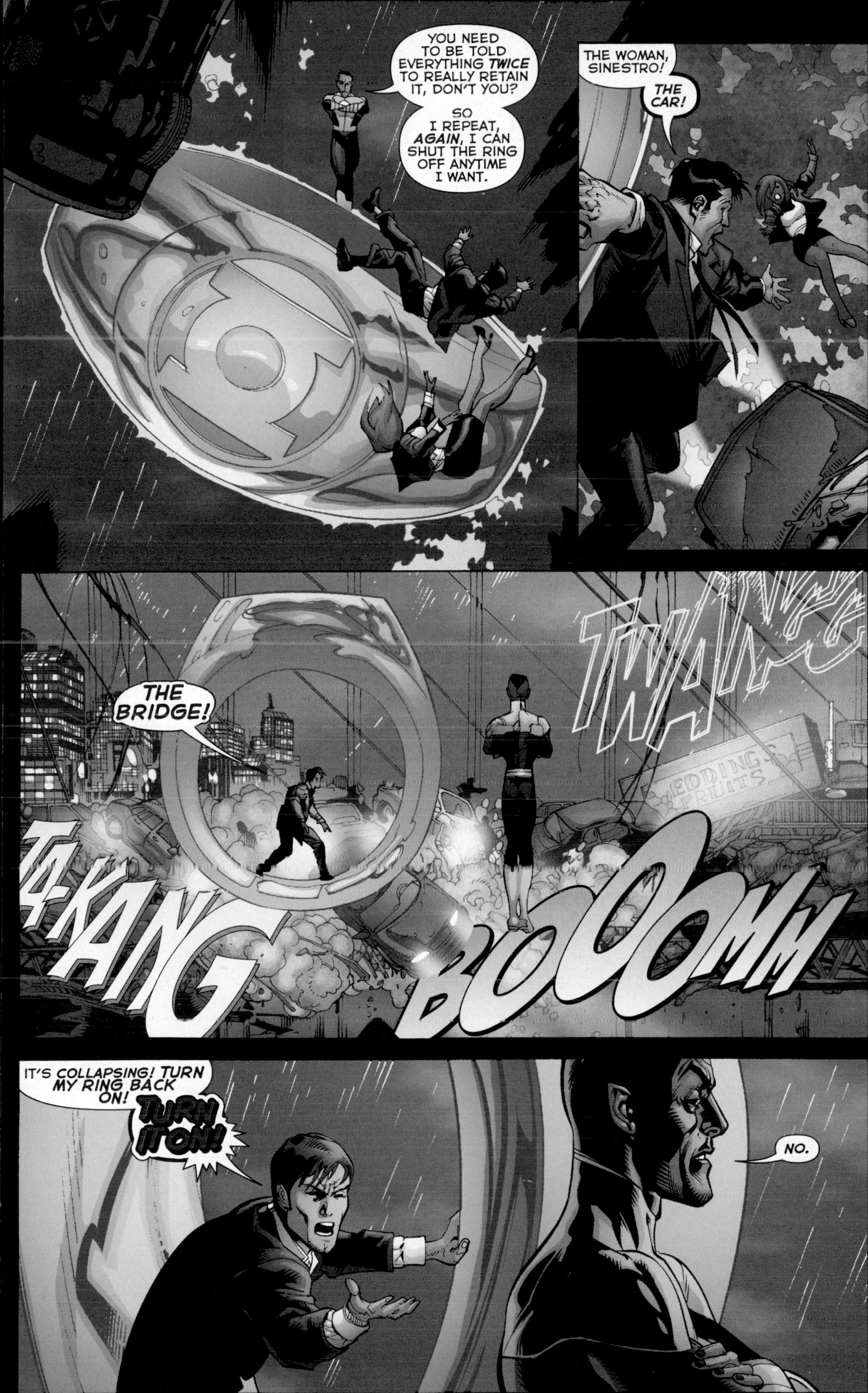
YOU NEED TO BE TOLD EVERYTHING *TWICE* TO REALLY RETAIN IT, DON'T YOU?
SO I REPEAT, *AGAIN*, I CAN SHUT THE RING OFF ANYTIME I WANT.
THE WOMAN, SINESTRO!
THE CAR!
THE BRIDGE!
TWANG
TA-KANG
BOOOOMM
EDDING FRUITS
IT'S COLLAPSING! TURN MY RING BACK ON!
TURN IT ON!!
NO.

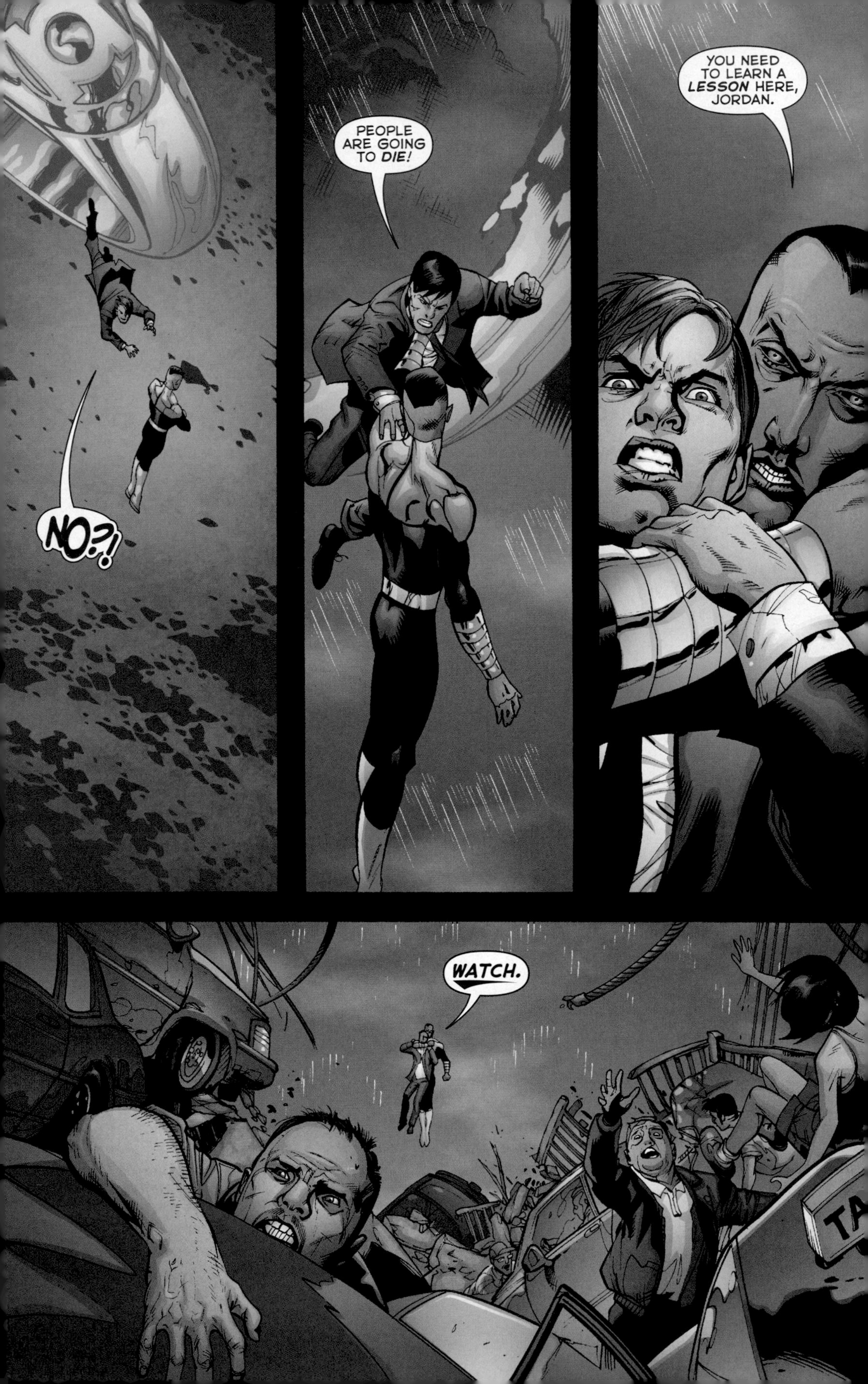
NO?!
PEOPLE ARE GOING TO DIE!
YOU NEED TO LEARN A LESSON HERE, JORDAN.
WATCH.

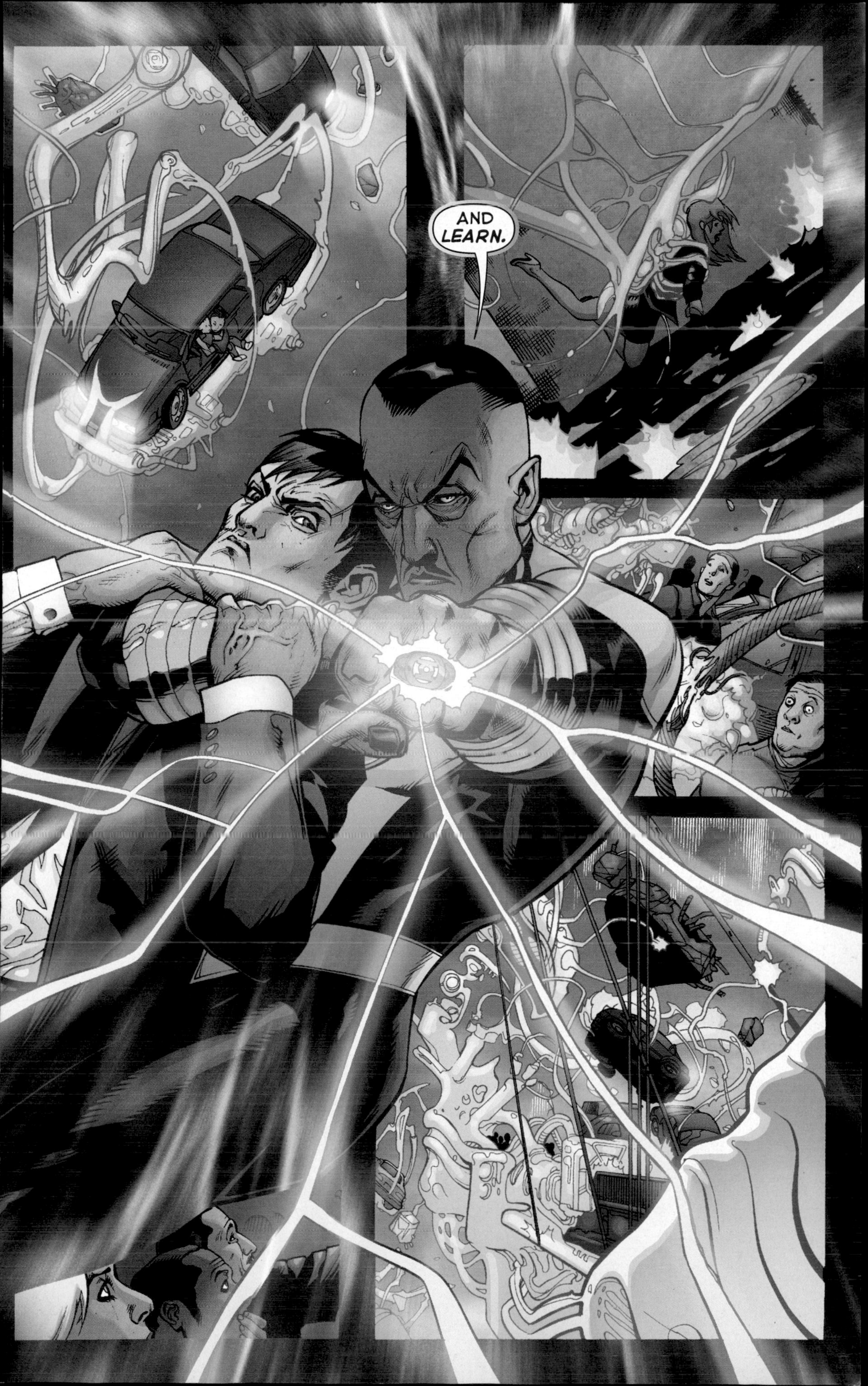
AND LEARN.

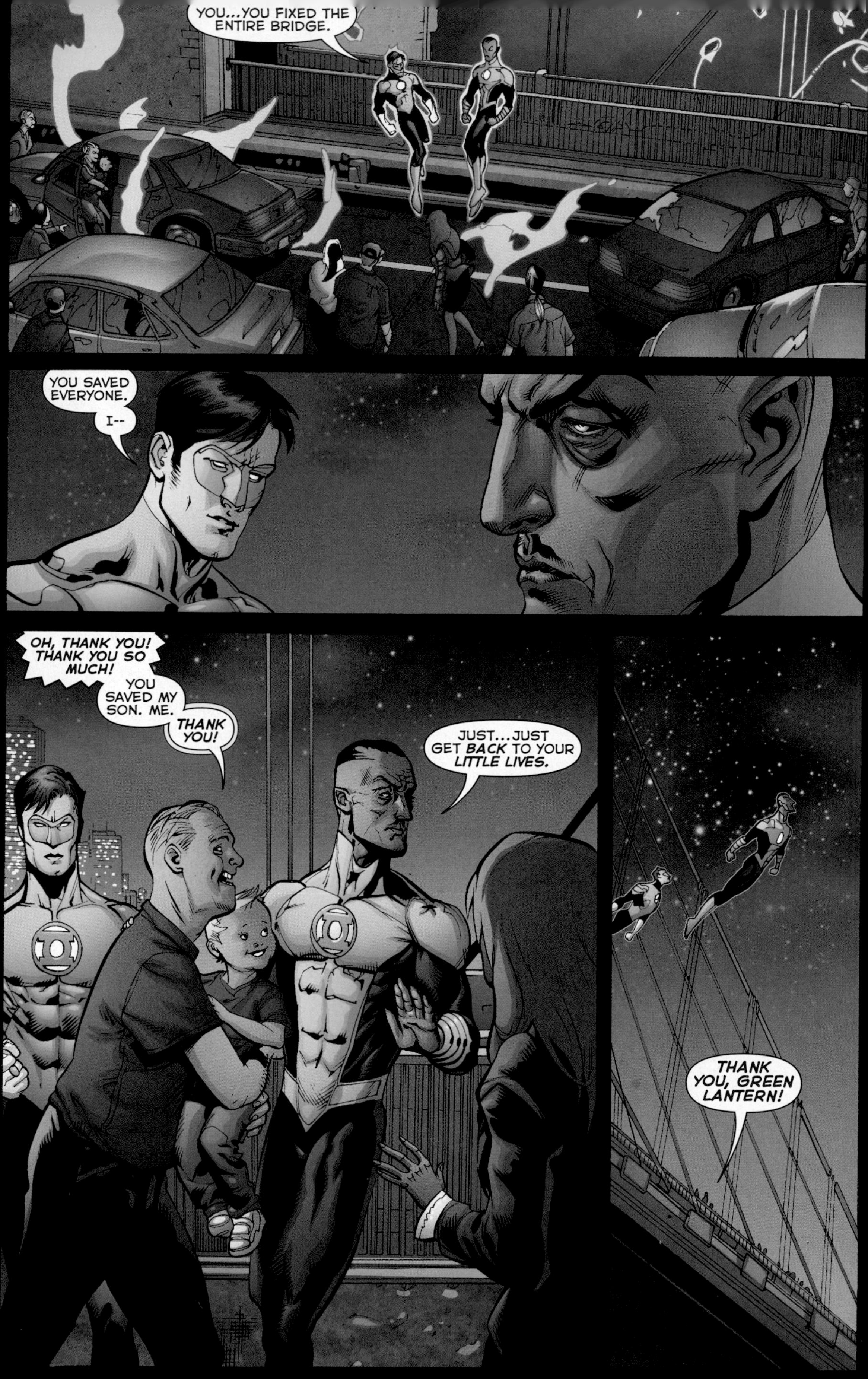
YOU...YOU FIXED THE ENTIRE BRIDGE.
YOU SAVED EVERYONE.
I--
OH, THANK YOU! THANK YOU SO MUCH!
YOU SAVED MY SON. ME.
THANK YOU!
JUST...JUST GET BACK TO YOUR LITTLE LIVES.
THANK YOU, GREEN LANTERN!

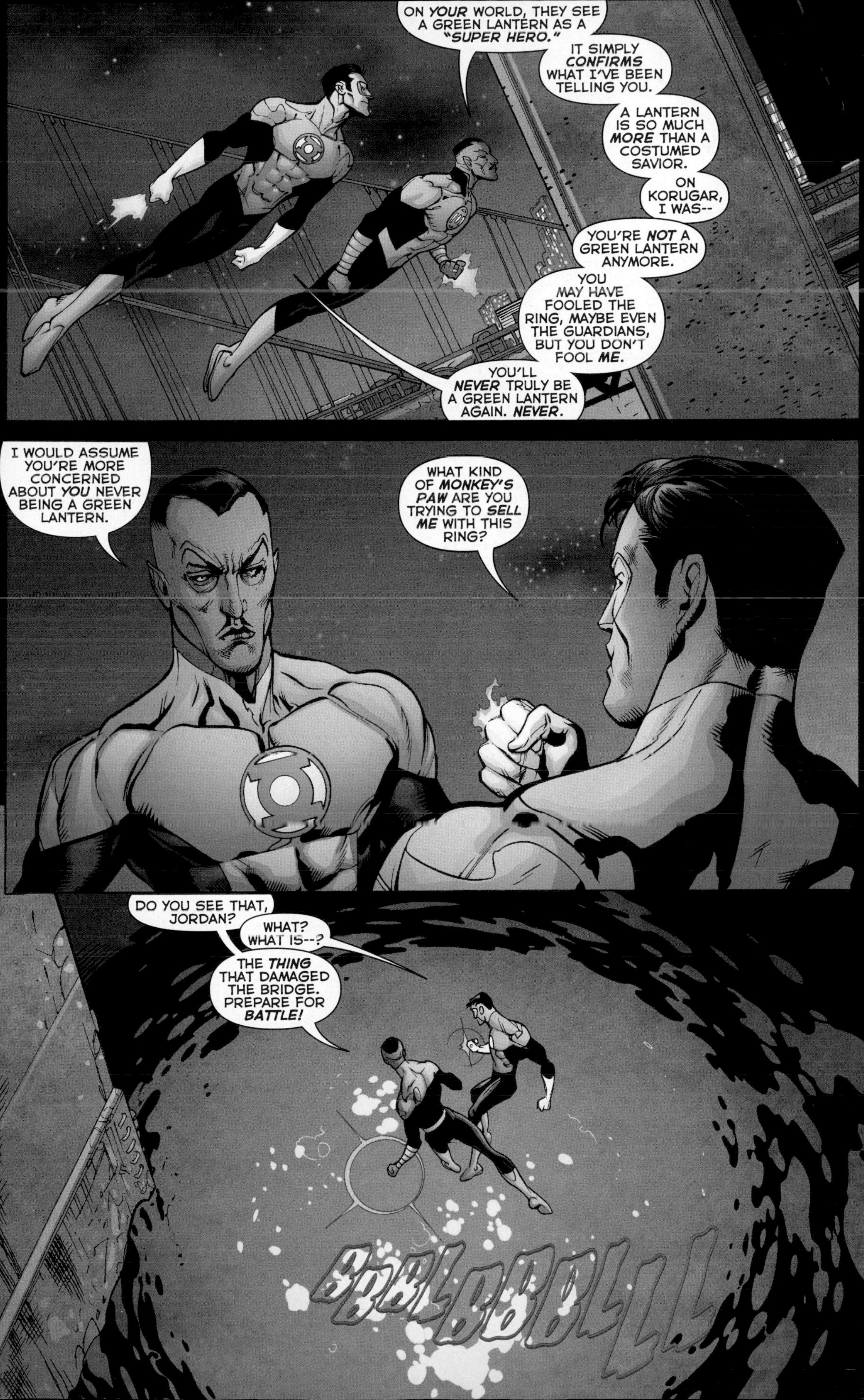
ON YOUR WORLD, THEY SEE A GREEN LANTERN AS A "SUPER HERO."
IT SIMPLY CONFIRMS WHAT I'VE BEEN TELLING YOU.
A LANTERN IS SO MUCH MORE THAN A COSTUMED SAVIOR.
ON KORUGAR, I WAS--
YOU'RE NOT A GREEN LANTERN ANYMORE.
YOU MAY HAVE FOOLED THE RING, MAYBE EVEN THE GUARDIANS, BUT YOU DON'T FOOL ME.
YOU'LL NEVER TRULY BE A GREEN LANTERN AGAIN. NEVER.
I WOULD ASSUME YOU'RE MORE CONCERNED ABOUT YOU NEVER BEING A GREEN LANTERN.
WHAT KIND OF MONKEY'S PAW ARE YOU TRYING TO SELL ME WITH THIS RING?
DO YOU SEE THAT, JORDAN?
WHAT? WHAT IS--?
THE THING THAT DAMAGED THE BRIDGE. PREPARE FOR BATTLE!
BBBLBBBLLL

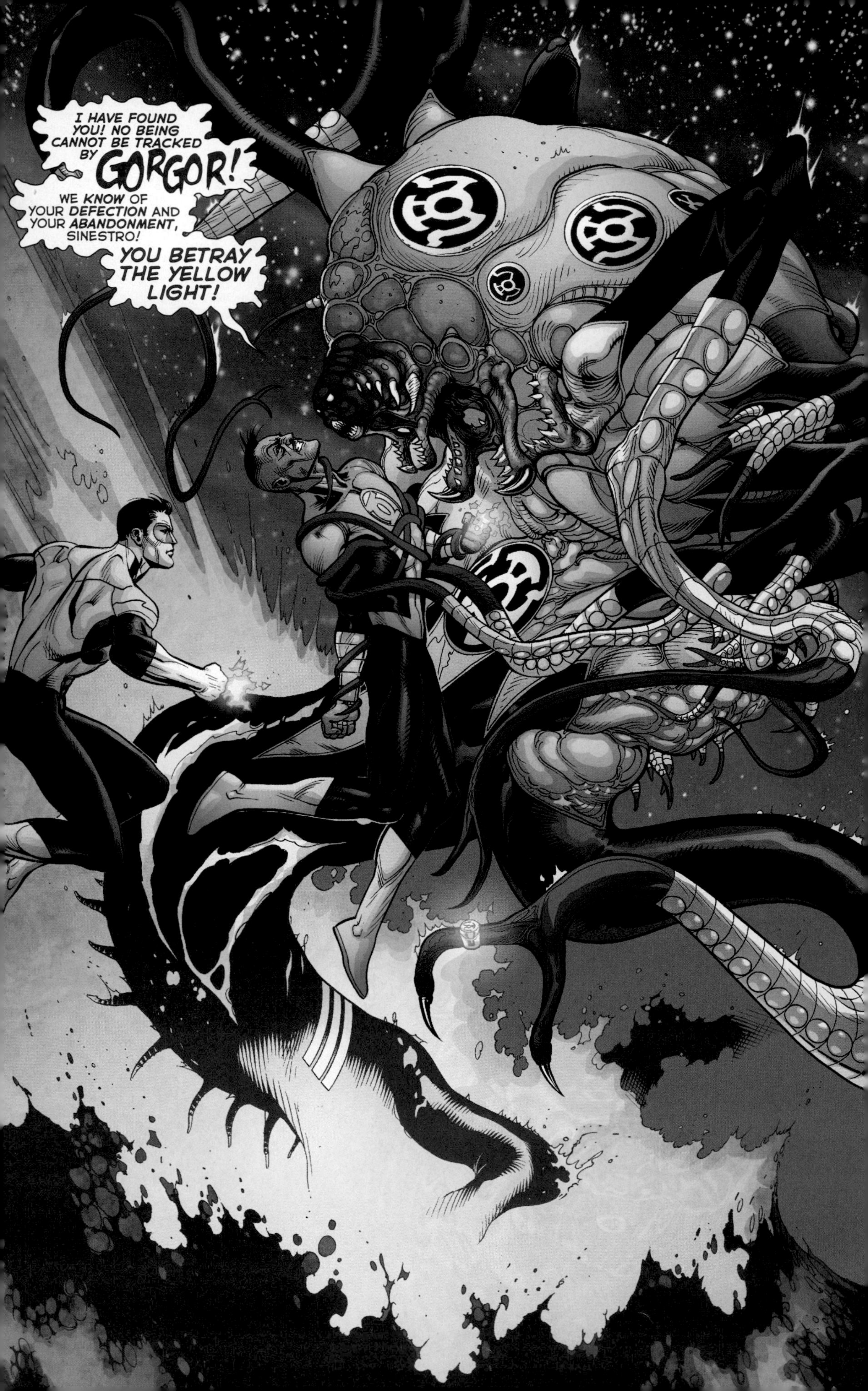
I HAVE FOUND YOU! NO BEING CANNOT BE TRACKED BY GORGOR!
WE KNOW OF YOUR DEFECTION AND YOUR ABANDONMENT, SINESTRO!
YOU BETRAY THE YELLOW LIGHT!

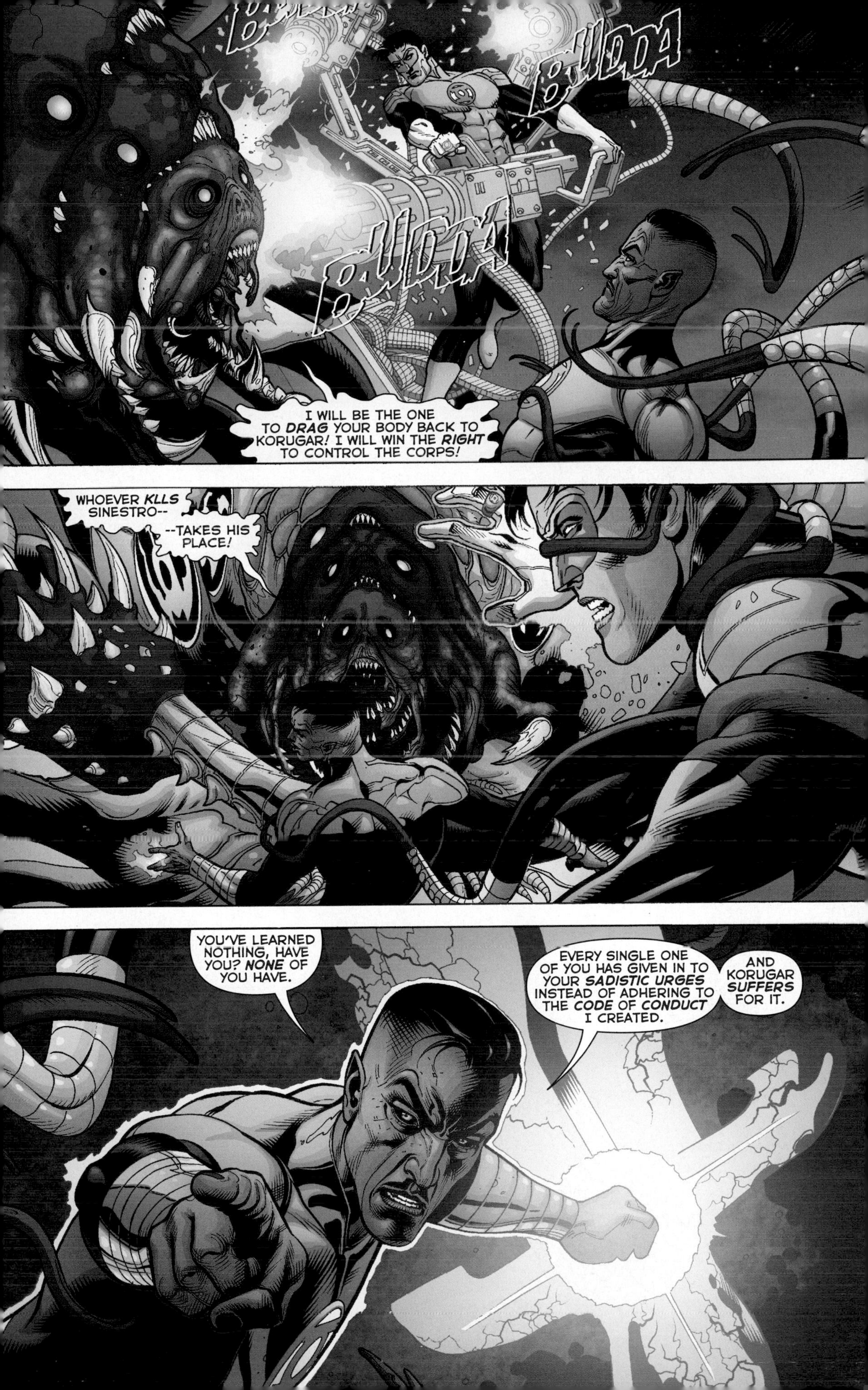
BUDDA
BUDDA
BUDDA
I WILL BE THE ONE TO DRAG YOUR BODY BACK TO KORUGAR! I WILL WIN THE RIGHT TO CONTROL THE CORPS!
WHOEVER KLLS SINESTRO--
--TAKES HIS PLACE!
YOU'VE LEARNED NOTHING, HAVE YOU? NONE OF YOU HAVE.
EVERY SINGLE ONE OF YOU HAS GIVEN IN TO YOUR SADISTIC URGES INSTEAD OF ADHERING TO THE CODE OF CONDUCT I CREATED.
AND KORUGAR SUFFERS FOR IT.

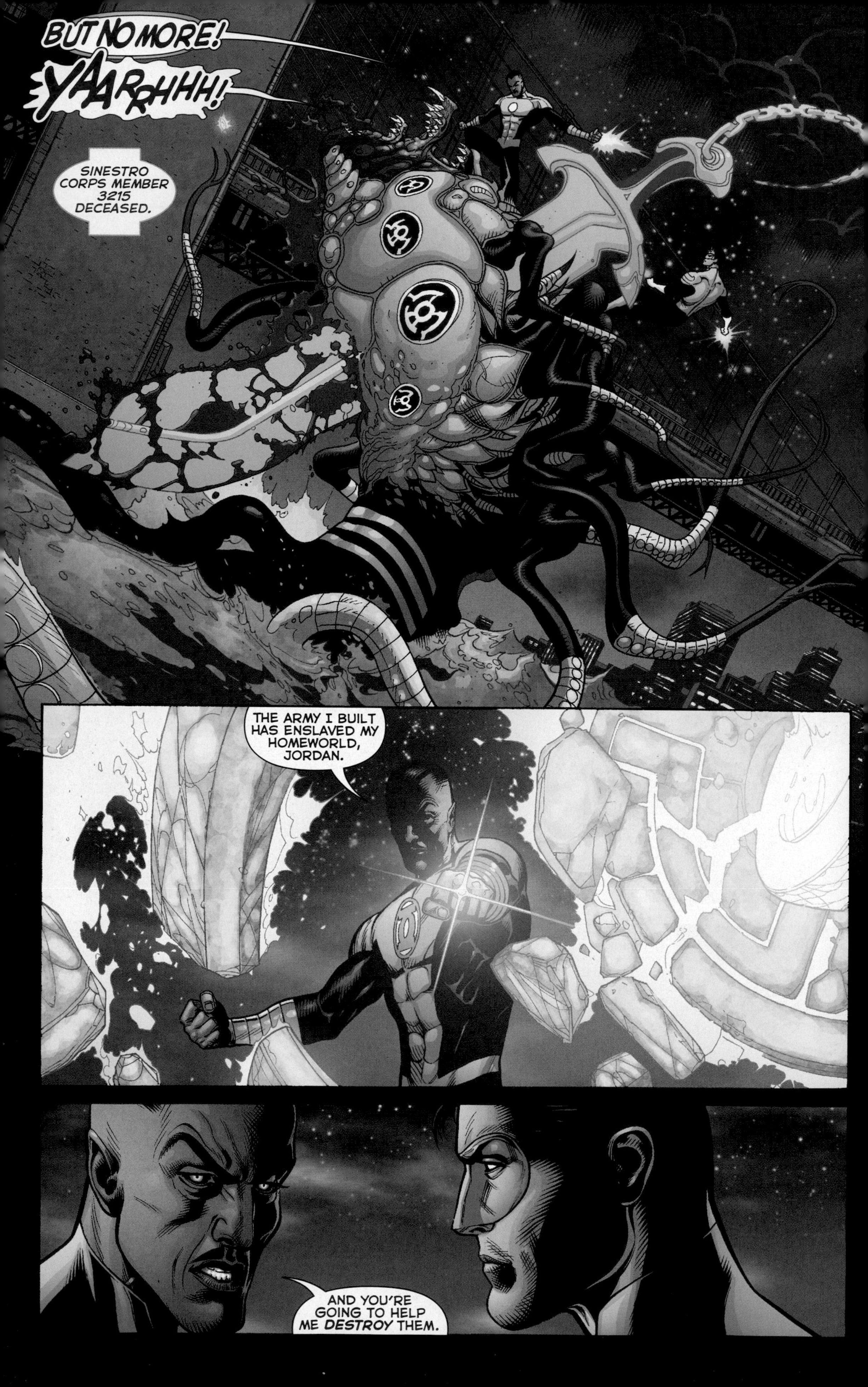
BUT NO MORE!
YAARRHHH!
SINESTRO CORPS MEMBER 3215 DECEASED.
THE ARMY I BUILT HAS ENSLAVED MY HOMEWORLD, JORDAN.
AND YOU'RE GOING TO HELP ME DESTROY THEM.

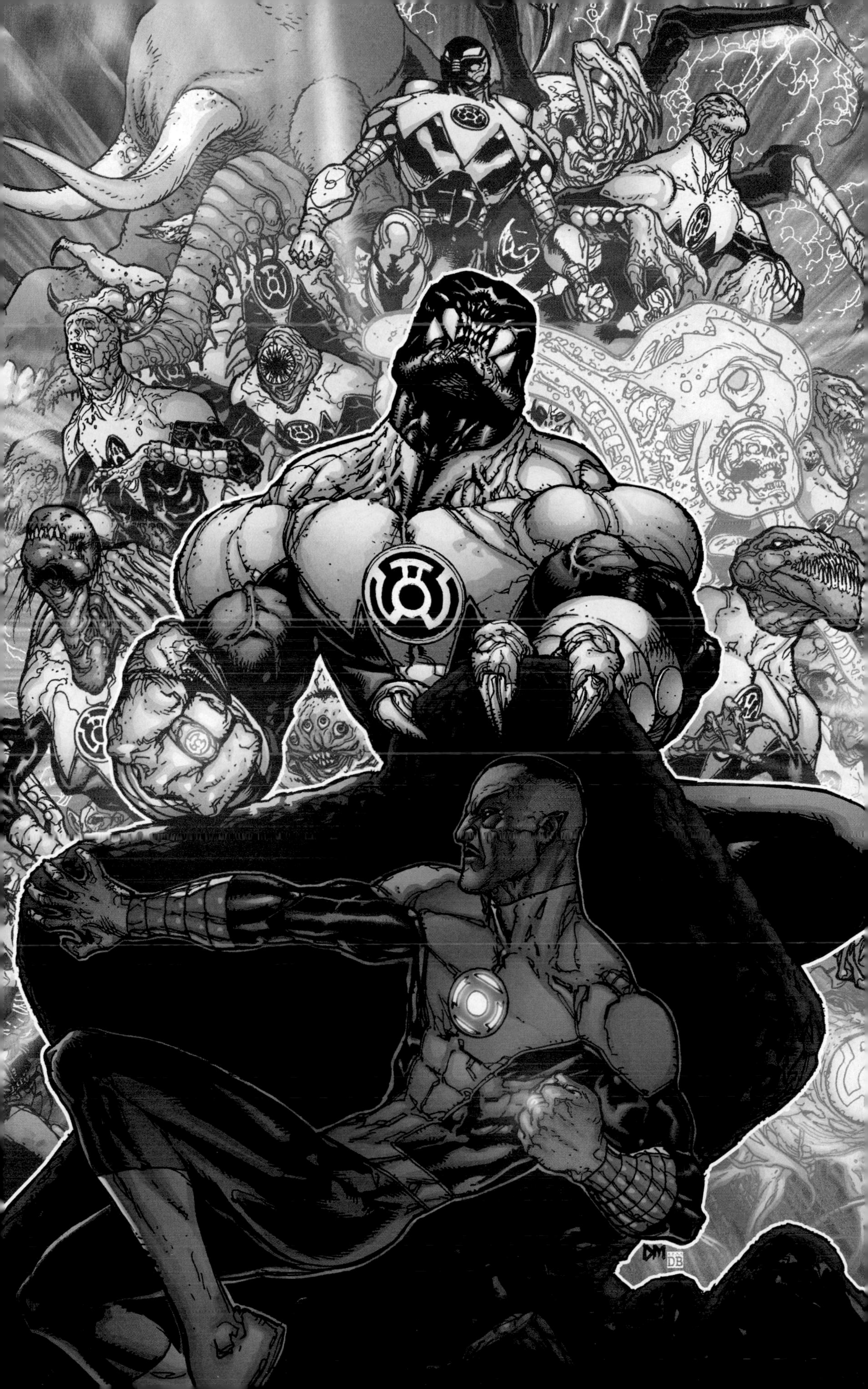

Doug Mahnke & David Baron

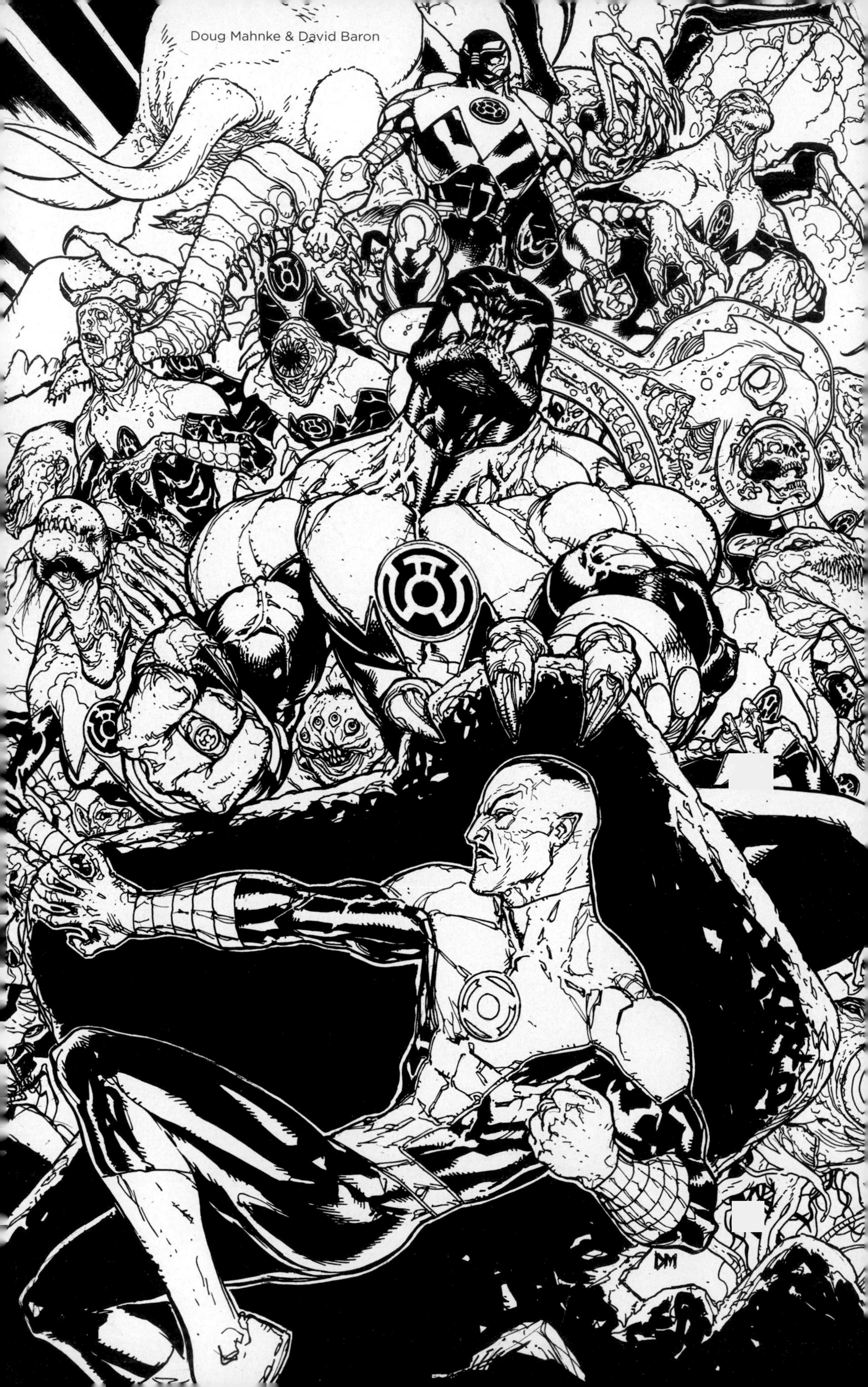

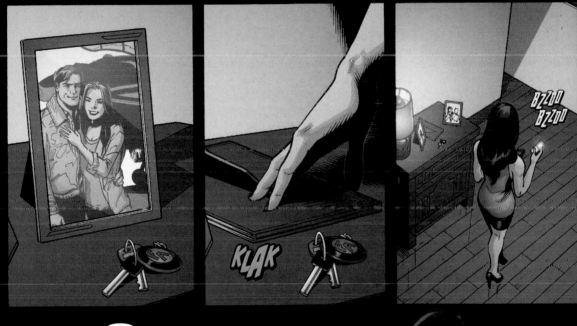

BZZOO
BZZOO

KLAK

HAL?

UH, NO, MISS FERRIS. IT'S TOM KALMAKU.

TOM? YOU SOUND WORRIED. WHAT'S WRONG? DID HAL CALL YOU ABOUT TONIGHT?

IS YOUR TV ON?

NO.

TURN IT ON. CHANNEL FOUR.

BUT--

YOU GOTTA SEE THIS!

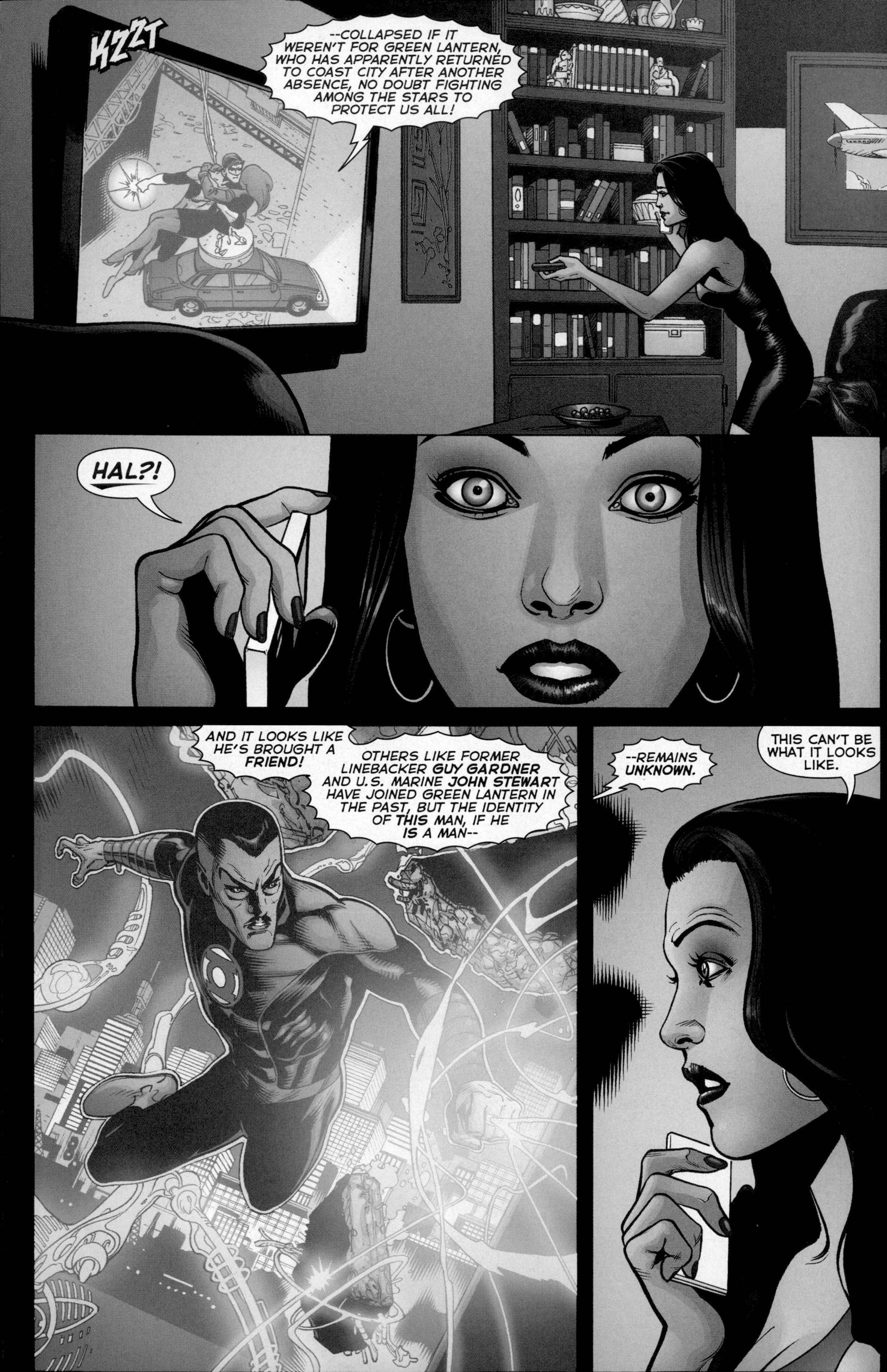
KZZT
--COLLAPSED IF IT WEREN'T FOR GREEN LANTERN, WHO HAS APPARENTLY RETURNED TO COAST CITY AFTER ANOTHER ABSENCE, NO DOUBT FIGHTING AMONG THE STARS TO PROTECT US ALL!
HAL?!
AND IT LOOKS LIKE HE'S BROUGHT A FRIEND!
OTHERS LIKE FORMER LINEBACKER GUY GARDNER AND U.S. MARINE JOHN STEWART HAVE JOINED GREEN LANTERN IN THE PAST, BUT THE IDENTITY OF THIS MAN, IF HE IS A MAN--
--REMAINS UNKNOWN.
THIS CAN'T BE WHAT IT LOOKS LIKE.

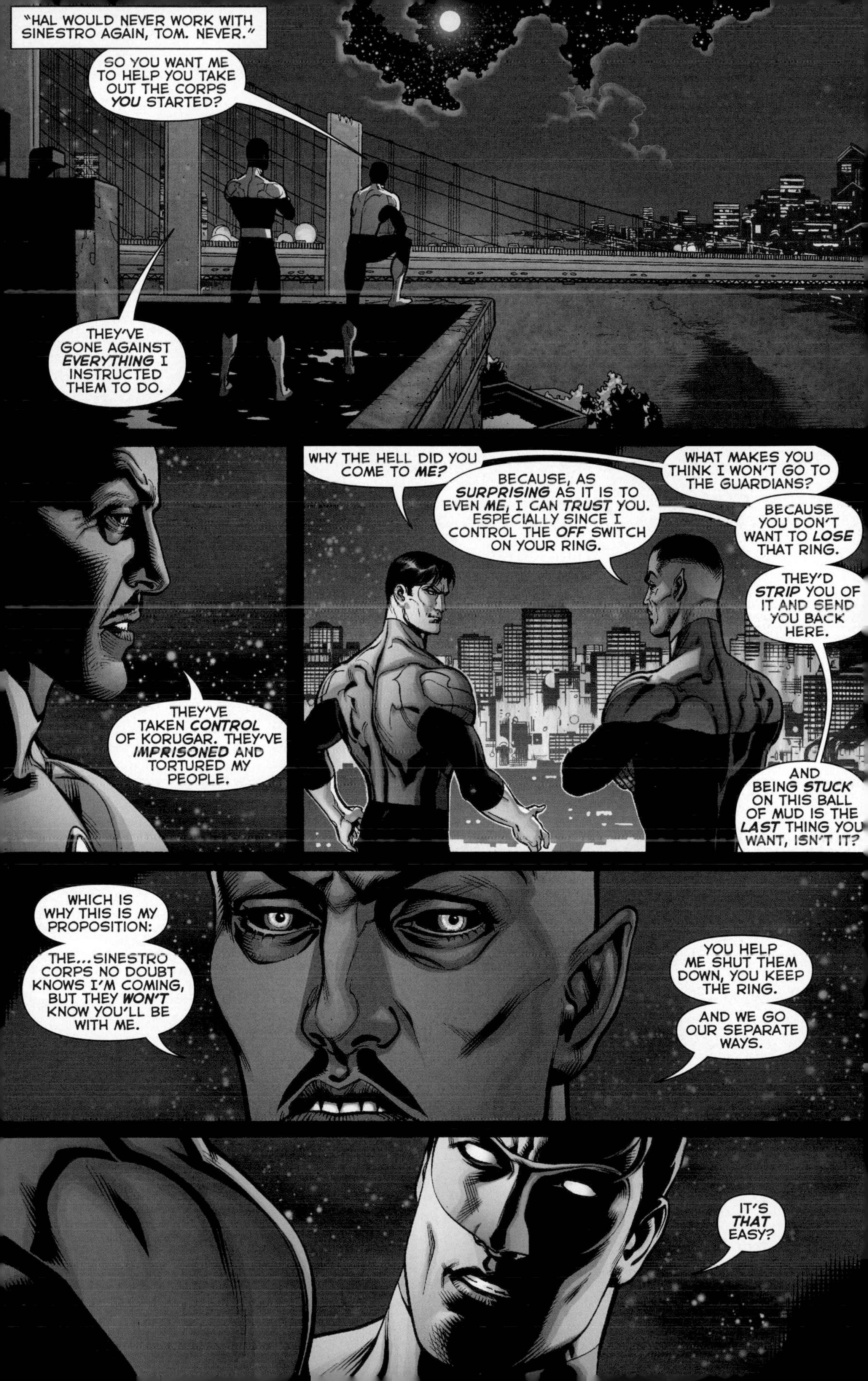
"HAL WOULD NEVER WORK WITH SINESTRO AGAIN, TOM. NEVER."
SO YOU WANT ME TO HELP YOU TAKE OUT THE CORPS YOU STARTED?
THEY'VE GONE AGAINST EVERYTHING I INSTRUCTED THEM TO DO.
THEY'VE TAKEN CONTROL OF KORUGAR. THEY'VE IMPRISONED AND TORTURED MY PEOPLE.
WHY THE HELL DID YOU COME TO ME?
BECAUSE, AS SURPRISING AS IT IS TO EVEN ME, I CAN TRUST YOU. ESPECIALLY SINCE I CONTROL THE OFF SWITCH ON YOUR RING.
WHAT MAKES YOU THINK I WON'T GO TO THE GUARDIANS?
BECAUSE YOU DON'T WANT TO LOSE THAT RING.
THEY'D STRIP YOU OF IT AND SEND YOU BACK HERE.
AND BEING STUCK ON THIS BALL OF MUD IS THE LAST THING YOU WANT, ISN'T IT?
WHICH IS WHY THIS IS MY PROPOSITION:
THE...SINESTRO CORPS NO DOUBT KNOWS I'M COMING, BUT THEY WON'T KNOW YOU'LL BE WITH ME.
YOU HELP ME SHUT THEM DOWN, YOU KEEP THE RING.
AND WE GO OUR SEPARATE WAYS.
IT'S THAT EASY?

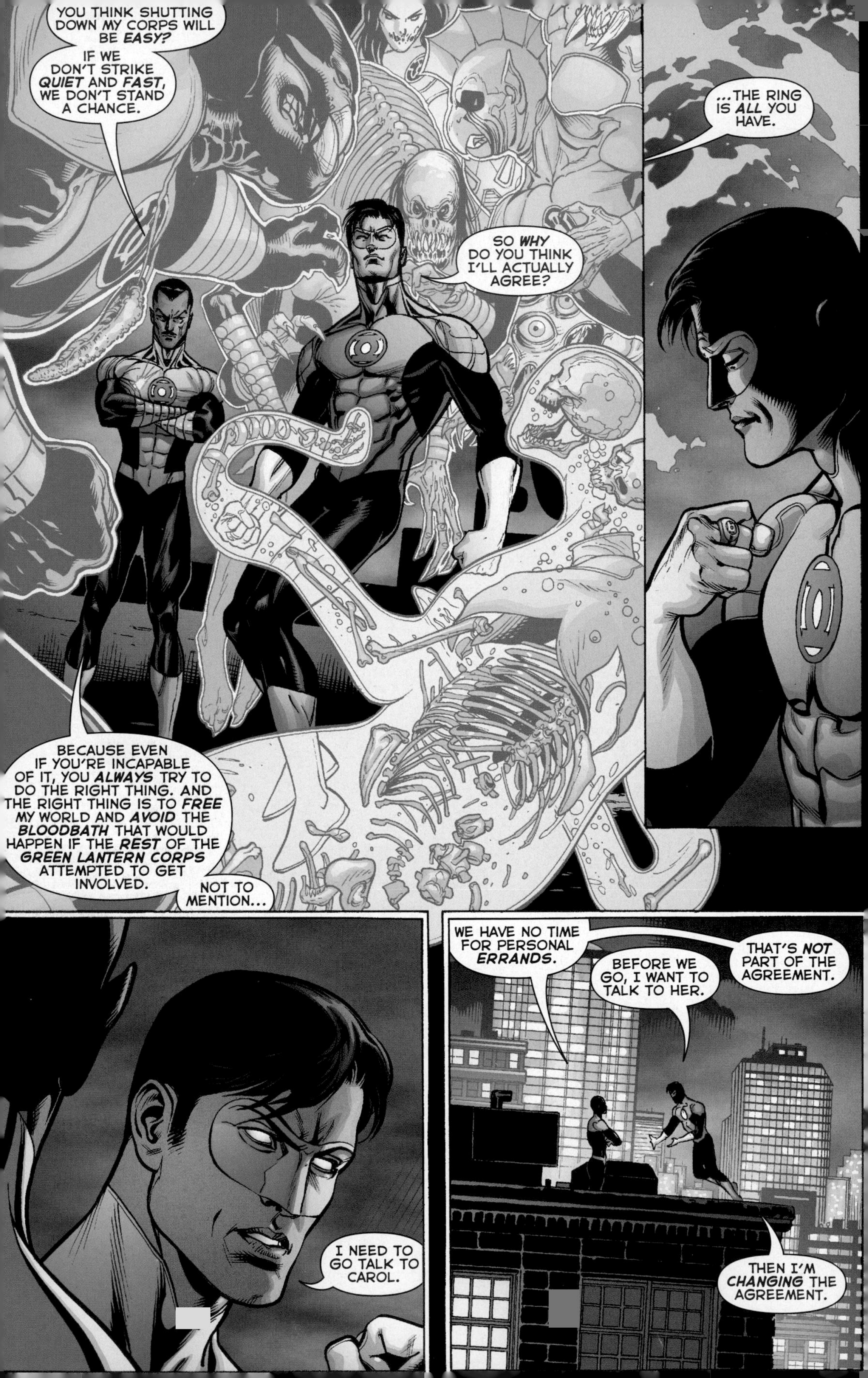
YOU THINK SHUTTING DOWN MY CORPS WILL BE EASY?
IF WE DON'T STRIKE QUIET AND FAST, WE DON'T STAND A CHANCE.
SO WHY DO YOU THINK I'LL ACTUALLY AGREE?
...THE RING IS ALL YOU HAVE.
BECAUSE EVEN IF YOU'RE INCAPABLE OF IT, YOU ALWAYS TRY TO DO THE RIGHT THING. AND THE RIGHT THING IS TO FREE MY WORLD AND AVOID THE BLOODBATH THAT WOULD HAPPEN IF THE REST OF THE GREEN LANTERN CORPS ATTEMPTED TO GET INVOLVED.
NOT TO MENTION...
I NEED TO GO TALK TO CAROL.
WE HAVE NO TIME FOR PERSONAL ERRANDS.
BEFORE WE GO, I WANT TO TALK TO HER.
THAT'S NOT PART OF THE AGREEMENT.
THEN I'M CHANGING THE AGREEMENT.

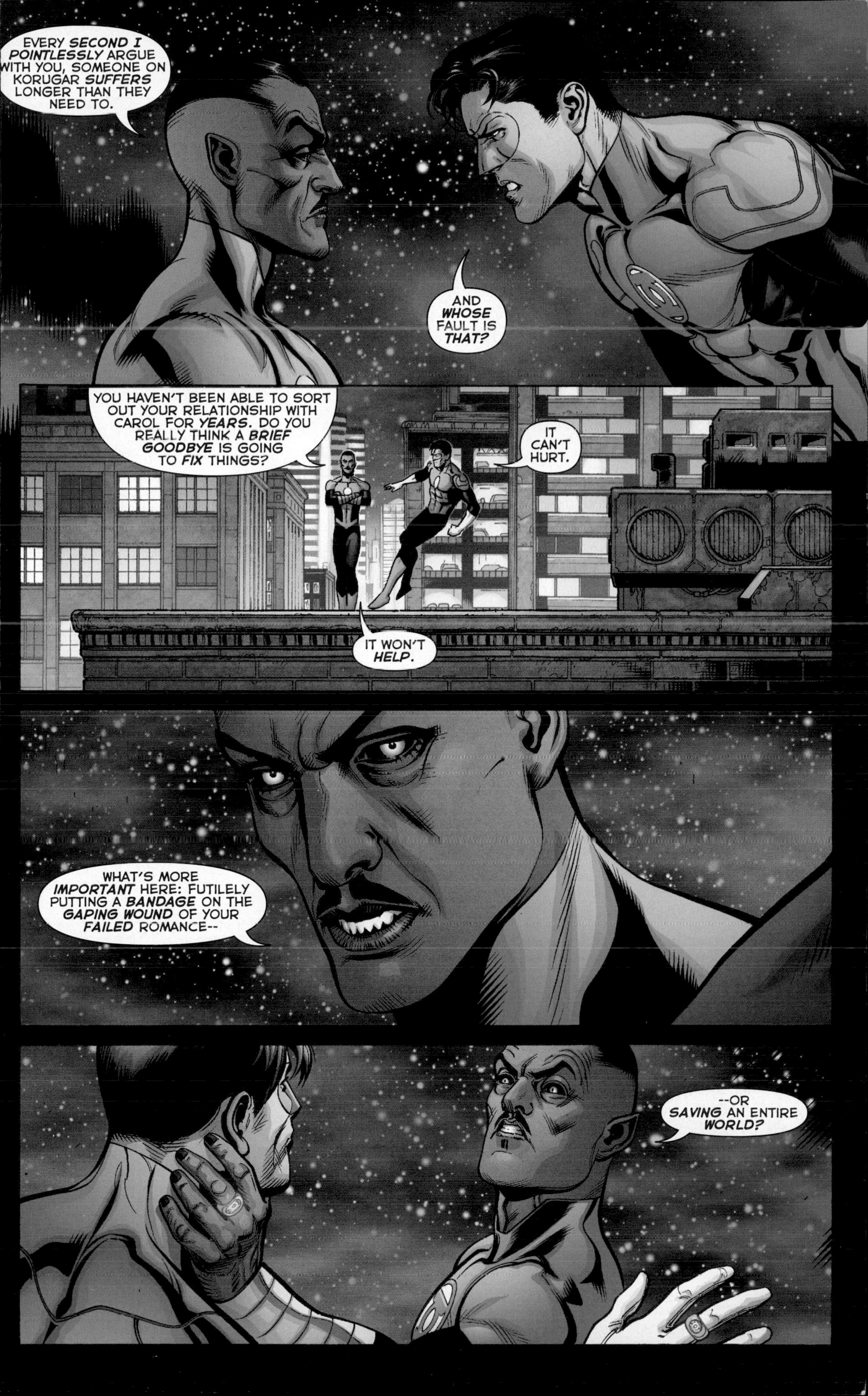
EVERY SECOND I POINTLESSLY ARGUE WITH YOU, SOMEONE ON KORUGAR SUFFERS LONGER THAN THEY NEED TO.
AND WHOSE FAULT IS THAT?
YOU HAVEN'T BEEN ABLE TO SORT OUT YOUR RELATIONSHIP WITH CAROL FOR YEARS. DO YOU REALLY THINK A BRIEF GOODBYE IS GOING TO FIX THINGS?
IT CAN'T HURT.
IT WON'T HELP.
WHAT'S MORE IMPORTANT HERE: FUTILELY PUTTING A BANDAGE ON THE GAPING WOUND OF YOUR FAILED ROMANCE--
--OR SAVING AN ENTIRE WORLD?

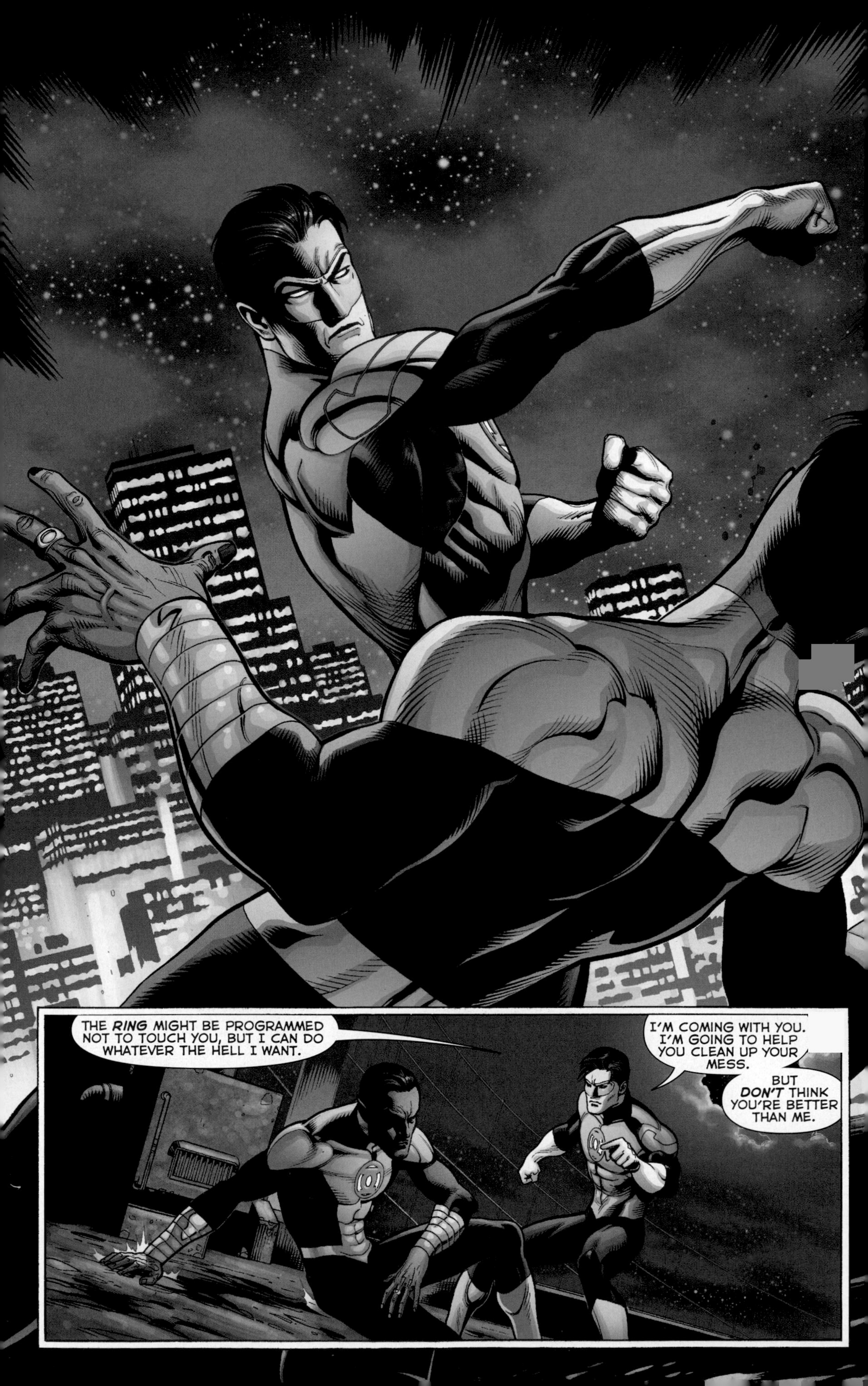
THE RING MIGHT BE PROGRAMMED NOT TO TOUCH YOU, BUT I CAN DO WHATEVER THE HELL I WANT.
I'M COMING WITH YOU. I'M GOING TO HELP YOU CLEAN UP YOUR MESS.
BUT DON'T THINK YOU'RE BETTER THAN ME.

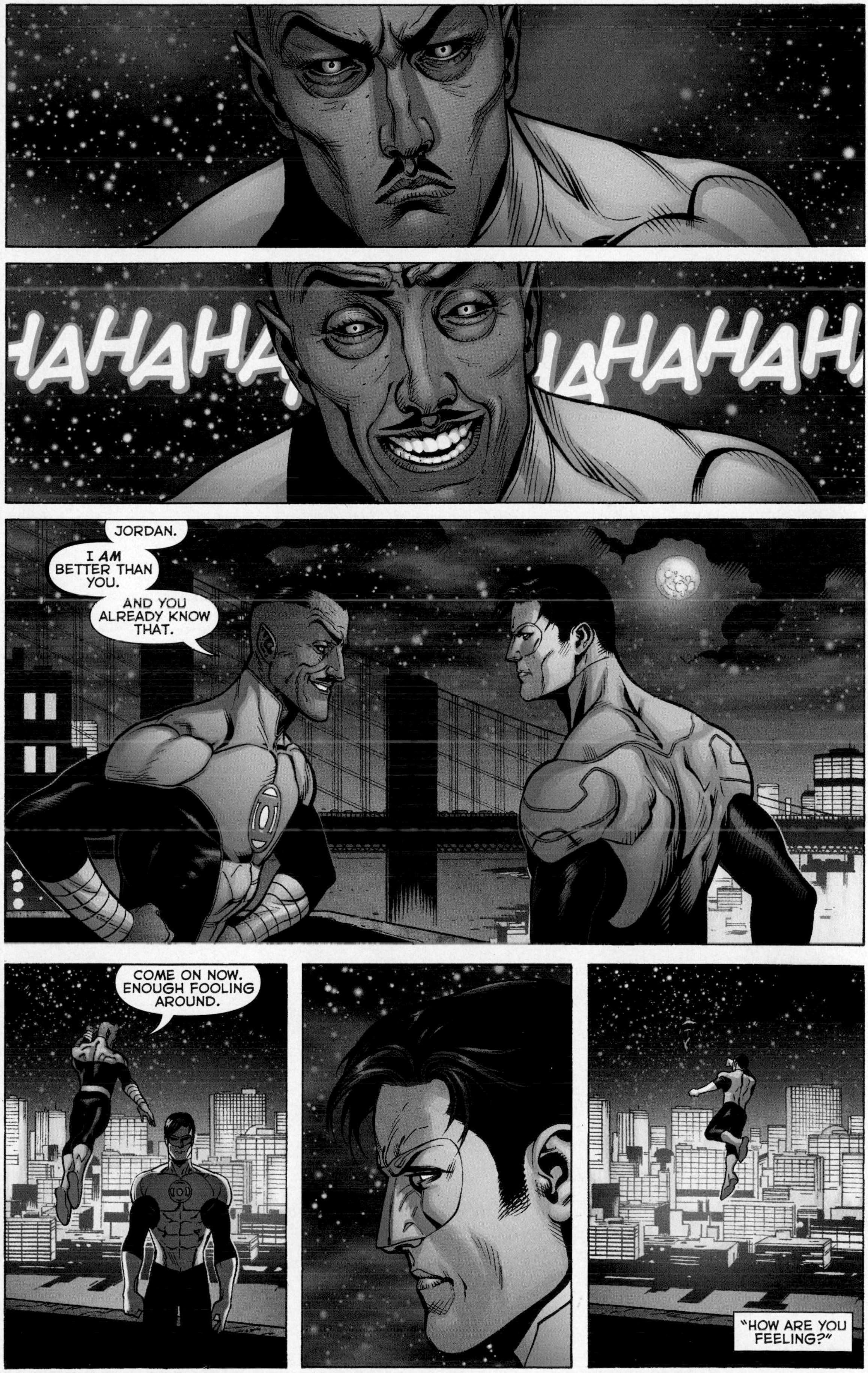
HAHAHAHAHAHAHAHAHAH
JORDAN.
I AM BETTER THAN YOU.
AND YOU ALREADY KNOW THAT.
COME ON NOW. ENOUGH FOOLING AROUND.
"HOW ARE YOU FEELING?"

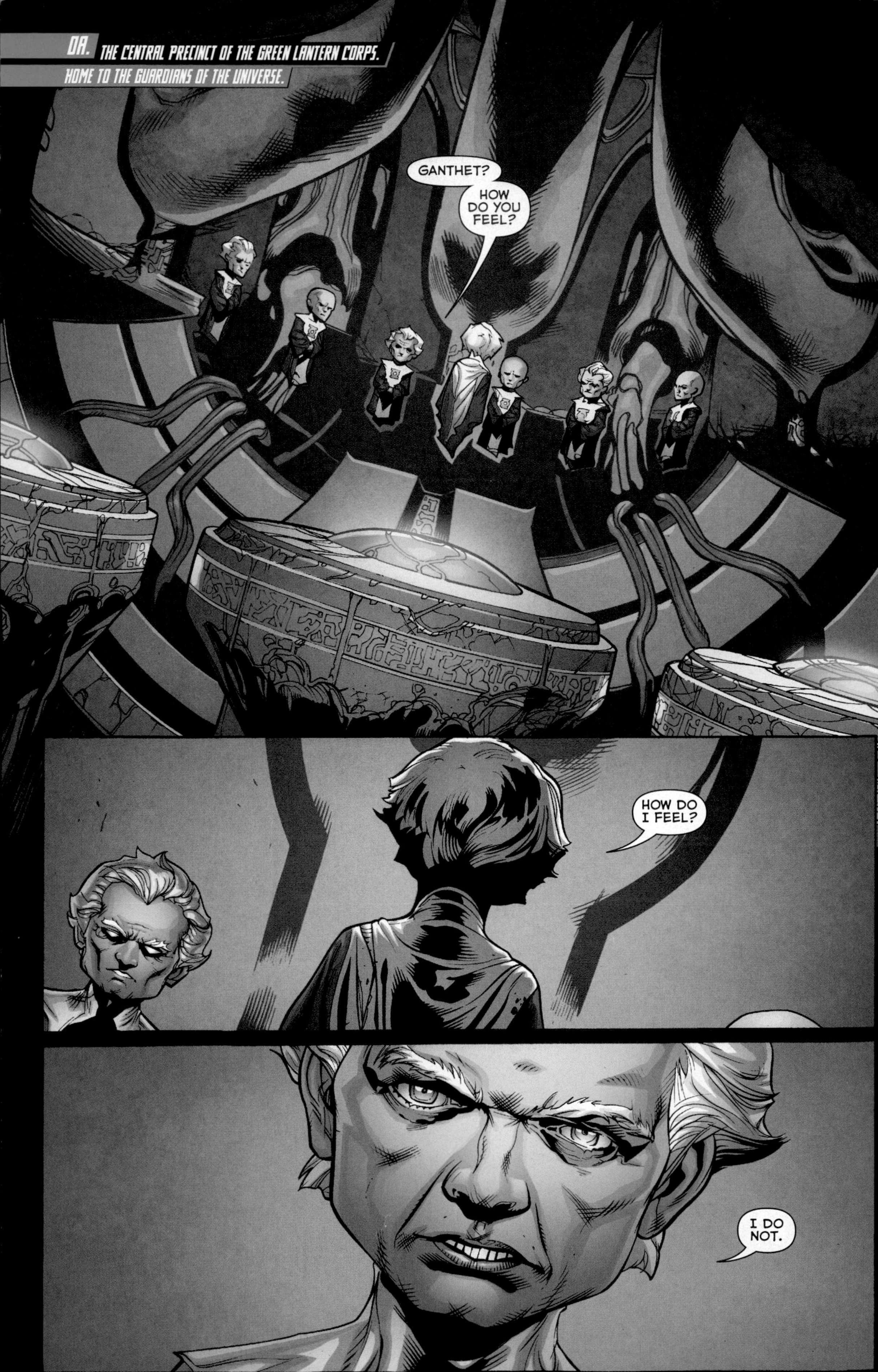
OA. THE CENTRAL PRECINCT OF THE GREEN LANTERN CORPS.
HOME TO THE GUARDIANS OF THE UNIVERSE.
GANTHET?
HOW DO YOU FEEL?
HOW DO I FEEL?
I DO NOT.

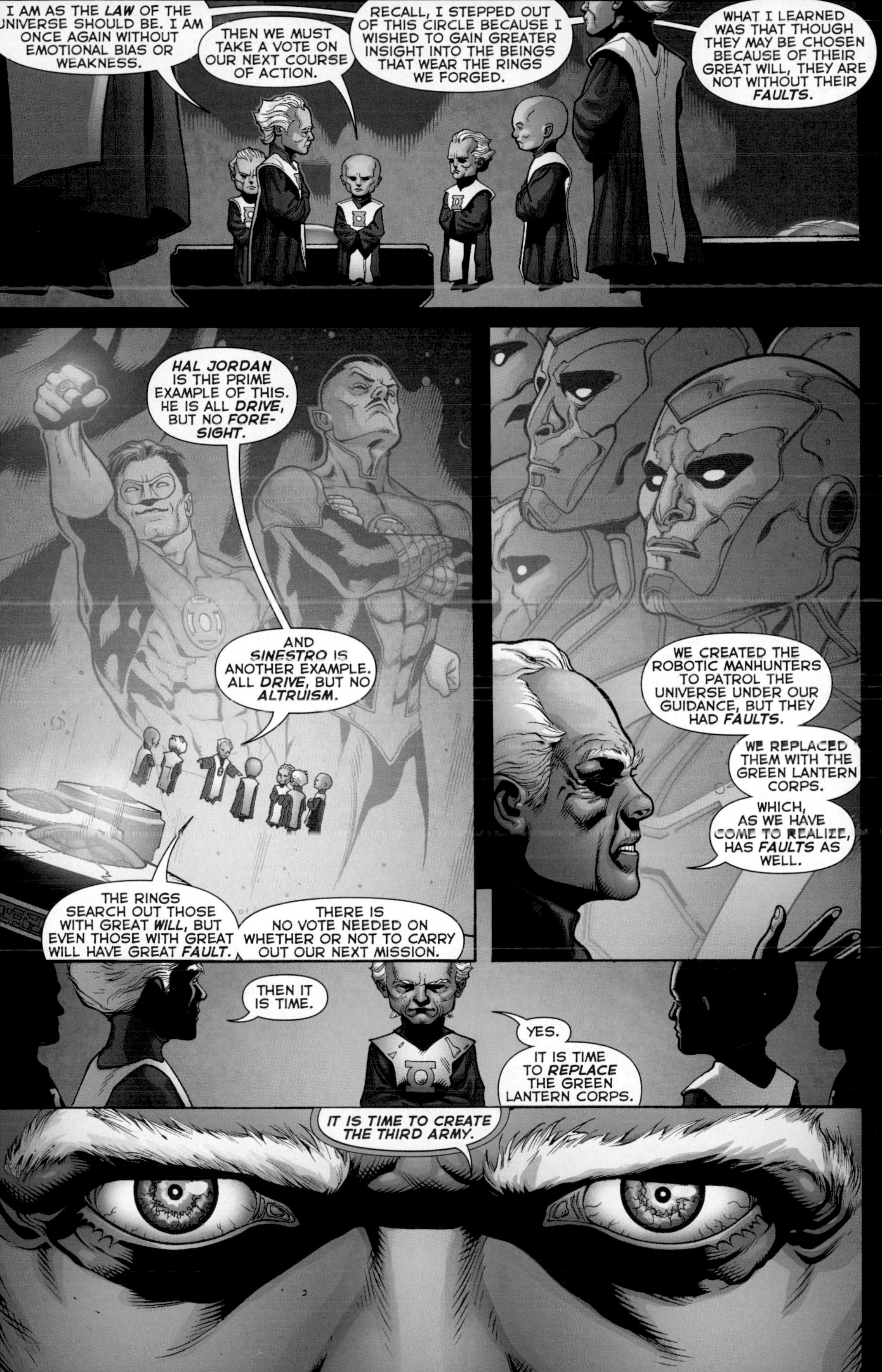
I AM AS THE LAW OF THE UNIVERSE SHOULD BE. I AM ONCE AGAIN WITHOUT EMOTIONAL BIAS OR WEAKNESS.
THEN WE MUST TAKE A VOTE ON OUR NEXT COURSE OF ACTION.
RECALL, I STEPPED OUT OF THIS CIRCLE BECAUSE I WISHED TO GAIN GREATER INSIGHT INTO THE BEINGS THAT WEAR THE RINGS WE FORGED.
WHAT I LEARNED WAS THAT THOUGH THEY MAY BE CHOSEN BECAUSE OF THEIR GREAT WILL, THEY ARE NOT WITHOUT THEIR FAULTS.
HAL JORDAN IS THE PRIME EXAMPLE OF THIS. HE IS ALL DRIVE, BUT NO FORE-SIGHT.
AND SINESTRO IS ANOTHER EXAMPLE. ALL DRIVE, BUT NO ALTRUISM.
THE RINGS SEARCH OUT THOSE WITH GREAT WILL, BUT EVEN THOSE WITH GREAT WILL HAVE GREAT FAULT.
WE CREATED THE ROBOTIC MANHUNTERS TO PATROL THE UNIVERSE UNDER OUR GUIDANCE, BUT THEY HAD FAULTS.
WE REPLACED THEM WITH THE GREEN LANTERN CORPS.
WHICH, AS WE HAVE COME TO REALIZE, HAS FAULTS AS WELL.
THERE IS NO VOTE NEEDED ON WHETHER OR NOT TO CARRY OUT OUR NEXT MISSION.
THEN IT IS TIME.
YES.
IT IS TIME TO REPLACE THE GREEN LANTERN CORPS.
IT IS TIME TO CREATE THE THIRD ARMY.

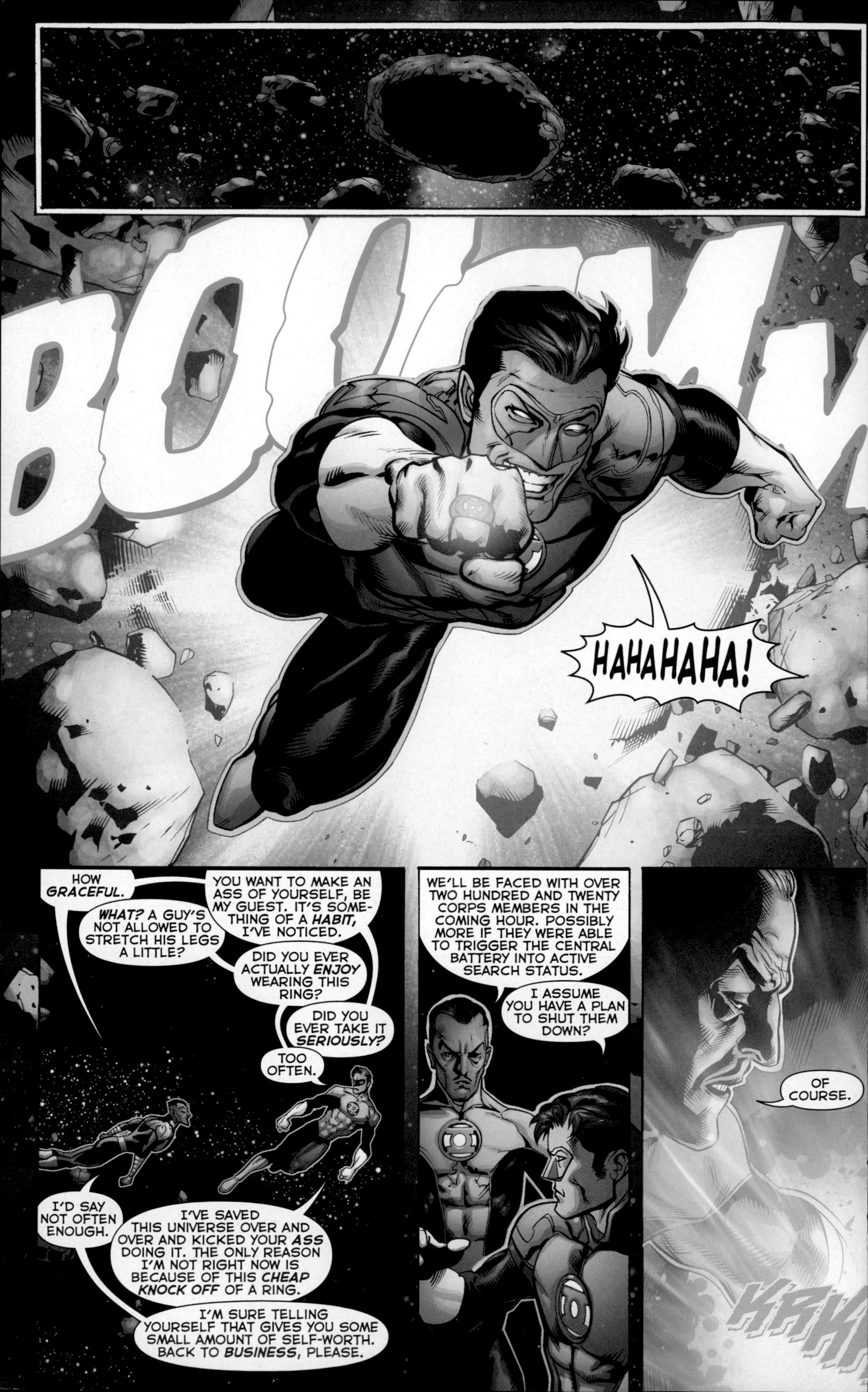
HAHAHAHA!
HOW GRACEFUL.
WHAT? A GUY'S NOT ALLOWED TO STRETCH HIS LEGS A LITTLE?
YOU WANT TO MAKE AN ASS OF YOURSELF, BE MY GUEST. IT'S SOMETHING OF A HABIT, I'VE NOTICED.
DID YOU EVER ACTUALLY ENJOY WEARING THIS RING?
DID YOU EVER TAKE IT SERIOUSLY?
TOO OFTEN.
I'D SAY NOT OFTEN ENOUGH.
I'VE SAVED THIS UNIVERSE OVER AND OVER AND KICKED YOUR ASS DOING IT. THE ONLY REASON I'M NOT RIGHT NOW IS BECAUSE OF THIS CHEAP KNOCK OFF OF A RING.
I'M SURE TELLING YOURSELF THAT GIVES YOU SOME SMALL AMOUNT OF SELF-WORTH. BACK TO BUSINESS, PLEASE.
WE'LL BE FACED WITH OVER TWO HUNDRED AND TWENTY CORPS MEMBERS IN THE COMING HOUR. POSSIBLY MORE IF THEY WERE ABLE TO TRIGGER THE CENTRAL BATTERY INTO ACTIVE SEARCH STATUS.
I ASSUME YOU HAVE A PLAN TO SHUT THEM DOWN?
OF COURSE.

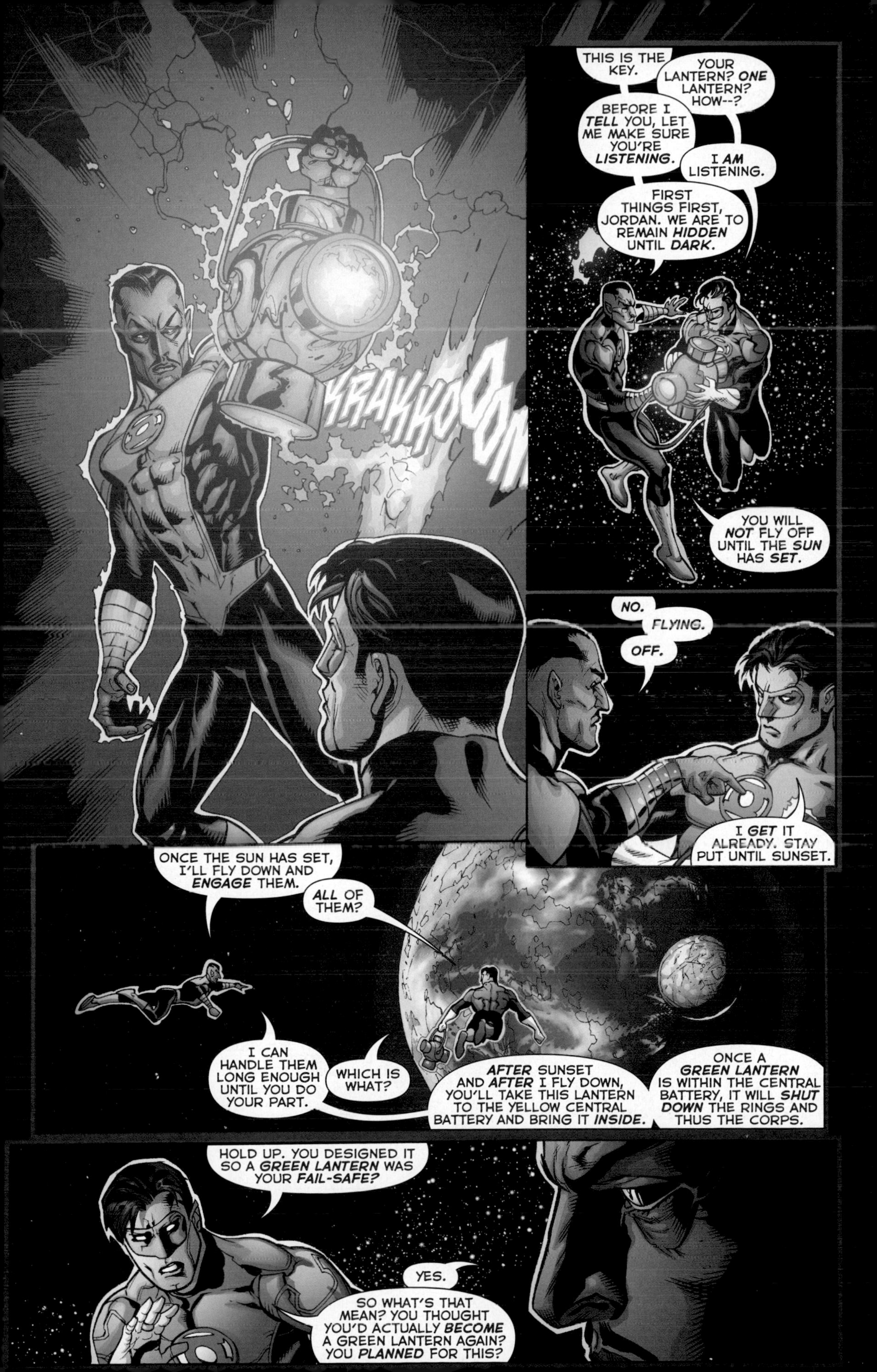
KRAKKOOOM
THIS IS THE KEY.
YOUR LANTERN? ONE LANTERN? HOW--?
BEFORE I TELL YOU, LET ME MAKE SURE YOU'RE LISTENING.
I AM LISTENING.
FIRST THINGS FIRST, JORDAN. WE ARE TO REMAIN HIDDEN UNTIL DARK.
YOU WILL NOT FLY OFF UNTIL THE SUN HAS SET.
NO.
FLYING.
OFF.
I GET IT ALREADY. STAY PUT UNTIL SUNSET.
ONCE THE SUN HAS SET, I'LL FLY DOWN AND ENGAGE THEM.
ALL OF THEM?
I CAN HANDLE THEM LONG ENOUGH UNTIL YOU DO YOUR PART.
WHICH IS WHAT?
AFTER SUNSET AND AFTER I FLY DOWN, YOU'LL TAKE THIS LANTERN TO THE YELLOW CENTRAL BATTERY AND BRING IT INSIDE.
ONCE A GREEN LANTERN IS WITHIN THE CENTRAL BATTERY, IT WILL SHUT DOWN THE RINGS AND THUS THE CORPS.
HOLD UP. YOU DESIGNED IT SO A GREEN LANTERN WAS YOUR FAIL-SAFE?
YES.
SO WHAT'S THAT MEAN? YOU THOUGHT YOU'D ACTUALLY BECOME A GREEN LANTERN AGAIN? YOU PLANNED FOR THIS?

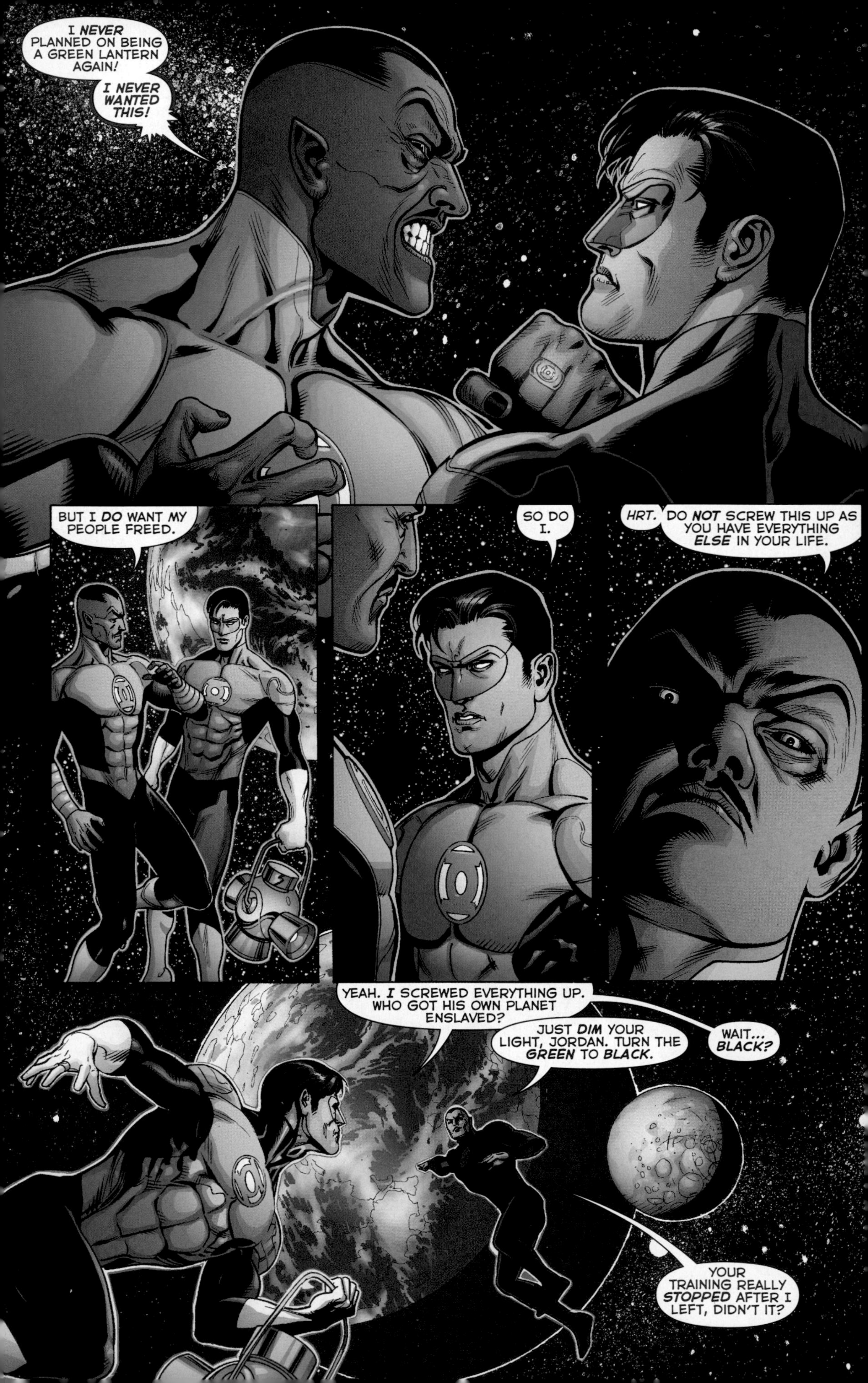
I NEVER PLANNED ON BEING A GREEN LANTERN AGAIN!
I NEVER WANTED THIS!
BUT I DO WANT MY PEOPLE FREED.
SO DO I.
HRT.
DO NOT SCREW THIS UP AS YOU HAVE EVERYTHING ELSE IN YOUR LIFE.
YEAH. I SCREWED EVERYTHING UP. WHO GOT HIS OWN PLANET ENSLAVED?
JUST DIM YOUR LIGHT, JORDAN. TURN THE GREEN TO BLACK.
WAIT... BLACK?
YOUR TRAINING REALLY STOPPED AFTER I LEFT, DIDN'T IT?

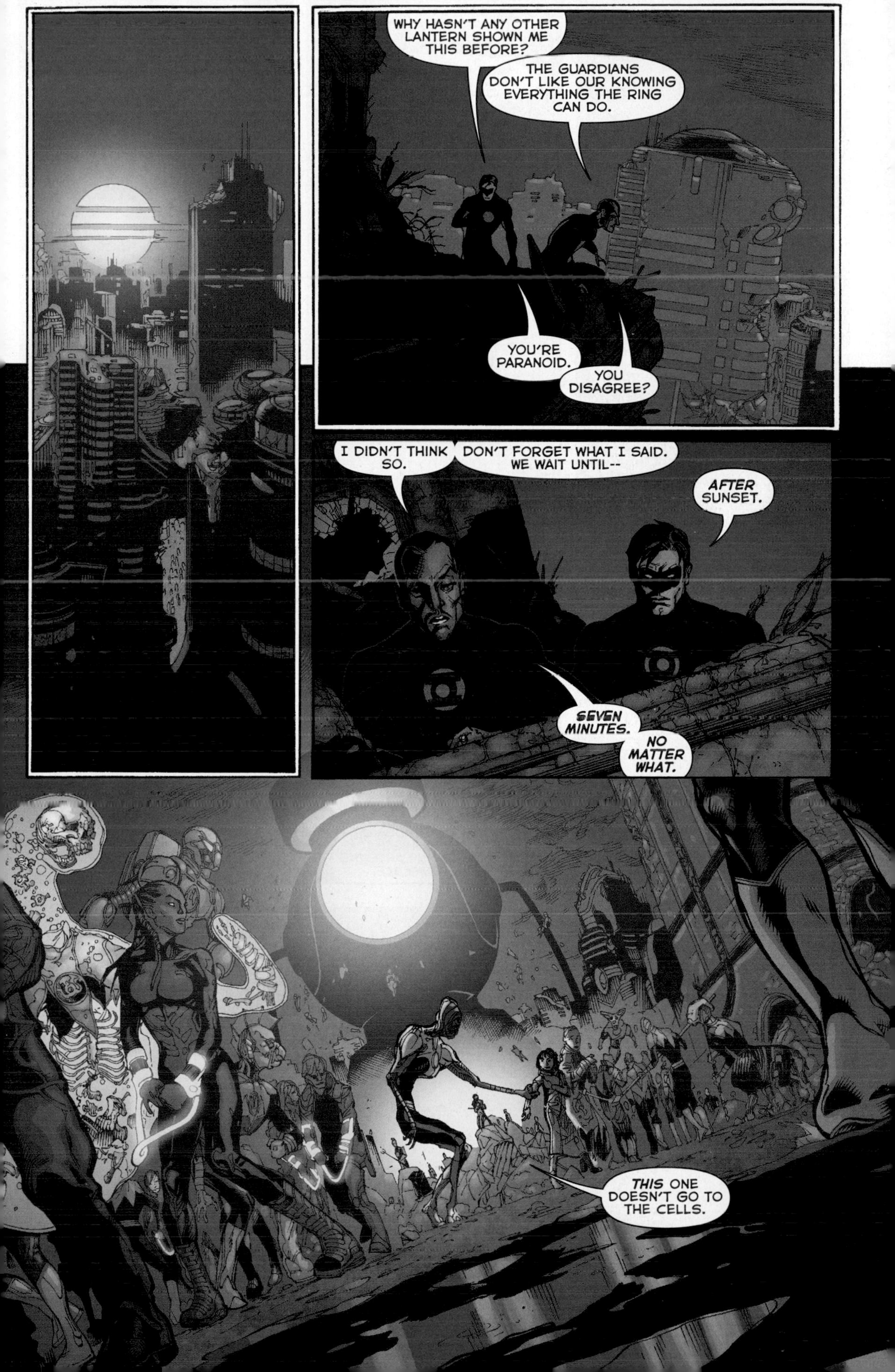
WHY HASN'T ANY OTHER LANTERN SHOWN ME THIS BEFORE?
THE GUARDIANS DON'T LIKE OUR KNOWING EVERYTHING THE RING CAN DO.
YOU'RE PARANOID.
YOU DISAGREE?
I DIDN'T THINK SO.
DON'T FORGET WHAT I SAID. WE WAIT UNTIL--
AFTER SUNSET.
SEVEN MINUTES.
NO MATTER WHAT.
THIS ONE DOESN'T GO TO THE CELLS.

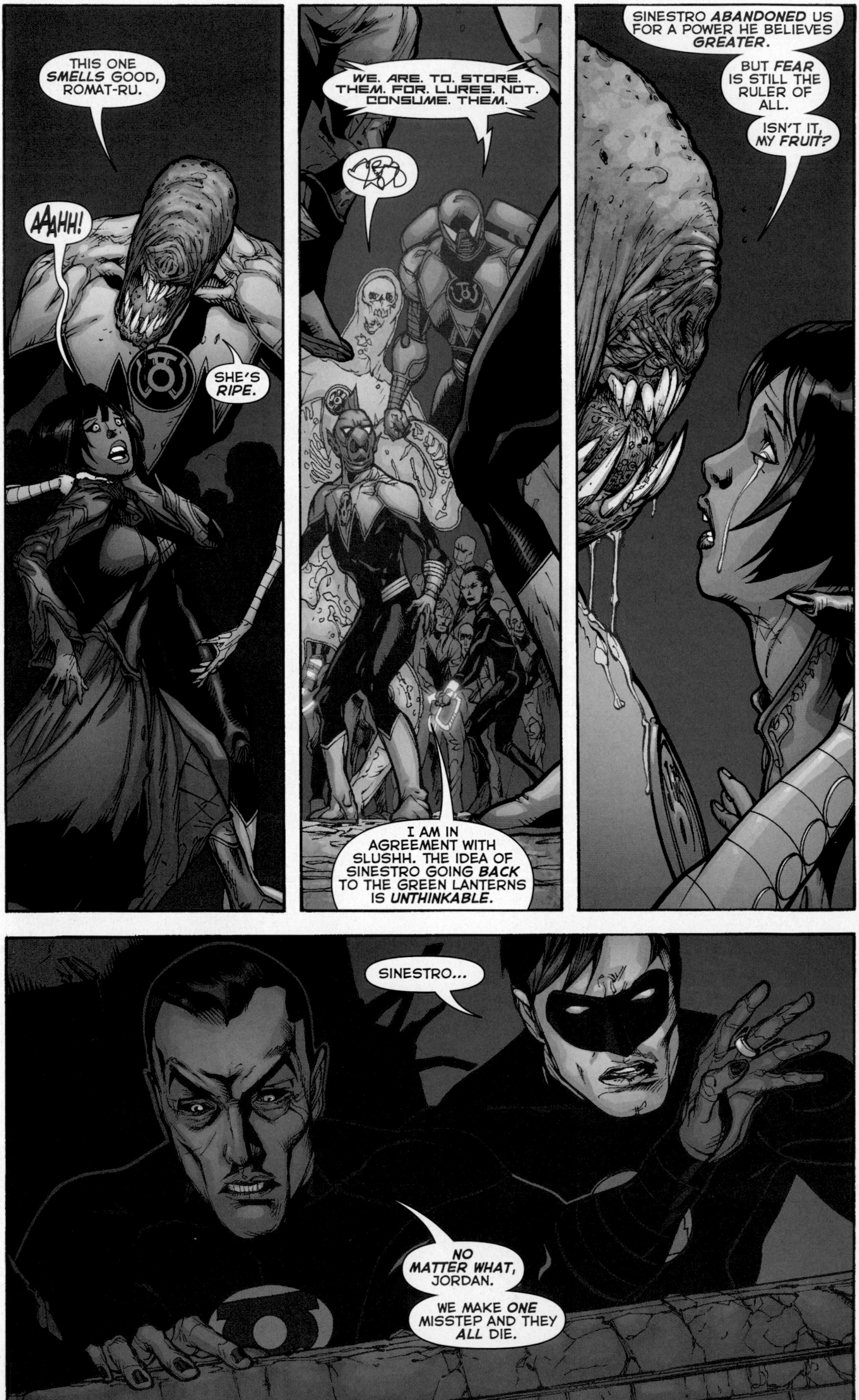
THIS ONE SMELLS GOOD, ROMAT-RU.
AAAHH!
SHE'S RIPE.
WE. ARE. TO. STORE. THEM. FOR. LURES. NOT. CONSUME. THEM.
I AM IN AGREEMENT WITH SLUSHH. THE IDEA OF SINESTRO GOING BACK TO THE GREEN LANTERNS IS UNTHINKABLE.
SINESTRO ABANDONED US FOR A POWER HE BELIEVES GREATER.
BUT FEAR IS STILL THE RULER OF ALL.
ISN'T IT, MY FRUIT?
SINESTRO...
NO MATTER WHAT, JORDAN.
WE MAKE ONE MISSTEP AND THEY ALL DIE.

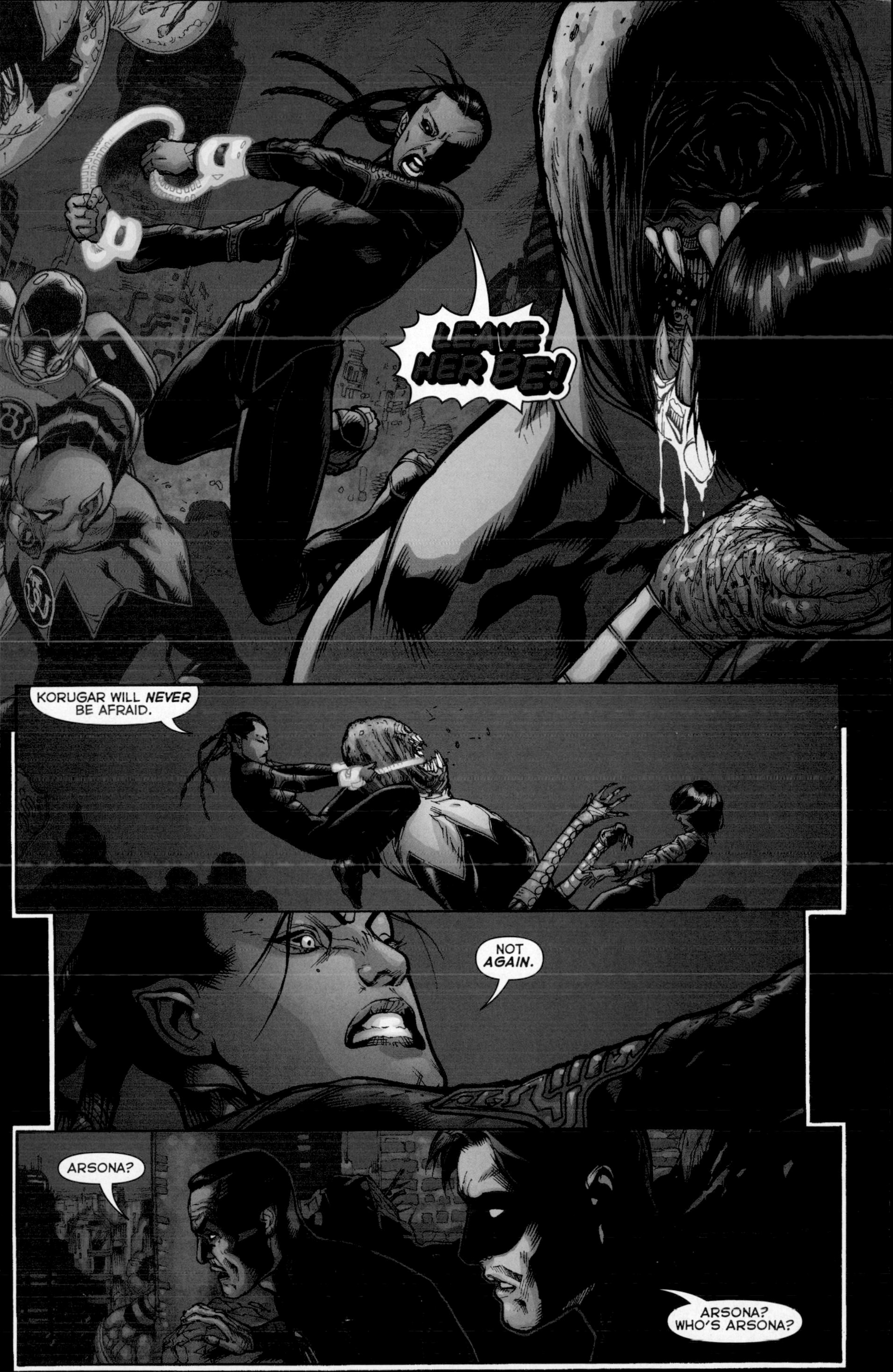
LEAVE HER BE!
KORUGAR WILL NEVER BE AFRAID.
NOT AGAIN.
ARSONA?
ARSONA? WHO'S ARSONA?

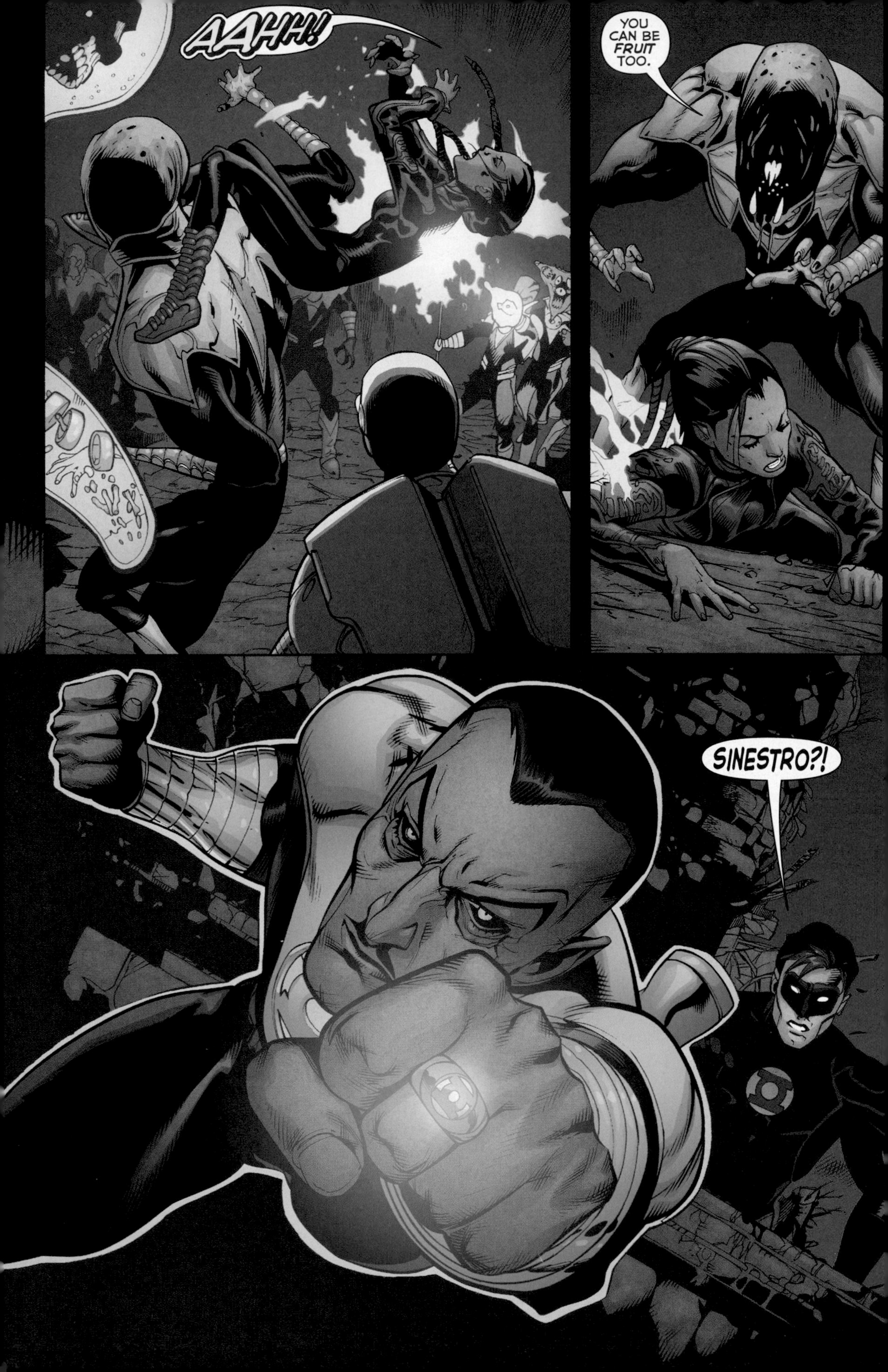
AAHH!
YOU CAN BE FRUIT TOO.
SINESTRO?!

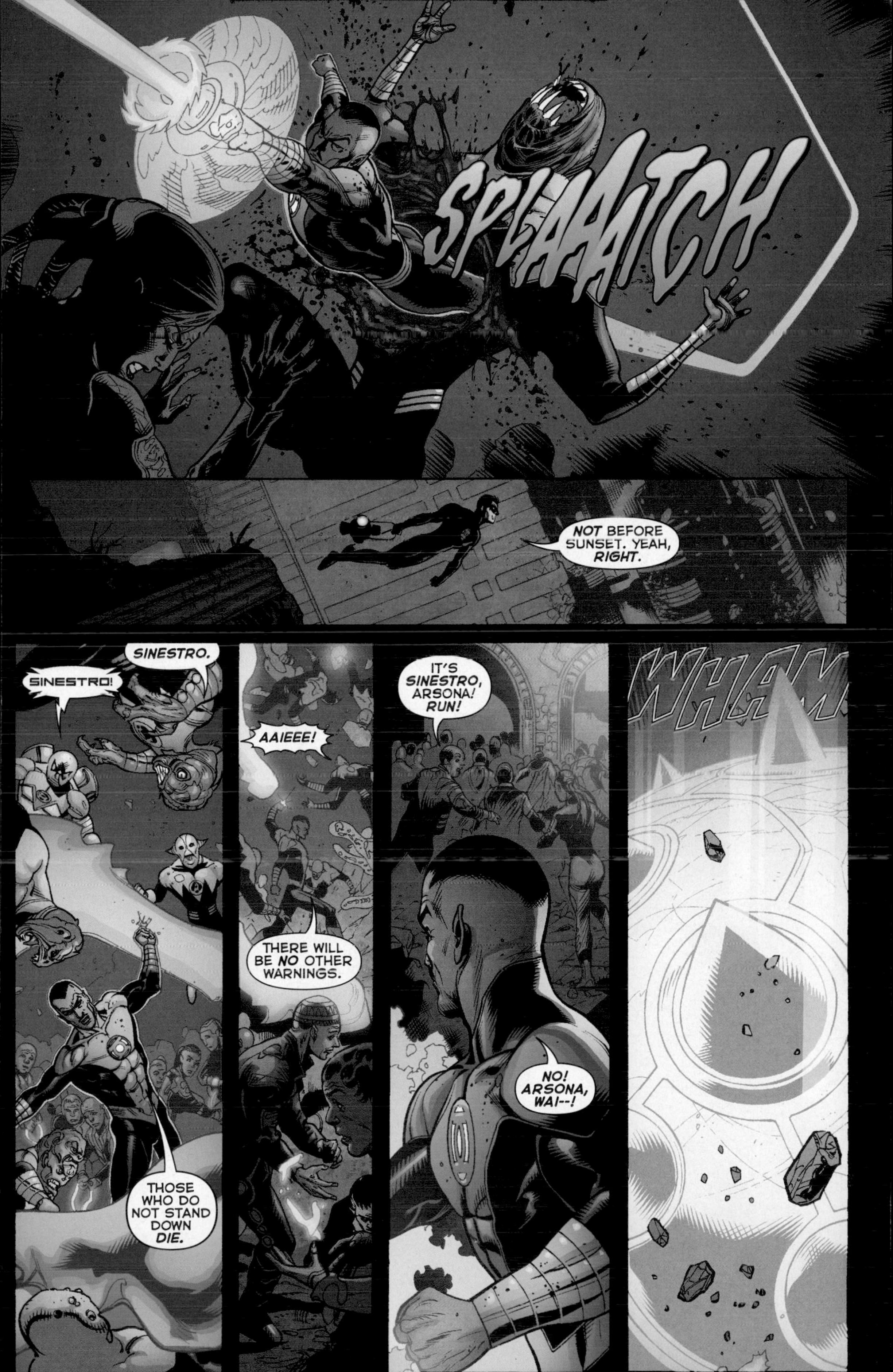
SPLAAATCH
NOT BEFORE SUNSET. YEAH, RIGHT.
SINESTRO.
SINESTRO!
THOSE WHO DO NOT STAND DOWN DIE.
AAIEEE!
THERE WILL BE NO OTHER WARNINGS.
IT'S SINESTRO, ARSONA! RUN!
NO! ARSONA, WAI--!

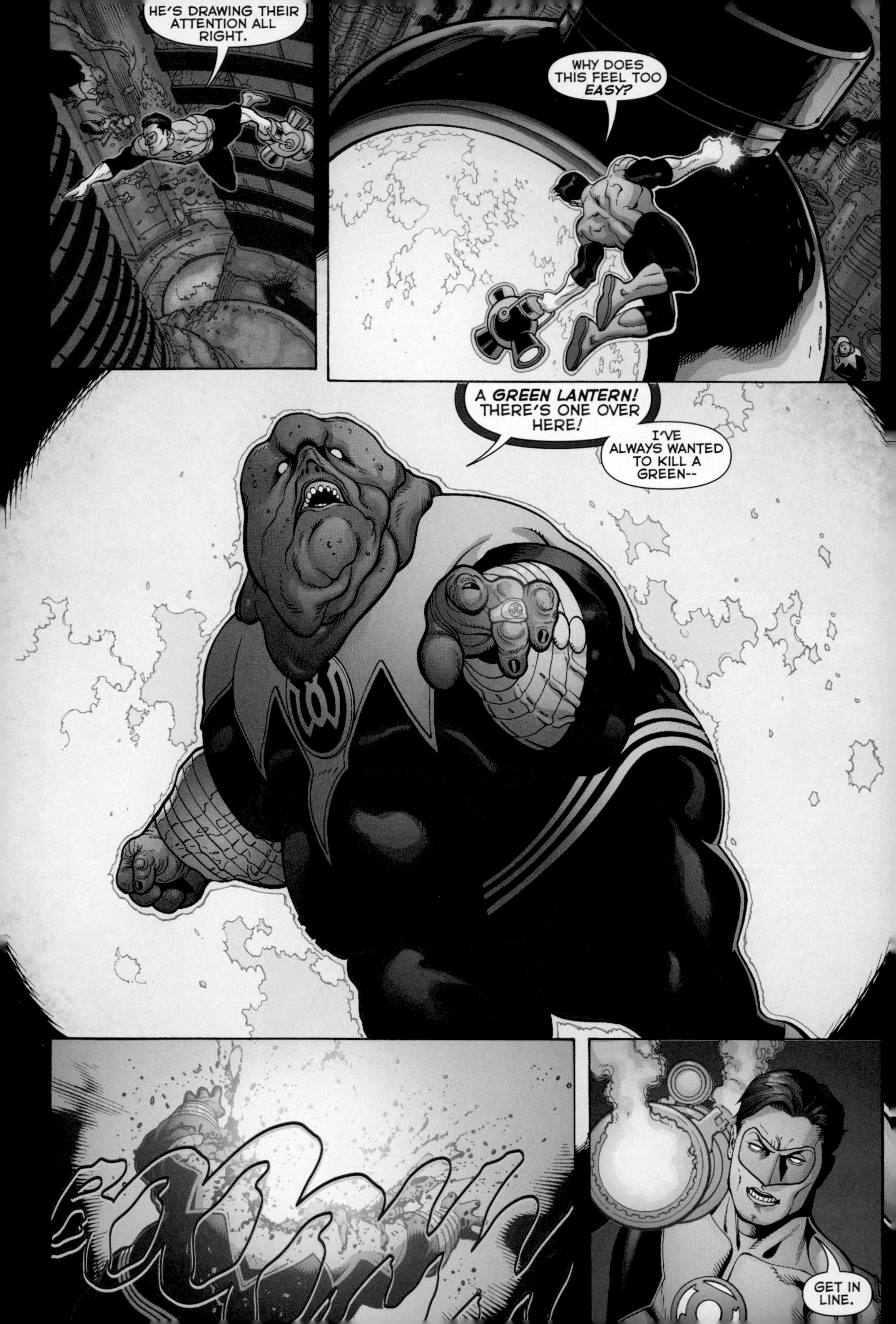
HE'S DRAWING THEIR ATTENTION ALL RIGHT.
WHY DOES THIS FEEL TOO *EASY?*
A *GREEN LANTERN!* THERE'S ONE OVER HERE!
I'VE ALWAYS WANTED TO KILL A GREEN--
GET IN LINE.

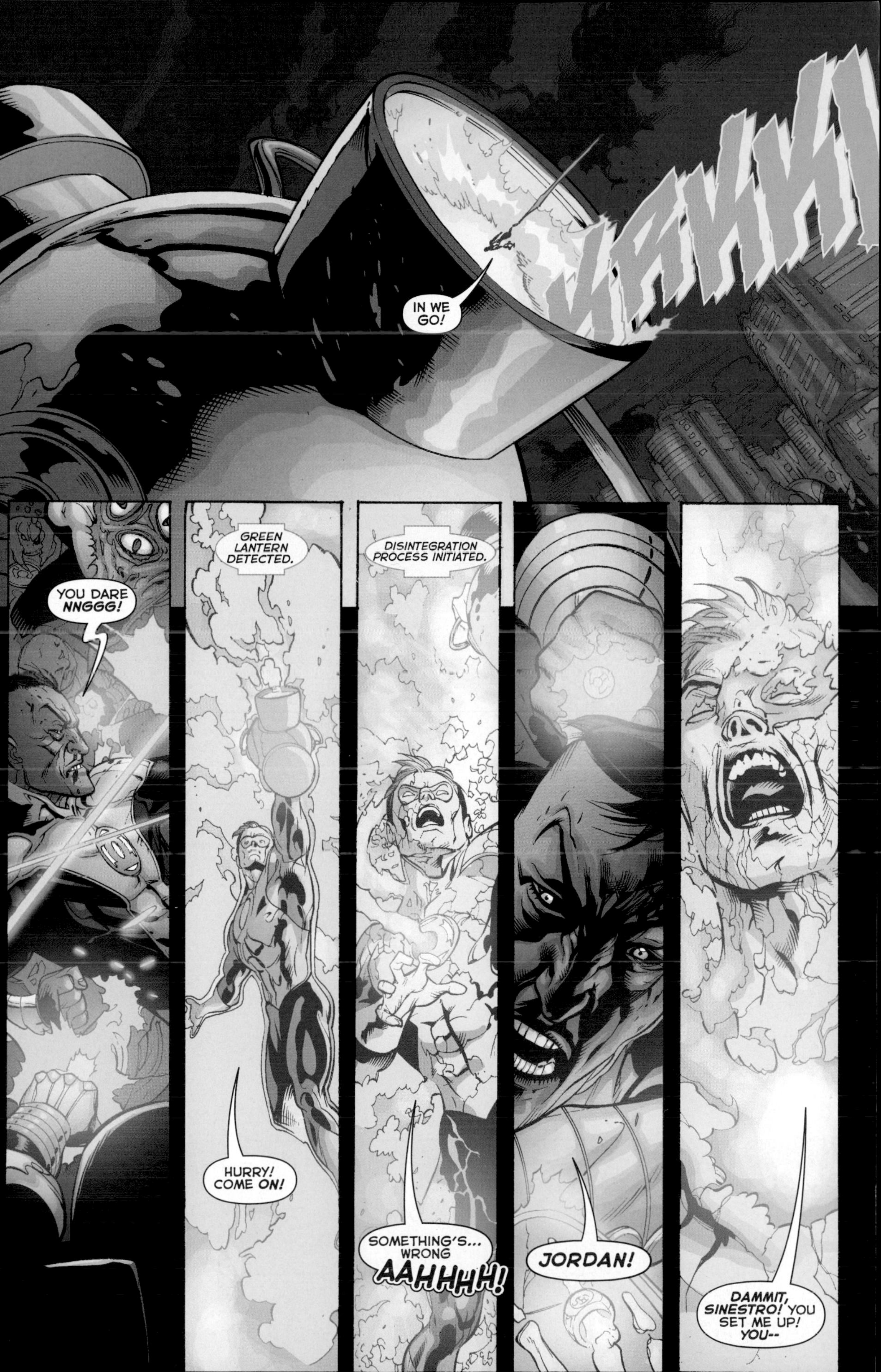
IN WE GO!
YOU DARE NNGGG!
GREEN LANTERN DETECTED.
HURRY! COME ON!
DISINTEGRATION PROCESS INITIATED.
SOMETHING'S... WRONG
AAHHHH!
JORDAN!
DAMMIT, SINESTRO! YOU SET ME UP! YOU--

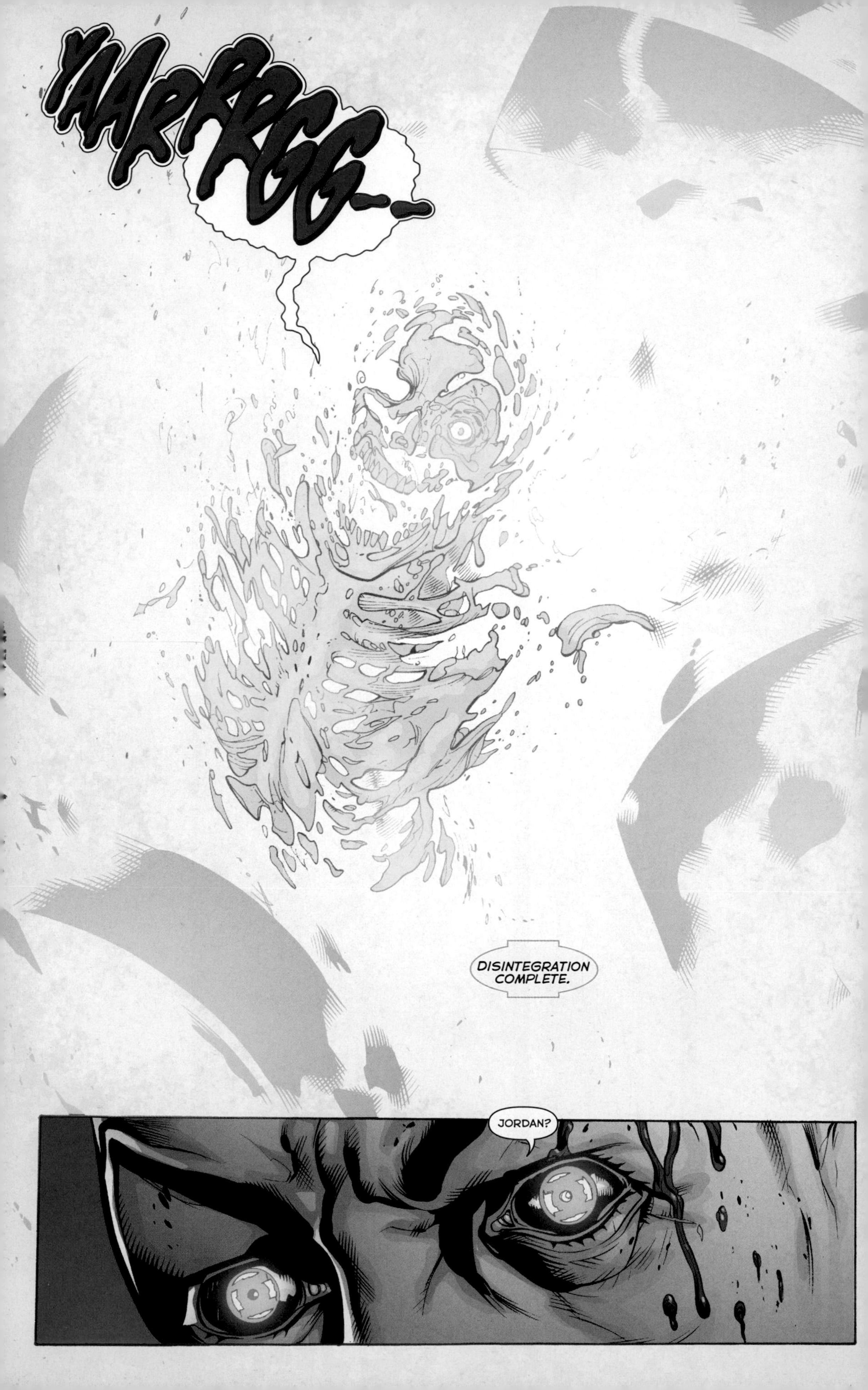
YAARRGG--
DISINTEGRATION COMPLETE.
JORDAN?

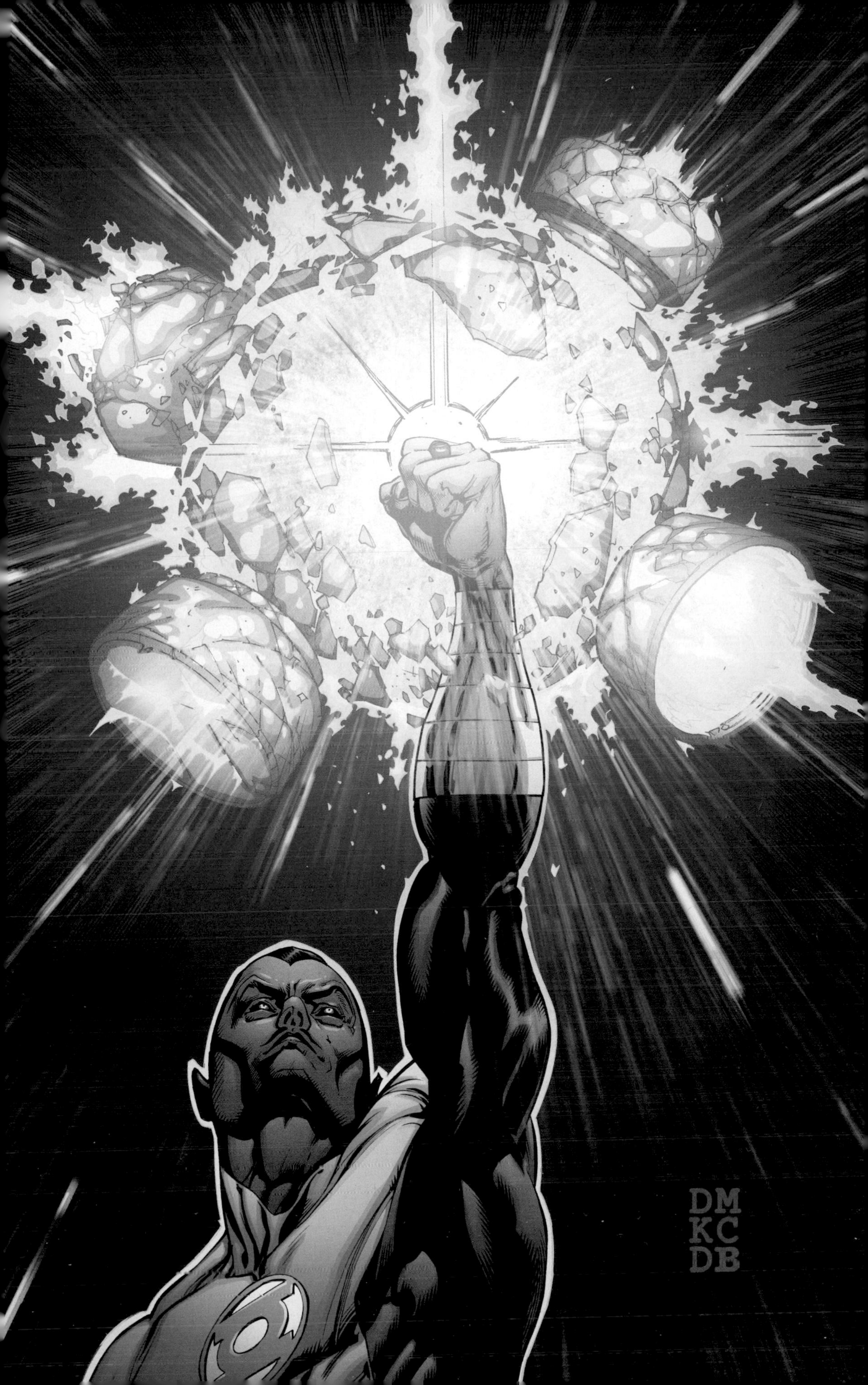
DM
KC
DB

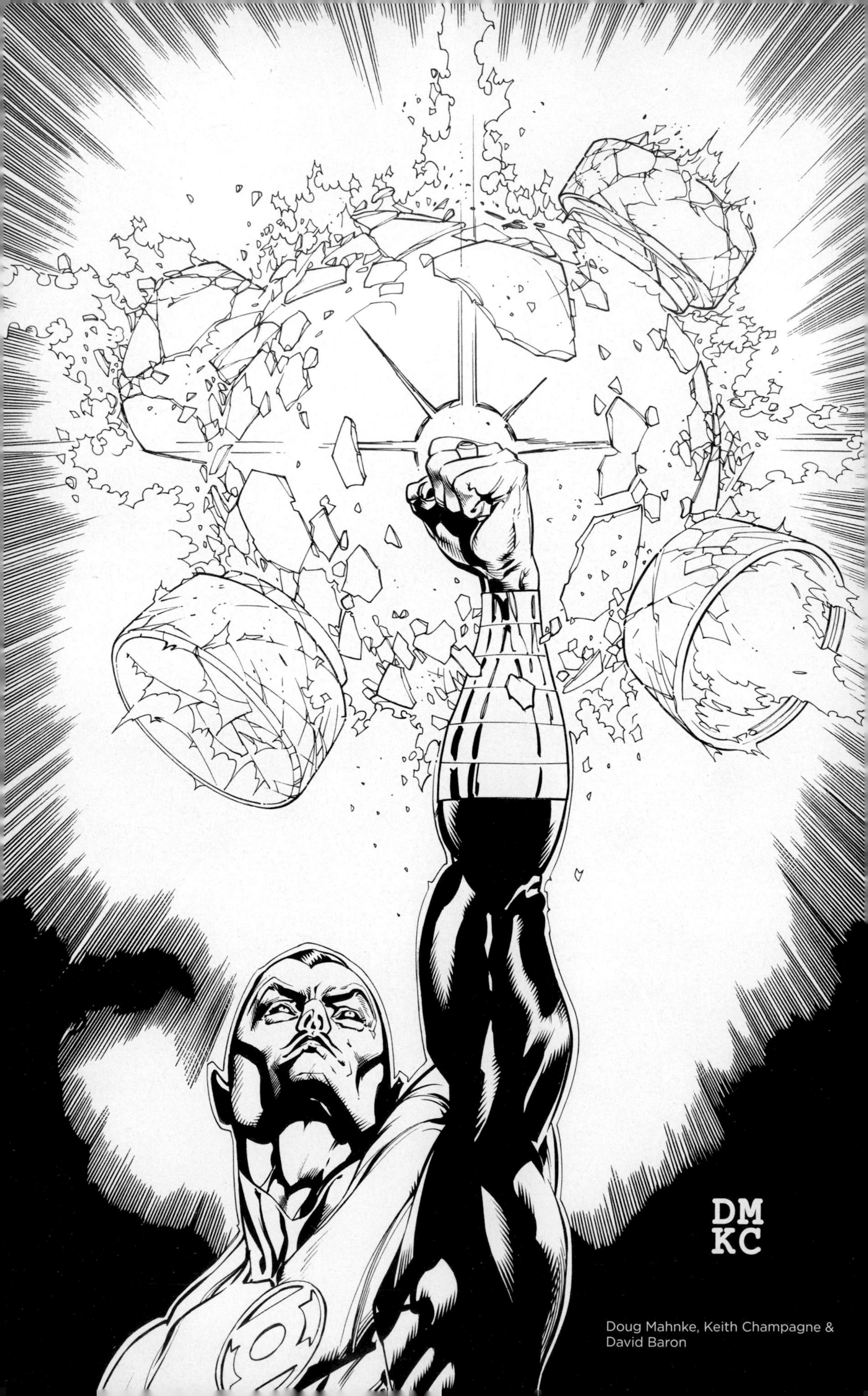
DM
KC

Doug Mahnke, Keith Champagne &
David Baron

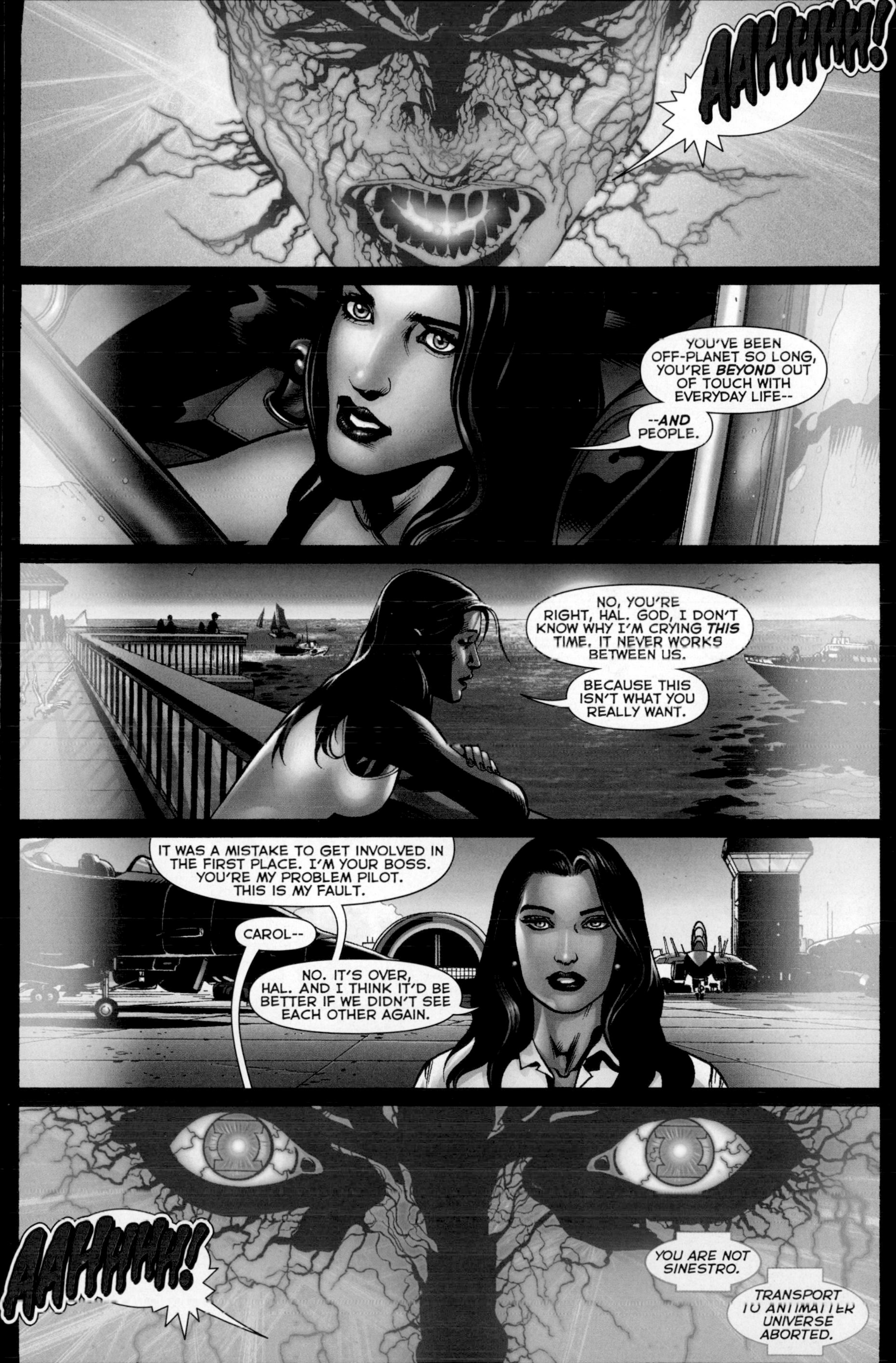
AAHHHHH!
YOU'VE BEEN OFF-PLANET SO LONG, YOU'RE BEYOND OUT OF TOUCH WITH EVERYDAY LIFE--
--AND PEOPLE.
NO, YOU'RE RIGHT, HAL. GOD, I DON'T KNOW WHY I'M CRYING THIS TIME. IT NEVER WORKS BETWEEN US.
BECAUSE THIS ISN'T WHAT YOU REALLY WANT.
IT WAS A MISTAKE TO GET INVOLVED IN THE FIRST PLACE. I'M YOUR BOSS. YOU'RE MY PROBLEM PILOT. THIS IS MY FAULT.
CAROL--
NO. IT'S OVER, HAL. AND I THINK IT'D BE BETTER IF WE DIDN'T SEE EACH OTHER AGAIN.
AAHHHHH!
YOU ARE NOT SINESTRO.
TRANSPORT TO ANTIMATTER UNIVERSE ABORTED.

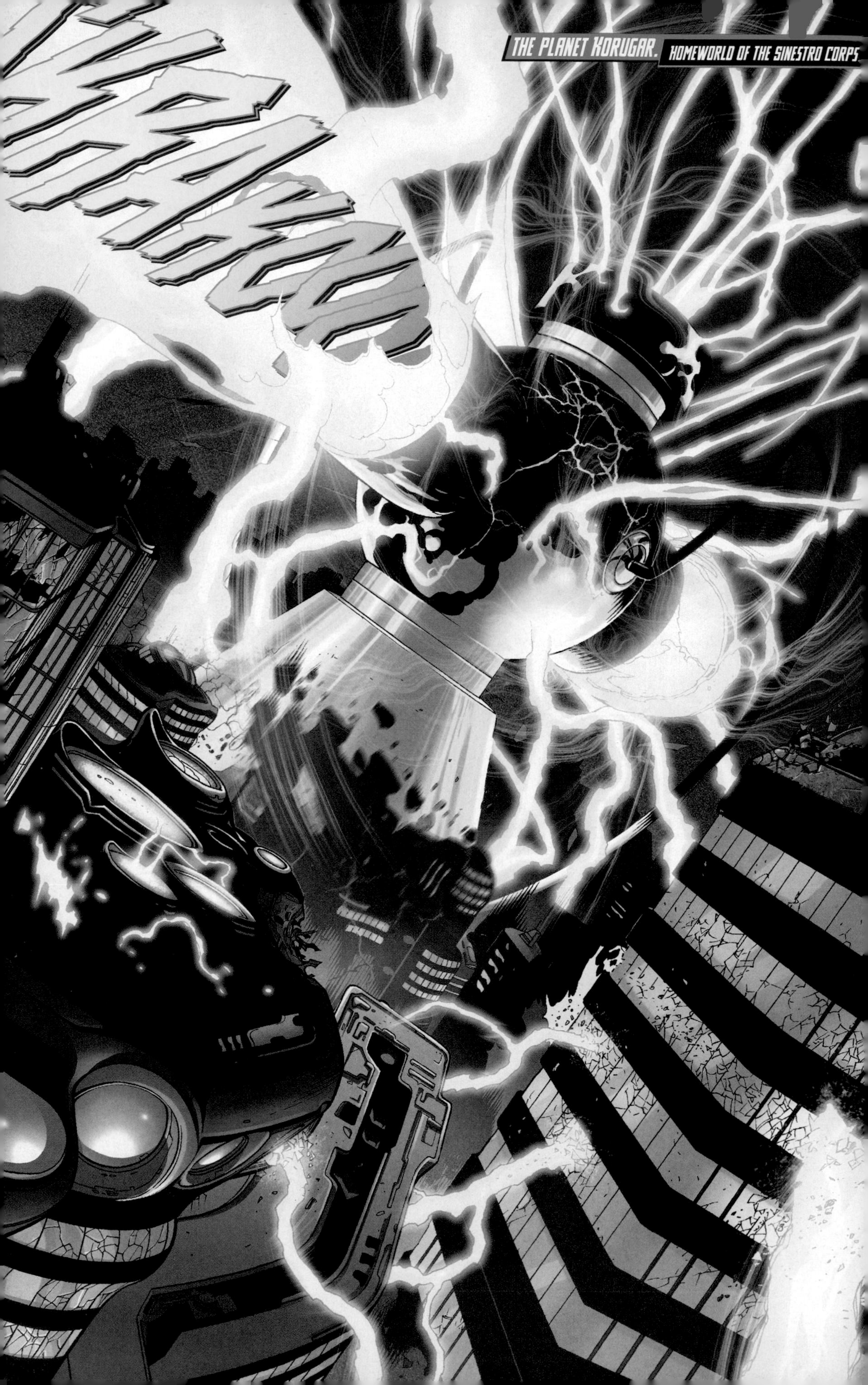
THE PLANET KORUGAR.
HOMEWORLD OF THE SINESTRO CORPS.

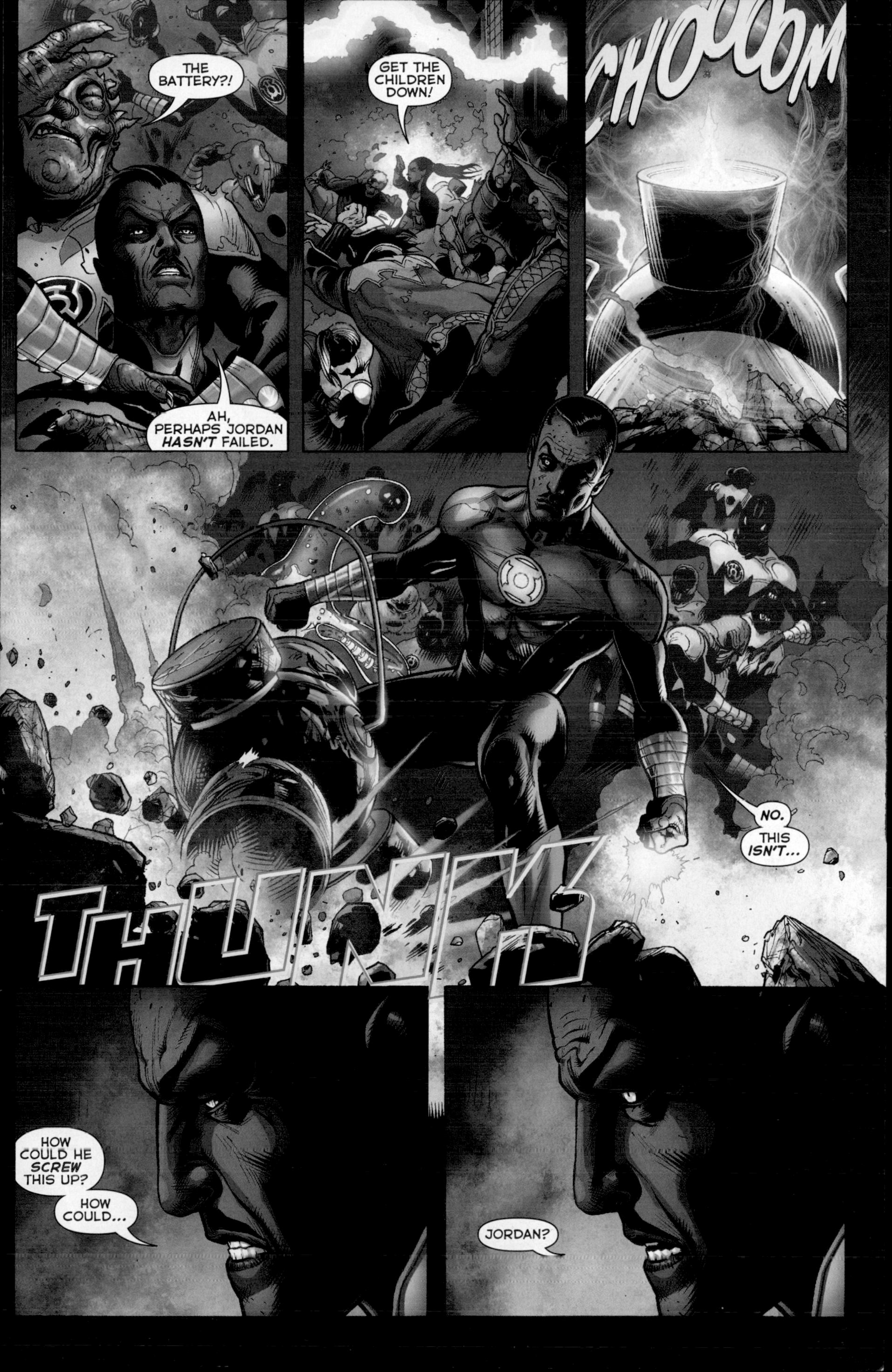

THE BATTERY?!
AH, PERHAPS JORDAN HASN'T FAILED.
GET THE CHILDREN DOWN!
CHOOOOM
NO. THIS ISN'T...
THUMPF
HOW COULD HE SCREW THIS UP?
HOW COULD...
JORDAN?

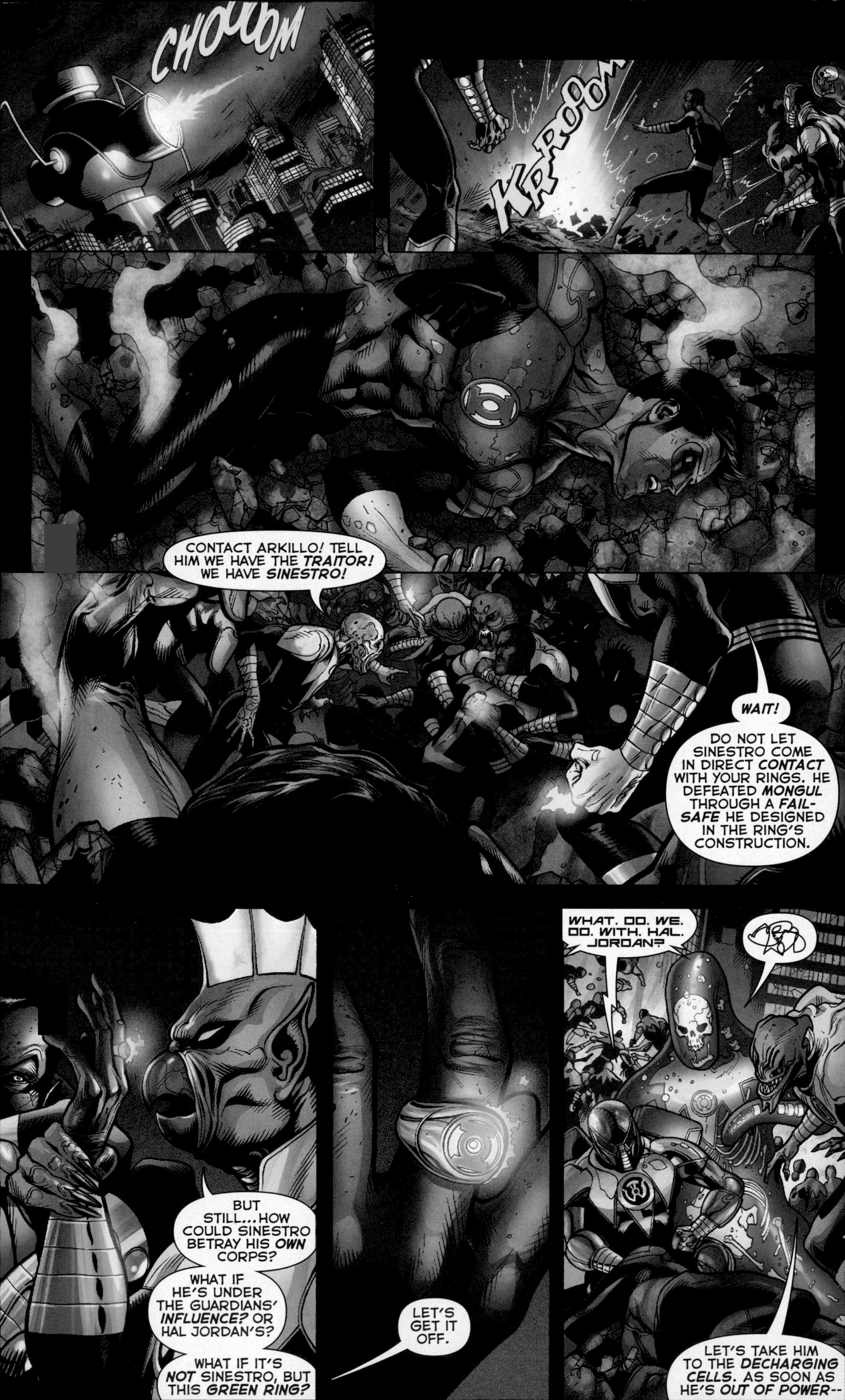
CHOOOM
KRROOOOM
CONTACT ARKILLO! TELL HIM WE HAVE THE *TRAITOR!* WE HAVE *SINESTRO!*
WAIT!
DO NOT LET SINESTRO COME IN DIRECT *CONTACT* WITH YOUR RINGS. HE DEFEATED *MONGUL* THROUGH A *FAIL-SAFE* HE DESIGNED IN THE RING'S CONSTRUCTION.
BUT STILL...HOW COULD SINESTRO BETRAY HIS *OWN* CORPS?
WHAT IF HE'S UNDER THE GUARDIANS' *INFLUENCE?* OR HAL JORDAN'S?
WHAT IF IT'S *NOT* SINESTRO, BUT THIS *GREEN RING?*
LET'S GET IT OFF.
WHAT. DO. WE. DO. WITH. HAL. JORDAN?
LET'S TAKE HIM TO THE *DECHARGING CELLS.* AS SOON AS HE'S *OUT OF POWER--*

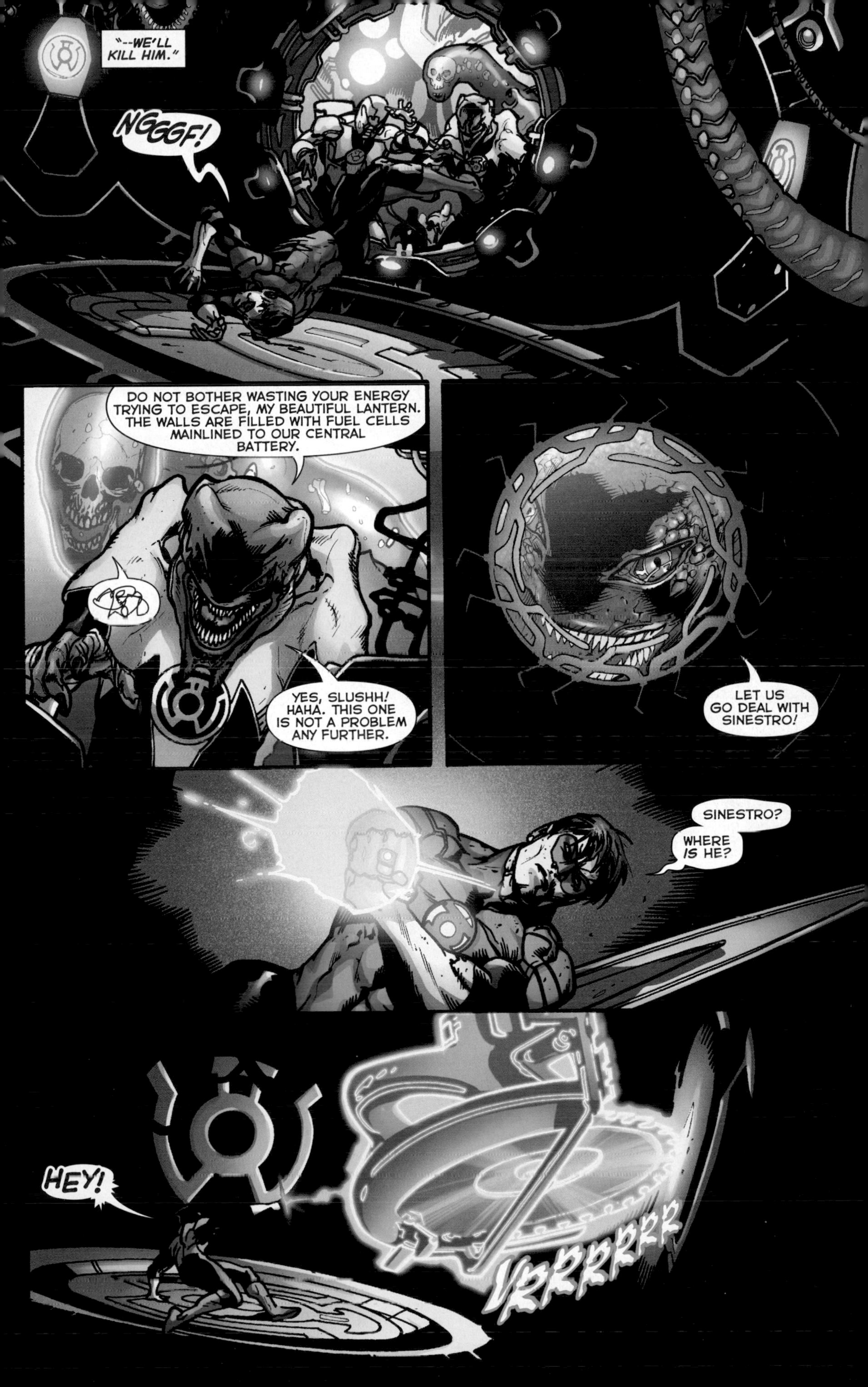
"--WE'LL KILL HIM."
NGGGF!
DO NOT BOTHER WASTING YOUR ENERGY TRYING TO ESCAPE, MY BEAUTIFUL LANTERN. THE WALLS ARE FILLED WITH FUEL CELLS MAINLINED TO OUR CENTRAL BATTERY.
YES, SLUSHH! HAHA. THIS ONE IS NOT A PROBLEM ANY FURTHER.
LET US GO DEAL WITH SINESTRO!
SINESTRO?
WHERE IS HE?
HEY!
VRRRRRR

KRRAKSH

BRKKKK

COME ON!

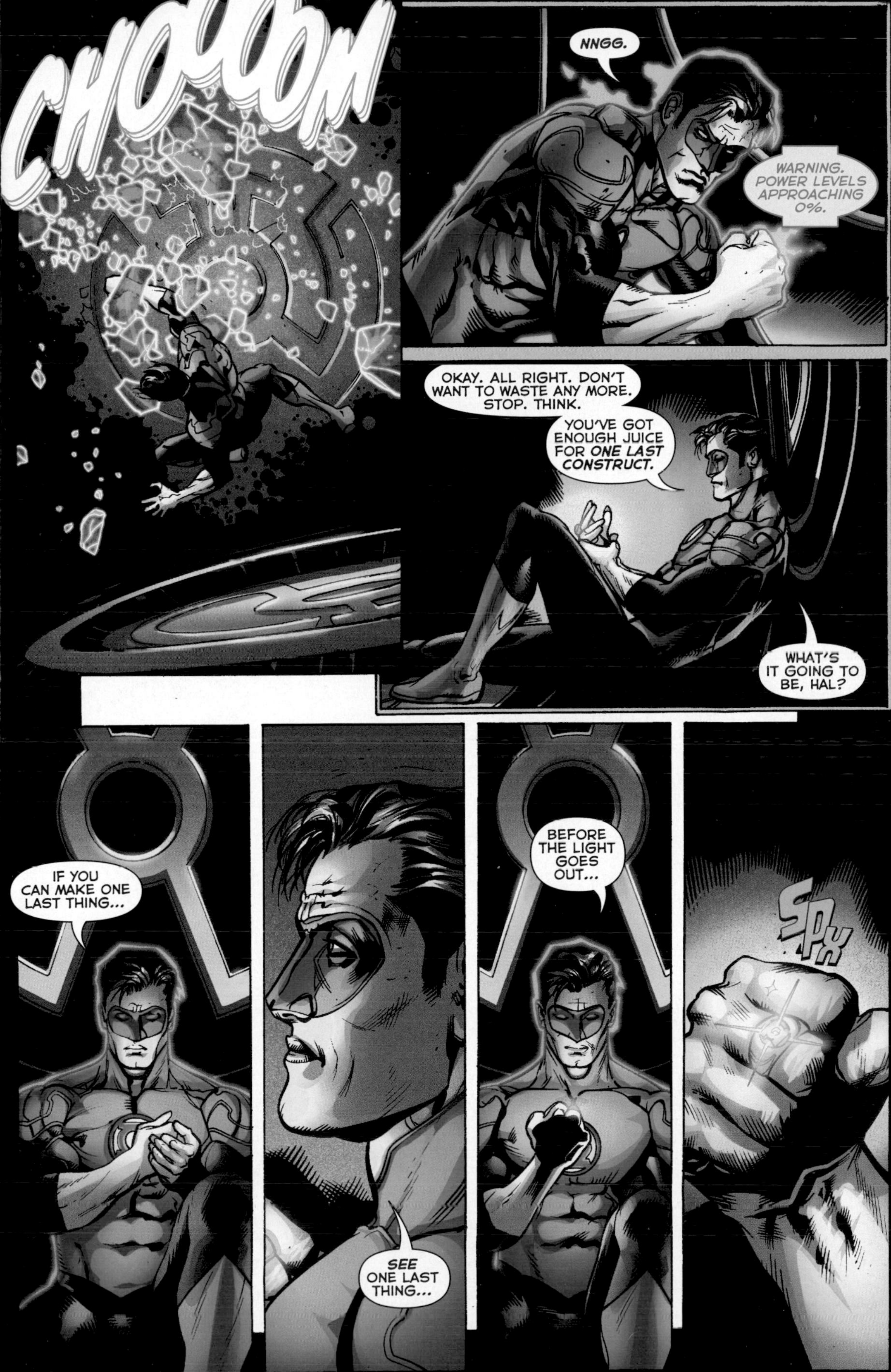
CHOOOOM
NNGG.
WARNING. POWER LEVELS APPROACHING 0%.
OKAY. ALL RIGHT. DON'T WANT TO WASTE ANY MORE. STOP. THINK.
YOU'VE GOT ENOUGH JUICE FOR *ONE LAST CONSTRUCT.*
WHAT'S IT GOING TO BE, HAL?
IF YOU CAN MAKE ONE LAST THING...
SEE ONE LAST THING...
BEFORE THE LIGHT GOES OUT...
SPX

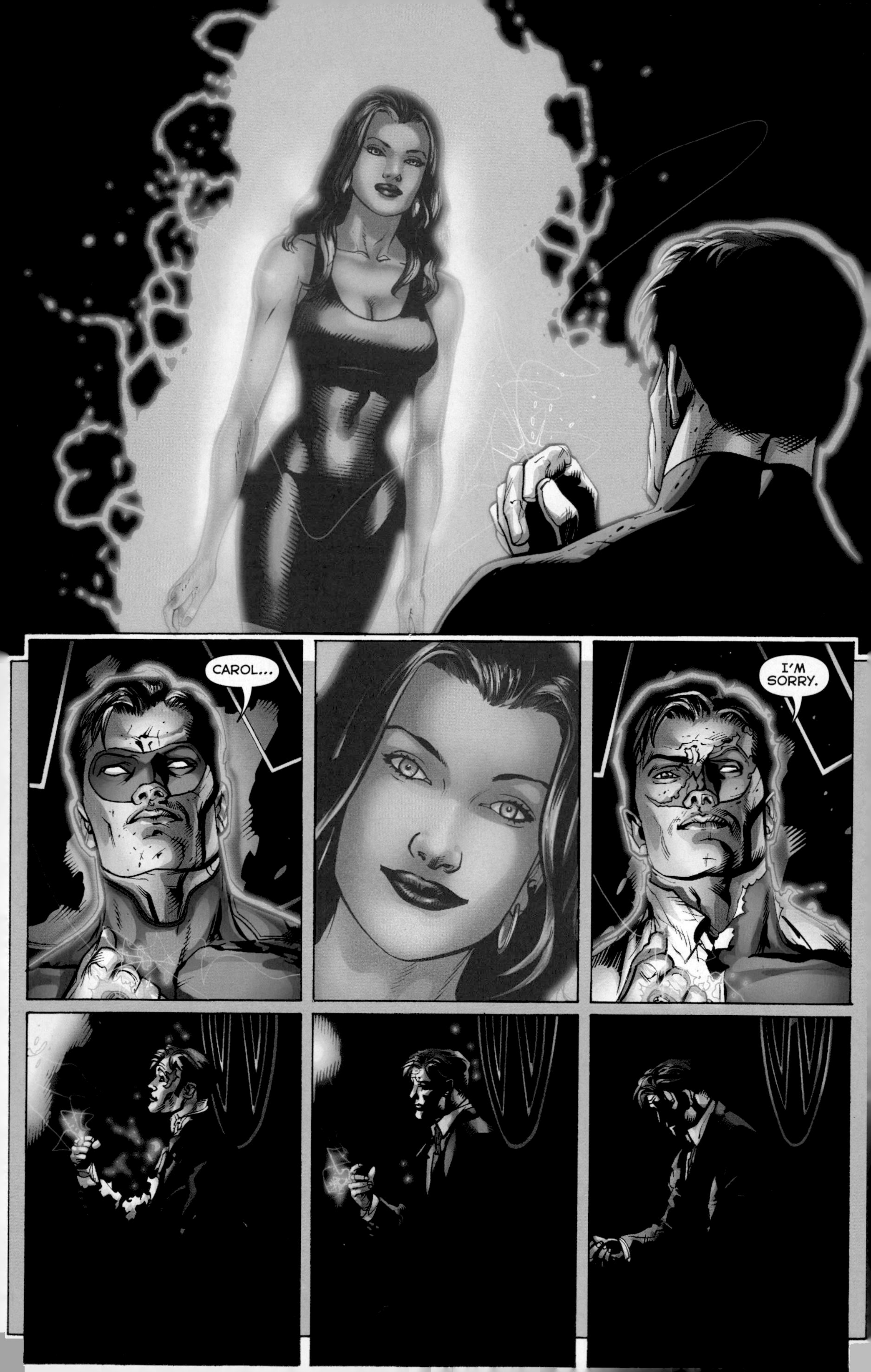
CAROL...
I'M SORRY.

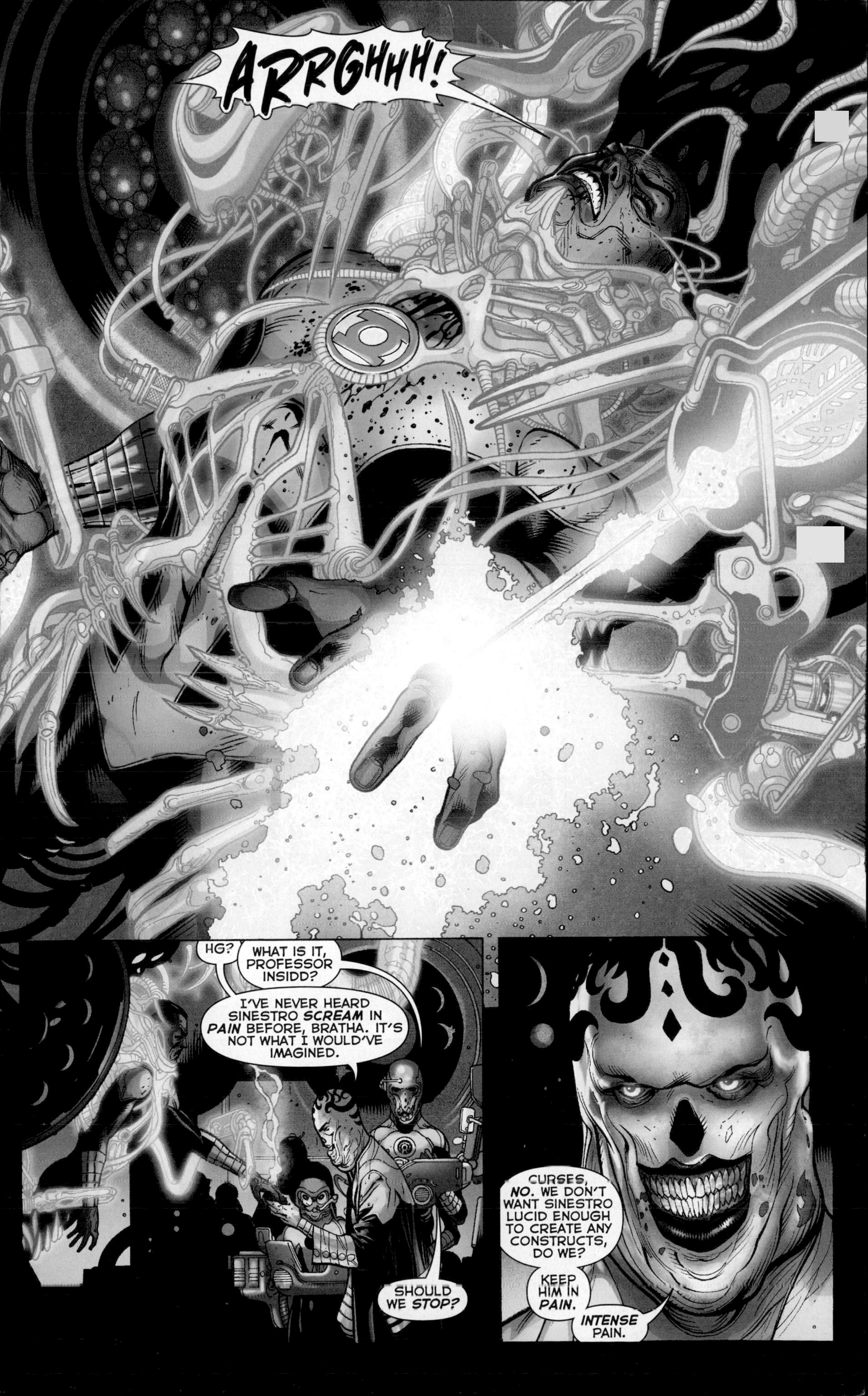
ARRGHHH!
HG?
WHAT IS IT, PROFESSOR INSIDD?
I'VE NEVER HEARD SINESTRO SCREAM IN PAIN BEFORE, BRATHA. IT'S NOT WHAT I WOULD'VE IMAGINED.
SHOULD WE STOP?
CURSES, NO. WE DON'T WANT SINESTRO LUCID ENOUGH TO CREATE ANY CONSTRUCTS, DO WE?
KEEP HIM IN PAIN.
INTENSE PAIN.

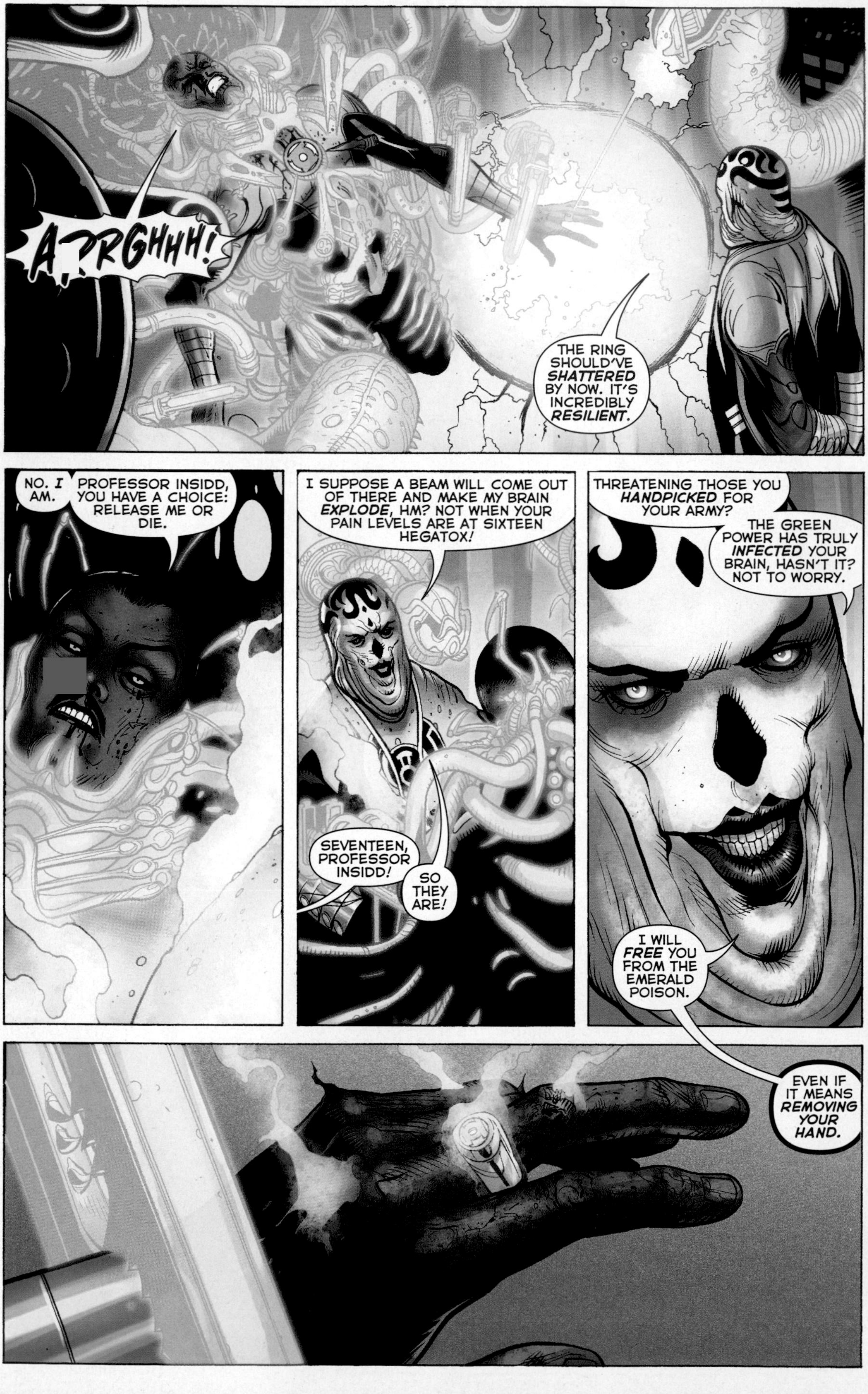
ARGHHH!
THE RING SHOULD'VE SHATTERED BY NOW. IT'S INCREDIBLY RESILIENT.
NO. I AM.
PROFESSOR INSIDD, YOU HAVE A CHOICE: RELEASE ME OR DIE.
I SUPPOSE A BEAM WILL COME OUT OF THERE AND MAKE MY BRAIN EXPLODE, HM? NOT WHEN YOUR PAIN LEVELS ARE AT SIXTEEN HEGATOX!
SEVENTEEN, PROFESSOR INSIDD!
SO THEY ARE!
THREATENING THOSE YOU HANDPICKED FOR YOUR ARMY?
THE GREEN POWER HAS TRULY INFECTED YOUR BRAIN, HASN'T IT? NOT TO WORRY.
I WILL FREE YOU FROM THE EMERALD POISON.
EVEN IF IT MEANS REMOVING YOUR HAND.

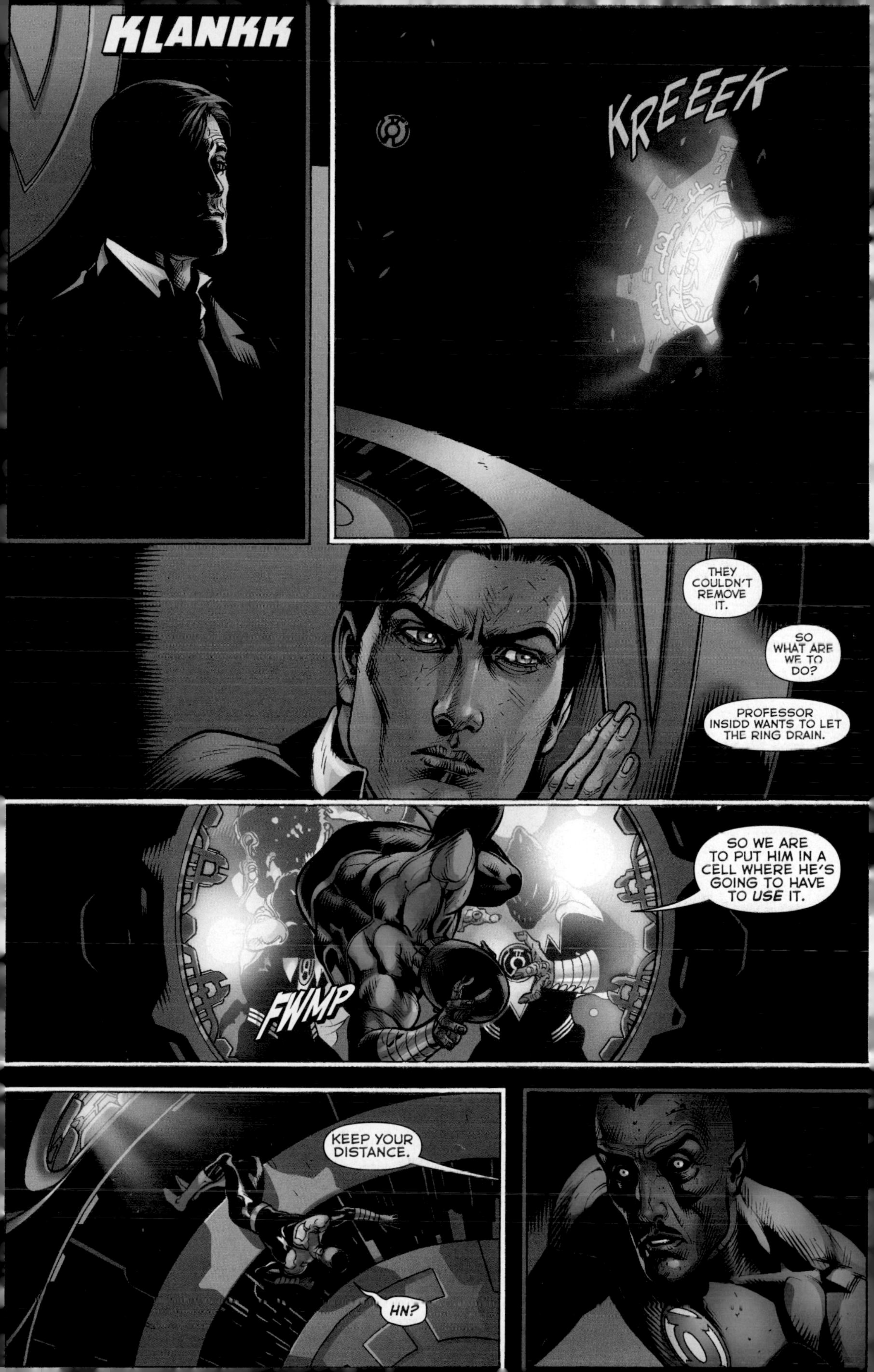
KLANKK
KREEEK
THEY COULDN'T REMOVE IT.
SO WHAT ARE WE TO DO?
PROFESSOR INSIDD WANTS TO LET THE RING DRAIN.
SO WE ARE TO PUT HIM IN A CELL WHERE HE'S GOING TO HAVE TO *USE* IT.
FWMP
KEEP YOUR DISTANCE.
HN?

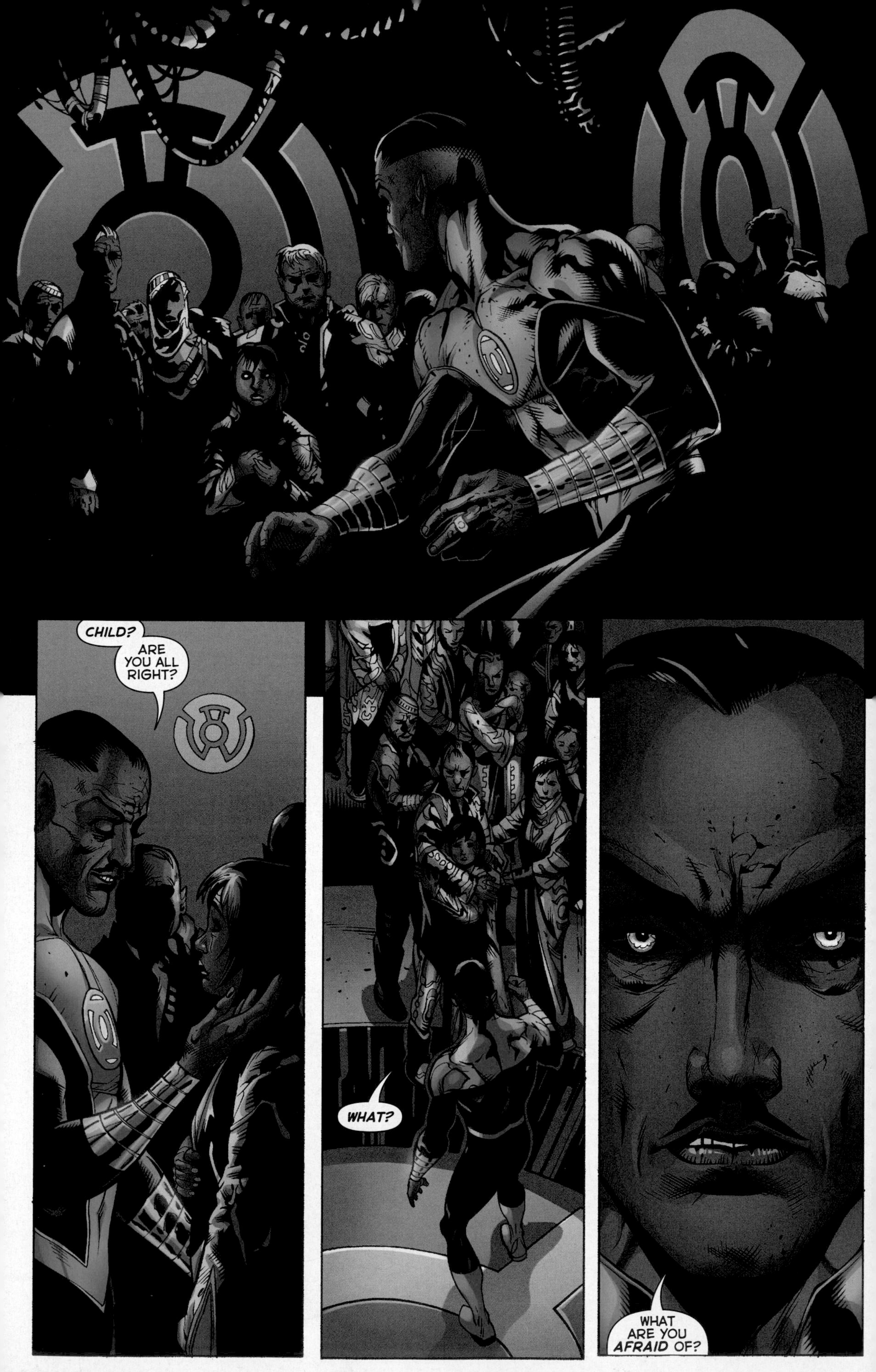
CHILD?
ARE YOU ALL RIGHT?
WHAT?
WHAT ARE YOU AFRAID OF?

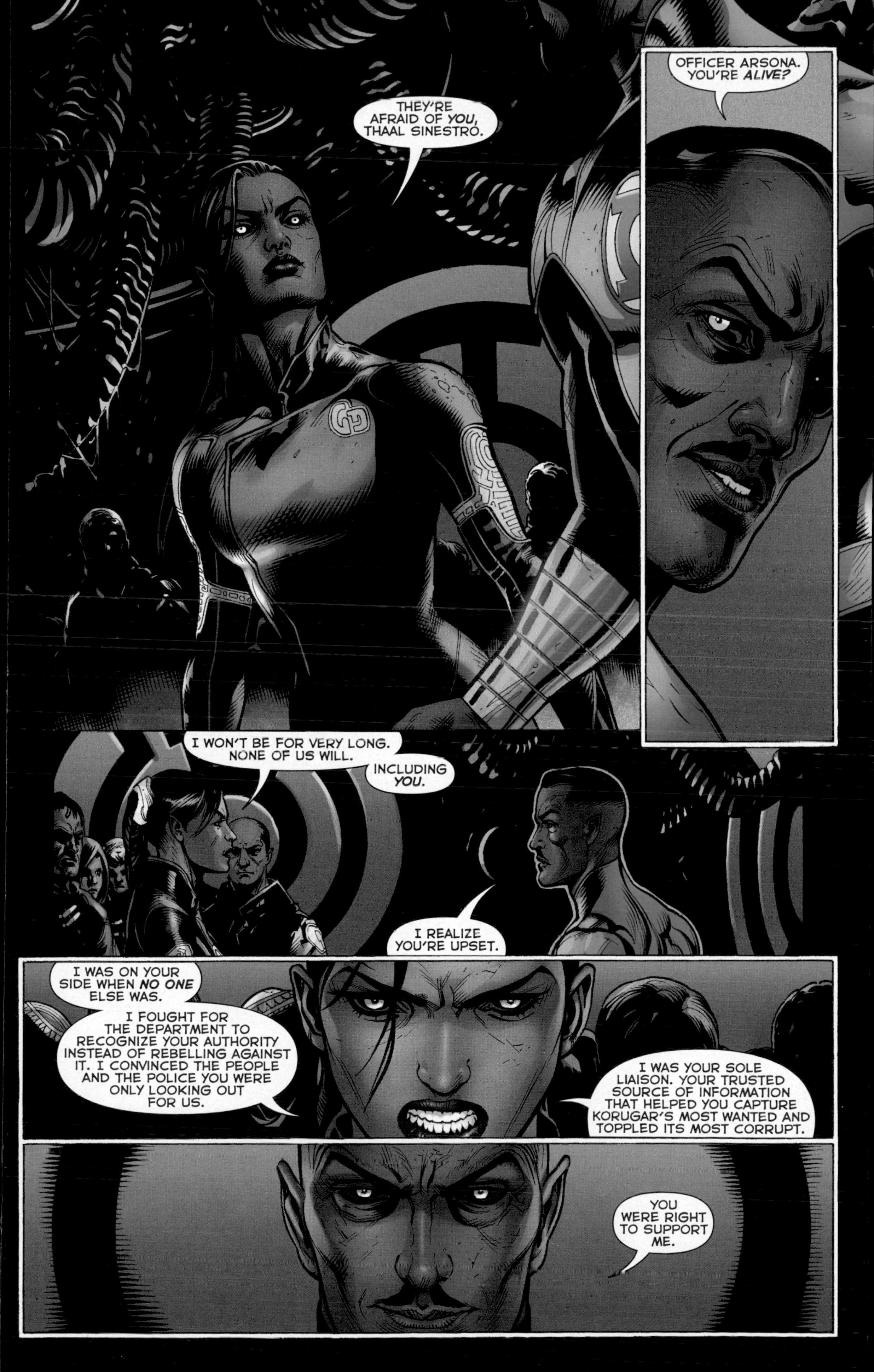
THEY'RE AFRAID OF *YOU*, THAAL SINESTRO.
OFFICER ARSONA. YOU'RE *ALIVE?*
I WON'T BE FOR VERY LONG. NONE OF US WILL.
INCLUDING *YOU*.
I REALIZE YOU'RE UPSET.
I WAS ON YOUR SIDE WHEN *NO ONE* ELSE WAS.
I FOUGHT FOR THE DEPARTMENT TO RECOGNIZE YOUR AUTHORITY INSTEAD OF REBELLING AGAINST IT. I CONVINCED THE PEOPLE AND THE POLICE YOU WERE ONLY LOOKING OUT FOR US.
I WAS YOUR SOLE LIAISON. YOUR TRUSTED SOURCE OF INFORMATION THAT HELPED YOU CAPTURE KORUGAR'S MOST WANTED AND TOPPLED ITS MOST CORRUPT.
YOU WERE RIGHT TO SUPPORT ME.

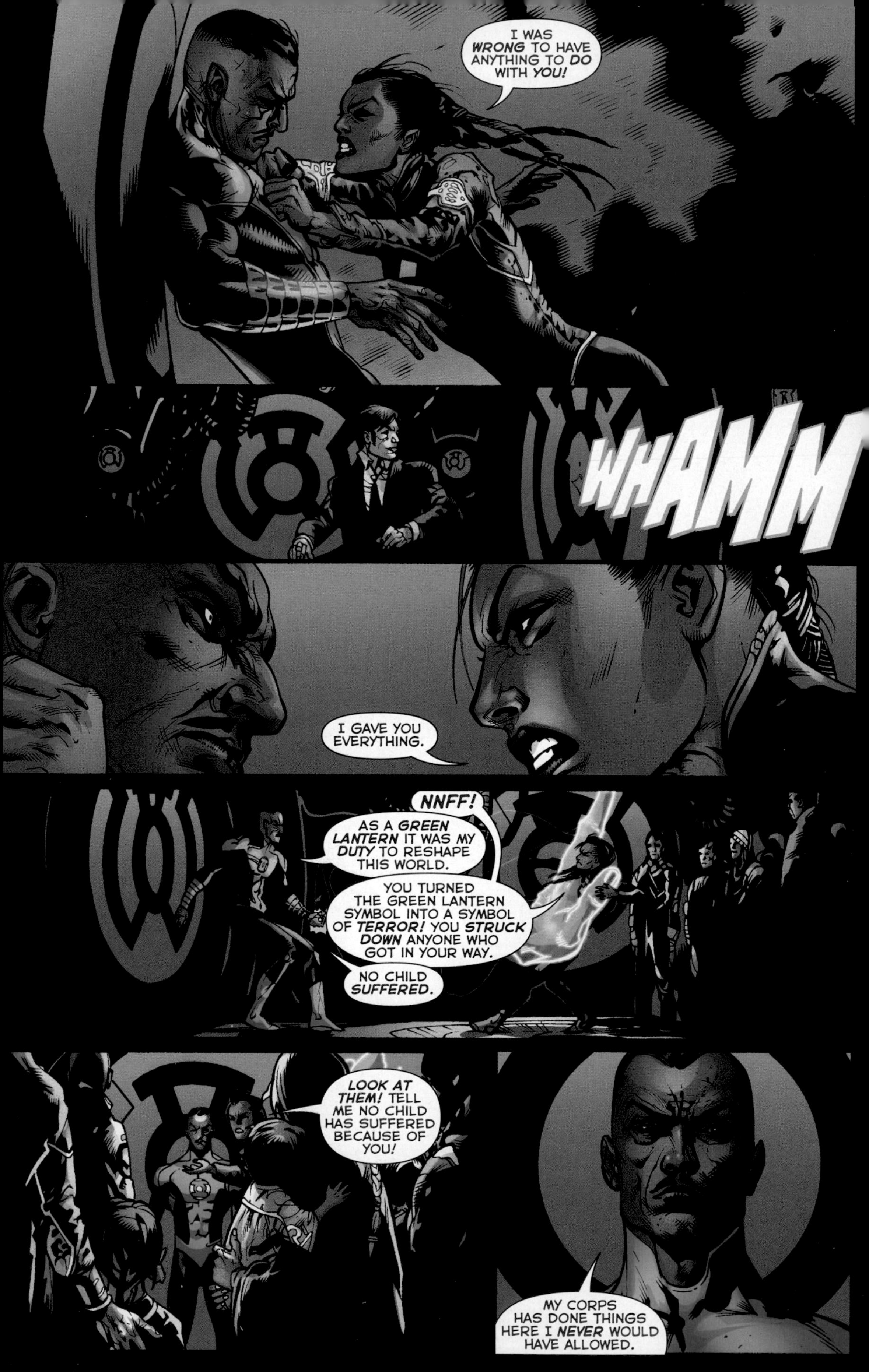
I WAS WRONG TO HAVE ANYTHING TO DO WITH YOU!
WHAMM
I GAVE YOU EVERYTHING.
NNFF!
AS A GREEN LANTERN IT WAS MY DUTY TO RESHAPE THIS WORLD.
YOU TURNED THE GREEN LANTERN SYMBOL INTO A SYMBOL OF TERROR! YOU STRUCK DOWN ANYONE WHO GOT IN YOUR WAY.
NO CHILD SUFFERED.
LOOK AT THEM! TELL ME NO CHILD HAS SUFFERED BECAUSE OF YOU!
MY CORPS HAS DONE THINGS HERE I NEVER WOULD HAVE ALLOWED.

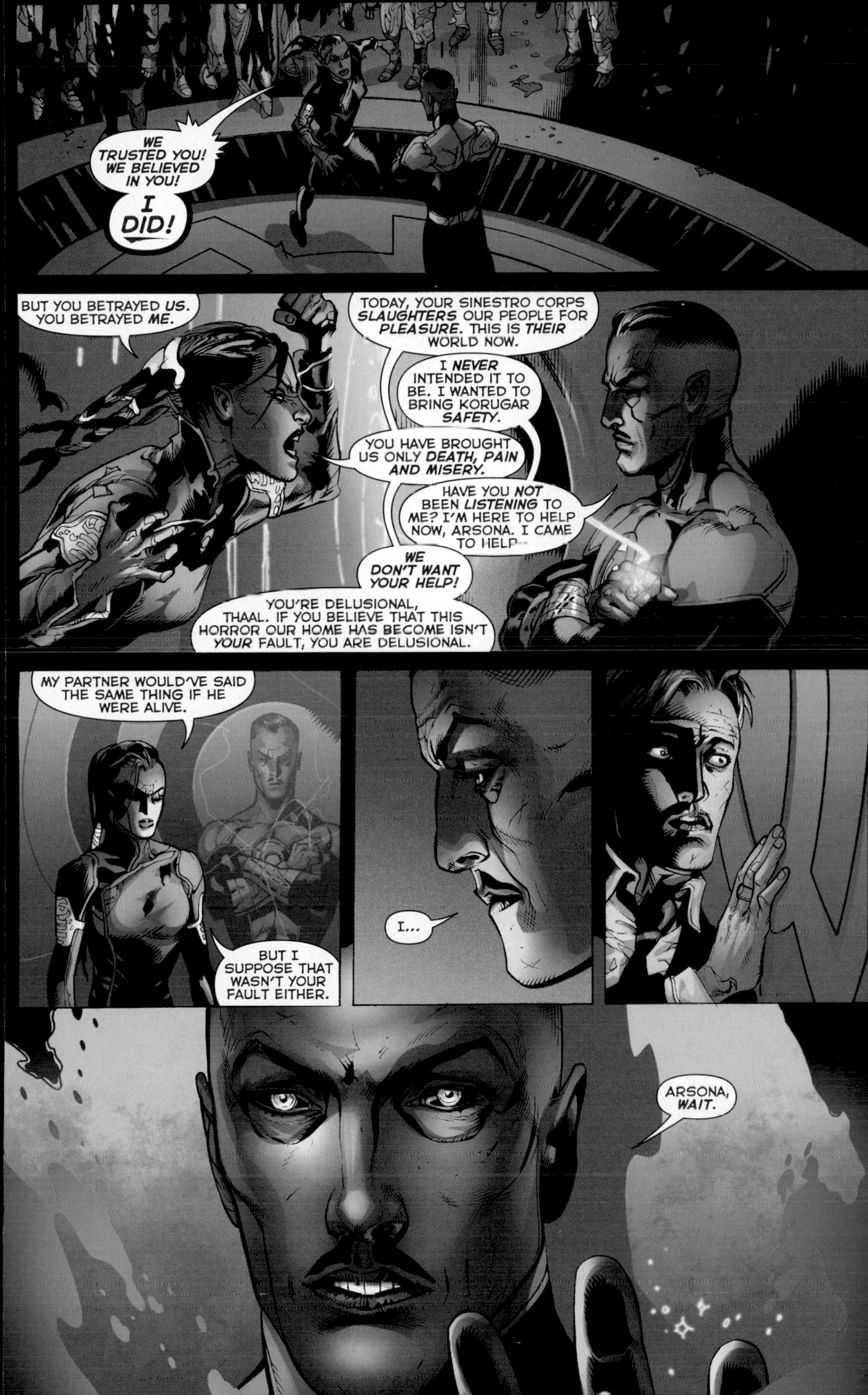
WE TRUSTED YOU! WE BELIEVED IN YOU!
I DID!
BUT YOU BETRAYED US. YOU BETRAYED ME.
TODAY, YOUR SINESTRO CORPS SLAUGHTERS OUR PEOPLE FOR PLEASURE. THIS IS THEIR WORLD NOW.
I NEVER INTENDED IT TO BE. I WANTED TO BRING KORUGAR SAFETY.
YOU HAVE BROUGHT US ONLY DEATH, PAIN AND MISERY.
HAVE YOU NOT BEEN LISTENING TO ME? I'M HERE TO HELP NOW, ARSONA. I CAME TO HELP--
WE DON'T WANT YOUR HELP!
YOU'RE DELUSIONAL, THAAL. IF YOU BELIEVE THAT THIS HORROR OUR HOME HAS BECOME ISN'T YOUR FAULT, YOU ARE DELUSIONAL.
MY PARTNER WOULD'VE SAID THE SAME THING IF HE WERE ALIVE.
BUT I SUPPOSE THAT WASN'T YOUR FAULT EITHER.
I...
ARSONA, WAIT.

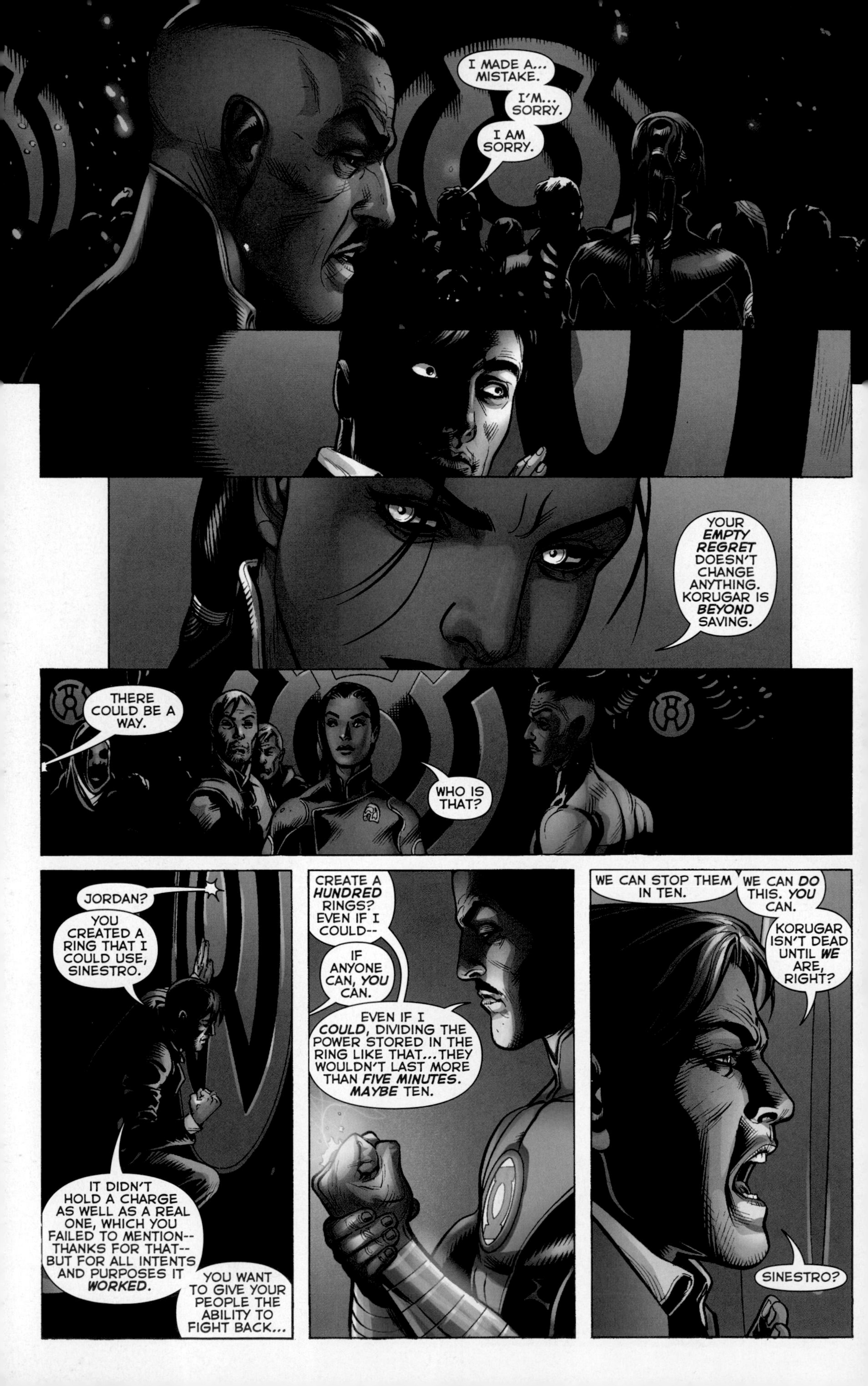
I MADE A... MISTAKE.
I'M... SORRY.
I AM SORRY.
YOUR EMPTY REGRET DOESN'T CHANGE ANYTHING. KORUGAR IS BEYOND SAVING.
THERE COULD BE A WAY.
WHO IS THAT?
JORDAN?
YOU CREATED A RING THAT I COULD USE, SINESTRO.
IT DIDN'T HOLD A CHARGE AS WELL AS A REAL ONE, WHICH YOU FAILED TO MENTION-- THANKS FOR THAT-- BUT FOR ALL INTENTS AND PURPOSES IT WORKED.
YOU WANT TO GIVE YOUR PEOPLE THE ABILITY TO FIGHT BACK...
CREATE A HUNDRED RINGS? EVEN IF I COULD--
IF ANYONE CAN, YOU CAN.
EVEN IF I COULD, DIVIDING THE POWER STORED IN THE RING LIKE THAT...THEY WOULDN'T LAST MORE THAN FIVE MINUTES. MAYBE TEN.
WE CAN STOP THEM IN TEN.
WE CAN DO THIS. YOU CAN.
KORUGAR ISN'T DEAD UNTIL WE ARE, RIGHT?
SINESTRO?

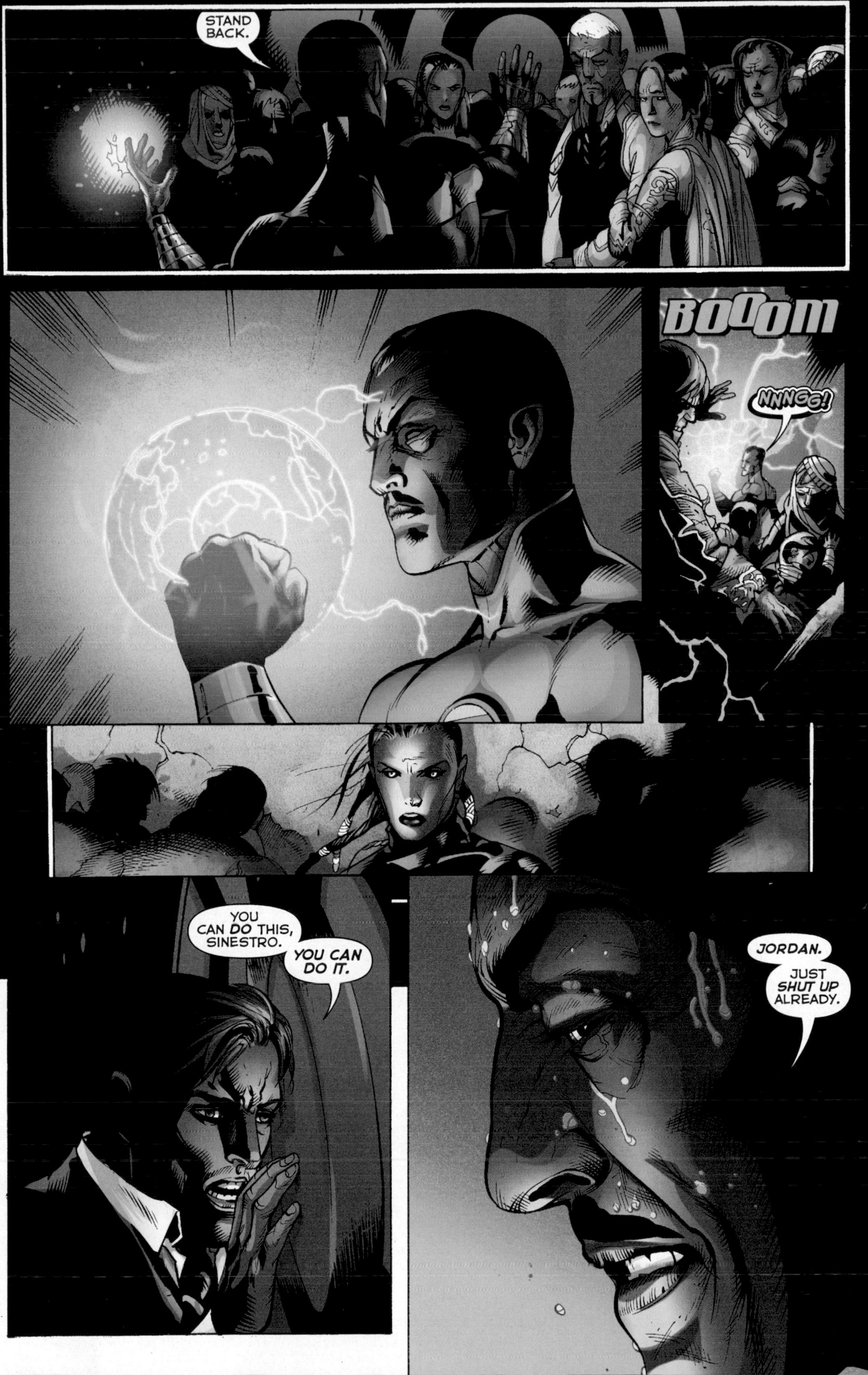
STAND BACK.
BOOOOM
NNNGG!
YOU CAN DO THIS, SINESTRO.
YOU CAN DO IT.
JORDAN.
JUST SHUT UP ALREADY.

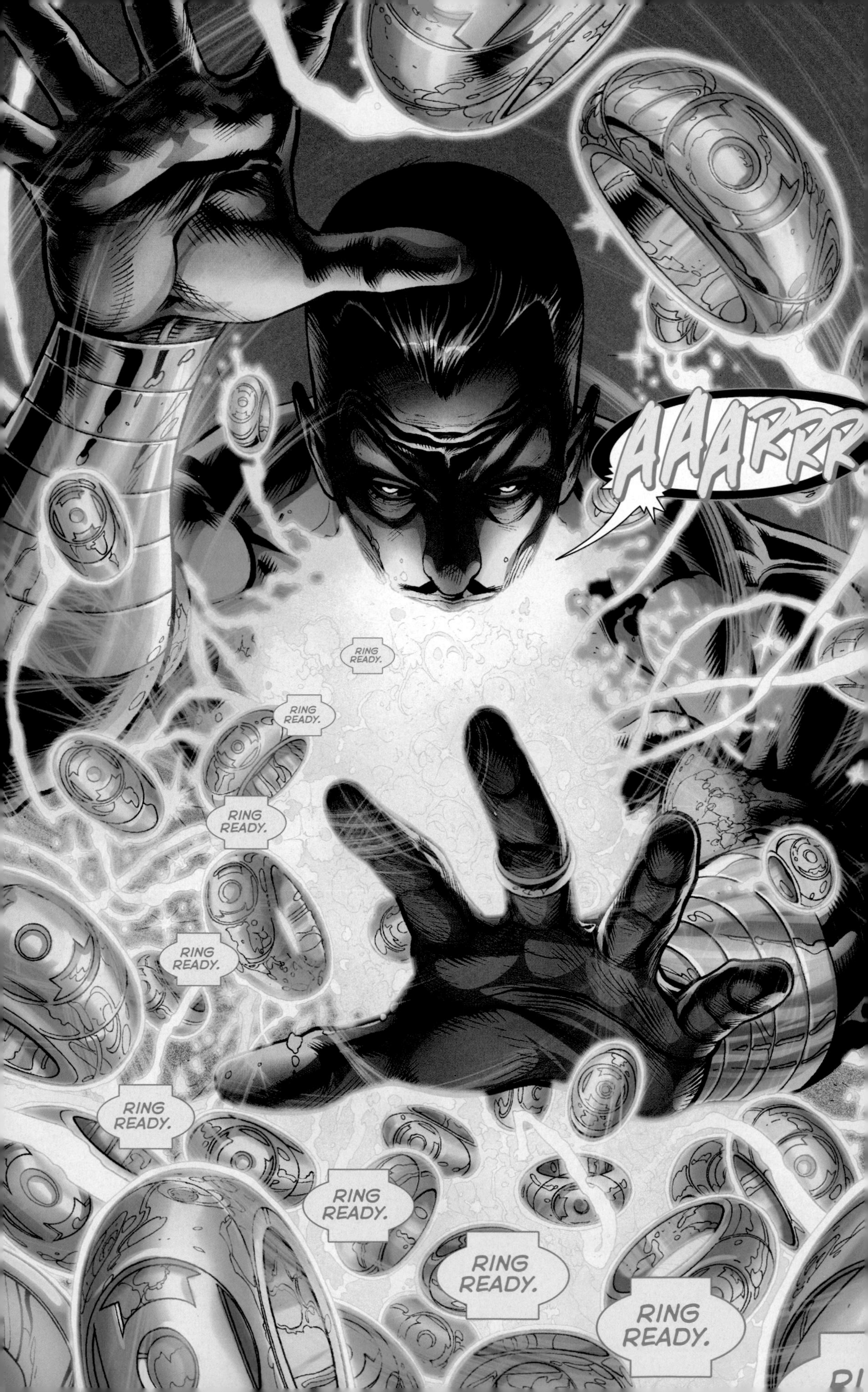
AAARRR
RING READY.
RING READY.
RING READY.
RING READY.
RING READY.
RING READY.
RING READY.
RING READY.

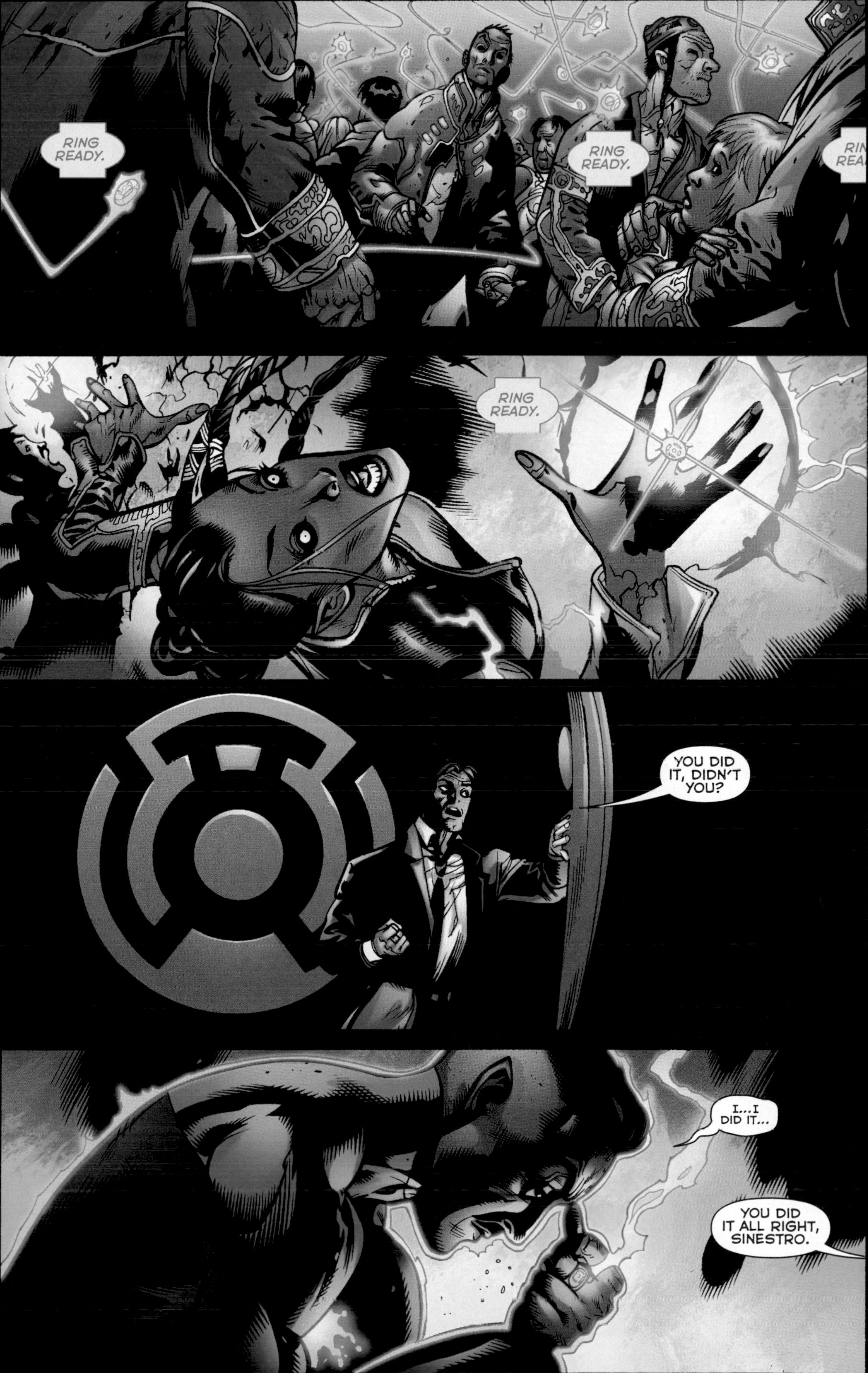

RING READY.
RING READY.
RING READY.
YOU DID IT, DIDN'T YOU?
I...I DID IT...
YOU DID IT ALL RIGHT, SINESTRO.

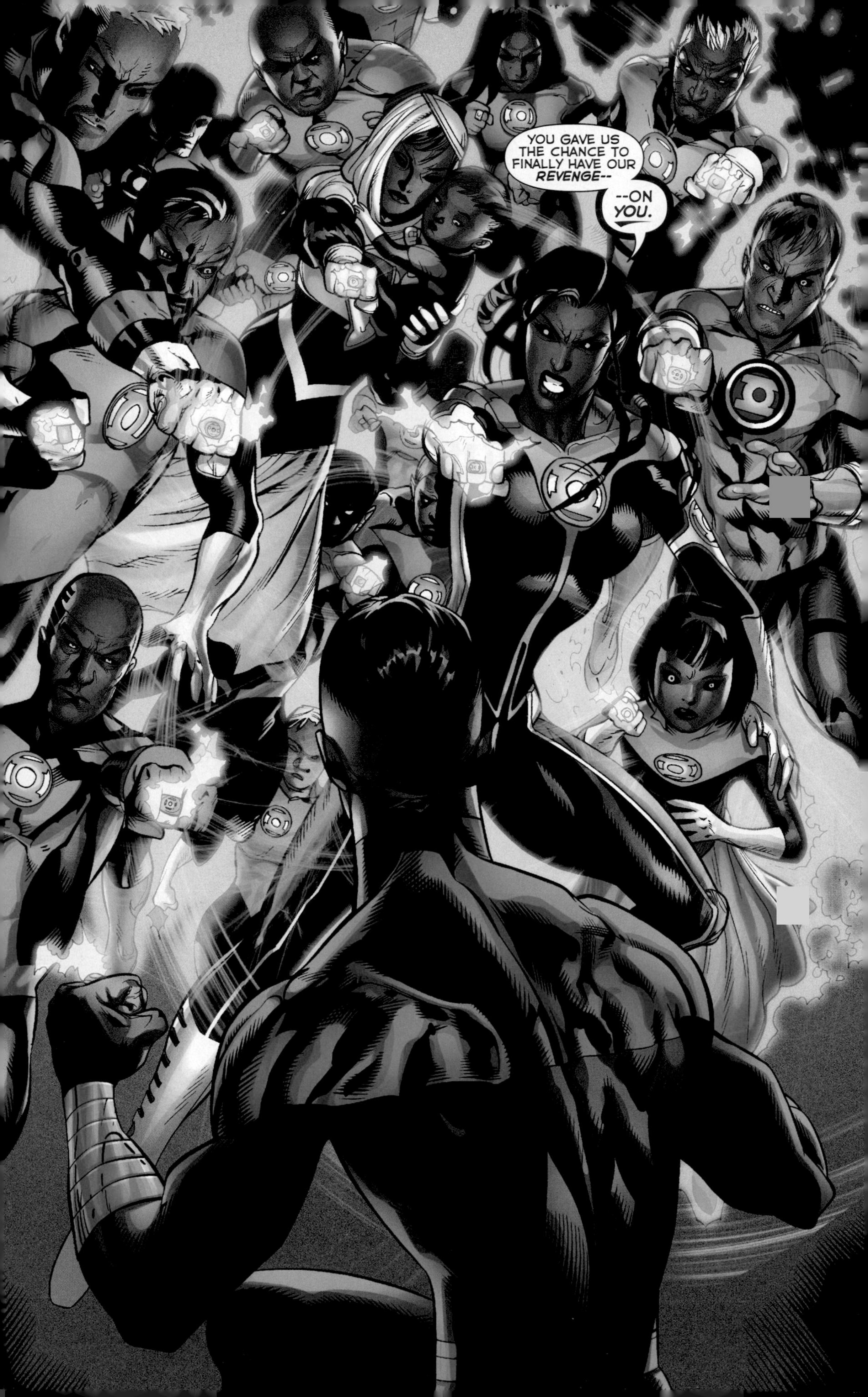
YOU GAVE US THE CHANCE TO FINALLY HAVE OUR *REVENGE*--
--ON *YOU*.

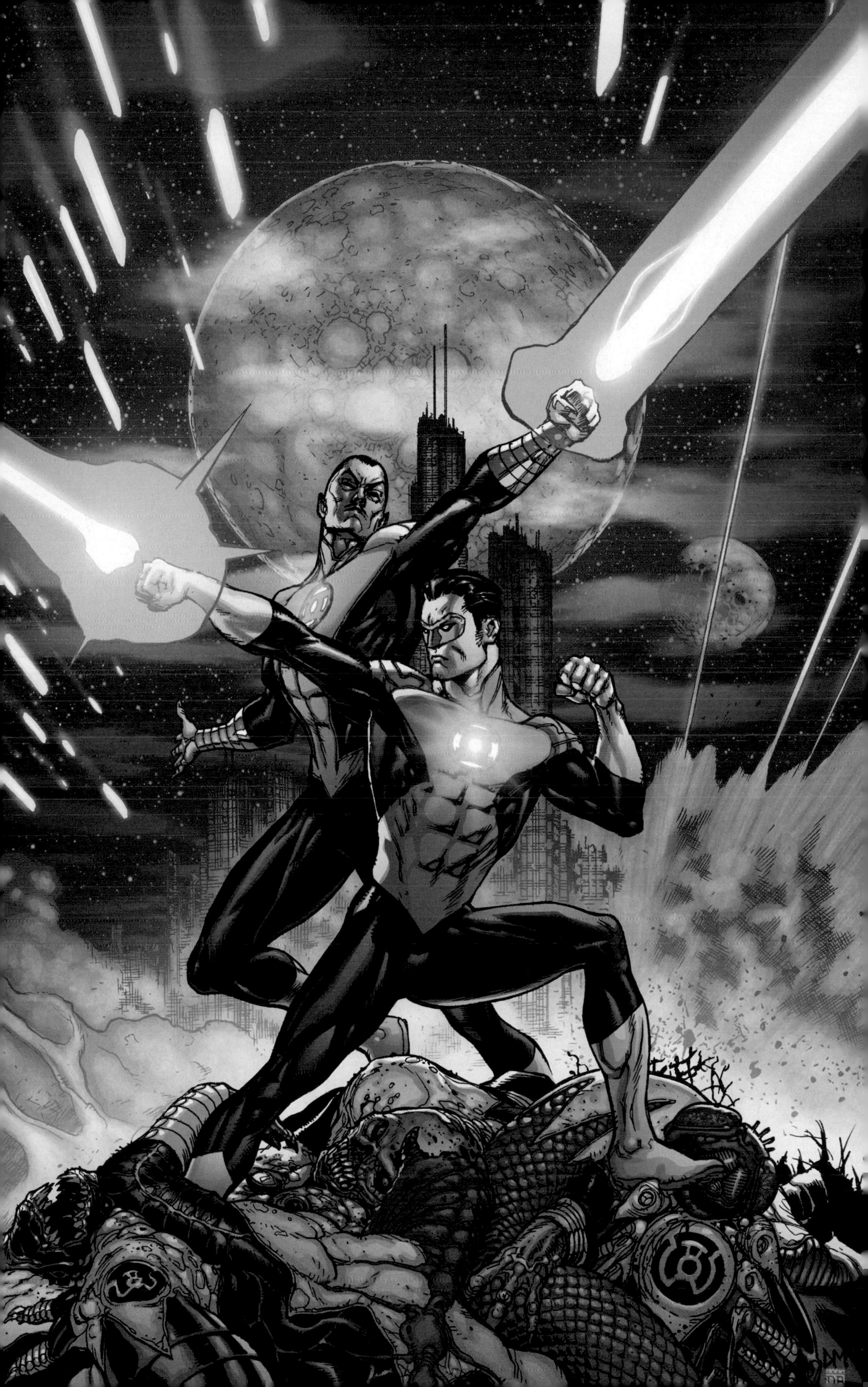

Doug Mahnke & David Baron

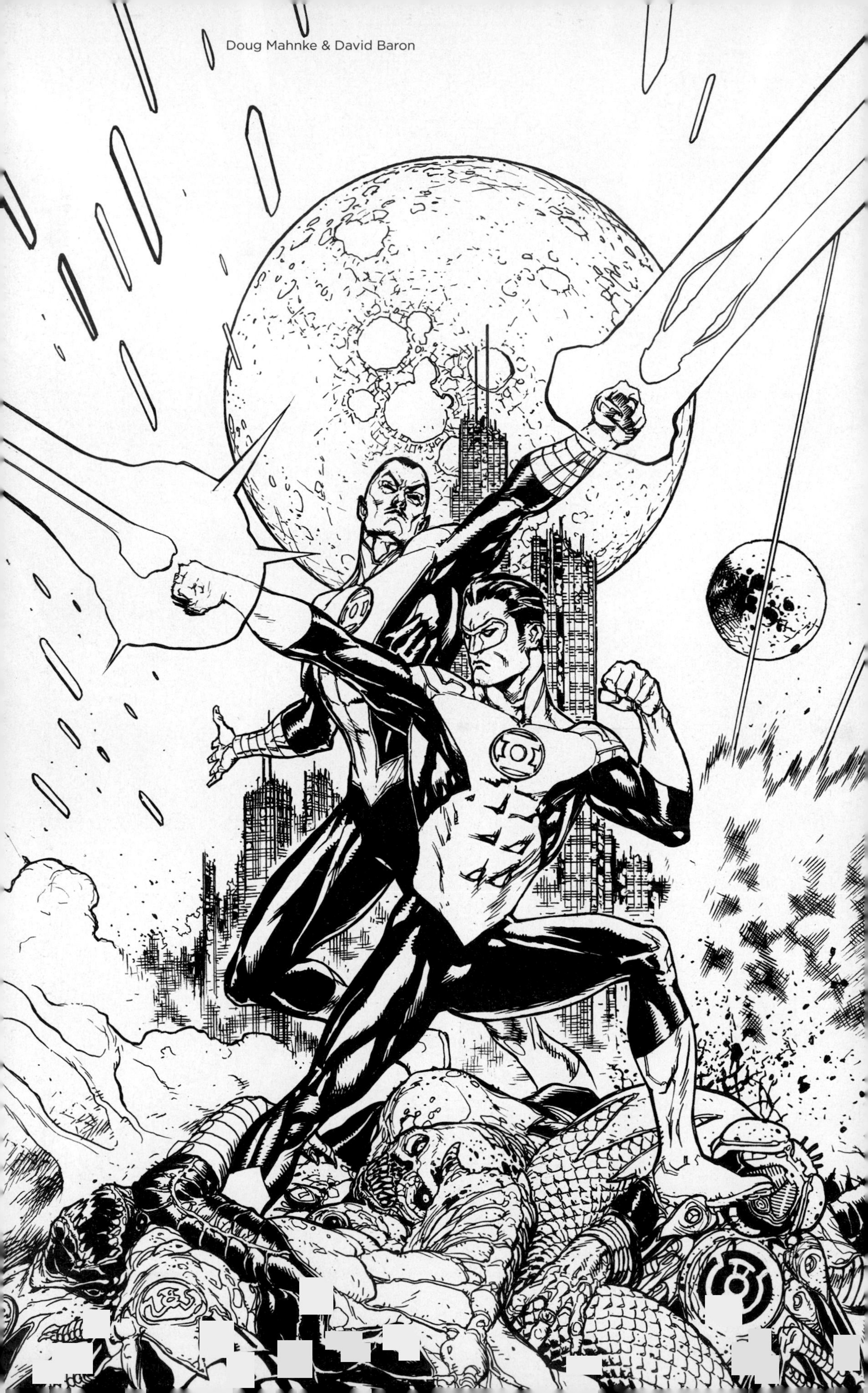

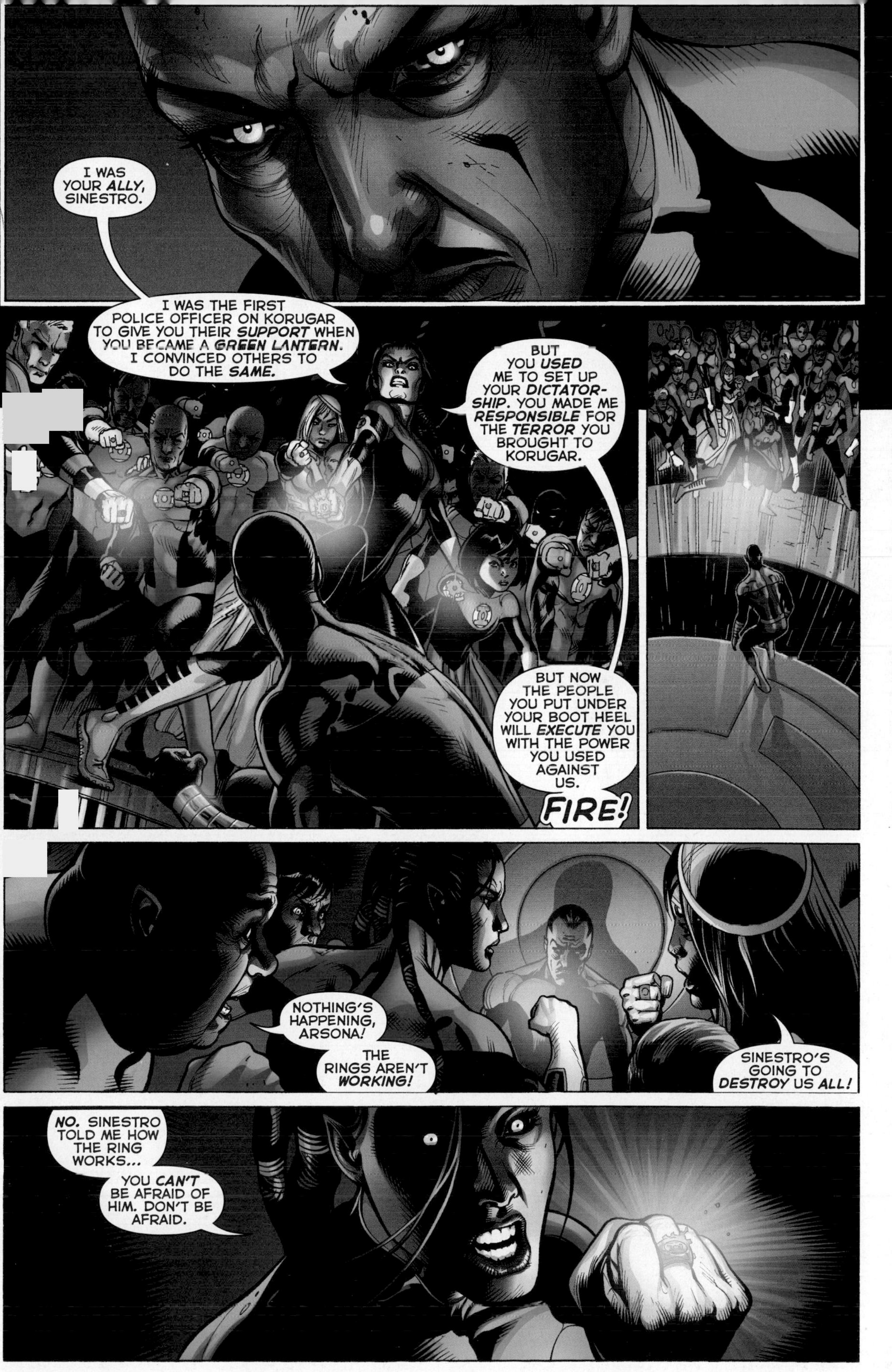
I WAS YOUR *ALLY,* SINESTRO.
I WAS THE FIRST POLICE OFFICER ON KORUGAR TO GIVE YOU THEIR *SUPPORT* WHEN YOU BECAME A *GREEN LANTERN.* I CONVINCED OTHERS TO DO THE *SAME.*
BUT YOU *USED* ME TO SET UP YOUR *DICTATORSHIP.* YOU MADE ME *RESPONSIBLE* FOR THE *TERROR* YOU BROUGHT TO KORUGAR.
BUT NOW THE PEOPLE YOU PUT UNDER YOUR BOOT HEEL WILL *EXECUTE* YOU WITH THE POWER YOU USED AGAINST US.
FIRE!
NOTHING'S HAPPENING, ARSONA!
THE RINGS AREN'T *WORKING!*
SINESTRO'S GOING TO *DESTROY* US *ALL!*
NO. SINESTRO TOLD ME HOW THE RING WORKS...
YOU *CAN'T* BE AFRAID OF HIM. DON'T BE AFRAID.

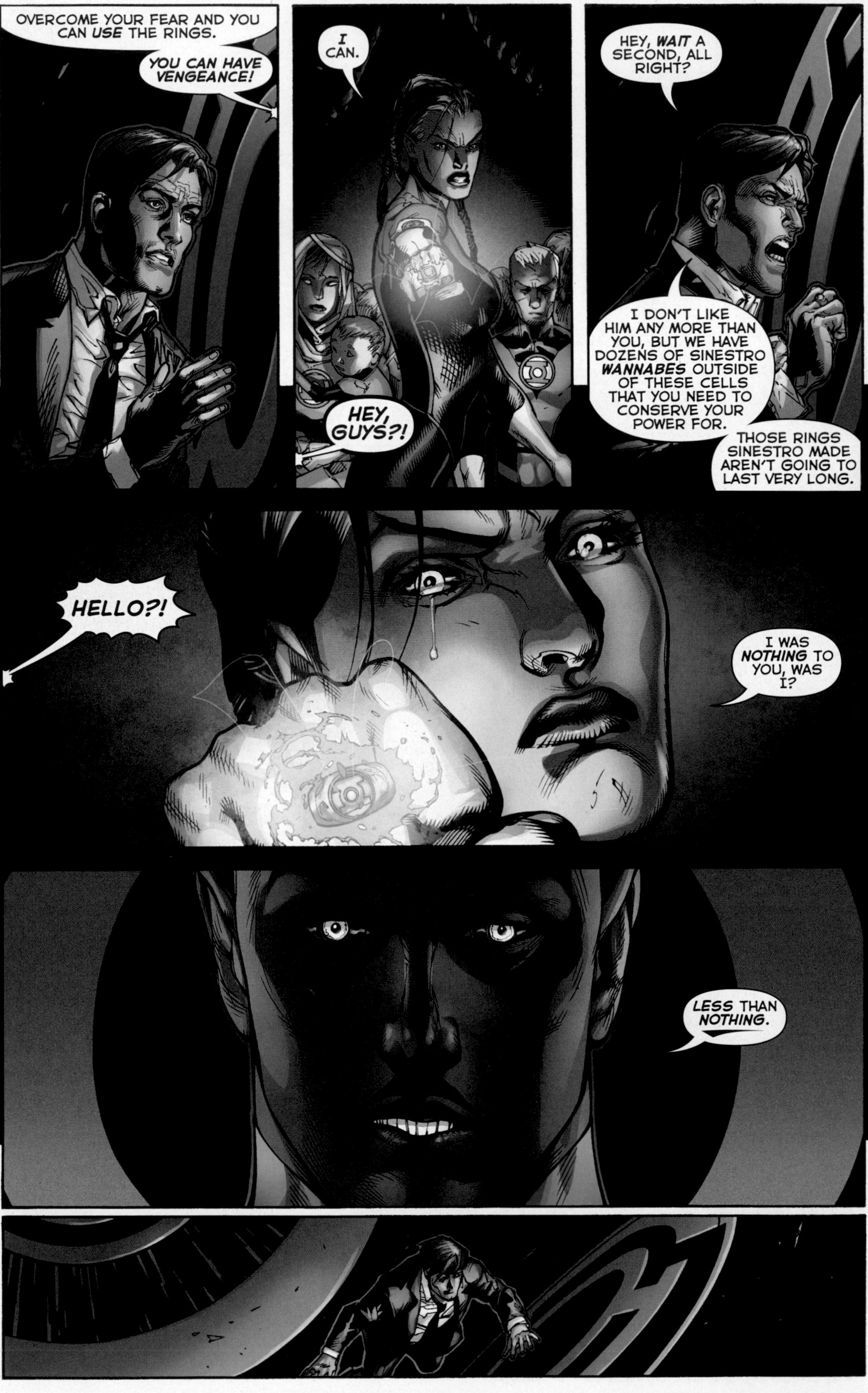
OVERCOME YOUR FEAR AND YOU CAN USE THE RINGS.
YOU CAN HAVE VENGEANCE!
I CAN.
HEY, GUYS?!
HEY, WAIT A SECOND, ALL RIGHT?
I DON'T LIKE HIM ANY MORE THAN YOU, BUT WE HAVE DOZENS OF SINESTRO WANNABES OUTSIDE OF THESE CELLS THAT YOU NEED TO CONSERVE YOUR POWER FOR.
THOSE RINGS SINESTRO MADE AREN'T GOING TO LAST VERY LONG.
HELLO?!
I WAS NOTHING TO YOU, WAS I?
LESS THAN NOTHING.

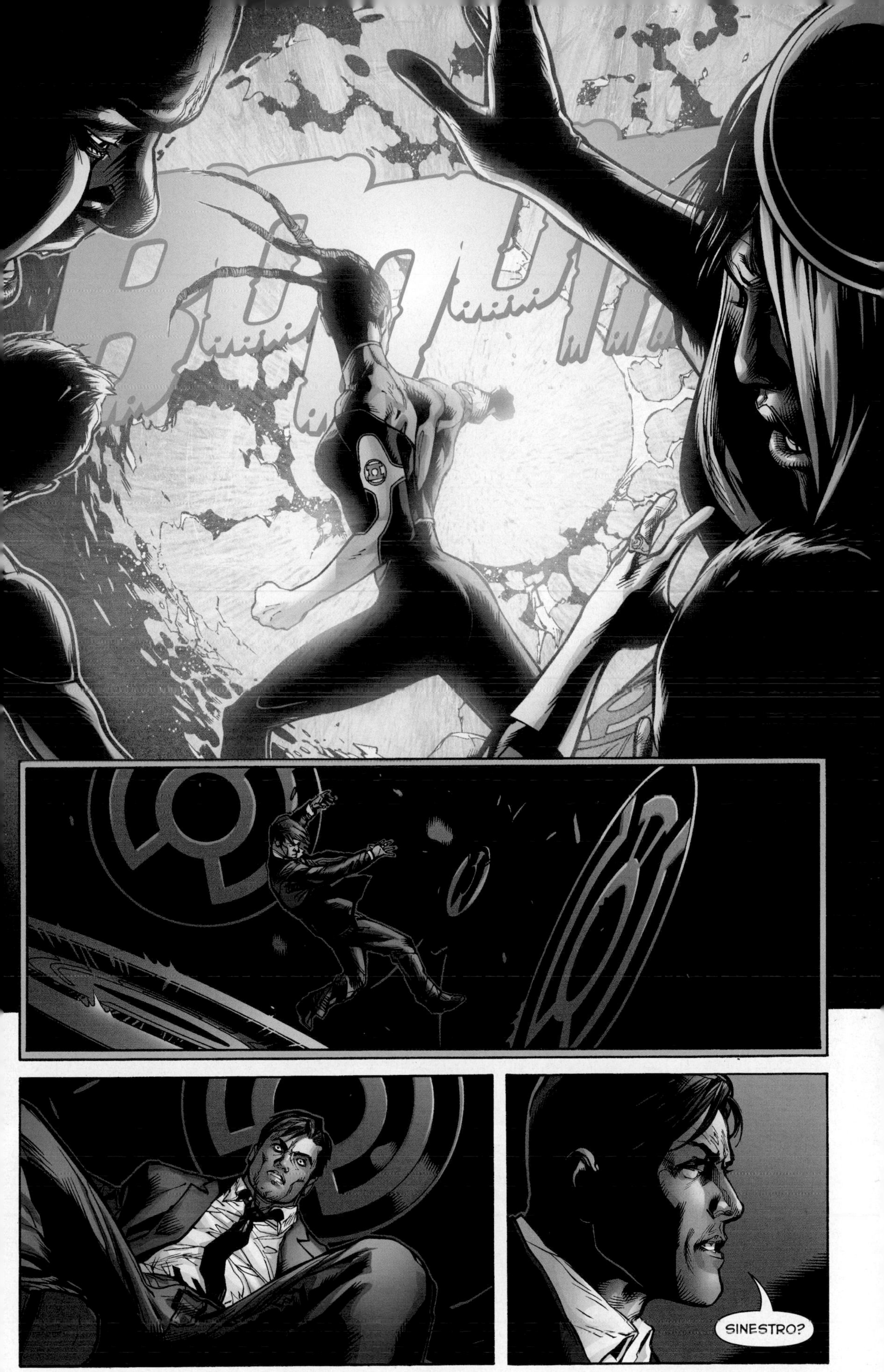
SINESTRO?

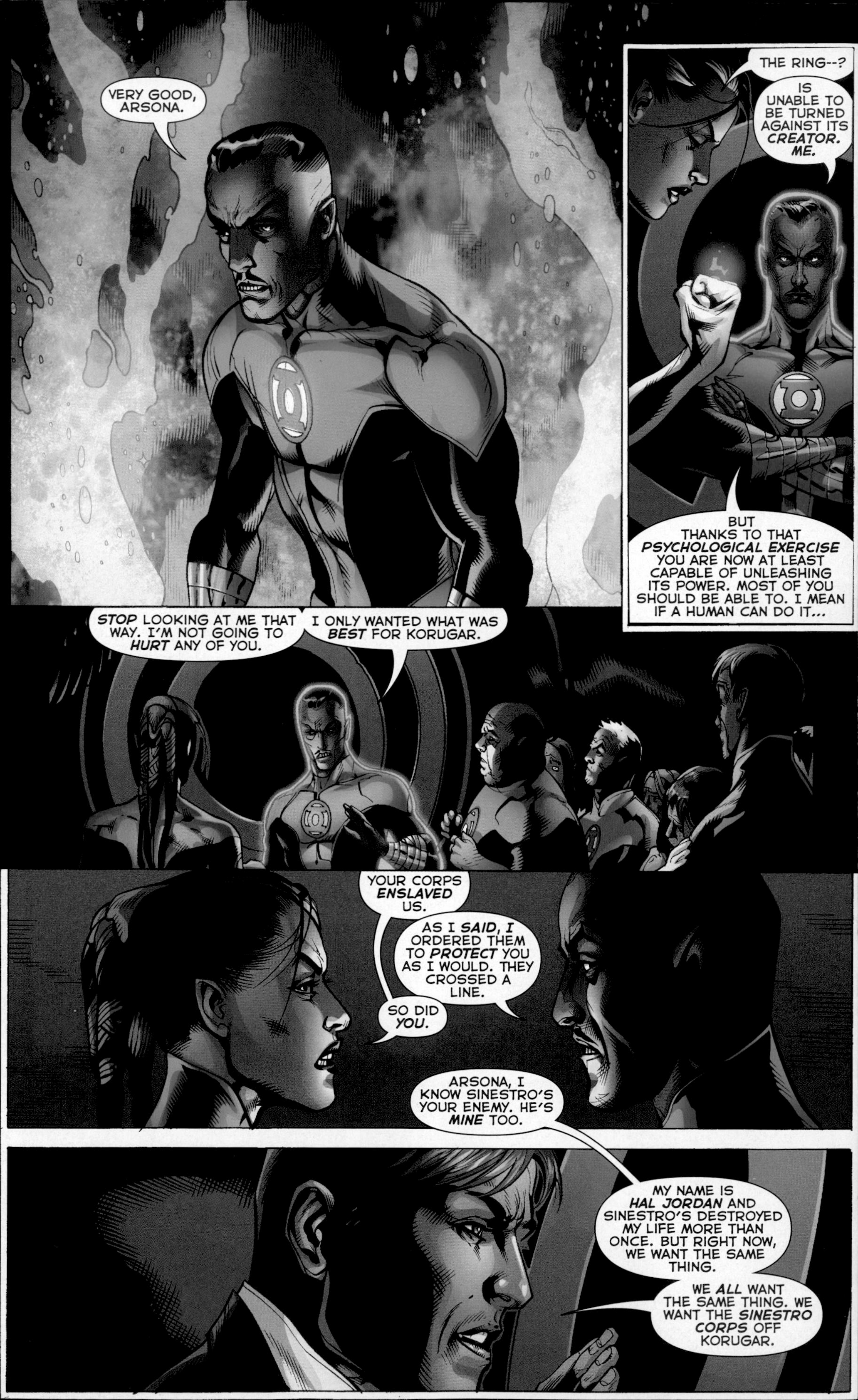
VERY GOOD, ARSONA.
THE RING--?
IS UNABLE TO BE TURNED AGAINST ITS *CREATOR. ME.*
BUT THANKS TO THAT *PSYCHOLOGICAL EXERCISE* YOU ARE NOW AT LEAST CAPABLE OF UNLEASHING ITS POWER. MOST OF YOU SHOULD BE ABLE TO. I MEAN IF A HUMAN CAN DO IT...
STOP LOOKING AT ME THAT WAY. I'M NOT GOING TO *HURT* ANY OF YOU.
I ONLY WANTED WHAT WAS *BEST* FOR KORUGAR.
YOUR CORPS *ENSLAVED* US.
AS I *SAID, I* ORDERED THEM TO *PROTECT* YOU AS I WOULD. THEY CROSSED A LINE.
SO DID *YOU.*
ARSONA, I KNOW SINESTRO'S YOUR ENEMY. HE'S *MINE* TOO.
MY NAME IS *HAL JORDAN* AND SINESTRO'S DESTROYED MY LIFE MORE THAN ONCE. BUT RIGHT NOW, WE WANT THE SAME THING.
WE *ALL* WANT THE SAME THING. WE WANT THE *SINESTRO CORPS* OFF KORUGAR.

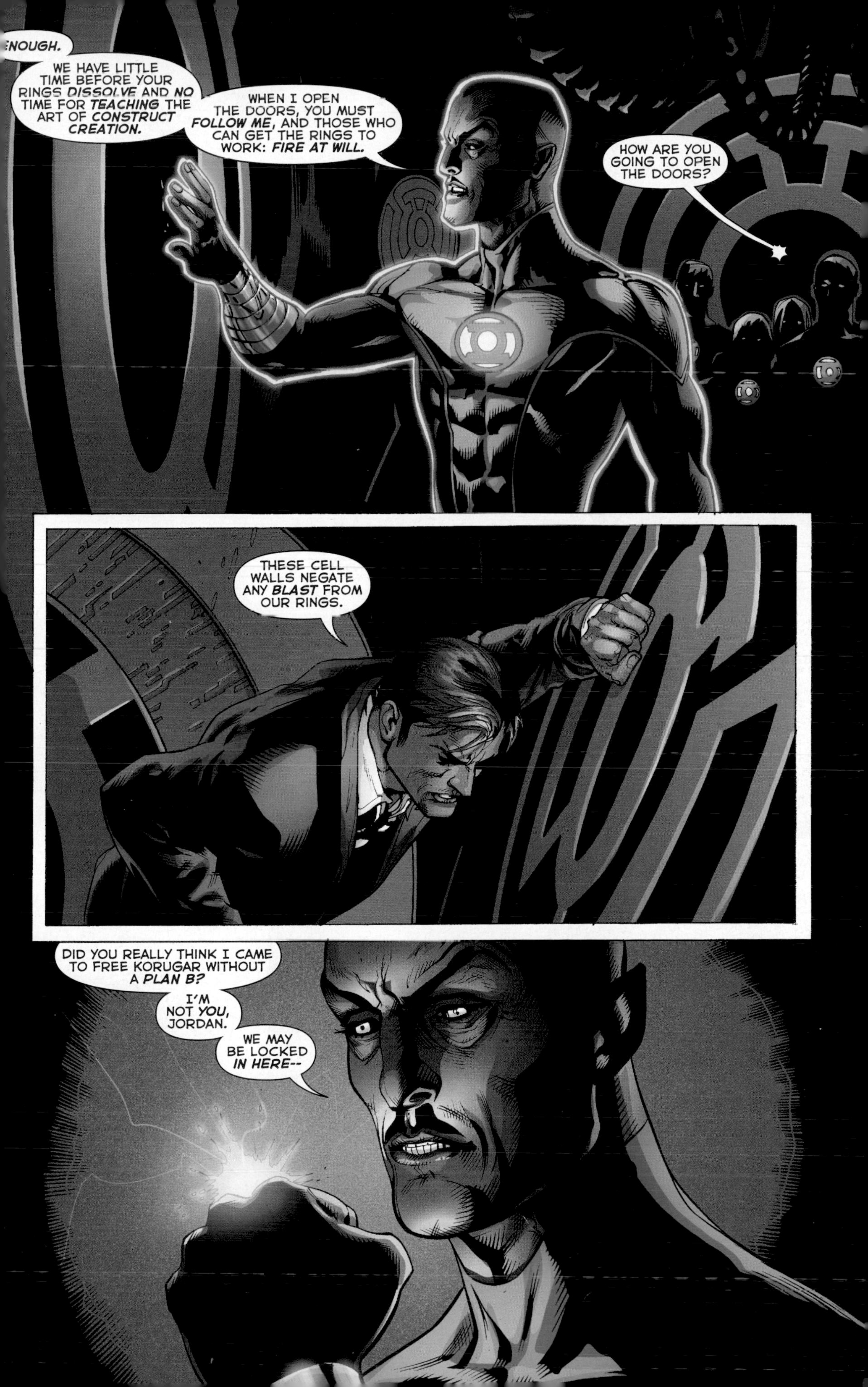
ENOUGH.
WE HAVE LITTLE TIME BEFORE YOUR RINGS DISSOLVE AND NO TIME FOR TEACHING THE ART OF CONSTRUCT CREATION.
WHEN I OPEN THE DOORS, YOU MUST FOLLOW ME, AND THOSE WHO CAN GET THE RINGS TO WORK: FIRE AT WILL.
HOW ARE YOU GOING TO OPEN THE DOORS?
THESE CELL WALLS NEGATE ANY BLAST FROM OUR RINGS.
DID YOU REALLY THINK I CAME TO FREE KORUGAR WITHOUT A PLAN B?
I'M NOT YOU, JORDAN.
WE MAY BE LOCKED IN HERE--

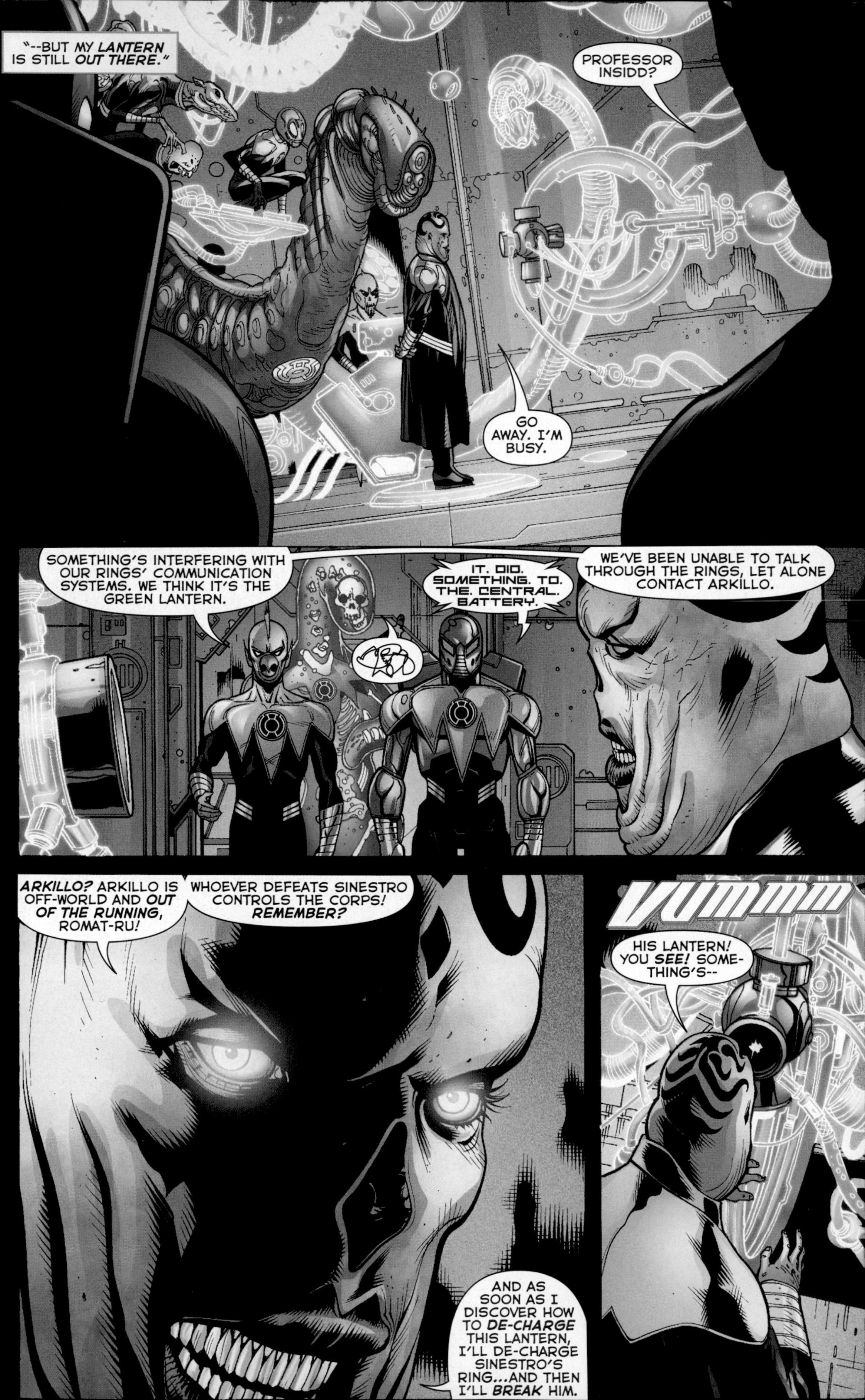
"--BUT MY *LANTERN* IS STILL *OUT THERE."*
PROFESSOR INSIDD?
GO AWAY. I'M BUSY.
SOMETHING'S INTERFERING WITH OUR RINGS' COMMUNICATION SYSTEMS. WE THINK IT'S THE GREEN LANTERN.
IT. DID. SOMETHING. TO. THE. CENTRAL. BATTERY.
WE'VE BEEN UNABLE TO TALK THROUGH THE RINGS, LET ALONE CONTACT ARKILLO.
ARKILLO? ARKILLO IS OFF-WORLD AND *OUT OF THE RUNNING,* ROMAT-RU!
WHOEVER DEFEATS SINESTRO CONTROLS THE CORPS! *REMEMBER?*
AND AS SOON AS I DISCOVER HOW TO *DE-CHARGE* THIS LANTERN, I'LL DE-CHARGE SINESTRO'S RING...AND THEN I'LL *BREAK* HIM.
VUMMM
HIS LANTERN! YOU *SEE!* SOME-THING'S--

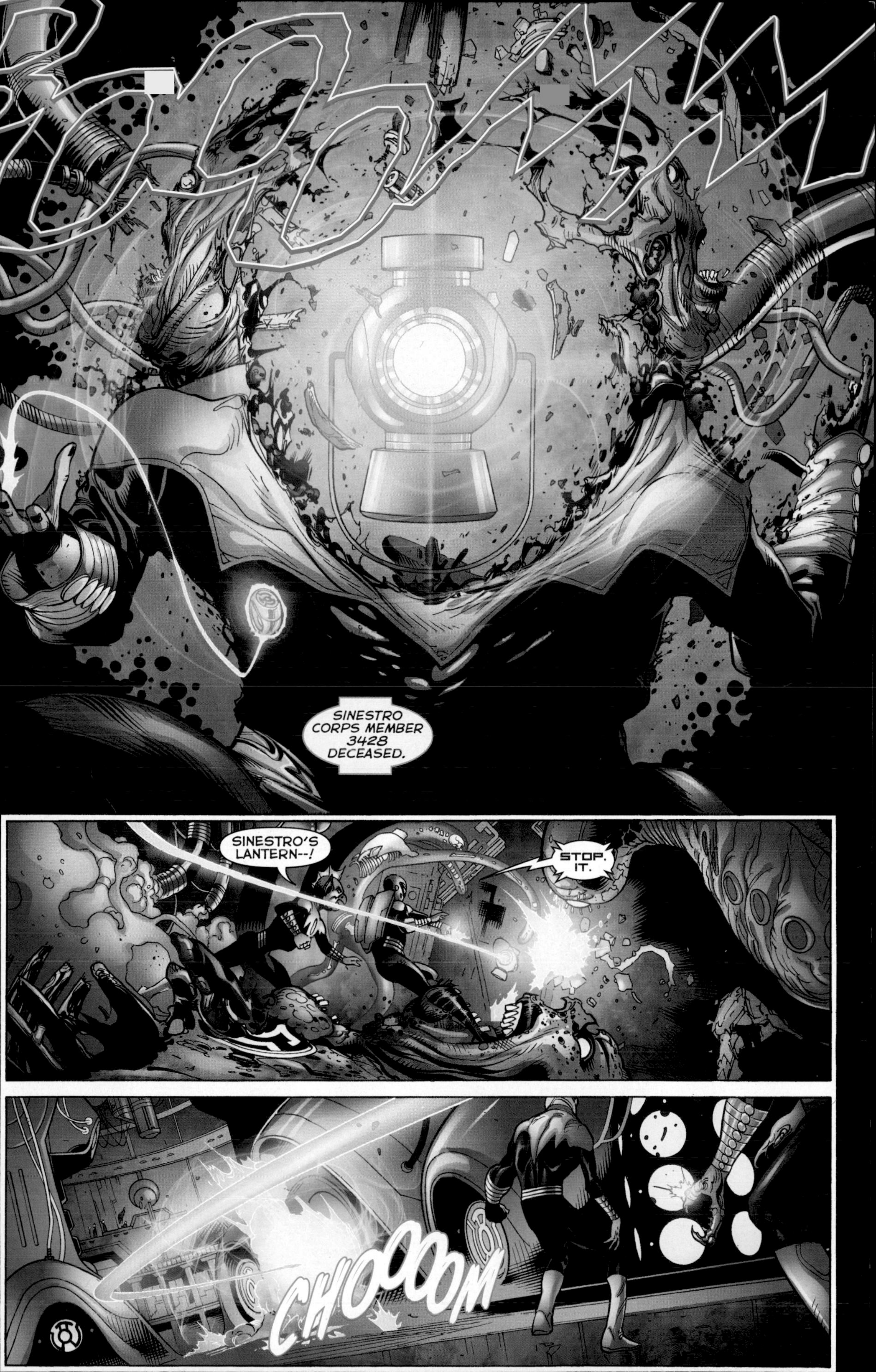
SINESTRO CORPS MEMBER 3428 DECEASED.
SINESTRO'S LANTERN--!
STOP. IT.
CHOOOOM

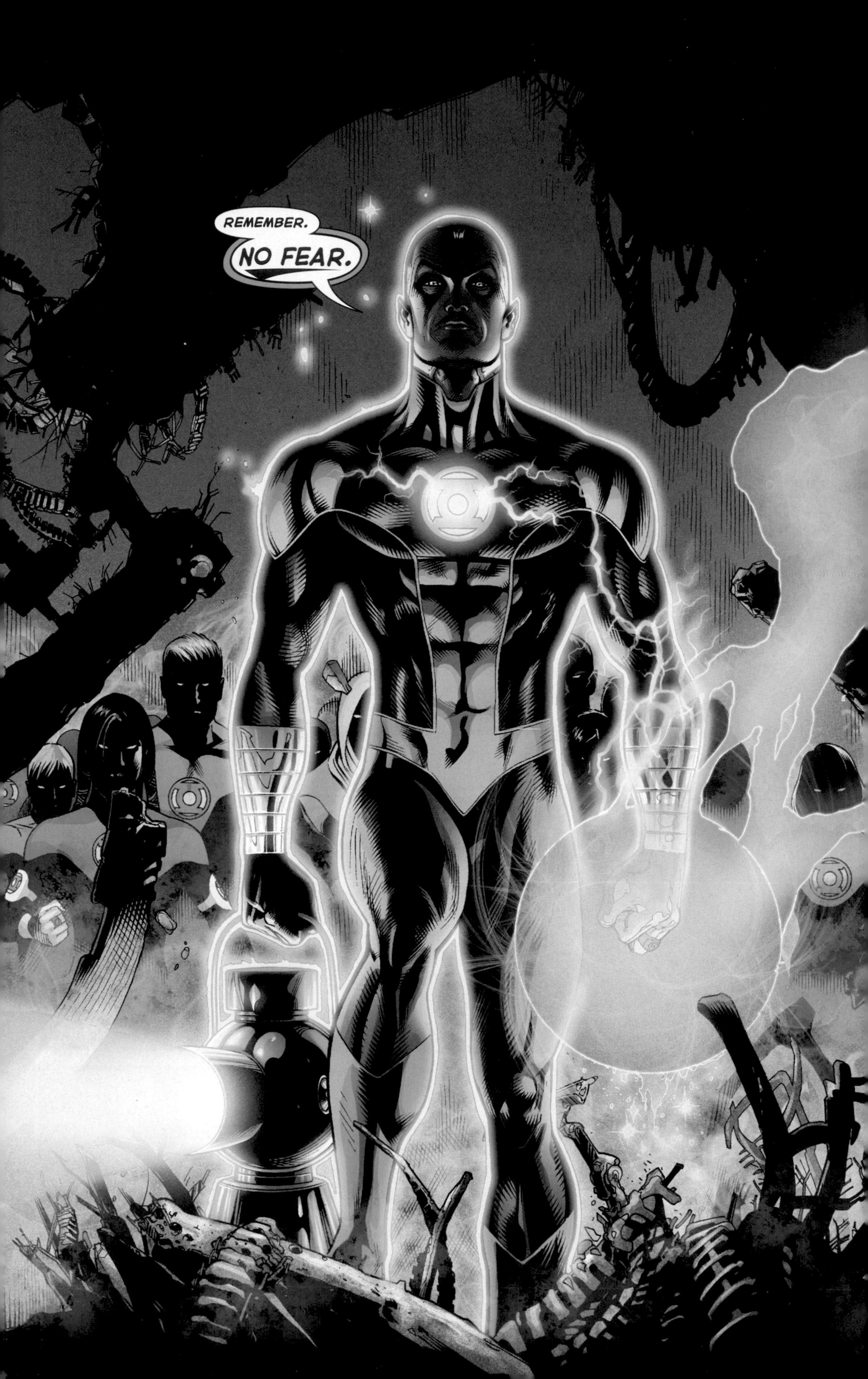
REMEMBER.
NO FEAR.

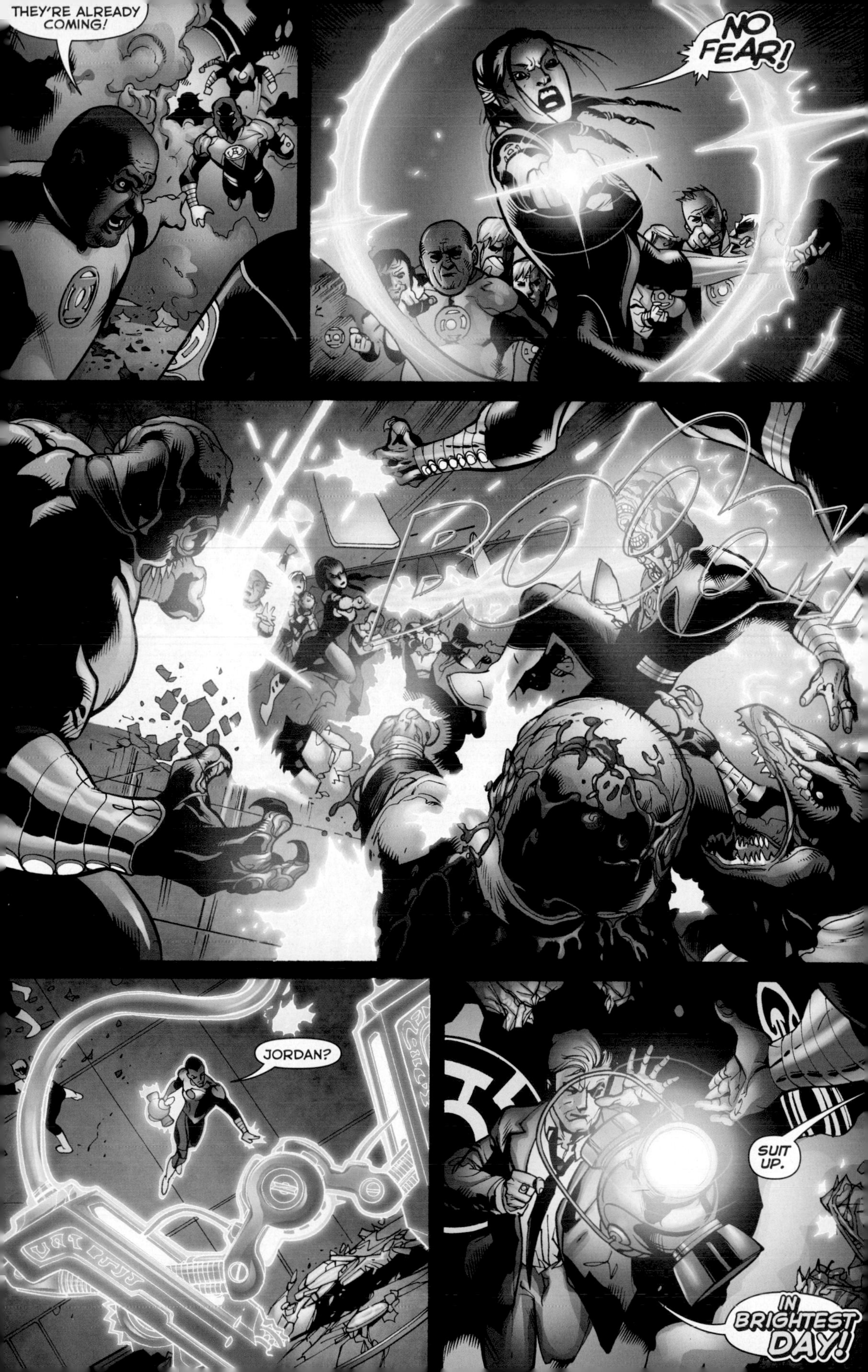
THEY'RE ALREADY COMING!
NO FEAR!
BOOM
JORDAN?
SUIT UP.
IN BRIGHTEST DAY!

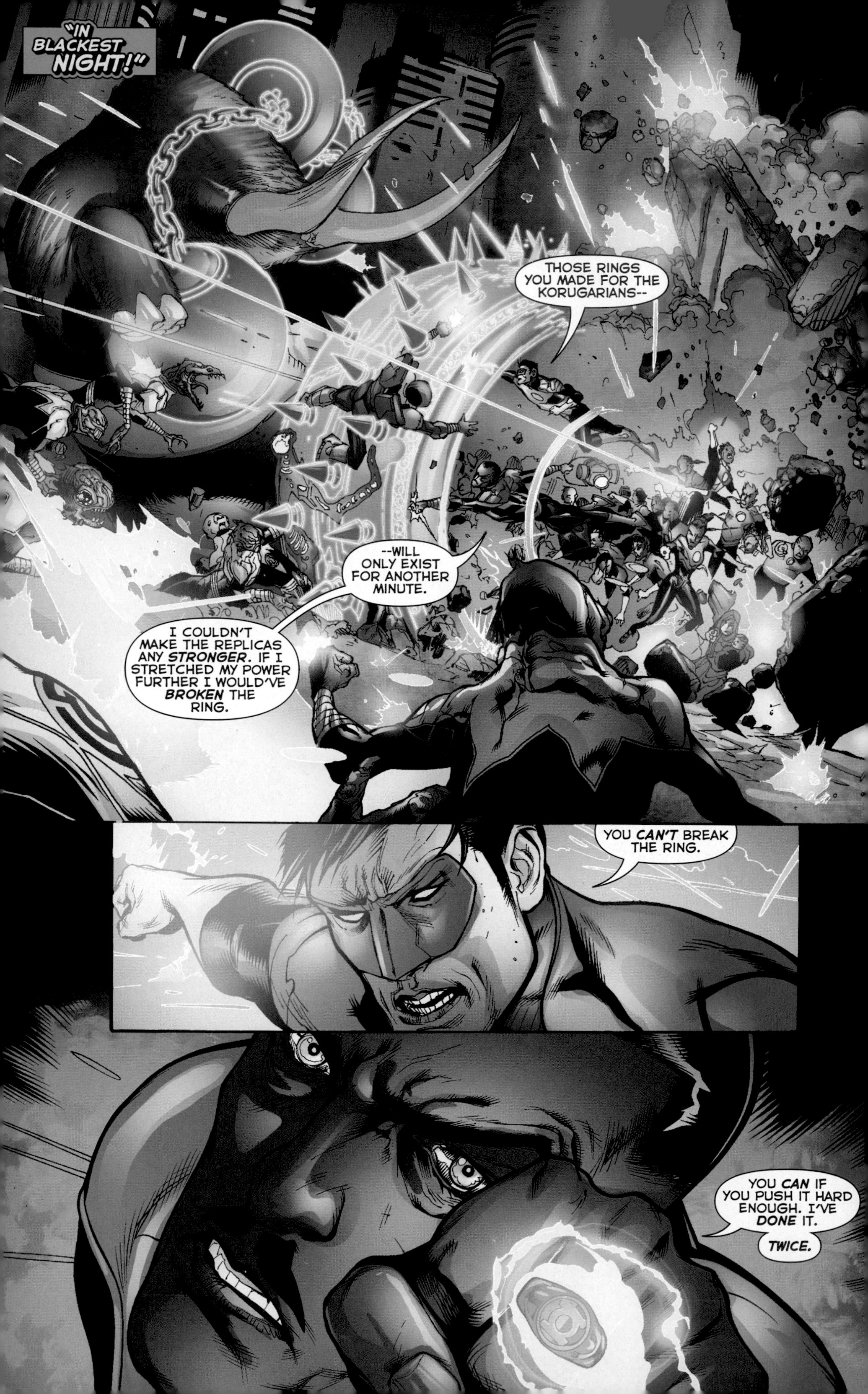
"IN BLACKEST NIGHT!"
THOSE RINGS YOU MADE FOR THE KORUGARIANS--
--WILL ONLY EXIST FOR ANOTHER MINUTE.
I COULDN'T MAKE THE REPLICAS ANY STRONGER. IF I STRETCHED MY POWER FURTHER I WOULD'VE BROKEN THE RING.
YOU CAN'T BREAK THE RING.
YOU CAN IF YOU PUSH IT HARD ENOUGH. I'VE DONE IT.
TWICE.

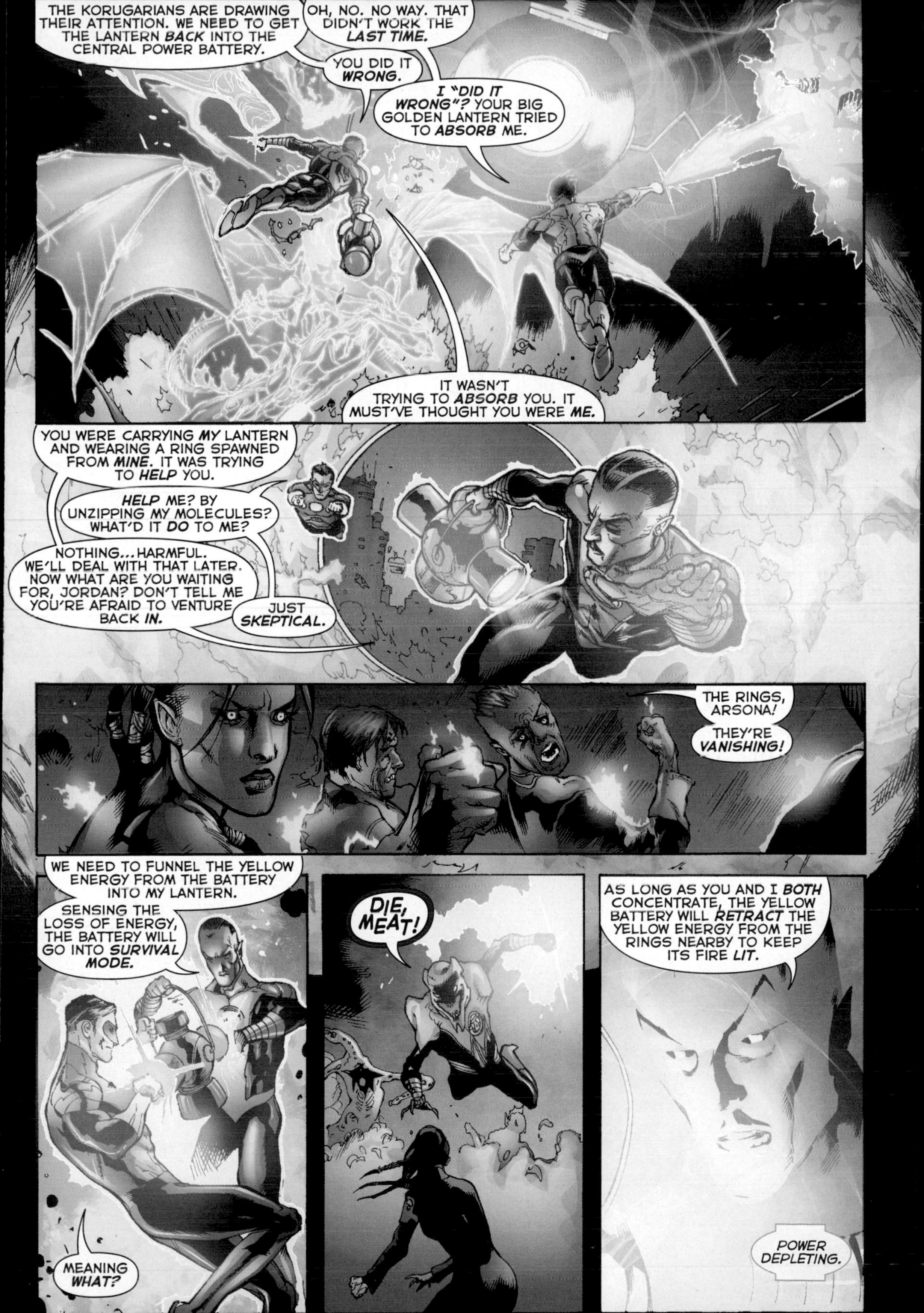
THE KORUGARIANS ARE DRAWING THEIR ATTENTION. WE NEED TO GET THE LANTERN BACK INTO THE CENTRAL POWER BATTERY.
OH, NO. NO WAY. THAT DIDN'T WORK THE LAST TIME.
YOU DID IT WRONG.
I "DID IT WRONG"? YOUR BIG GOLDEN LANTERN TRIED TO ABSORB ME.
IT WASN'T TRYING TO ABSORB YOU. IT MUST'VE THOUGHT YOU WERE ME.
YOU WERE CARRYING MY LANTERN AND WEARING A RING SPAWNED FROM MINE. IT WAS TRYING TO HELP YOU.
HELP ME? BY UNZIPPING MY MOLECULES? WHAT'D IT DO TO ME?
NOTHING... HARMFUL. WE'LL DEAL WITH THAT LATER. NOW WHAT ARE YOU WAITING FOR, JORDAN? DON'T TELL ME YOU'RE AFRAID TO VENTURE BACK IN.
JUST SKEPTICAL.
THE RINGS, ARSONA!
THEY'RE VANISHING!
WE NEED TO FUNNEL THE YELLOW ENERGY FROM THE BATTERY INTO MY LANTERN.
SENSING THE LOSS OF ENERGY, THE BATTERY WILL GO INTO SURVIVAL MODE.
MEANING WHAT?
DIE, MEAT!
AS LONG AS YOU AND I BOTH CONCENTRATE, THE YELLOW BATTERY WILL RETRACT THE YELLOW ENERGY FROM THE RINGS NEARBY TO KEEP ITS FIRE LIT.
POWER DEPLETING.

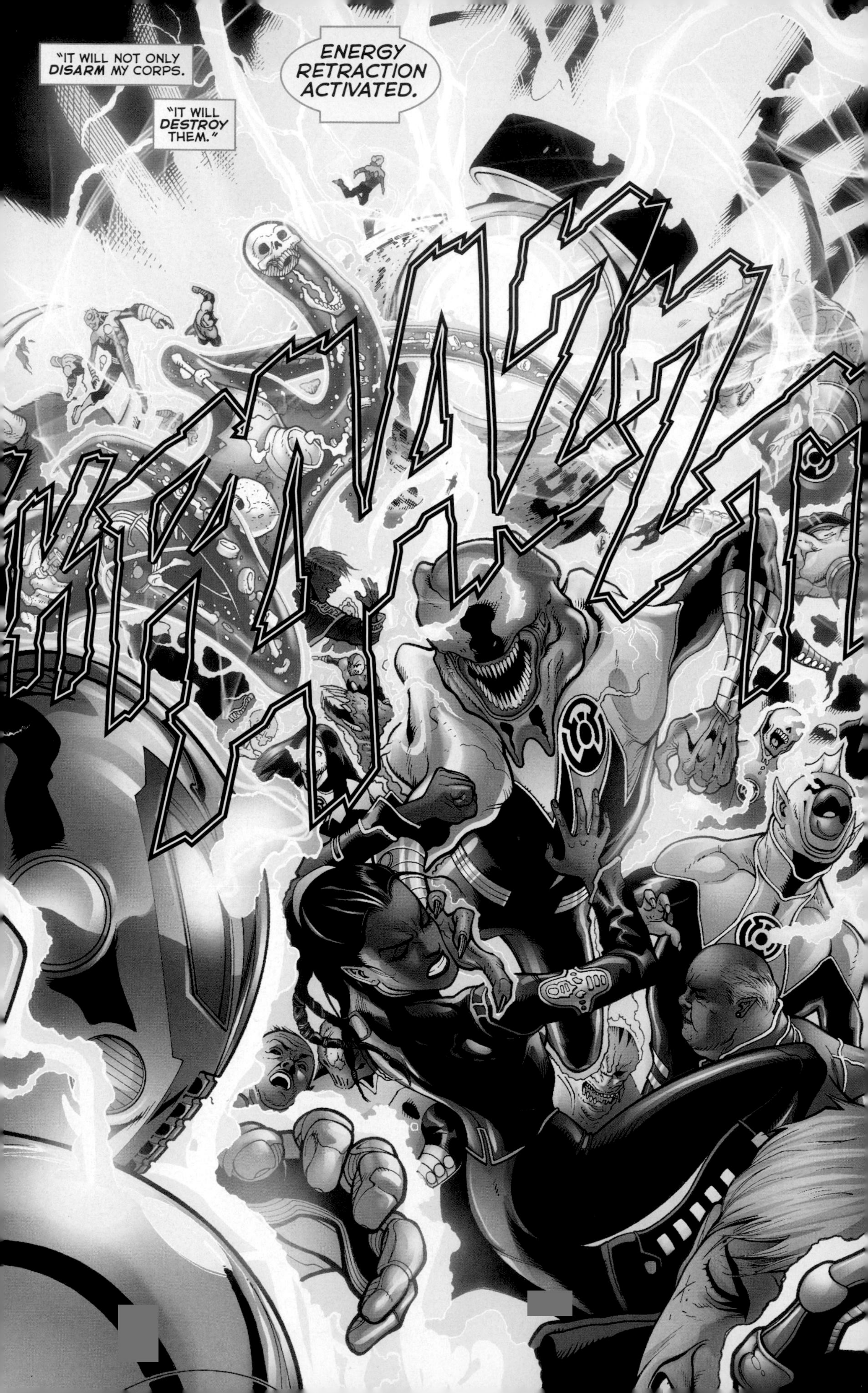
"IT WILL NOT ONLY DISARM MY CORPS.
"IT WILL DESTROY THEM."
ENERGY RETRACTION ACTIVATED.

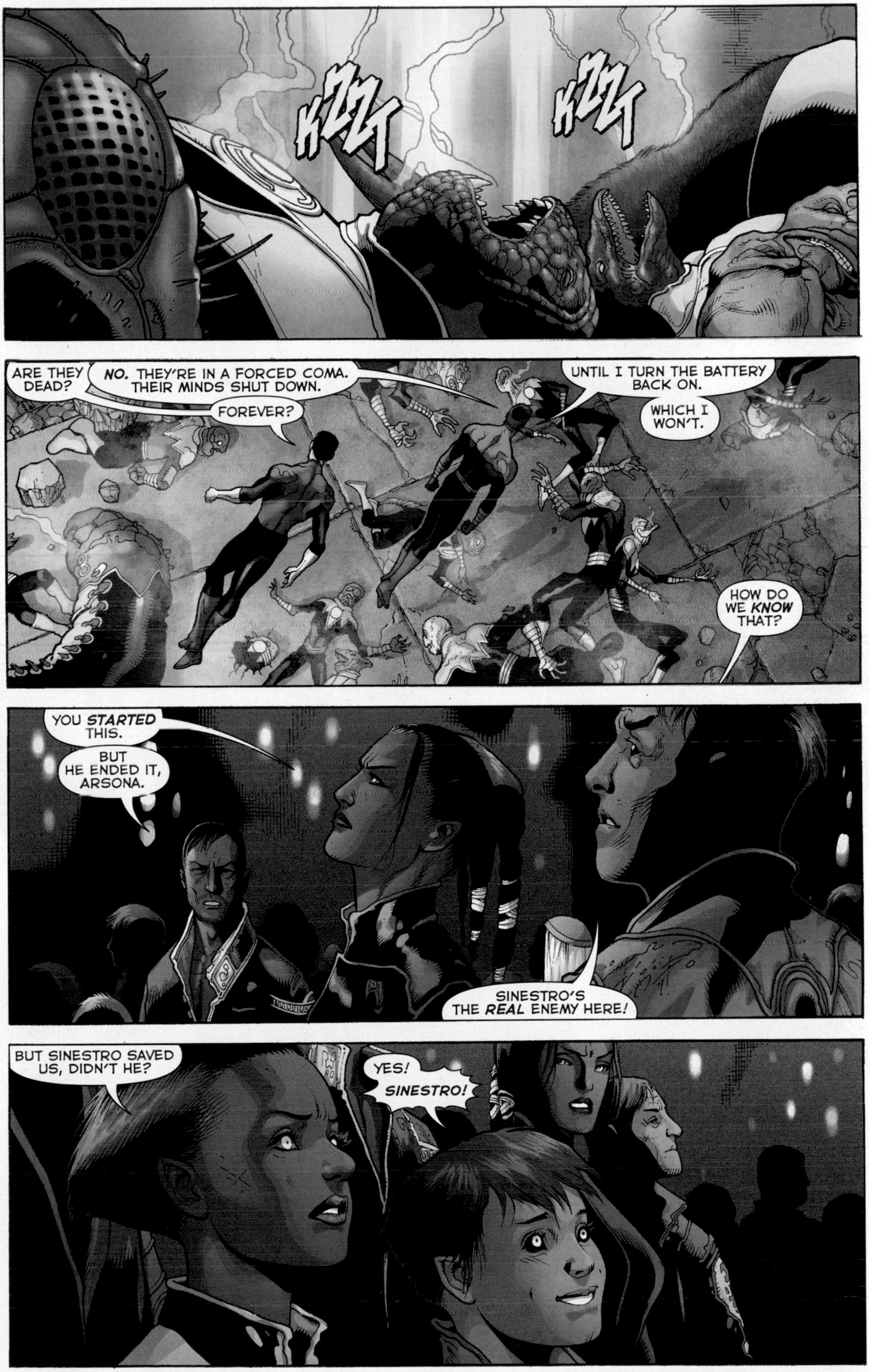
KZZT
KZZT
ARE THEY DEAD?
NO. THEY'RE IN A FORCED COMA. THEIR MINDS SHUT DOWN.
FOREVER?
UNTIL I TURN THE BATTERY BACK ON.
WHICH I WON'T.
HOW DO WE KNOW THAT?
YOU STARTED THIS.
BUT HE ENDED IT, ARSONA.
SINESTRO'S THE REAL ENEMY HERE!
BUT SINESTRO SAVED US, DIDN'T HE?
YES! SINESTRO!

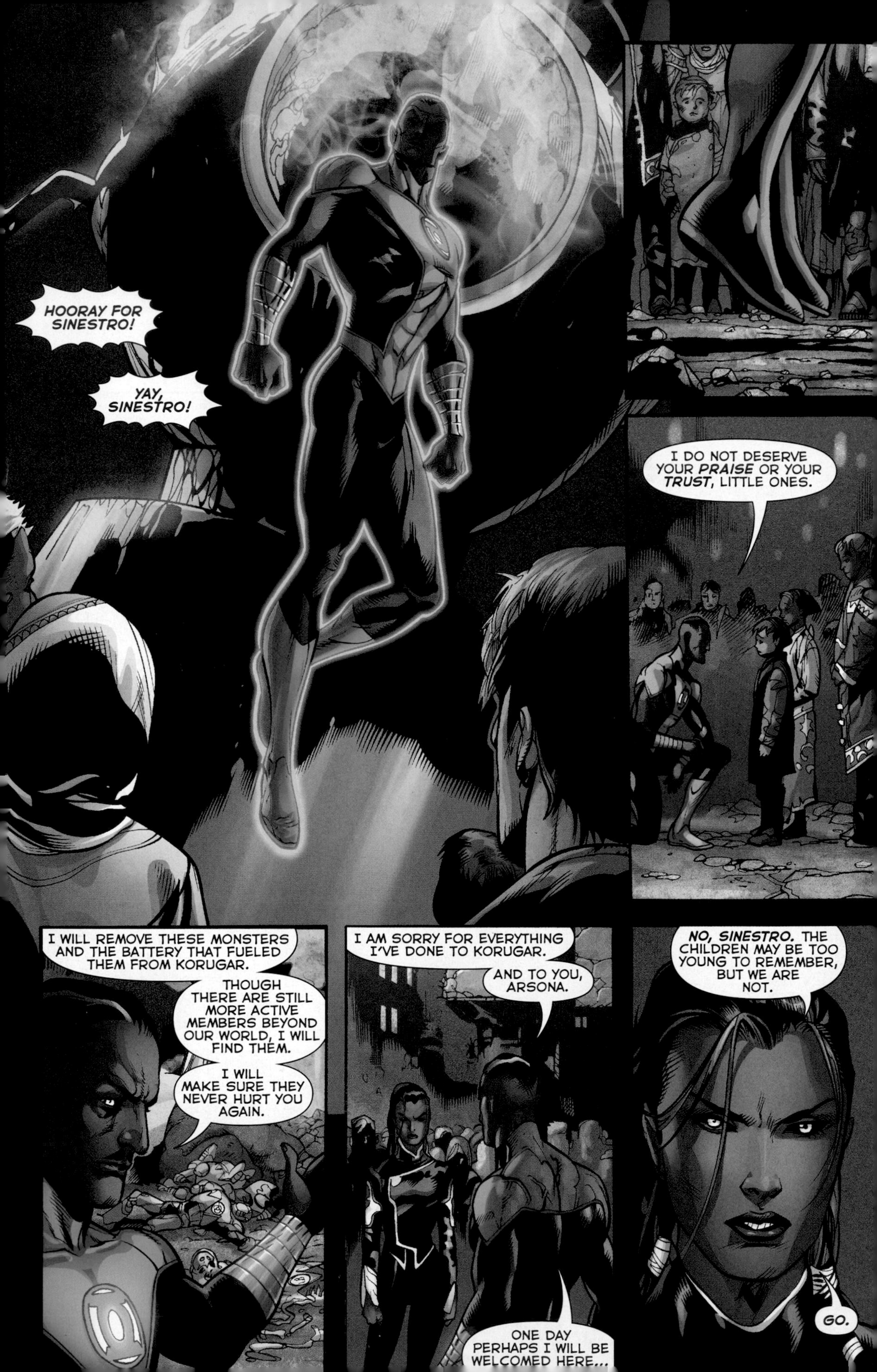
HOORAY FOR SINESTRO!
YAY, SINESTRO!
I DO NOT DESERVE YOUR PRAISE OR YOUR TRUST, LITTLE ONES.
I WILL REMOVE THESE MONSTERS AND THE BATTERY THAT FUELED THEM FROM KORUGAR.
THOUGH THERE ARE STILL MORE ACTIVE MEMBERS BEYOND OUR WORLD, I WILL FIND THEM.
I WILL MAKE SURE THEY NEVER HURT YOU AGAIN.
I AM SORRY FOR EVERYTHING I'VE DONE TO KORUGAR.
AND TO YOU, ARSONA.
ONE DAY PERHAPS I WILL BE WELCOMED HERE...
NO, SINESTRO. THE CHILDREN MAY BE TOO YOUNG TO REMEMBER, BUT WE ARE NOT.
GO.

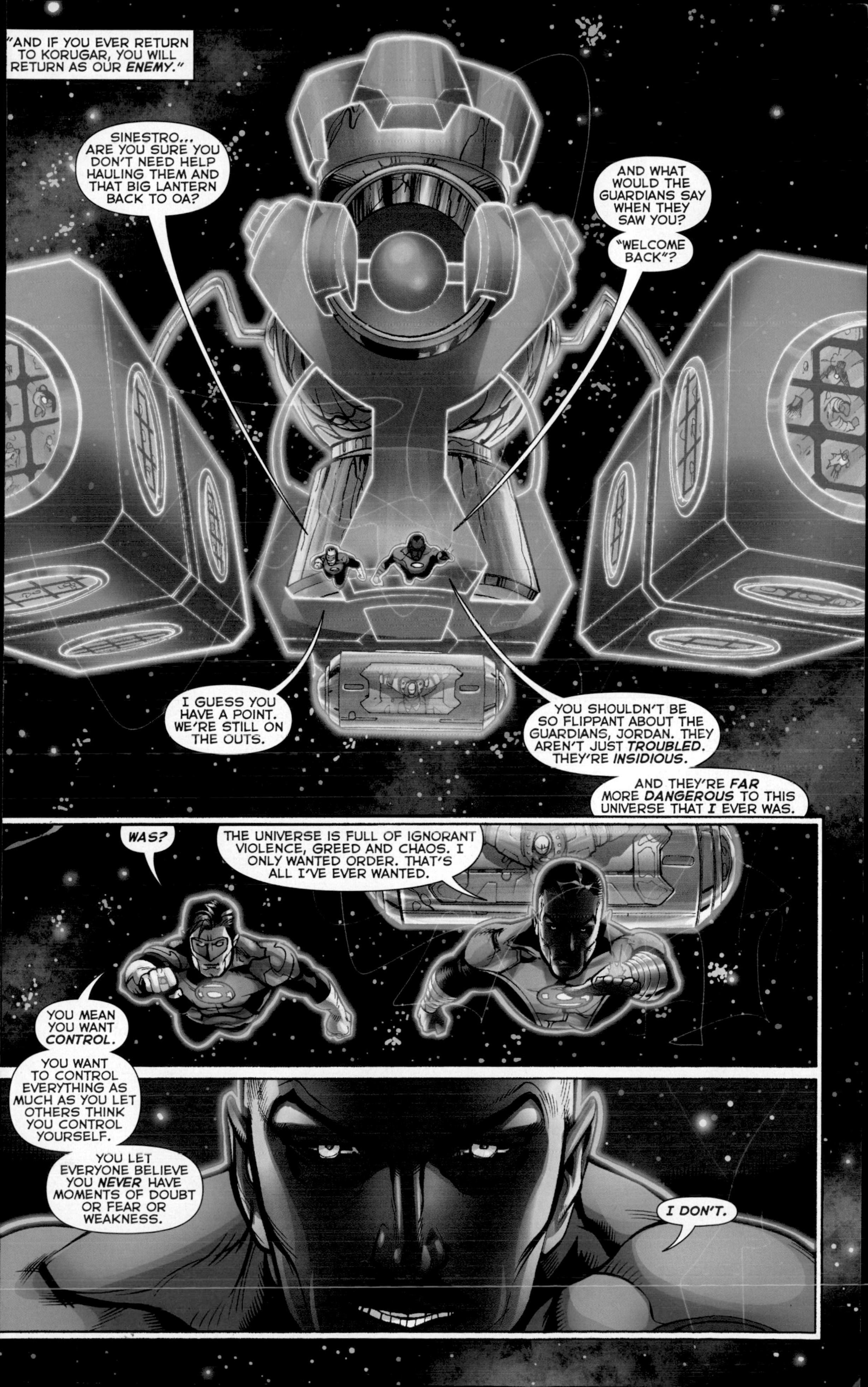
"AND IF YOU EVER RETURN TO KORUGAR, YOU WILL RETURN AS OUR *ENEMY*."
SINESTRO... ARE YOU SURE YOU DON'T NEED HELP HAULING THEM AND THAT BIG LANTERN BACK TO OA?
AND WHAT WOULD THE GUARDIANS SAY WHEN THEY SAW YOU?
"WELCOME BACK"?
I GUESS YOU HAVE A POINT. WE'RE STILL ON THE OUTS.
YOU SHOULDN'T BE SO FLIPPANT ABOUT THE GUARDIANS, JORDAN. THEY AREN'T JUST *TROUBLED*. THEY'RE *INSIDIOUS*.
AND THEY'RE *FAR* MORE *DANGEROUS* TO THIS UNIVERSE THAT *I* EVER WAS.
WAS?
THE UNIVERSE IS FULL OF IGNORANT VIOLENCE, GREED AND CHAOS. I ONLY WANTED ORDER. THAT'S ALL I'VE EVER WANTED.
YOU MEAN YOU WANT *CONTROL*.
YOU WANT TO CONTROL EVERYTHING AS MUCH AS YOU LET OTHERS THINK YOU CONTROL YOURSELF.
YOU LET EVERYONE BELIEVE YOU *NEVER* HAVE MOMENTS OF DOUBT OR FEAR OR WEAKNESS.
I DON'T.

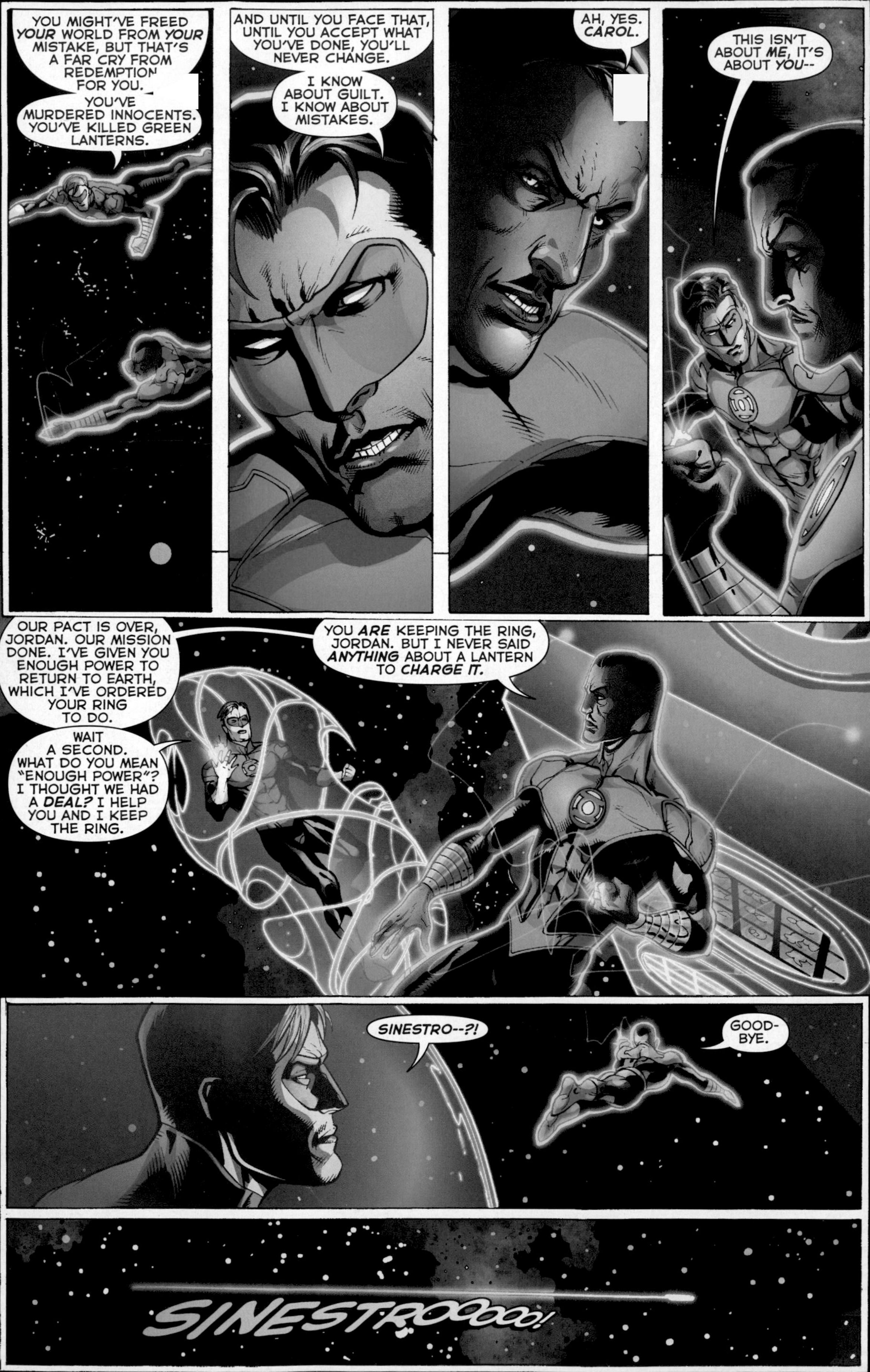
YOU MIGHT'VE FREED YOUR WORLD FROM YOUR MISTAKE, BUT THAT'S A FAR CRY FROM REDEMPTION FOR YOU.
YOU'VE MURDERED INNOCENTS. YOU'VE KILLED GREEN LANTERNS.
AND UNTIL YOU FACE THAT, UNTIL YOU ACCEPT WHAT YOU'VE DONE, YOU'LL NEVER CHANGE.
I KNOW ABOUT GUILT. I KNOW ABOUT MISTAKES.
AH, YES. CAROL.
THIS ISN'T ABOUT ME, IT'S ABOUT YOU--
OUR PACT IS OVER, JORDAN. OUR MISSION DONE. I'VE GIVEN YOU ENOUGH POWER TO RETURN TO EARTH, WHICH I'VE ORDERED YOUR RING TO DO.
WAIT A SECOND. WHAT DO YOU MEAN "ENOUGH POWER"? I THOUGHT WE HAD A DEAL? I HELP YOU AND I KEEP THE RING.
YOU ARE KEEPING THE RING, JORDAN. BUT I NEVER SAID ANYTHING ABOUT A LANTERN TO CHARGE IT.
SINESTRO--?!
GOOD-BYE.
SINESTROOOOOO!

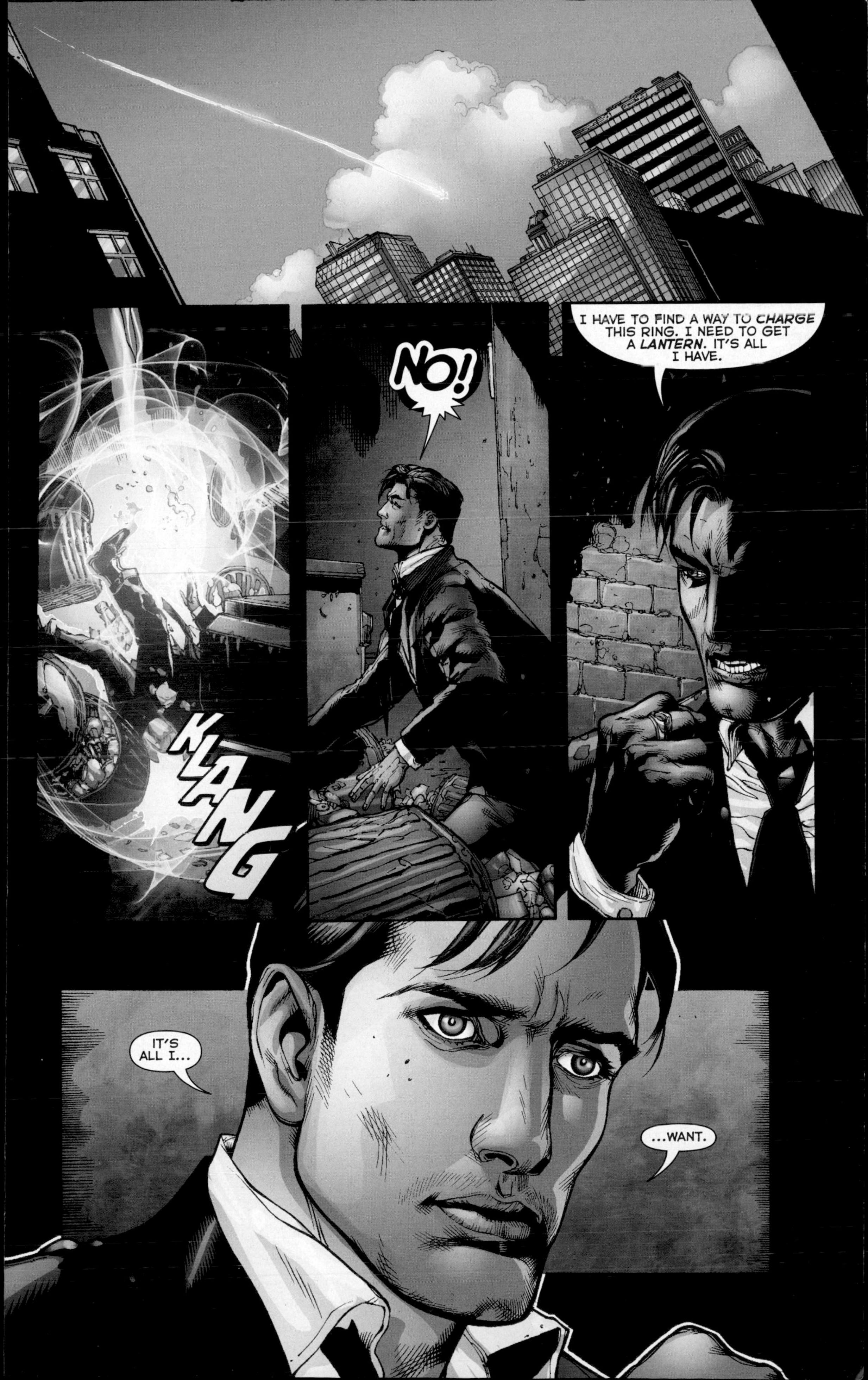
KLANG
NO!
I HAVE TO FIND A WAY TO CHARGE THIS RING. I NEED TO GET A LANTERN. IT'S ALL I HAVE.
IT'S ALL I...
...WANT.

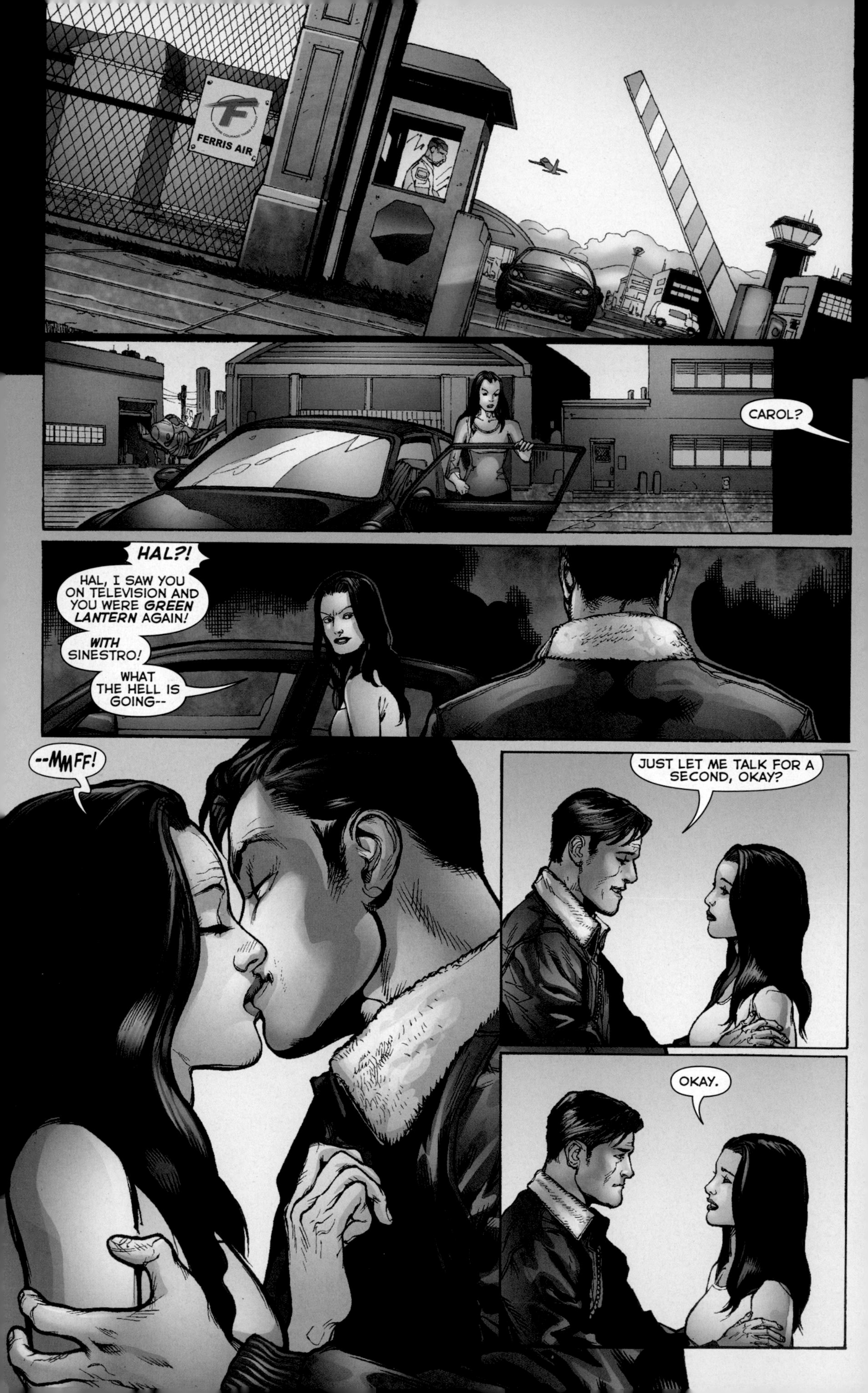
FERRIS AIR
CAROL?
HAL?!
HAL, I SAW YOU ON TELEVISION AND YOU WERE GREEN LANTERN AGAIN!
WITH SINESTRO!
WHAT THE HELL IS GOING--
--MMFF!
JUST LET ME TALK FOR A SECOND, OKAY?
OKAY.

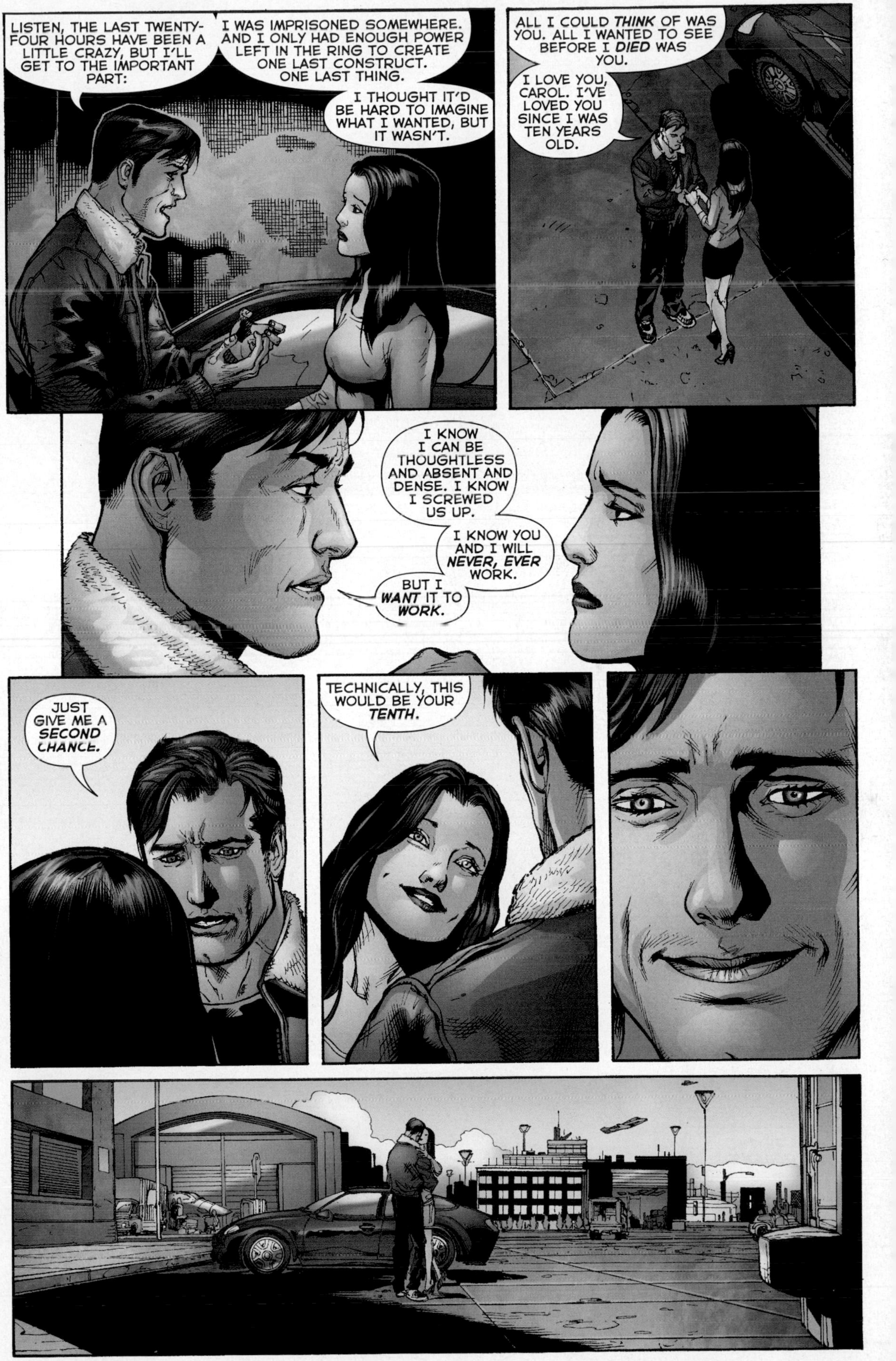
LISTEN, THE LAST TWENTY-FOUR HOURS HAVE BEEN A LITTLE CRAZY, BUT I'LL GET TO THE IMPORTANT PART:
I WAS IMPRISONED SOMEWHERE. AND I ONLY HAD ENOUGH POWER LEFT IN THE RING TO CREATE ONE LAST CONSTRUCT. ONE LAST THING.
I THOUGHT IT'D BE HARD TO IMAGINE WHAT I WANTED, BUT IT WASN'T.
ALL I COULD *THINK* OF WAS YOU. ALL I WANTED TO SEE BEFORE I *DIED* WAS YOU.
I LOVE YOU, CAROL. I'VE LOVED YOU SINCE I WAS TEN YEARS OLD.
I KNOW I CAN BE THOUGHTLESS AND ABSENT AND DENSE. I KNOW I SCREWED US UP.
I KNOW YOU AND I WILL *NEVER, EVER* WORK.
BUT I *WANT* IT TO *WORK.*
JUST GIVE ME A *SECOND CHANCE.*
TECHNICALLY, THIS WOULD BE YOUR *TENTH.*

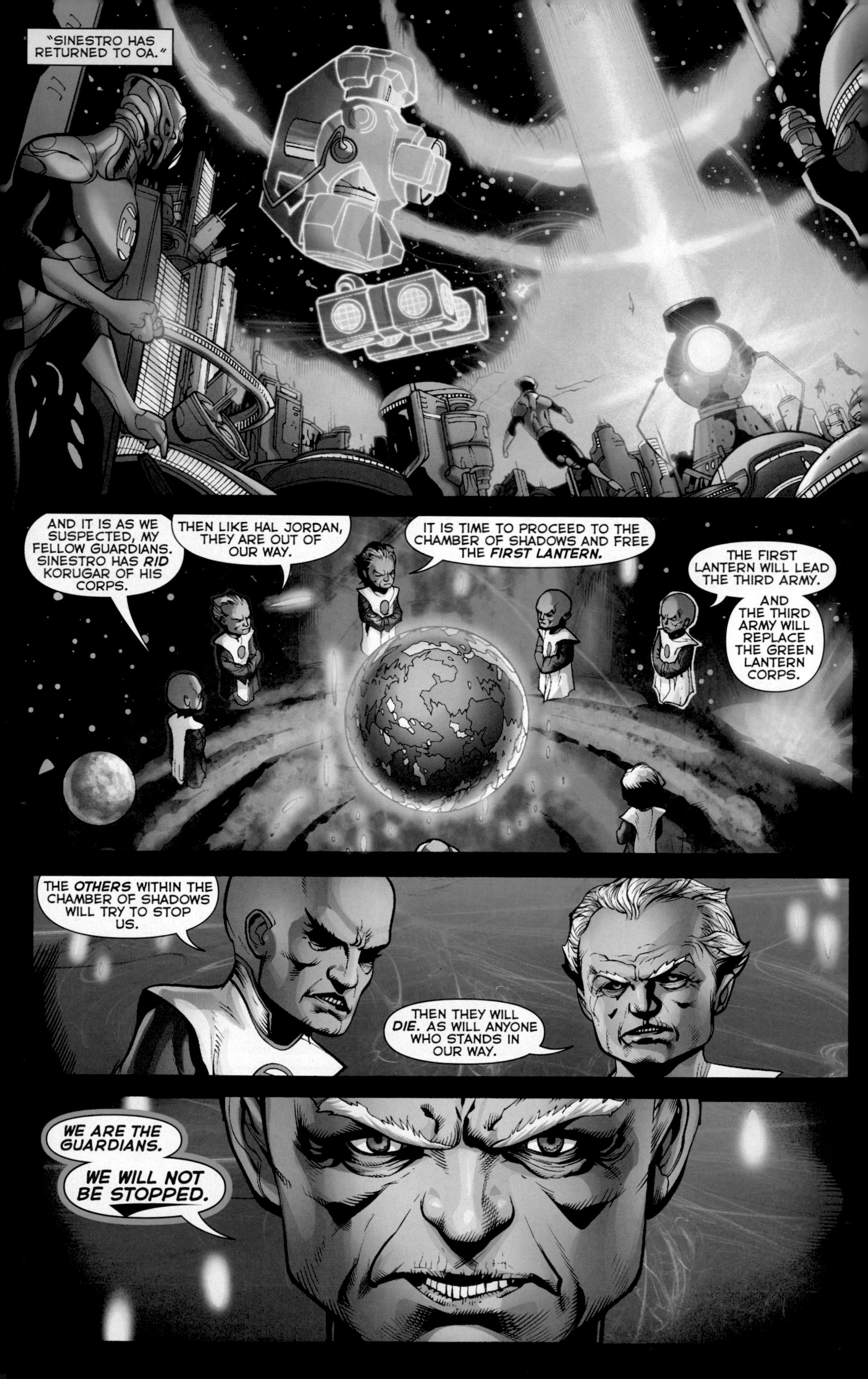
"SINESTRO HAS RETURNED TO OA."
AND IT IS AS WE SUSPECTED, MY FELLOW GUARDIANS. SINESTRO HAS *RID* KORUGAR OF HIS CORPS.
THEN LIKE HAL JORDAN, THEY ARE OUT OF OUR WAY.
IT IS TIME TO PROCEED TO THE CHAMBER OF SHADOWS AND FREE THE *FIRST LANTERN.*
THE FIRST LANTERN WILL LEAD THE THIRD ARMY.
AND THE THIRD ARMY WILL REPLACE THE GREEN LANTERN CORPS.
THE *OTHERS* WITHIN THE CHAMBER OF SHADOWS WILL TRY TO STOP US.
THEN THEY WILL *DIE*. AS WILL ANYONE WHO STANDS IN OUR WAY.
WE ARE THE GUARDIANS.
WE WILL NOT BE STOPPED.

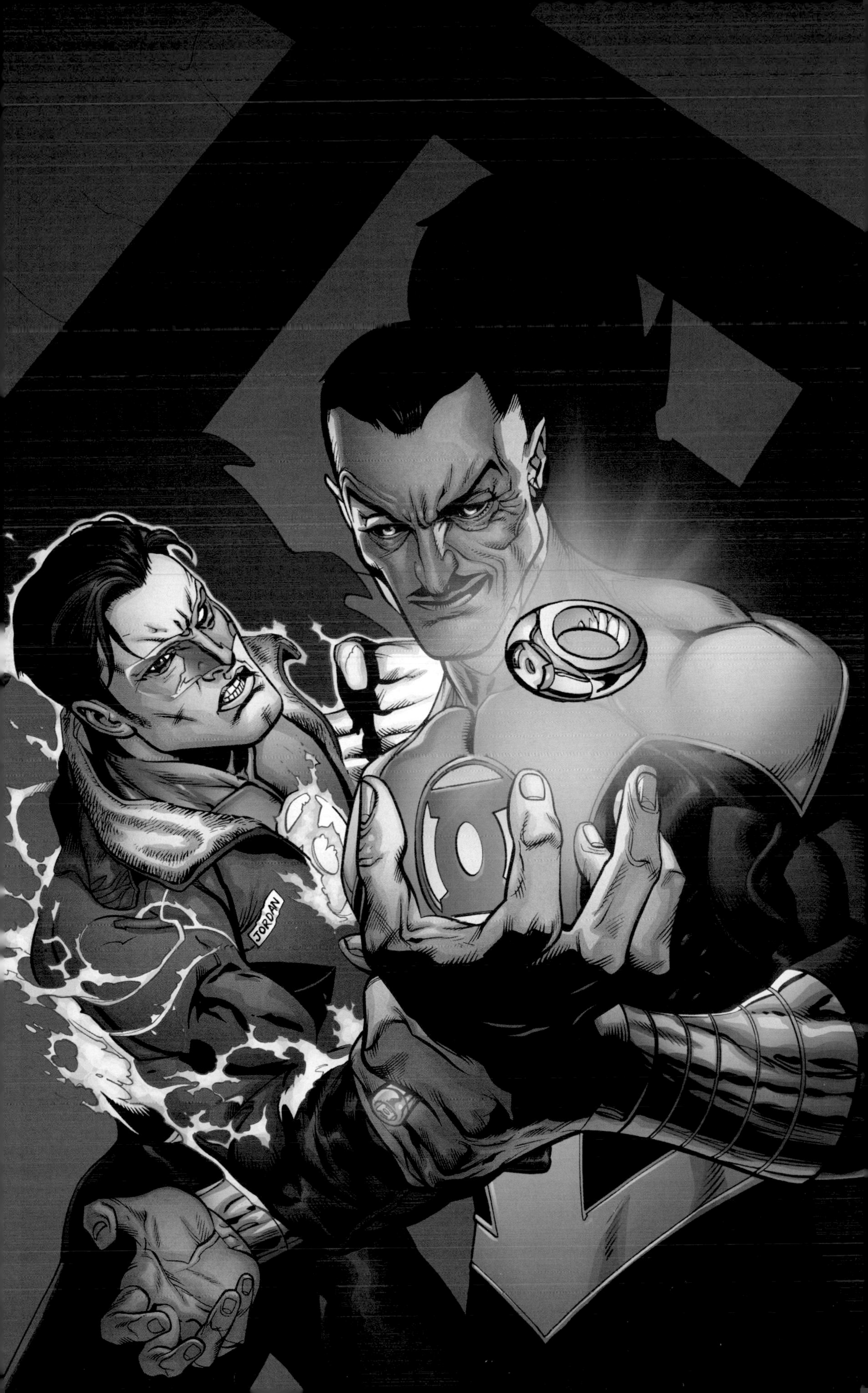
JORDAN

Doug Mahnke, Keith Champagne & David Baron

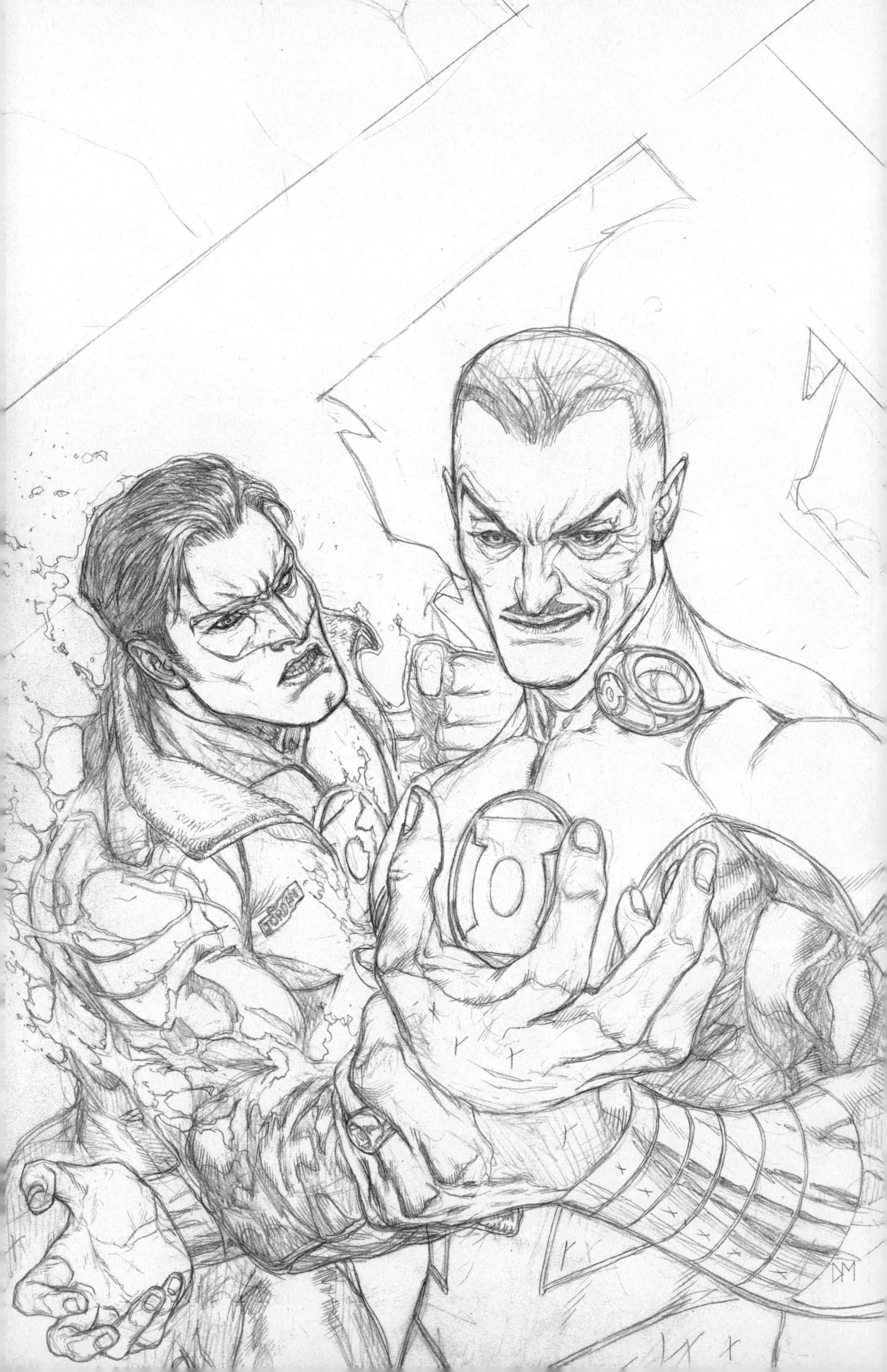
JORDAN

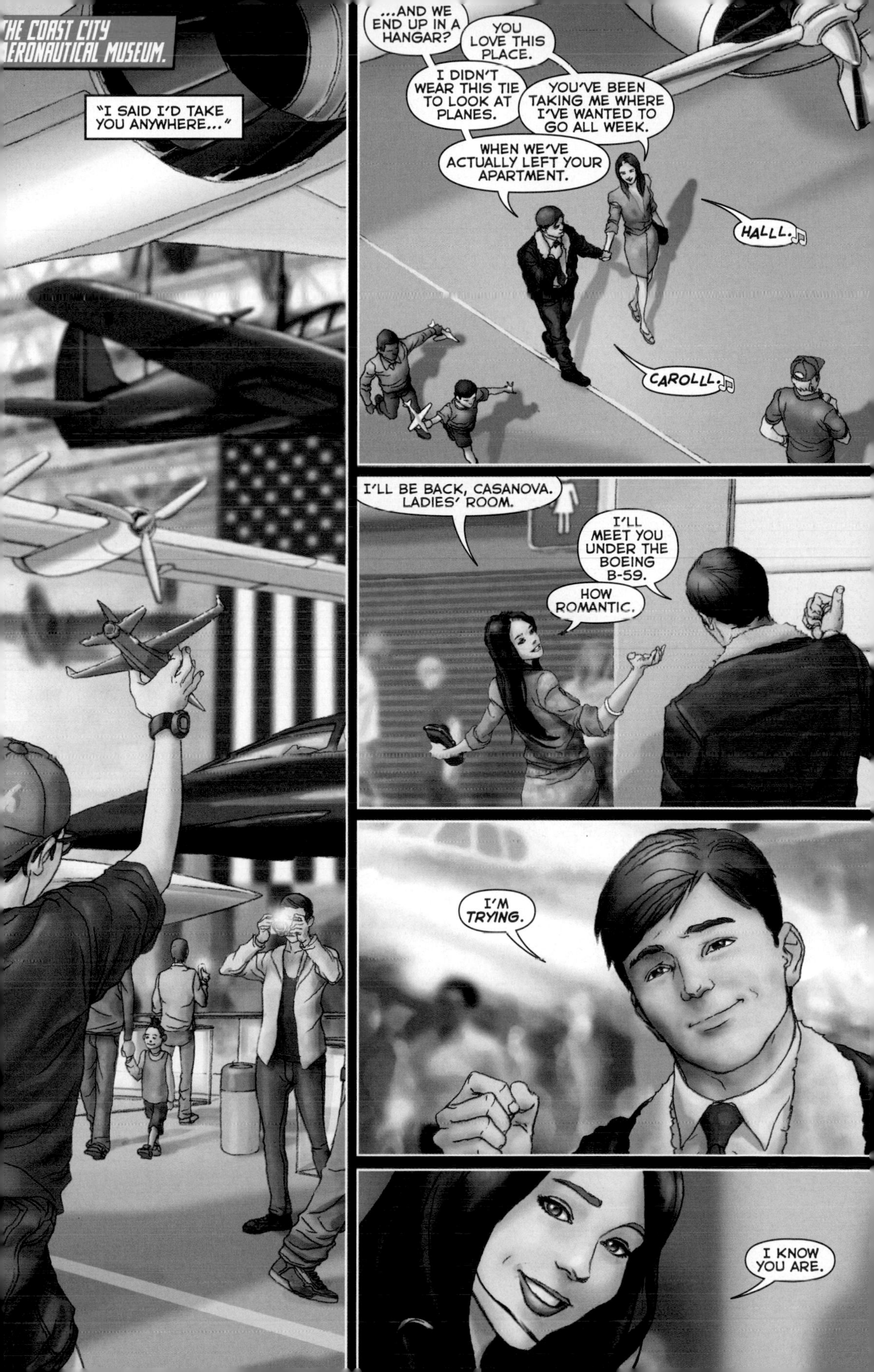
THE COAST CITY AERONAUTICAL MUSEUM.
"I SAID I'D TAKE YOU ANYWHERE..."
...AND WE END UP IN A HANGAR?
YOU LOVE THIS PLACE.
I DIDN'T WEAR THIS TIE TO LOOK AT PLANES.
YOU'VE BEEN TAKING ME WHERE I'VE WANTED TO GO ALL WEEK.
WHEN WE'VE ACTUALLY LEFT YOUR APARTMENT.
HALLL.
CAROLLL.
I'LL BE BACK, CASANOVA. LADIES' ROOM.
I'LL MEET YOU UNDER THE BOEING B-59.
HOW ROMANTIC.
I'M TRYING.
I KNOW YOU ARE.

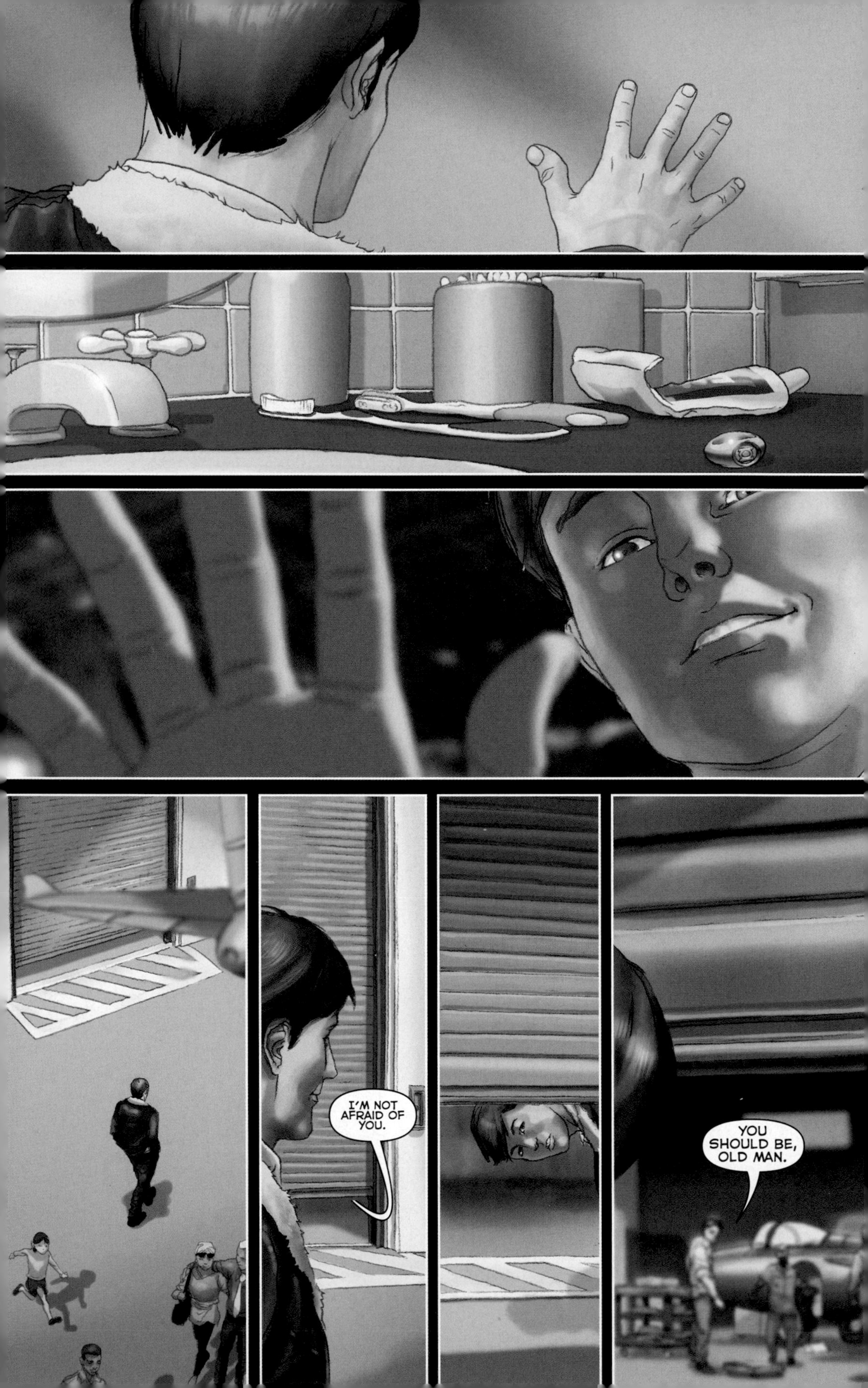
I'M NOT AFRAID OF YOU.
YOU SHOULD BE, OLD MAN.

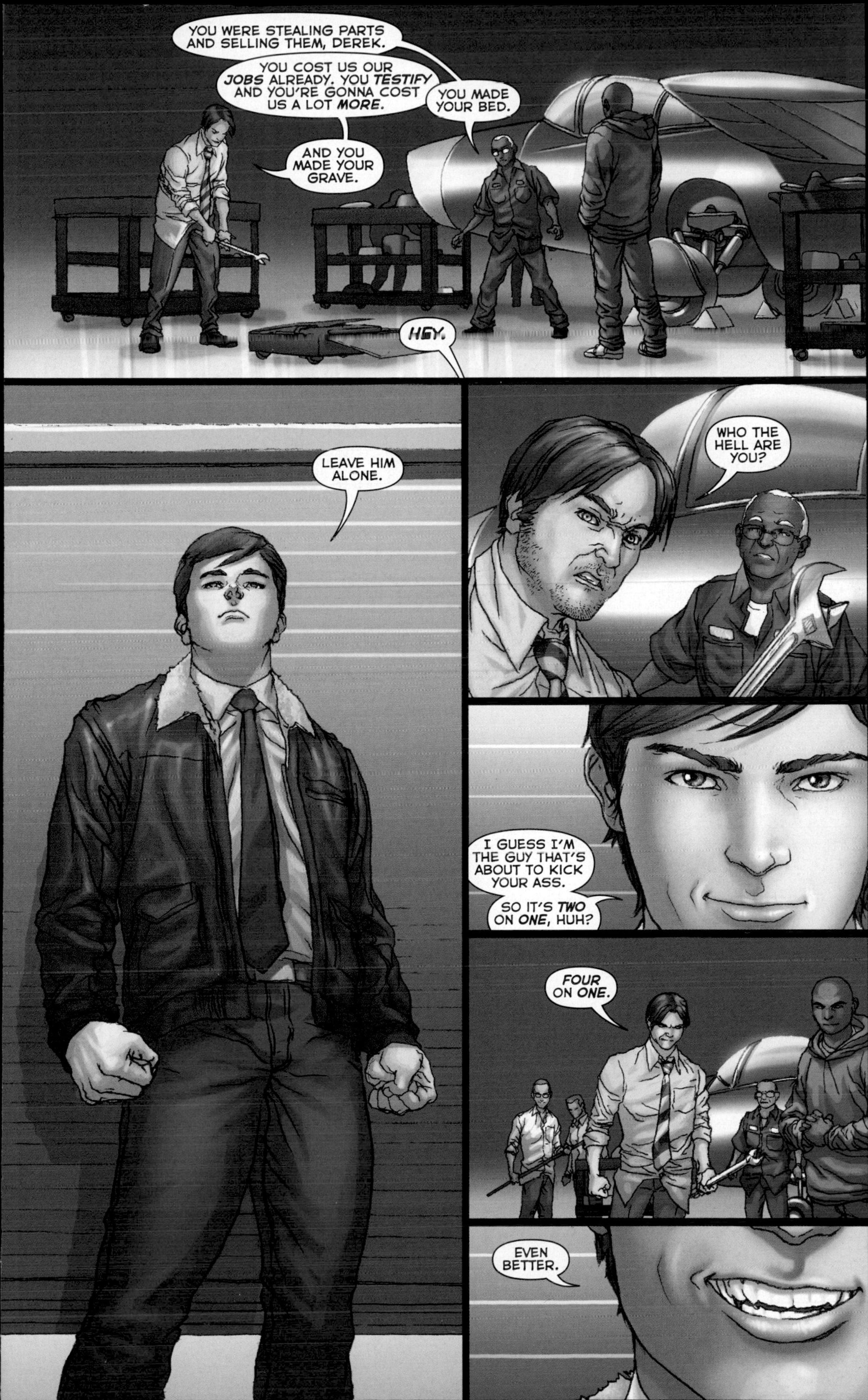

YOU WERE STEALING PARTS AND SELLING THEM, DEREK.
YOU COST US OUR JOBS ALREADY. YOU TESTIFY AND YOU'RE GONNA COST US A LOT MORE.
YOU MADE YOUR BED.
AND YOU MADE YOUR GRAVE.
HEY.
LEAVE HIM ALONE.
WHO THE HELL ARE YOU?
I GUESS I'M THE GUY THAT'S ABOUT TO KICK YOUR ASS.
SO IT'S TWO ON ONE, HUH?
FOUR ON ONE.
EVEN BETTER.

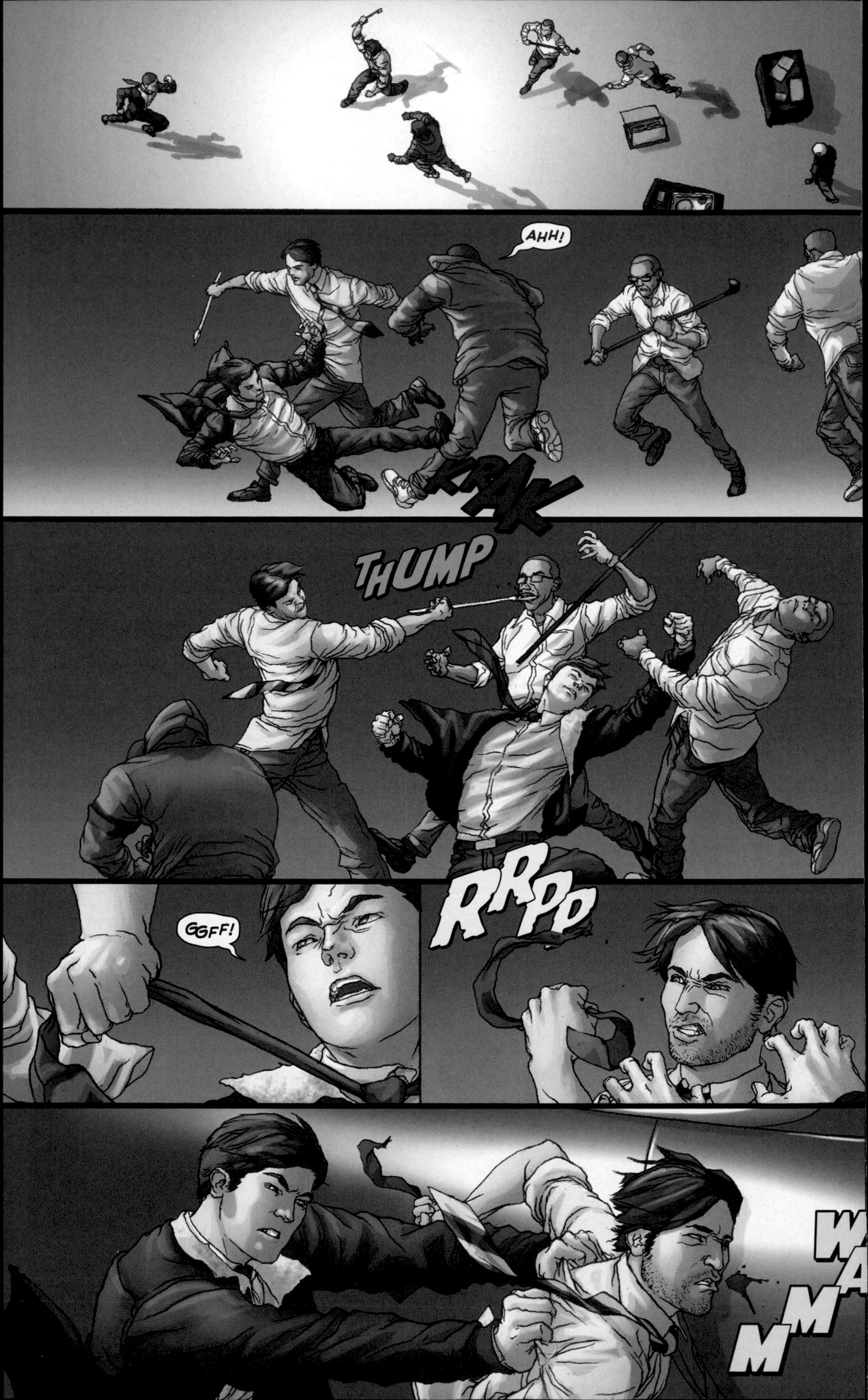
AHH!
KRAK
THUMP
GGFF!
RRPD
WAMMM

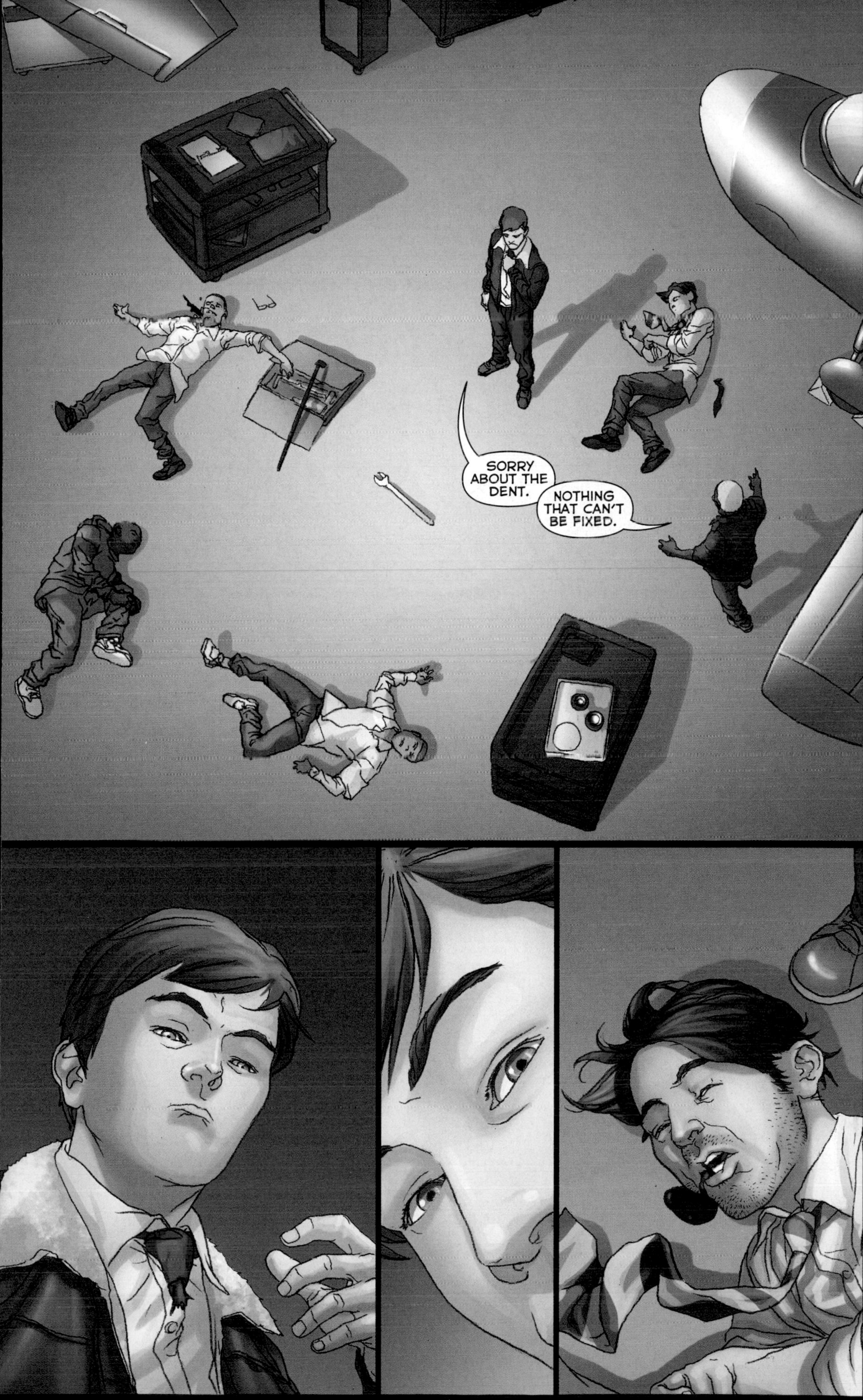
SORRY ABOUT THE DENT.
NOTHING THAT CAN'T BE FIXED.

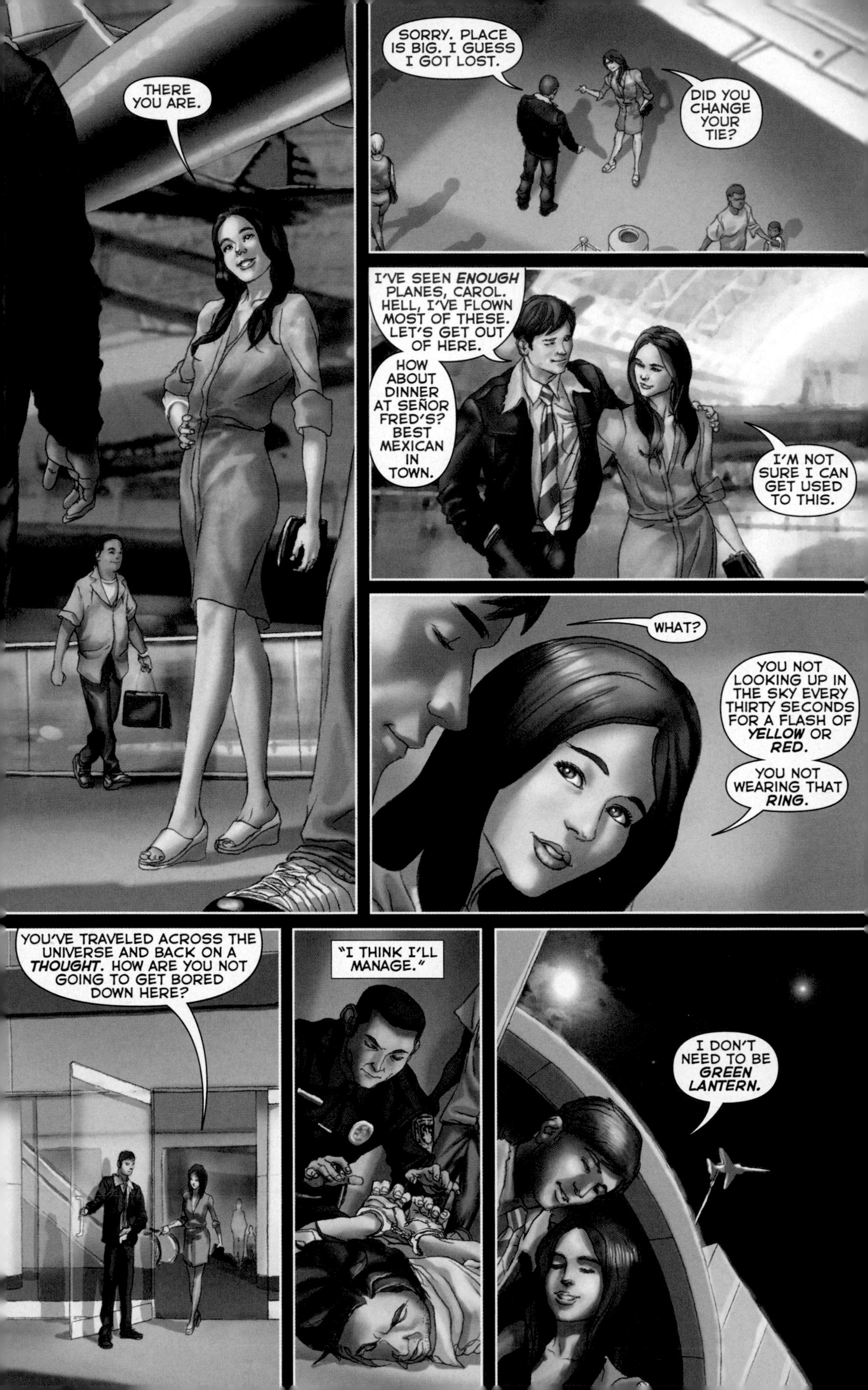
THERE YOU ARE.
SORRY. PLACE IS BIG. I GUESS I GOT LOST.
DID YOU CHANGE YOUR TIE?
I'VE SEEN ENOUGH PLANES, CAROL. HELL, I'VE FLOWN MOST OF THESE. LET'S GET OUT OF HERE.
HOW ABOUT DINNER AT SEÑOR FRED'S? BEST MEXICAN IN TOWN.
I'M NOT SURE I CAN GET USED TO THIS.
WHAT?
YOU NOT LOOKING UP IN THE SKY EVERY THIRTY SECONDS FOR A FLASH OF YELLOW OR RED.
YOU NOT WEARING THAT RING.
YOU'VE TRAVELED ACROSS THE UNIVERSE AND BACK ON A THOUGHT. HOW ARE YOU NOT GOING TO GET BORED DOWN HERE?
"I THINK I'LL MANAGE."
I DON'T NEED TO BE GREEN LANTERN.

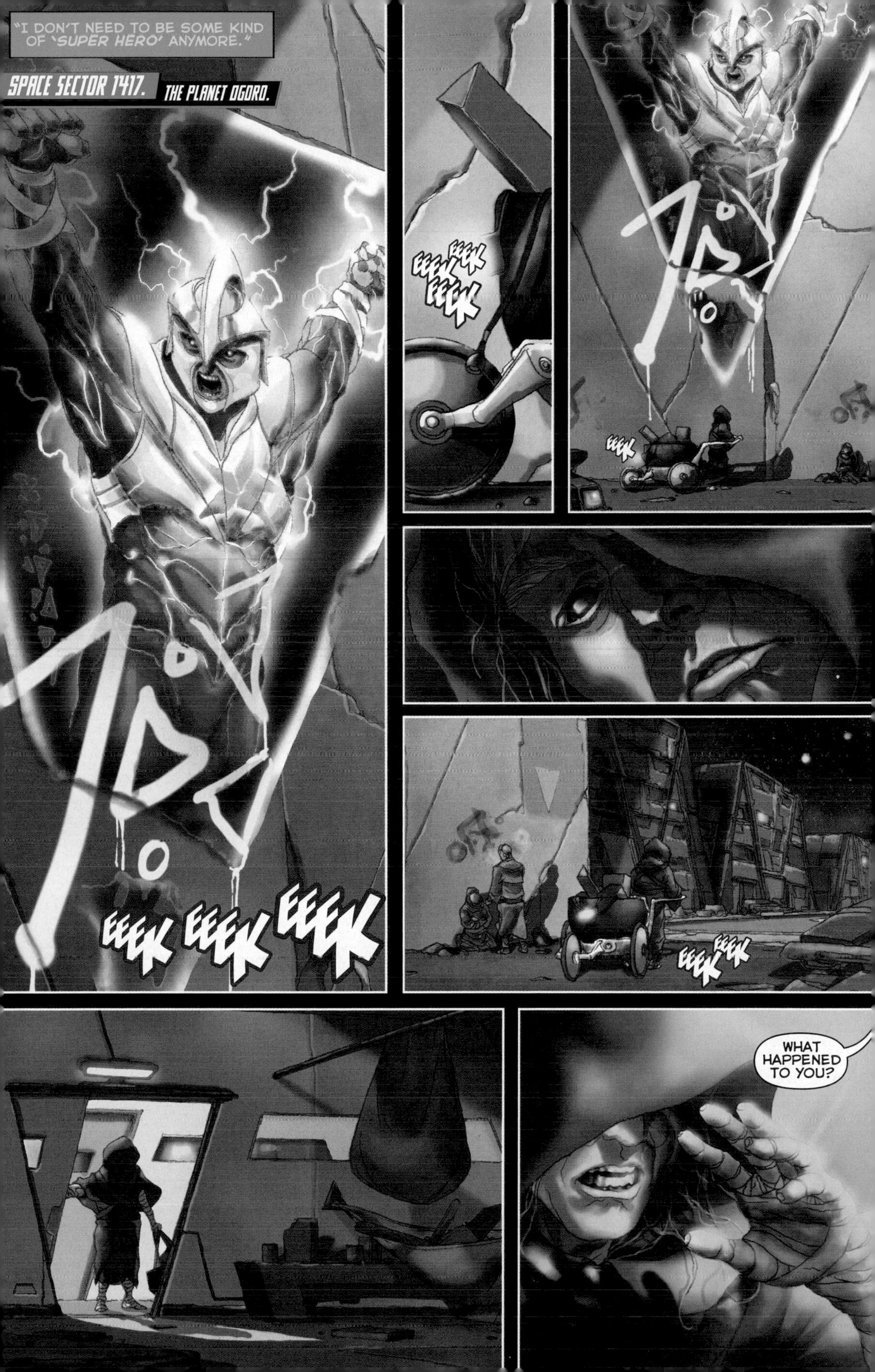
"I DON'T NEED TO BE SOME KIND OF 'SUPER HERO' ANYMORE."
SPACE SECTOR 1417.
THE PLANET OGORO.
EEEK EEEK EEEK
EEEK EEEK EEEK
EEEK
EEEK EEEK
WHAT HAPPENED TO YOU?

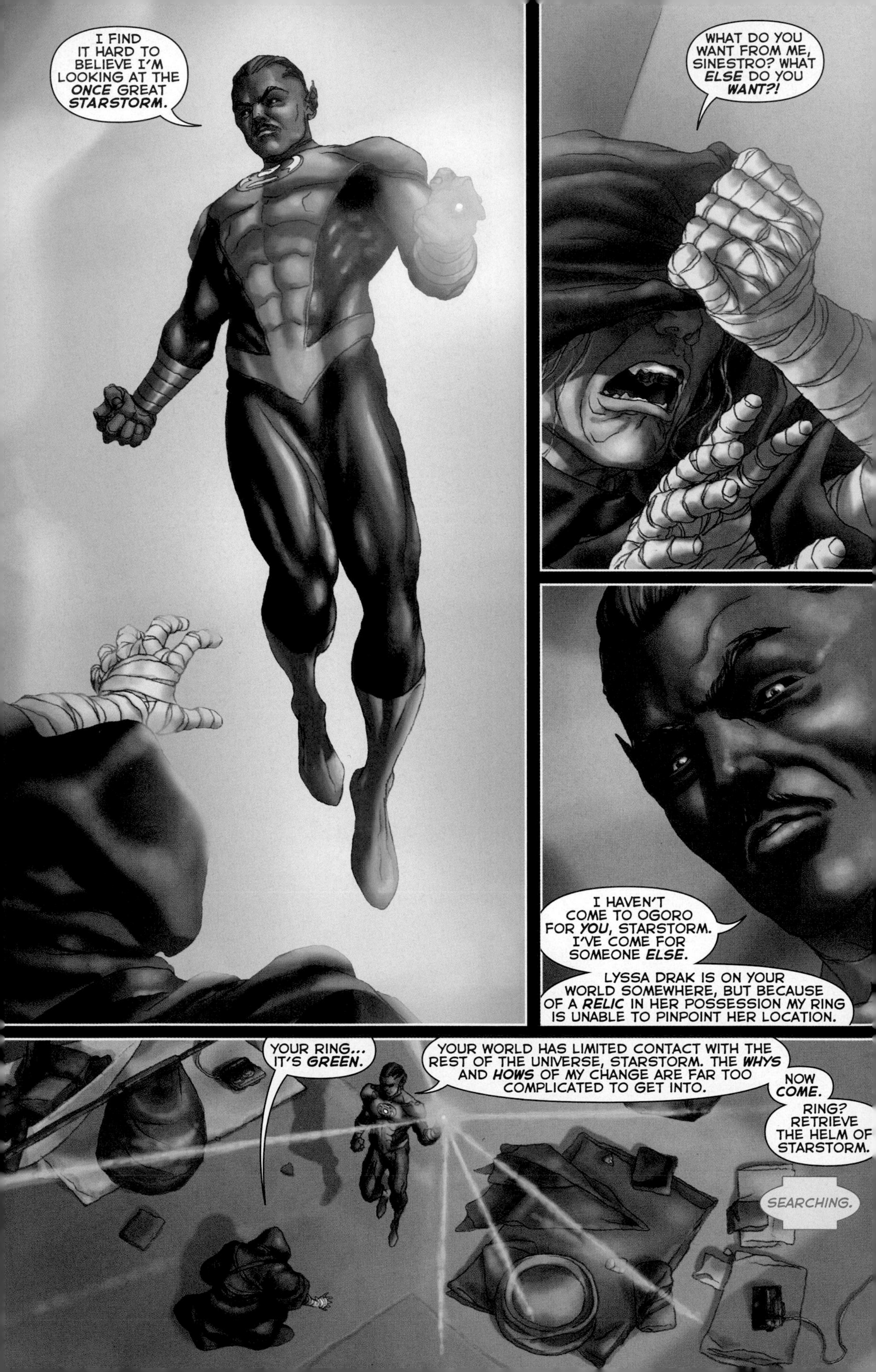

I FIND IT HARD TO BELIEVE I'M LOOKING AT THE ONCE GREAT STARSTORM.
WHAT DO YOU WANT FROM ME, SINESTRO? WHAT ELSE DO YOU WANT?!
I HAVEN'T COME TO OGORO FOR YOU, STARSTORM. I'VE COME FOR SOMEONE ELSE.
LYSSA DRAK IS ON YOUR WORLD SOMEWHERE, BUT BECAUSE OF A RELIC IN HER POSSESSION MY RING IS UNABLE TO PINPOINT HER LOCATION.
YOUR RING... IT'S GREEN.
YOUR WORLD HAS LIMITED CONTACT WITH THE REST OF THE UNIVERSE, STARSTORM. THE WHYS AND HOWS OF MY CHANGE ARE FAR TOO COMPLICATED TO GET INTO.
NOW COME.
RING? RETRIEVE THE HELM OF STARSTORM.
SEARCHING.

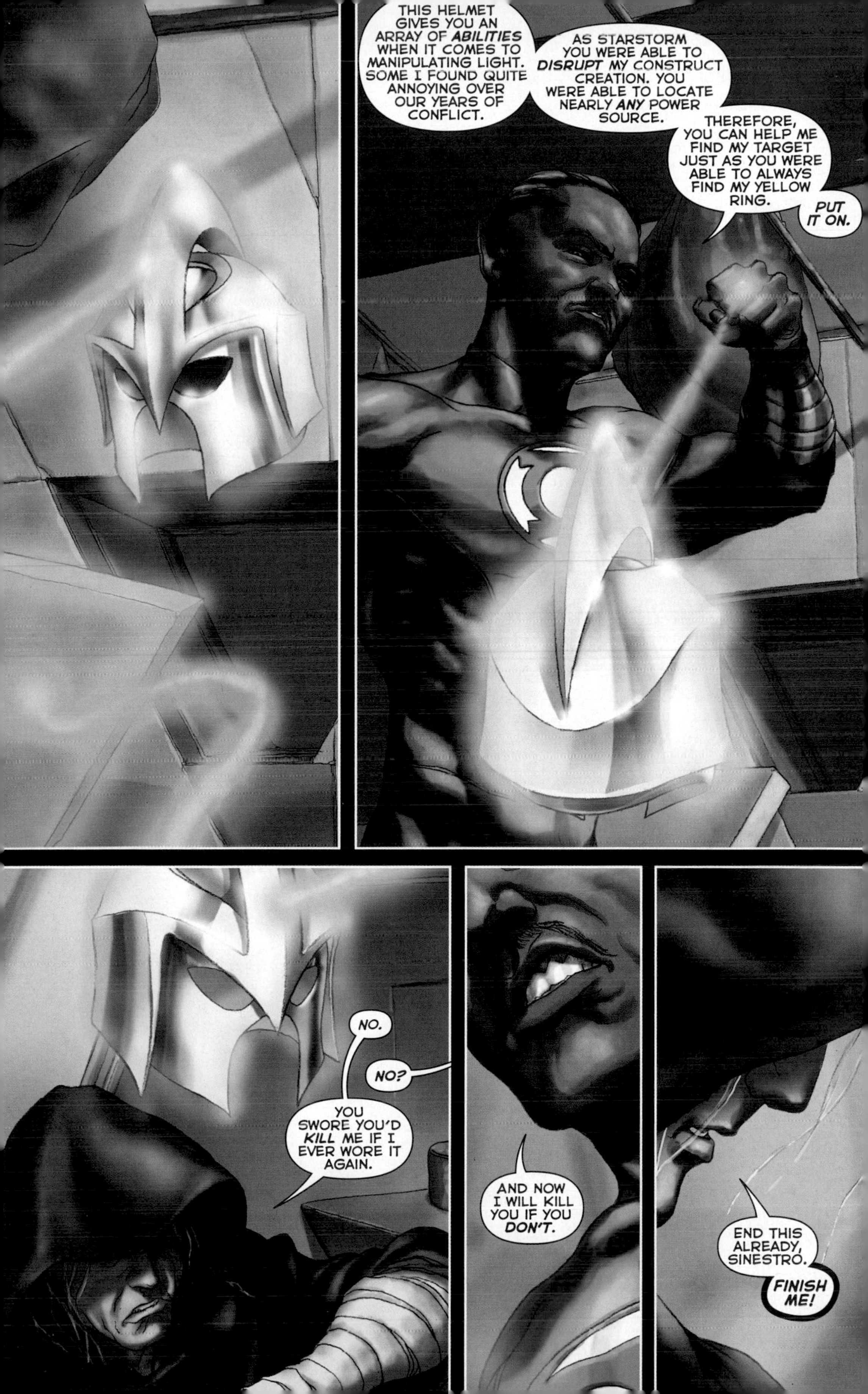
THIS HELMET GIVES YOU AN ARRAY OF ABILITIES WHEN IT COMES TO MANIPULATING LIGHT. SOME I FOUND QUITE ANNOYING OVER OUR YEARS OF CONFLICT.
AS STARSTORM YOU WERE ABLE TO DISRUPT MY CONSTRUCT CREATION. YOU WERE ABLE TO LOCATE NEARLY ANY POWER SOURCE.
THEREFORE, YOU CAN HELP ME FIND MY TARGET JUST AS YOU WERE ABLE TO ALWAYS FIND MY YELLOW RING.
PUT IT ON.
NO.
NO?
YOU SWORE YOU'D KILL ME IF I EVER WORE IT AGAIN.
AND NOW I WILL KILL YOU IF YOU DON'T.
END THIS ALREADY, SINESTRO.
FINISH ME!

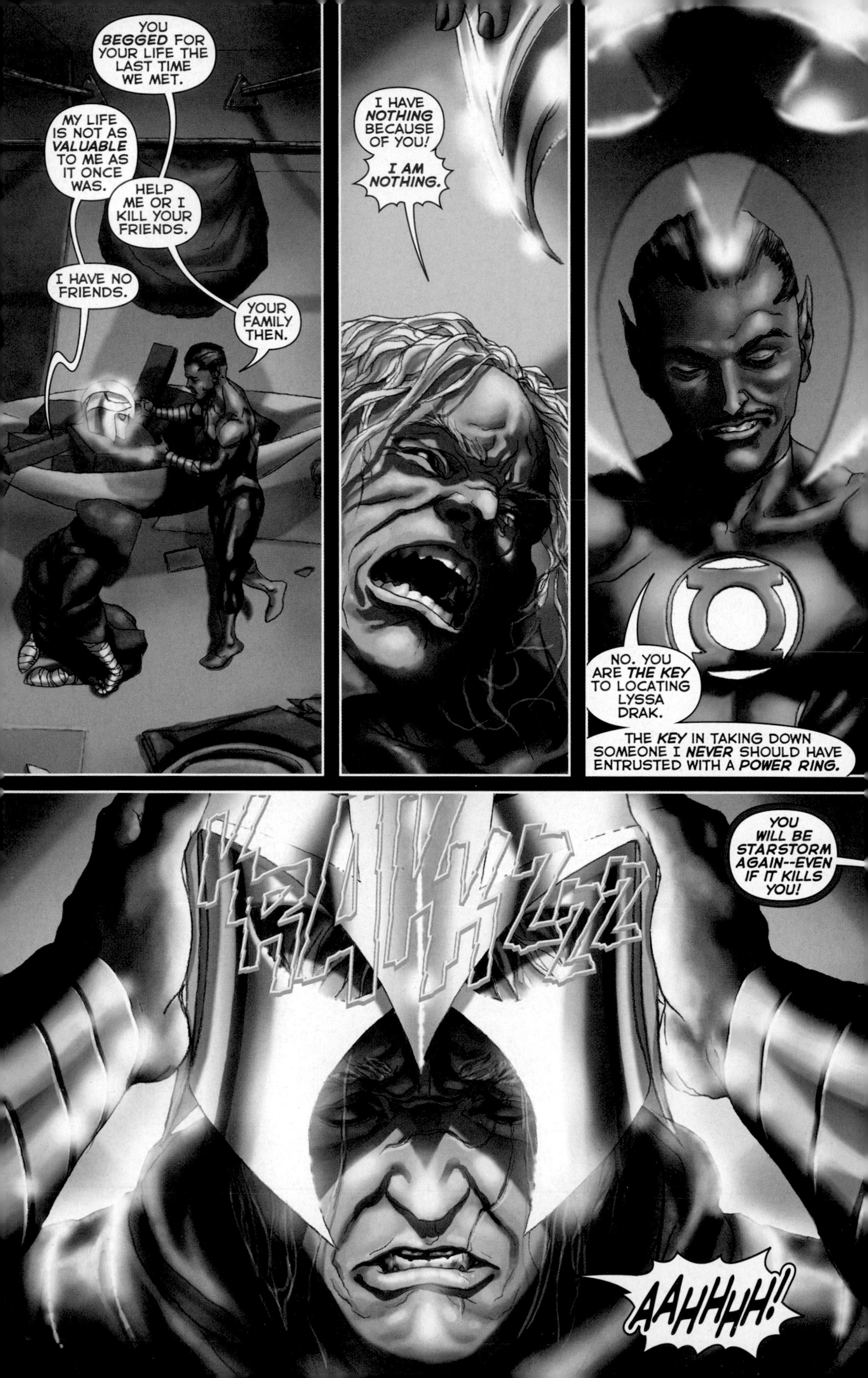
YOU *BEGGED* FOR YOUR LIFE THE LAST TIME WE MET.
MY LIFE IS NOT AS *VALUABLE* TO ME AS IT ONCE WAS.
HELP ME OR I KILL YOUR FRIENDS.
I HAVE NO FRIENDS.
YOUR FAMILY THEN.
I HAVE *NOTHING* BECAUSE OF YOU!
I AM NOTHING.
NO. YOU ARE *THE KEY* TO LOCATING LYSSA DRAK.
THE *KEY* IN TAKING DOWN SOMEONE I *NEVER* SHOULD HAVE ENTRUSTED WITH A *POWER RING.*
KRAKKZZ
YOU WILL BE STARSTORM AGAIN--EVEN IF IT KILLS YOU!
AAHHHH!

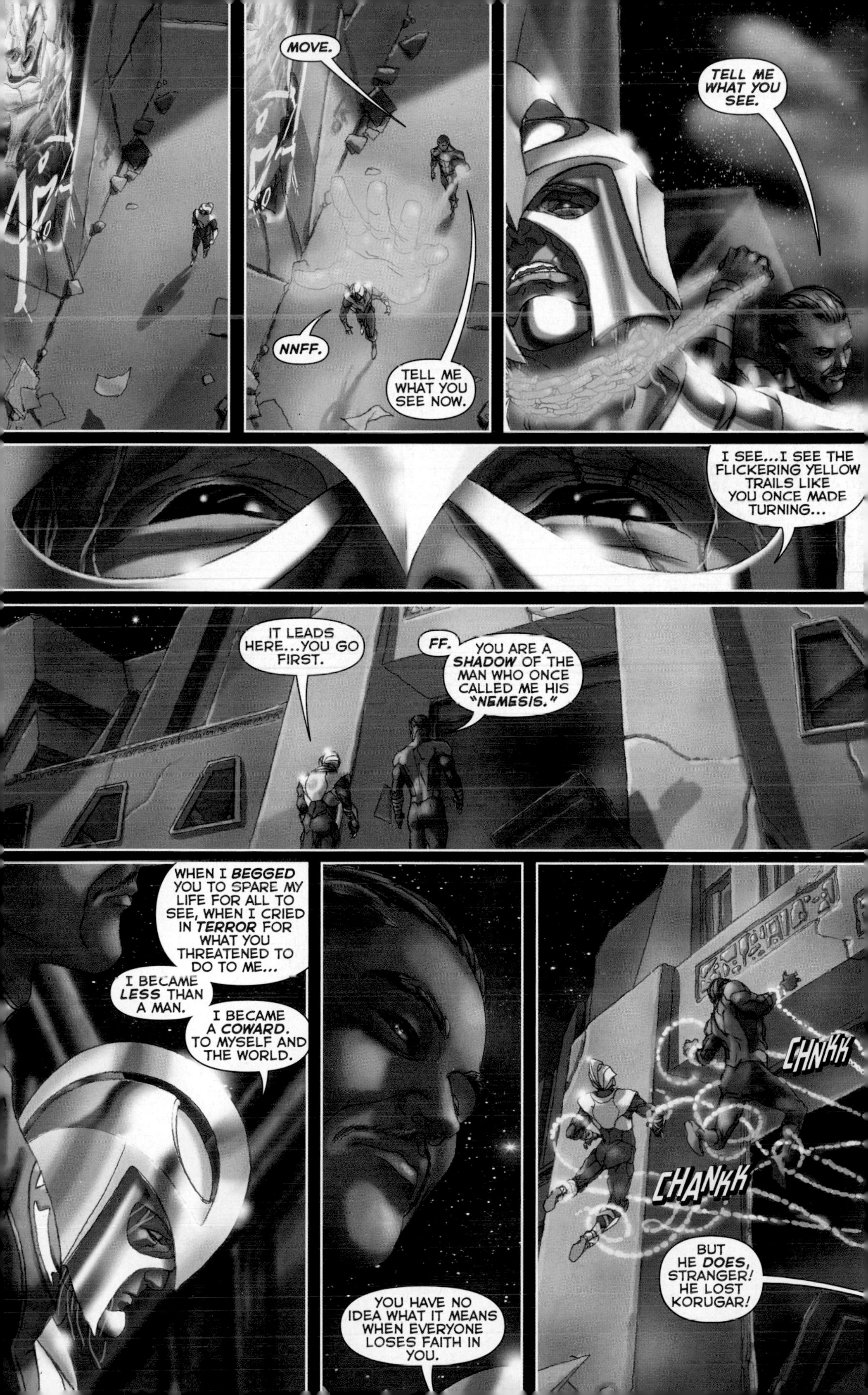
MOVE.
NNFF.
TELL ME WHAT YOU SEE NOW.
TELL ME WHAT YOU SEE.
I SEE...I SEE THE FLICKERING YELLOW TRAILS LIKE YOU ONCE MADE TURNING...
IT LEADS HERE...YOU GO FIRST.
FF.
YOU ARE A SHADOW OF THE MAN WHO ONCE CALLED ME HIS "NEMESIS."
WHEN I BEGGED YOU TO SPARE MY LIFE FOR ALL TO SEE, WHEN I CRIED IN TERROR FOR WHAT YOU THREATENED TO DO TO ME...
I BECAME LESS THAN A MAN.
I BECAME A COWARD. TO MYSELF AND THE WORLD.
YOU HAVE NO IDEA WHAT IT MEANS WHEN EVERYONE LOSES FAITH IN YOU.
CHNKK
CHANKK
BUT HE DOES, STRANGER! HE LOST KORUGAR!

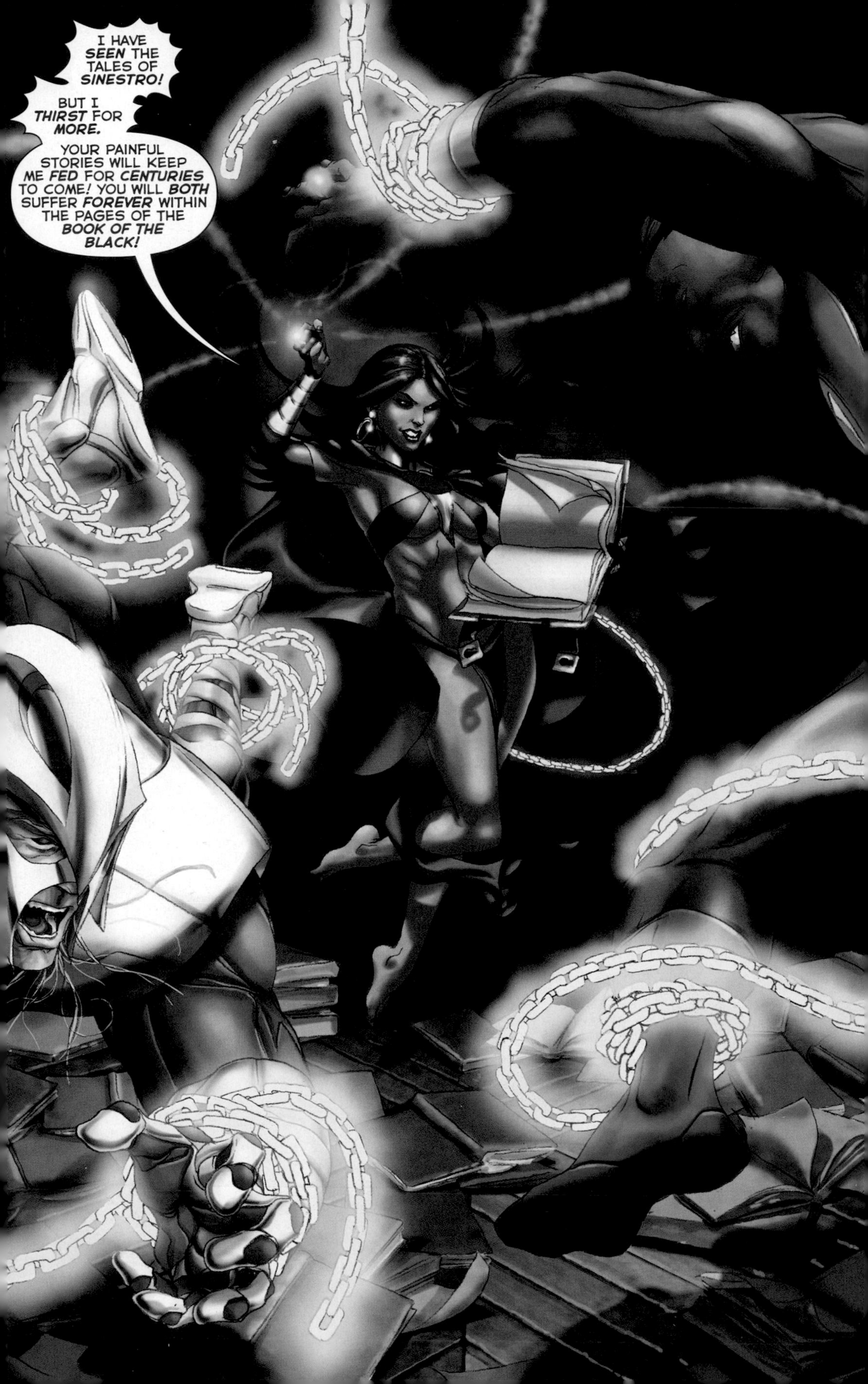
I HAVE SEEN THE TALES OF SINESTRO!
BUT I THIRST FOR MORE.
YOUR PAINFUL STORIES WILL KEEP ME FED FOR CENTURIES TO COME! YOU WILL BOTH SUFFER FOREVER WITHIN THE PAGES OF THE BOOK OF THE BLACK!

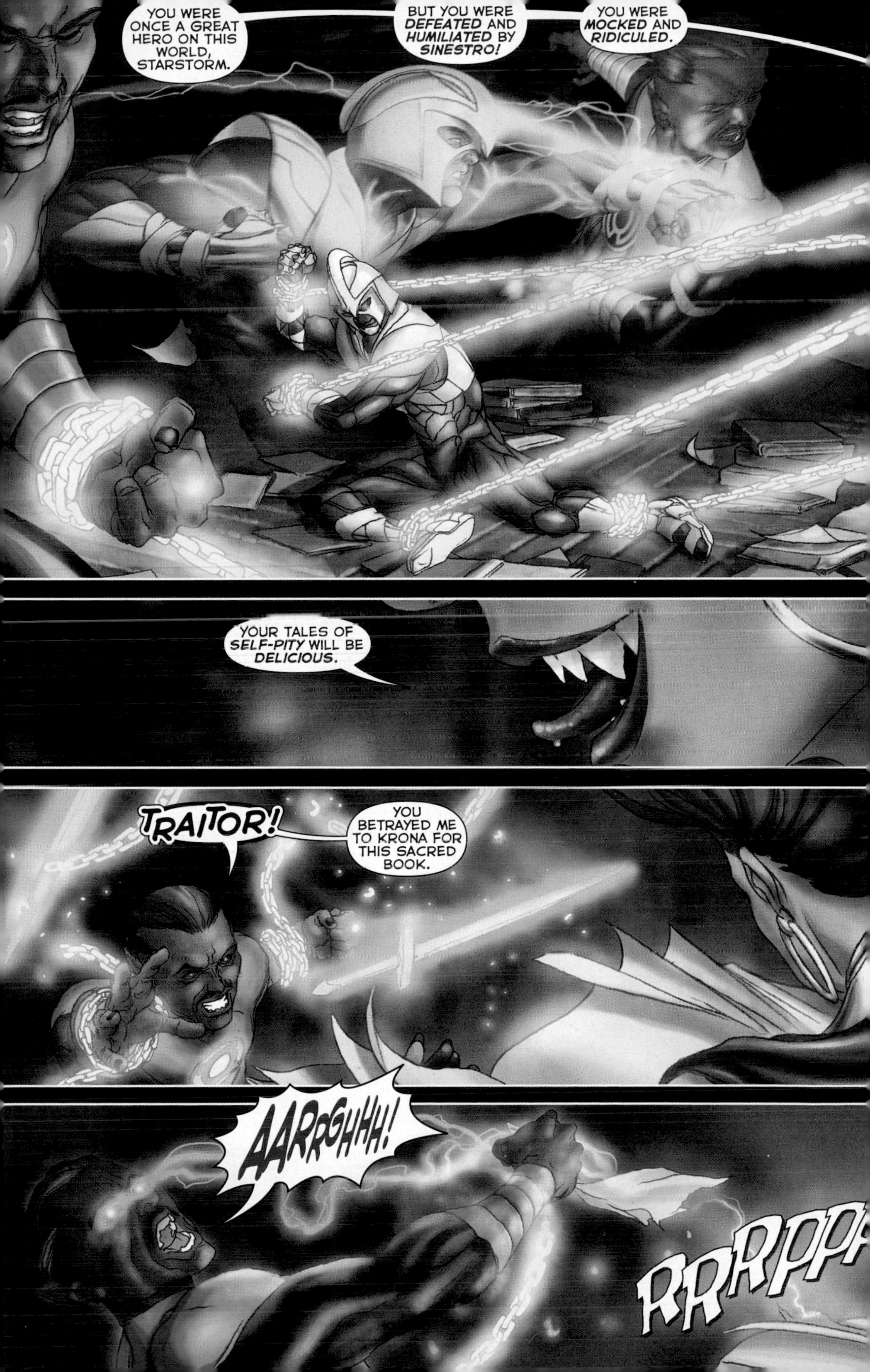
YOU WERE ONCE A GREAT HERO ON THIS WORLD, STARSTORM.
BUT YOU WERE *DEFEATED* AND *HUMILIATED* BY *SINESTRO!*
YOU WERE *MOCKED* AND *RIDICULED*.
YOUR TALES OF *SELF-PITY* WILL BE *DELICIOUS*.
TRAITOR!
YOU BETRAYED ME TO KRONA FOR THIS SACRED BOOK.
AARRGHHH!
RRRPPP

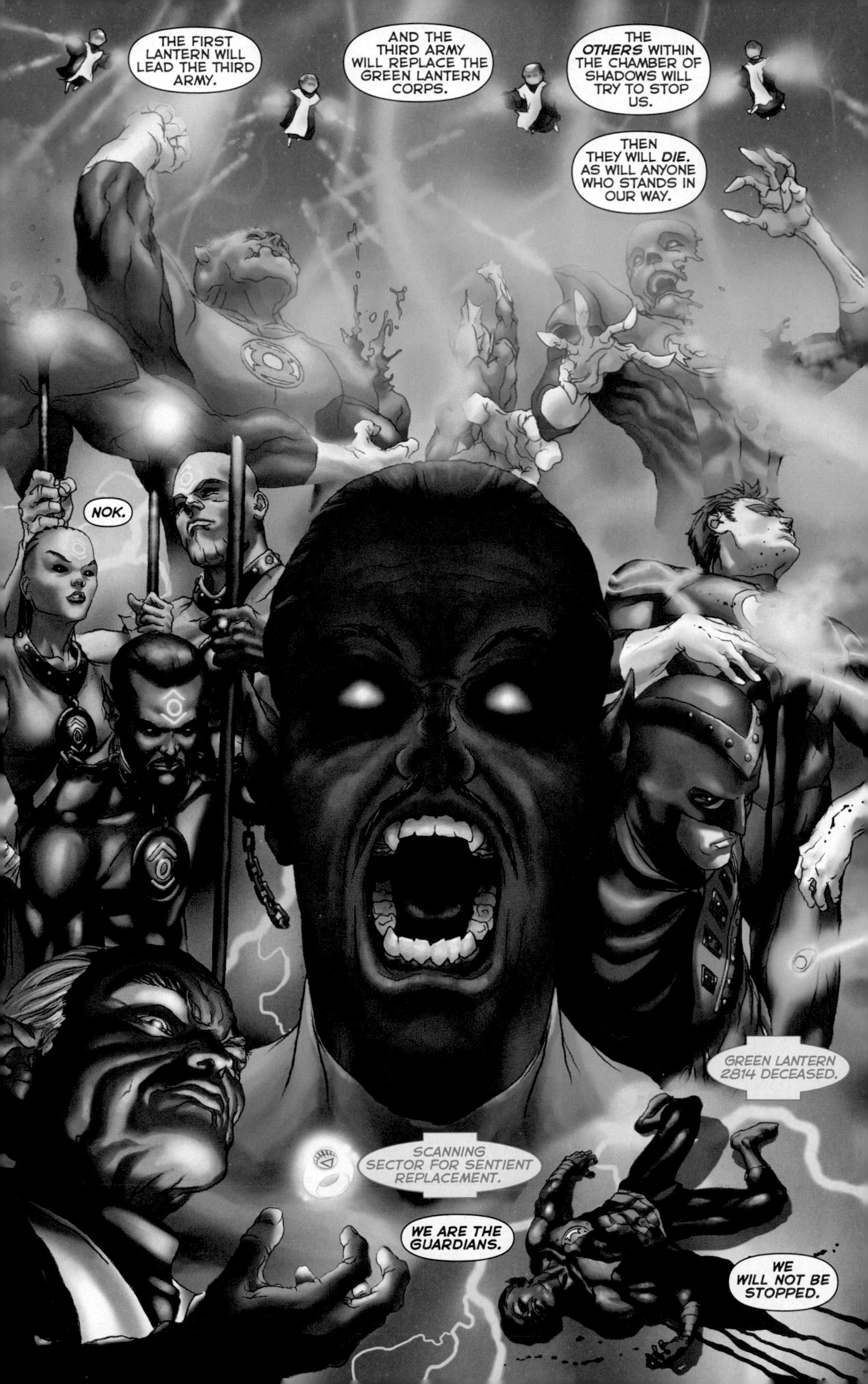

THE FIRST LANTERN WILL LEAD THE THIRD ARMY.
AND THE THIRD ARMY WILL REPLACE THE GREEN LANTERN CORPS.
THE OTHERS WITHIN THE CHAMBER OF SHADOWS WILL TRY TO STOP US.
THEN THEY WILL DIE. AS WILL ANYONE WHO STANDS IN OUR WAY.
NOK.
GREEN LANTERN 2814 DECEASED.
SCANNING SECTOR FOR SENTIENT REPLACEMENT.
WE ARE THE GUARDIANS.
WE WILL NOT BE STOPPED.

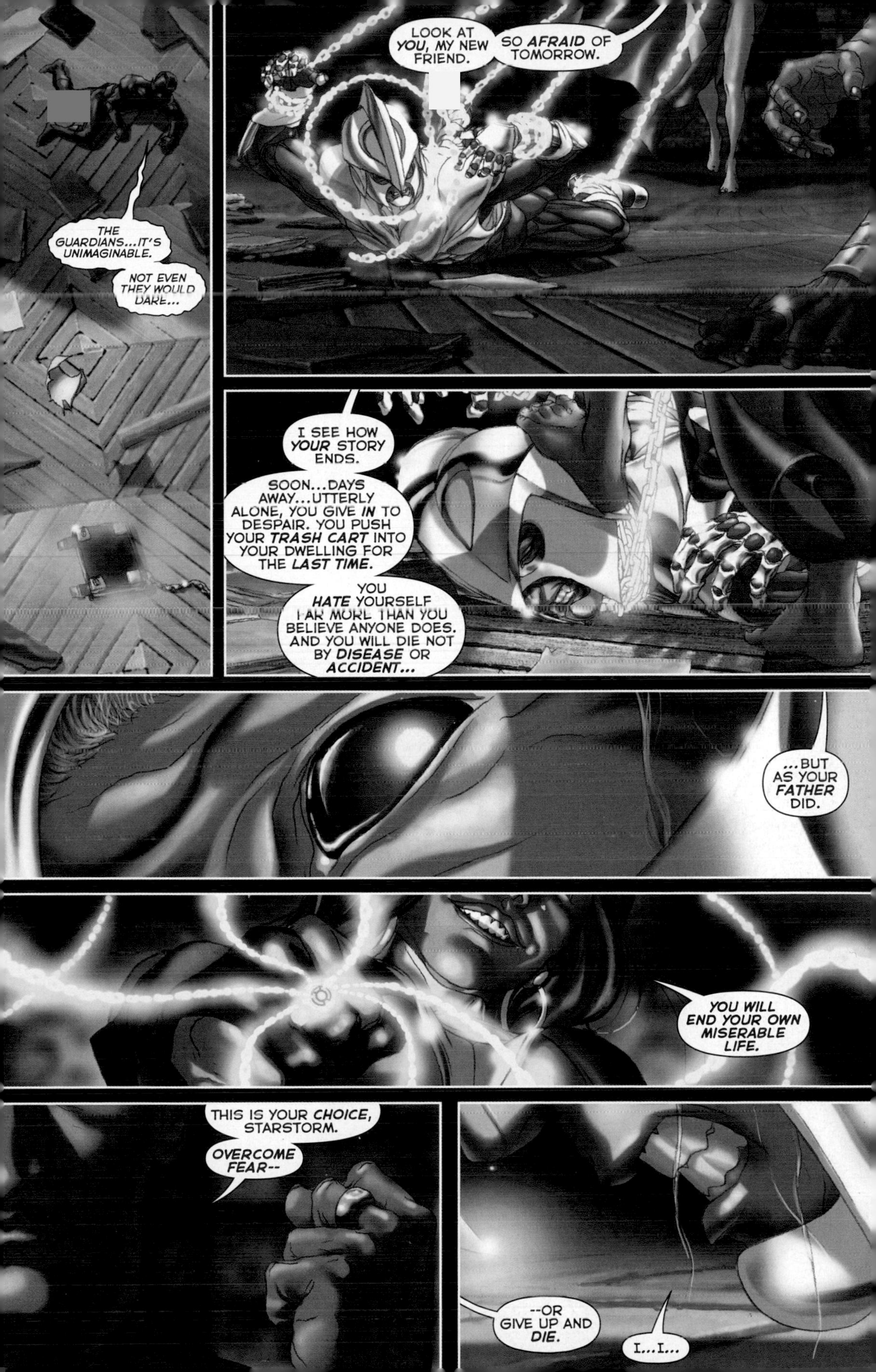
THE GUARDIANS...IT'S UNIMAGINABLE.
NOT EVEN THEY WOULD DARE...
LOOK AT *YOU*, MY NEW FRIEND.
SO *AFRAID* OF TOMORROW.
I SEE HOW *YOUR* STORY ENDS.
SOON...DAYS AWAY...UTTERLY ALONE, YOU GIVE *IN* TO DESPAIR. YOU PUSH YOUR *TRASH CART* INTO YOUR DWELLING FOR THE *LAST TIME.*
YOU *HATE* YOURSELF FAR MORE THAN YOU BELIEVE ANYONE DOES. AND YOU WILL DIE NOT BY *DISEASE* OR *ACCIDENT...*
...BUT AS YOUR *FATHER* DID.
YOU WILL END YOUR OWN MISERABLE LIFE.
THIS IS YOUR *CHOICE,* STARSTORM.
OVERCOME FEAR--
--OR GIVE UP AND *DIE.*
I...I...

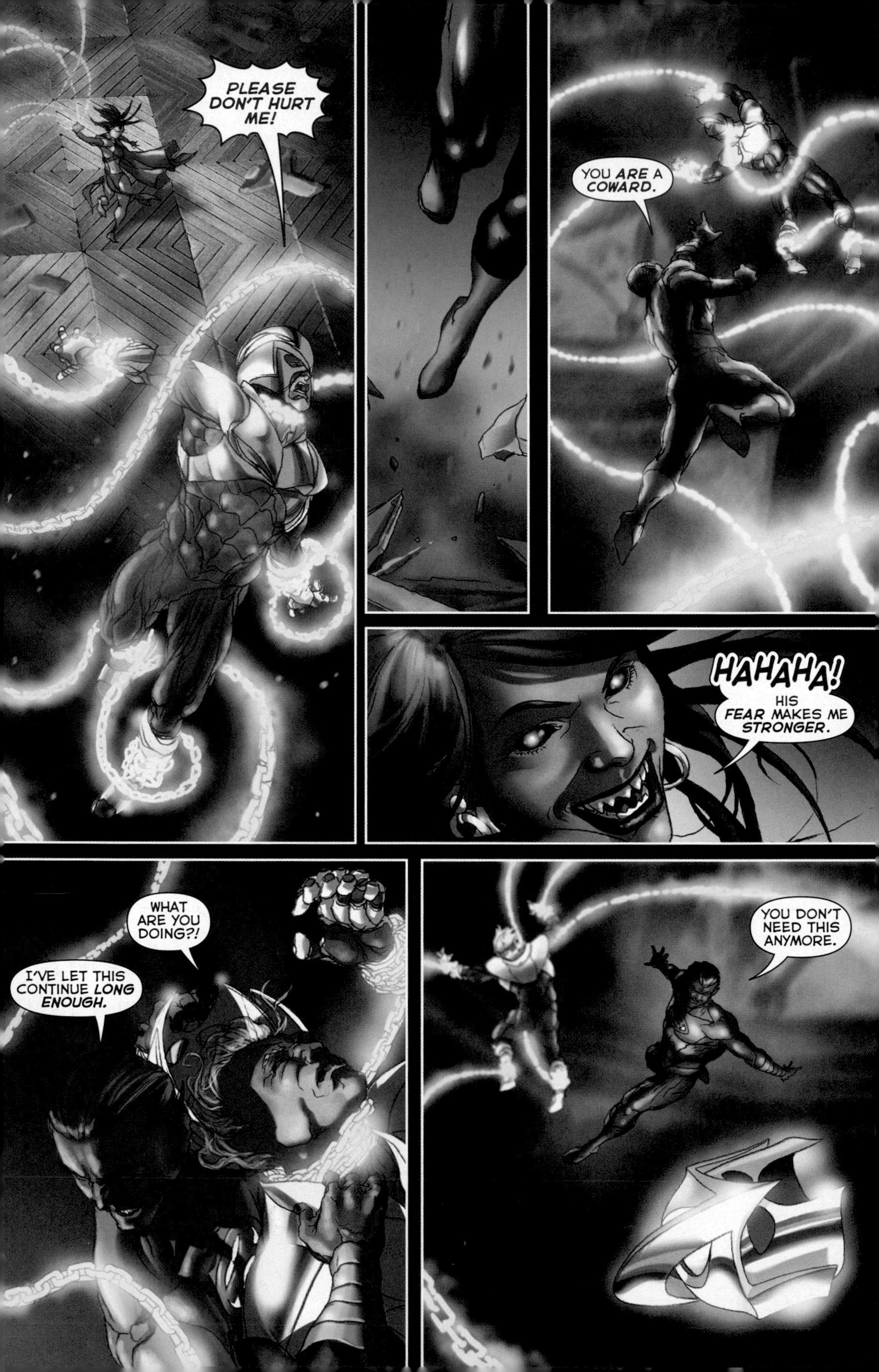
PLEASE DON'T HURT ME!
YOU ARE A COWARD.
HAHAHA!
HIS FEAR MAKES ME STRONGER.
WHAT ARE YOU DOING?!
I'VE LET THIS CONTINUE LONG ENOUGH.
YOU DON'T NEED THIS ANYMORE.

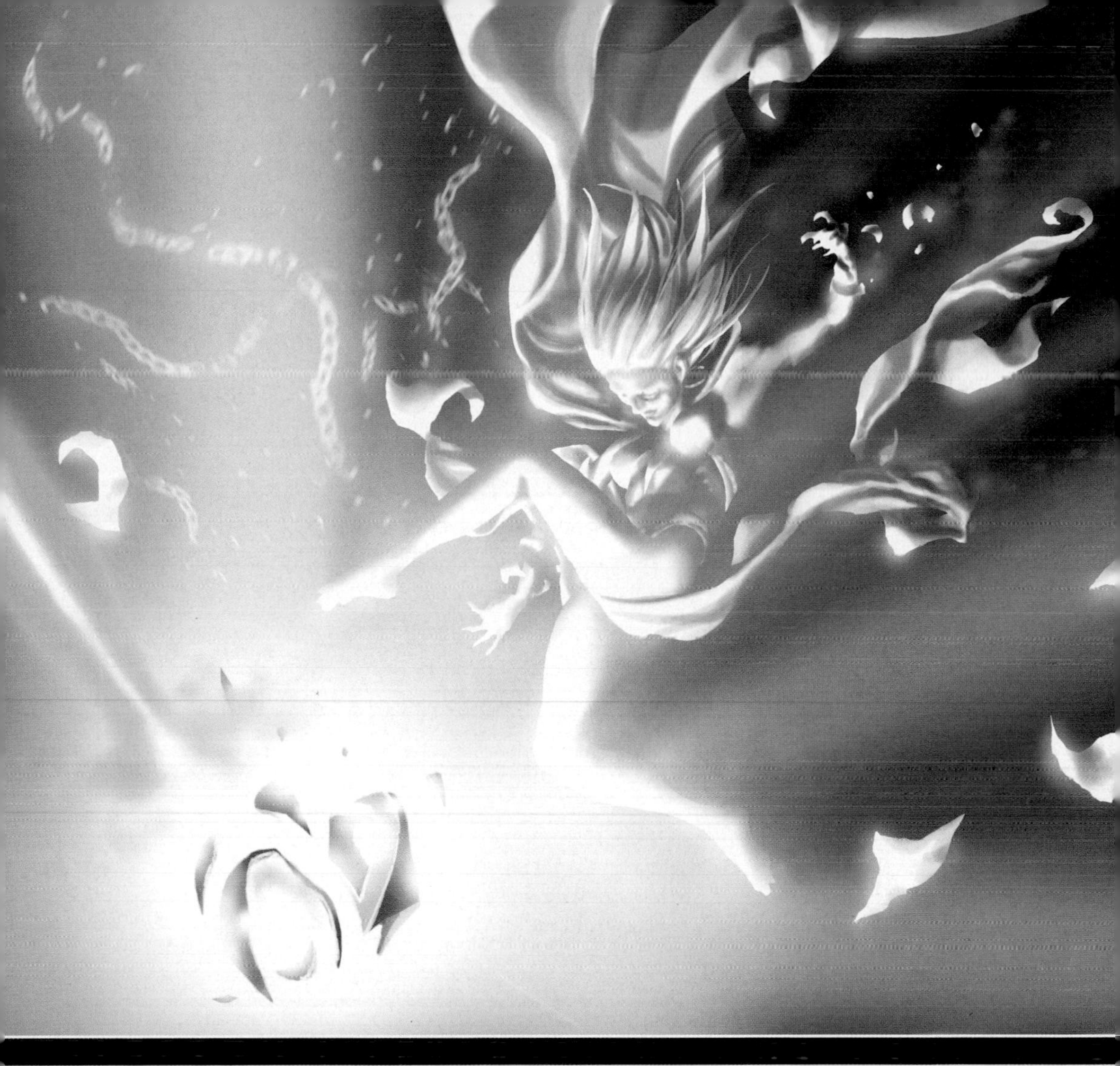

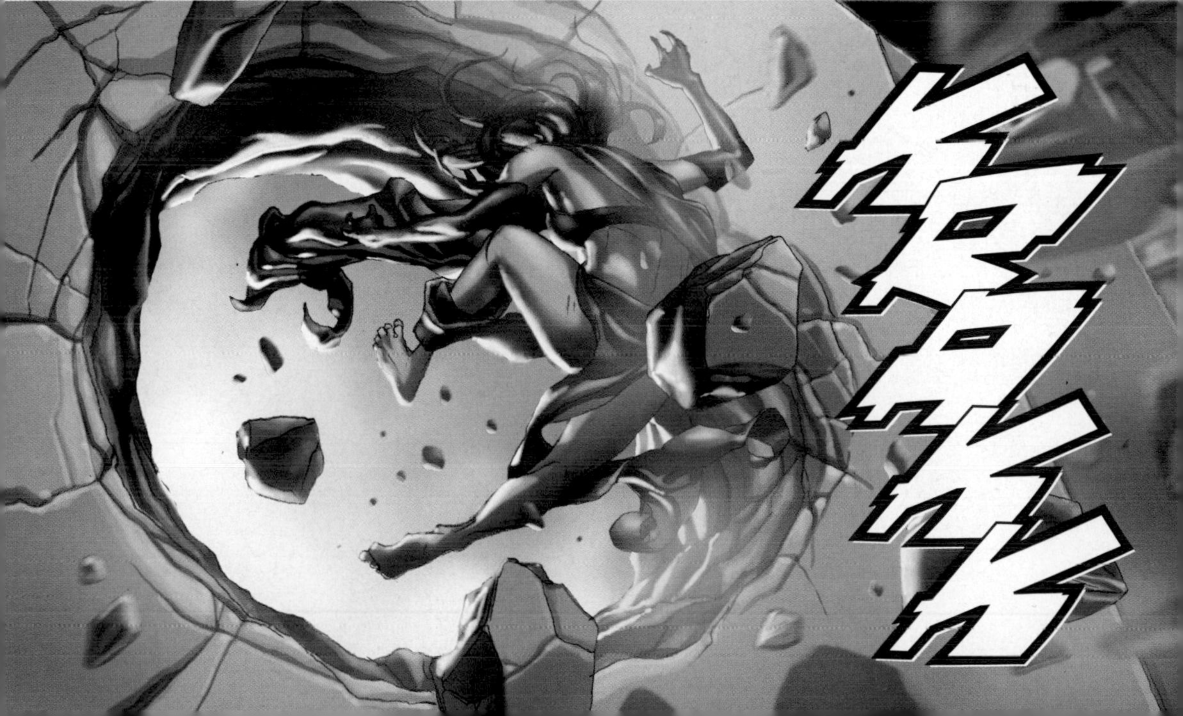
KRAKK

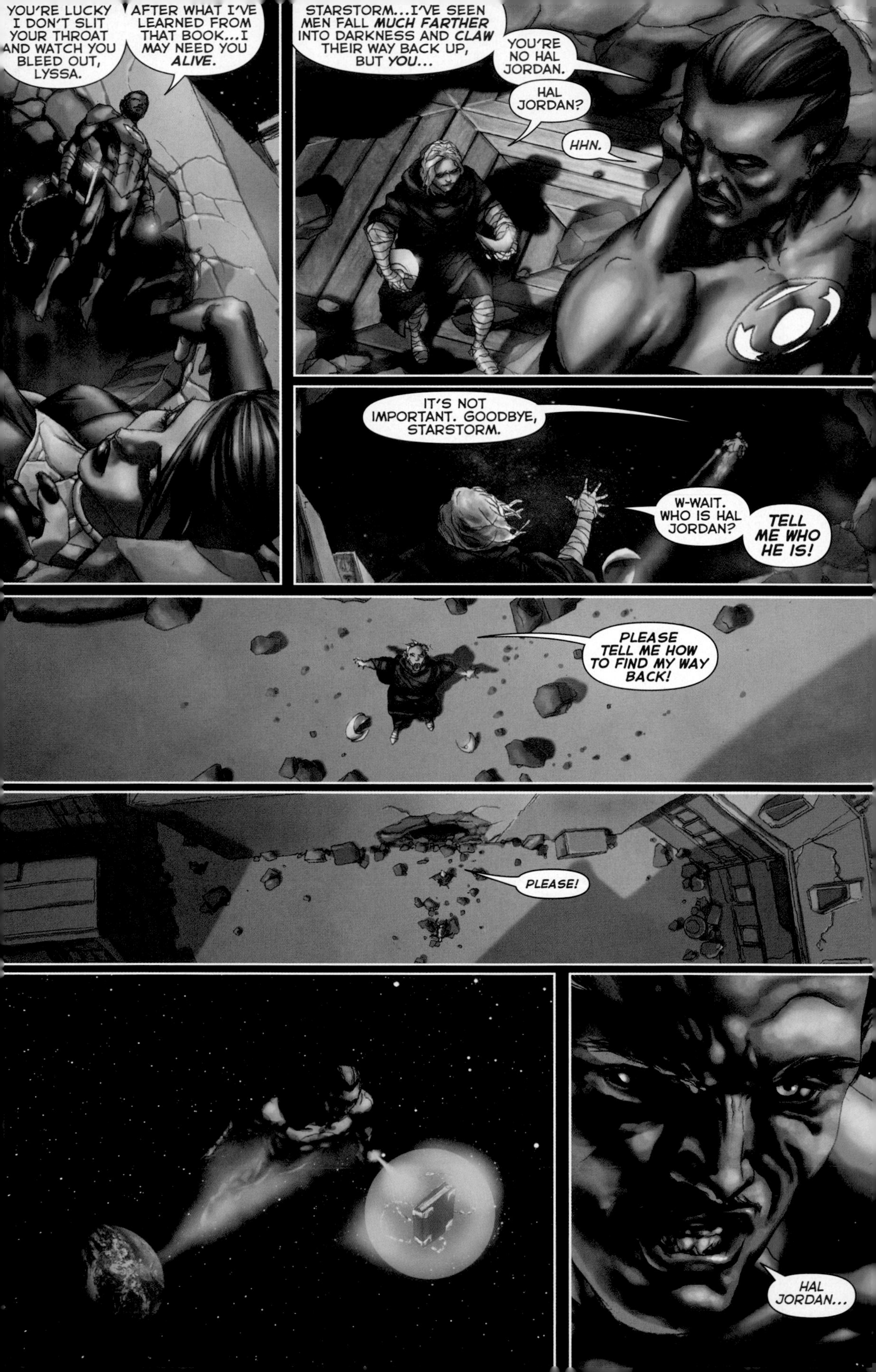
YOU'RE LUCKY I DON'T SLIT YOUR THROAT AND WATCH YOU BLEED OUT, LYSSA.
AFTER WHAT I'VE LEARNED FROM THAT BOOK...I MAY NEED YOU ALIVE.
STARSTORM...I'VE SEEN MEN FALL MUCH FARTHER INTO DARKNESS AND CLAW THEIR WAY BACK UP, BUT YOU...
YOU'RE NO HAL JORDAN.
HAL JORDAN?
HHN.
IT'S NOT IMPORTANT. GOODBYE, STARSTORM.
W-WAIT. WHO IS HAL JORDAN?
TELL ME WHO HE IS!
PLEASE TELL ME HOW TO FIND MY WAY BACK!
PLEASE!
HAL JORDAN...

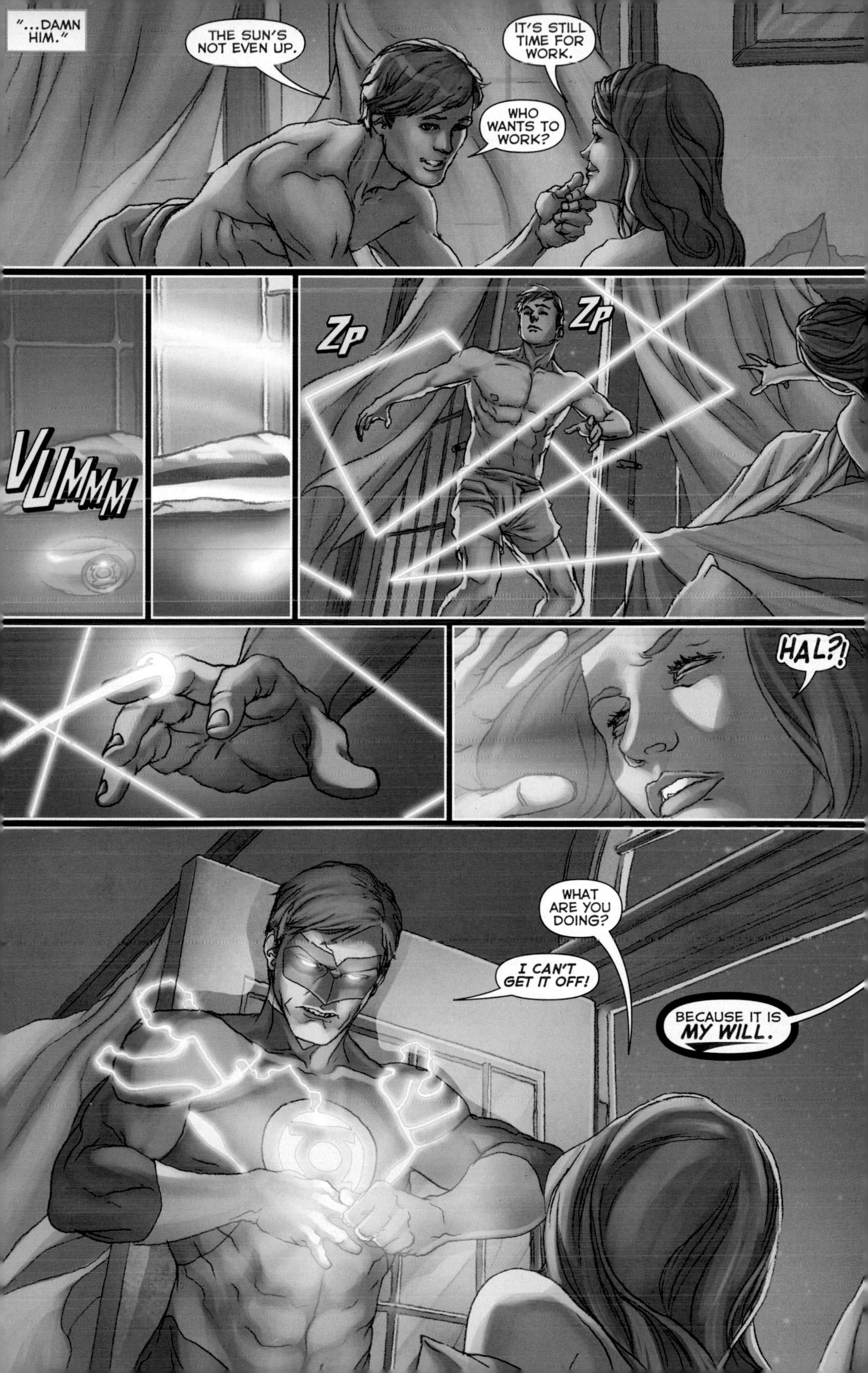
"...DAMN HIM."
THE SUN'S NOT EVEN UP.
IT'S STILL TIME FOR WORK.
WHO WANTS TO WORK?
VUMMMM
ZP
ZP
HAL?!
WHAT ARE YOU DOING?
I CAN'T GET IT OFF!
BECAUSE IT IS MY WILL.

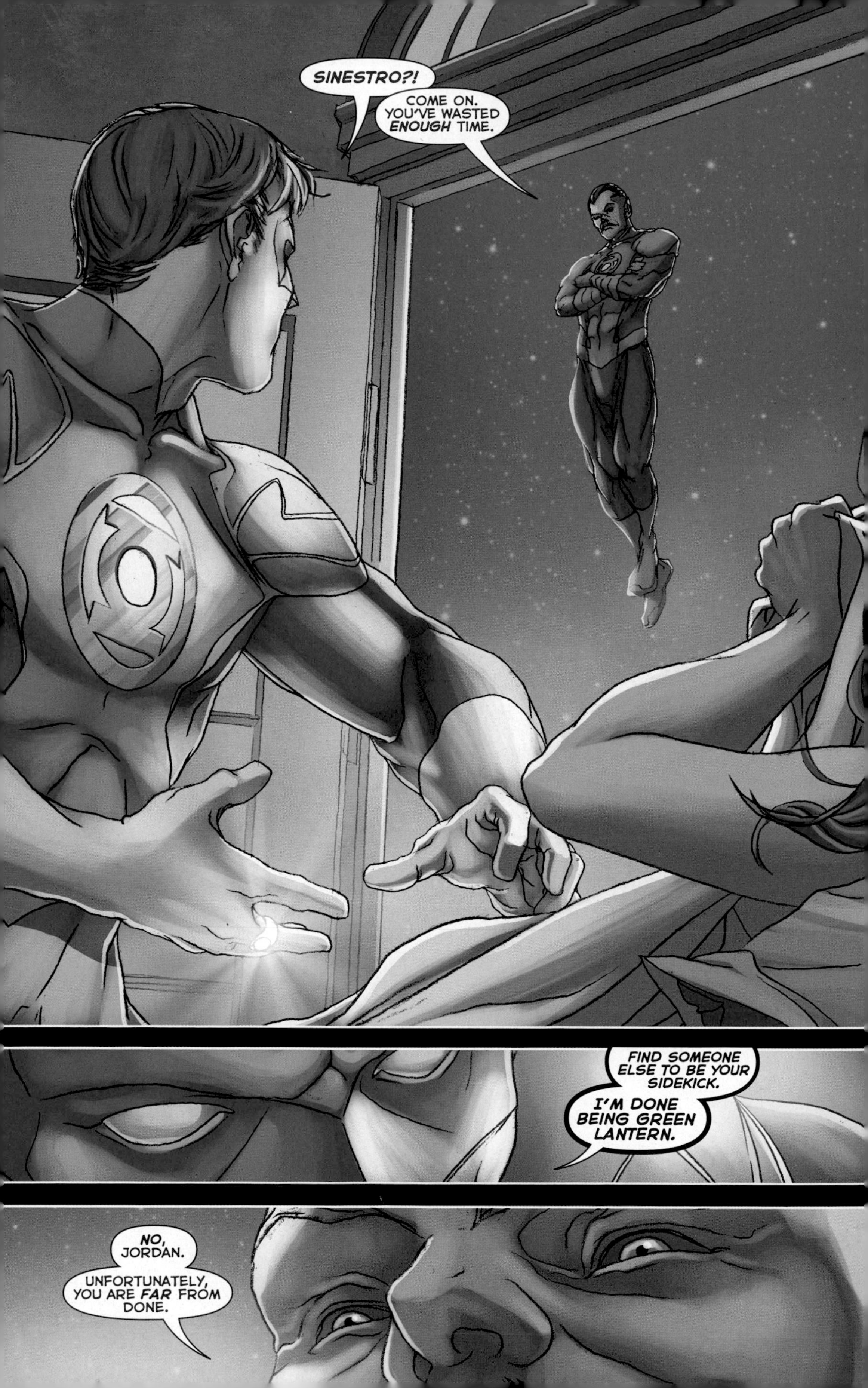
SINESTRO?!
COME ON. YOU'VE WASTED ENOUGH TIME.
FIND SOMEONE ELSE TO BE YOUR SIDEKICK.
I'M DONE BEING GREEN LANTERN.
NO, JORDAN.
UNFORTUNATELY, YOU ARE FAR FROM DONE.

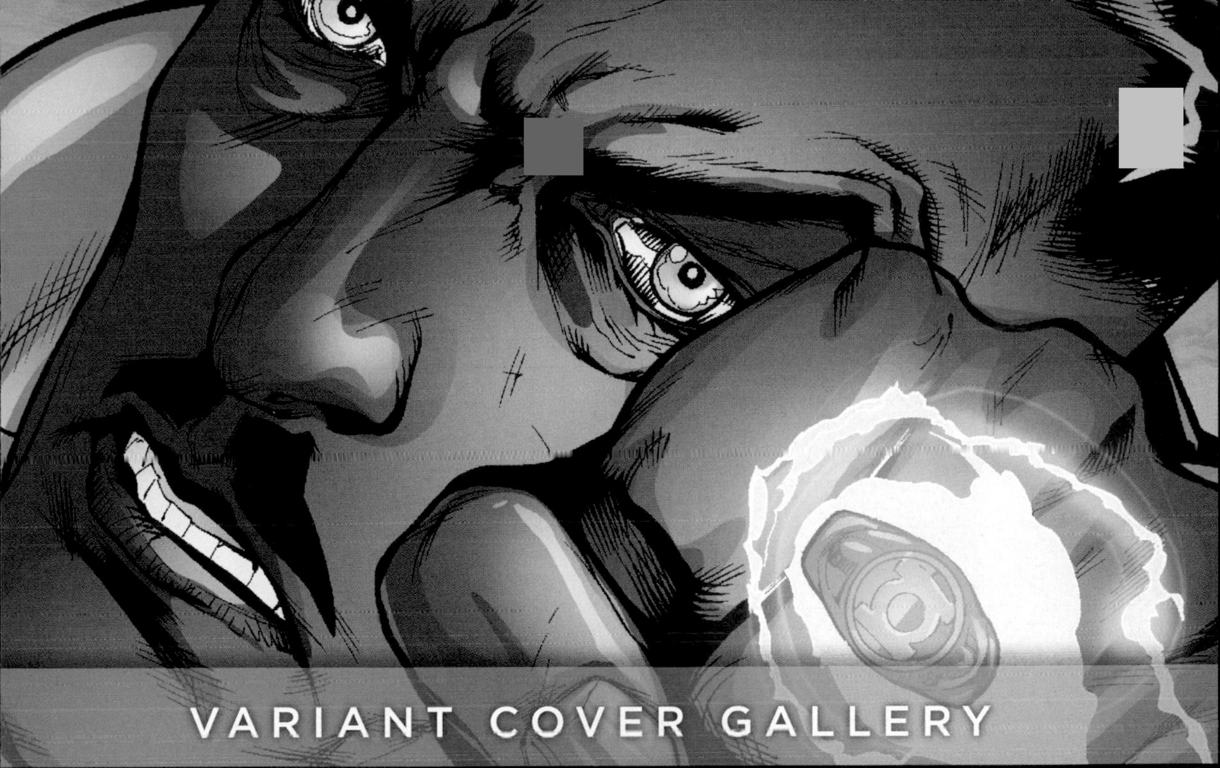

VARIANT COVER GALLERY

GREEN LANTERN 1
by Greg Capullo

GREEN LANTERN 2
by David Finch, Richard Friend & Peter Steigerwald

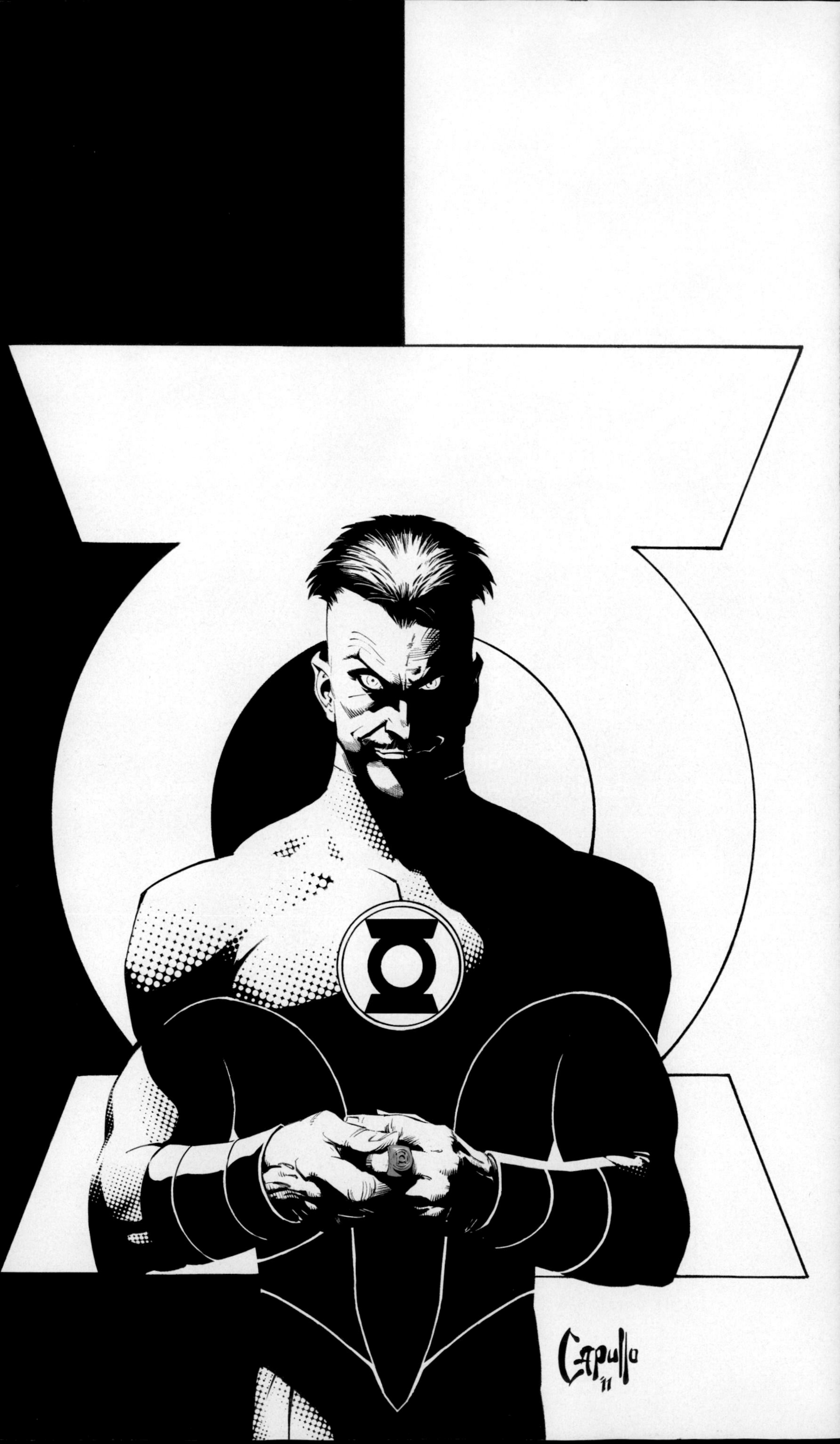
Capullo '11

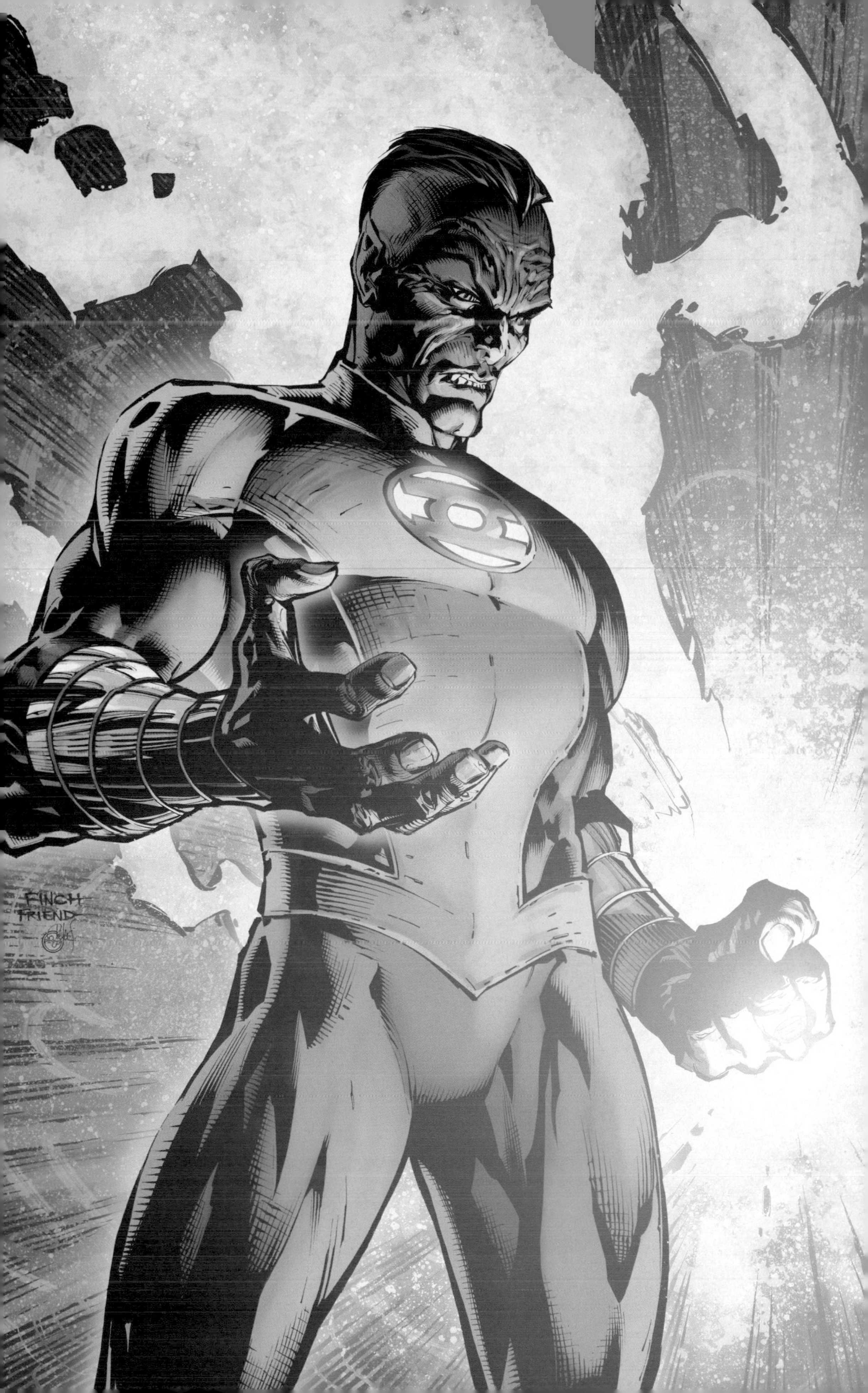
FINCH
FRIEND

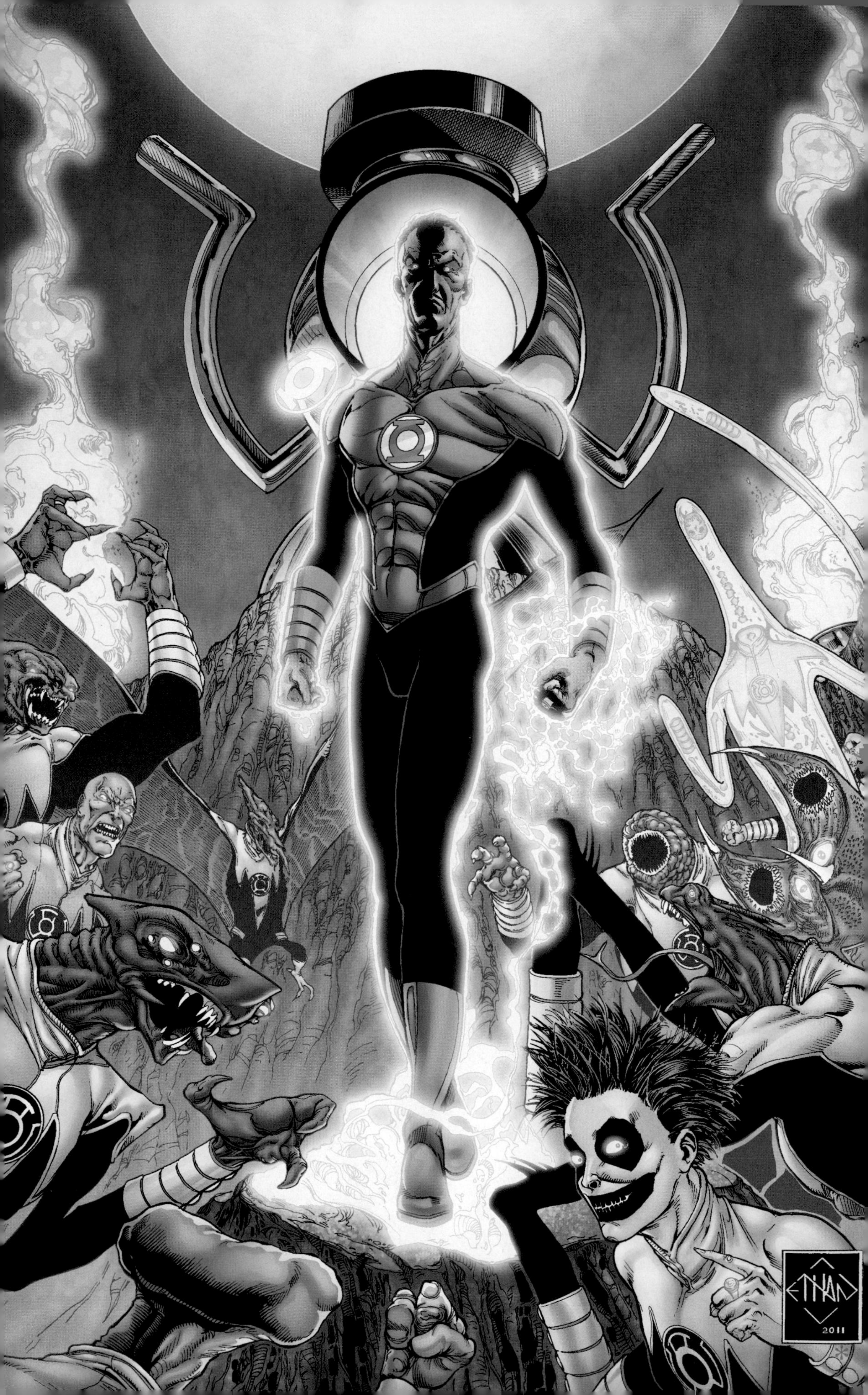
2011

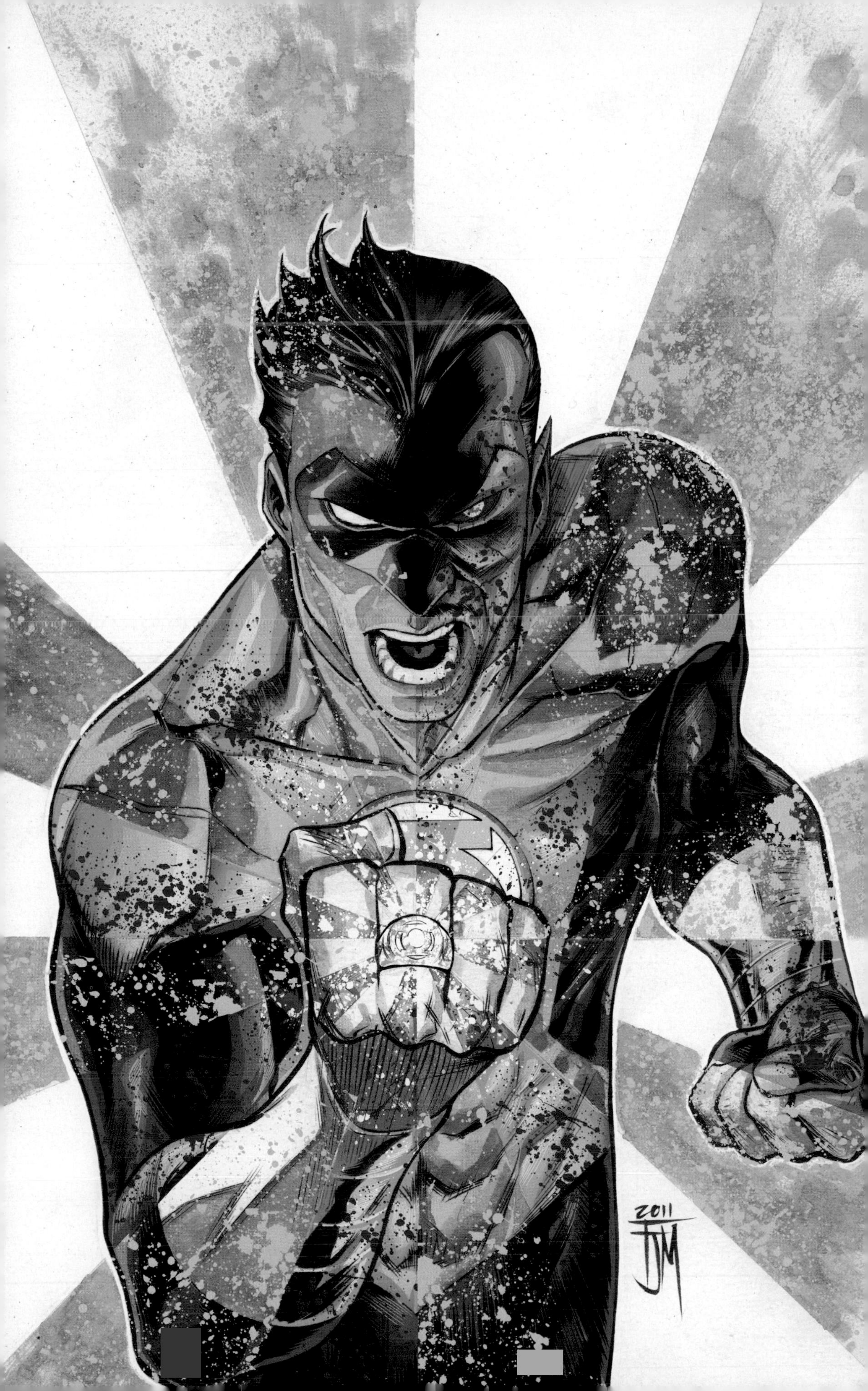
2011

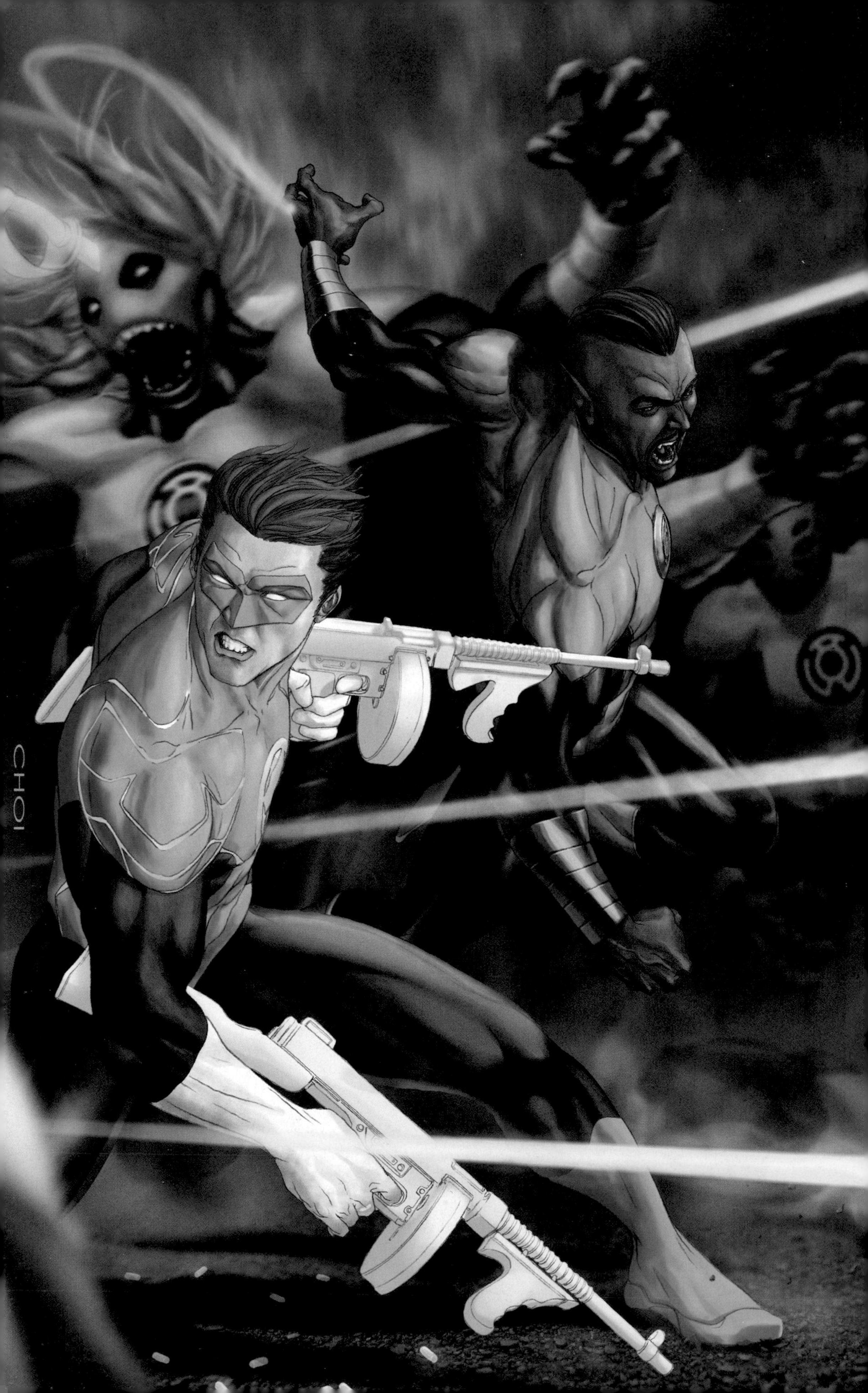
CHOI

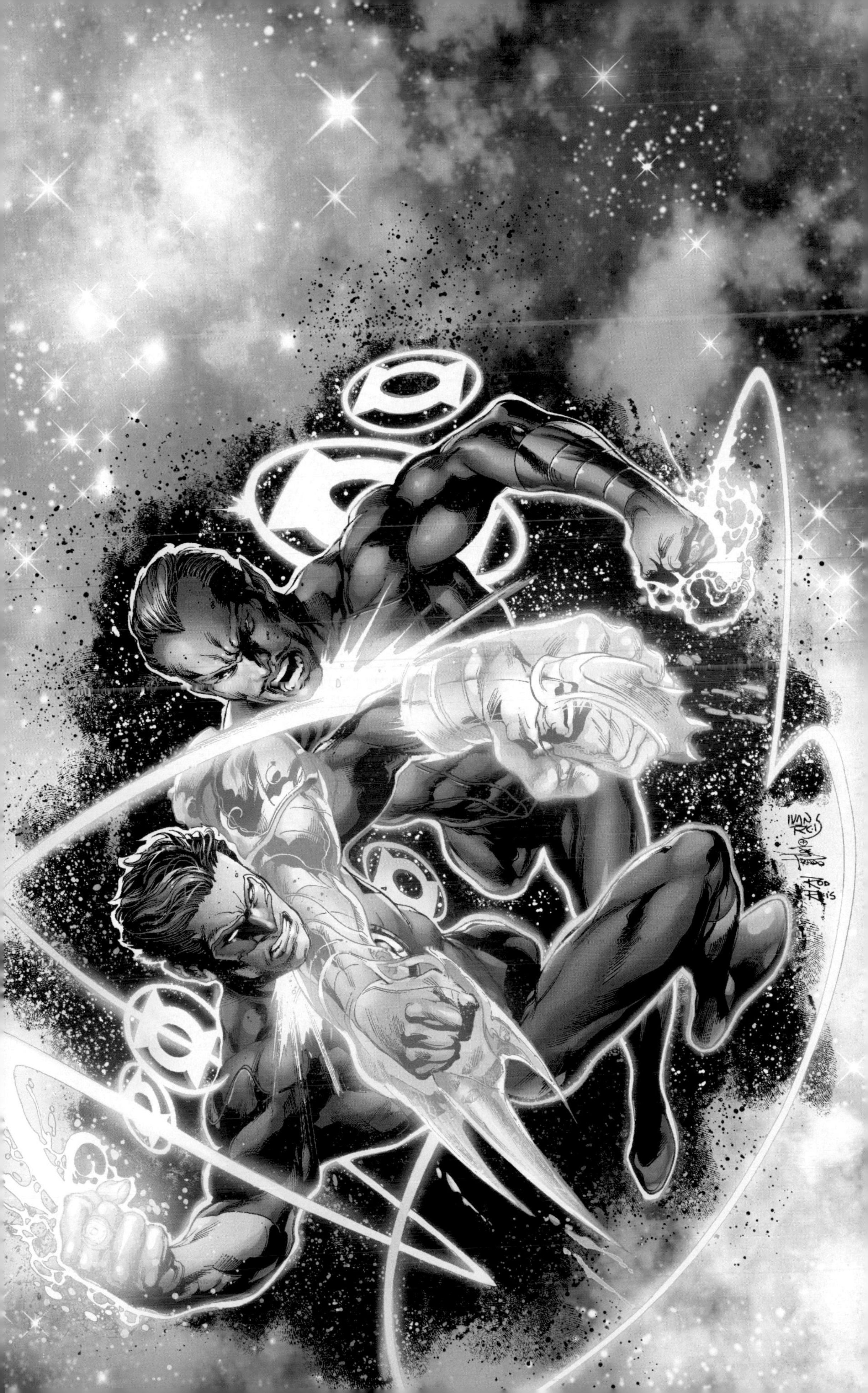

GREEN LANTERN
COVER SKETCHES BY DOUG MAHNKE

1

2

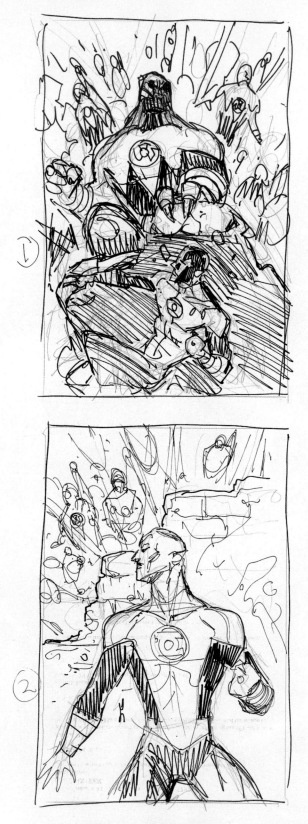

GREEN LANTERN #3

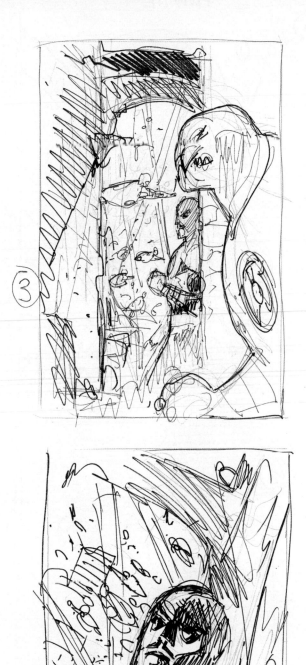

GREEN LANTERN #3

FAVORITE

1

2

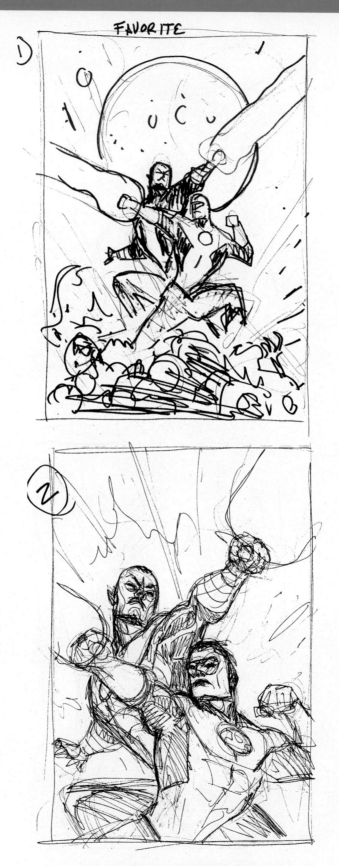

GREEN LANTERN #5

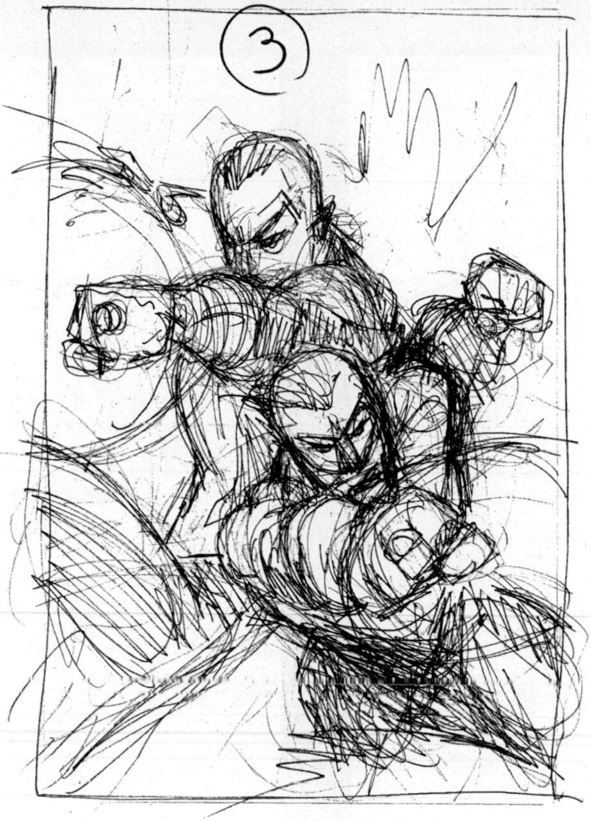
3

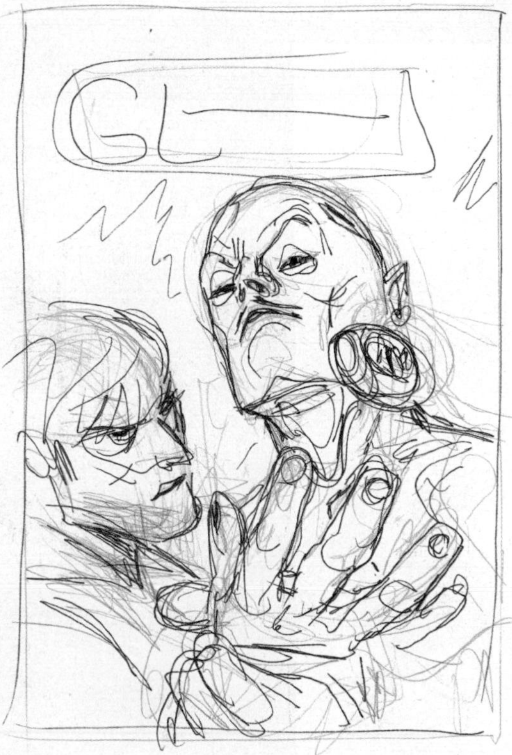
GL

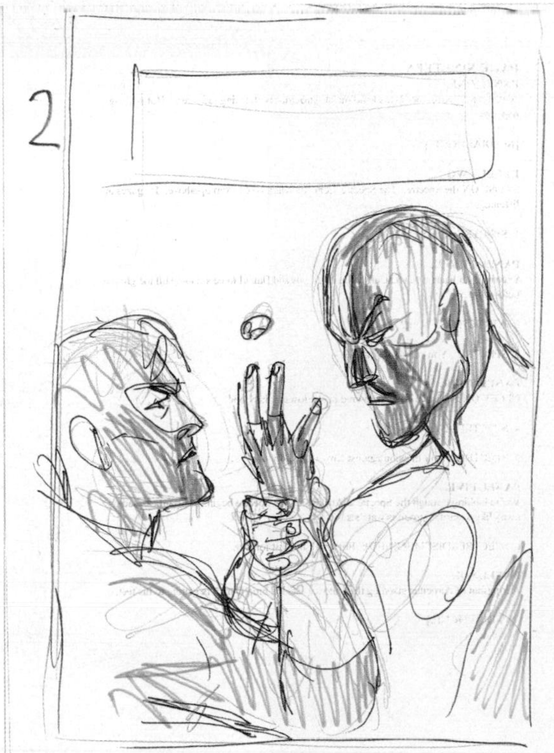
2

GREEN LANTERN #6

GREEN LANTERN

#1 PAGE ROUGHS BY DOUG MAHNKE

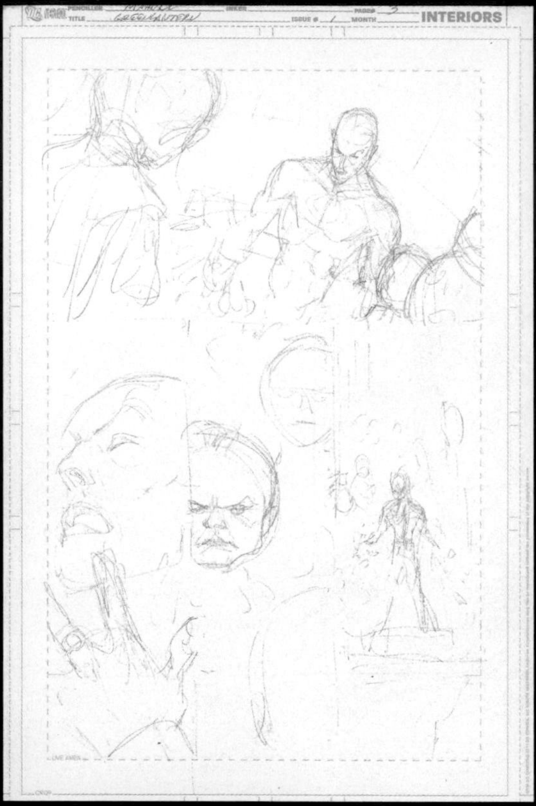
INTERIORS

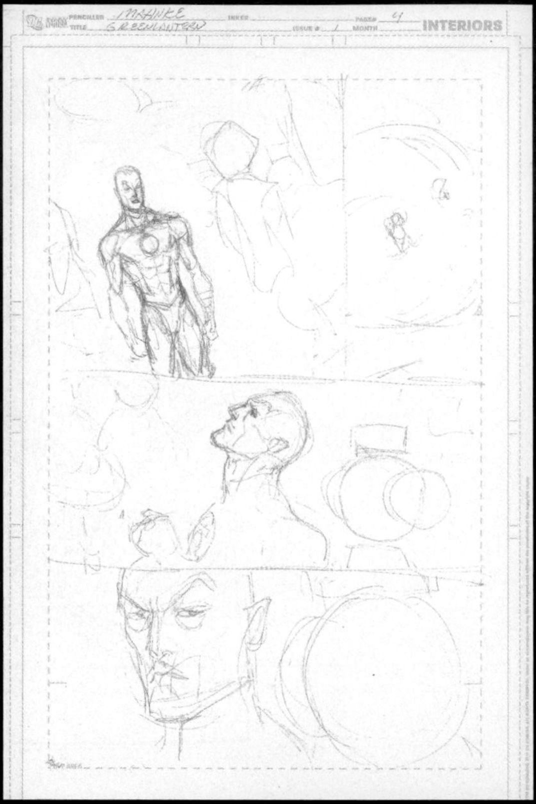
INTERIORS

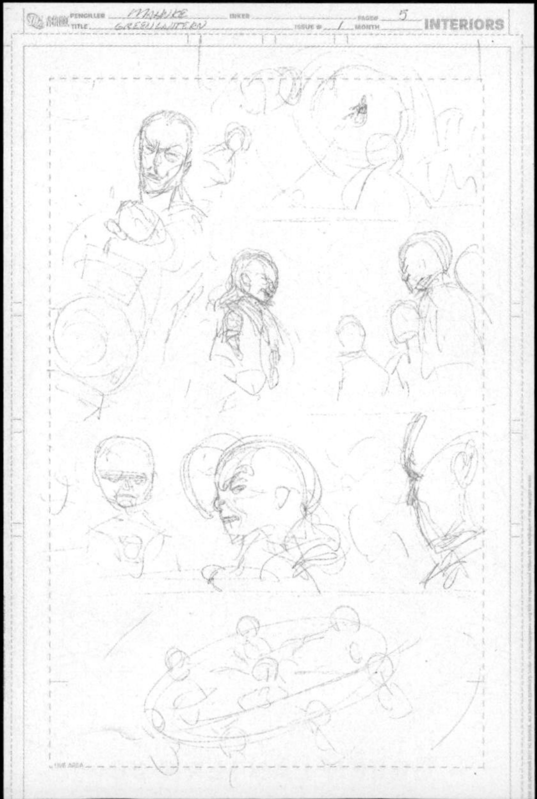
INTERIORS

GREEN LANTERN
#1 PAGE PENCILS BY DOUG MAHNKE

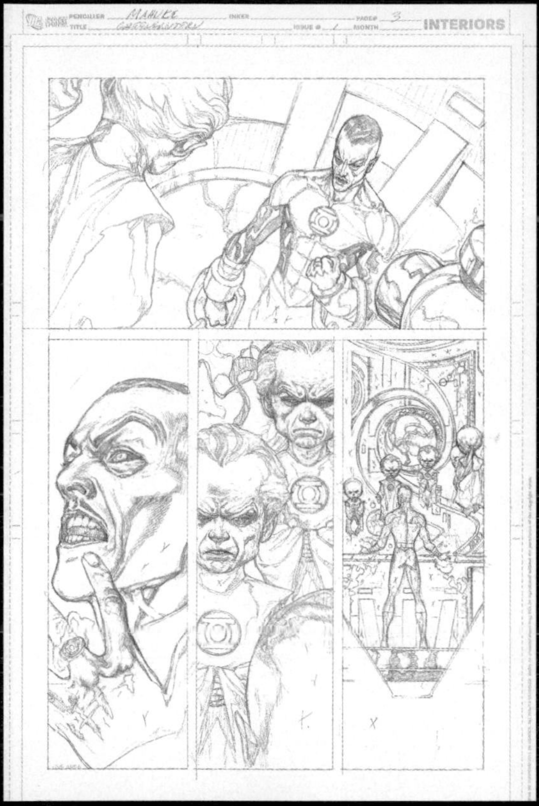
INTERIORS

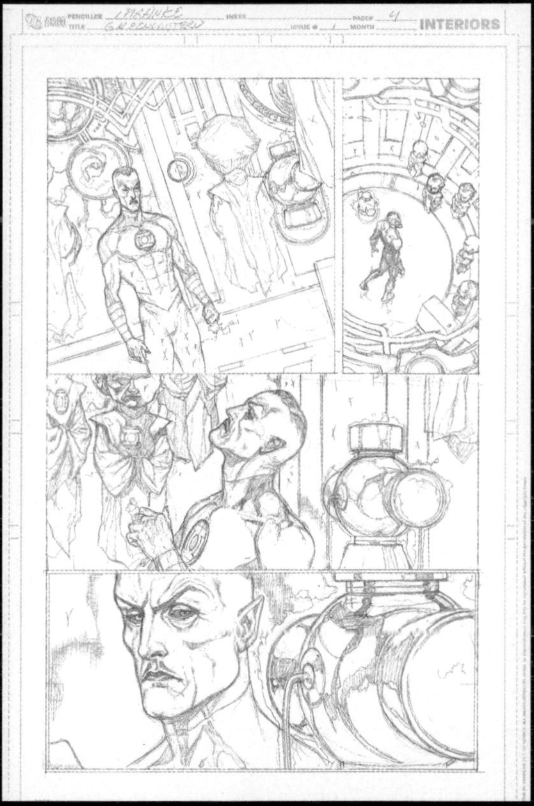
INTERIORS

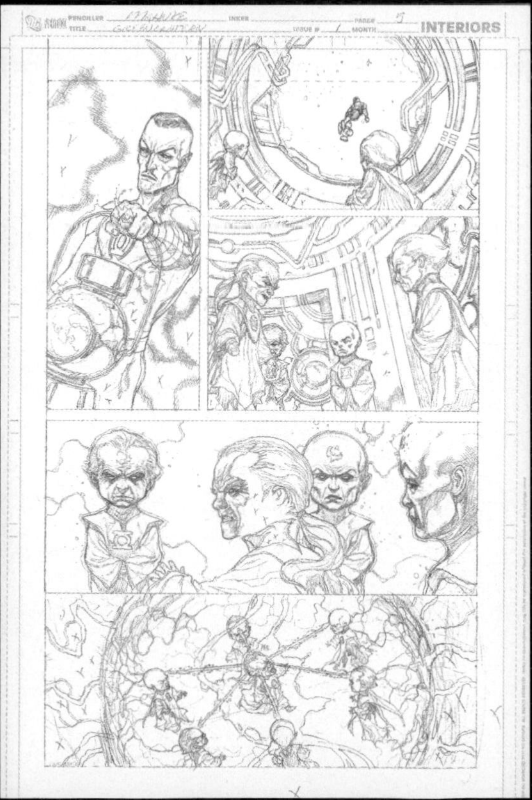
INTERIORS

GREEN LANTERN
#1 PAGE ROUGHS BY DOUG MAHNKE

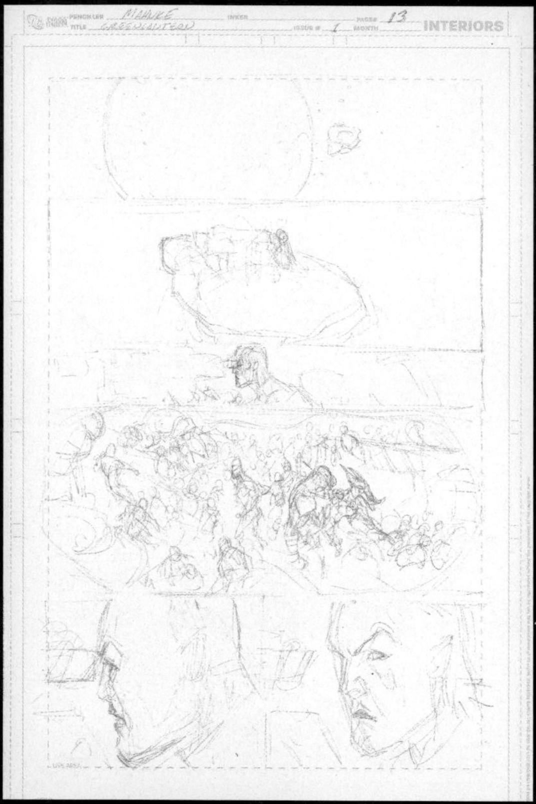
PENCILLER MAHNKE
TITLE GREEN LANTERN
PAGE# 13
ISSUE # 1
INTERIORS

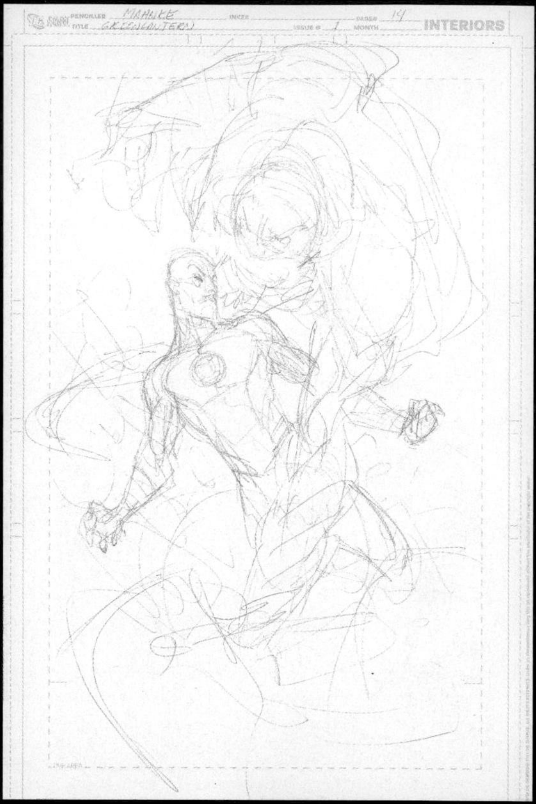
PENCILLER MAHNKE
PAGE# 14
ISSUE # 1
INTERIORS

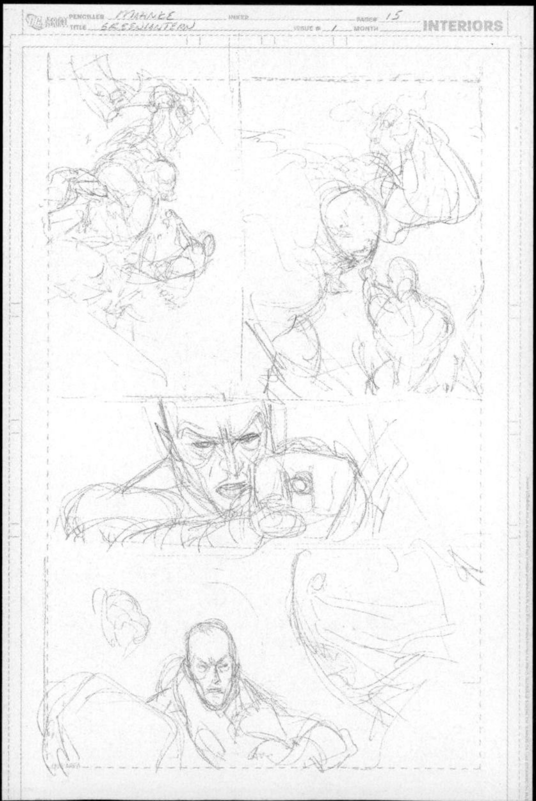
PENCILLER MAHNKE
PAGE# 15
ISSUE # 1
INTERIORS

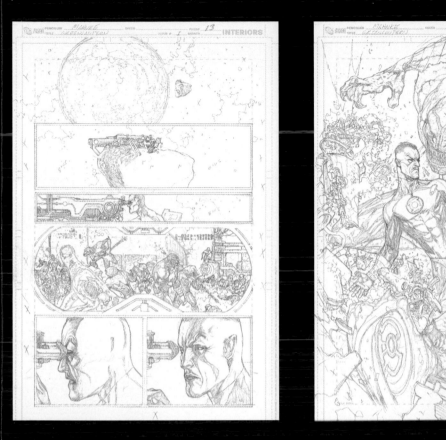

GREEN LANTERN

#2 PAGE ROUGHS BY DOUG MAHNKE

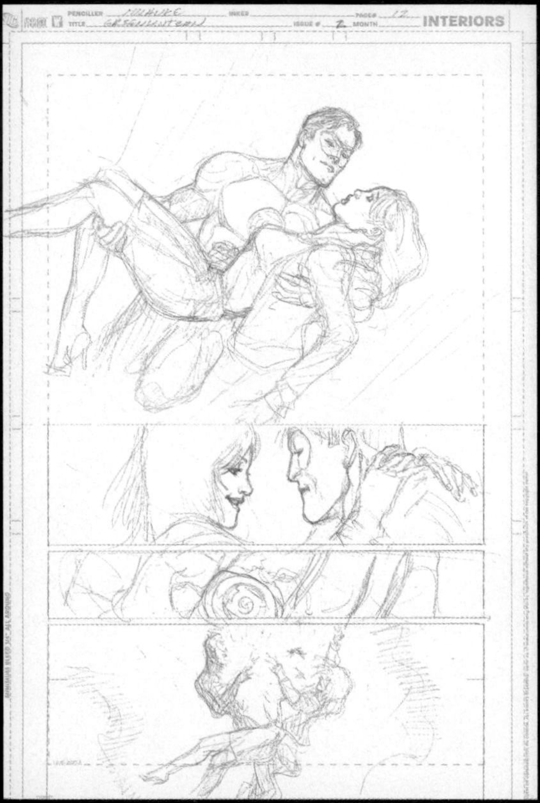
INTERIORS

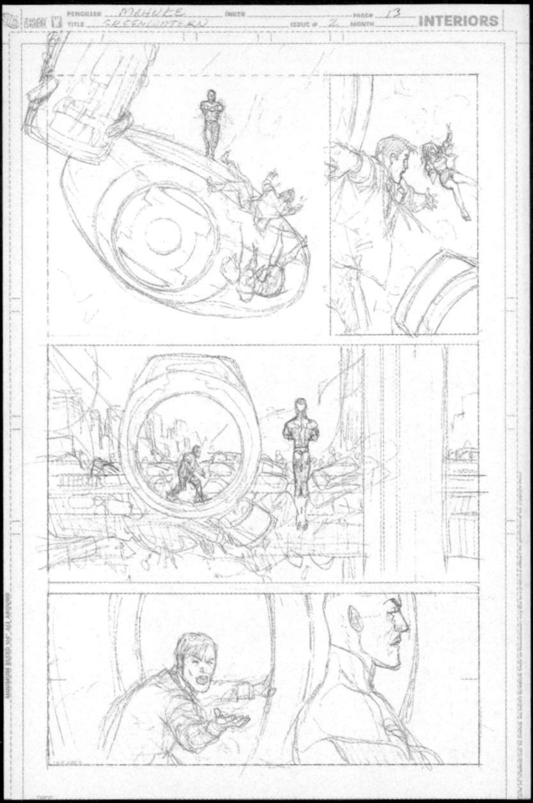
INTERIORS

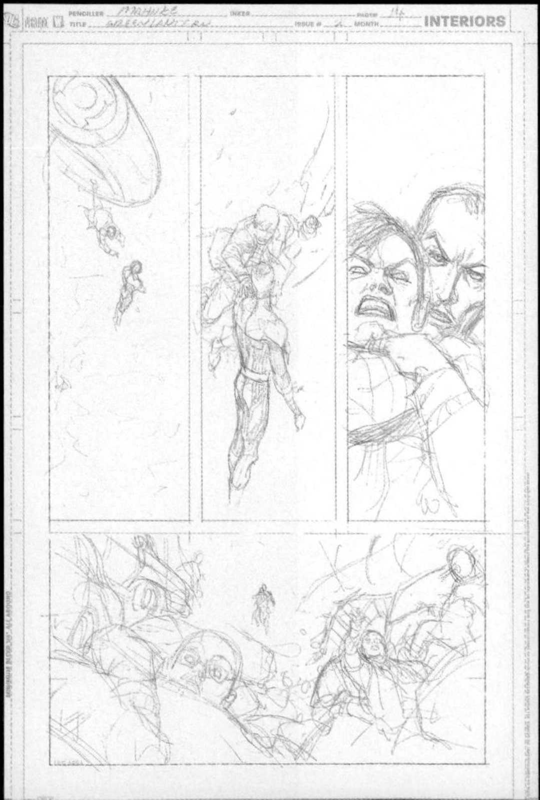
INTERIORS

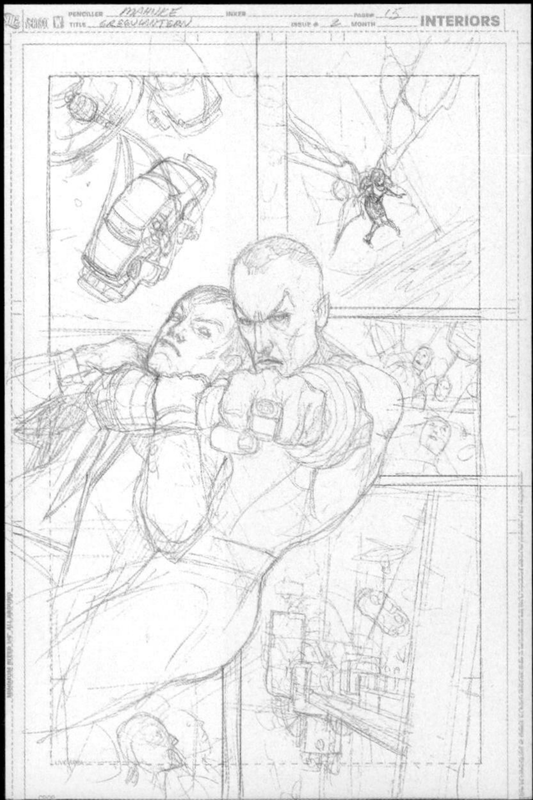
INTERIORS

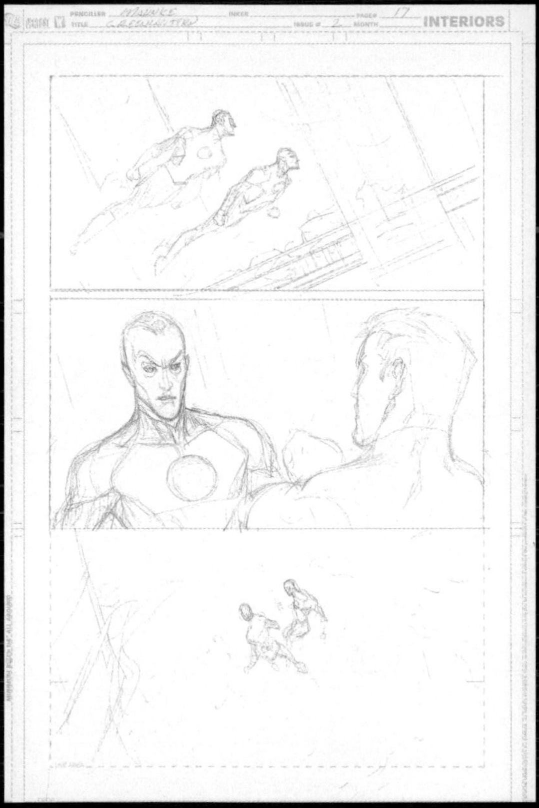
INTERIORS

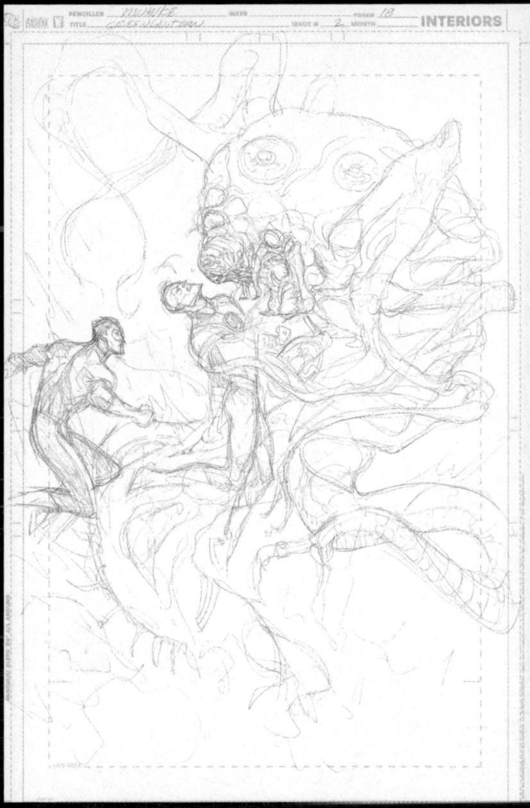
INTERIORS

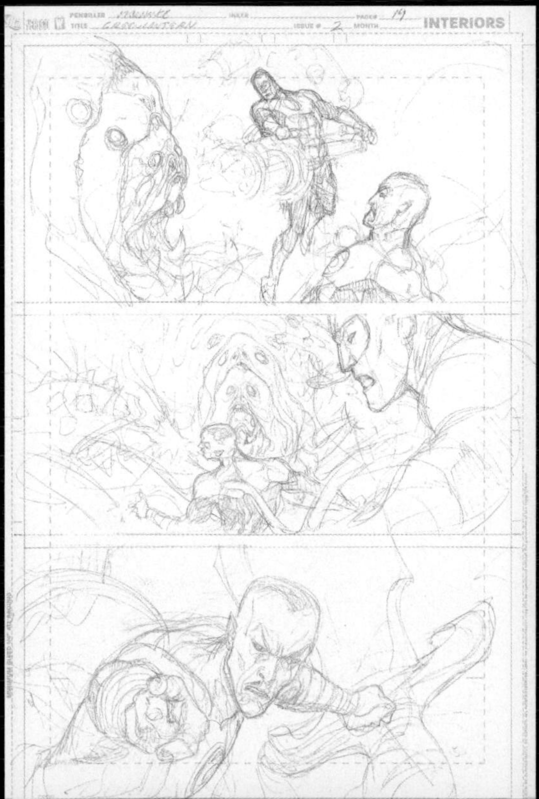
INTERIORS

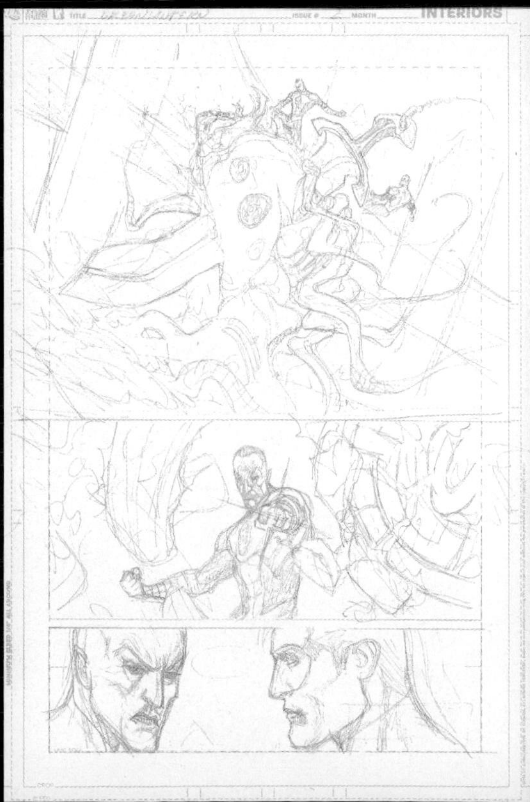
INTERIORS

GREEN LANTERN
#3 PAGE PENCILS BY DOUG MAHNKE

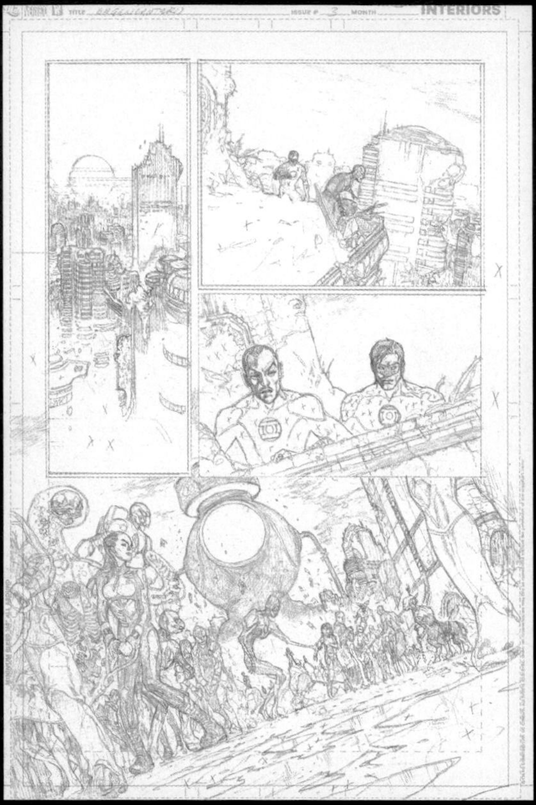
INTERIORS

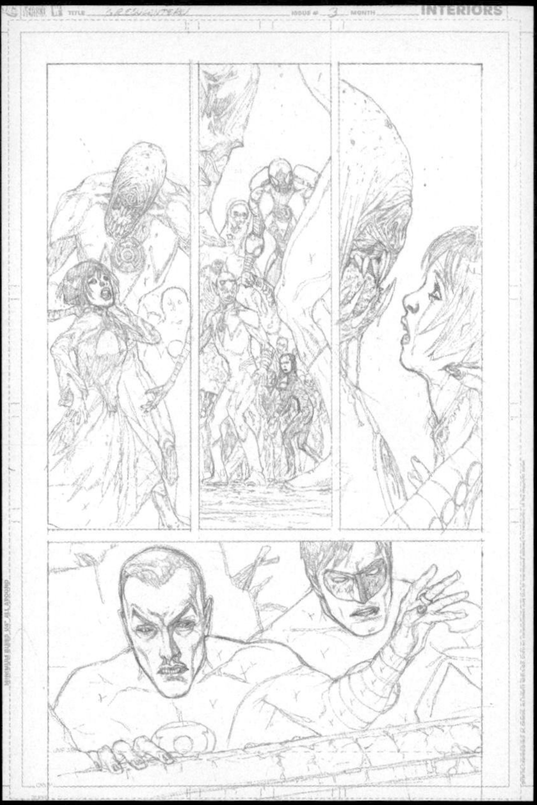
INTERIORS

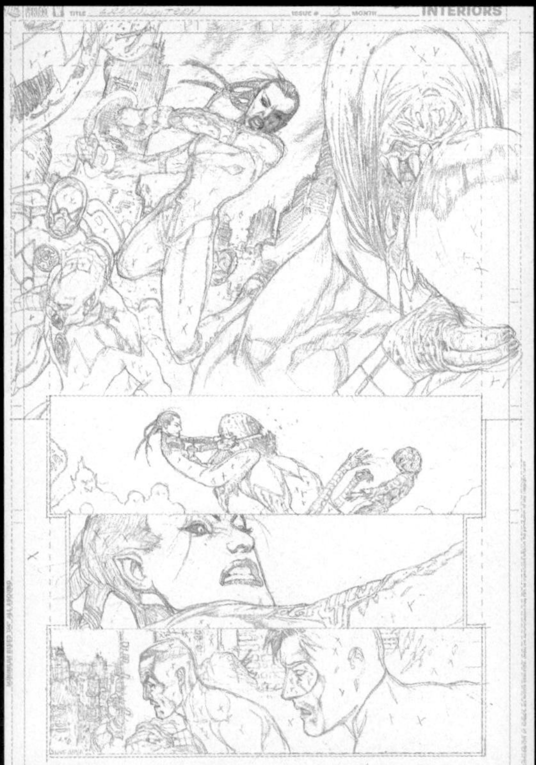
INTERIORS

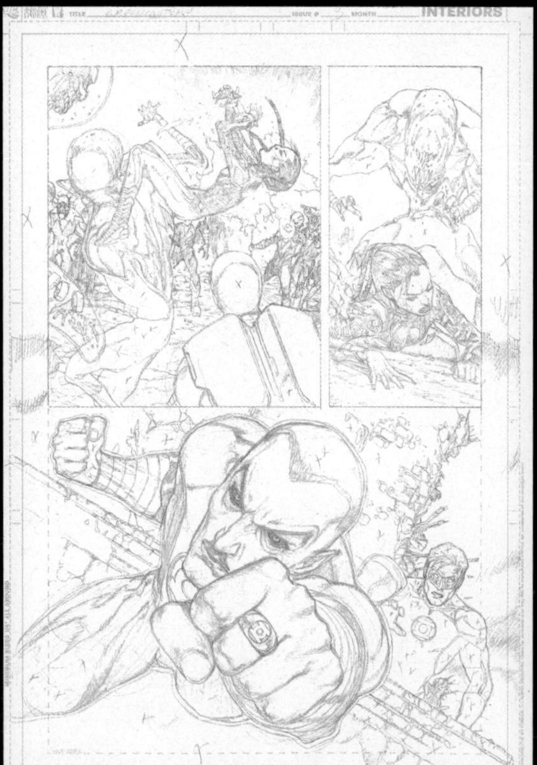
INTERIORS

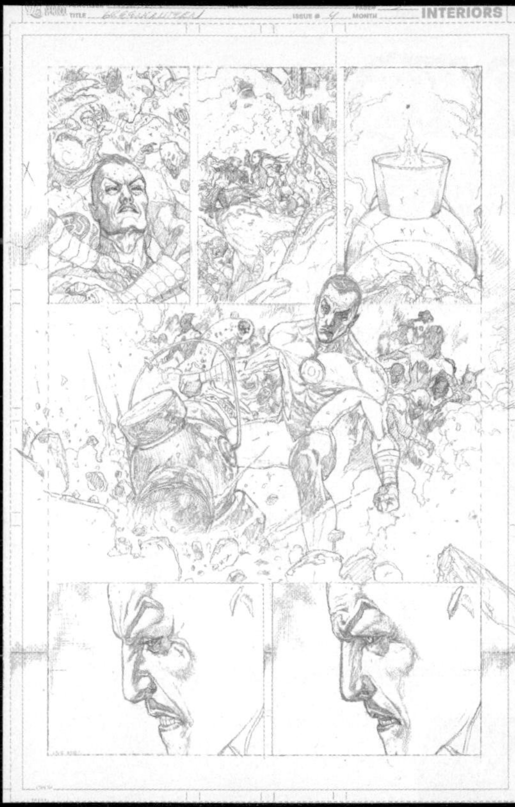
TITLE
ISSUE # 4
MONTH
INTERIORS

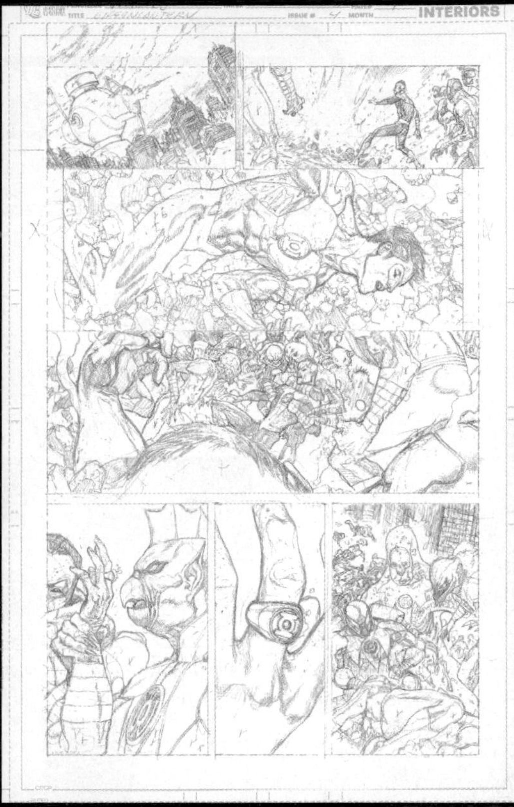
TITLE
ISSUE # 4
MONTH
INTERIORS

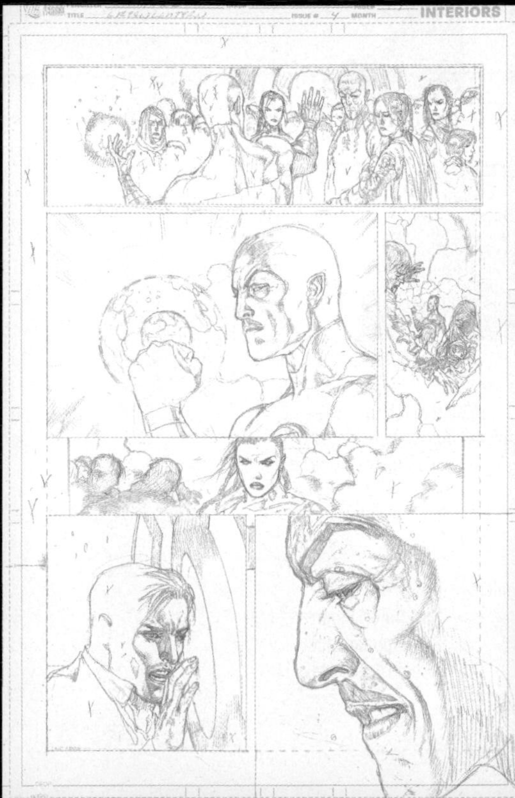
TITLE
ISSUE # 4
MONTH
INTERIORS

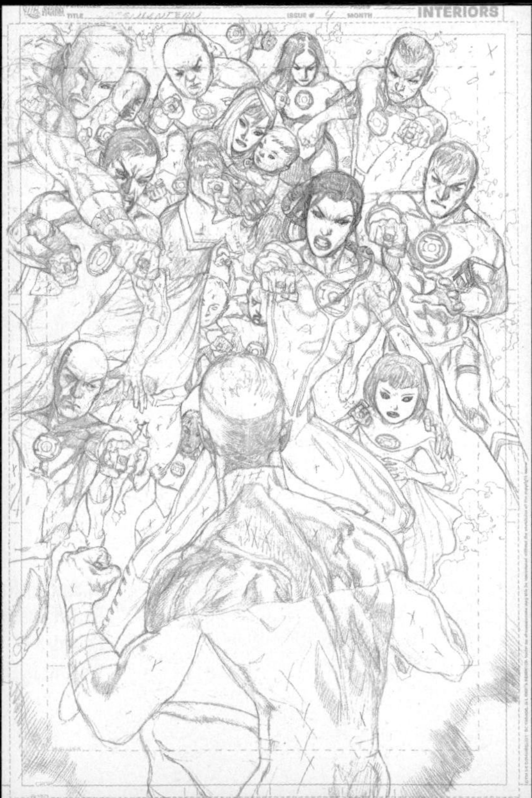
TITLE
ISSUE # 4
MONTH
INTERIORS

Character Chest Emblem

Costume Details & Call-Outs

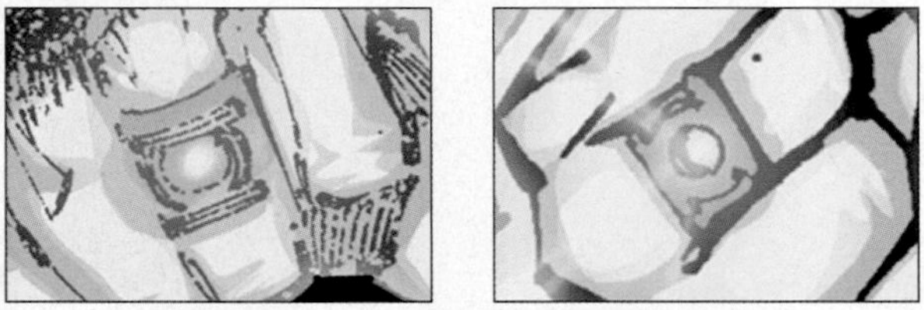

Concept art by Cully Hamner

Based on designs by Jim Lee

Note that on costume, the ring surrounding the emblem is the same thickness as the emblem.

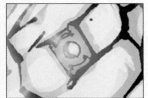

Ring: Negative area in the center of the ring glows continuously and more intensely when active.

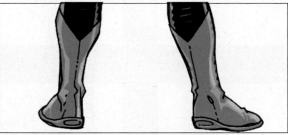

Boots: Hal's boots are made of a soft, lightweight leathery material and feature rubber sneaker-like soles.

Chest Area: The chest emblem on Green Lantern's costume glows continuously even when inactive. It radiates a green plasma-like energy when active or engaging in combat. The lines running through the upper shoulders and the chest also glow like the emblem although with slightly less intensity since there is less surface area. The linear detail maintains a faint glow when Hal's powers are inactive.

Character Name: Green Lantern
Real Name: Hal Jordan
Height: 6' 2"
Weight: 186 lbs.

Eye Color: Brown
Hair Color: Brown
First Appearance:
Justice League #1 (2011)

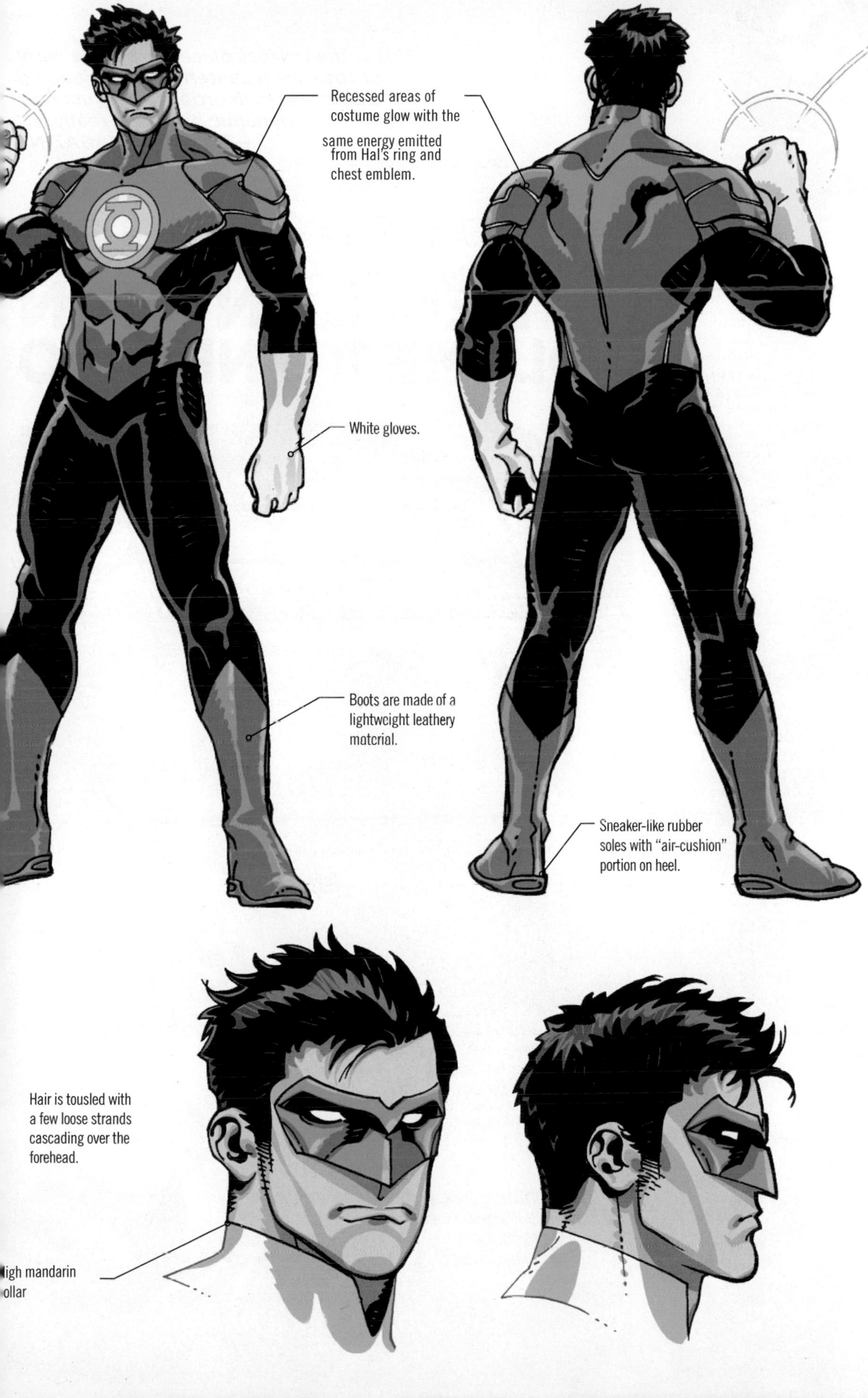
Recessed areas of costume glow with the same energy emitted from Hal's ring and chest emblem.
White gloves.
Boots are made of a lightweight leathery material.
Sneaker-like rubber soles with "air-cushion" portion on heel.
Hair is tousled with a few loose strands cascading over the forehead.
igh mandarin ollar

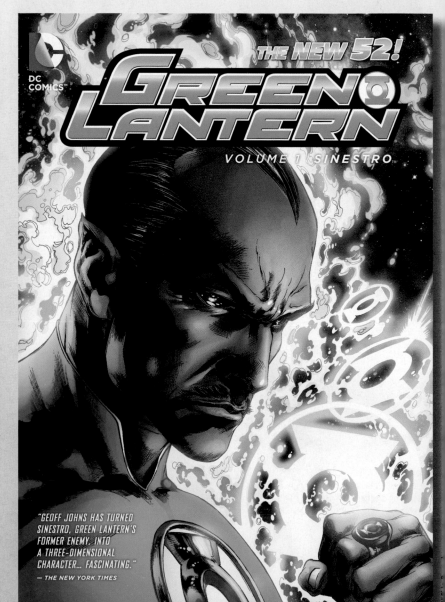

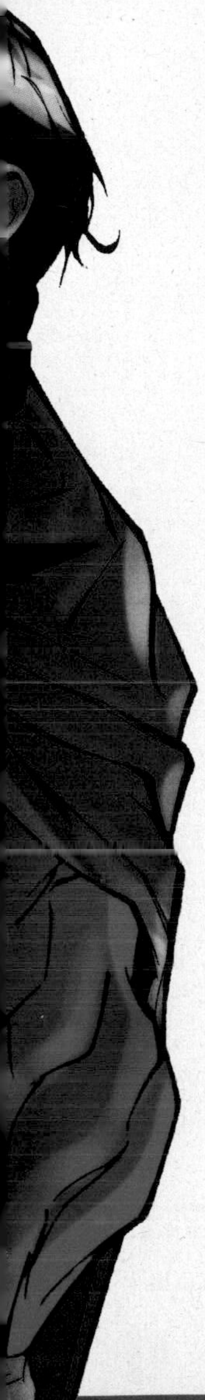

Alan Burnett
Writer

Dustin Nguyen
Pencils

Derek Fridolfs
Inks

Rob Leigh
Letters

Randy Mayor
Colors

Dustin Nguyen & Derek Fridolfs
Original Series Covers

Batman created by Bob Kane

Superman created by Jerry Siegel and Joe Shuster

SUPERMAN BATMAN

TORMENT

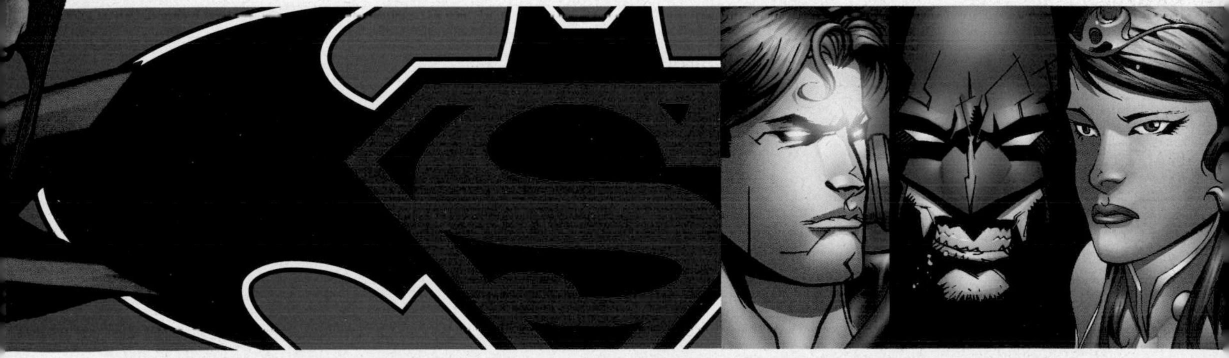

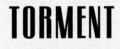

DAN DIDIO Senior VP-Executive Editor   EDDIE BERGANZA Editor-original series   ADAM SCHLAGMAN Assistant Editor-original series   BOB JOY Editor-collected edition
ROBBIN BROSTERMAN Senior Art Director   PAUL LEVITZ President & Publisher   GEORG BREWER VP-Design & DC Direct Creative   RICHARD BRUNING Senior VP-Creative Director
PATRICK CALDON Executive VP-Finance & Operations   CHRIS CARAMALIS VP-Finance   JOHN CUNNINGHAM VP-Marketing   TERRI CUNNINGHAM VP-Managing Editor   ALISON GILL VP-Manufacturing
DAVID HYDE VP-Publicity   HANK KANALZ VP-General Manager, WildStorm   JIM LEE Editorial Director-WildStorm   PAULA LOWITT Senior VP-Business & Legal Affairs
MARYELLEN MCLAUGHLIN VP-Advertising & Custom Publishing   JOHN NEE Senior VP-Business Development   GREGORY NOVECK Senior VP-Creative Affairs   SUE POHJA VP-Book Trade Sales
STEVE ROTTERDAM Senior VP-Sales & Marketing   CHERYL RUBIN Senior VP-Brand Management   JEFF TROJAN VP-Business Development, DC Direct   BOB WAYNE VP-Sales

Cover art by Dustin Nguyen / Derek Fridolfs

SUPERMAN/BATMAN: TORMENT
Published by DC Comics. Cover and compilation Copyright © 2008 DC Comics. All Rights Reserved.
Originally published in single magazine form as SUPERMAN/BATMAN 37-42 Copyright © 2007, 2008 DC Comics. All Rights Reserved. All characters, their distinctive likenesses and related elements featured
in this publication are trademarks of DC Comics. The stories, characters and incidents featured in this publication are entirely fictional. DC Comics does not read or accept unsolicited submissions of
ideas, stories or artwork.

DC Comics, 1700 Broadway, New York, NY 10019. A Warner Bros. Entertainment Company. Second Printing. ISBN: 978-1-4012-1740-2
Printed by Quad/Graphics, Montreal, Qc, Canada. 01/14/11.

Fiber used in this product line meets the
sourcing requirements of the SFI program
www.sfiprogram.org SGS-SFICOC-0130

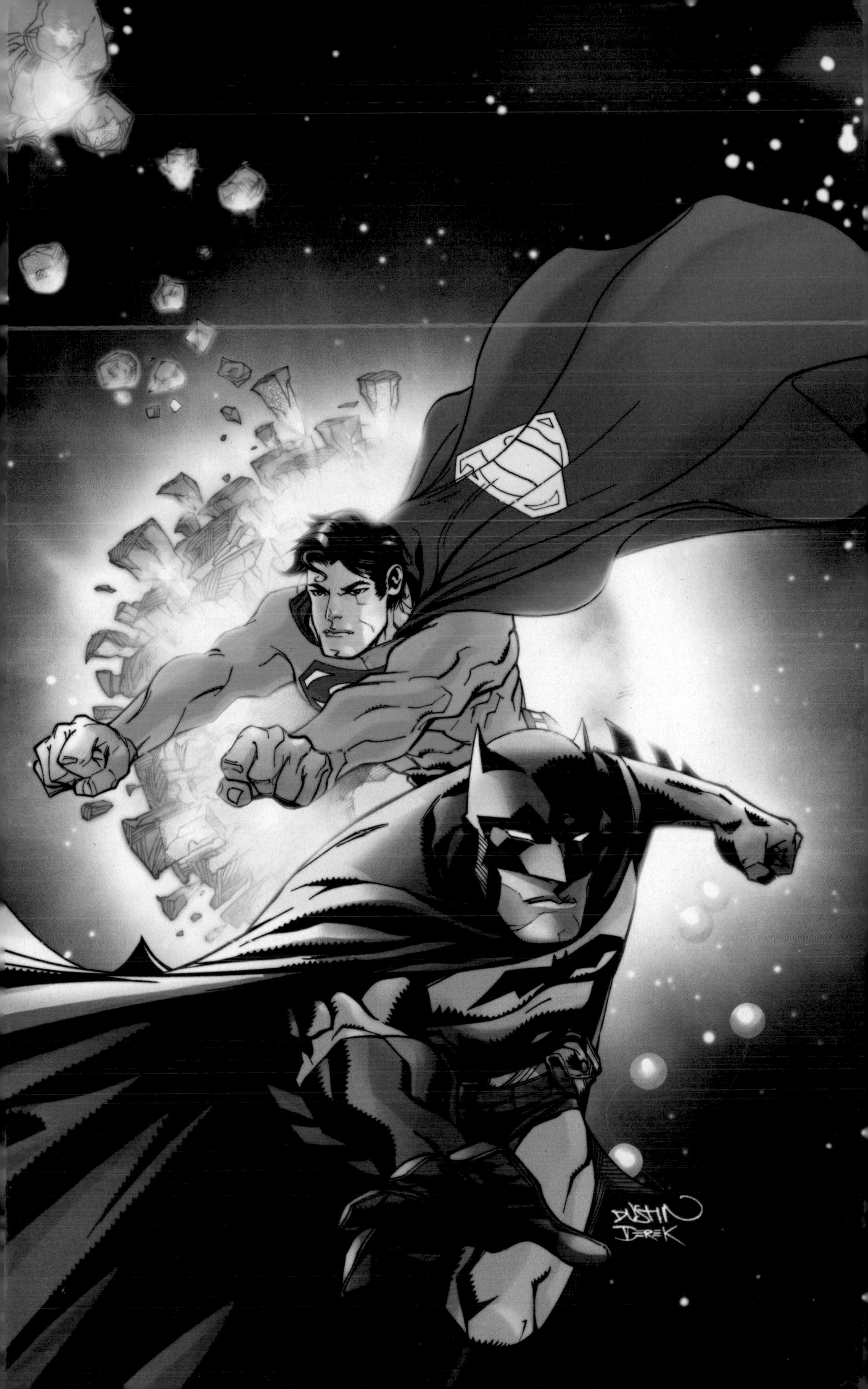
DUSTIN
DEREK

TORMENT: PART ONE

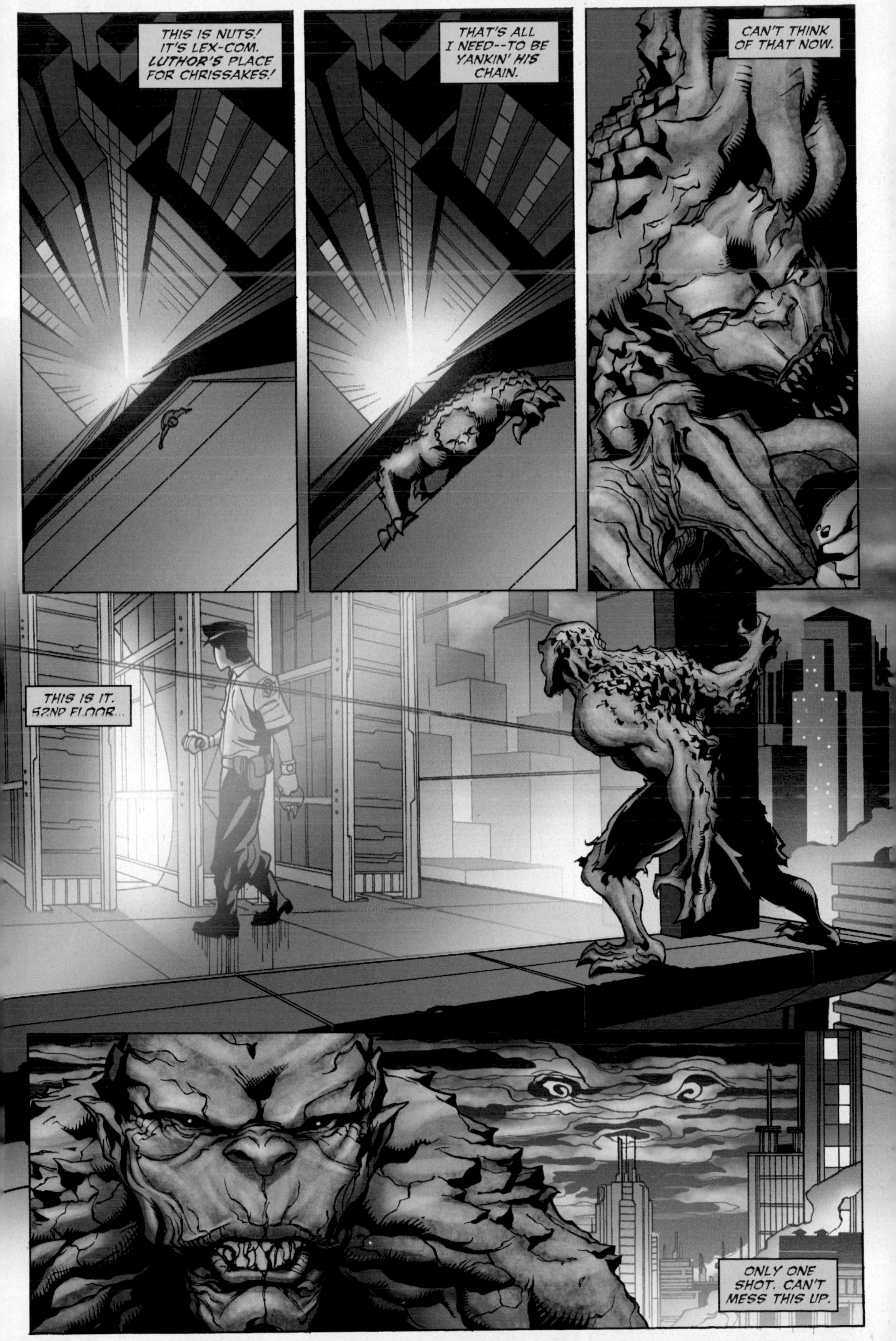
THIS IS NUTS! IT'S LEX-COM. LUTHOR'S PLACE FOR CHRISSAKES!
THAT'S ALL I NEED--TO BE YANKIN' HIS CHAIN.
CAN'T THINK OF THAT NOW.
THIS IS IT. 52ND FLOOR...
ONLY ONE SHOT. CAN'T MESS THIS UP.

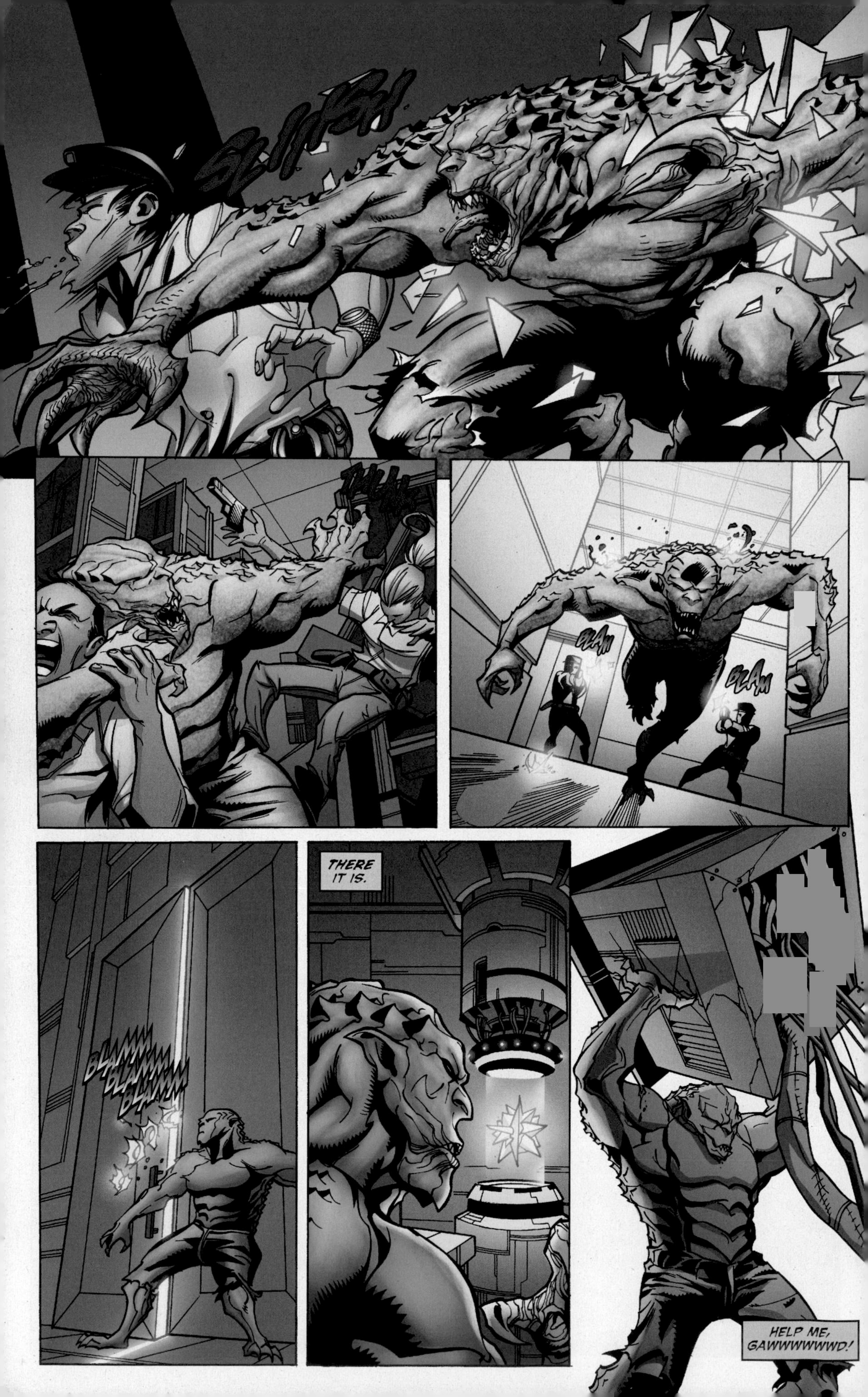
BLAM
BLAM
THERE IT IS.
HELP ME, GAWWWWWWD!

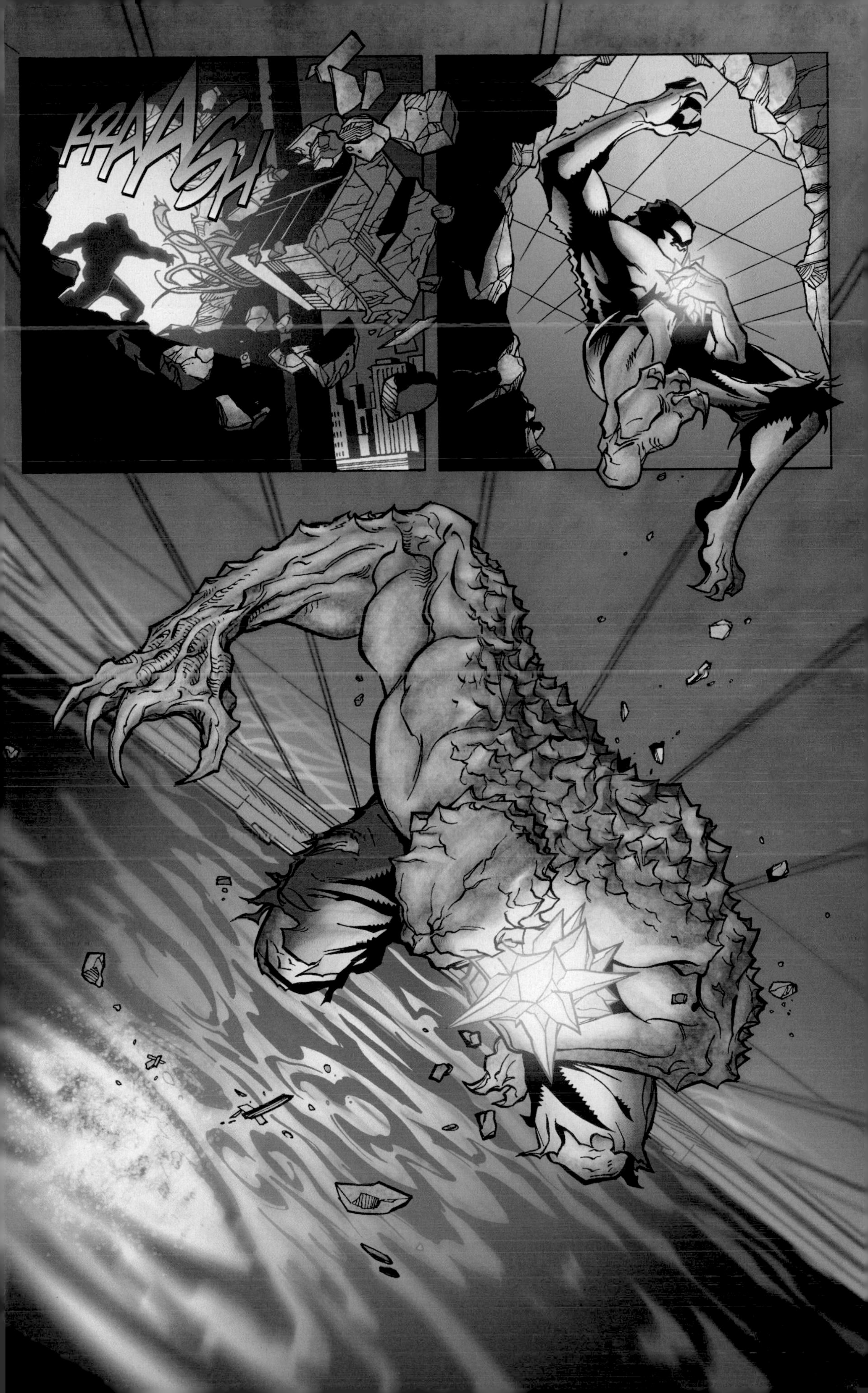
KRAASH

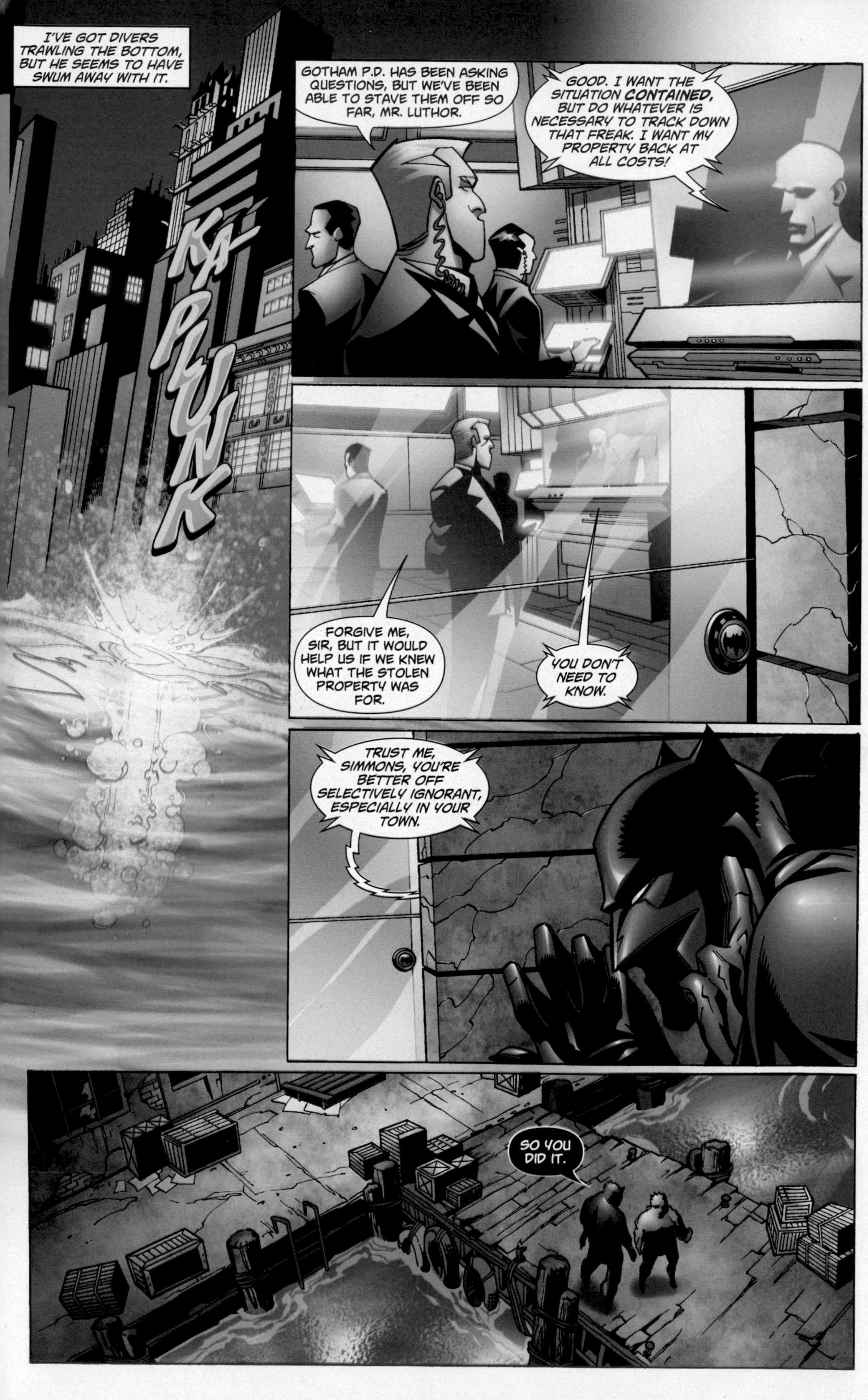
I'VE GOT DIVERS TRAWLING THE BOTTOM, BUT HE SEEMS TO HAVE SWUM AWAY WITH IT.
KA-PLUNK
GOTHAM P.D. HAS BEEN ASKING QUESTIONS, BUT WE'VE BEEN ABLE TO STAVE THEM OFF SO FAR, MR. LUTHOR.
GOOD. I WANT THE SITUATION CONTAINED, BUT DO WHATEVER IS NECESSARY TO TRACK DOWN THAT FREAK. I WANT MY PROPERTY BACK AT ALL COSTS!
FORGIVE ME, SIR, BUT IT WOULD HELP US IF WE KNEW WHAT THE STOLEN PROPERTY WAS FOR.
YOU DON'T NEED TO KNOW.
TRUST ME, SIMMONS, YOU'RE BETTER OFF SELECTIVELY IGNORANT, ESPECIALLY IN YOUR TOWN.
SO YOU DID IT.

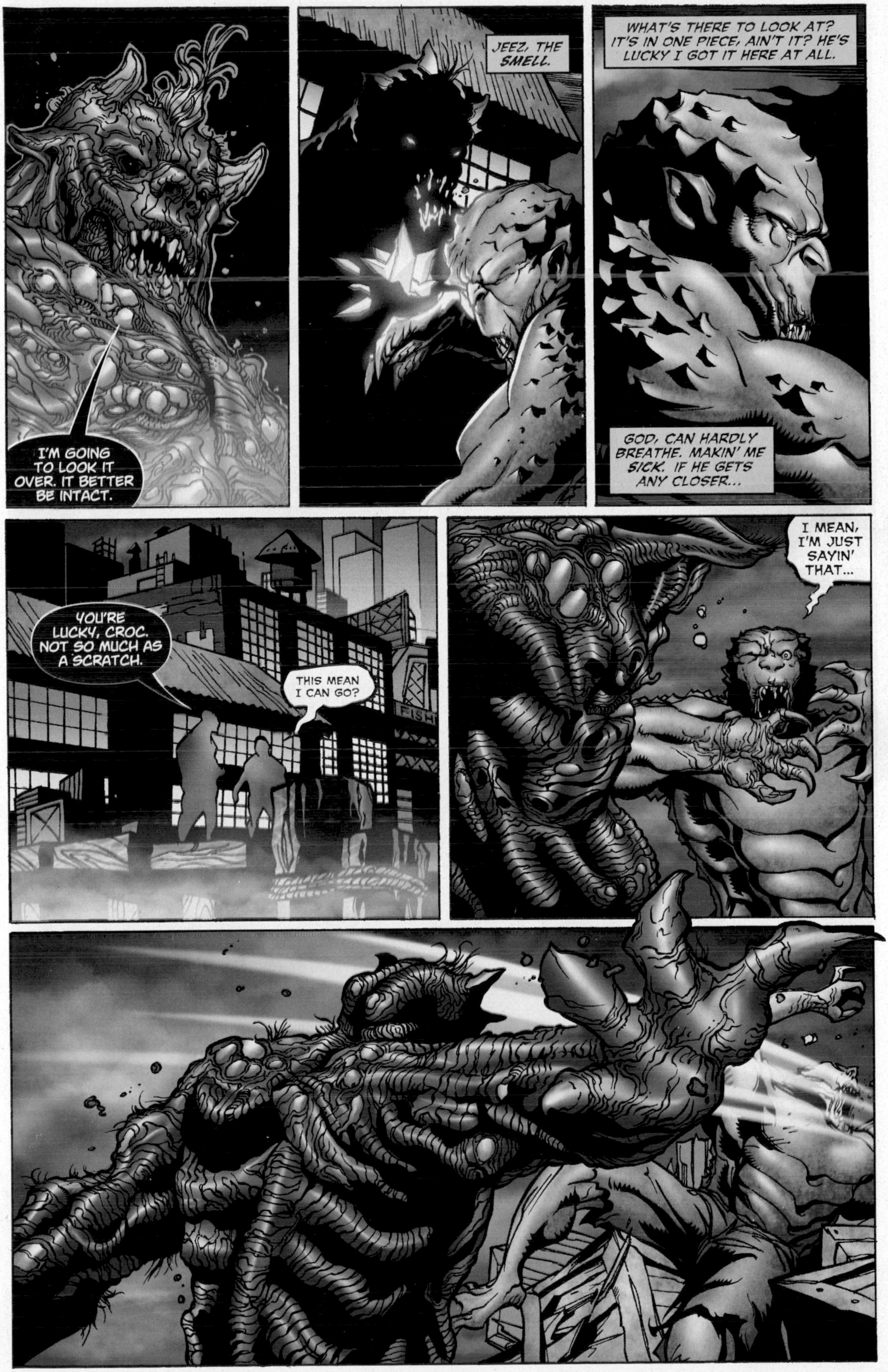
I'M GOING TO LOOK IT OVER. IT BETTER BE INTACT.
JEEZ, THE SMELL.
WHAT'S THERE TO LOOK AT? IT'S IN ONE PIECE, AIN'T IT? HE'S LUCKY I GOT IT HERE AT ALL.
GOD, CAN HARDLY BREATHE. MAKIN' ME SICK. IF HE GETS ANY CLOSER...
YOU'RE LUCKY, CROC. NOT SO MUCH AS A SCRATCH.
THIS MEAN I CAN GO?
FISH
I MEAN, I'M JUST SAYIN' THAT...

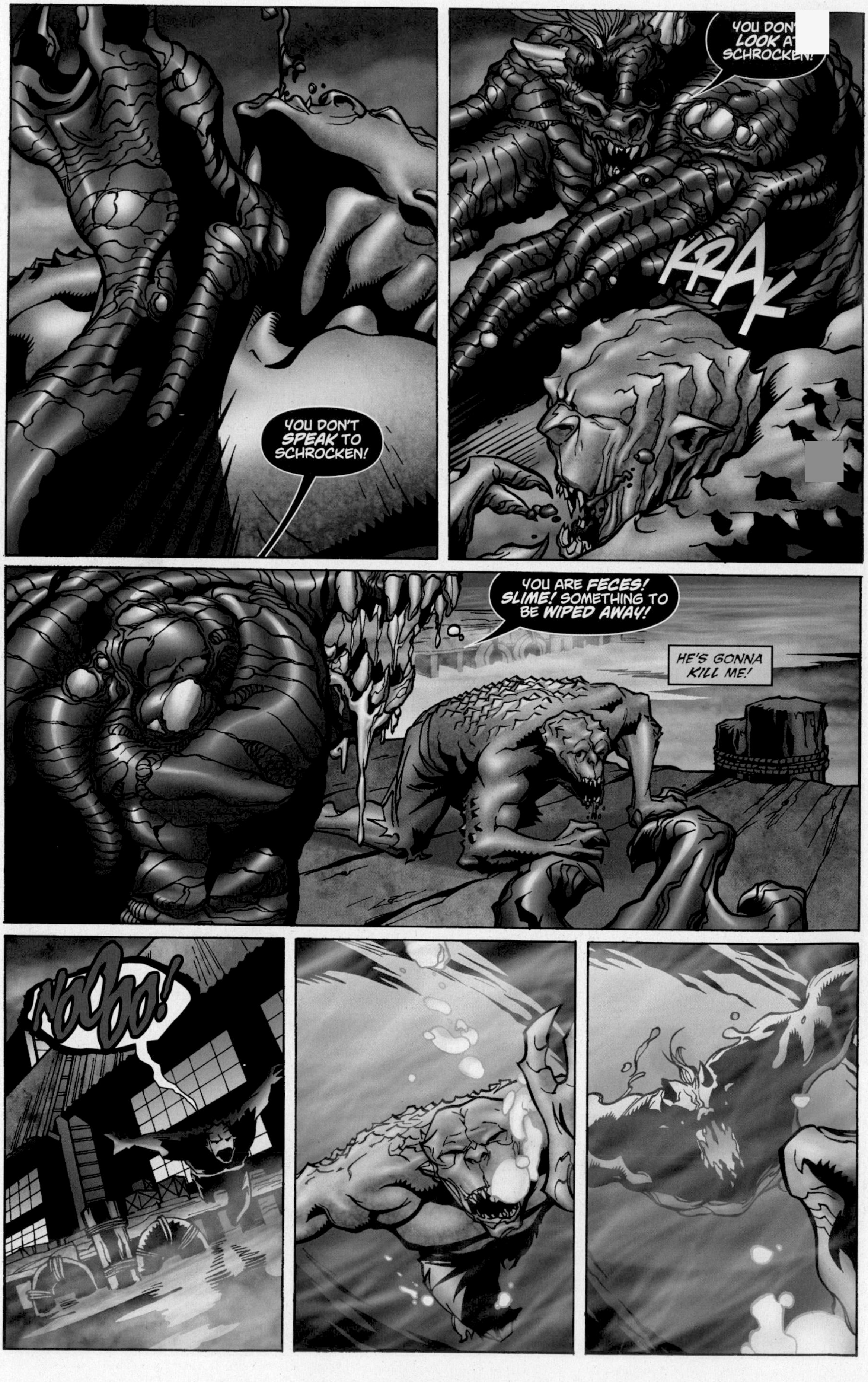
YOU DON'T SPEAK TO SCHROCKEN!
YOU DON' LOOK A SCHROCKEN!
KRAK
YOU ARE FECES! SLIME! SOMETHING TO BE WIPED AWAY!
HE'S GONNA KILL ME!
NOOOO!

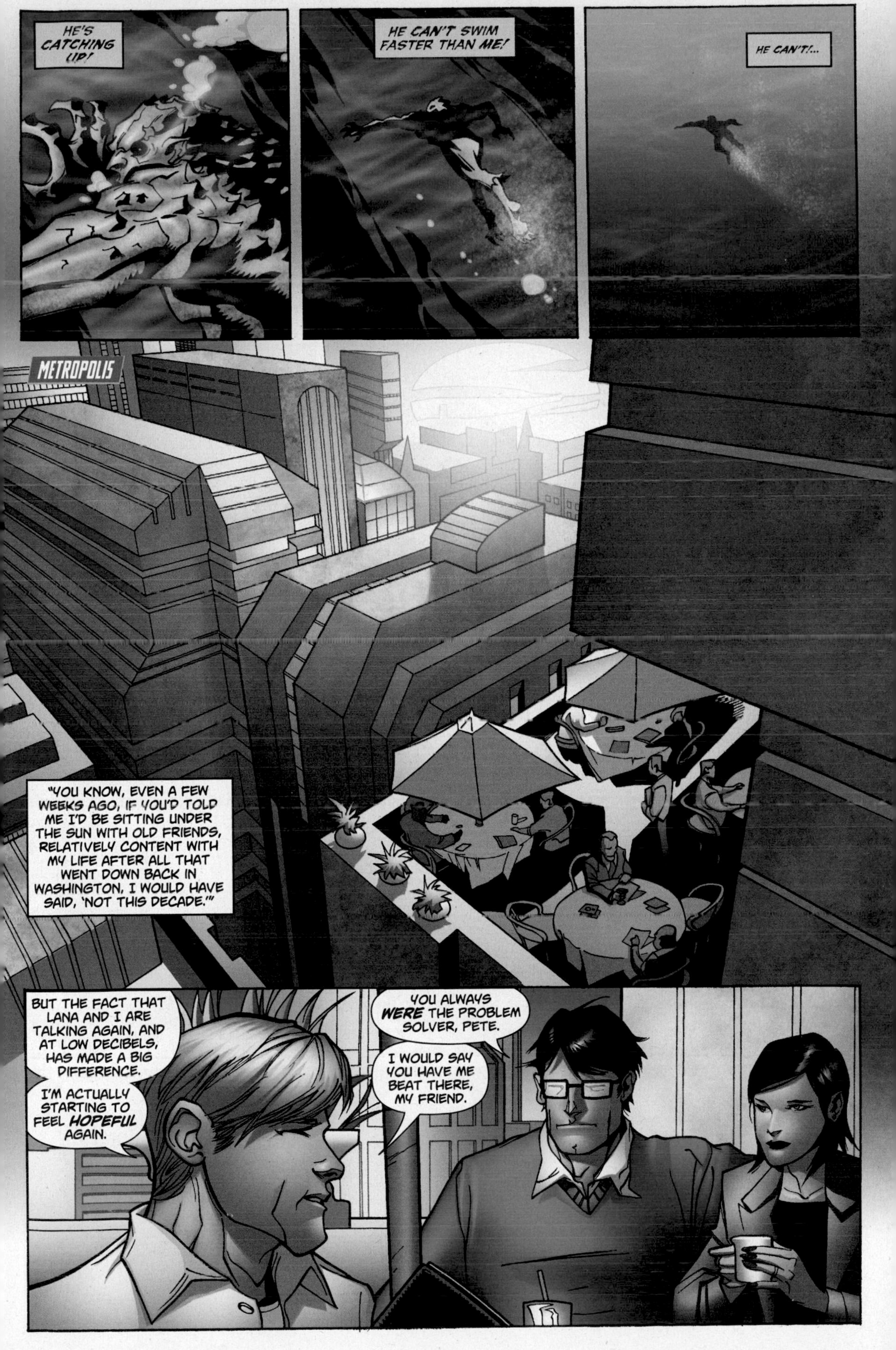
HE'S CATCHING UP!
HE CAN'T SWIM FASTER THAN ME!
HE CAN'T!...
METROPOLIS
"YOU KNOW, EVEN A FEW WEEKS AGO, IF YOU'D TOLD ME I'D BE SITTING UNDER THE SUN WITH OLD FRIENDS, RELATIVELY CONTENT WITH MY LIFE AFTER ALL THAT WENT DOWN BACK IN WASHINGTON, I WOULD HAVE SAID, 'NOT THIS DECADE.'"
BUT THE FACT THAT LANA AND I ARE TALKING AGAIN, AND AT LOW DECIBELS, HAS MADE A BIG DIFFERENCE.
I'M ACTUALLY STARTING TO FEEL HOPEFUL AGAIN.
YOU ALWAYS WERE THE PROBLEM SOLVER, PETE.
I WOULD SAY YOU HAVE ME BEAT THERE, MY FRIEND.

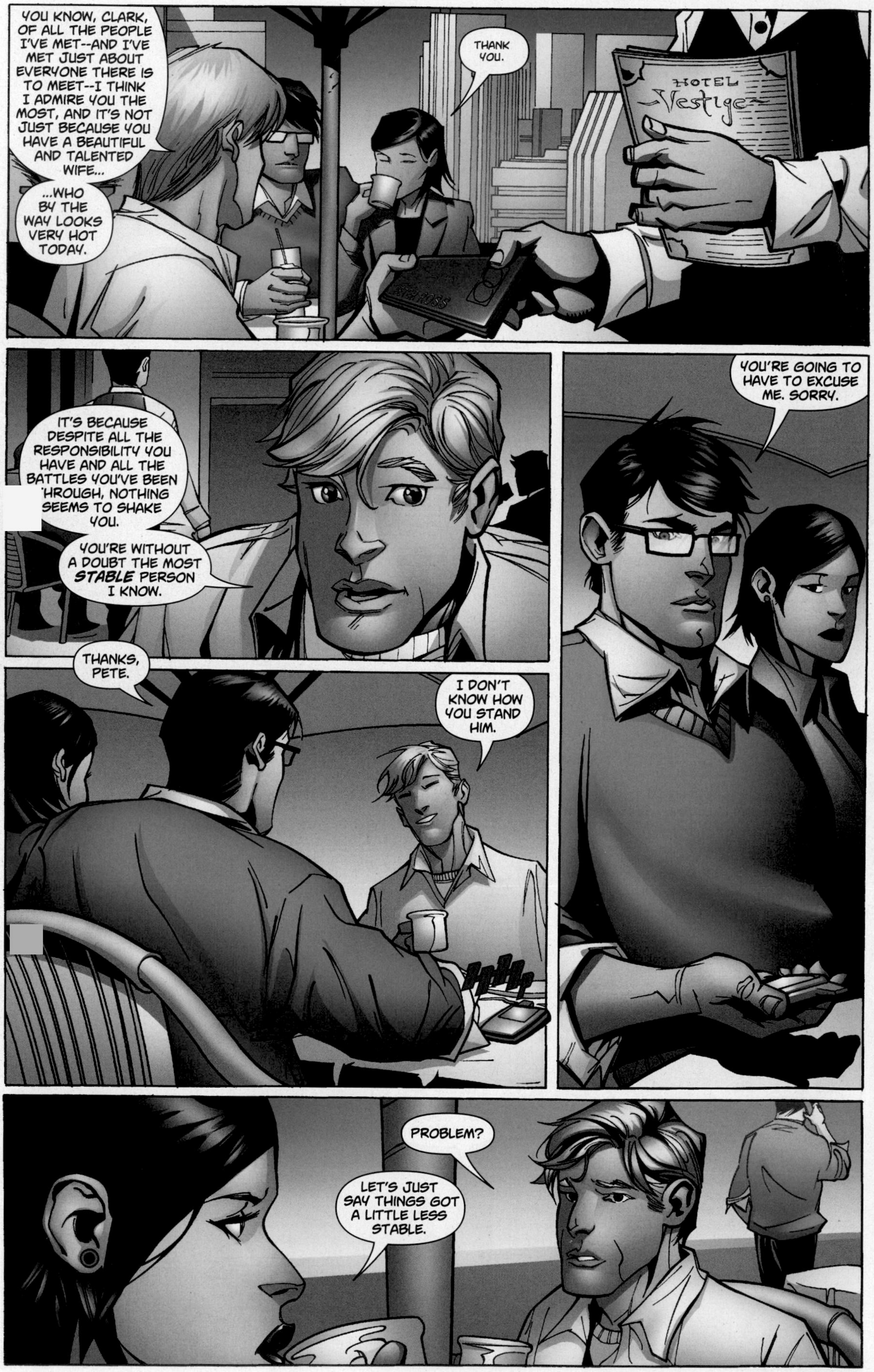
YOU KNOW, CLARK, OF ALL THE PEOPLE I'VE MET--AND I'VE MET JUST ABOUT EVERYONE THERE IS TO MEET--I THINK I ADMIRE YOU THE MOST, AND IT'S NOT JUST BECAUSE YOU HAVE A BEAUTIFUL AND TALENTED WIFE...
...WHO BY THE WAY LOOKS VERY HOT TODAY.
THANK YOU.
HOTEL Vestige
IT'S BECAUSE DESPITE ALL THE RESPONSIBILITY YOU HAVE AND ALL THE BATTLES YOU'VE BEEN THROUGH, NOTHING SEEMS TO SHAKE YOU.
YOU'RE WITHOUT A DOUBT THE MOST STABLE PERSON I KNOW.
THANKS, PETE.
I DON'T KNOW HOW YOU STAND HIM.
YOU'RE GOING TO HAVE TO EXCUSE ME. SORRY.
PROBLEM?
LET'S JUST SAY THINGS GOT A LITTLE LESS STABLE.

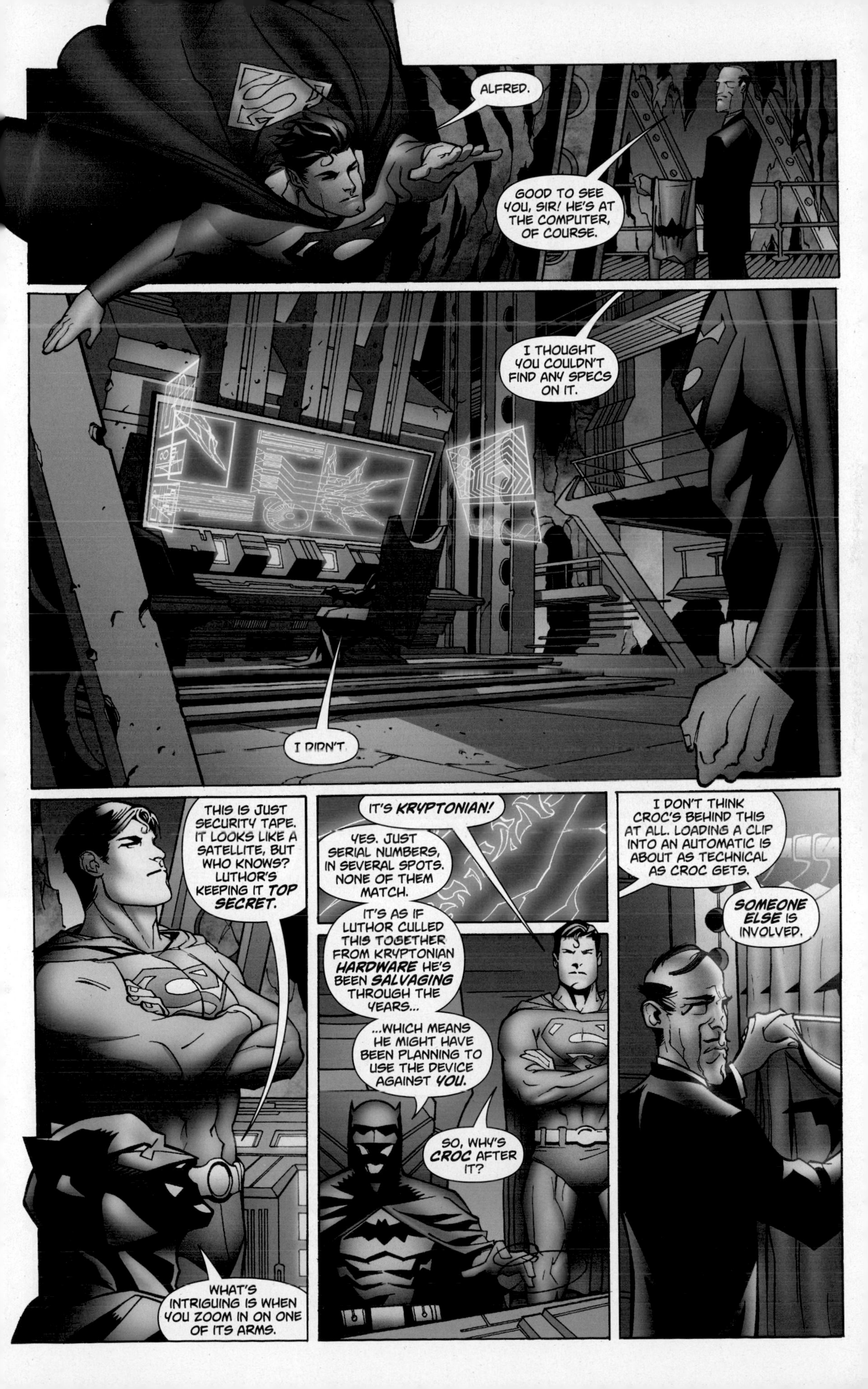
ALFRED.
GOOD TO SEE YOU, SIR! HE'S AT THE COMPUTER, OF COURSE.
I THOUGHT YOU COULDN'T FIND ANY SPECS ON IT.
I DIDN'T.
THIS IS JUST SECURITY TAPE. IT LOOKS LIKE A SATELLITE, BUT WHO KNOWS? LUTHOR'S KEEPING IT TOP SECRET.
WHAT'S INTRIGUING IS WHEN YOU ZOOM IN ON ONE OF ITS ARMS.
IT'S KRYPTONIAN!
YES. JUST SERIAL NUMBERS, IN SEVERAL SPOTS. NONE OF THEM MATCH.
IT'S AS IF LUTHOR CULLED THIS TOGETHER FROM KRYPTONIAN HARDWARE HE'S BEEN SALVAGING THROUGH THE YEARS...
...WHICH MEANS HE MIGHT HAVE BEEN PLANNING TO USE THE DEVICE AGAINST YOU.
SO, WHY'S CROC AFTER IT?
I DON'T THINK CROC'S BEHIND THIS AT ALL. LOADING A CLIP INTO AN AUTOMATIC IS ABOUT AS TECHNICAL AS CROC GETS.
SOMEONE ELSE IS INVOLVED.

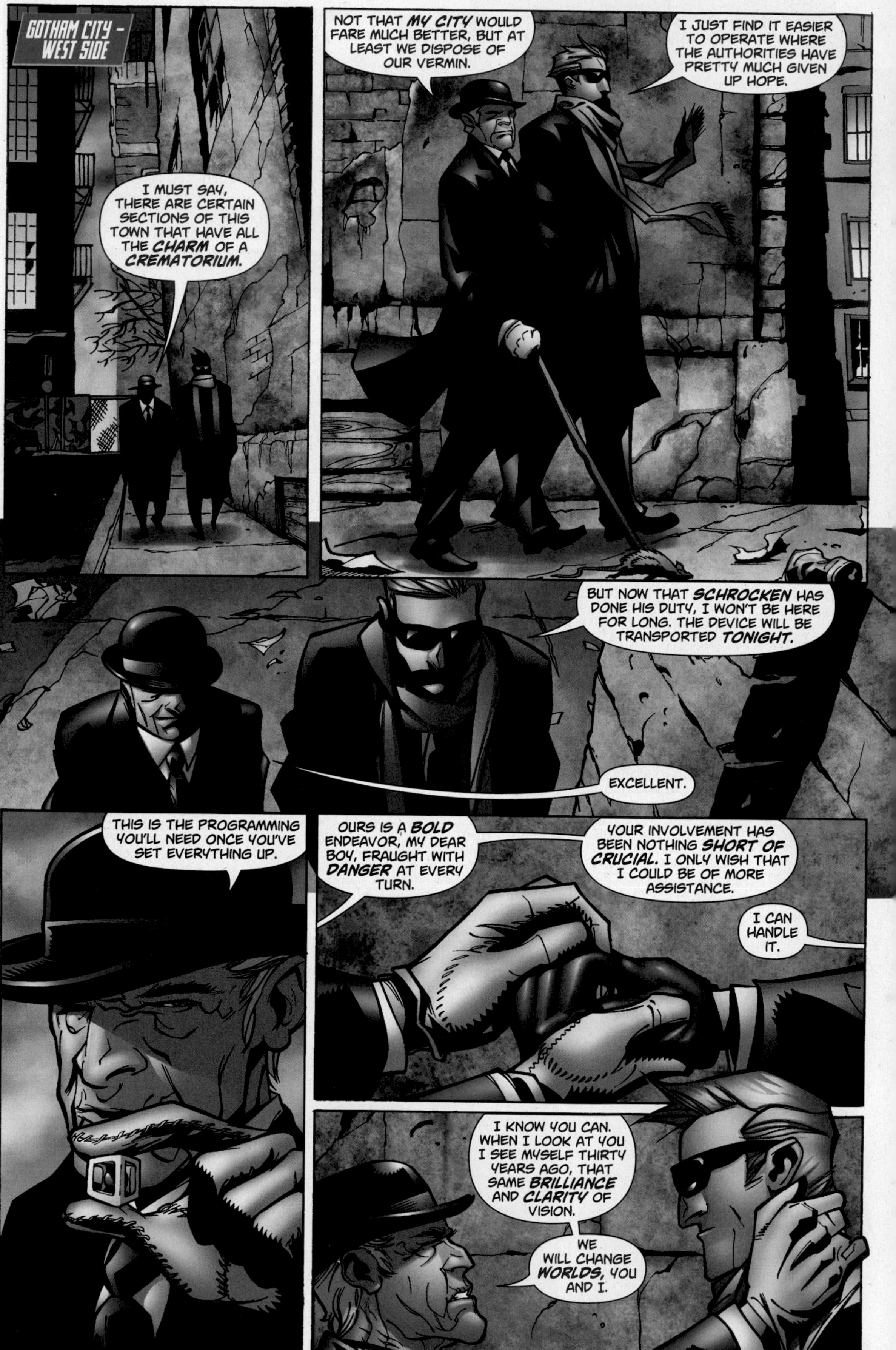
GOTHAM CITY - WEST SIDE
I MUST SAY, THERE ARE CERTAIN SECTIONS OF THIS TOWN THAT HAVE ALL THE CHARM OF A CREMATORIUM.
NOT THAT MY CITY WOULD FARE MUCH BETTER, BUT AT LEAST WE DISPOSE OF OUR VERMIN.
I JUST FIND IT EASIER TO OPERATE WHERE THE AUTHORITIES HAVE PRETTY MUCH GIVEN UP HOPE.
BUT NOW THAT SCHROCKEN HAS DONE HIS DUTY, I WON'T BE HERE FOR LONG. THE DEVICE WILL BE TRANSPORTED TONIGHT.
EXCELLENT.
THIS IS THE PROGRAMMING YOU'LL NEED ONCE YOU'VE SET EVERYTHING UP.
OURS IS A BOLD ENDEAVOR, MY DEAR BOY, FRAUGHT WITH DANGER AT EVERY TURN.
YOUR INVOLVEMENT HAS BEEN NOTHING SHORT OF CRUCIAL. I ONLY WISH THAT I COULD BE OF MORE ASSISTANCE.
I CAN HANDLE IT.
I KNOW YOU CAN. WHEN I LOOK AT YOU I SEE MYSELF THIRTY YEARS AGO, THAT SAME BRILLIANCE AND CLARITY OF VISION.
WE WILL CHANGE WORLDS, YOU AND I.

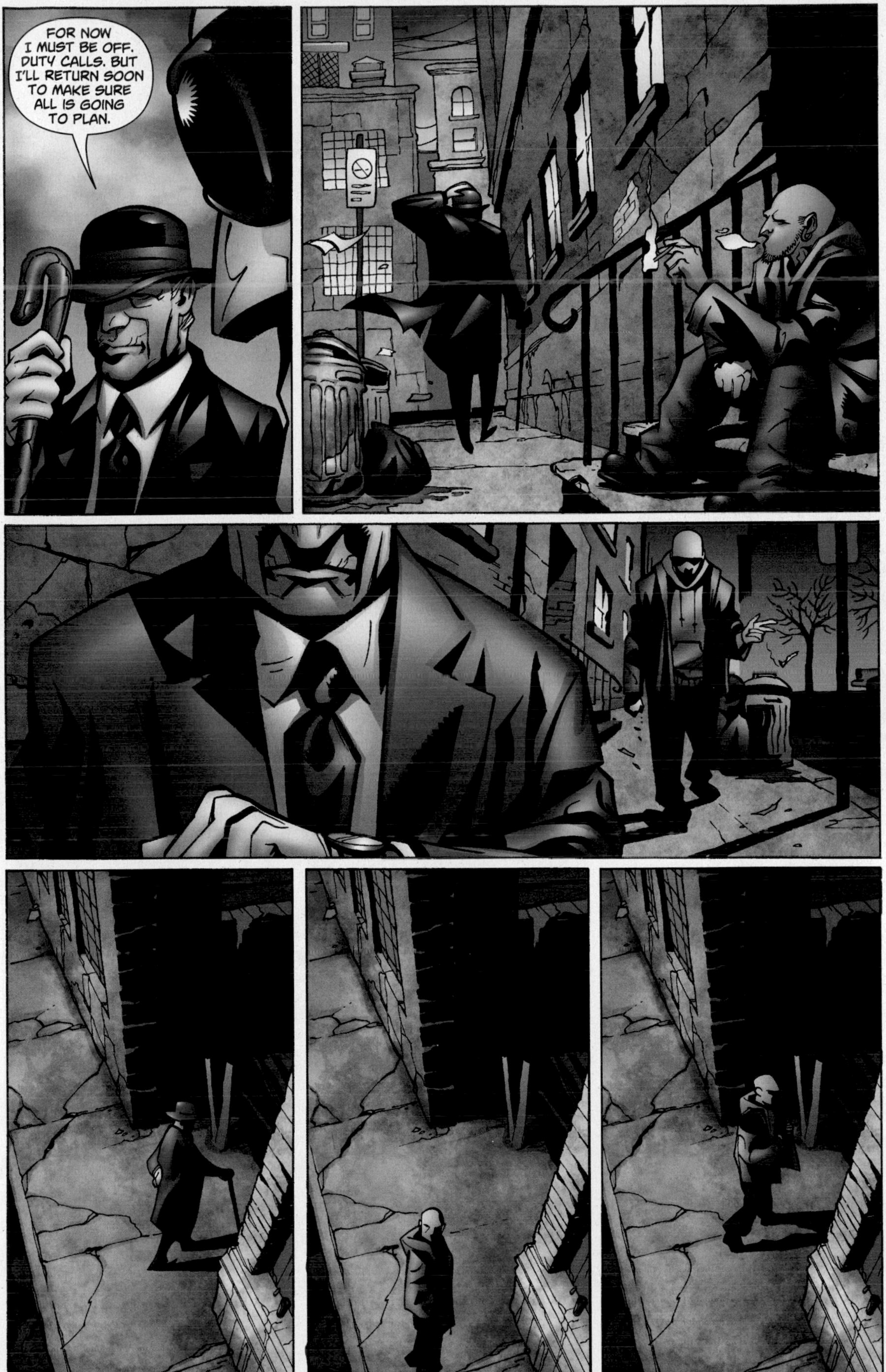
FOR NOW I MUST BE OFF. DUTY CALLS. BUT I'LL RETURN SOON TO MAKE SURE ALL IS GOING TO PLAN.

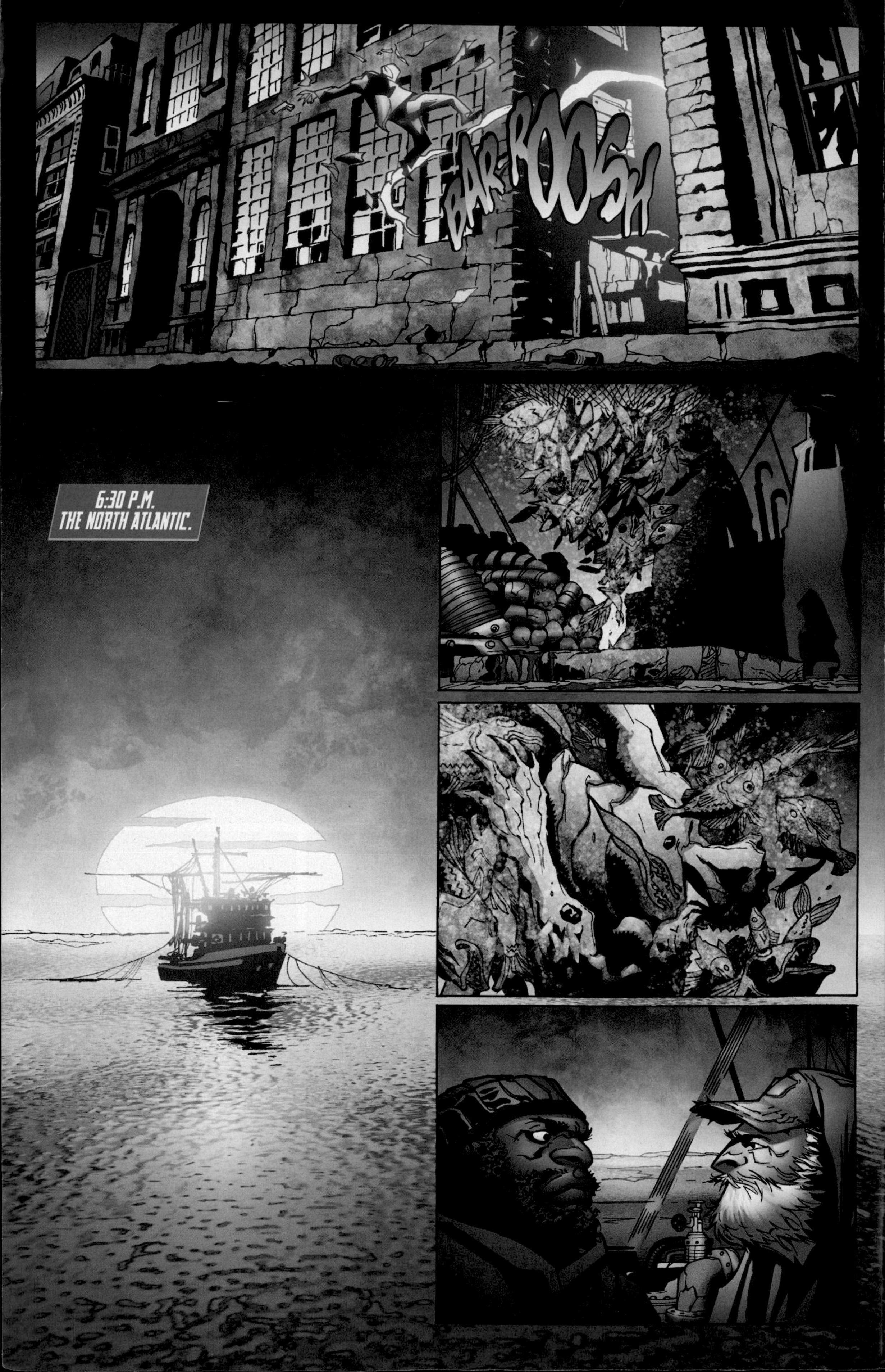
BAR-ROOSH
6:30 P.M.
THE NORTH ATLANTIC.

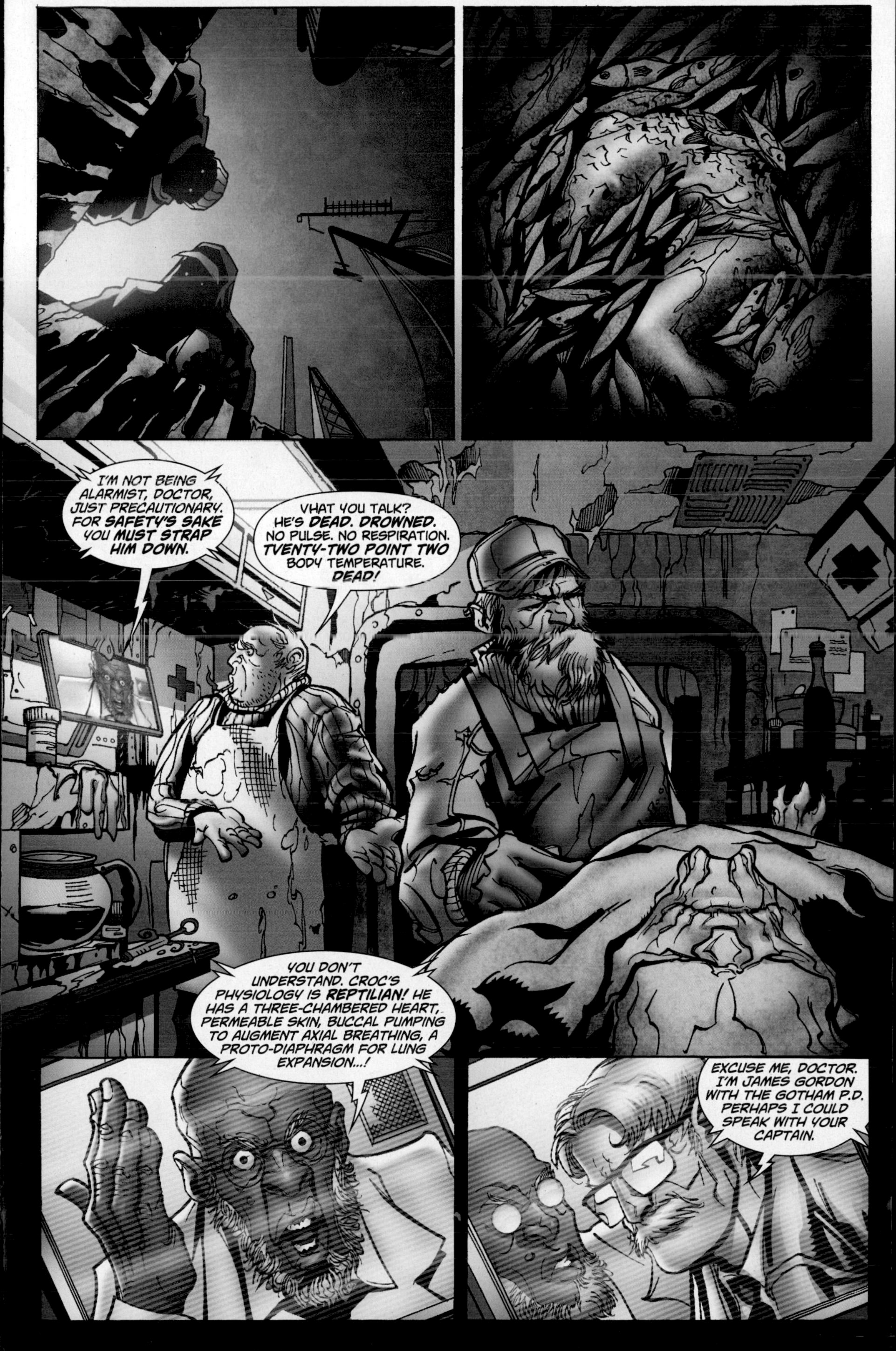
I'M NOT BEING ALARMIST, DOCTOR, JUST PRECAUTIONARY. FOR SAFETY'S SAKE YOU MUST STRAP HIM DOWN.
VHAT YOU TALK? HE'S DEAD. DROWNED. NO PULSE. NO RESPIRATION. TVENTY-TWO POINT TWO BODY TEMPERATURE. DEAD!
YOU DON'T UNDERSTAND. CROC'S PHYSIOLOGY IS REPTILIAN! HE HAS A THREE-CHAMBERED HEART, PERMEABLE SKIN, BUCCAL PUMPING TO AUGMENT AXIAL BREATHING, A PROTO-DIAPHRAGM FOR LUNG EXPANSION...!
EXCUSE ME, DOCTOR. I'M JAMES GORDON WITH THE GOTHAM P.D. PERHAPS I COULD SPEAK WITH YOUR CAPTAIN.

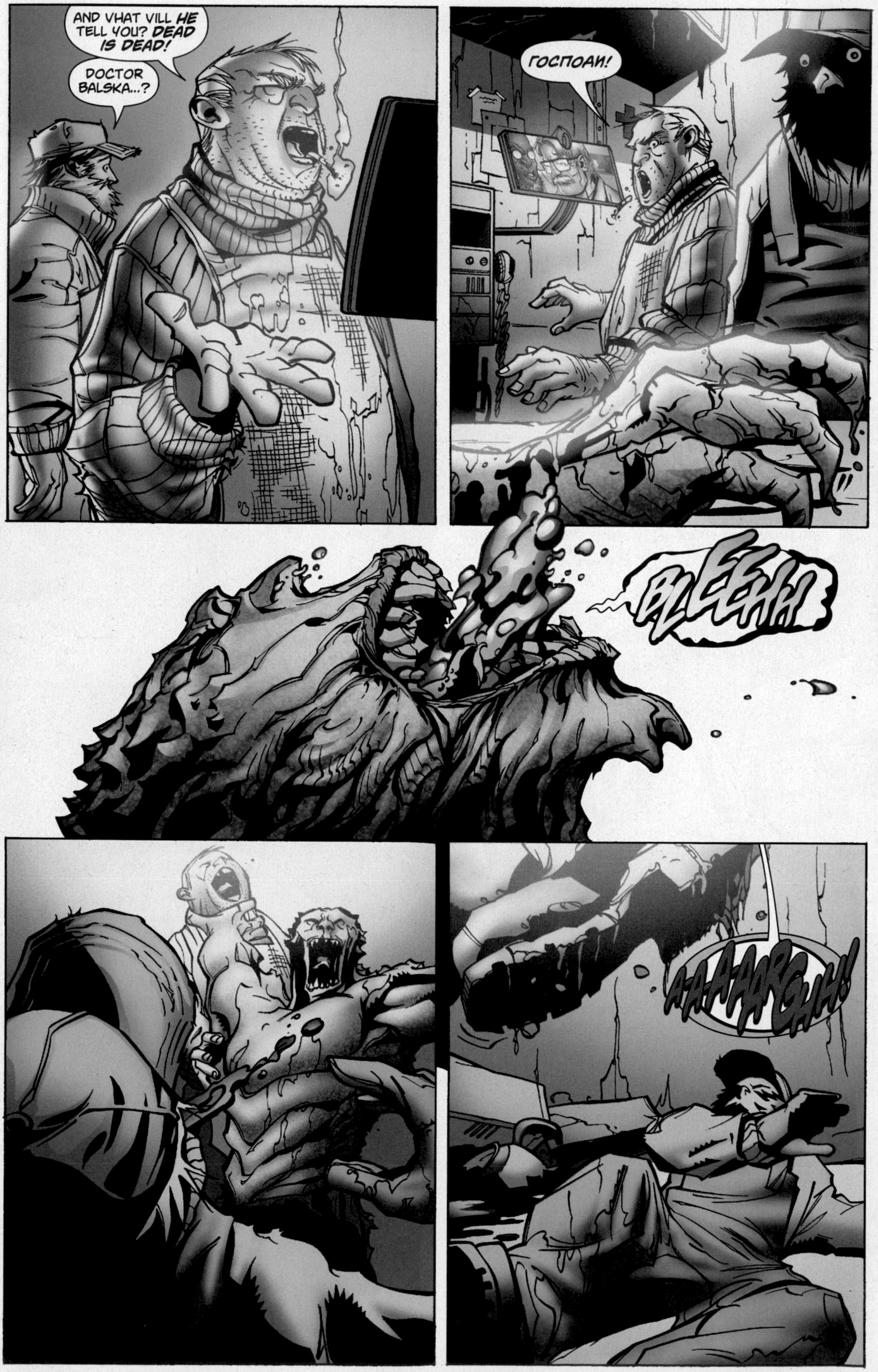
AND VHAT VILL HE TELL YOU? DEAD IS DEAD!
DOCTOR BALSKA...?
ГОСПОАИ!
BLEEHH
A-A-A-AARGHH!

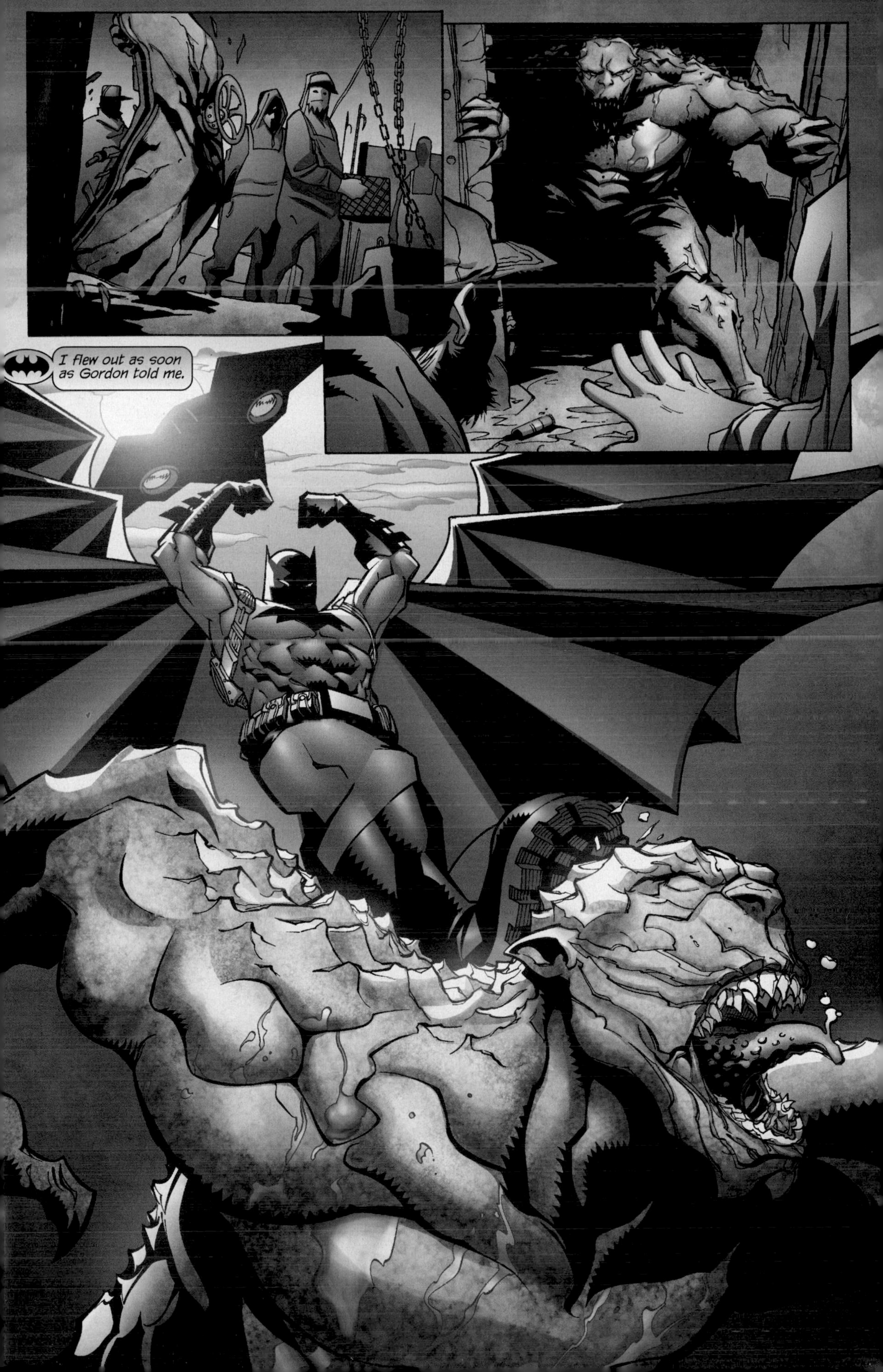
I flew out as soon as Gordon told me.

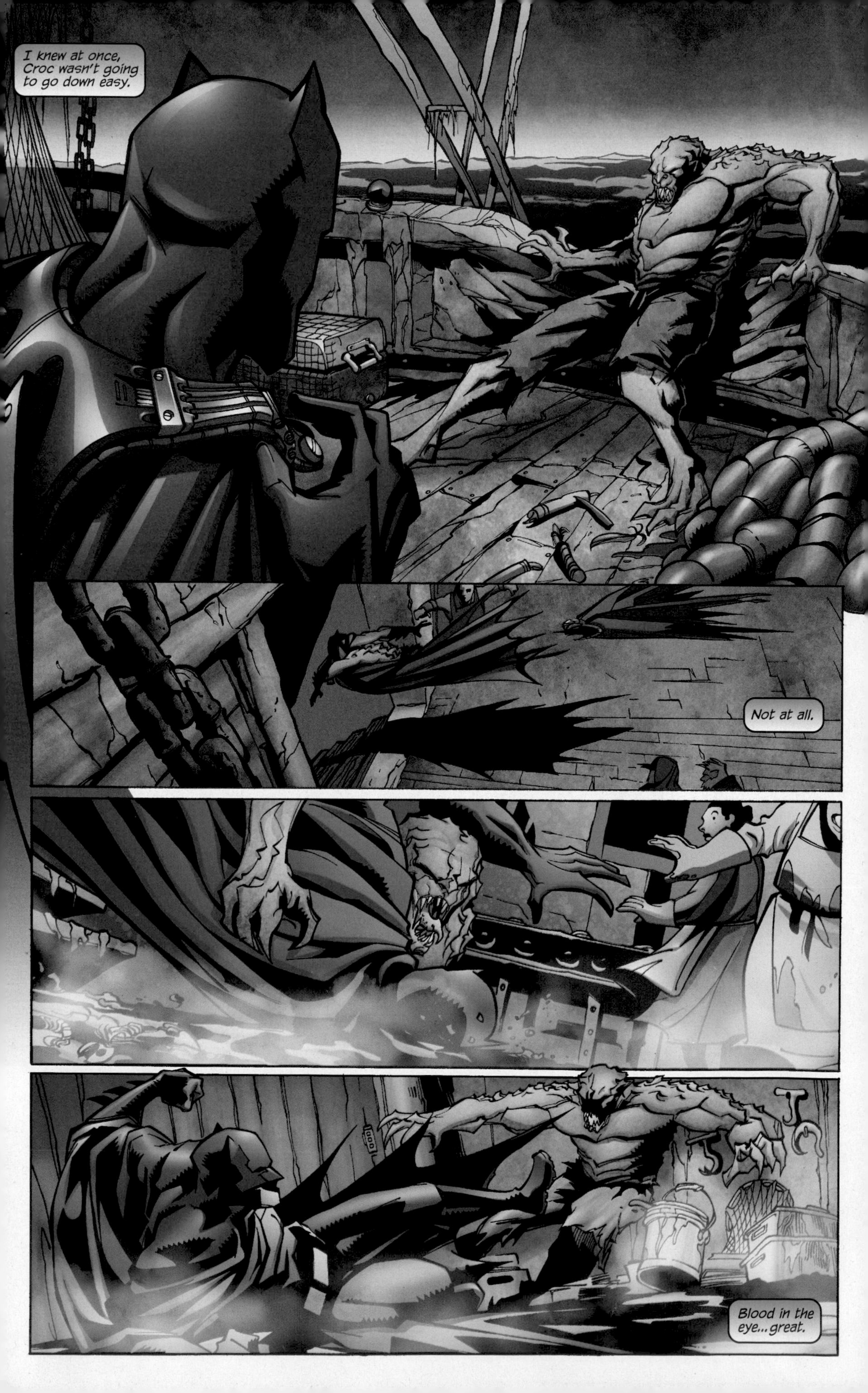
I knew at once, Croc wasn't going to go down easy.
Not at all.
Blood in the eye...great.

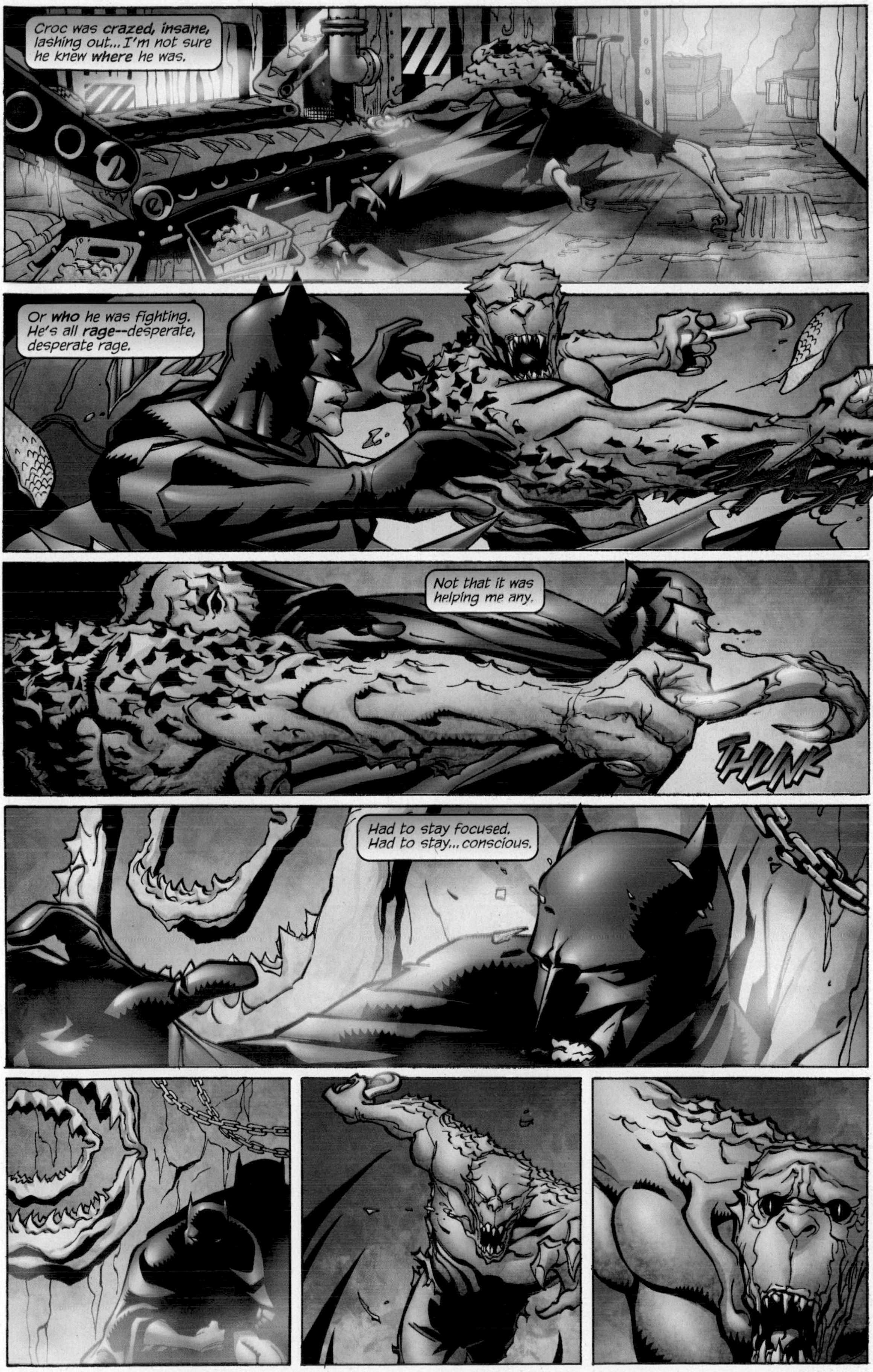
Croc was crazed, insane, lashing out... I'm not sure he knew where he was.
Or who he was fighting. He's all rage--desperate, desperate rage.
SHAKK
Not that it was helping me any.
THUNK
Had to stay focused. Had to stay... conscious.

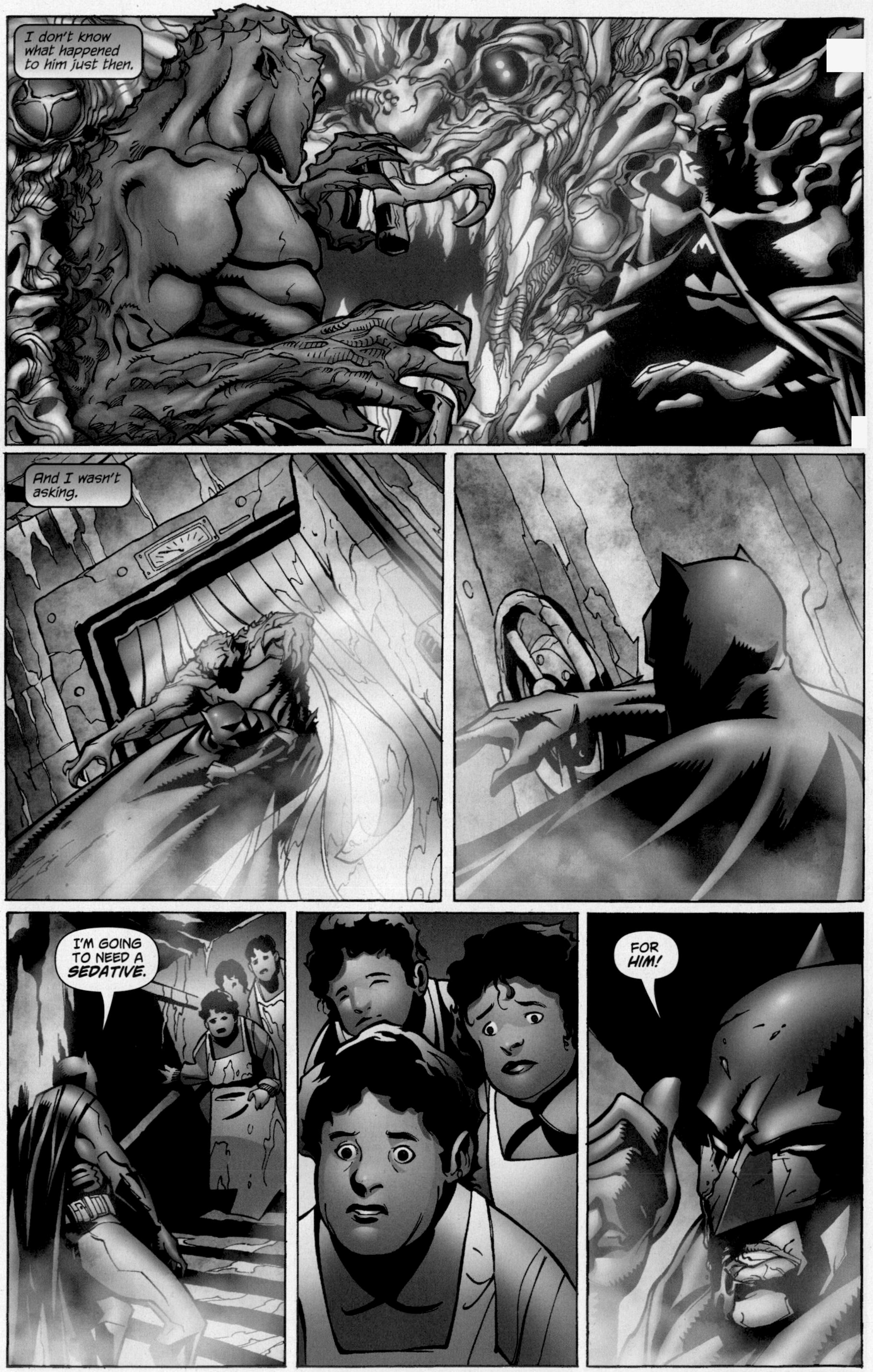
I don't know what happened to him just then.
And I wasn't asking.
I'M GOING TO NEED A SEDATIVE.
FOR HIM!

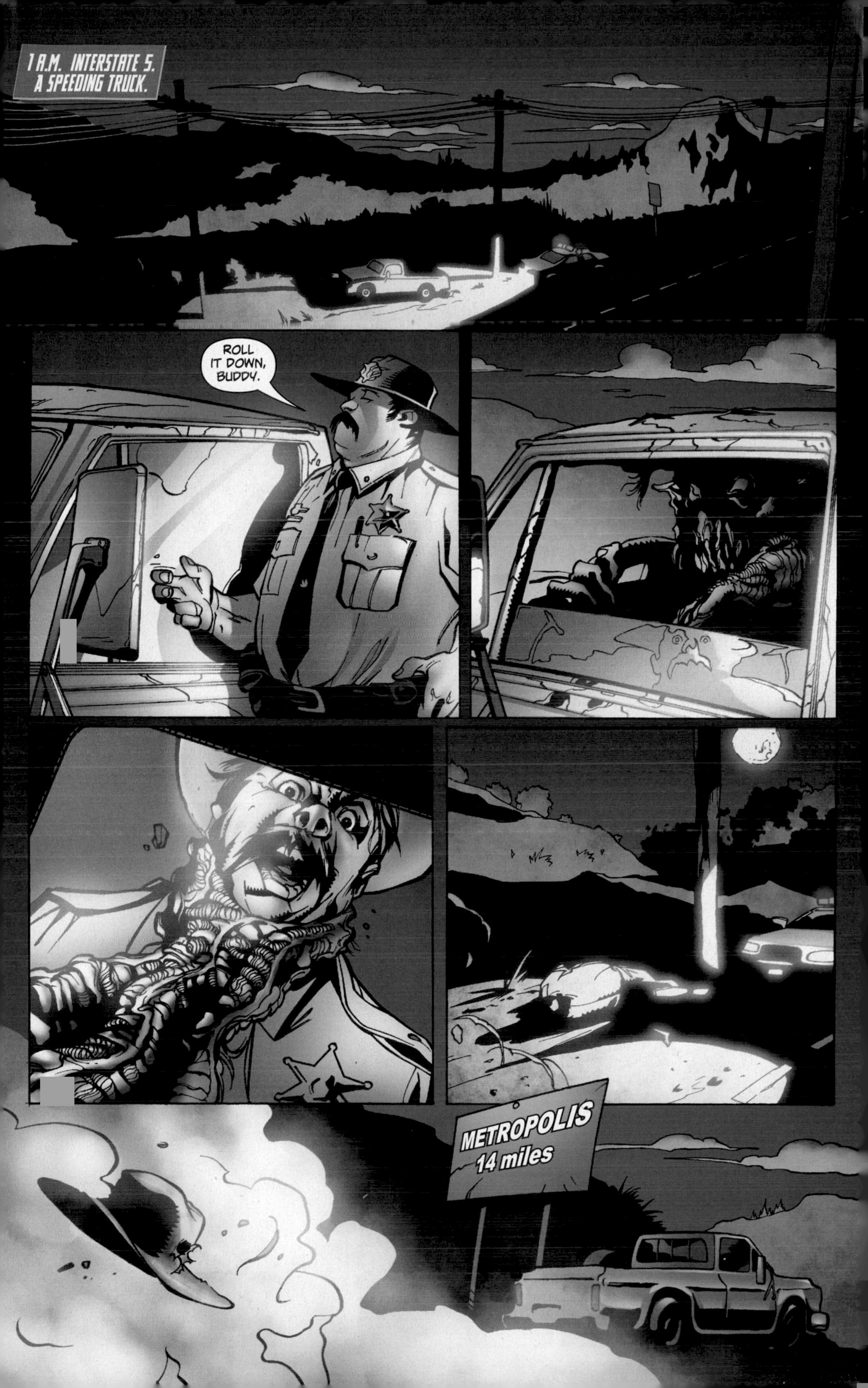
1 A.M. INTERSTATE 5. A SPEEDING TRUCK.
ROLL IT DOWN, BUDDY.
METROPOLIS
14 miles

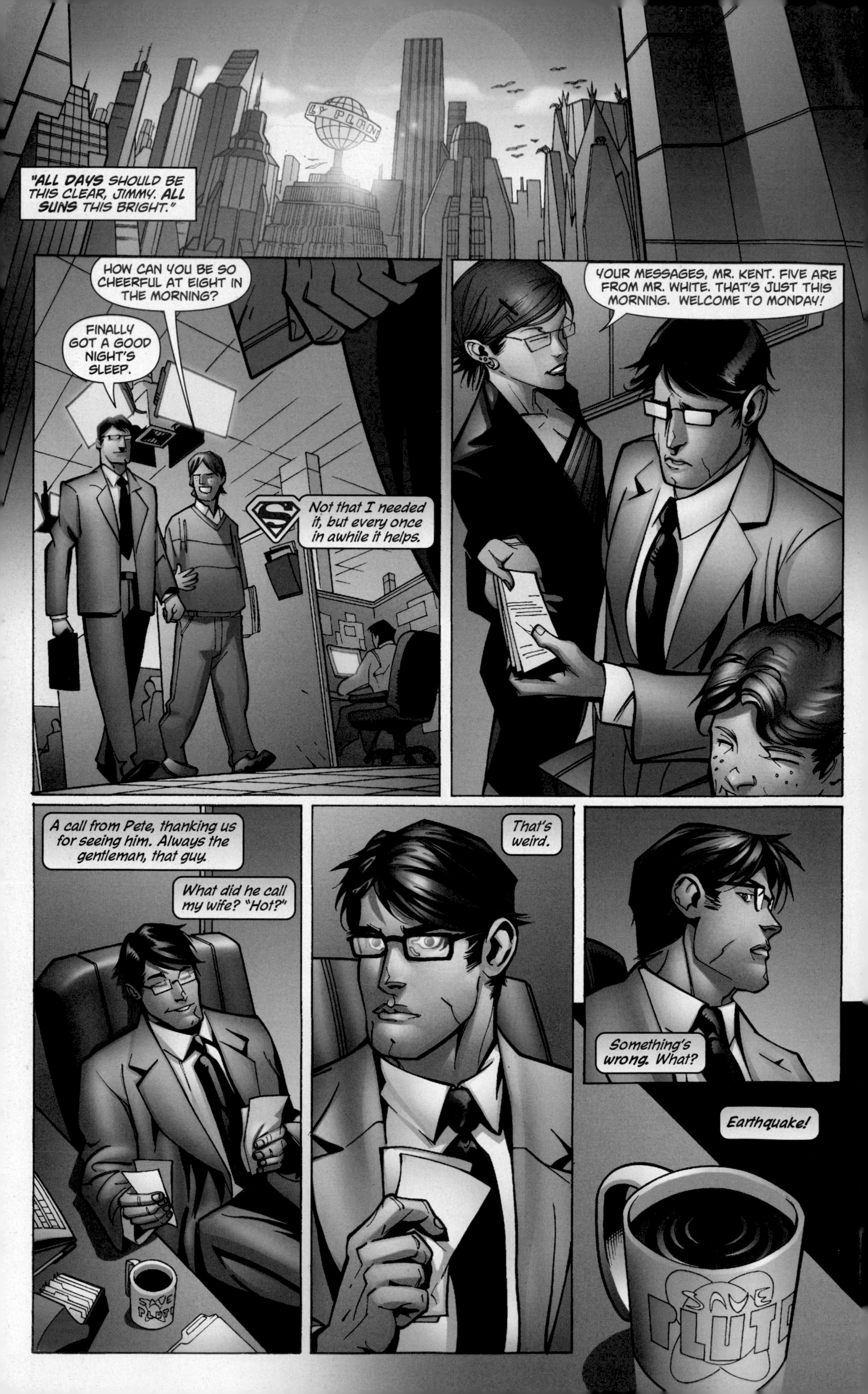
"ALL DAYS SHOULD BE THIS CLEAR, JIMMY. ALL SUNS THIS BRIGHT."
HOW CAN YOU BE SO CHEERFUL AT EIGHT IN THE MORNING?
FINALLY GOT A GOOD NIGHT'S SLEEP.
Not that I needed it, but every once in awhile it helps.
YOUR MESSAGES, MR. KENT. FIVE ARE FROM MR. WHITE. THAT'S JUST THIS MORNING. WELCOME TO MONDAY!
A call from Pete, thanking us for seeing him. Always the gentleman, that guy.
What did he call my wife? "Hot?"
That's weird.
Something's wrong. What?
Earthquake!
SAVE PLUTO

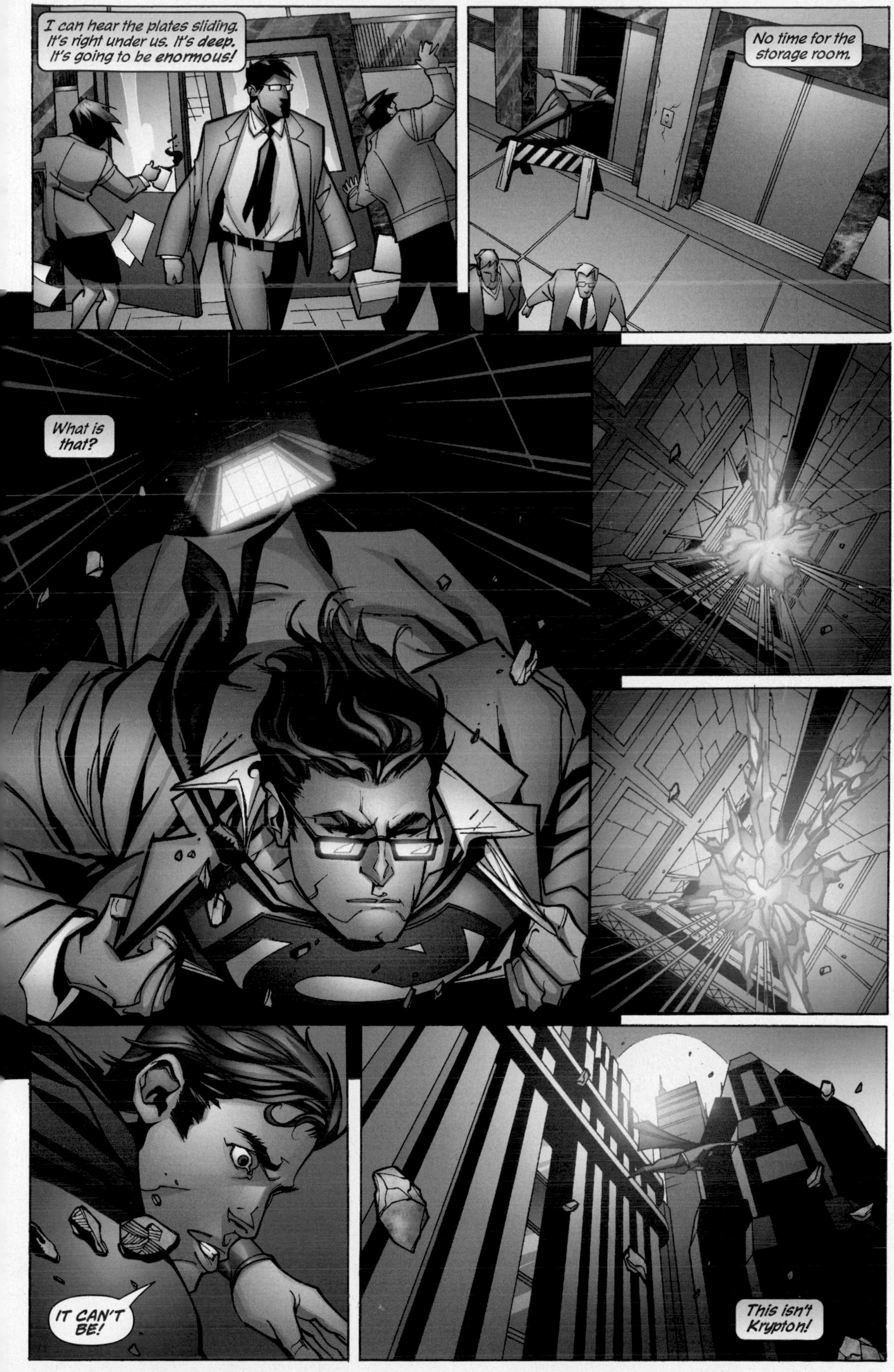
I can hear the plates sliding. It's right under us. It's deep. It's going to be enormous!
No time for the storage room.
What is that?
IT CAN'T BE!
This isn't Krypton!

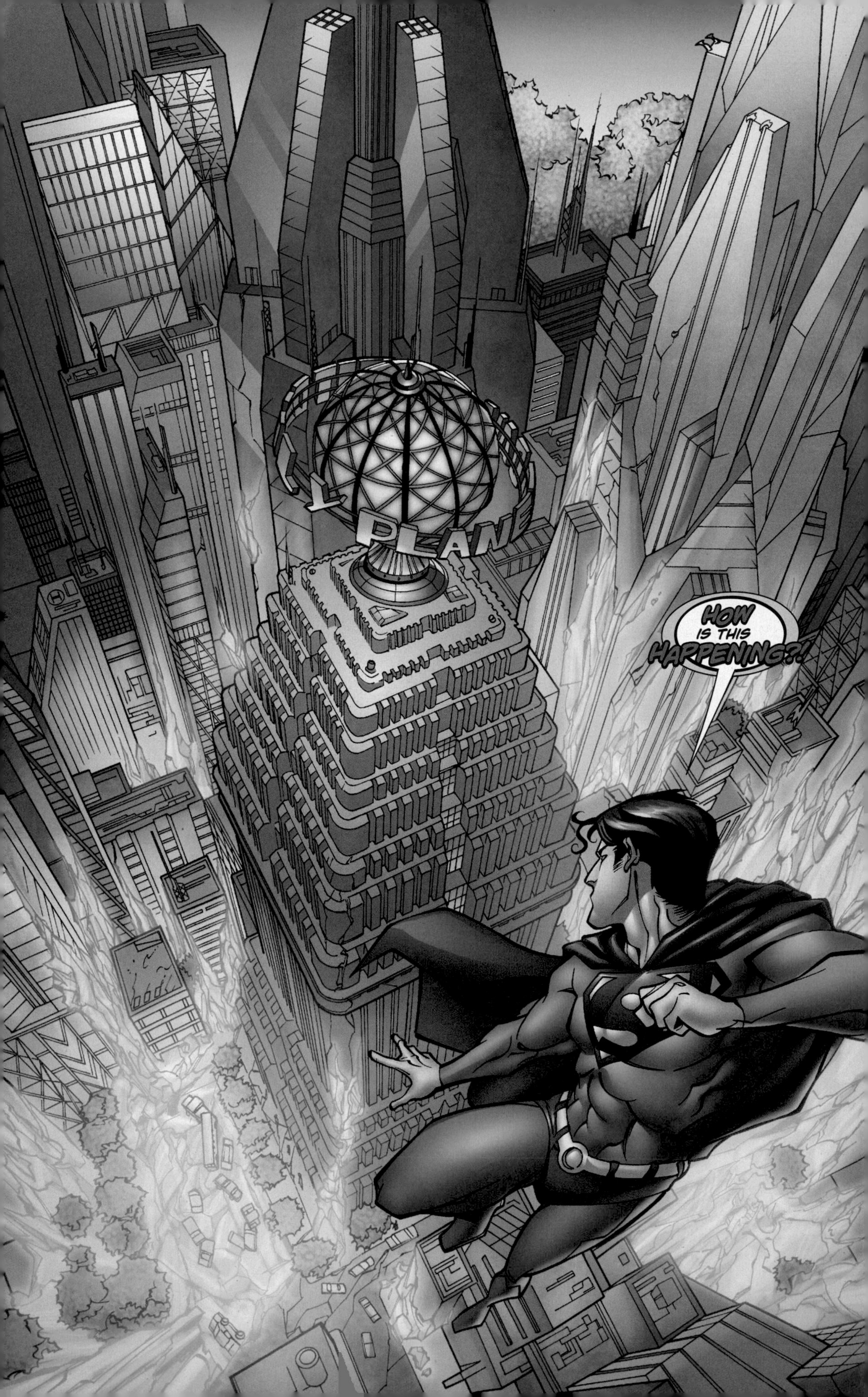
PLANE
HOW IS THIS HAPPENING?!

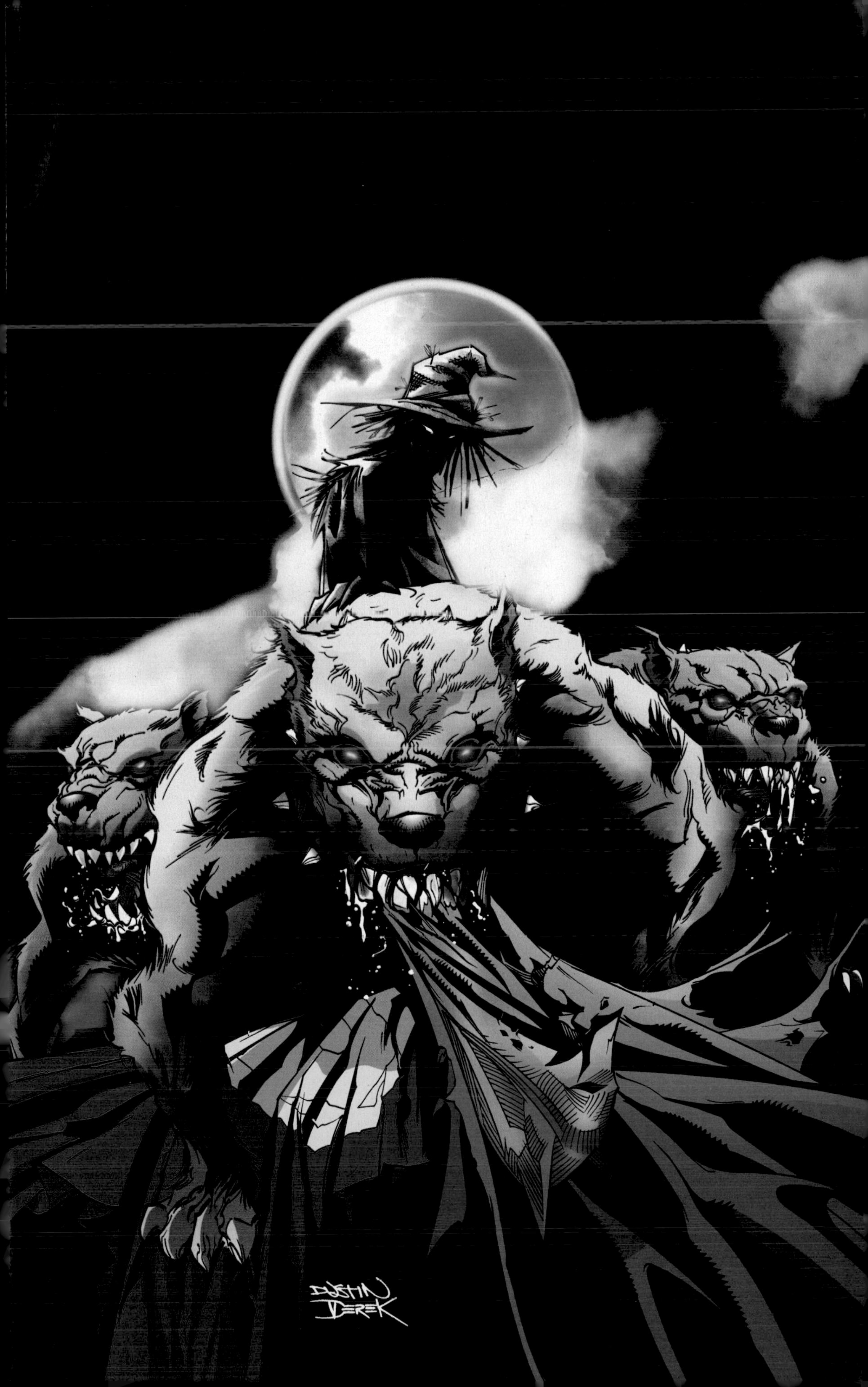
DUSTIN
DEREK

TORMENT: PART TWO
CRACK-UP

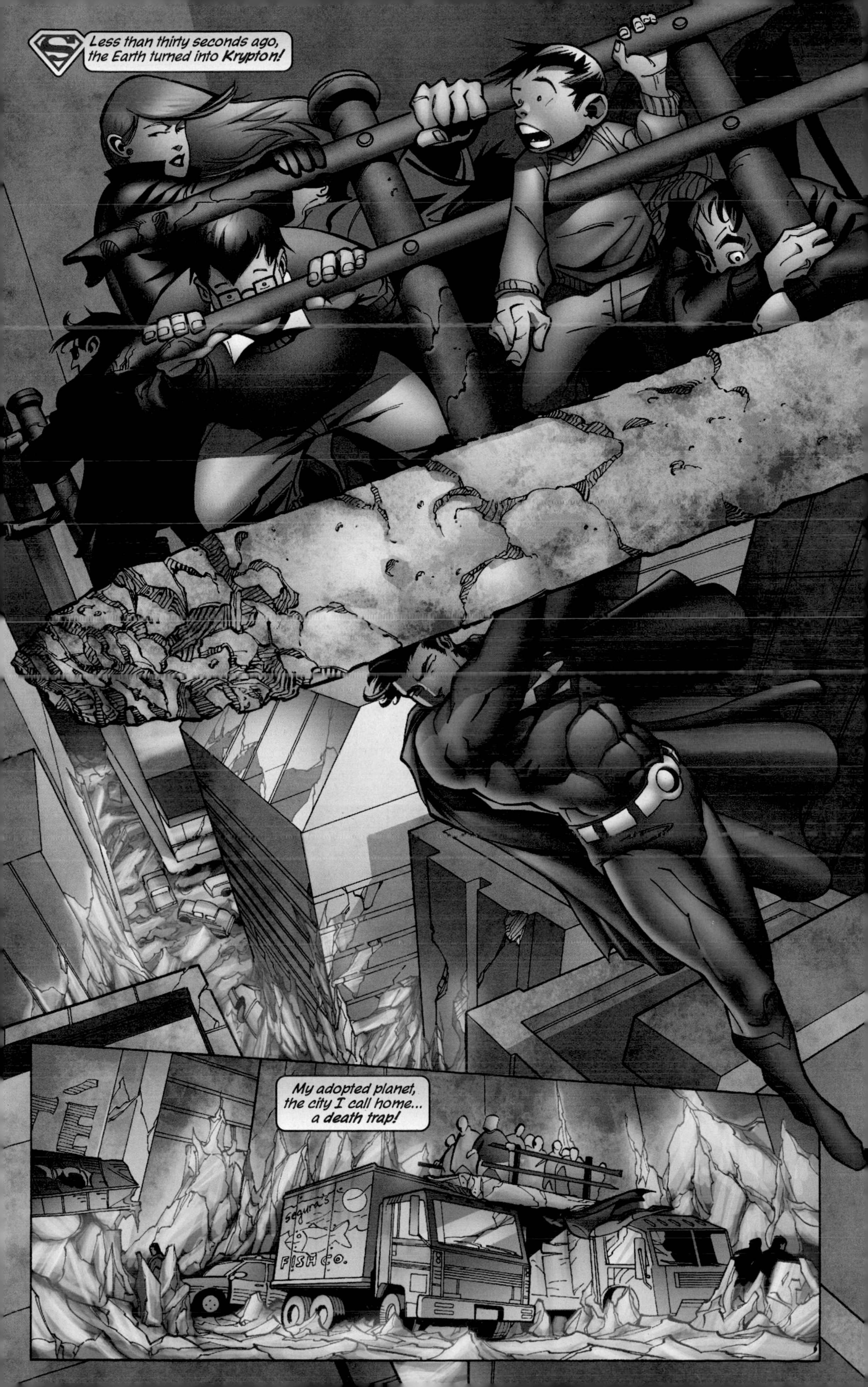
Less than thirty seconds ago, the Earth turned into Krypton!
My adopted planet, the city I call home... a death trap!
Segura's
FISH Co.

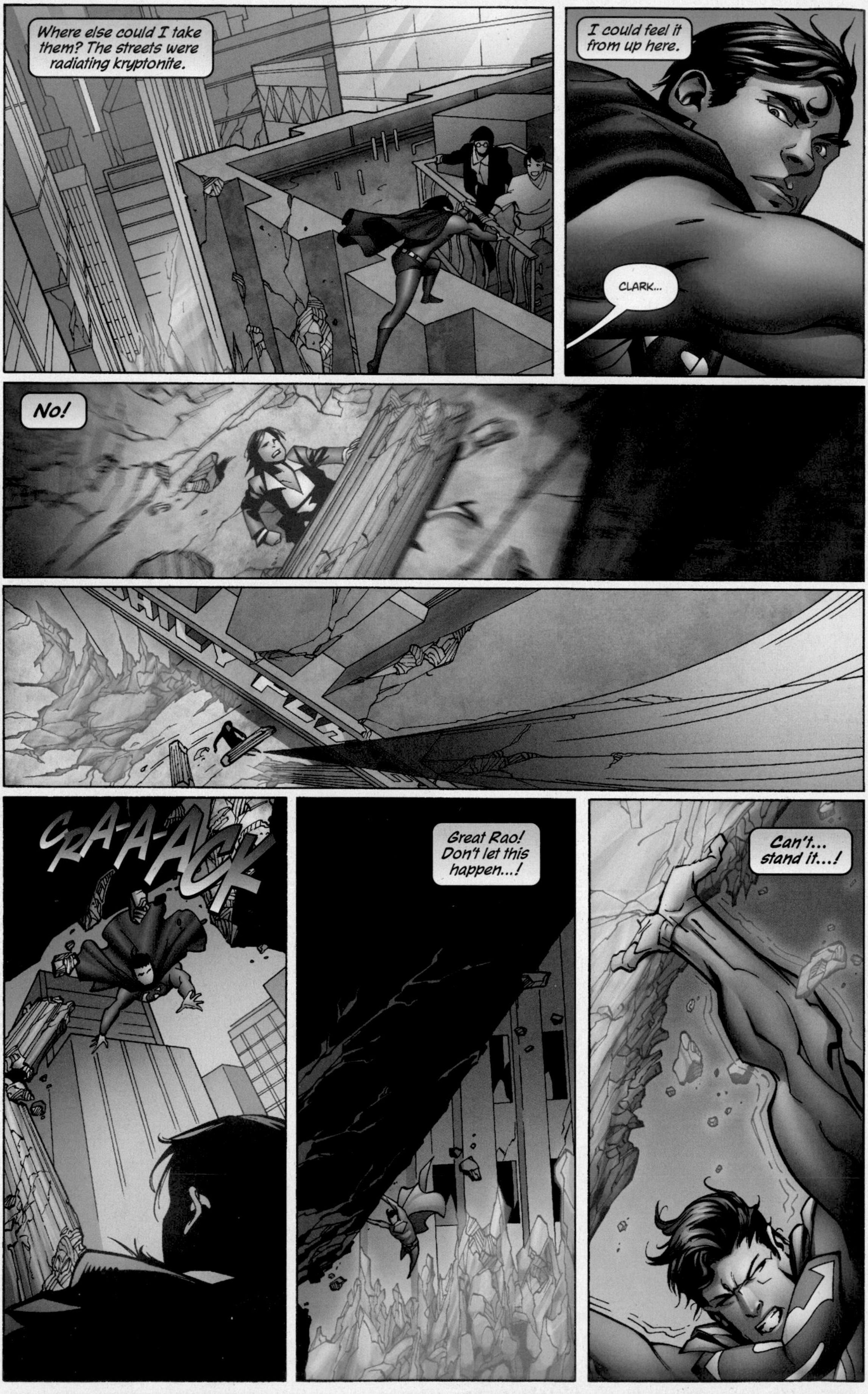
Where else could I take them? The streets were radiating kryptonite.
I could feel it from up here.
CLARK...
No!
CRA-A-ACK
Great Rao! Don't let this happen...!
Can't... stand it...!

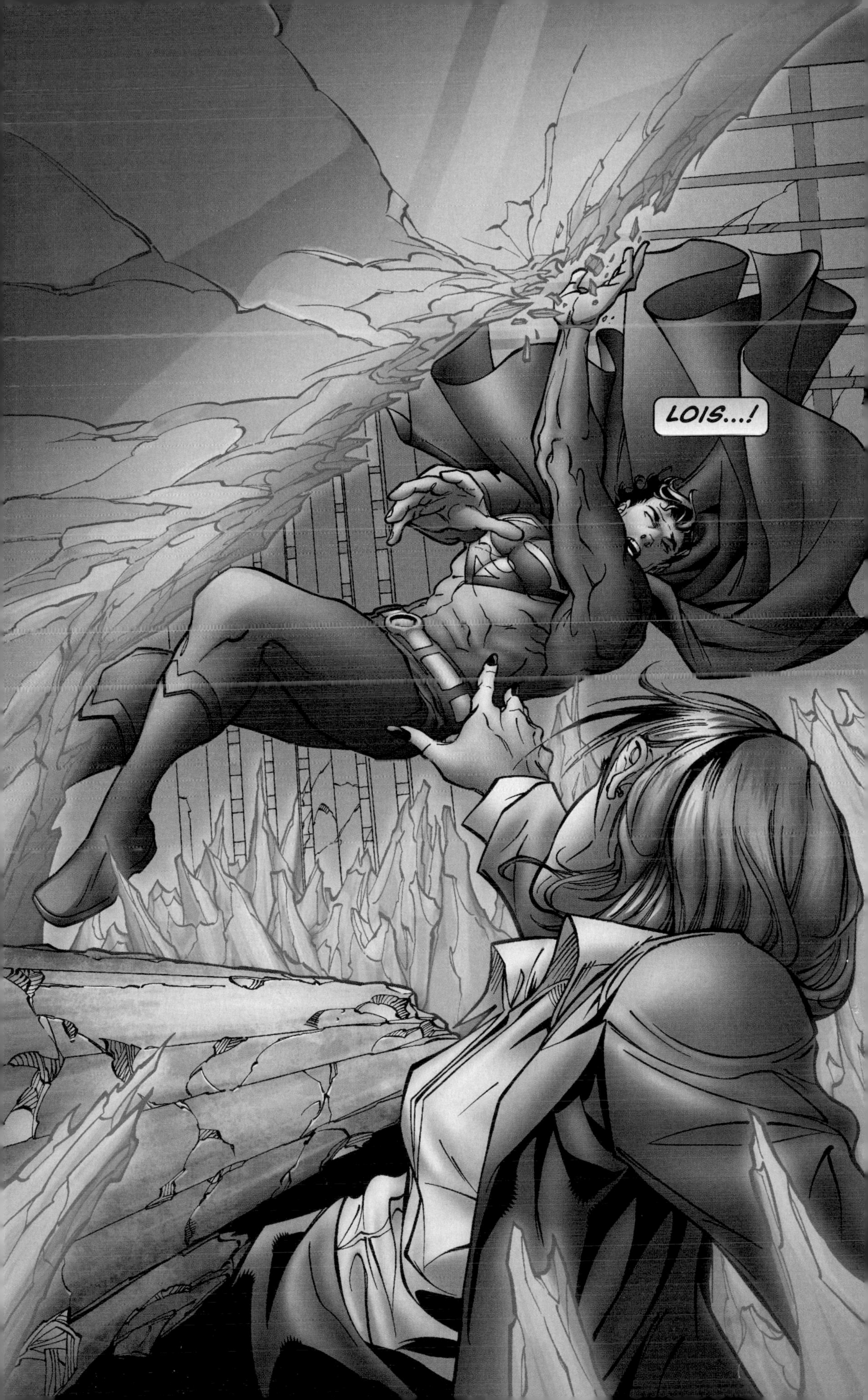
LOIS...!

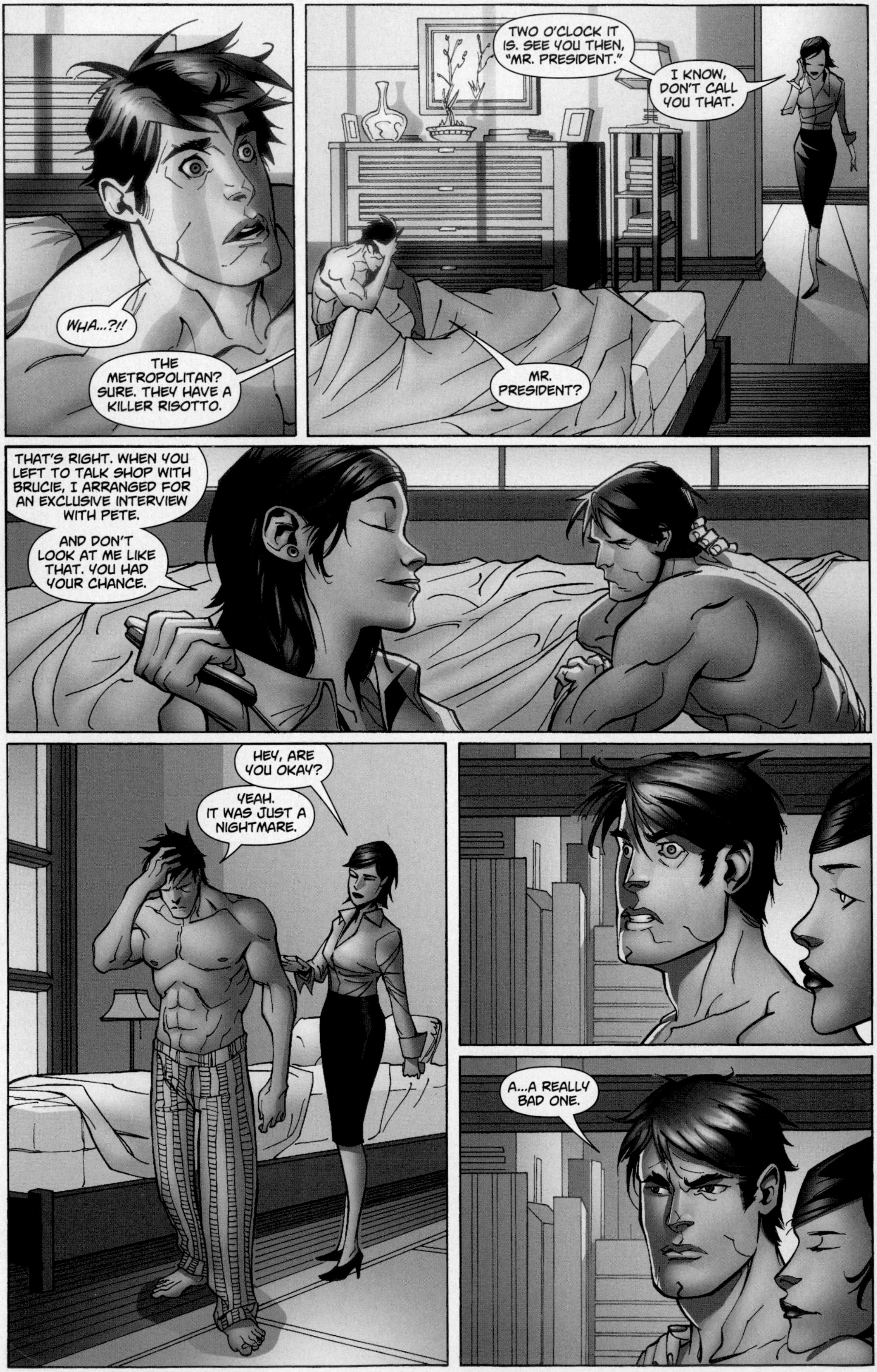
WHA...?!!
THE METROPOLITAN? SURE. THEY HAVE A KILLER RISOTTO.
TWO O'CLOCK IT IS. SEE YOU THEN, "MR. PRESIDENT."
I KNOW, DON'T CALL YOU THAT.
MR. PRESIDENT?
THAT'S RIGHT. WHEN YOU LEFT TO TALK SHOP WITH BRUCIE, I ARRANGED FOR AN EXCLUSIVE INTERVIEW WITH PETE.
AND DON'T LOOK AT ME LIKE THAT. YOU HAD YOUR CHANCE.
HEY, ARE YOU OKAY?
YEAH. IT WAS JUST A NIGHTMARE.
A...A REALLY BAD ONE.

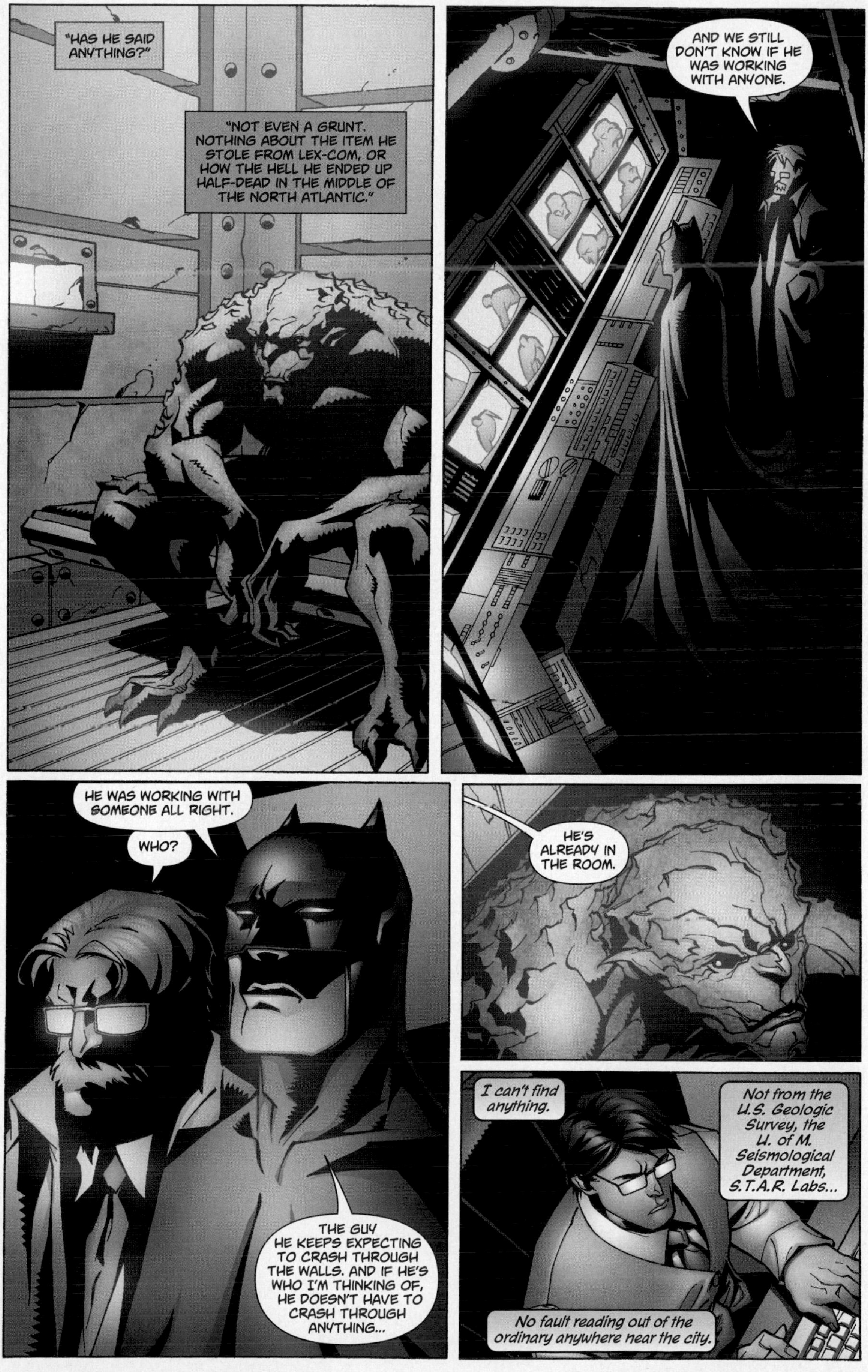
"HAS HE SAID ANYTHING?"
"NOT EVEN A GRUNT. NOTHING ABOUT THE ITEM HE STOLE FROM LEX-COM, OR HOW THE HELL HE ENDED UP HALF-DEAD IN THE MIDDLE OF THE NORTH ATLANTIC."
AND WE STILL DON'T KNOW IF HE WAS WORKING WITH ANYONE.
HE WAS WORKING WITH SOMEONE ALL RIGHT.
WHO?
THE GUY HE KEEPS EXPECTING TO CRASH THROUGH THE WALLS. AND IF HE'S WHO I'M THINKING OF, HE DOESN'T HAVE TO CRASH THROUGH ANYTHING...
HE'S ALREADY IN THE ROOM.
I can't find anything.
Not from the U.S. Geologic Survey, the U. of M. Seismological Department, S.T.A.R. Labs...
No fault reading out of the ordinary anywhere near the city.

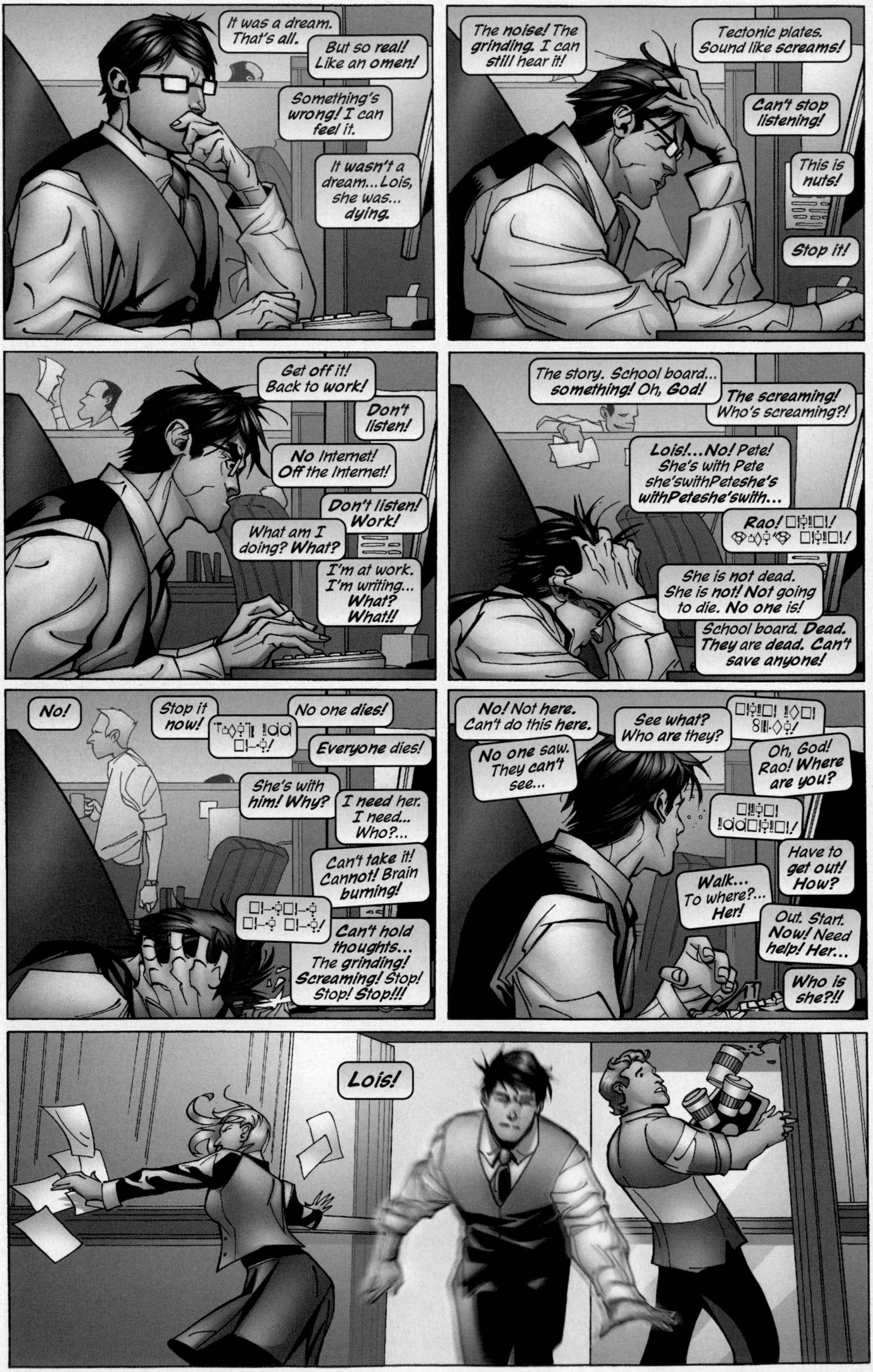

It was a dream. That's all.
But so real! Like an omen!
Something's wrong! I can feel it.
It wasn't a dream...Lois, she was... dying.
The noise! The grinding. I can still hear it!
Tectonic plates. Sound like screams!
Can't stop listening!
This is nuts!
Stop it!
Get off it! Back to work!
Don't listen!
No Internet! Off the Internet!
Don't listen! Work!
What am I doing? What?
I'm at work. I'm writing... What? What!!
The story. School board... something! Oh, God!
The screaming! Who's screaming?!
Lois!...No! Pete! She's with Pete she'swithPeteshe's withPeteshe'swith...
Rao!
She is not dead. She is not! Not going to die. No one is!
School board. Dead. They are dead. Can't save anyone!
No!
Stop it now!
No one dies!
Everyone dies!
She's with him! Why?
I need her. I need... Who?...
Can't take it! Cannot! Brain burning!
Can't hold thoughts... The grinding! Screaming! Stop! Stop! Stop!!!
No! Not here. Can't do this here.
See what? Who are they?
No one saw. They can't see...
Oh, God! Rao! Where are you?
Have to get out! How?
Walk... To where?... Her!
Out. Start. Now! Need help! Her...
Who is she?!!
Lois!

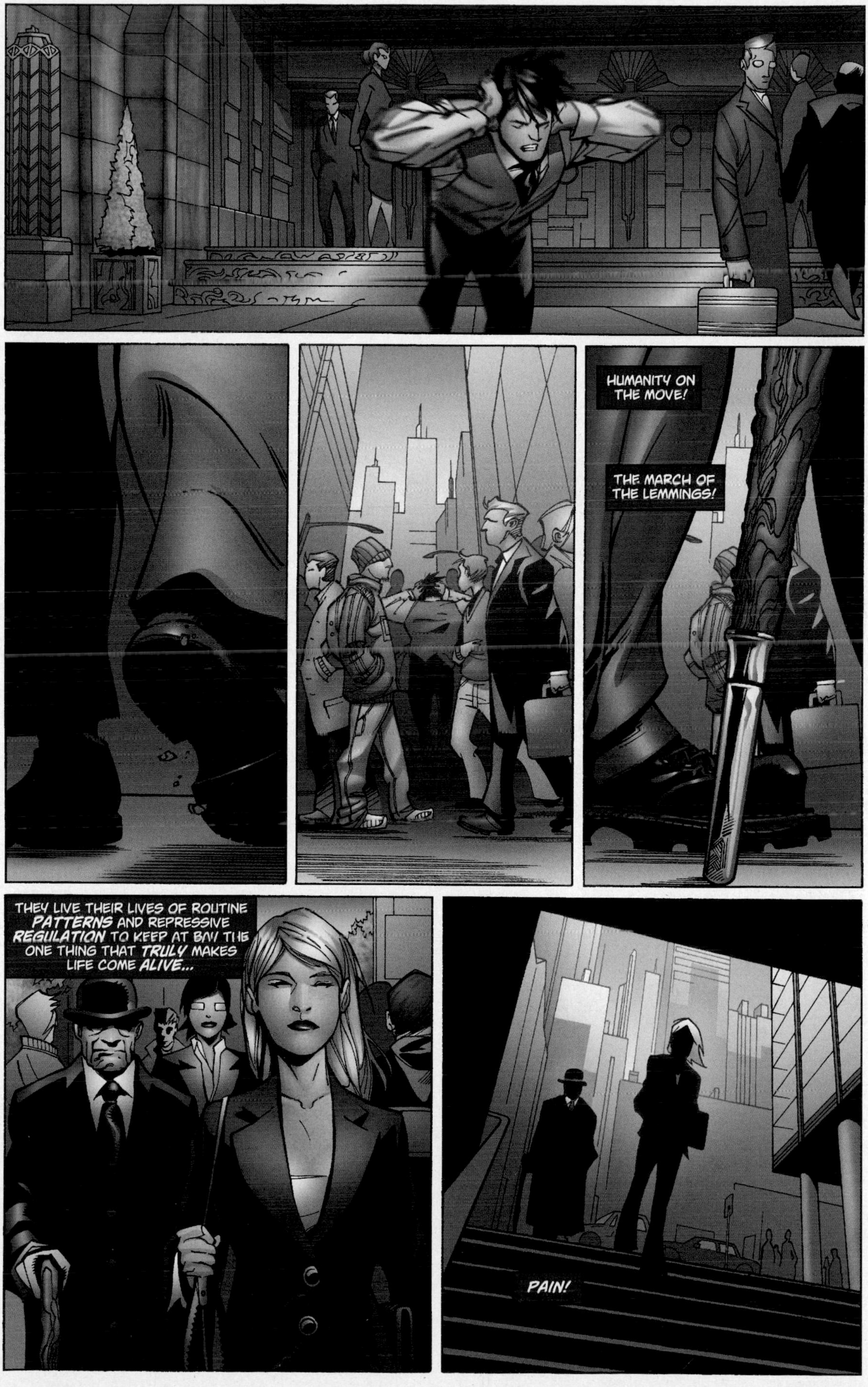
HUMANITY ON THE MOVE!
THE MARCH OF THE LEMMINGS!
THEY LIVE THEIR LIVES OF ROUTINE *PATTERNS* AND REPRESSIVE *REGULATION* TO KEEP AT BAY THE ONE THING THAT *TRULY* MAKES LIFE COME *ALIVE*...
PAIN!

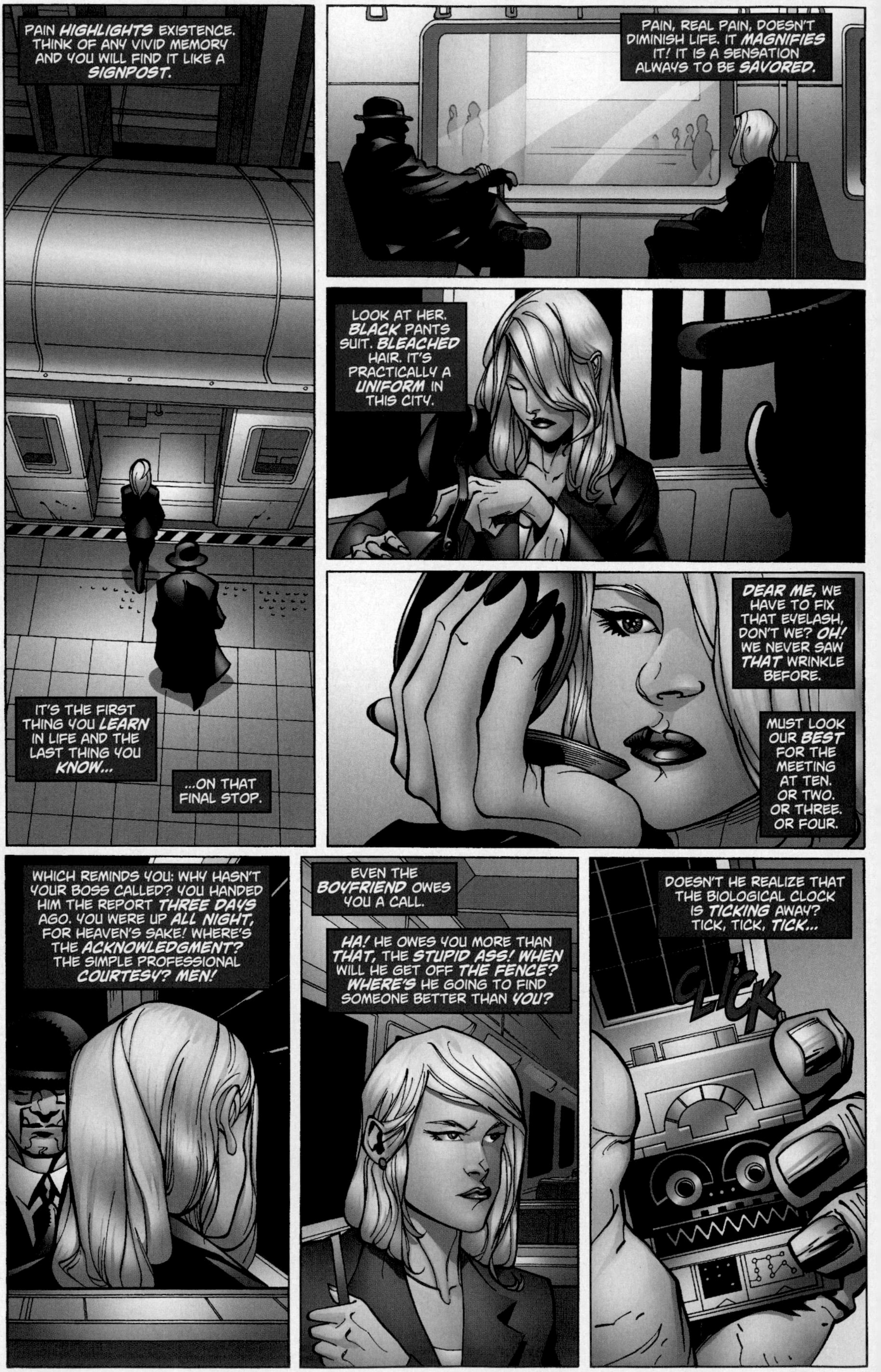
PAIN HIGHLIGHTS EXISTENCE. THINK OF ANY VIVID MEMORY AND YOU WILL FIND IT LIKE A SIGNPOST.
IT'S THE FIRST THING YOU LEARN IN LIFE AND THE LAST THING YOU KNOW...
...ON THAT FINAL STOP.
PAIN, REAL PAIN, DOESN'T DIMINISH LIFE. IT MAGNIFIES IT! IT IS A SENSATION ALWAYS TO BE SAVORED.
LOOK AT HER. BLACK PANTS SUIT. BLEACHED HAIR. IT'S PRACTICALLY A UNIFORM IN THIS CITY.
DEAR ME, WE HAVE TO FIX THAT EYELASH, DON'T WE? OH! WE NEVER SAW THAT WRINKLE BEFORE.
MUST LOOK OUR BEST FOR THE MEETING AT TEN. OR TWO. OR THREE. OR FOUR.
WHICH REMINDS YOU: WHY HASN'T YOUR BOSS CALLED? YOU HANDED HIM THE REPORT THREE DAYS AGO. YOU WERE UP ALL NIGHT, FOR HEAVEN'S SAKE! WHERE'S THE ACKNOWLEDGMENT? THE SIMPLE PROFESSIONAL COURTESY? MEN!
EVEN THE BOYFRIEND OWES YOU A CALL.
HA! HE OWES YOU MORE THAN THAT, THE STUPID ASS! WHEN WILL HE GET OFF THE FENCE? WHERE'S HE GOING TO FIND SOMEONE BETTER THAN YOU?
DOESN'T HE REALIZE THAT THE BIOLOGICAL CLOCK IS TICKING AWAY? TICK, TICK, TICK...
CLICK

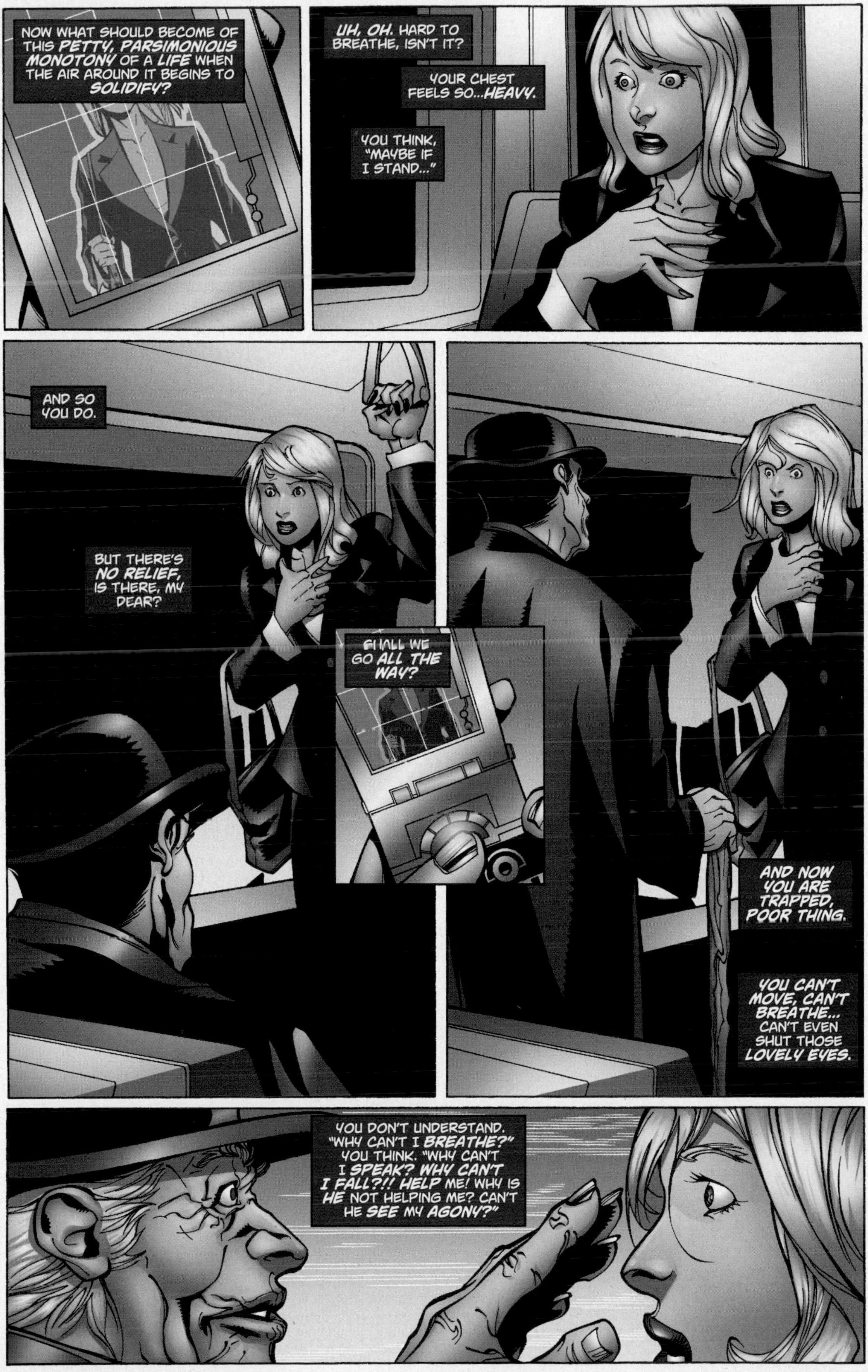

NOW WHAT SHOULD BECOME OF THIS PETTY, PARSIMONIOUS MONOTONY OF A LIFE WHEN THE AIR AROUND IT BEGINS TO SOLIDIFY?
UH, OH. HARD TO BREATHE, ISN'T IT?
YOUR CHEST FEELS SO...HEAVY.
YOU THINK, "MAYBE IF I STAND..."
AND SO YOU DO.
BUT THERE'S NO RELIEF, IS THERE, MY DEAR?
SHALL WE GO ALL THE WAY?
AND NOW YOU ARE TRAPPED, POOR THING.
YOU CAN'T MOVE, CAN'T BREATHE... CAN'T EVEN SHUT THOSE LOVELY EYES.
YOU DON'T UNDERSTAND. "WHY CAN'T I BREATHE?" YOU THINK. "WHY CAN'T I SPEAK? WHY CAN'T I FALL?!! HELP ME! WHY IS HE NOT HELPING ME? CAN'T HE SEE MY AGONY?"

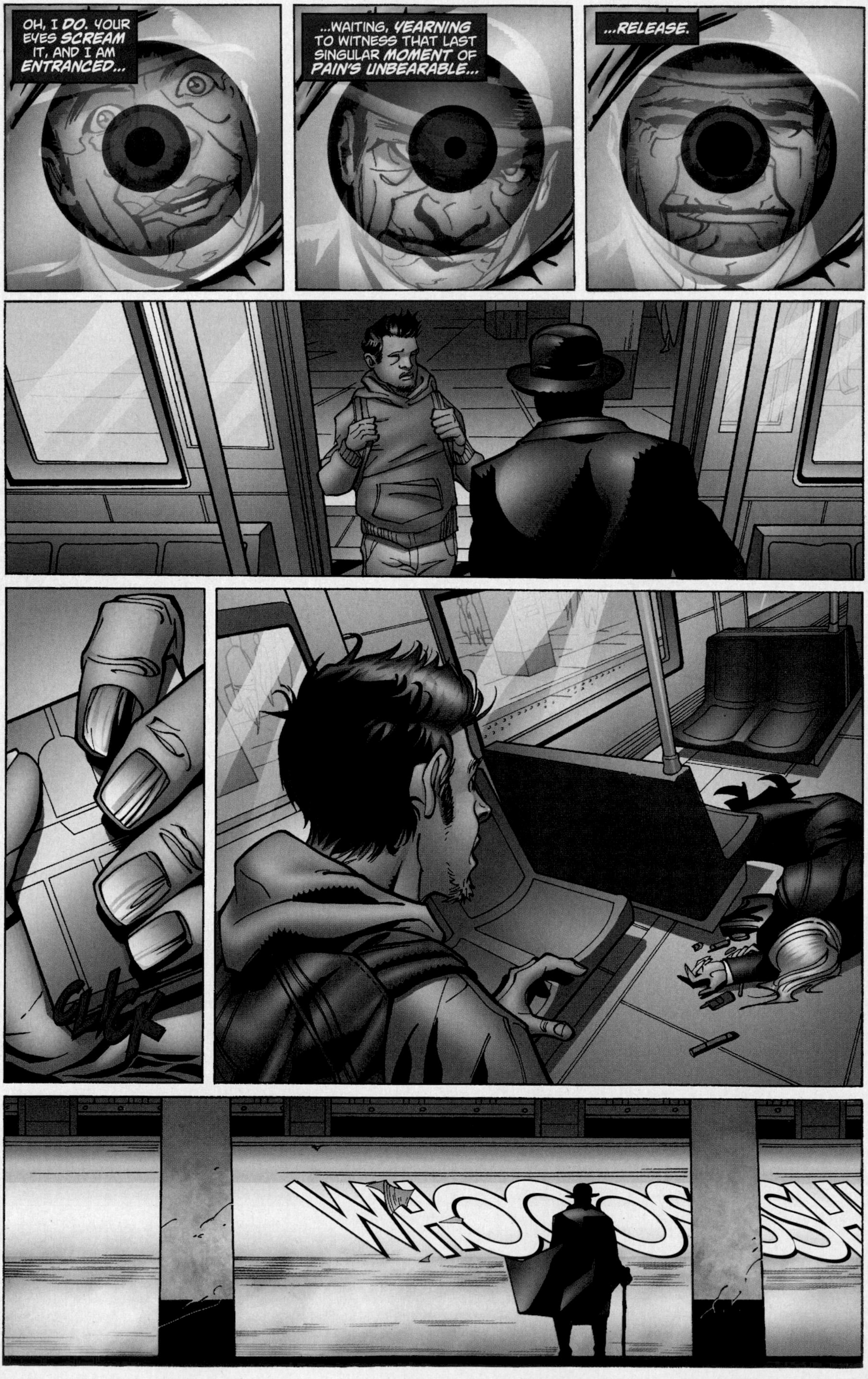
OH, I *DO*. YOUR EYES *SCREAM* IT, AND I AM *ENTRANCED...*
...WAITING, *YEARNING* TO WITNESS THAT LAST SINGULAR *MOMENT* OF *PAIN'S UNBEARABLE...*
...RELEASE.
CLICK
WHOOOSSH

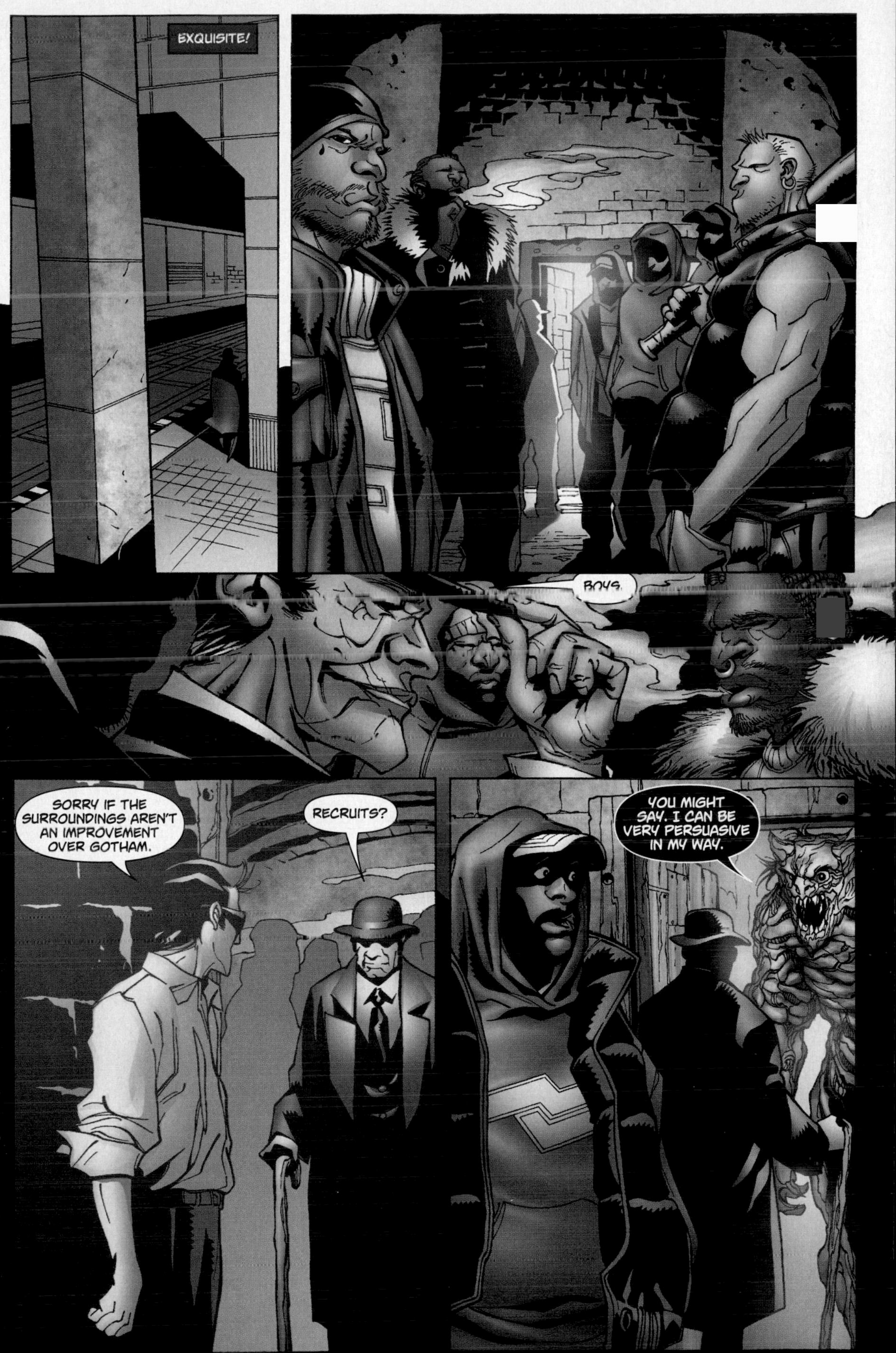
EXQUISITE!
BOYS.
SORRY IF THE SURROUNDINGS AREN'T AN IMPROVEMENT OVER GOTHAM.
RECRUITS?
YOU MIGHT SAY. I CAN BE VERY PERSUASIVE IN MY WAY.

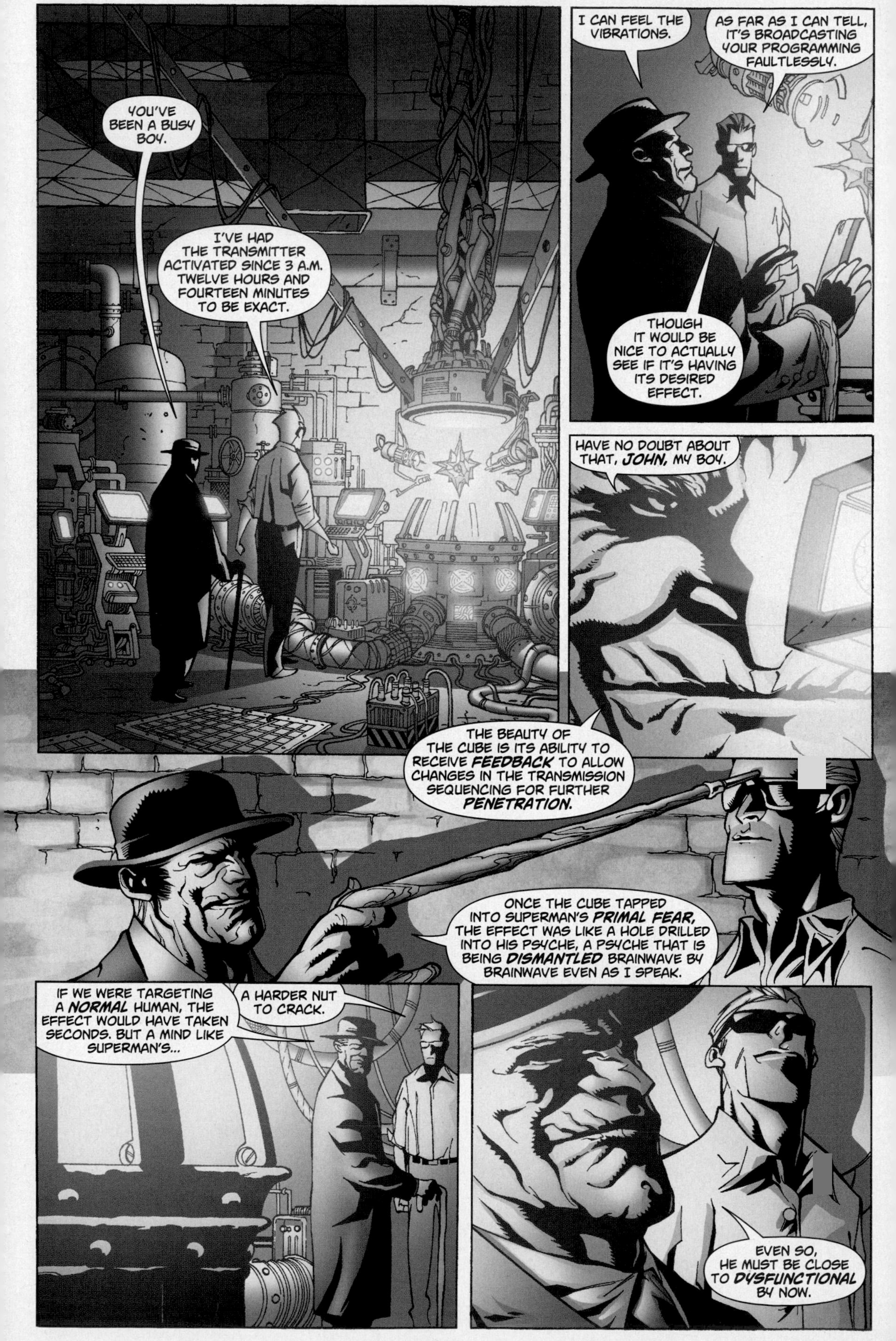
YOU'VE BEEN A BUSY BOY.
I'VE HAD THE TRANSMITTER ACTIVATED SINCE 3 A.M. TWELVE HOURS AND FOURTEEN MINUTES TO BE EXACT.
I CAN FEEL THE VIBRATIONS.
AS FAR AS I CAN TELL, IT'S BROADCASTING YOUR PROGRAMMING FAULTLESSLY.
THOUGH IT WOULD BE NICE TO ACTUALLY SEE IF IT'S HAVING ITS DESIRED EFFECT.
HAVE NO DOUBT ABOUT THAT, JOHN, MY BOY.
THE BEAUTY OF THE CUBE IS ITS ABILITY TO RECEIVE FEEDBACK TO ALLOW CHANGES IN THE TRANSMISSION SEQUENCING FOR FURTHER PENETRATION.
ONCE THE CUBE TAPPED INTO SUPERMAN'S PRIMAL FEAR, THE EFFECT WAS LIKE A HOLE DRILLED INTO HIS PSYCHE, A PSYCHE THAT IS BEING DISMANTLED BRAINWAVE BY BRAINWAVE EVEN AS I SPEAK.
IF WE WERE TARGETING A NORMAL HUMAN, THE EFFECT WOULD HAVE TAKEN SECONDS. BUT A MIND LIKE SUPERMAN'S...
A HARDER NUT TO CRACK.
EVEN SO, HE MUST BE CLOSE TO DYSFUNCTIONAL BY NOW.

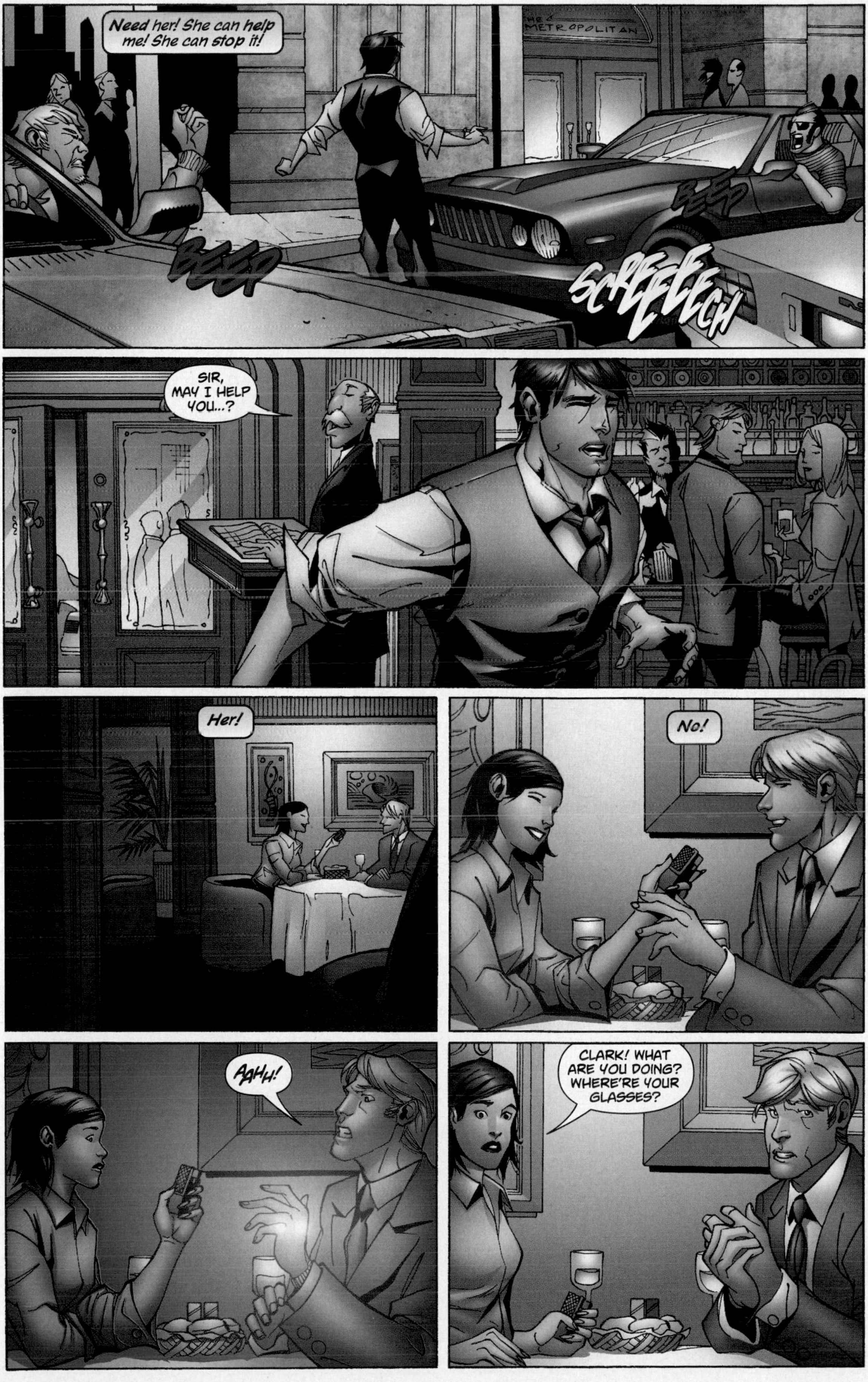
Need her! She can help me! She can stop it!
METROPOLITAN
BEEP
BEEP
SCREEEECH
SIR, MAY I HELP YOU...?
Her!
No!
AAHH!
CLARK! WHAT ARE YOU DOING? WHERE'RE YOUR GLASSES?

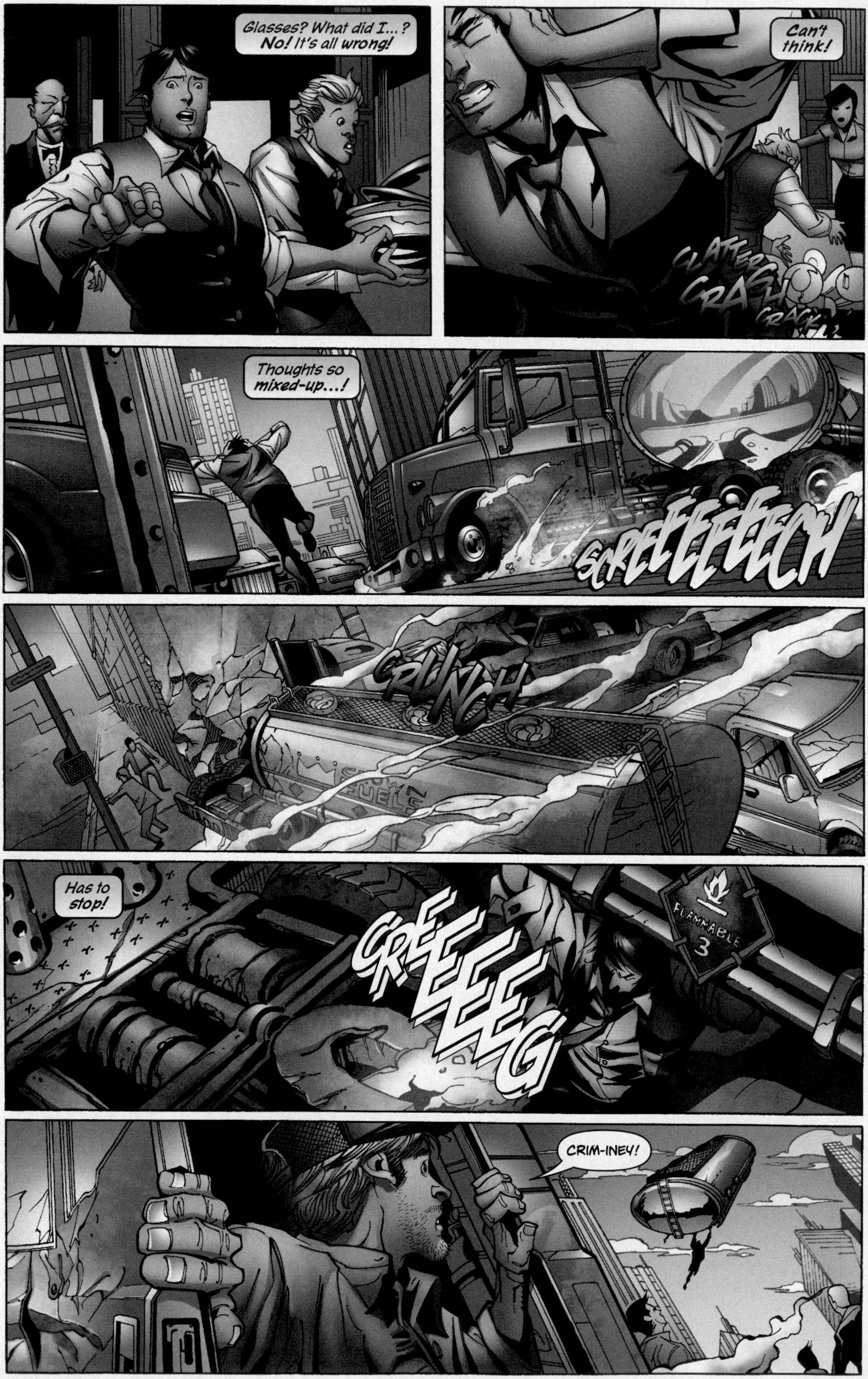
Glasses? What did I...? No! It's all wrong!
Can't think!
CLATTER
CRASH
CRACKLE
Thoughts so mixed-up...!
SCREEEEEECH
CRUNCH
Has to stop!
FLAMMABLE 3
CREEEEEG
CRIM-INEY!

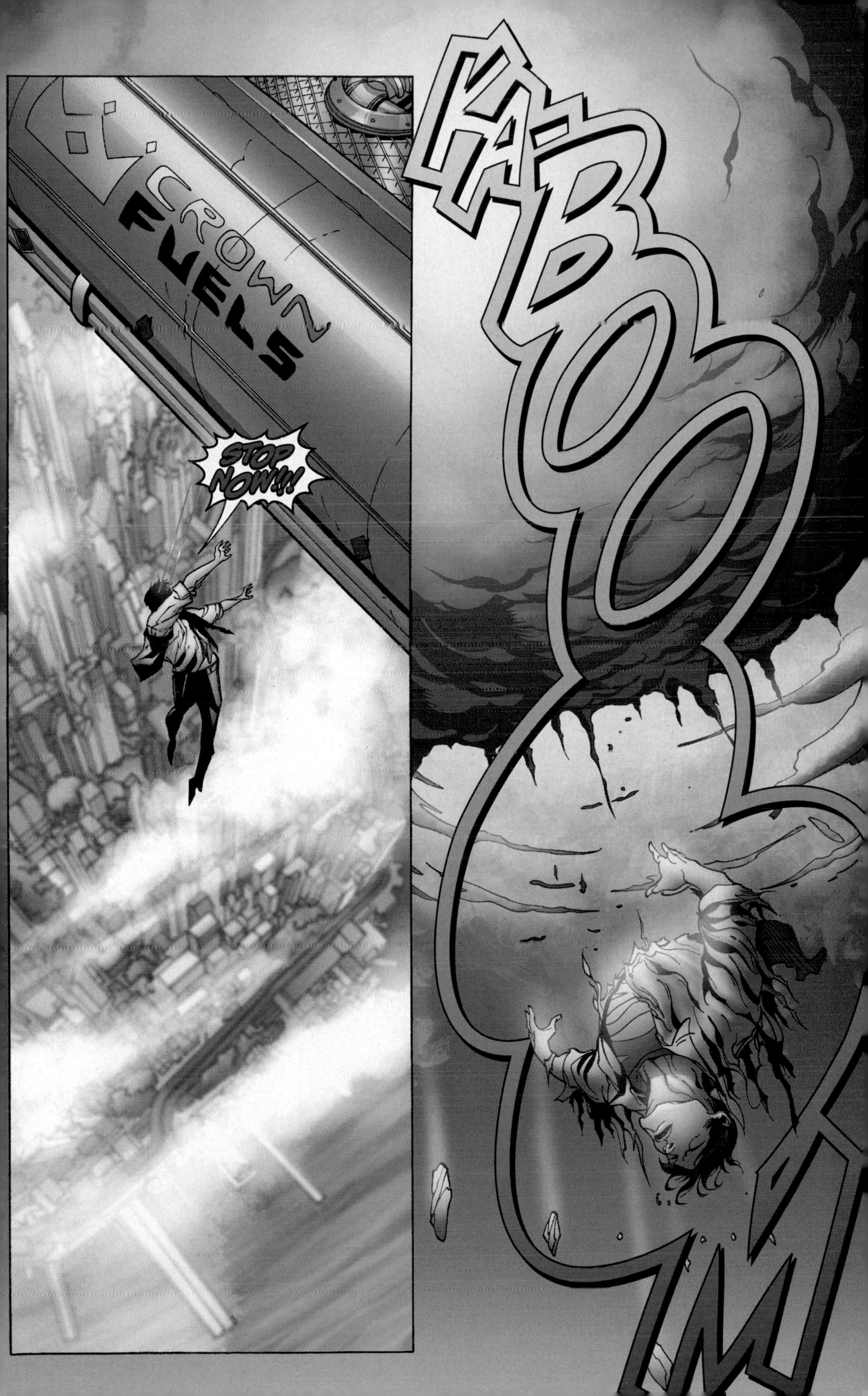
CROWN FUELS
STOP NOW!!!
KA-BOOOOM

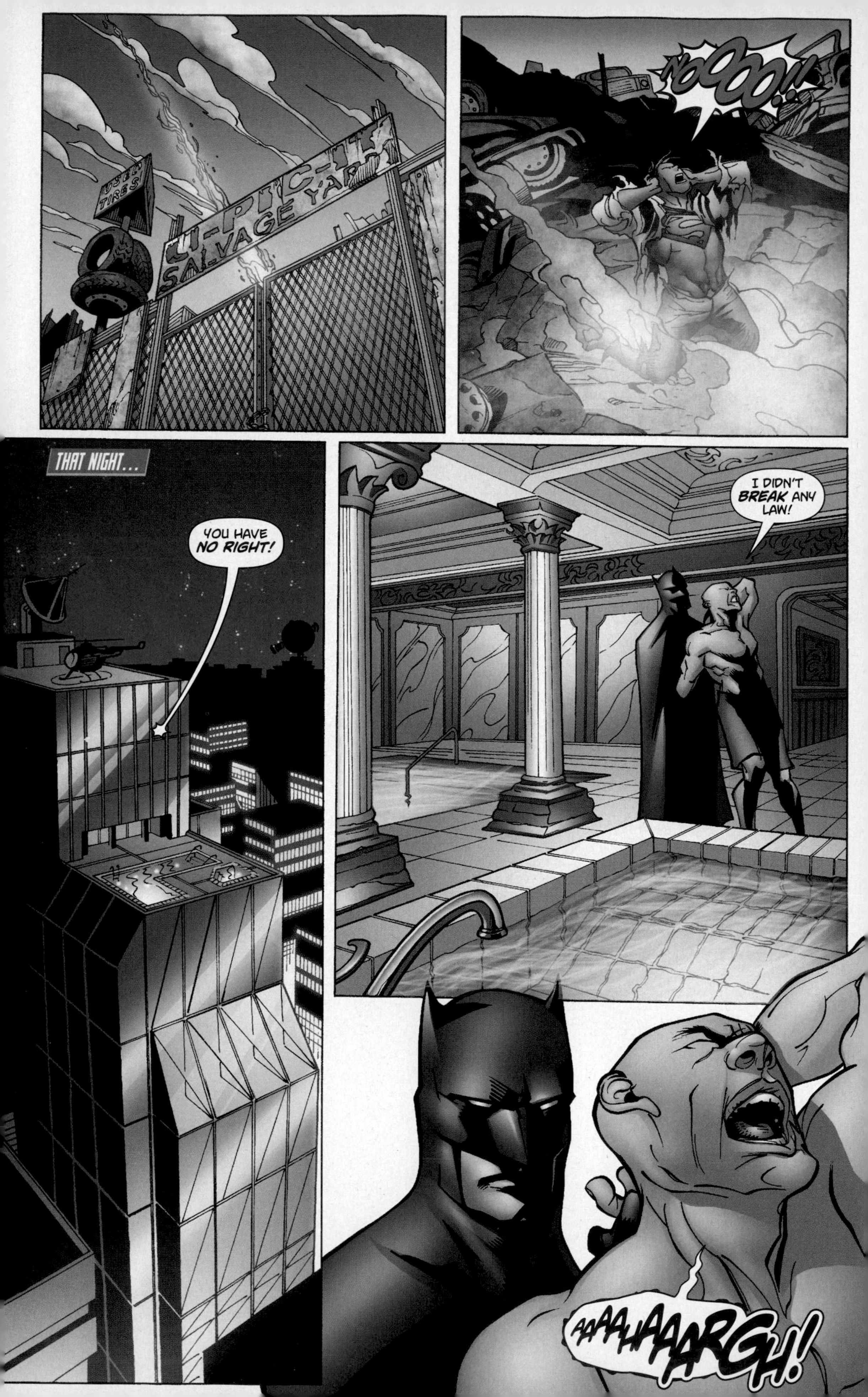
USED TIRES
U-PIC-IT
SALVAGE YAR
NOOOO!!
THAT NIGHT...
YOU HAVE NO RIGHT!
I DIDN'T BREAK ANY LAW!
AAAAHAAARGH!

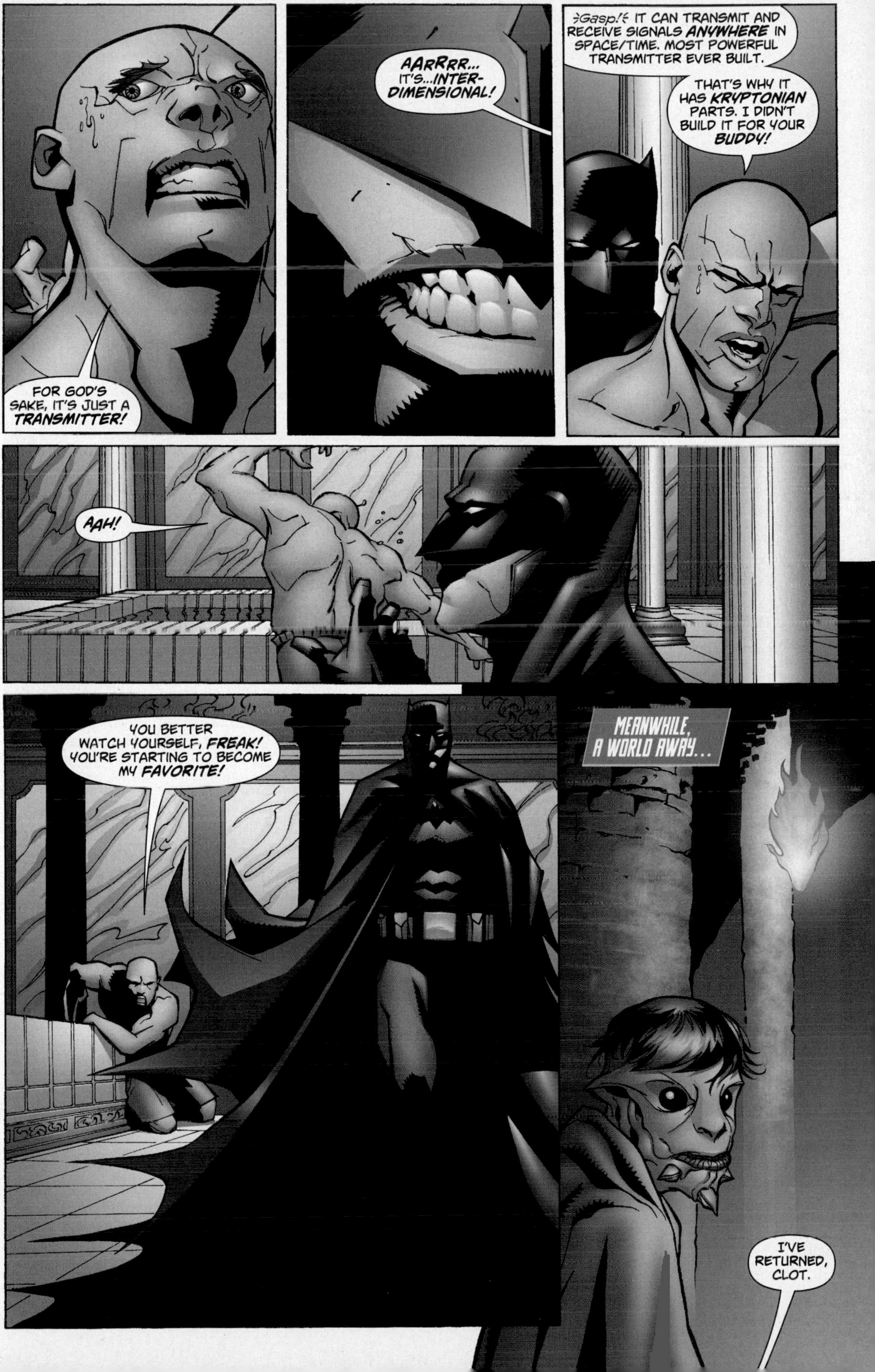
FOR GOD'S SAKE, IT'S JUST A TRANSMITTER!
AARRRR... IT'S...INTER-DIMENSIONAL!
Gasp! IT CAN TRANSMIT AND RECEIVE SIGNALS ANYWHERE IN SPACE/TIME. MOST POWERFUL TRANSMITTER EVER BUILT.
THAT'S WHY IT HAS KRYPTONIAN PARTS. I DIDN'T BUILD IT FOR YOUR BUDDY!
AAH!
YOU BETTER WATCH YOURSELF, FREAK! YOU'RE STARTING TO BECOME MY FAVORITE!
MEANWHILE, A WORLD AWAY...
I'VE RETURNED, CLOT.

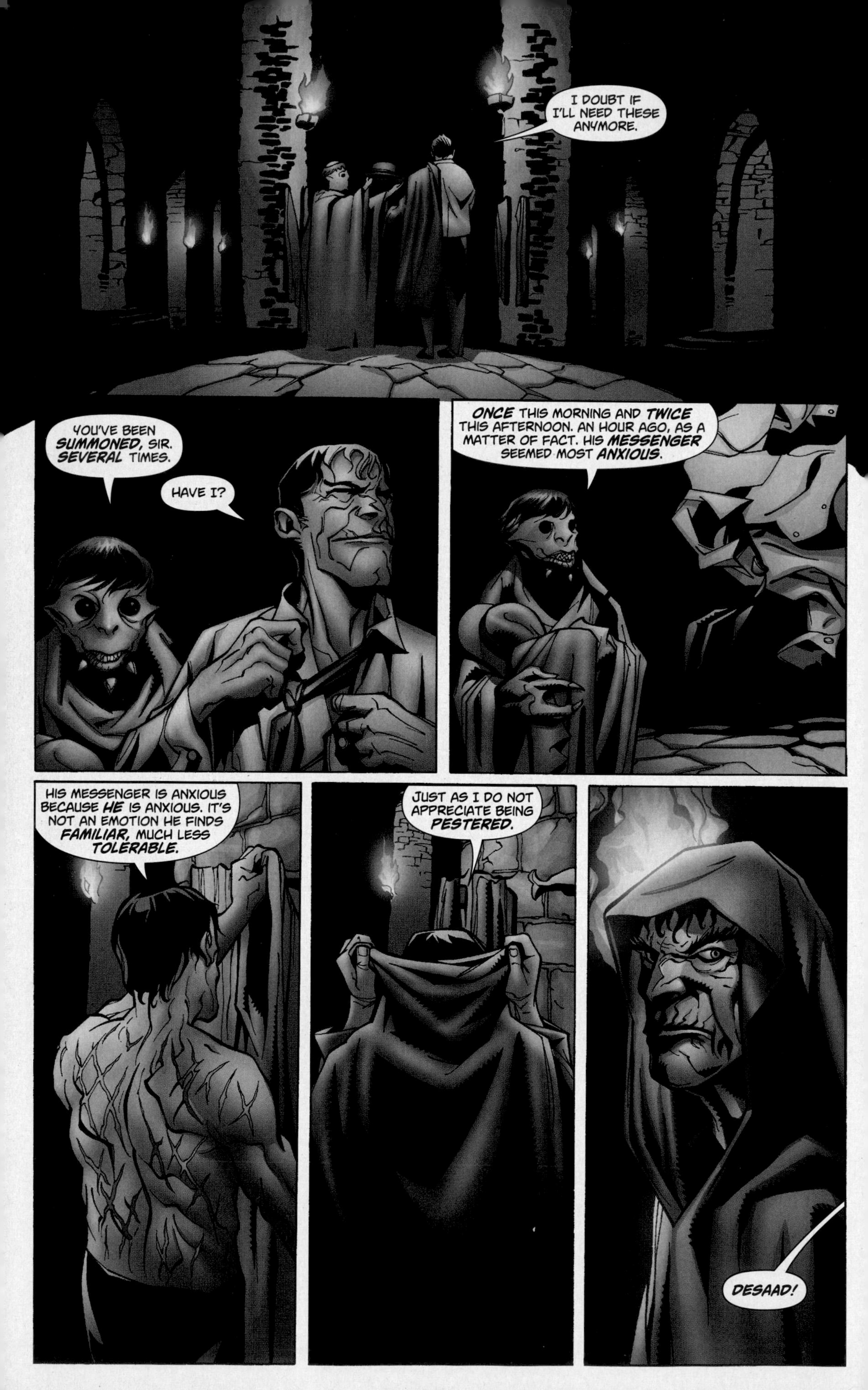
I DOUBT IF I'LL NEED THESE ANYMORE.
YOU'VE BEEN SUMMONED, SIR. SEVERAL TIMES.
HAVE I?
ONCE THIS MORNING AND TWICE THIS AFTERNOON. AN HOUR AGO, AS A MATTER OF FACT. HIS MESSENGER SEEMED MOST ANXIOUS.
HIS MESSENGER IS ANXIOUS BECAUSE HE IS ANXIOUS. IT'S NOT AN EMOTION HE FINDS FAMILIAR, MUCH LESS TOLERABLE.
JUST AS I DO NOT APPRECIATE BEING PESTERED.
DESAAD!

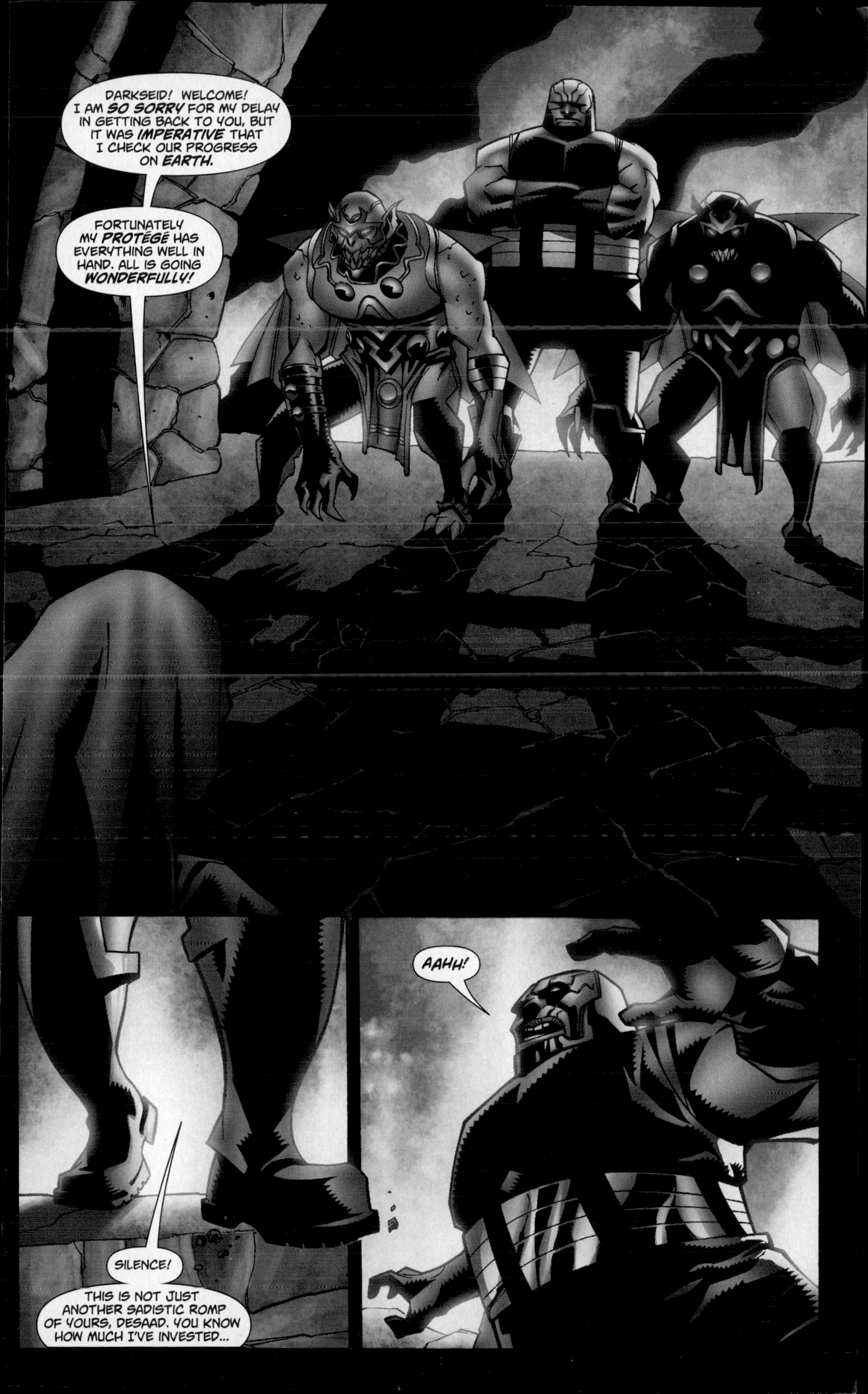
DARKSEID! WELCOME! I AM SO SORRY FOR MY DELAY IN GETTING BACK TO YOU, BUT IT WAS IMPERATIVE THAT I CHECK OUR PROGRESS ON EARTH.
FORTUNATELY MY PROTÉGÉ HAS EVERYTHING WELL IN HAND. ALL IS GOING WONDERFULLY!
SILENCE!
THIS IS NOT JUST ANOTHER SADISTIC ROMP OF YOURS, DESAAD. YOU KNOW HOW MUCH I'VE INVESTED...
AAHH!

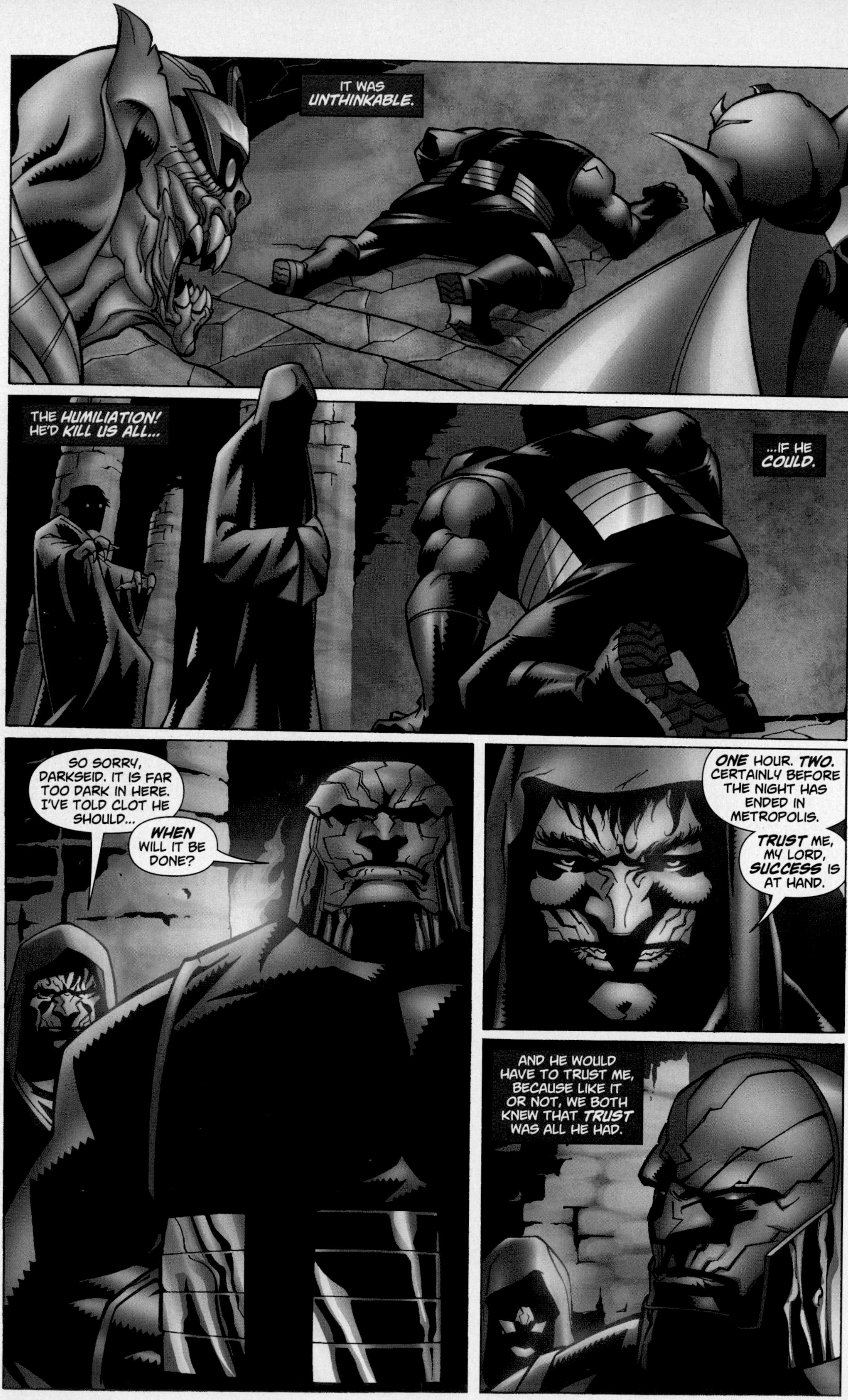

IT WAS UNTHINKABLE.
THE HUMILIATION! HE'D KILL US ALL...
...IF HE COULD.
SO SORRY, DARKSEID. IT IS FAR TOO DARK IN HERE. I'VE TOLD CLOT HE SHOULD...
WHEN WILL IT BE DONE?
ONE HOUR. TWO. CERTAINLY BEFORE THE NIGHT HAS ENDED IN METROPOLIS.
TRUST ME, MY LORD, SUCCESS IS AT HAND.
AND HE WOULD HAVE TO TRUST ME, BECAUSE LIKE IT OR NOT, WE BOTH KNEW THAT TRUST WAS ALL HE HAD.

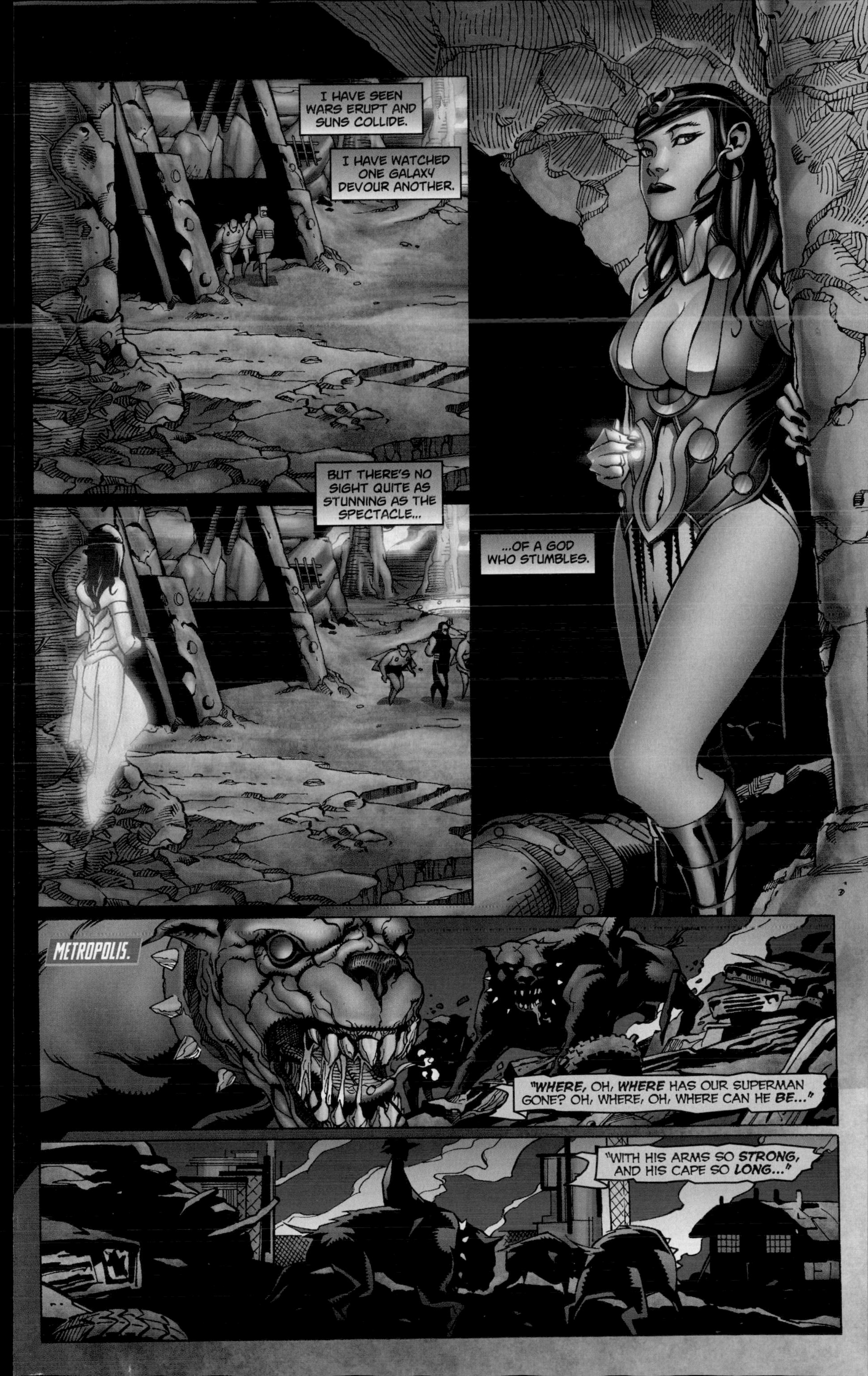

I HAVE SEEN WARS ERUPT AND SUNS COLLIDE.
I HAVE WATCHED ONE GALAXY DEVOUR ANOTHER.
BUT THERE'S NO SIGHT QUITE AS STUNNING AS THE SPECTACLE...
...OF A GOD WHO STUMBLES.
METROPOLIS.
"WHERE, OH, WHERE HAS OUR SUPERMAN GONE? OH, WHERE, OH, WHERE CAN HE BE..."
"WITH HIS ARMS SO STRONG, AND HIS CAPE SO LONG..."

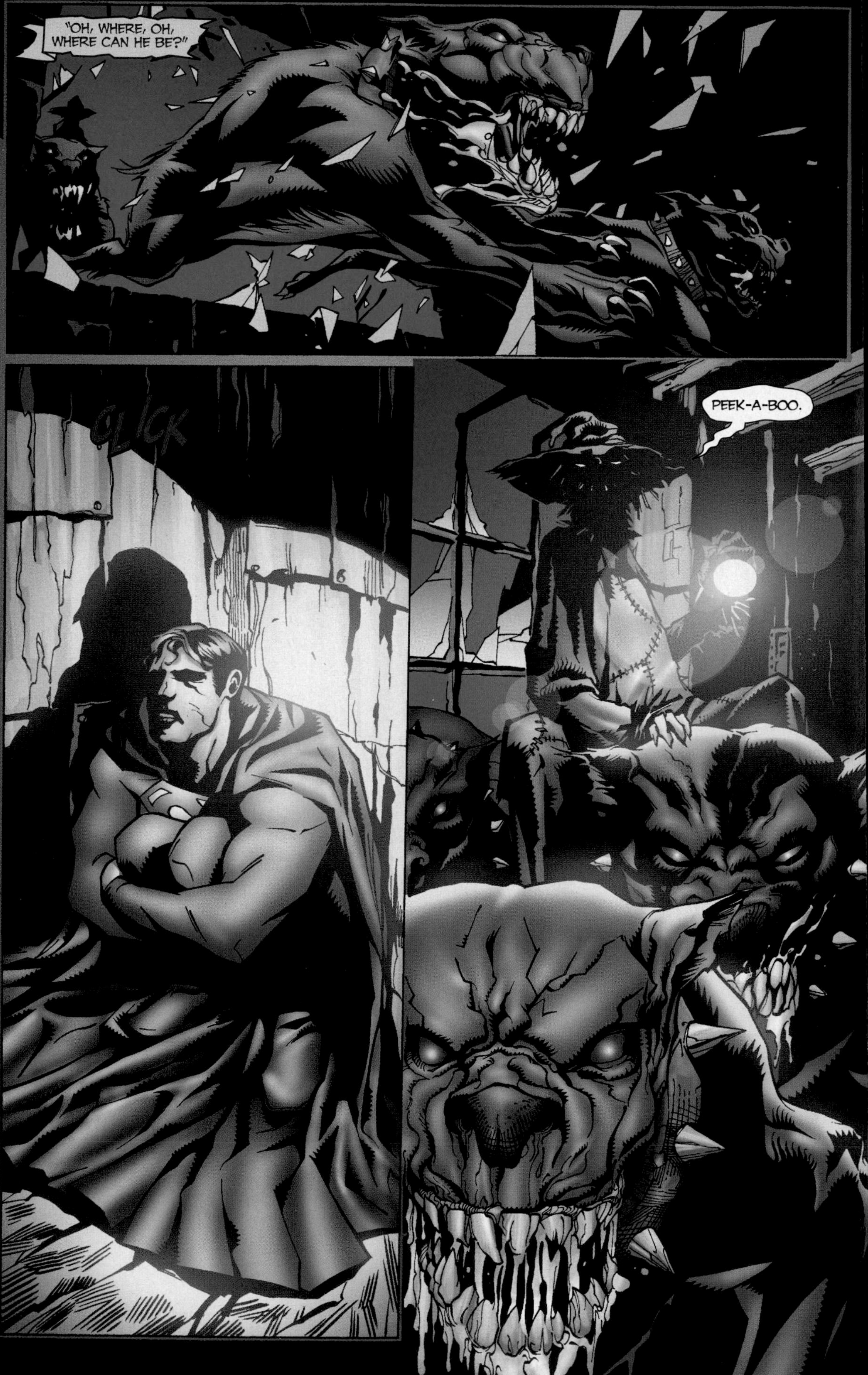
"OH, WHERE, OH, WHERE CAN HE BE?"
CLICK
PEEK-A-BOO.

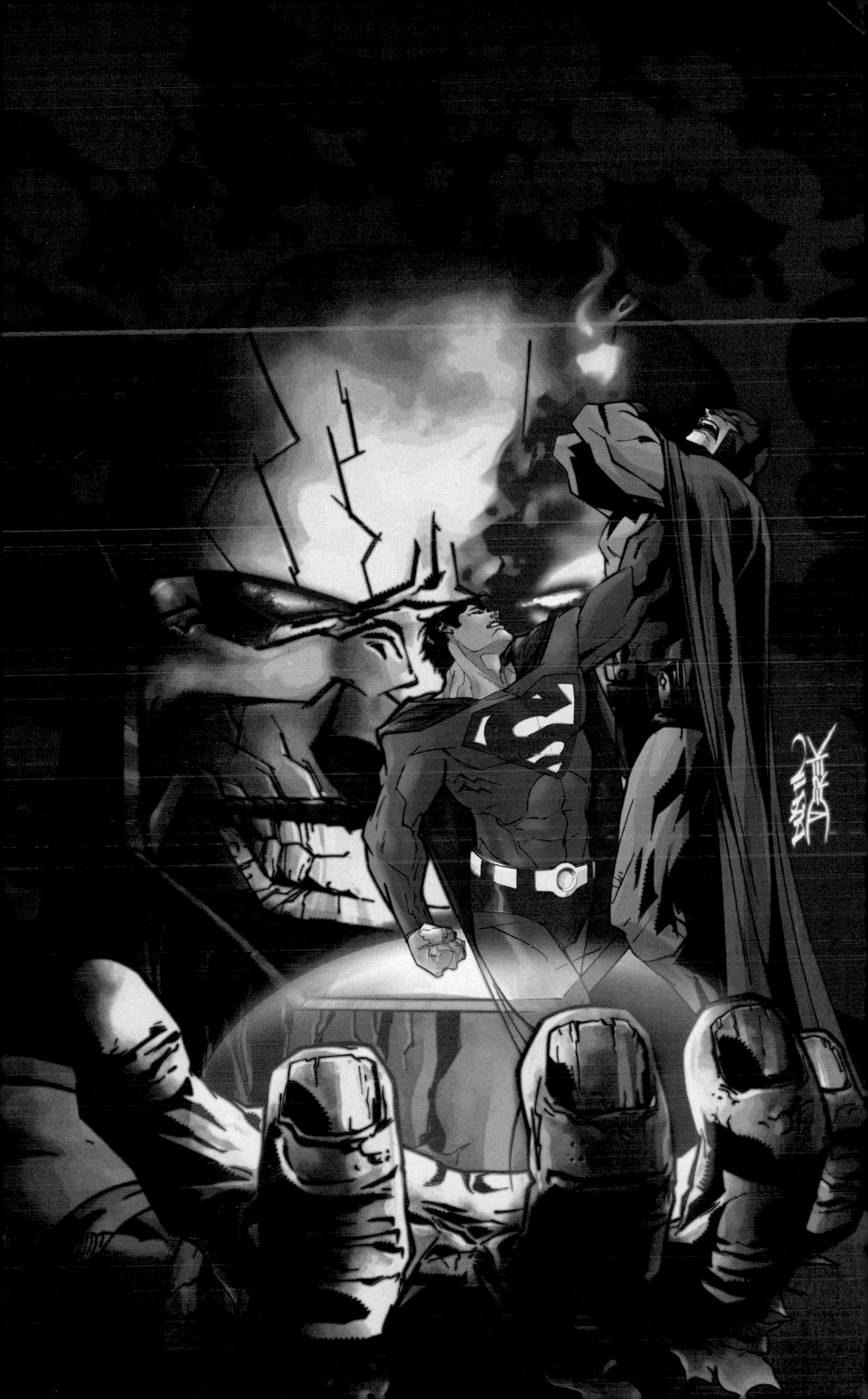

TORMENT: PART THREE
HELPLESS

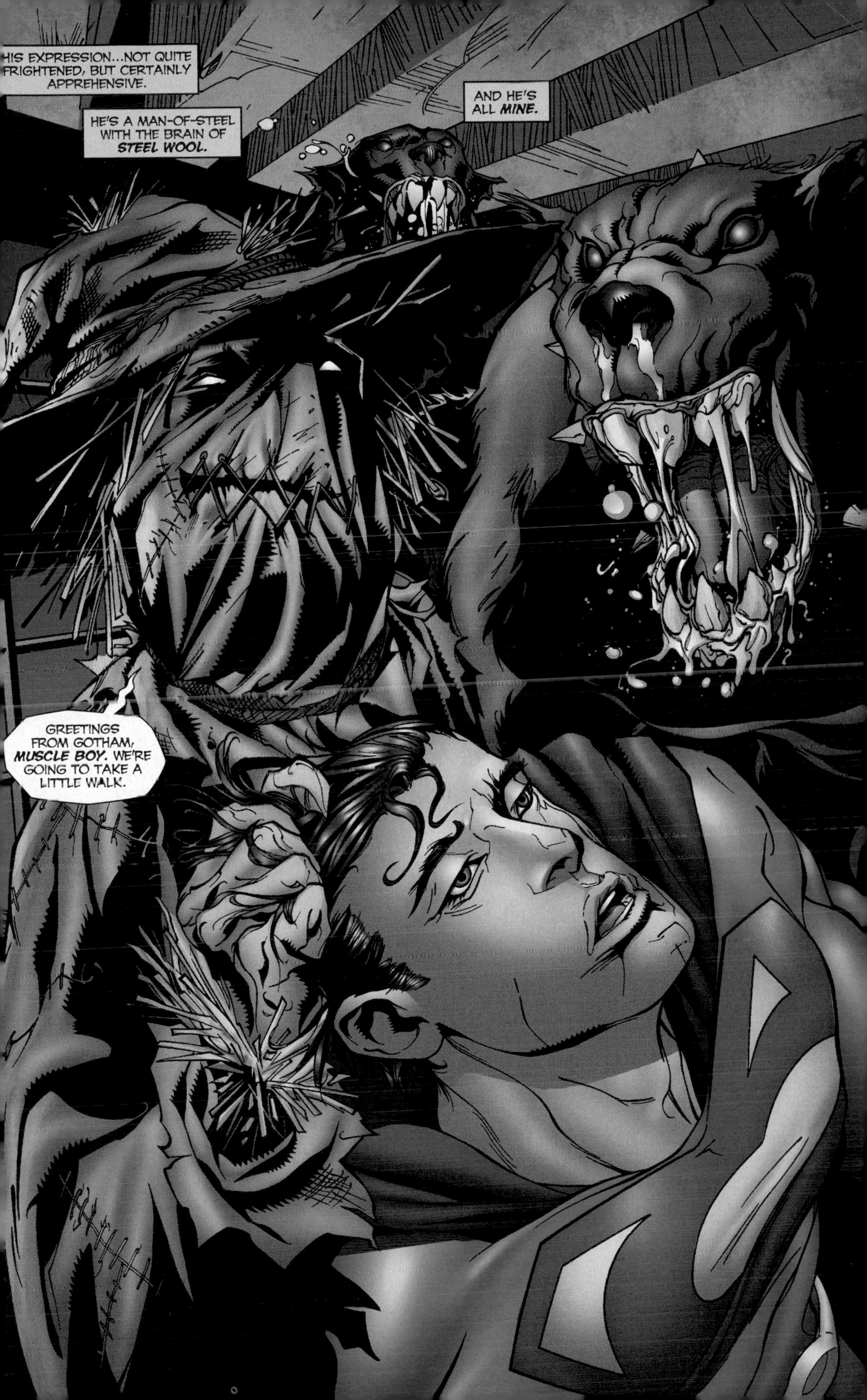
HIS EXPRESSION...NOT QUITE FRIGHTENED, BUT CERTAINLY APPREHENSIVE.
HE'S A MAN-OF-STEEL WITH THE BRAIN OF **STEEL WOOL.**
AND HE'S ALL **MINE.**
GREETINGS FROM GOTHAM, **MUSCLE BOY.** WE'RE GOING TO TAKE A LITTLE WALK.

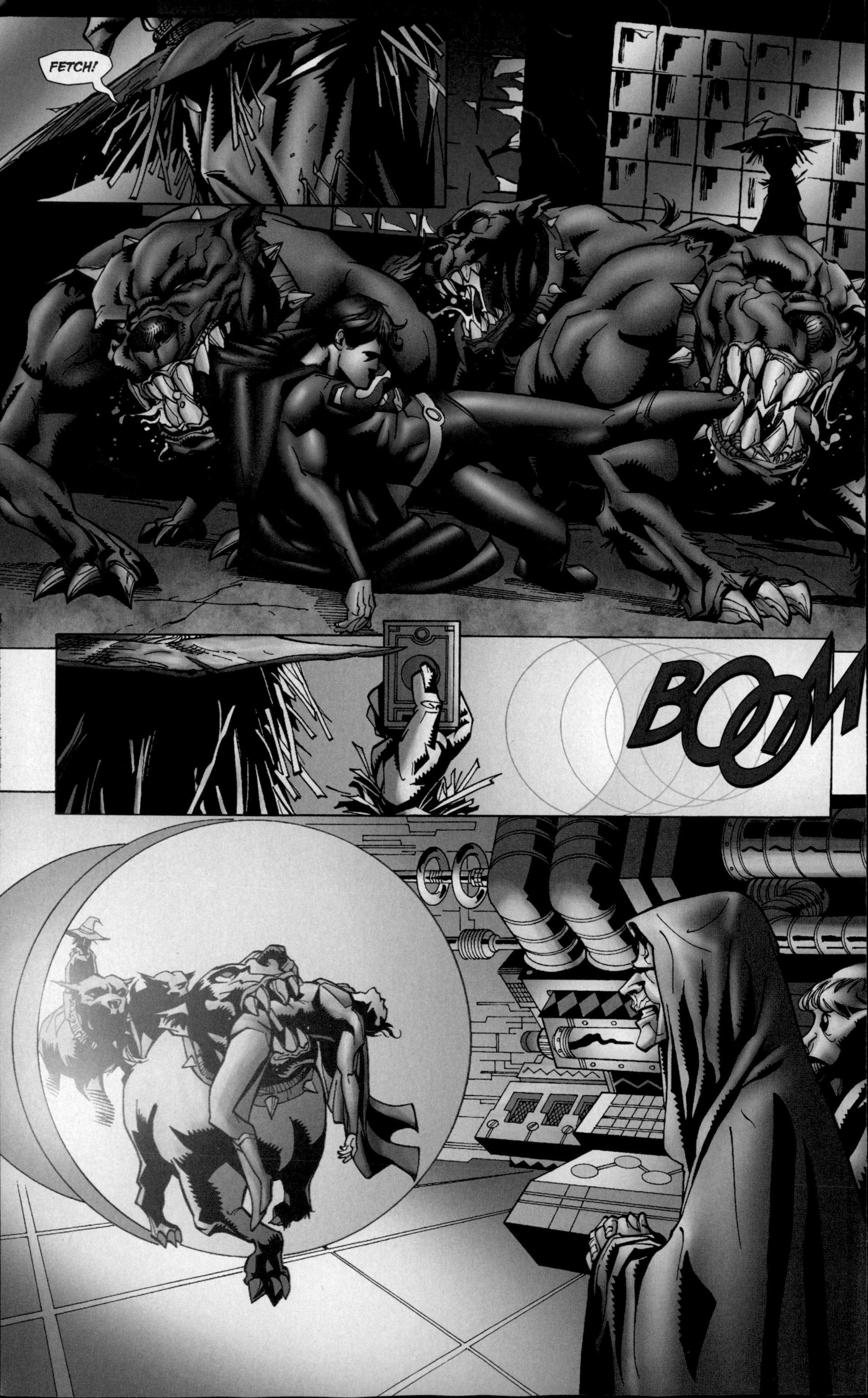
FETCH!
BOOM

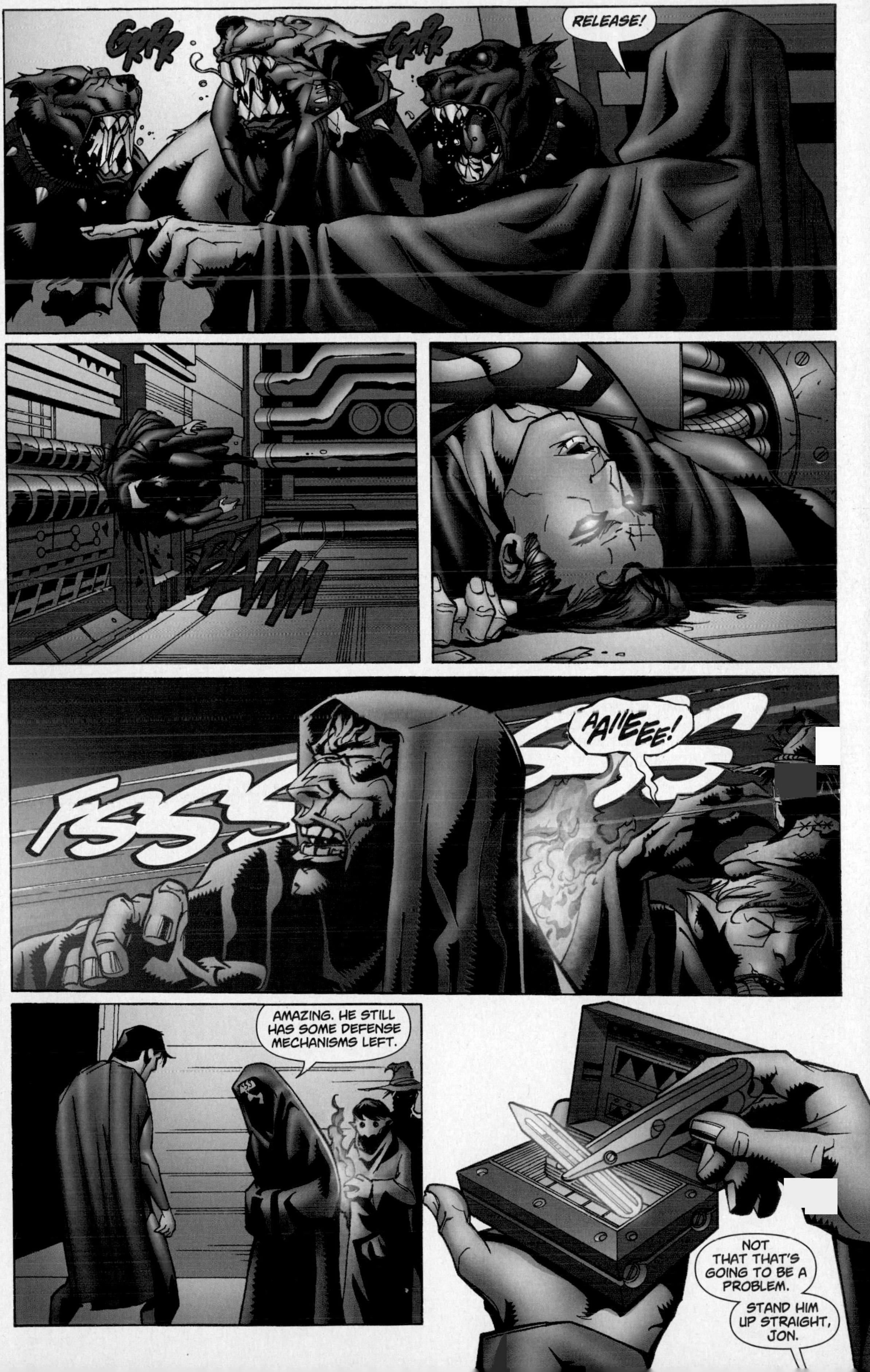
GRRR
GRRR
RELEASE!
BAMMM
FSSS
AAIIEEE!
AMAZING. HE STILL HAS SOME DEFENSE MECHANISMS LEFT.
NOT THAT THAT'S GOING TO BE A PROBLEM.
STAND HIM UP STRAIGHT, JON.

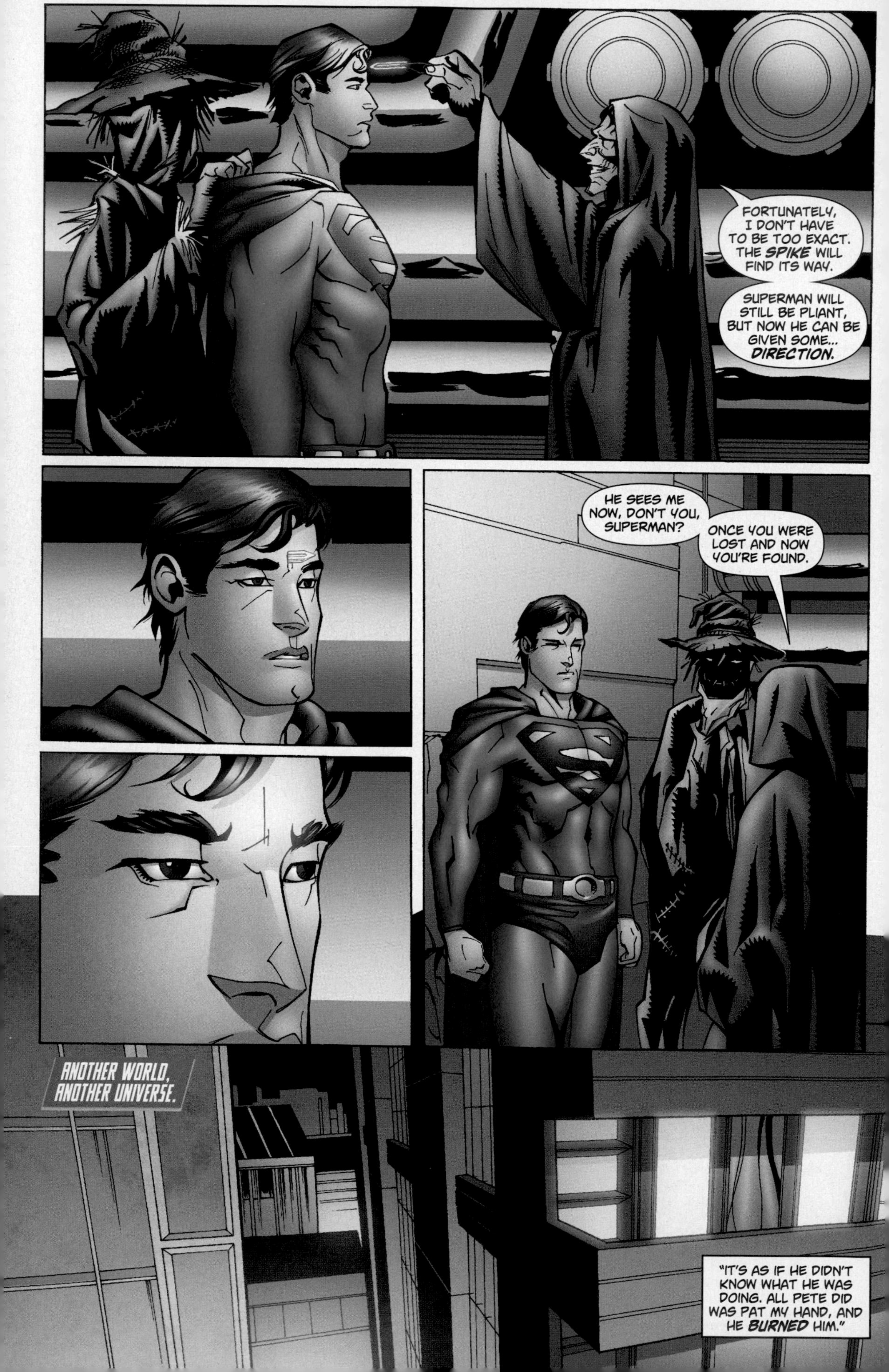
FORTUNATELY, I DON'T HAVE TO BE TOO EXACT. THE SPIKE WILL FIND ITS WAY.
SUPERMAN WILL STILL BE PLIANT, BUT NOW HE CAN BE GIVEN SOME... DIRECTION.
HE SEES ME NOW, DON'T YOU, SUPERMAN?
ONCE YOU WERE LOST AND NOW YOU'RE FOUND.
ANOTHER WORLD, ANOTHER UNIVERSE.
"IT'S AS IF HE DIDN'T KNOW WHAT HE WAS DOING. ALL PETE DID WAS PAT MY HAND, AND HE BURNED HIM."

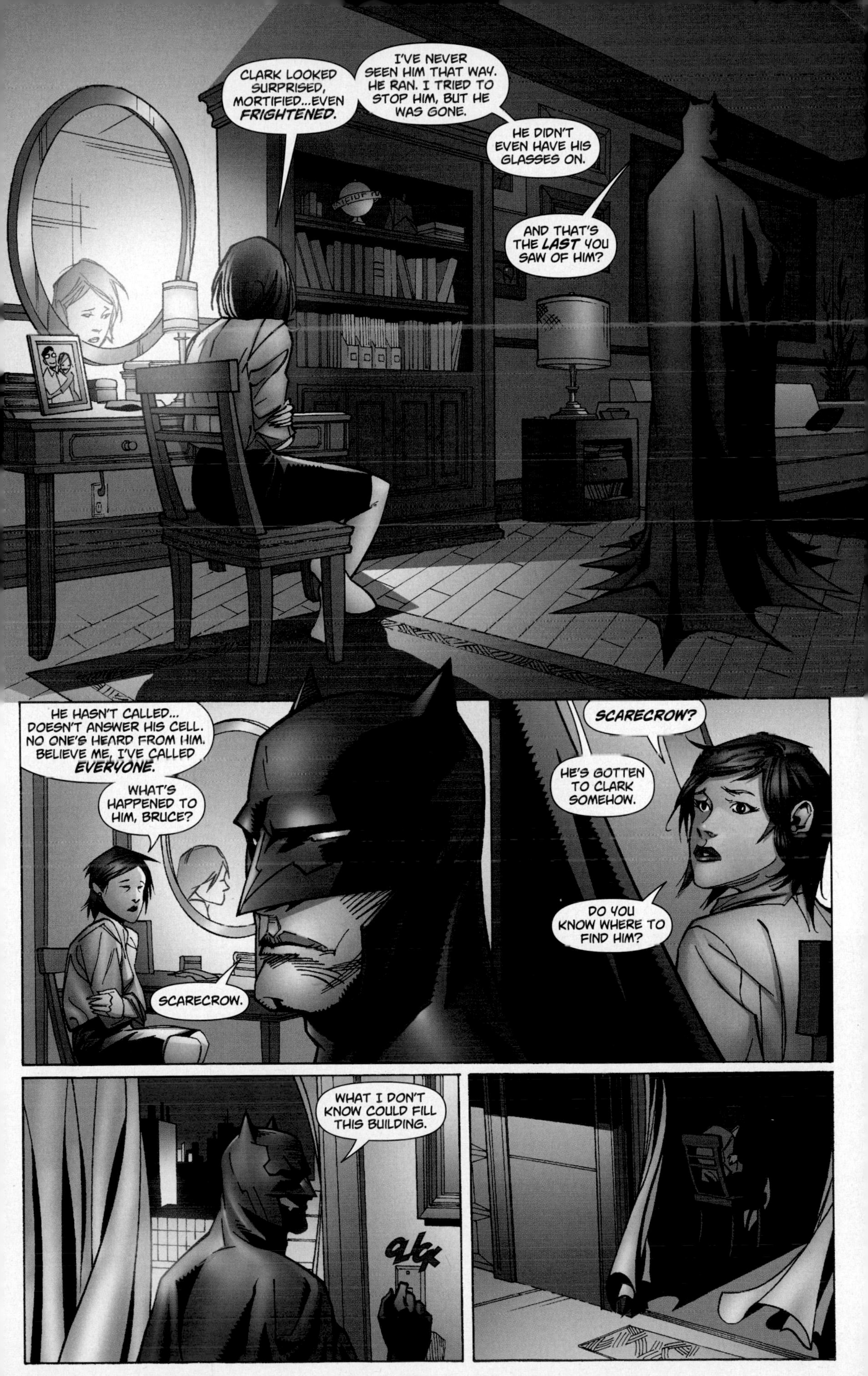
CLARK LOOKED SURPRISED, MORTIFIED...EVEN FRIGHTENED.
I'VE NEVER SEEN HIM THAT WAY. HE RAN. I TRIED TO STOP HIM, BUT HE WAS GONE.
HE DIDN'T EVEN HAVE HIS GLASSES ON.
AND THAT'S THE LAST YOU SAW OF HIM?
HE HASN'T CALLED... DOESN'T ANSWER HIS CELL. NO ONE'S HEARD FROM HIM. BELIEVE ME, I'VE CALLED EVERYONE.
WHAT'S HAPPENED TO HIM, BRUCE?
SCARECROW.
SCARECROW?
HE'S GOTTEN TO CLARK SOMEHOW.
DO YOU KNOW WHERE TO FIND HIM?
WHAT I DON'T KNOW COULD FILL THIS BUILDING.

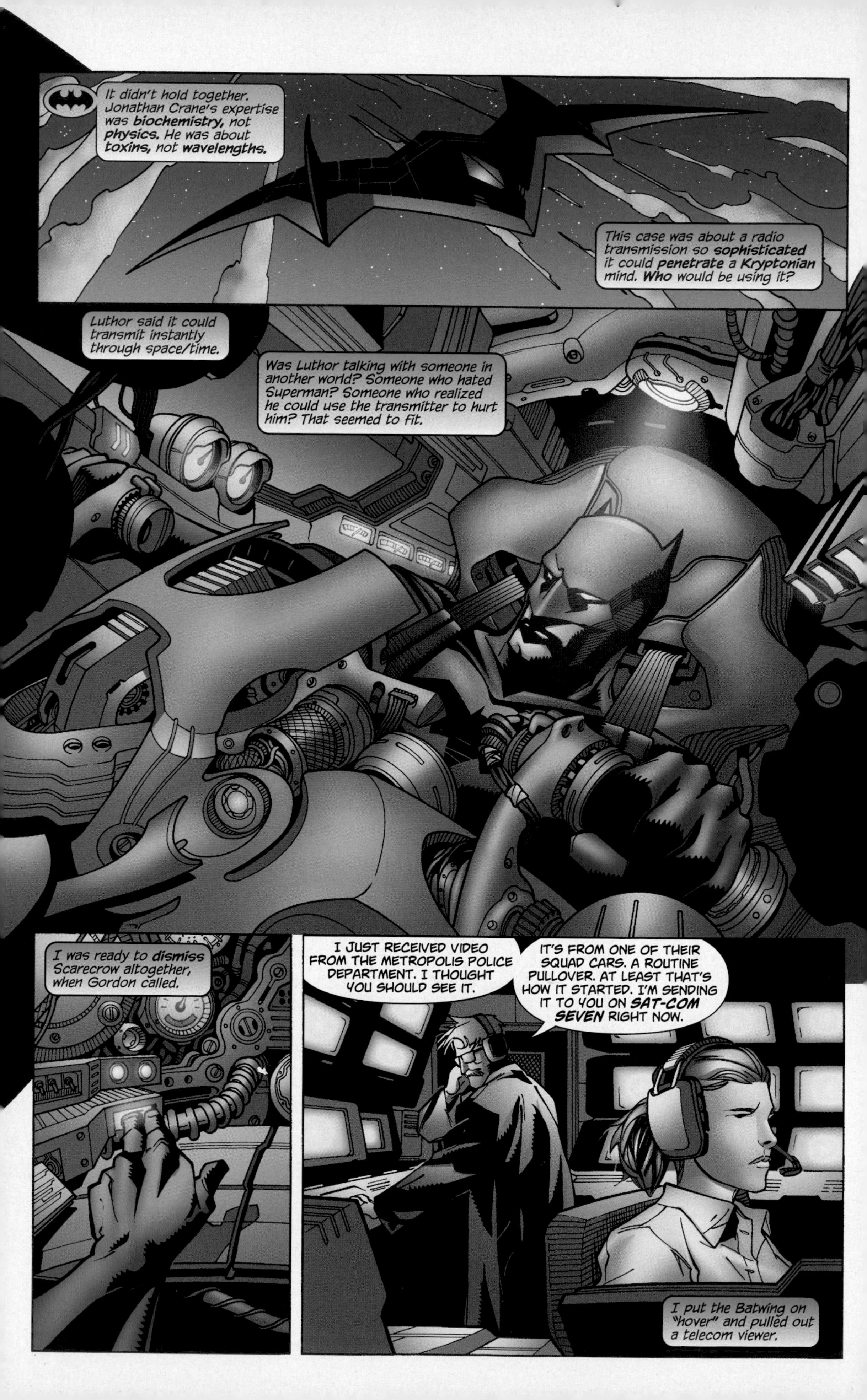
It didn't hold together. Jonathan Crane's expertise was biochemistry, not physics. He was about toxins, not wavelengths.
This case was about a radio transmission so sophisticated it could penetrate a Kryptonian mind. Who would be using it?
Luthor said it could transmit instantly through space/time.
Was Luthor talking with someone in another world? Someone who hated Superman? Someone who realized he could use the transmitter to hurt him? That seemed to fit.
I was ready to dismiss Scarecrow altogether, when Gordon called.
I JUST RECEIVED VIDEO FROM THE METROPOLIS POLICE DEPARTMENT. I THOUGHT YOU SHOULD SEE IT.
IT'S FROM ONE OF THEIR SQUAD CARS. A ROUTINE PULLOVER. AT LEAST THAT'S HOW IT STARTED. I'M SENDING IT TO YOU ON SAT-COM SEVEN RIGHT NOW.
I put the Batwing on "hover" and pulled out a telecom viewer.

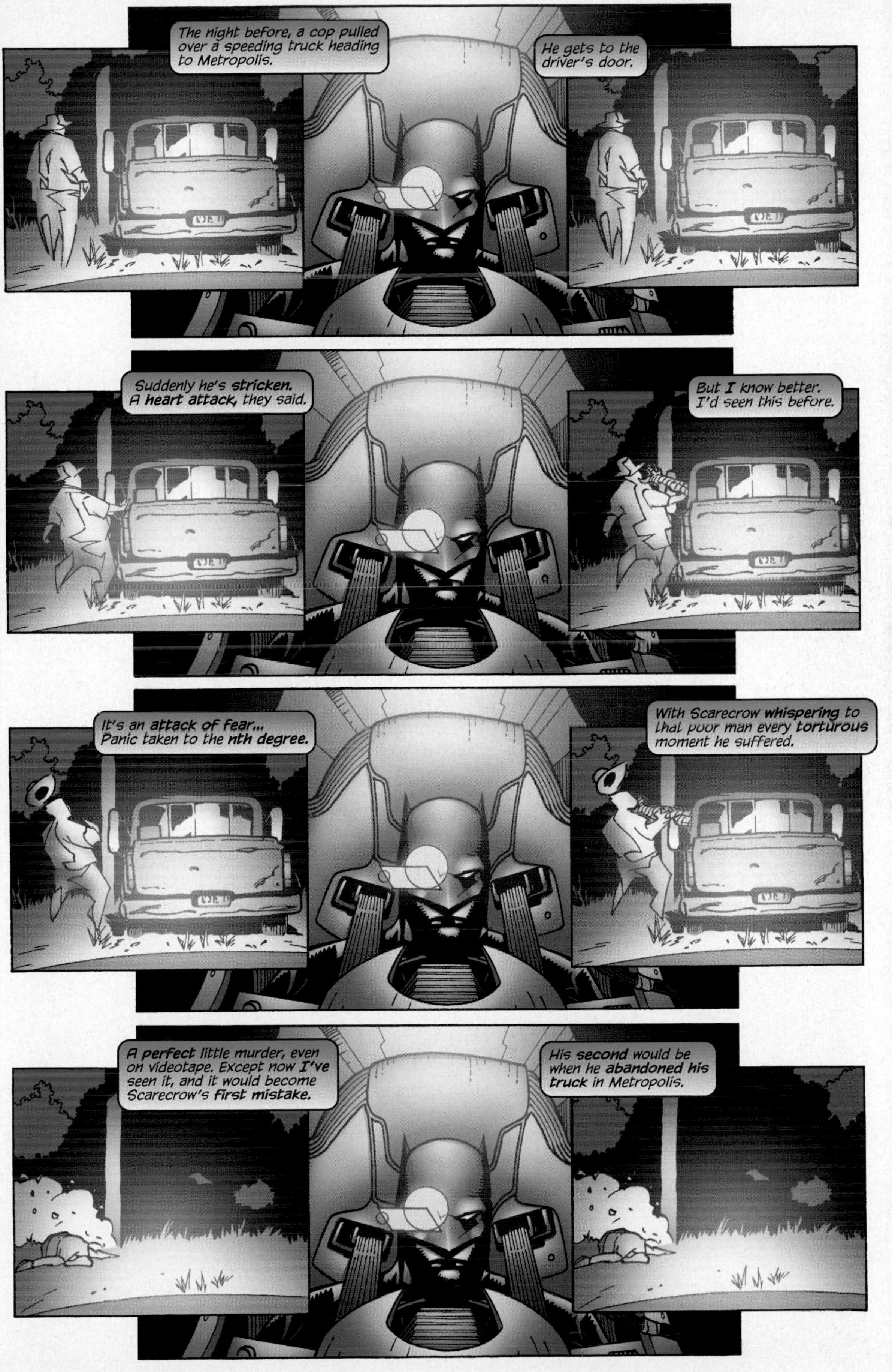
The night before, a cop pulled over a speeding truck heading to Metropolis.
He gets to the driver's door.
Suddenly he's stricken. A heart attack, they said.
But I know better. I'd seen this before.
It's an attack of fear... Panic taken to the nth degree.
With Scarecrow whispering to that poor man every torturous moment he suffered.
A perfect little murder, even on videotape. Except now I've seen it, and it would become Scarecrow's first mistake.
His second would be when he abandoned his truck in Metropolis.

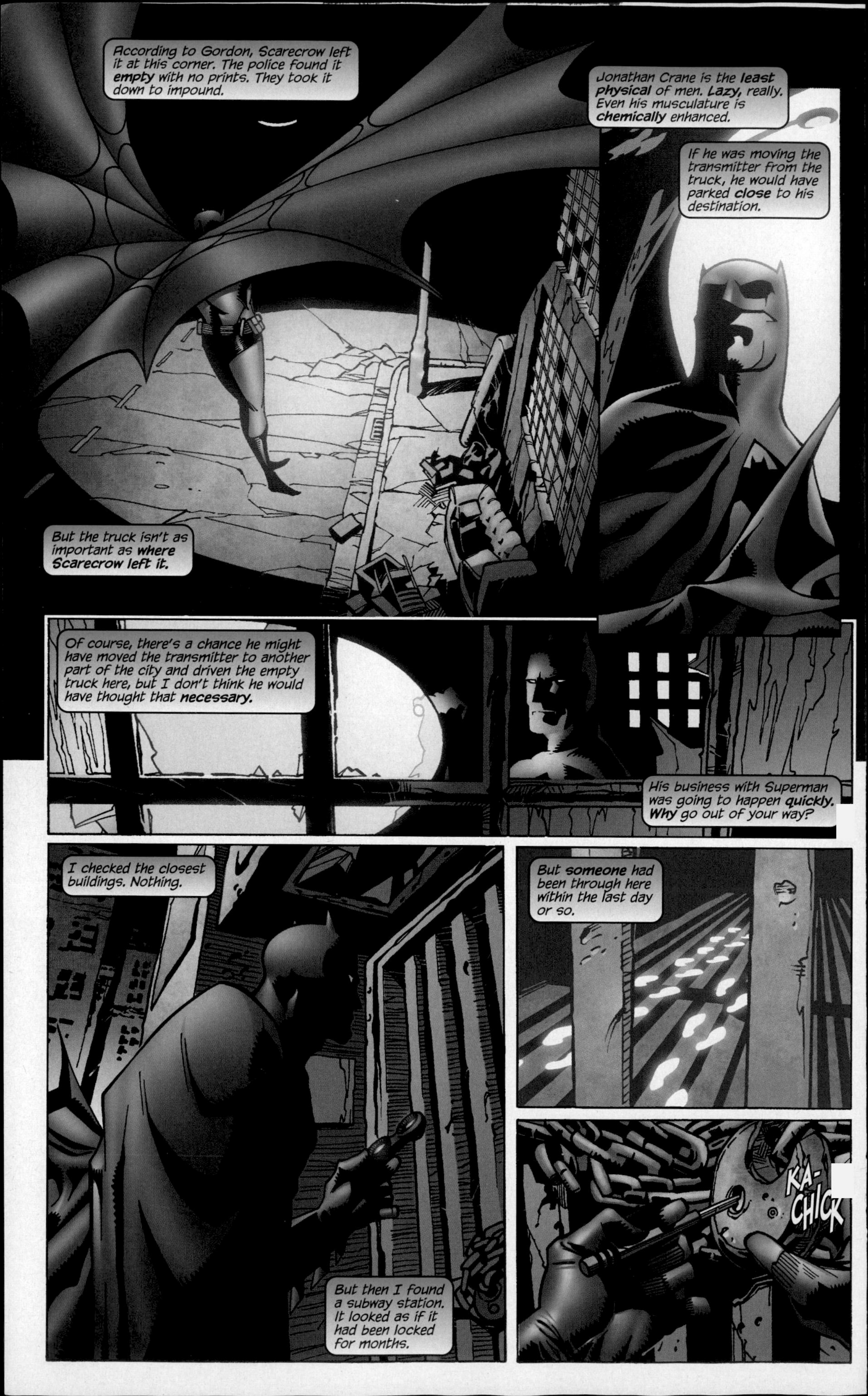
According to Gordon, Scarecrow left it at this corner. The police found it empty with no prints. They took it down to impound.
But the truck isn't as important as where Scarecrow left it.
Jonathan Crane is the least physical of men. Lazy, really. Even his musculature is chemically enhanced.
If he was moving the transmitter from the truck, he would have parked close to his destination.
Of course, there's a chance he might have moved the transmitter to another part of the city and driven the empty truck here, but I don't think he would have thought that necessary.
His business with Superman was going to happen quickly. Why go out of your way?
I checked the closest buildings. Nothing.
But then I found a subway station. It looked as if it had been locked for months.
But someone had been through here within the last day or so.
KA-CHICK

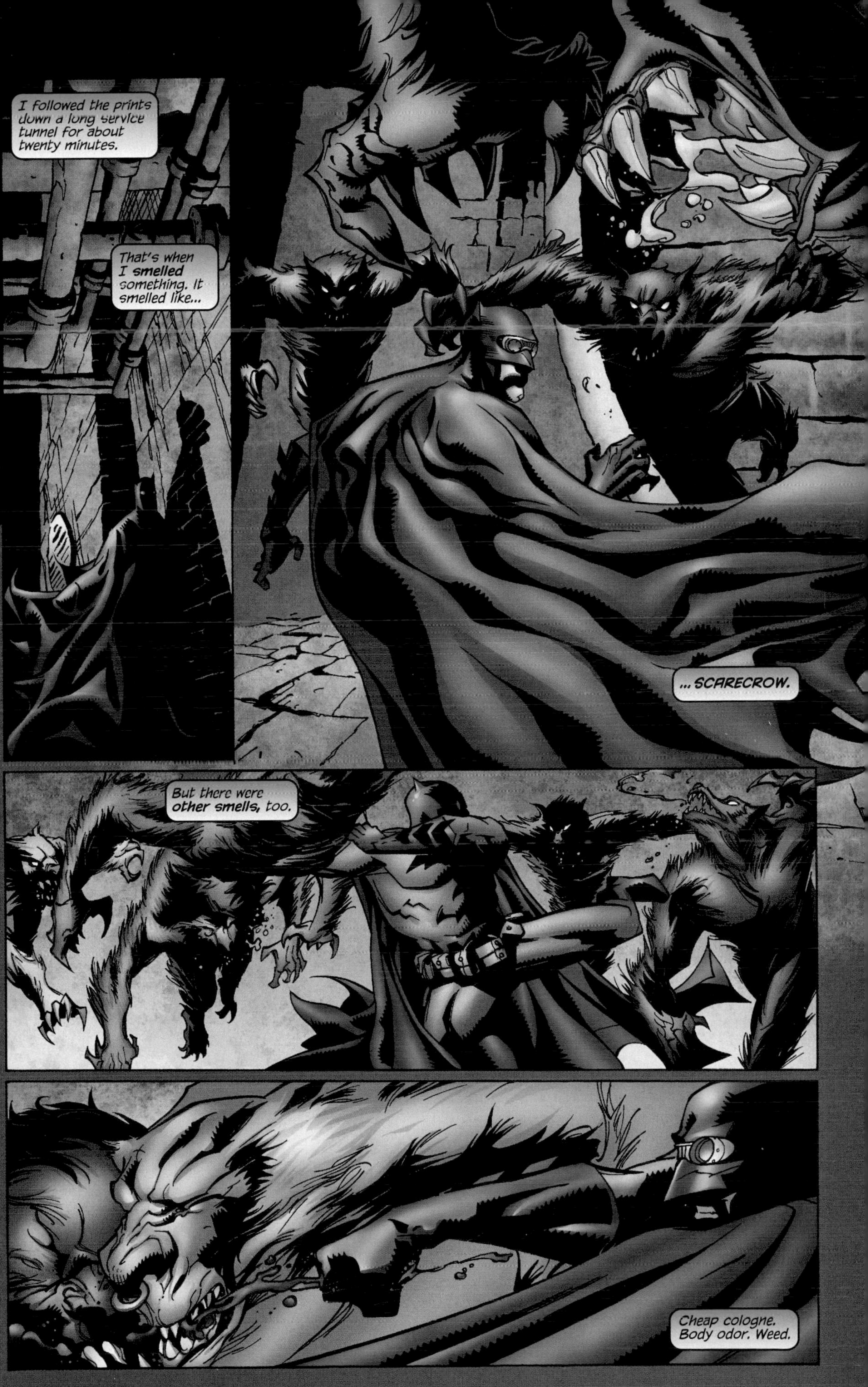
I followed the prints down a long service tunnel for about twenty minutes.
That's when I smelled something. It smelled like...
...SCARECROW.
But there were other smells, too.
Cheap cologne. Body odor. Weed.

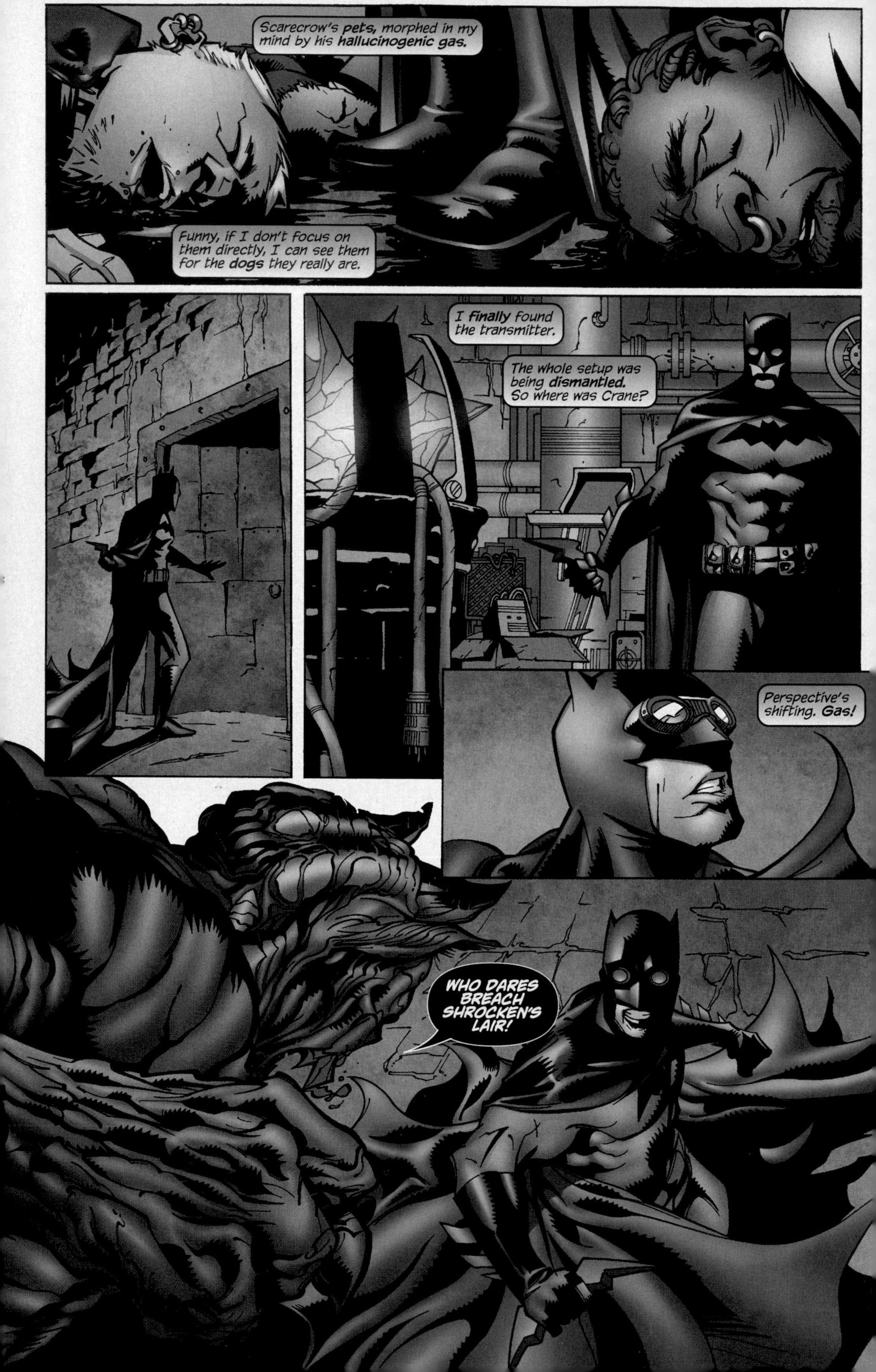

Scarecrow's **pets,** morphed in my mind by his **hallucinogenic gas.**
Funny, if I don't focus on them directly, I can see them for the **dogs** they really are.
I **finally** found the transmitter.
The whole setup was being **dismantled.** So where was Crane?
Perspective's shifting. **Gas!**
WHO DARES BREACH SHROCKEN'S LAIR!

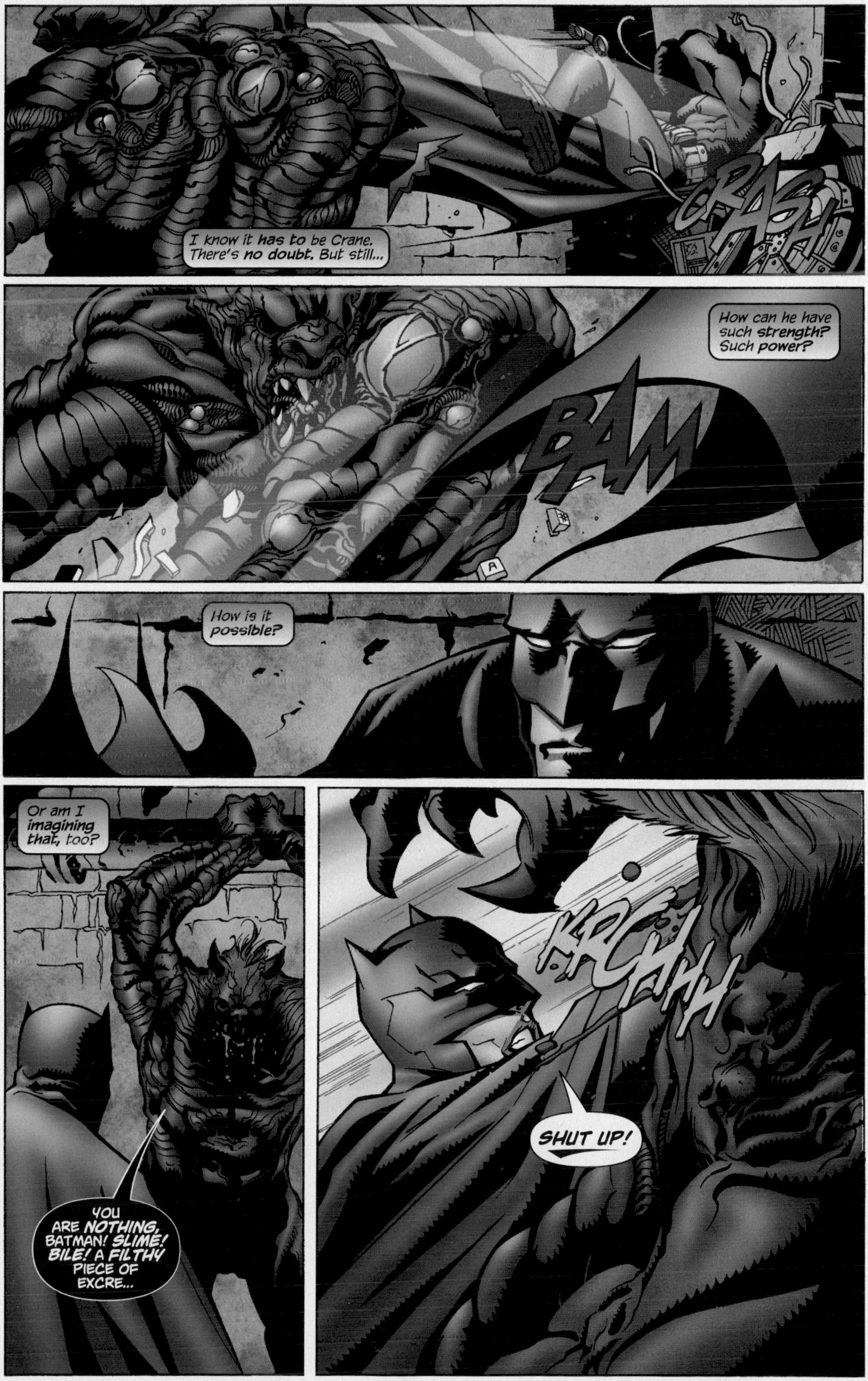
I know it has to be Crane. There's no doubt. But still...
CRASH
How can he have such strength? Such power?
BAM
How is it possible?
Or am I imagining that, too?
YOU ARE NOTHING, BATMAN! SLIME! BILE! A FILTHY PIECE OF EXCRE...
KRCHHH
SHUT UP!

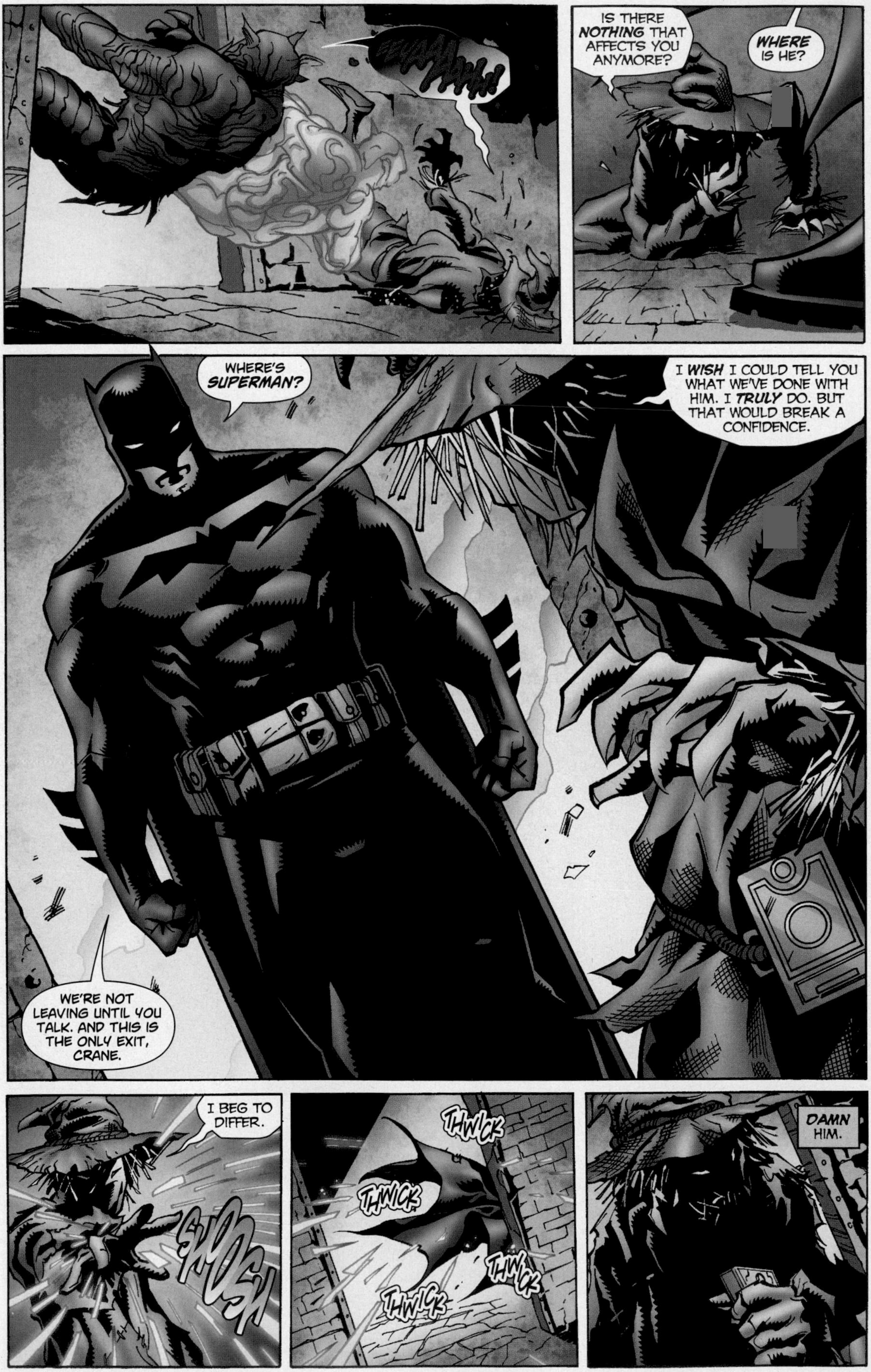
EEYAAAAHHH!
IS THERE NOTHING THAT AFFECTS YOU ANYMORE?
WHERE IS HE?
WHERE'S SUPERMAN?
I WISH I COULD TELL YOU WHAT WE'VE DONE WITH HIM. I TRULY DO. BUT THAT WOULD BREAK A CONFIDENCE.
WE'RE NOT LEAVING UNTIL YOU TALK. AND THIS IS THE ONLY EXIT, CRANE.
I BEG TO DIFFER.
SHOOSH
THWICK
THWICK
THWICK
THWICK
DAMN HIM.

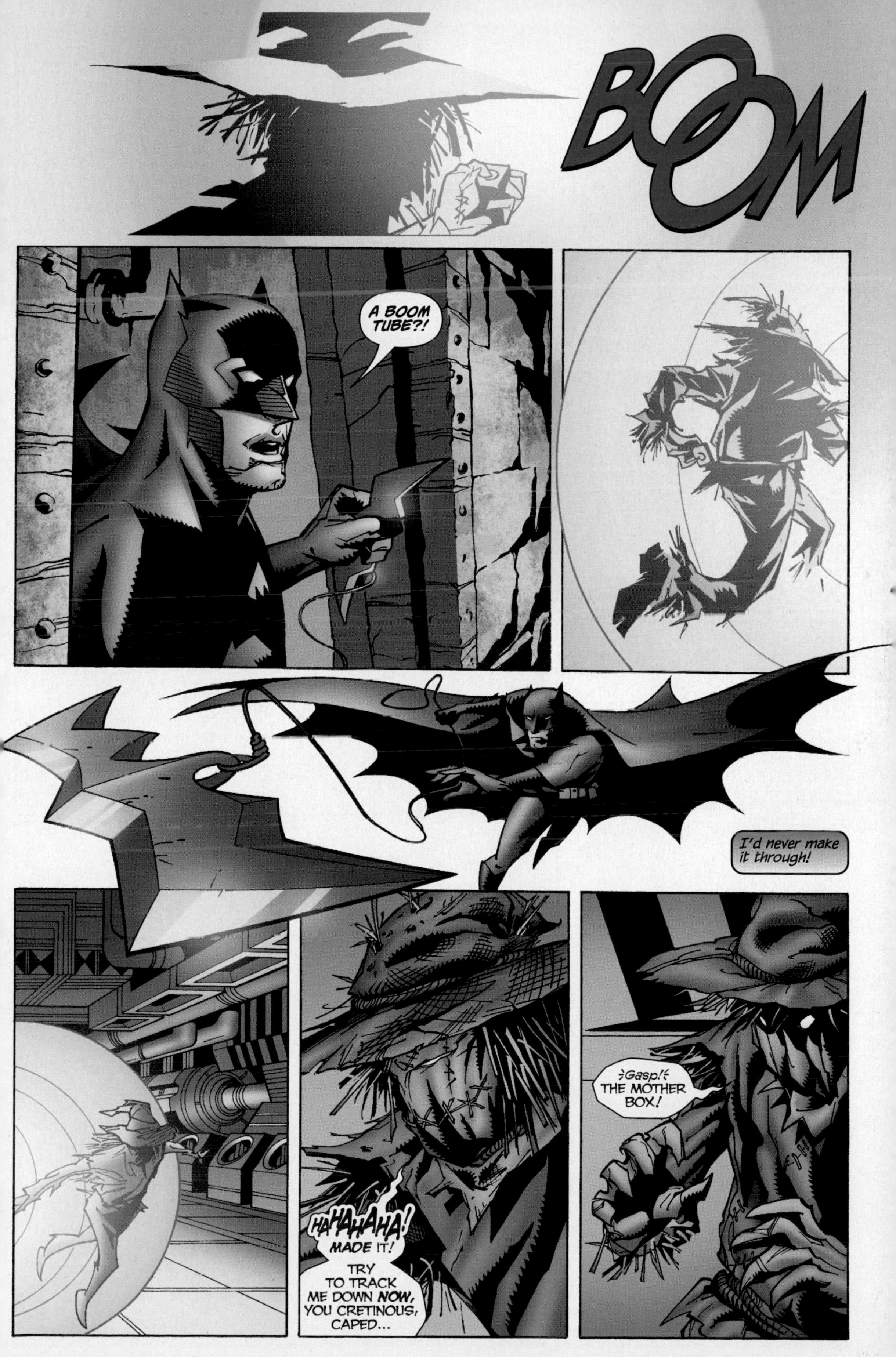
BOOM
A BOOM TUBE?!
I'd never make it through!
HAHAHAHA! MADE IT!
TRY TO TRACK ME DOWN NOW, YOU CRETINOUS, CAPED...
Gasp! THE MOTHER BOX!

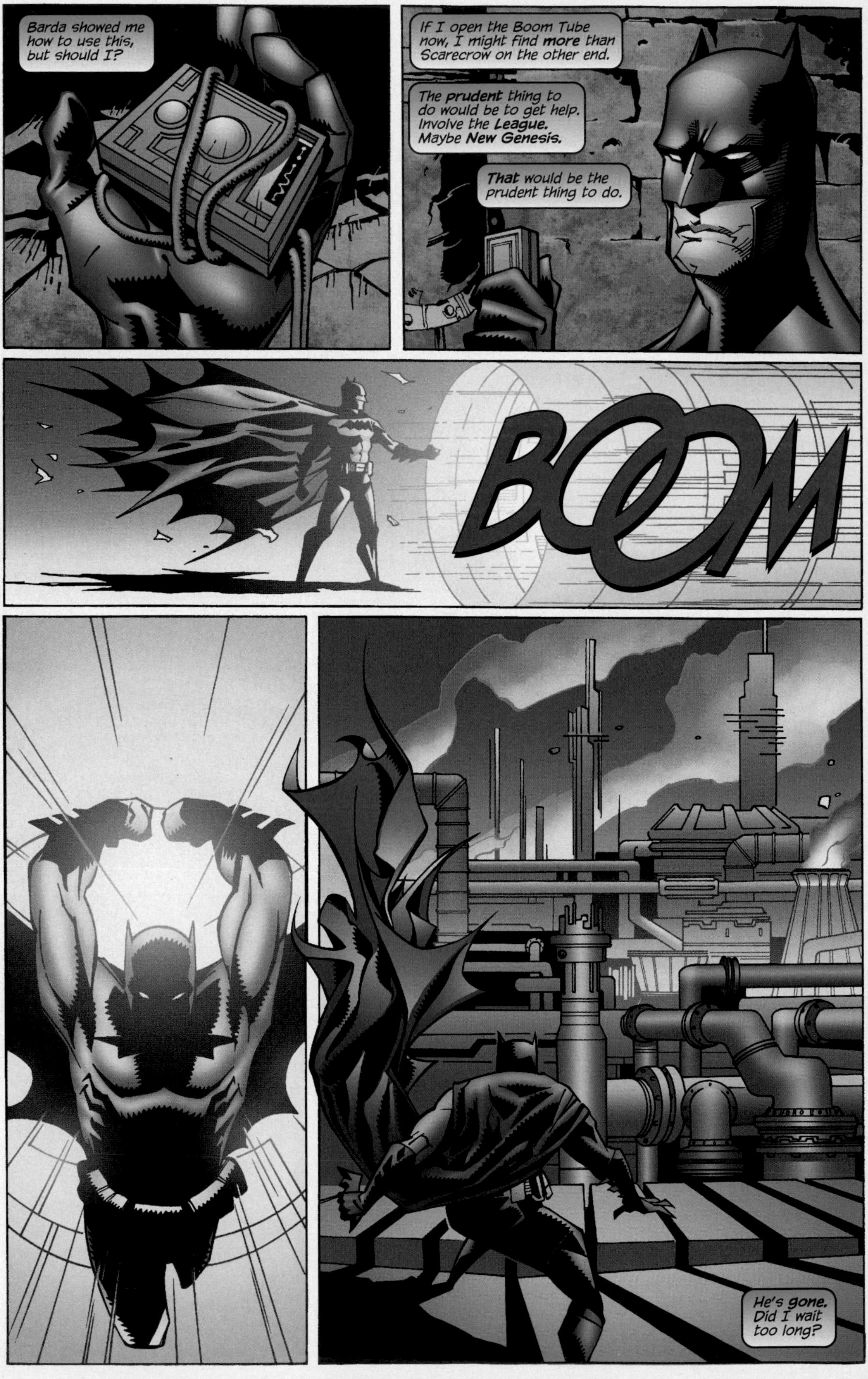
Barda showed me how to use this, but should I?
If I open the Boom Tube now, I might find more than Scarecrow on the other end.
The prudent thing to do would be to get help. Involve the League. Maybe New Genesis.
That would be the prudent thing to do.
BOOM
He's gone. Did I wait too long?

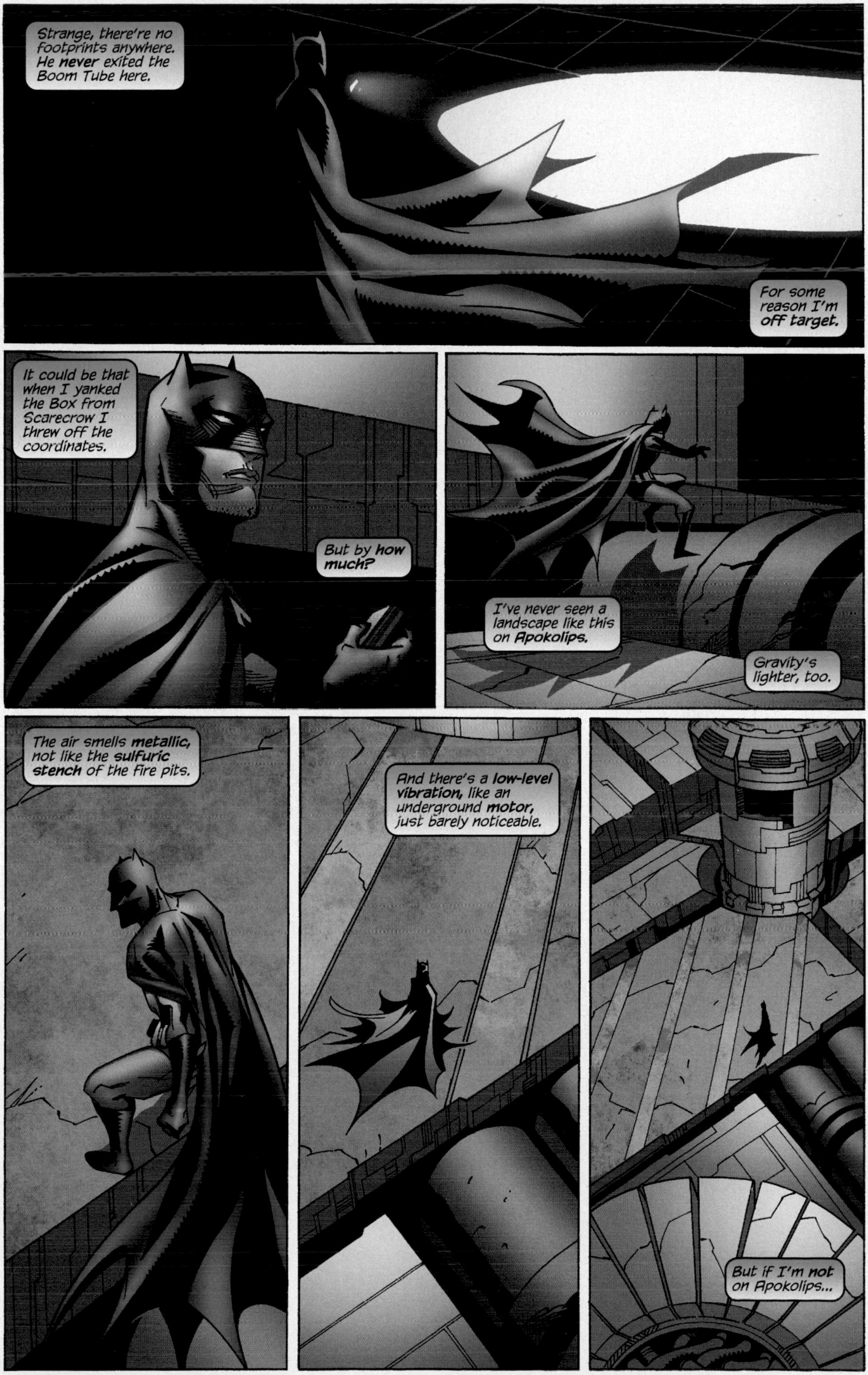
Strange, there're no footprints anywhere. He never exited the Boom Tube here.
For some reason I'm off target.
It could be that when I yanked the Box from Scarecrow I threw off the coordinates.
But by how much?
I've never seen a landscape like this on Apokolips.
Gravity's lighter, too.
The air smells metallic, not like the sulfuric stench of the fire pits.
And there's a low-level vibration, like an underground motor, just barely noticeable.
But if I'm not on Apokolips...

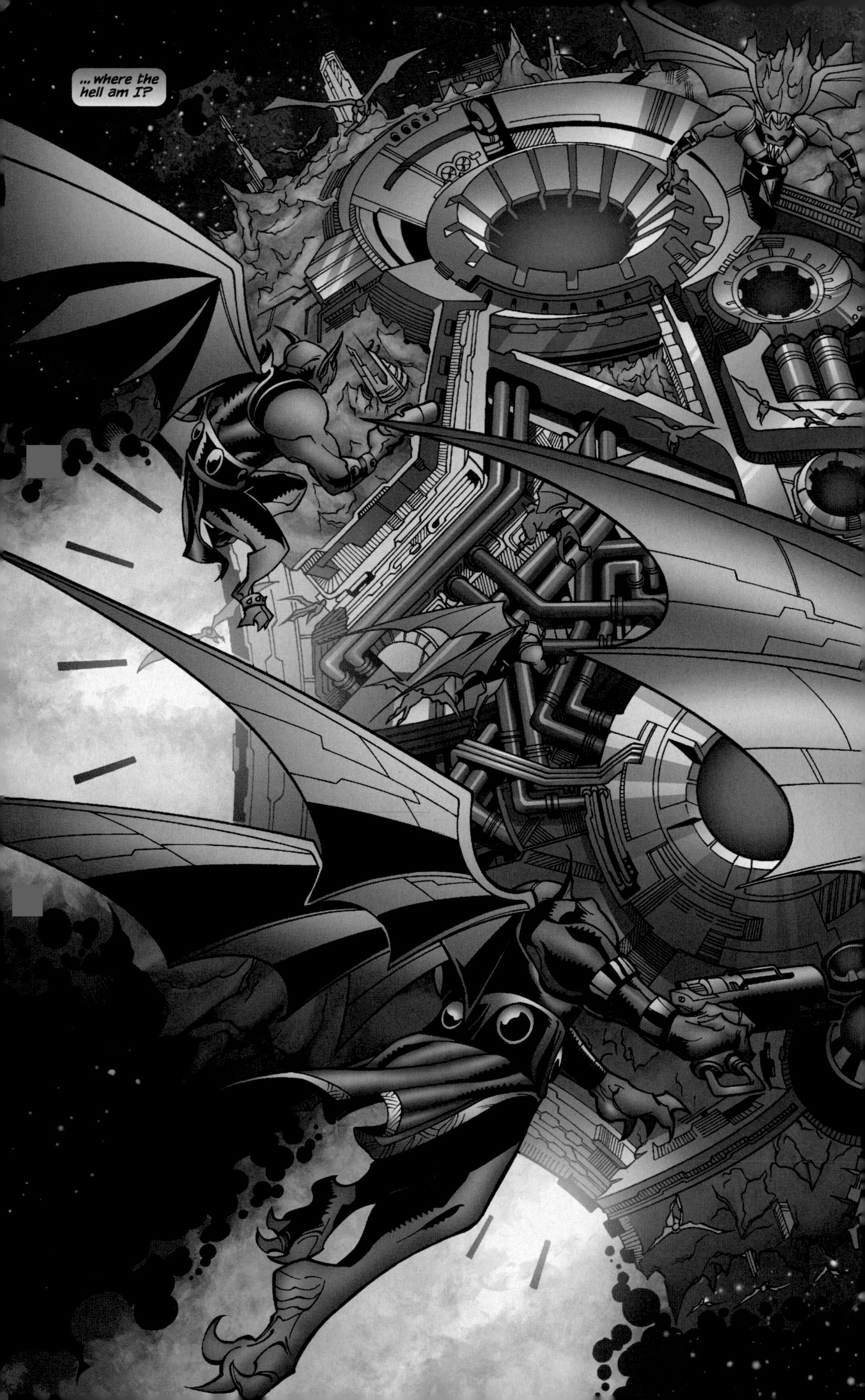
...where the hell am I?

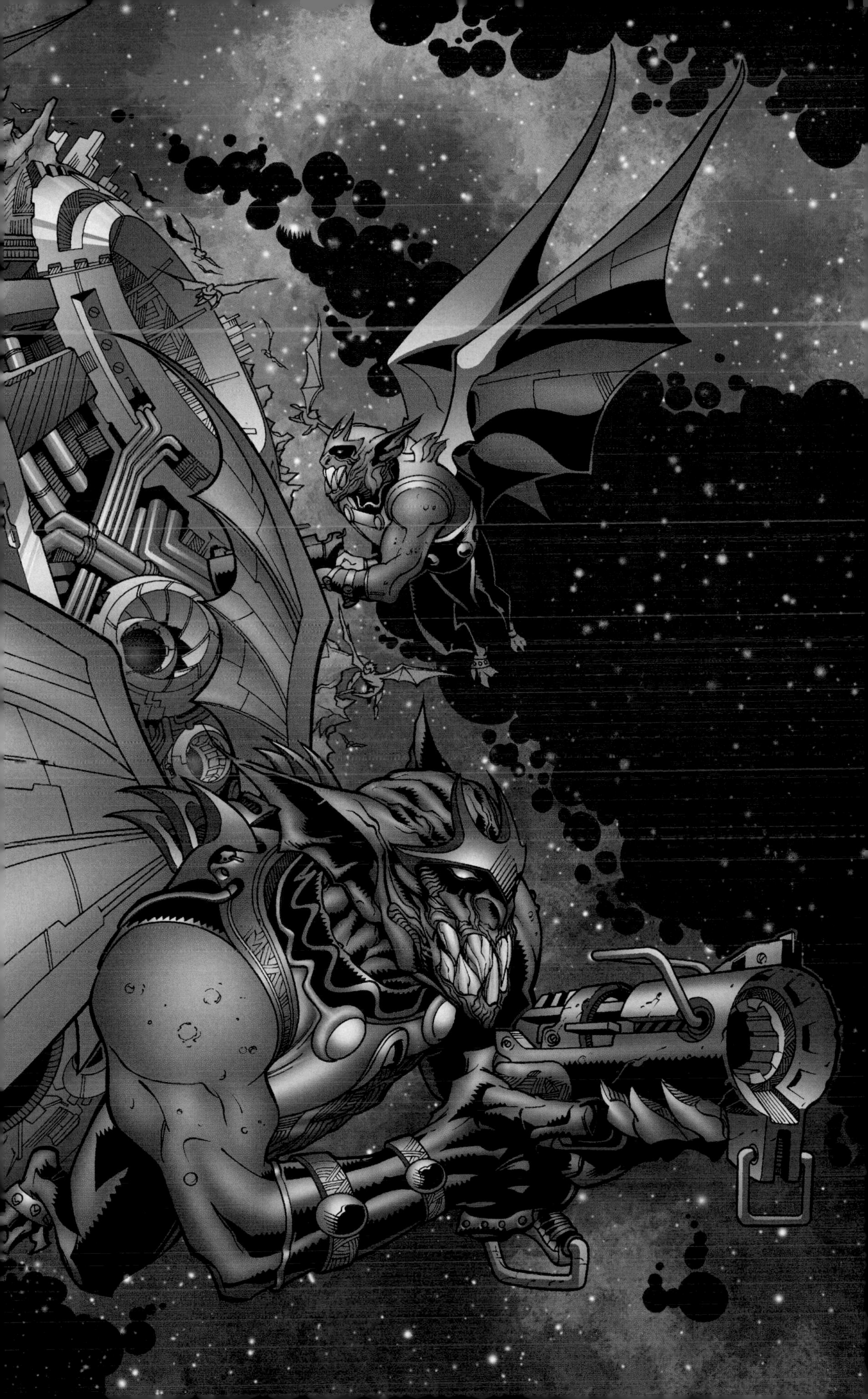

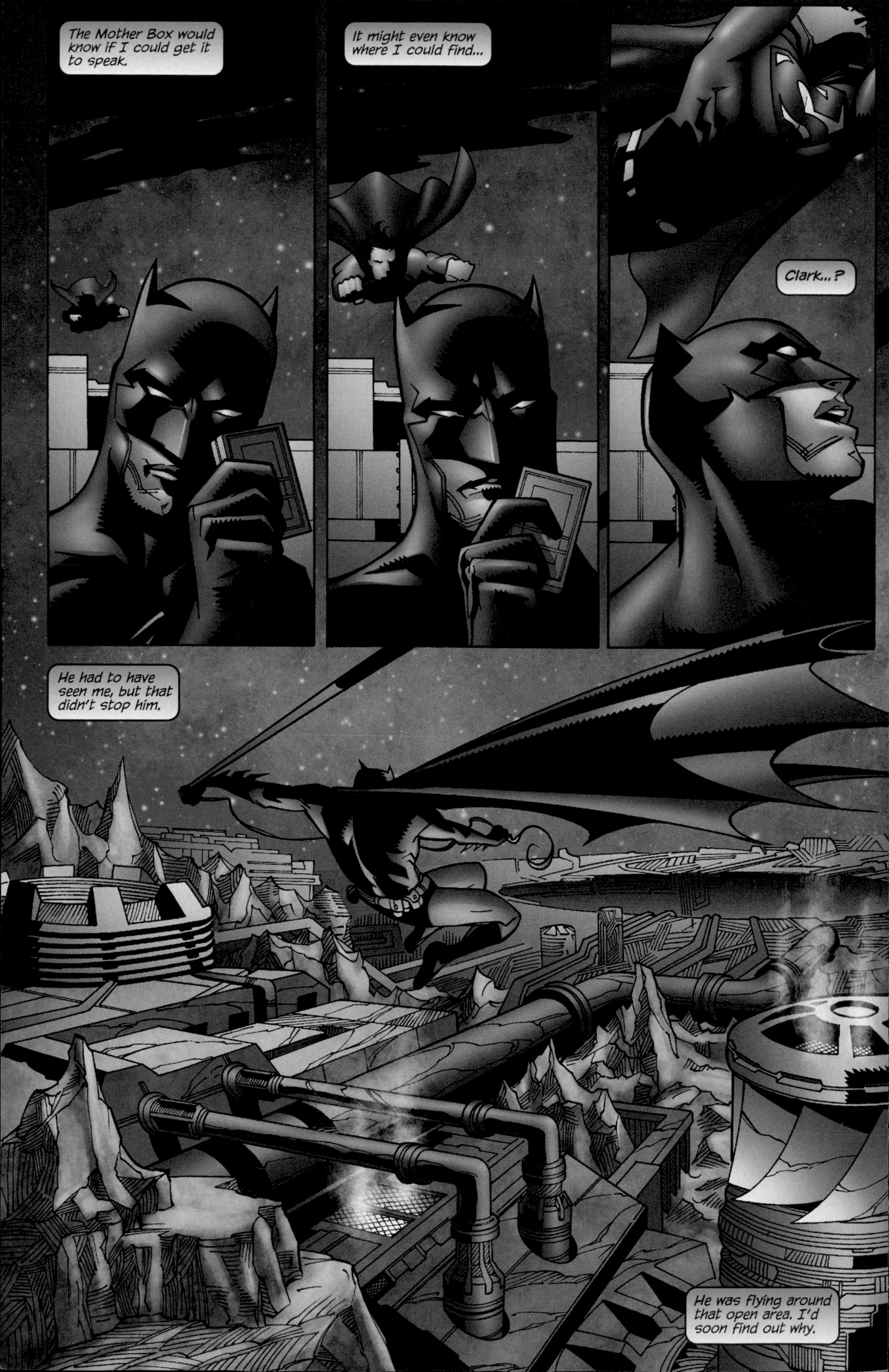
The Mother Box would know if I could get it to speak.
It might even know where I could find...
Clark...?
He had to have seen me, but that didn't stop him.
He was flying around that open area. I'd soon find out why.

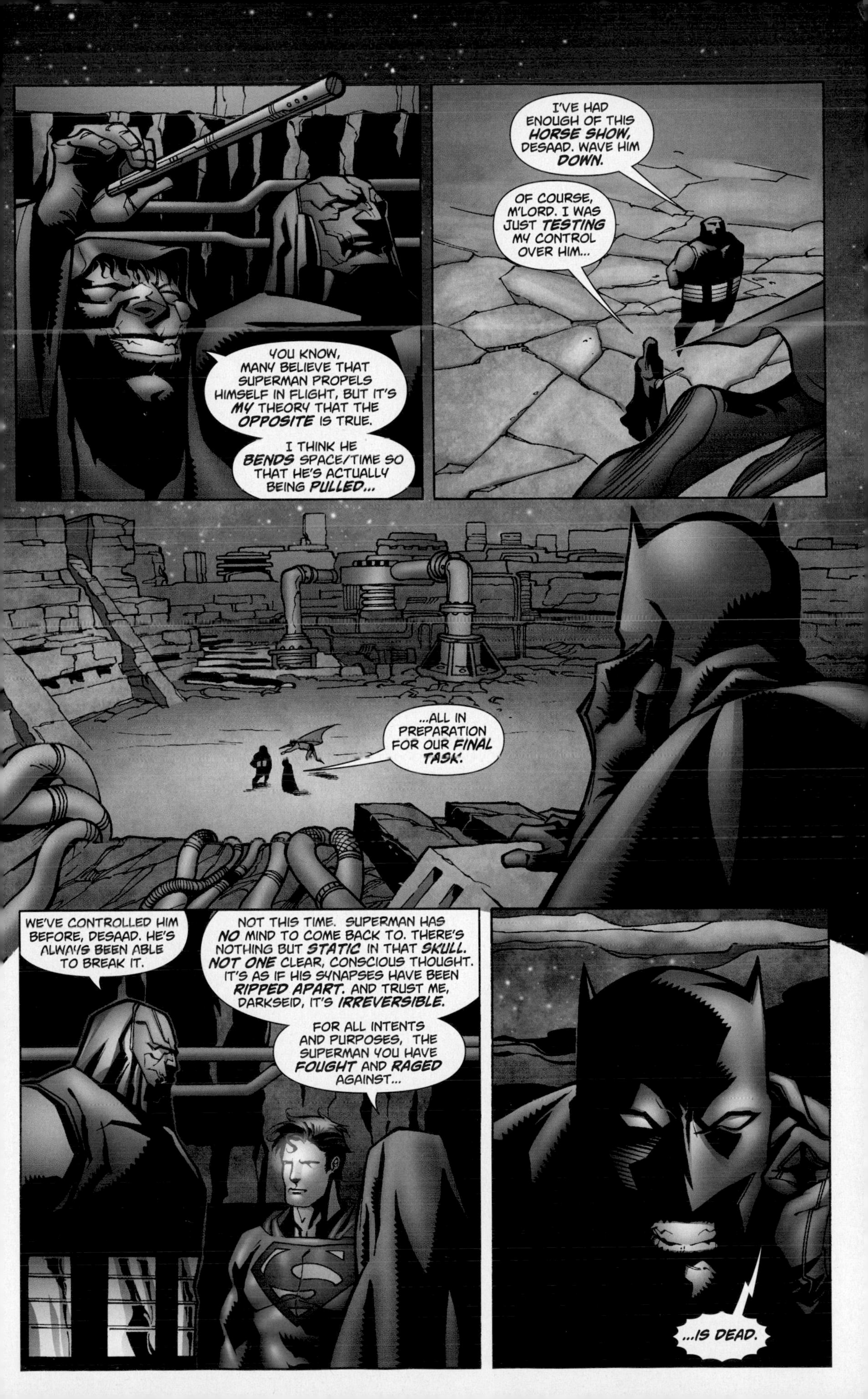
YOU KNOW, MANY BELIEVE THAT SUPERMAN PROPELS HIMSELF IN FLIGHT, BUT IT'S MY THEORY THAT THE OPPOSITE IS TRUE.
I THINK HE BENDS SPACE/TIME SO THAT HE'S ACTUALLY BEING PULLED...
I'VE HAD ENOUGH OF THIS HORSE SHOW, DESAAD. WAVE HIM DOWN.
OF COURSE, M'LORD. I WAS JUST TESTING MY CONTROL OVER HIM...
...ALL IN PREPARATION FOR OUR FINAL TASK.
WE'VE CONTROLLED HIM BEFORE, DESAAD. HE'S ALWAYS BEEN ABLE TO BREAK IT.
NOT THIS TIME. SUPERMAN HAS NO MIND TO COME BACK TO. THERE'S NOTHING BUT STATIC IN THAT SKULL. NOT ONE CLEAR, CONSCIOUS THOUGHT. IT'S AS IF HIS SYNAPSES HAVE BEEN RIPPED APART. AND TRUST ME, DARKSEID, IT'S IRREVERSIBLE.
FOR ALL INTENTS AND PURPOSES, THE SUPERMAN YOU HAVE FOUGHT AND RAGED AGAINST...
...IS DEAD.

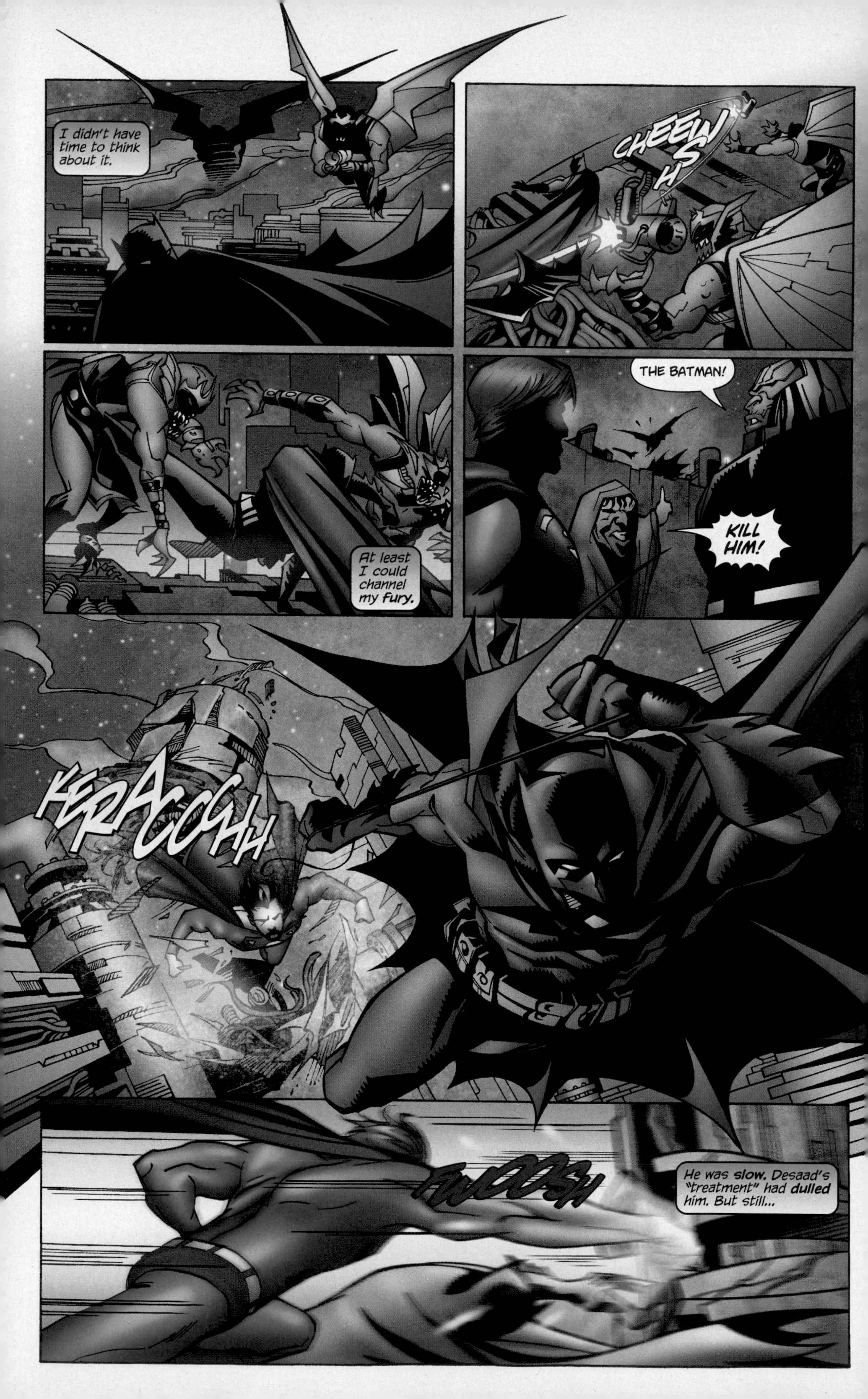
I didn't have time to think about it.
CHEEWSHH
At least I could channel my fury.
THE BATMAN!
KILL HIM!
KERACCOHH
FWOOSH
He was slow. Desaad's "treatment" had dulled him. But still...

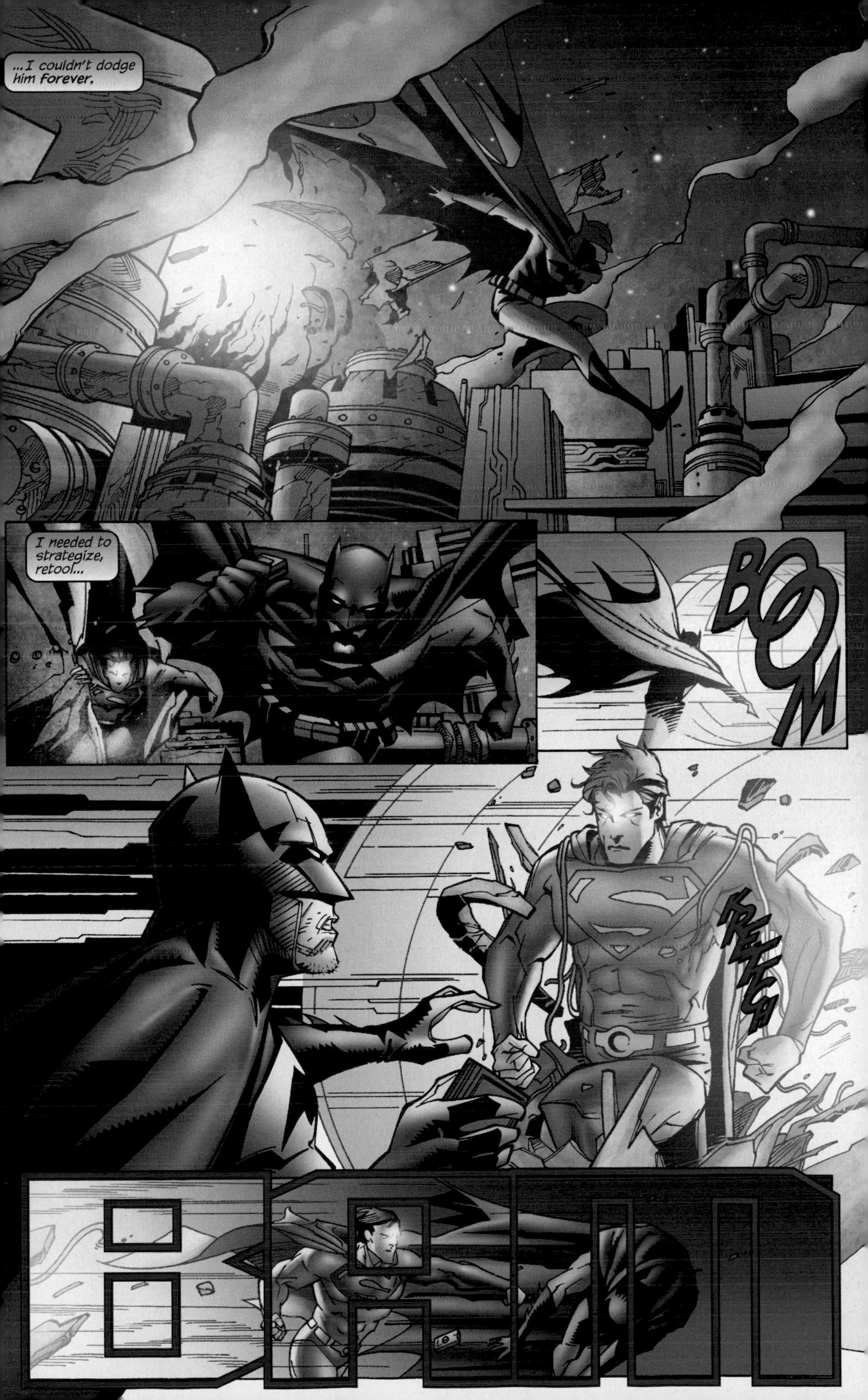
...I couldn't dodge him forever.
I needed to strategize, retool...
BOOM
KRETCH
BAM

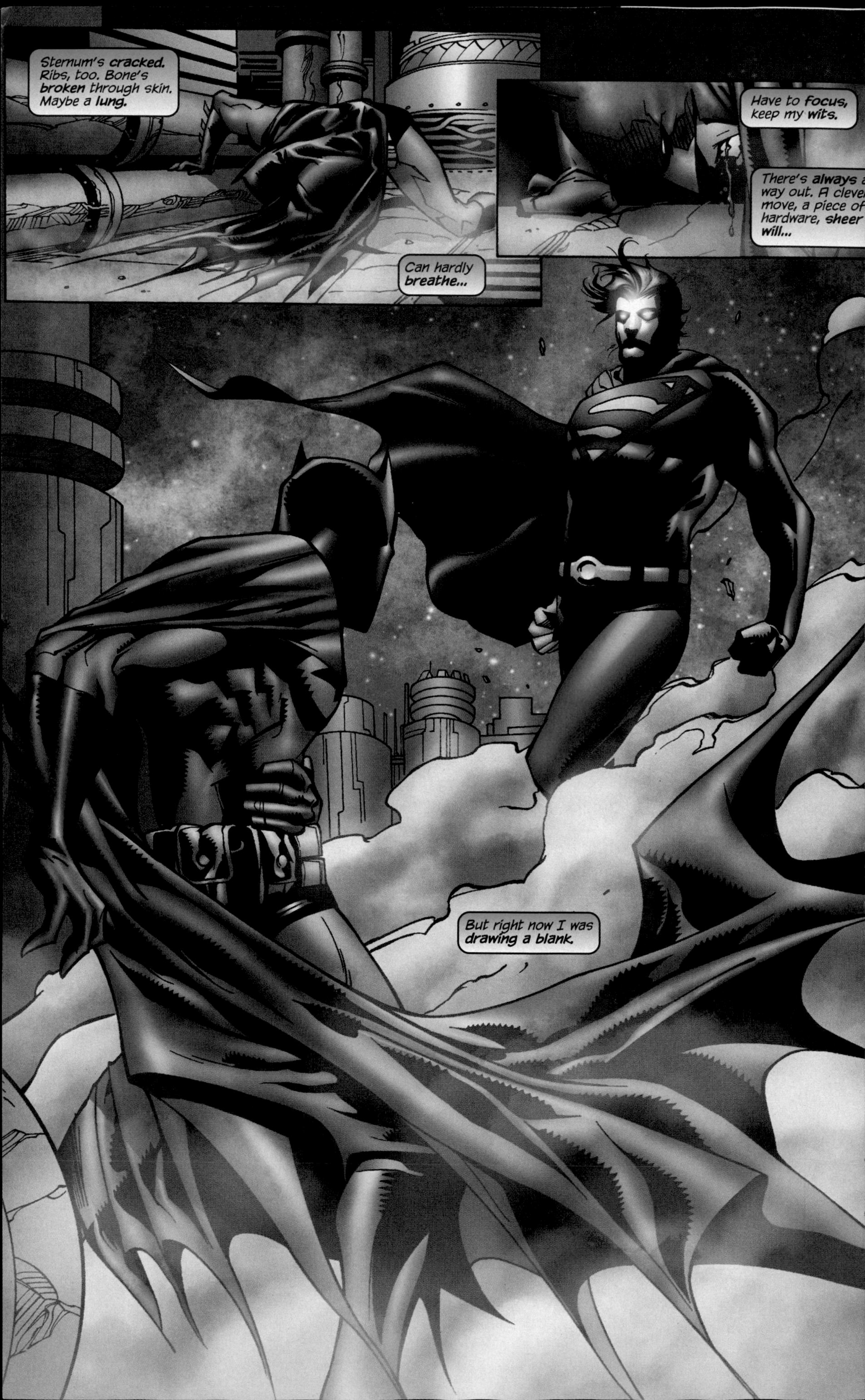
Sternum's cracked. Ribs, too. Bone's broken through skin. Maybe a lung.
Can hardly breathe...
Have to focus, keep my wits.
There's always a way out. A clever move, a piece of hardware, sheer will...
But right now I was drawing a blank.

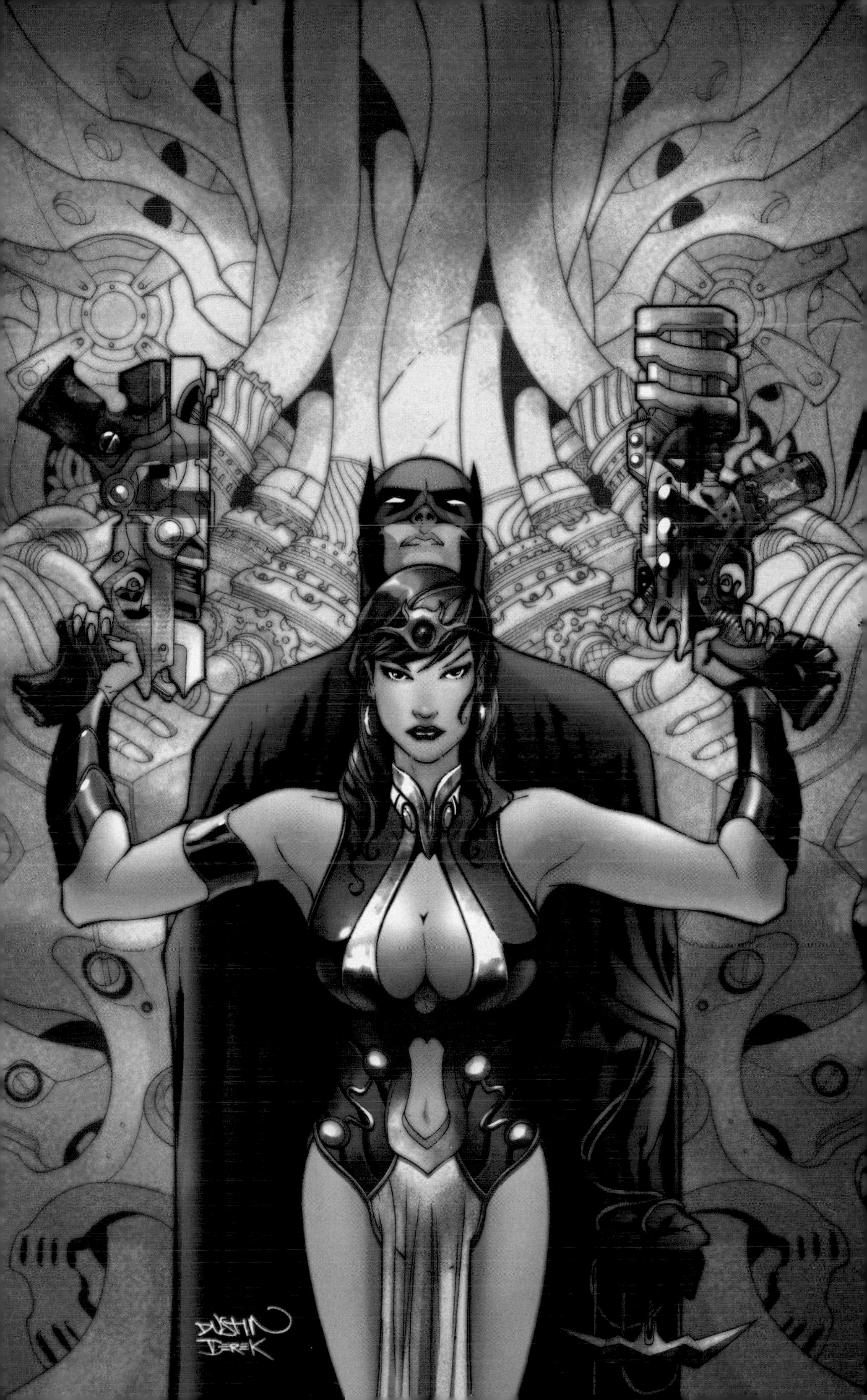
DUSTIN
DEREK

TORMENT: PART FOUR
TRAPPED

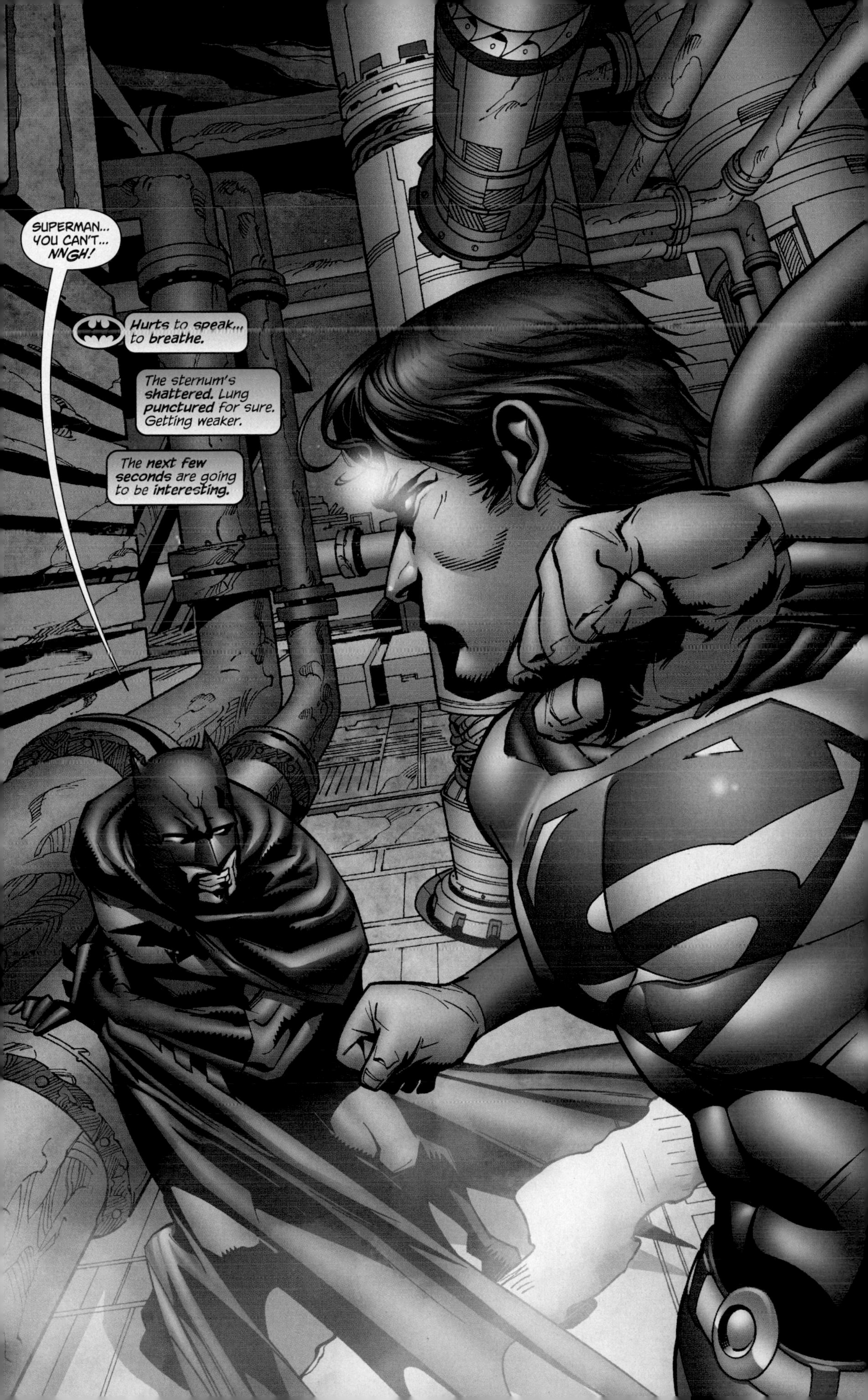
SUPERMAN... YOU CAN'T... NNGH!
Hurts to speak... to breathe.
The sternum's shattered. Lung punctured for sure. Getting weaker.
The next few seconds are going to be interesting.

And they are.

BOOSH

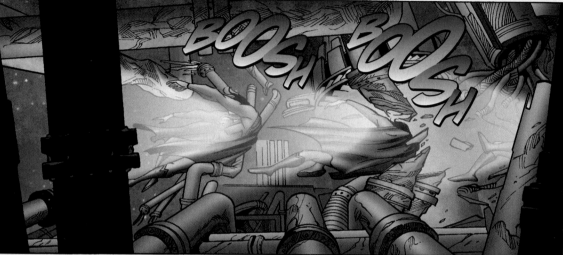

BOOSH BOOSH

STAY STILL.

I'M PHASING YOU OUT.

SWHOOSH

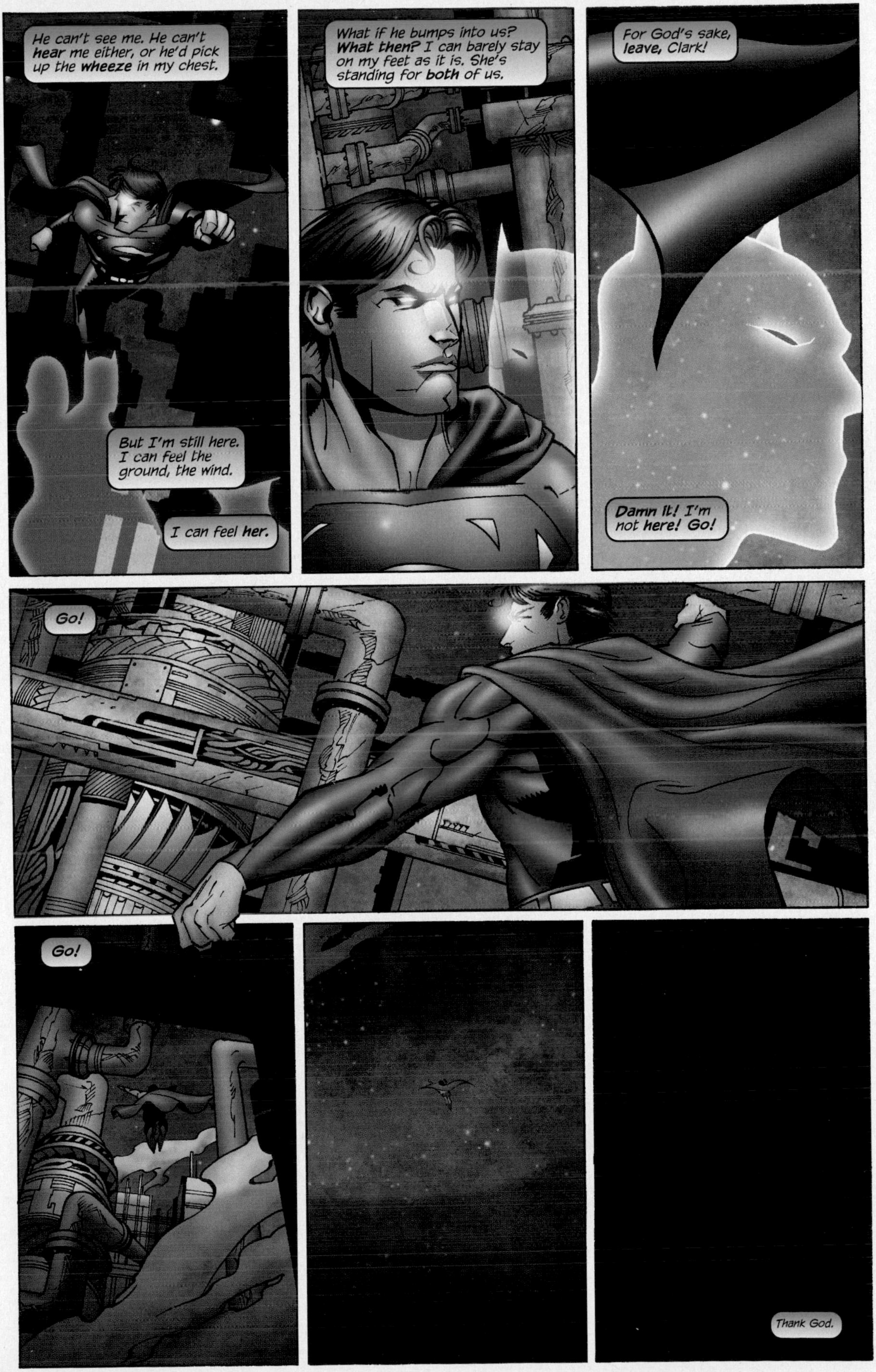
He can't see me. He can't hear me either, or he'd pick up the wheeze in my chest.
But I'm still here. I can feel the ground, the wind.
I can feel her.
What if he bumps into us? What then? I can barely stay on my feet as it is. She's standing for both of us.
For God's sake, leave, Clark!
Damn it! I'm not here! Go!
Go!
Go!
Thank God.

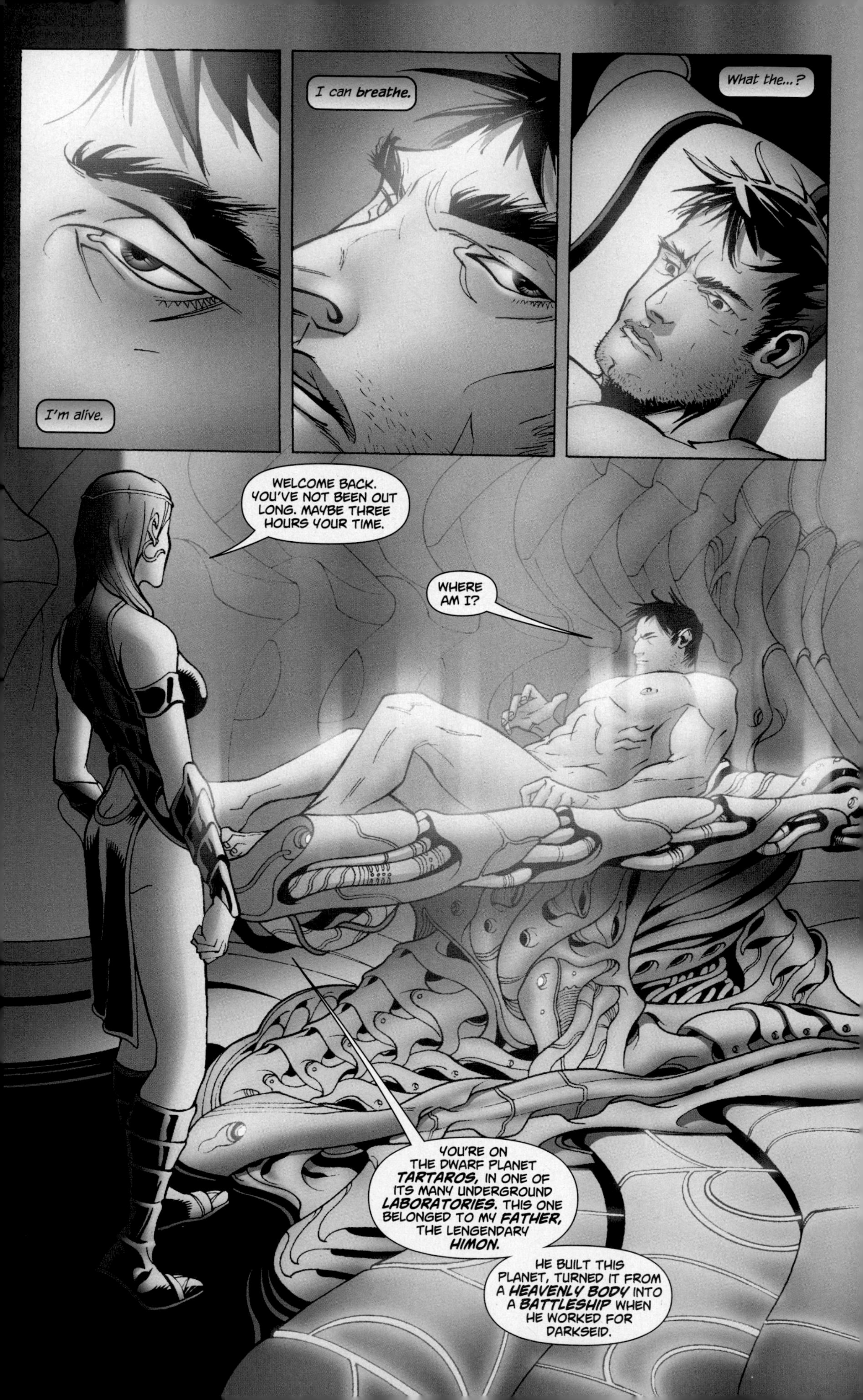
I'm alive.
I can breathe.
What the...?
WELCOME BACK. YOU'VE NOT BEEN OUT LONG. MAYBE THREE HOURS YOUR TIME.
WHERE AM I?
YOU'RE ON THE DWARF PLANET TARTAROS, IN ONE OF ITS MANY UNDERGROUND LABORATORIES. THIS ONE BELONGED TO MY FATHER, THE LENGENDARY HIMON.
HE BUILT THIS PLANET, TURNED IT FROM A HEAVENLY BODY INTO A BATTLESHIP WHEN HE WORKED FOR DARKSEID.

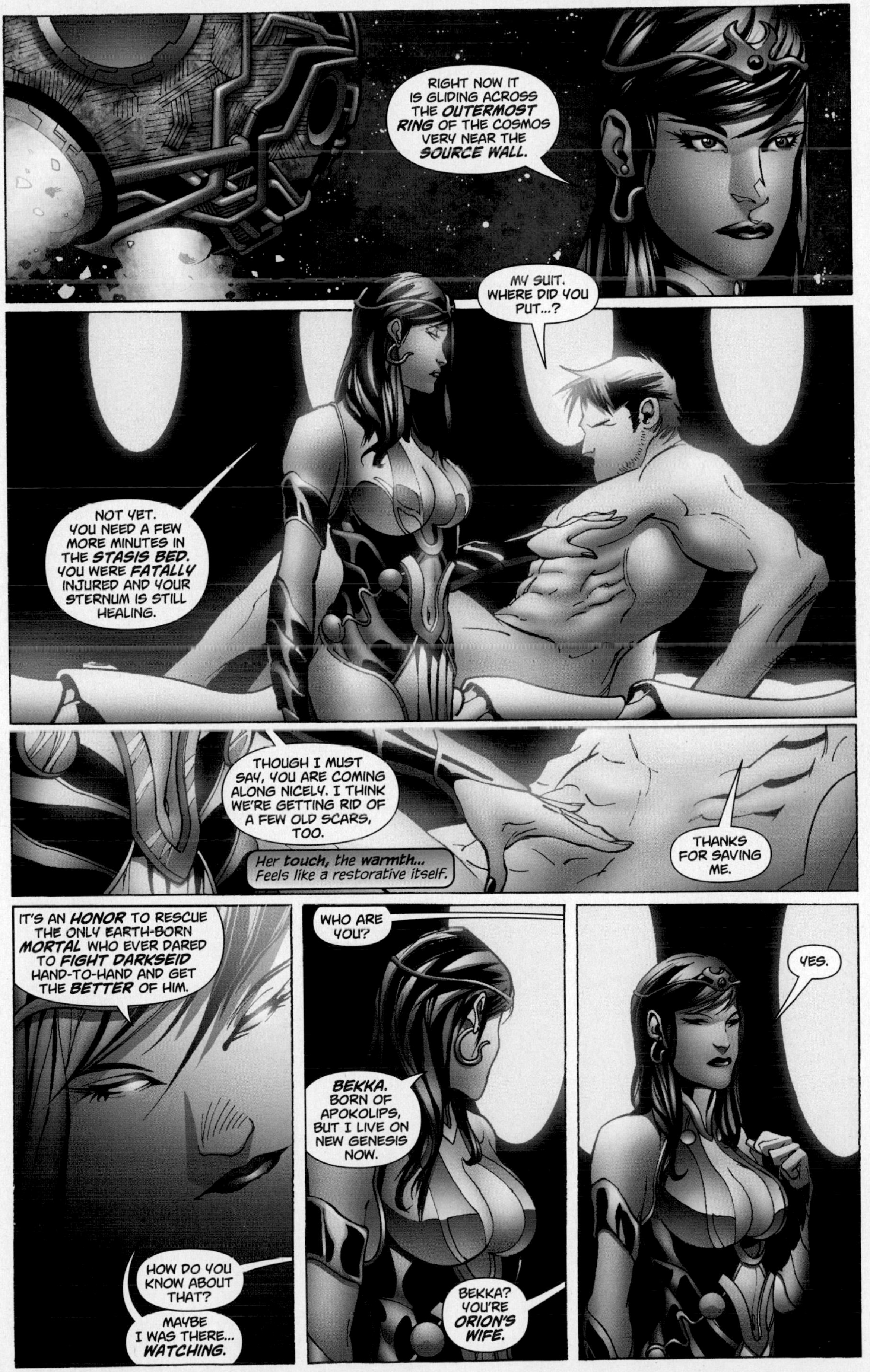
RIGHT NOW IT IS GLIDING ACROSS THE OUTERMOST RING OF THE COSMOS VERY NEAR THE SOURCE WALL.
MY SUIT. WHERE DID YOU PUT...?
NOT YET. YOU NEED A FEW MORE MINUTES IN THE STASIS BED. YOU WERE FATALLY INJURED AND YOUR STERNUM IS STILL HEALING.
THOUGH I MUST SAY, YOU ARE COMING ALONG NICELY. I THINK WE'RE GETTING RID OF A FEW OLD SCARS, TOO.
Her touch, the warmth... Feels like a restorative itself.
THANKS FOR SAVING ME.
IT'S AN HONOR TO RESCUE THE ONLY EARTH-BORN MORTAL WHO EVER DARED TO FIGHT DARKSEID HAND-TO-HAND AND GET THE BETTER OF HIM.
HOW DO YOU KNOW ABOUT THAT?
MAYBE I WAS THERE... WATCHING.
WHO ARE YOU?
BEKKA. BORN OF APOKOLIPS, BUT I LIVE ON NEW GENESIS NOW.
BEKKA? YOU'RE ORION'S WIFE.
YES.

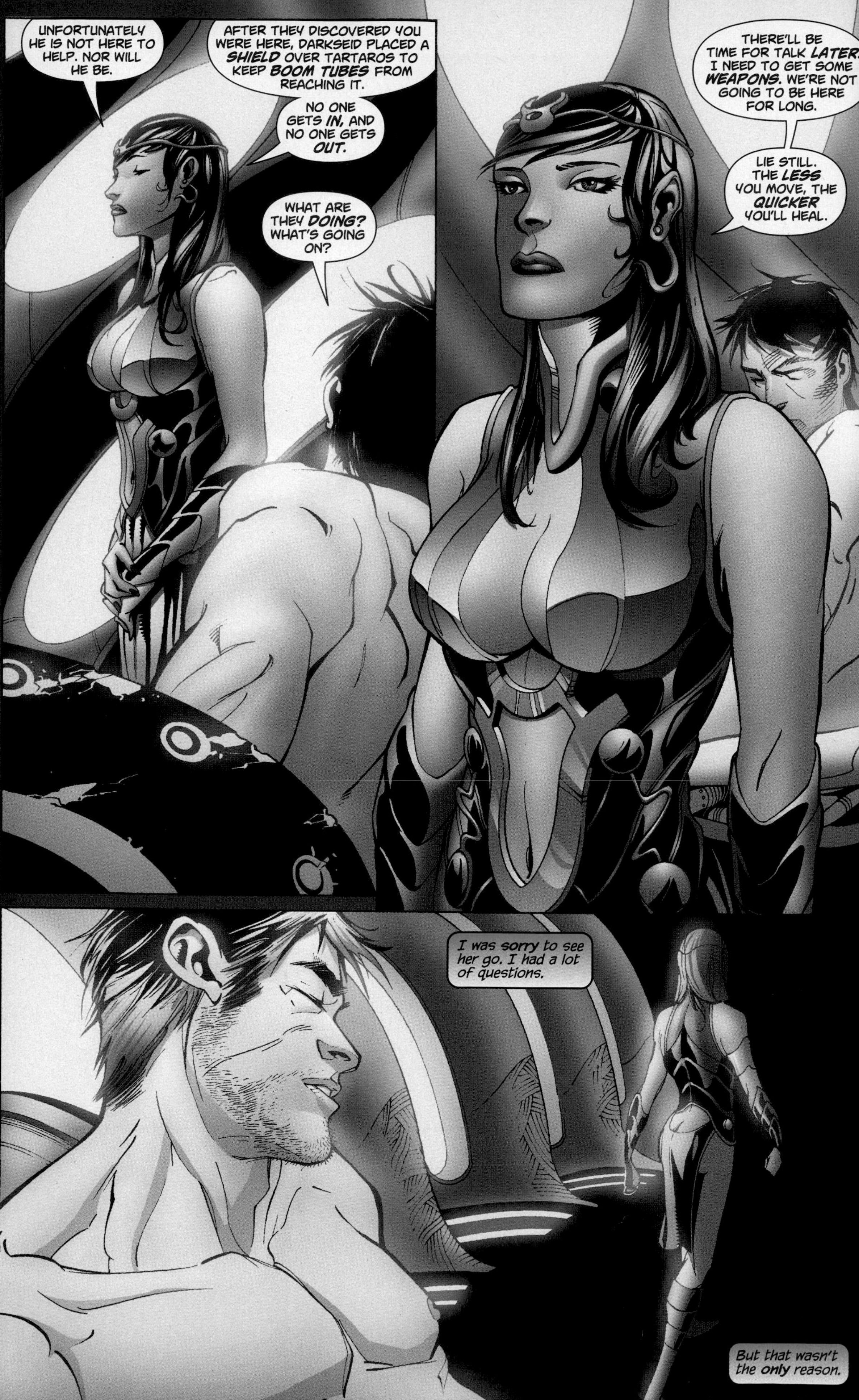

UNFORTUNATELY HE IS NOT HERE TO HELP. NOR WILL HE BE.
AFTER THEY DISCOVERED YOU WERE HERE, DARKSEID PLACED A SHIELD OVER TARTAROS TO KEEP BOOM TUBES FROM REACHING IT.
NO ONE GETS IN, AND NO ONE GETS OUT.
WHAT ARE THEY DOING? WHAT'S GOING ON?
THERE'LL BE TIME FOR TALK LATER. I NEED TO GET SOME WEAPONS. WE'RE NOT GOING TO BE HERE FOR LONG.
LIE STILL. THE LESS YOU MOVE, THE QUICKER YOU'LL HEAL.
I was sorry to see her go. I had a lot of questions.
But that wasn't the only reason.

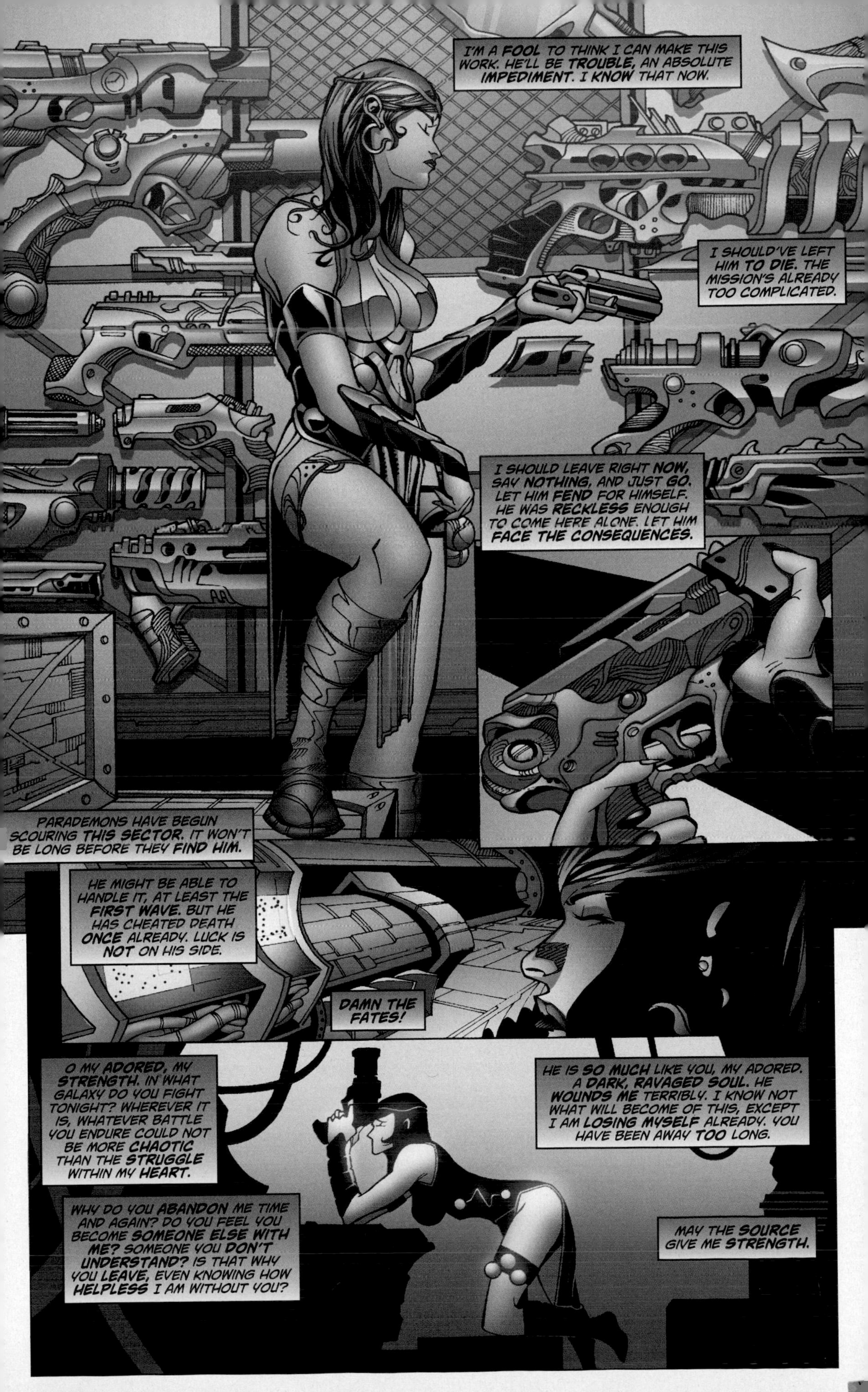
I'M A FOOL TO THINK I CAN MAKE THIS WORK. HE'LL BE TROUBLE, AN ABSOLUTE IMPEDIMENT. I KNOW THAT NOW.
I SHOULD'VE LEFT HIM TO DIE. THE MISSION'S ALREADY TOO COMPLICATED.
I SHOULD LEAVE RIGHT NOW, SAY NOTHING, AND JUST GO. LET HIM FEND FOR HIMSELF. HE WAS RECKLESS ENOUGH TO COME HERE ALONE. LET HIM FACE THE CONSEQUENCES.
PARADEMONS HAVE BEGUN SCOURING THIS SECTOR. IT WON'T BE LONG BEFORE THEY FIND HIM.
HE MIGHT BE ABLE TO HANDLE IT, AT LEAST THE FIRST WAVE. BUT HE HAS CHEATED DEATH ONCE ALREADY. LUCK IS NOT ON HIS SIDE.
DAMN THE FATES!
O MY ADORED, MY STRENGTH. IN WHAT GALAXY DO YOU FIGHT TONIGHT? WHEREVER IT IS, WHATEVER BATTLE YOU ENDURE COULD NOT BE MORE CHAOTIC THAN THE STRUGGLE WITHIN MY HEART.
WHY DO YOU ABANDON ME TIME AND AGAIN? DO YOU FEEL YOU BECOME SOMEONE ELSE WITH ME? SOMEONE YOU DON'T UNDERSTAND? IS THAT WHY YOU LEAVE, EVEN KNOWING HOW HELPLESS I AM WITHOUT YOU?
HE IS SO MUCH LIKE YOU, MY ADORED. A DARK, RAVAGED SOUL. HE WOUNDS ME TERRIBLY. I KNOW NOT WHAT WILL BECOME OF THIS, EXCEPT I AM LOSING MYSELF ALREADY. YOU HAVE BEEN AWAY TOO LONG.
MAY THE SOURCE GIVE ME STRENGTH.

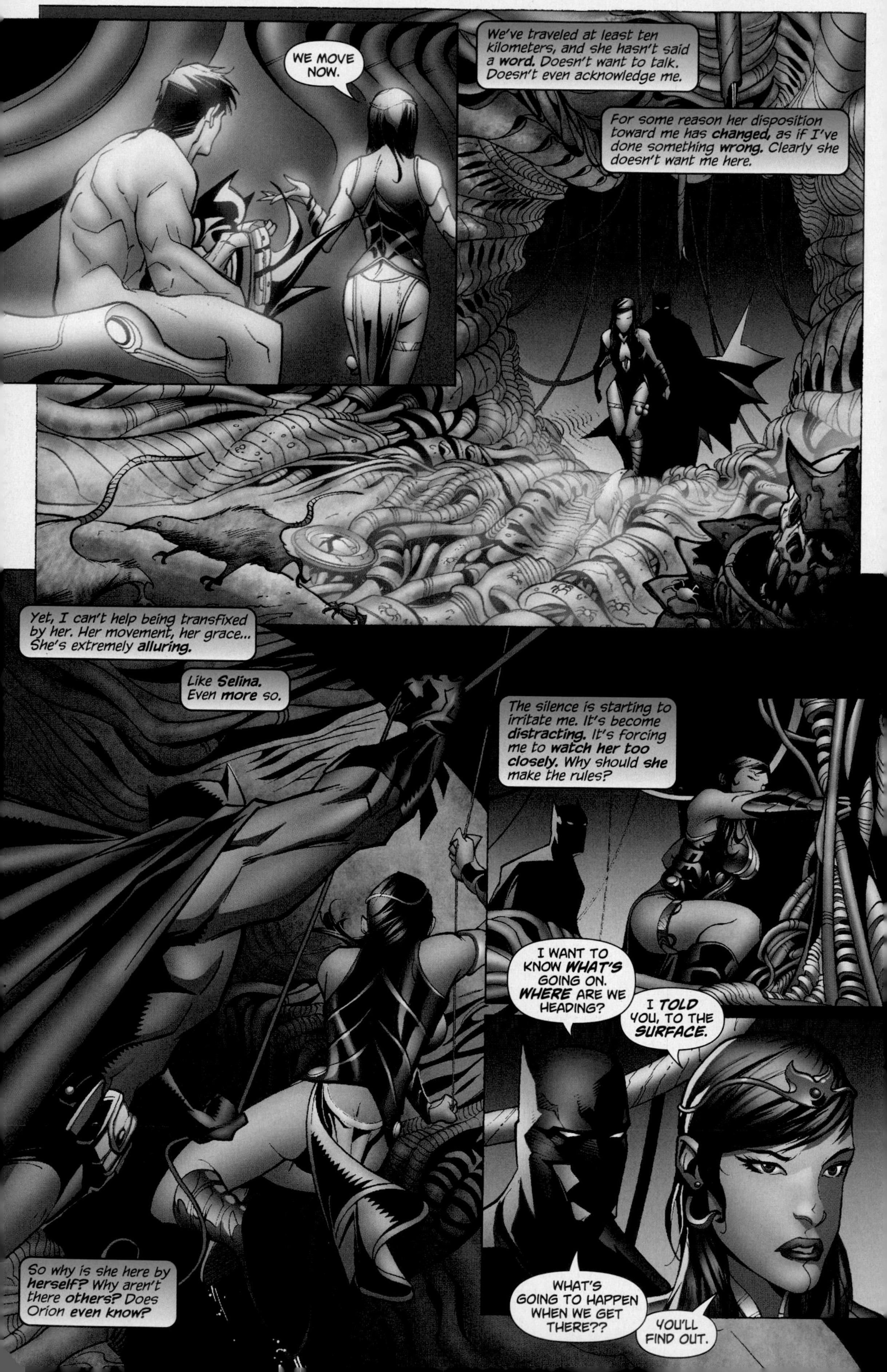
WE MOVE NOW.
We've traveled at least ten kilometers, and she hasn't said a **word.** Doesn't want to talk. Doesn't even acknowledge me.
For some reason her disposition toward me has **changed,** as if I've done something **wrong.** Clearly she doesn't want me here.
Yet, I can't help being transfixed by her. Her movement, her grace... She's extremely **alluring.**
Like **Selina.** Even **more** so.
So why is she here by **herself?** Why aren't there **others?** Does Orion **even know?**
The silence is starting to irritate me. It's become **distracting.** It's forcing me to **watch her too closely.** Why should **she** make the rules?
I WANT TO KNOW ***WHAT'S*** GOING ON. ***WHERE*** ARE WE HEADING?
I ***TOLD*** YOU, TO THE ***SURFACE.***
WHAT'S GOING TO HAPPEN WHEN WE GET THERE??
YOU'LL FIND OUT.

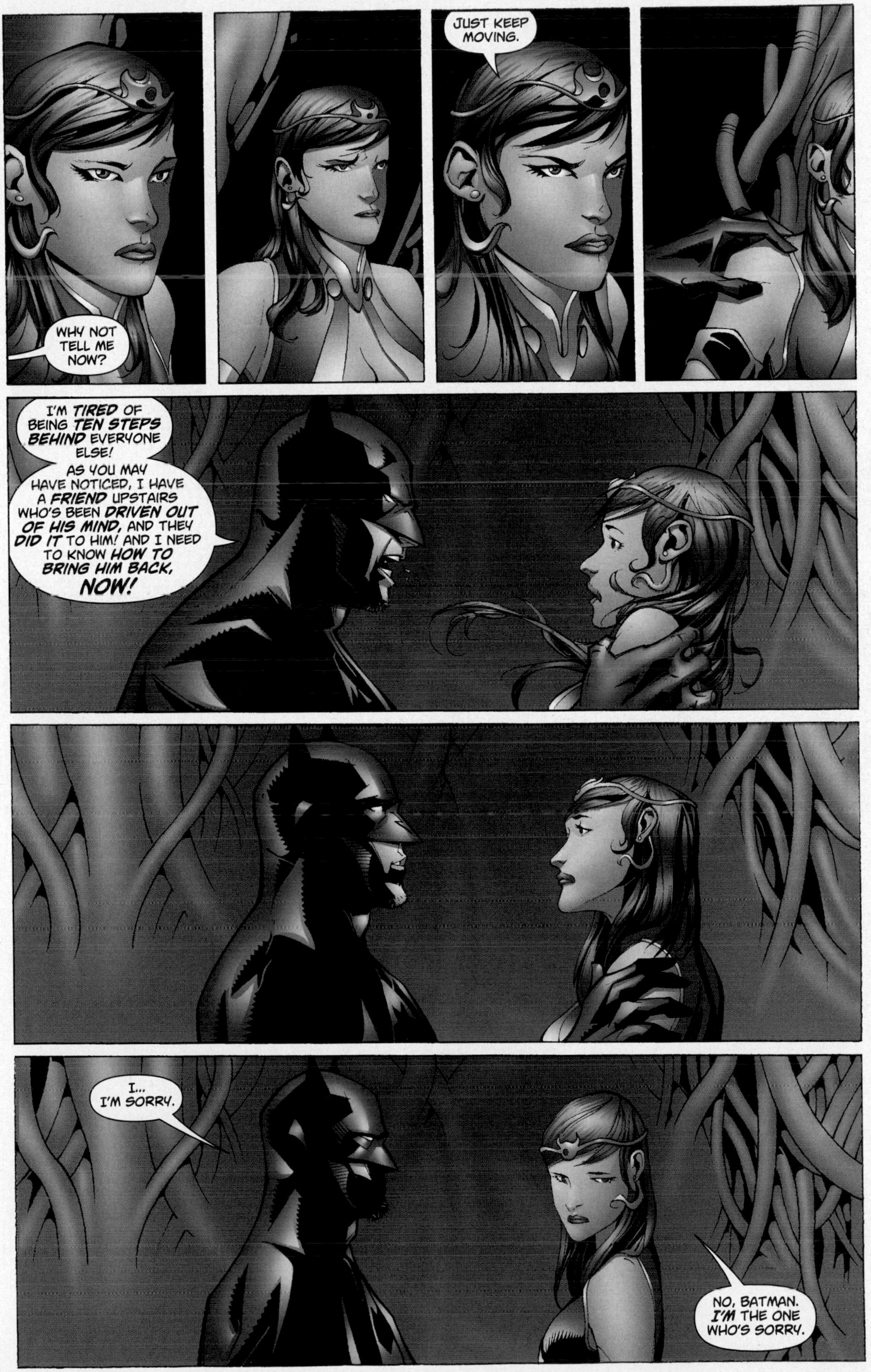
WHY NOT TELL ME NOW?
JUST KEEP MOVING.
I'M TIRED OF BEING TEN STEPS BEHIND EVERYONE ELSE!
AS YOU MAY HAVE NOTICED, I HAVE A FRIEND UPSTAIRS WHO'S BEEN DRIVEN OUT OF HIS MIND, AND THEY DID IT TO HIM! AND I NEED TO KNOW HOW TO BRING HIM BACK, NOW!
I... I'M SORRY.
NO, BATMAN. I'M THE ONE WHO'S SORRY.

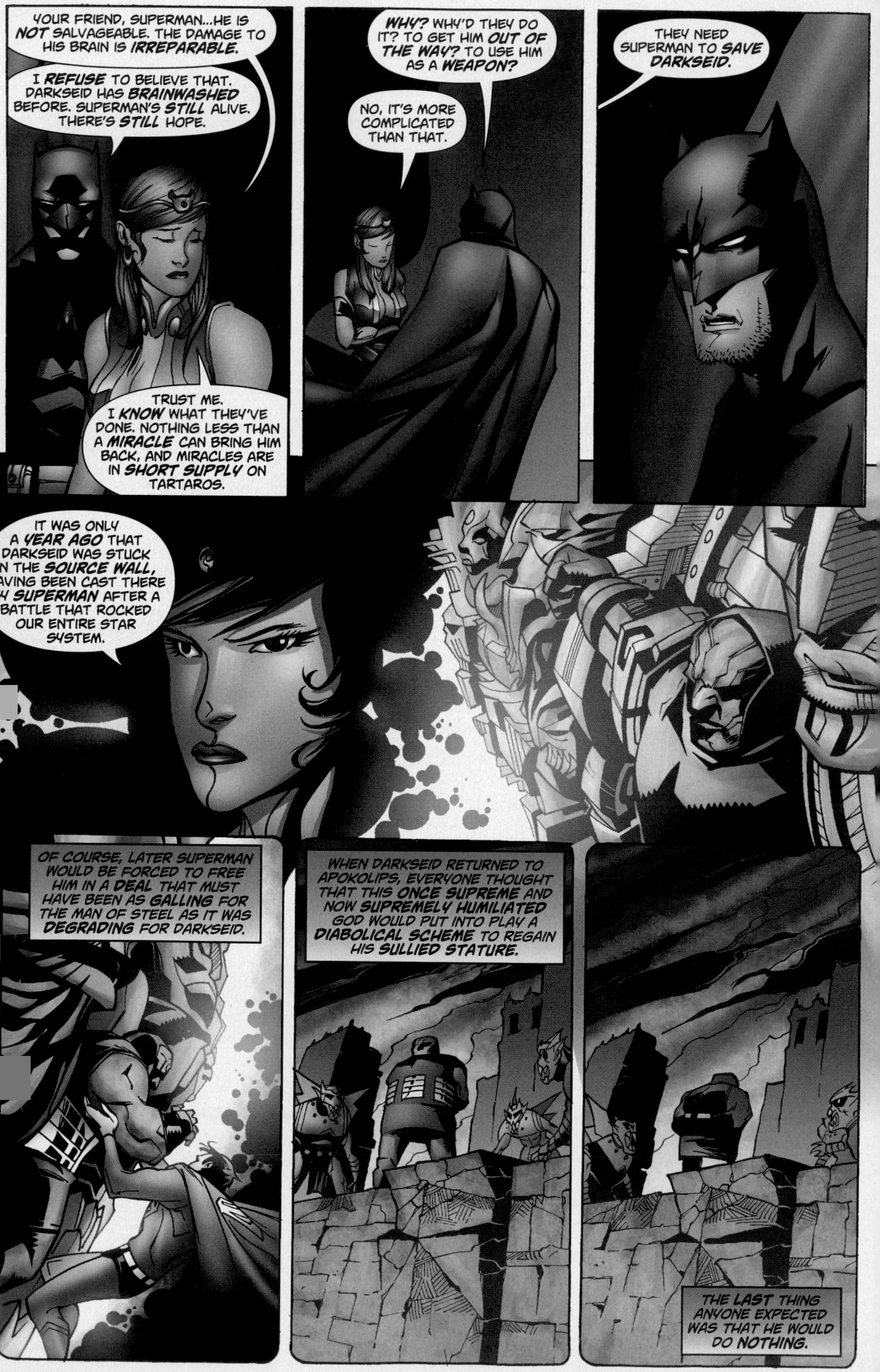
YOUR FRIEND, SUPERMAN...HE IS NOT SALVAGEABLE. THE DAMAGE TO HIS BRAIN IS IRREPARABLE.
I REFUSE TO BELIEVE THAT. DARKSEID HAS BRAINWASHED BEFORE. SUPERMAN'S STILL ALIVE. THERE'S STILL HOPE.
TRUST ME. I KNOW WHAT THEY'VE DONE. NOTHING LESS THAN A MIRACLE CAN BRING HIM BACK, AND MIRACLES ARE IN SHORT SUPPLY ON TARTAROS.
WHY? WHY'D THEY DO IT? TO GET HIM OUT OF THE WAY? TO USE HIM AS A WEAPON?
NO, IT'S MORE COMPLICATED THAN THAT.
THEY NEED SUPERMAN TO SAVE DARKSEID.
IT WAS ONLY A YEAR AGO THAT DARKSEID WAS STUCK IN THE SOURCE WALL, HAVING BEEN CAST THERE BY SUPERMAN AFTER A BATTLE THAT ROCKED OUR ENTIRE STAR SYSTEM.
OF COURSE, LATER SUPERMAN WOULD BE FORCED TO FREE HIM IN A DEAL THAT MUST HAVE BEEN AS GALLING FOR THE MAN OF STEEL AS IT WAS DEGRADING FOR DARKSEID.
WHEN DARKSEID RETURNED TO APOKOLIPS, EVERYONE THOUGHT THAT THIS ONCE SUPREME AND NOW SUPREMELY HUMILIATED GOD WOULD PUT INTO PLAY A DIABOLICAL SCHEME TO REGAIN HIS SULLIED STATURE.
THE LAST THING ANYONE EXPECTED WAS THAT HE WOULD DO NOTHING.

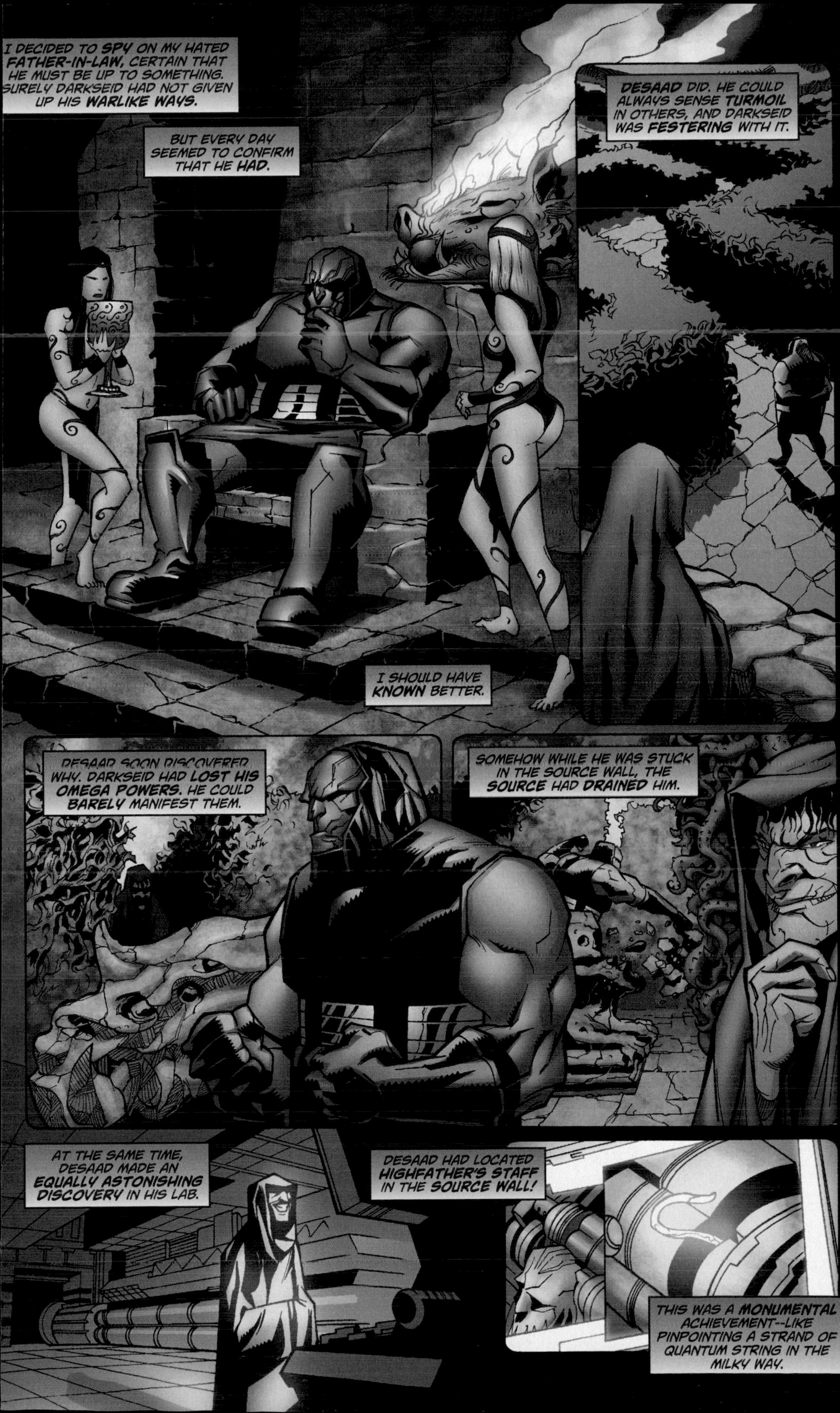
I DECIDED TO SPY ON MY HATED FATHER-IN-LAW, CERTAIN THAT HE MUST BE UP TO SOMETHING. SURELY DARKSEID HAD NOT GIVEN UP HIS WARLIKE WAYS.
BUT EVERY DAY SEEMED TO CONFIRM THAT HE HAD.
I SHOULD HAVE KNOWN BETTER.
DESAAD DID. HE COULD ALWAYS SENSE TURMOIL IN OTHERS, AND DARKSEID WAS FESTERING WITH IT.
DESAAD SOON DISCOVERED WHY. DARKSEID HAD LOST HIS OMEGA POWERS. HE COULD BARELY MANIFEST THEM.
SOMEHOW WHILE HE WAS STUCK IN THE SOURCE WALL, THE SOURCE HAD DRAINED HIM.
AT THE SAME TIME, DESAAD MADE AN EQUALLY ASTONISHING DISCOVERY IN HIS LAB.
DESAAD HAD LOCATED HIGHFATHER'S STAFF IN THE SOURCE WALL!
THIS WAS A MONUMENTAL ACHIEVEMENT--LIKE PINPOINTING A STRAND OF QUANTUM STRING IN THE MILKY WAY.

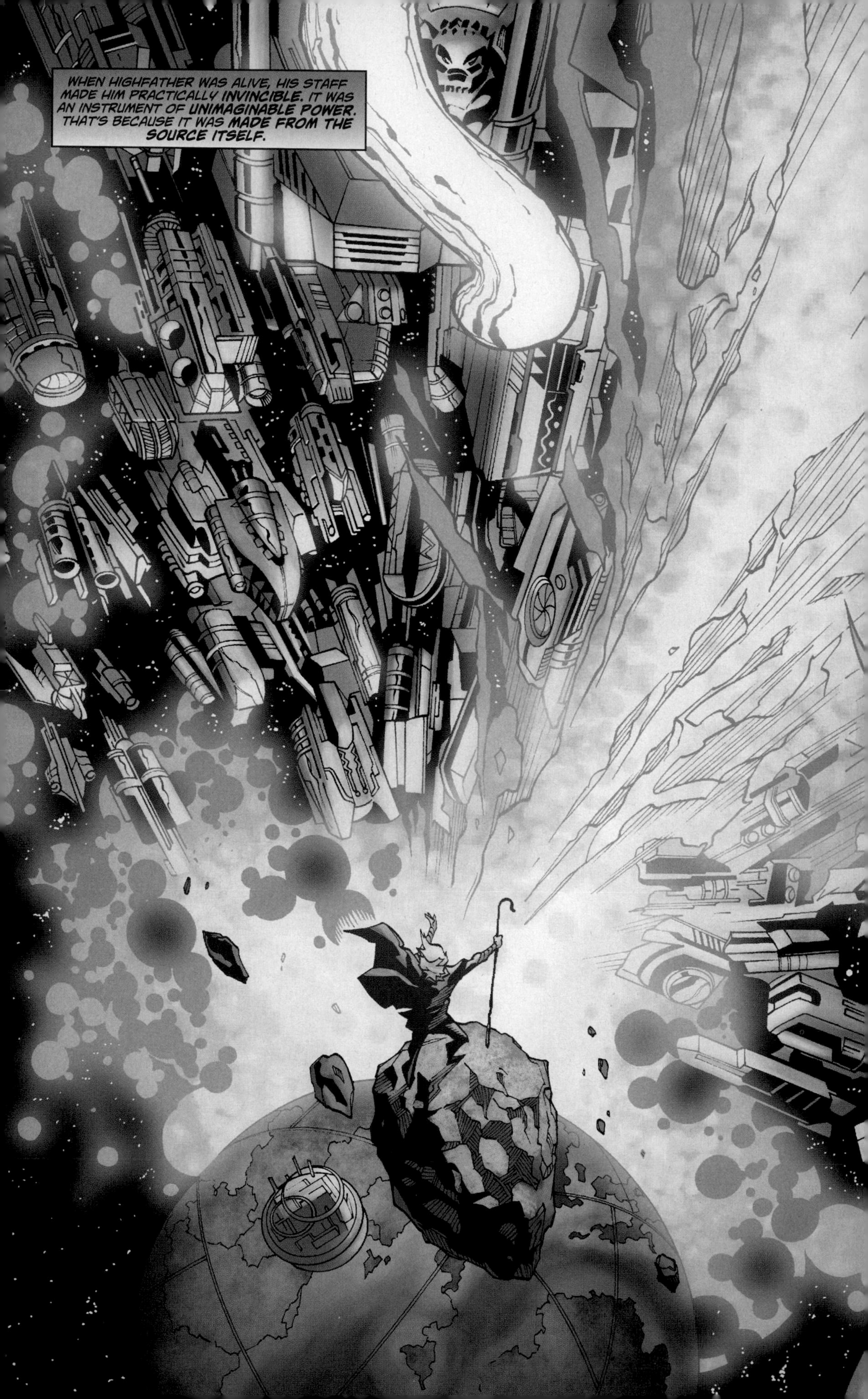
WHEN HIGHFATHER WAS ALIVE, HIS STAFF MADE HIM PRACTICALLY INVINCIBLE. IT WAS AN INSTRUMENT OF UNIMAGINABLE POWER. THAT'S BECAUSE IT WAS MADE FROM THE SOURCE ITSELF.

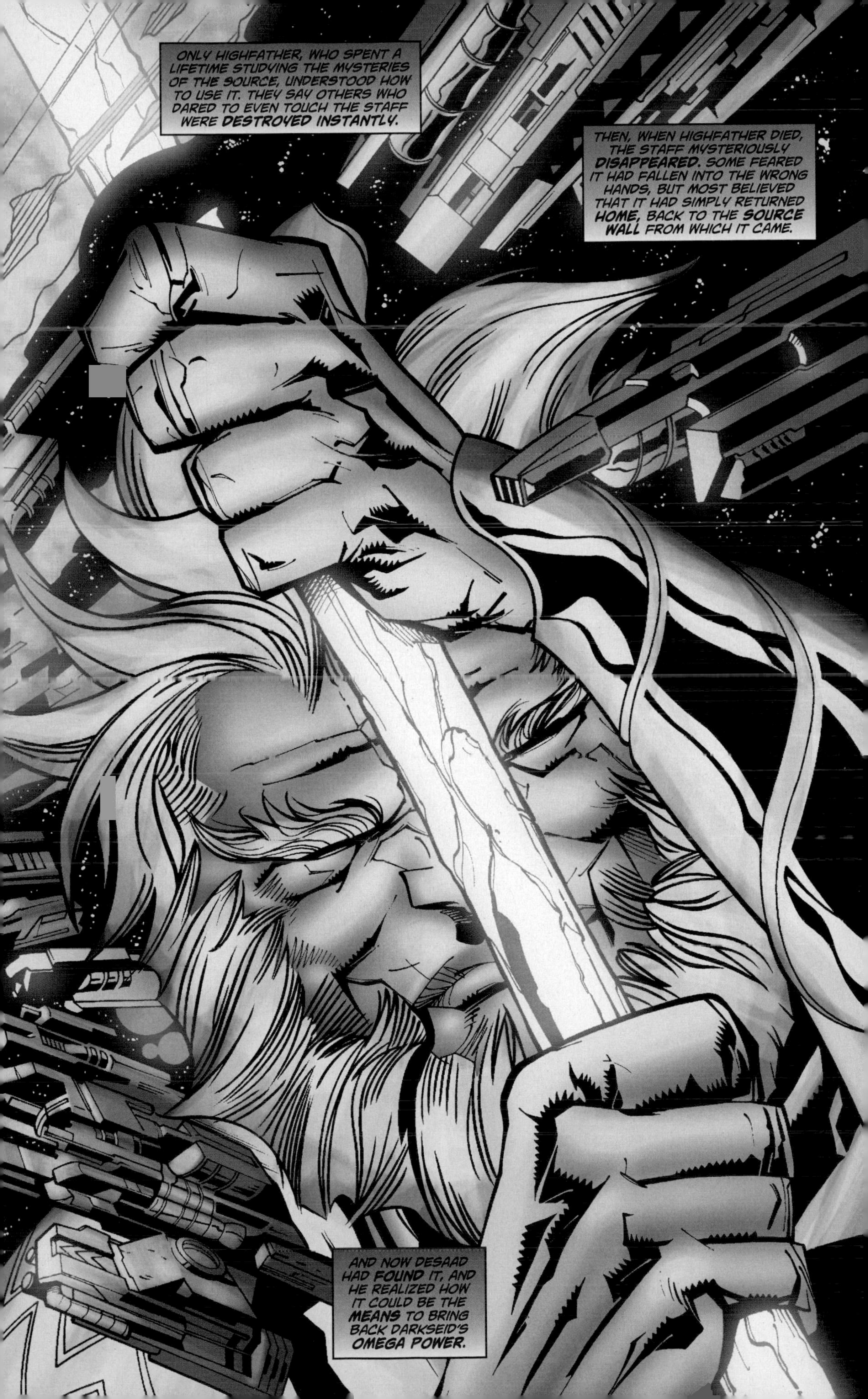
ONLY HIGHFATHER, WHO SPENT A LIFETIME STUDYING THE MYSTERIES OF THE SOURCE, UNDERSTOOD HOW TO USE IT. THEY SAY OTHERS WHO DARED TO EVEN TOUCH THE STAFF WERE DESTROYED INSTANTLY.
THEN, WHEN HIGHFATHER DIED, THE STAFF MYSTERIOUSLY DISAPPEARED. SOME FEARED IT HAD FALLEN INTO THE WRONG HANDS, BUT MOST BELIEVED THAT IT HAD SIMPLY RETURNED HOME, BACK TO THE SOURCE WALL FROM WHICH IT CAME.
AND NOW DESAAD HAD FOUND IT, AND HE REALIZED HOW IT COULD BE THE MEANS TO BRING BACK DARKSEID'S OMEGA POWER.

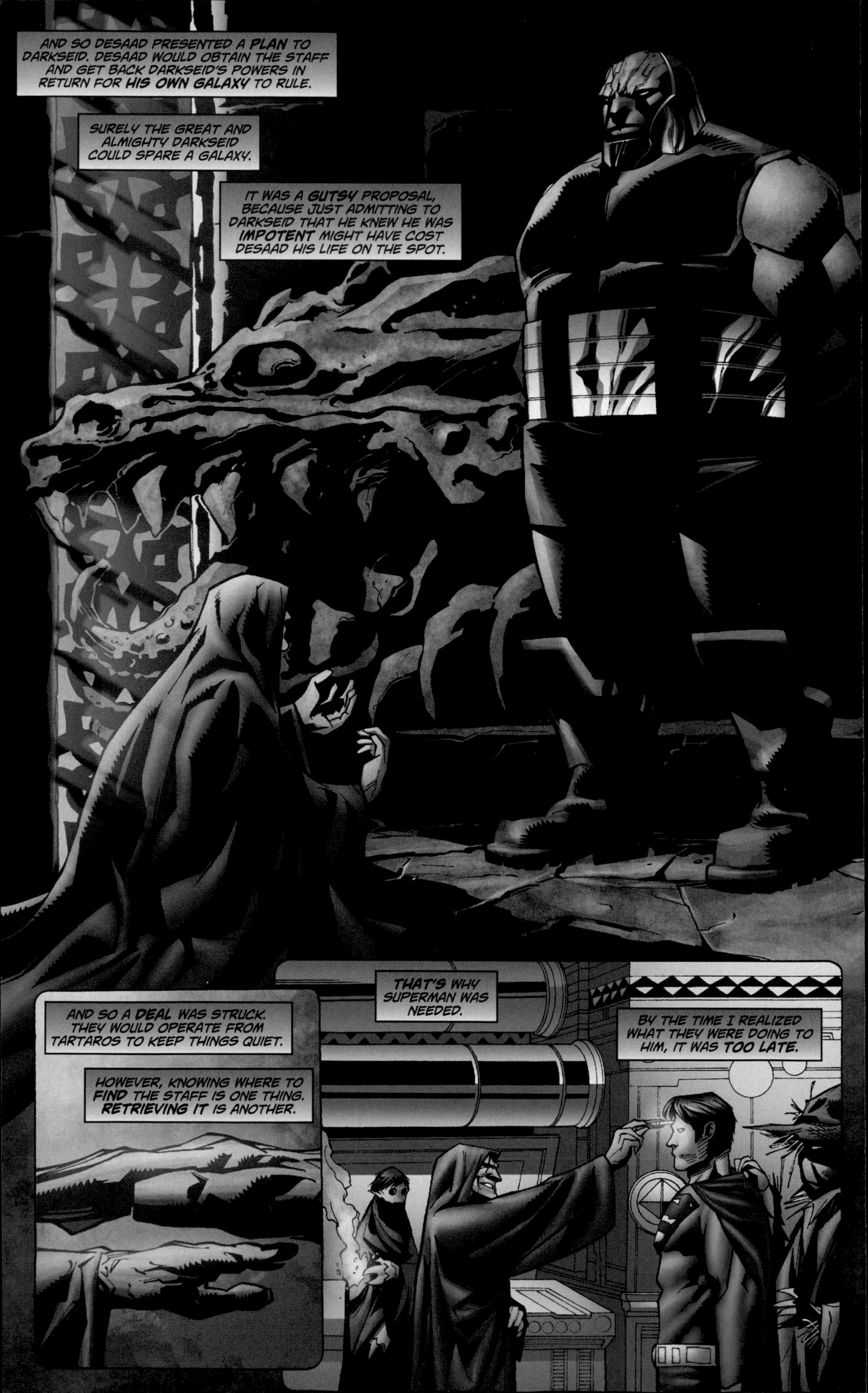
AND SO DESAAD PRESENTED A PLAN TO DARKSEID. DESAAD WOULD OBTAIN THE STAFF AND GET BACK DARKSEID'S POWERS IN RETURN FOR HIS OWN GALAXY TO RULE.
SURELY THE GREAT AND ALMIGHTY DARKSEID COULD SPARE A GALAXY.
IT WAS A GUTSY PROPOSAL, BECAUSE JUST ADMITTING TO DARKSEID THAT HE KNEW HE WAS IMPOTENT MIGHT HAVE COST DESAAD HIS LIFE ON THE SPOT.
AND SO A DEAL WAS STRUCK. THEY WOULD OPERATE FROM TARTAROS TO KEEP THINGS QUIET.
HOWEVER, KNOWING WHERE TO FIND THE STAFF IS ONE THING. RETRIEVING IT IS ANOTHER.
THAT'S WHY SUPERMAN WAS NEEDED.
BY THE TIME I REALIZED WHAT THEY WERE DOING TO HIM, IT WAS TOO LATE.

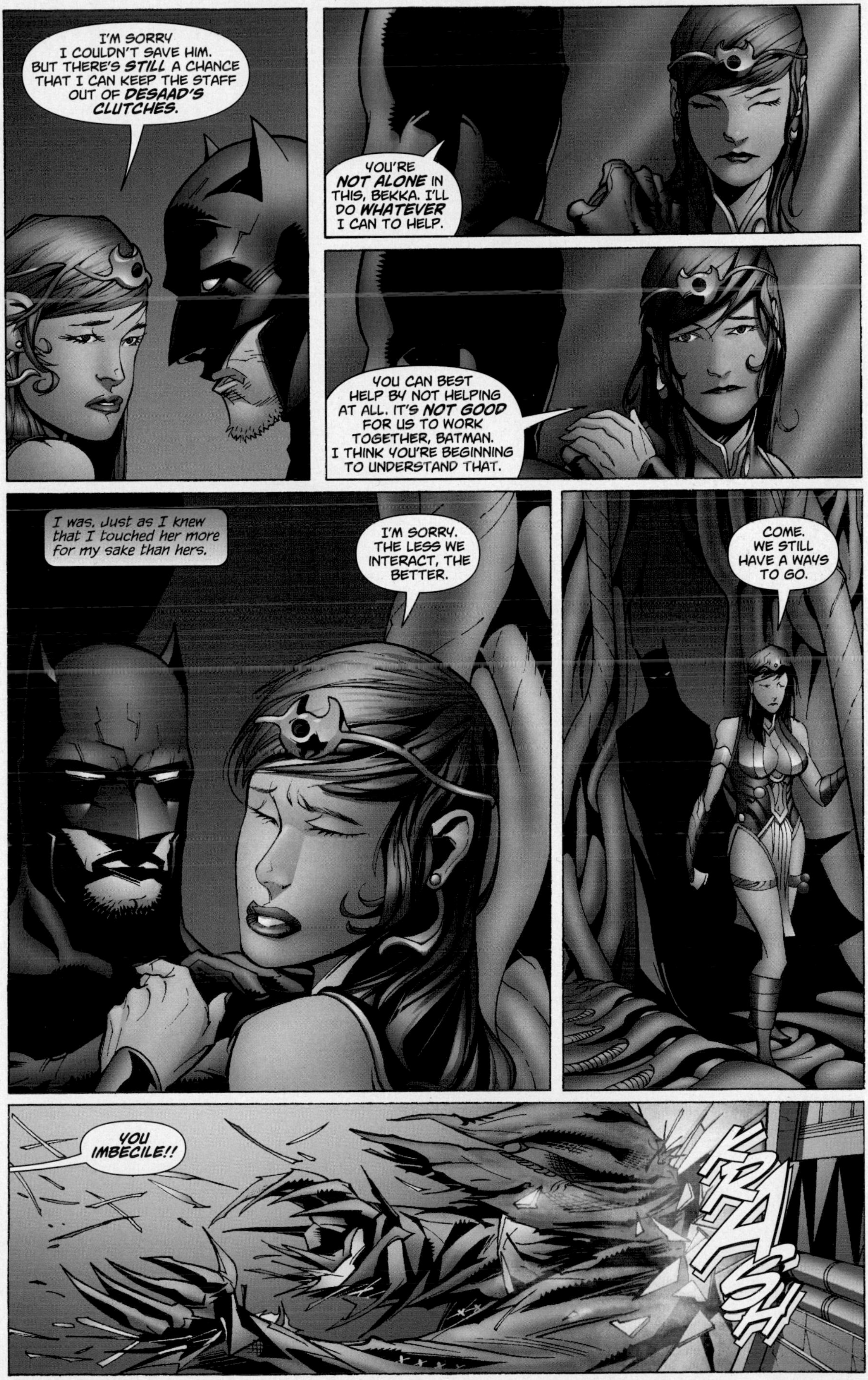
I'M SORRY I COULDN'T SAVE HIM. BUT THERE'S STILL A CHANCE THAT I CAN KEEP THE STAFF OUT OF DESAAD'S CLUTCHES.
YOU'RE NOT ALONE IN THIS, BEKKA. I'LL DO WHATEVER I CAN TO HELP.
YOU CAN BEST HELP BY NOT HELPING AT ALL. IT'S NOT GOOD FOR US TO WORK TOGETHER, BATMAN. I THINK YOU'RE BEGINNING TO UNDERSTAND THAT.
I was. Just as I knew that I touched her more for my sake than hers.
I'M SORRY. THE LESS WE INTERACT, THE BETTER.
COME. WE STILL HAVE A WAYS TO GO.
YOU IMBECILE!!
KRASSH

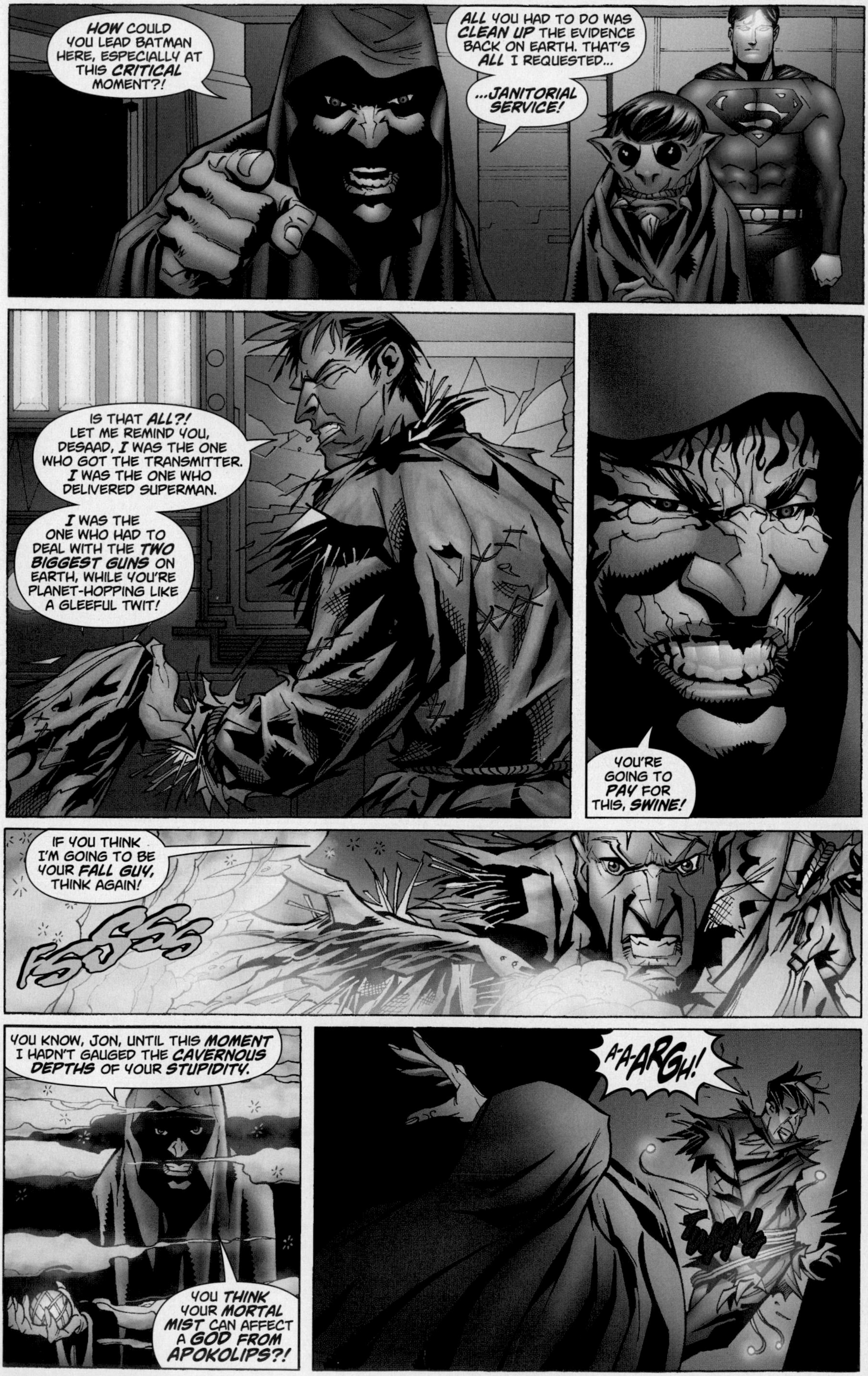
HOW COULD YOU LEAD BATMAN HERE, ESPECIALLY AT THIS CRITICAL MOMENT?!
ALL YOU HAD TO DO WAS CLEAN UP THE EVIDENCE BACK ON EARTH. THAT'S ALL I REQUESTED...
...JANITORIAL SERVICE!
IS THAT ALL?! LET ME REMIND YOU, DESAAD, I WAS THE ONE WHO GOT THE TRANSMITTER. I WAS THE ONE WHO DELIVERED SUPERMAN.
I WAS THE ONE WHO HAD TO DEAL WITH THE TWO BIGGEST GUNS ON EARTH, WHILE YOU'RE PLANET-HOPPING LIKE A GLEEFUL TWIT!
YOU'RE GOING TO PAY FOR THIS, SWINE!
IF YOU THINK I'M GOING TO BE YOUR FALL GUY, THINK AGAIN!
FSSSSS
YOU KNOW, JON, UNTIL THIS MOMENT I HADN'T GAUGED THE CAVERNOUS DEPTHS OF YOUR STUPIDITY.
YOU THINK YOUR MORTAL MIST CAN AFFECT A GOD FROM APOKOLIPS?!
A-A-ARGH!

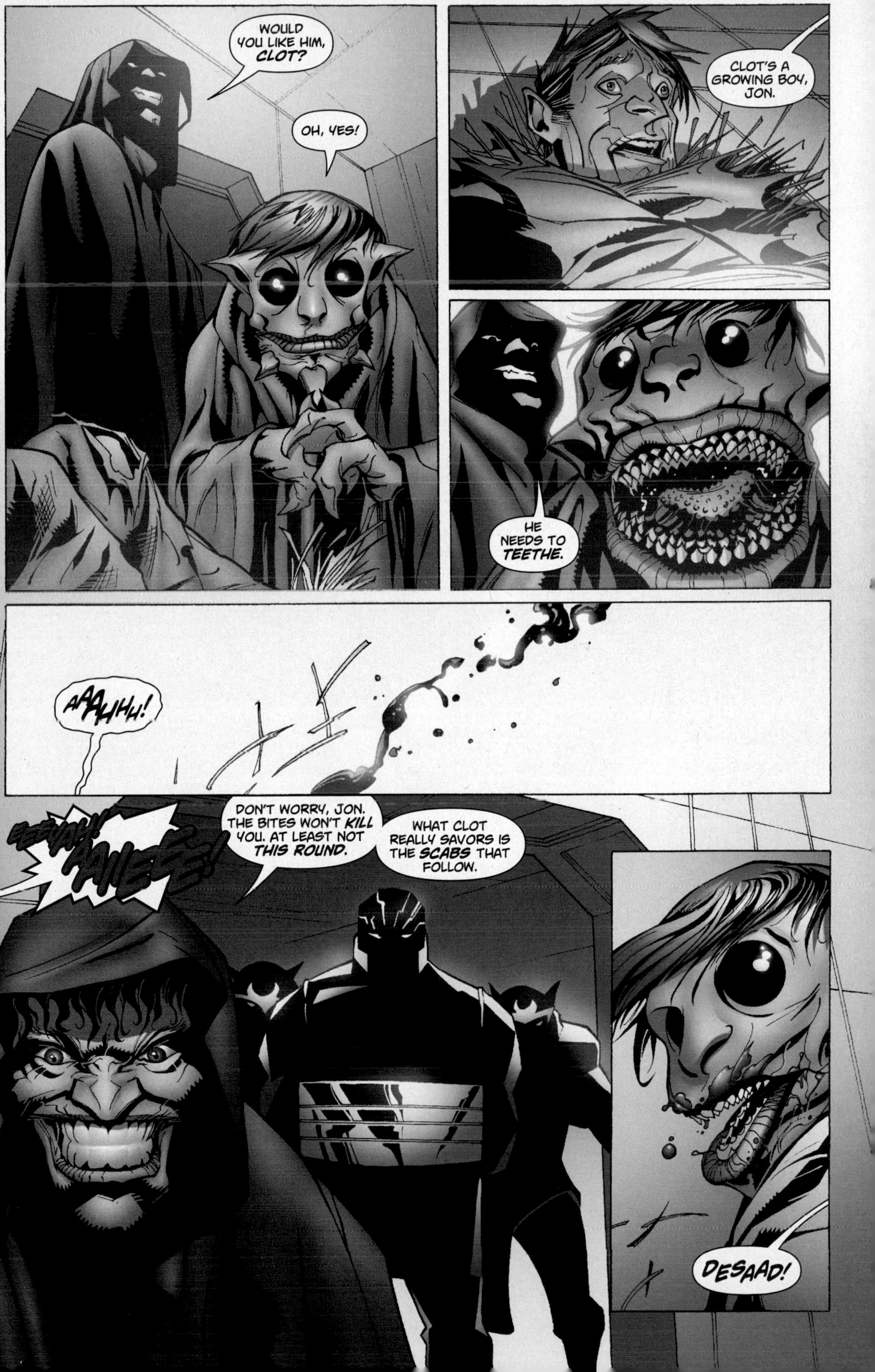
WOULD YOU LIKE HIM, CLOT?
OH, YES!
CLOT'S A GROWING BOY, JON.
HE NEEDS TO TEETHE.
AAAHHH!
DON'T WORRY, JON. THE BITES WON'T KILL YOU. AT LEAST NOT THIS ROUND.
WHAT CLOT REALLY SAVORS IS THE SCABS THAT FOLLOW.
DESAAD!

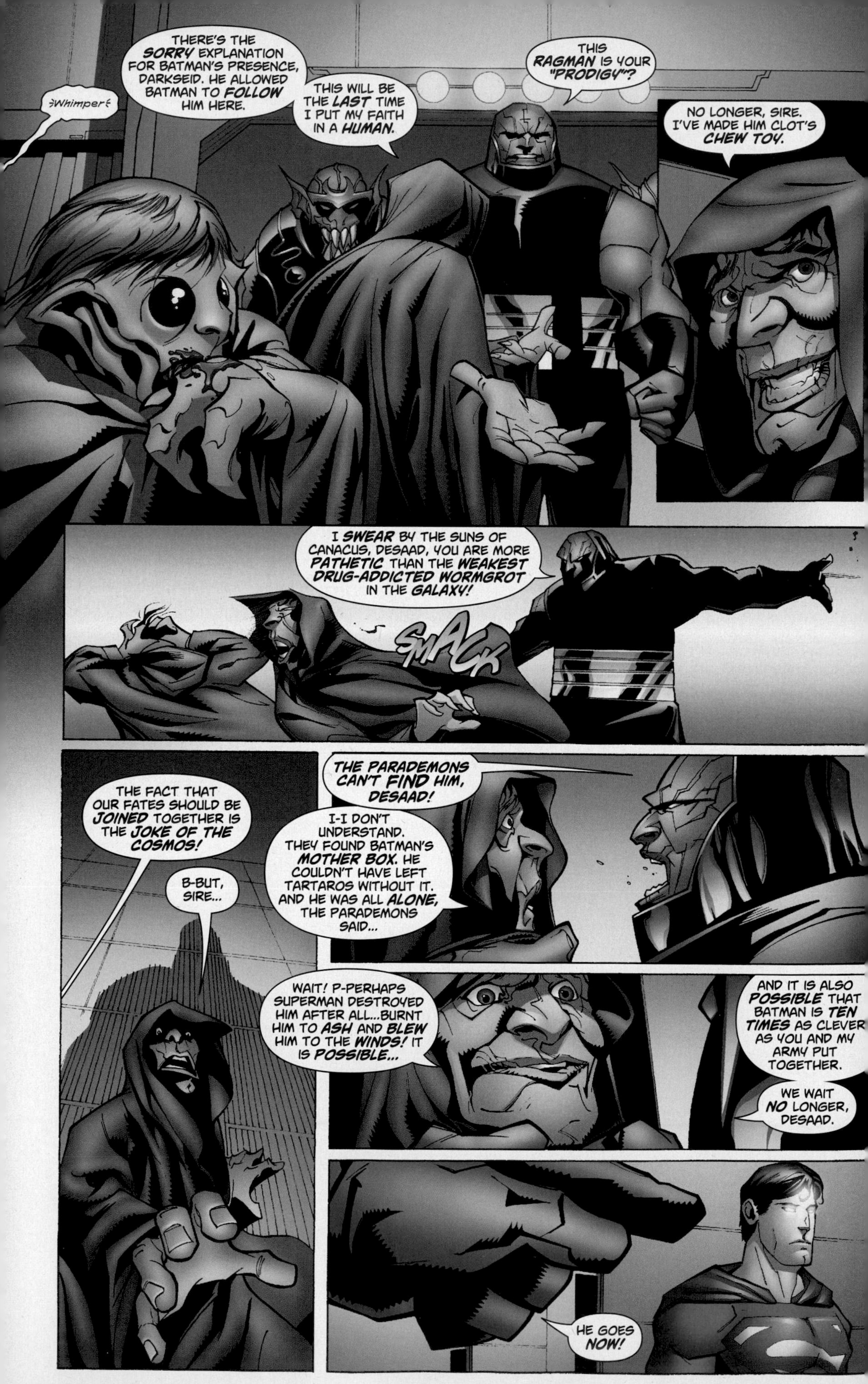

THERE'S THE SORRY EXPLANATION FOR BATMAN'S PRESENCE, DARKSEID. HE ALLOWED BATMAN TO FOLLOW HIM HERE.
Whimper
THIS WILL BE THE LAST TIME I PUT MY FAITH IN A HUMAN.
THIS RAGMAN IS YOUR "PRODIGY"?
NO LONGER, SIRE. I'VE MADE HIM CLOT'S CHEW TOY.
I SWEAR BY THE SUNS OF CANACUS, DESAAD, YOU ARE MORE PATHETIC THAN THE WEAKEST DRUG-ADDICTED WORMGROT IN THE GALAXY!
SMACK
THE FACT THAT OUR FATES SHOULD BE JOINED TOGETHER IS THE JOKE OF THE COSMOS!
B-BUT, SIRE...
THE PARADEMONS CAN'T FIND HIM, DESAAD!
I-I DON'T UNDERSTAND. THEY FOUND BATMAN'S MOTHER BOX. HE COULDN'T HAVE LEFT TARTAROS WITHOUT IT. AND HE WAS ALL ALONE, THE PARADEMONS SAID...
WAIT! P-PERHAPS SUPERMAN DESTROYED HIM AFTER ALL...BURNT HIM TO ASH AND BLEW HIM TO THE WINDS! IT IS POSSIBLE...
AND IT IS ALSO POSSIBLE THAT BATMAN IS TEN TIMES AS CLEVER AS YOU AND MY ARMY PUT TOGETHER.
WE WAIT NO LONGER, DESAAD.
HE GOES NOW!

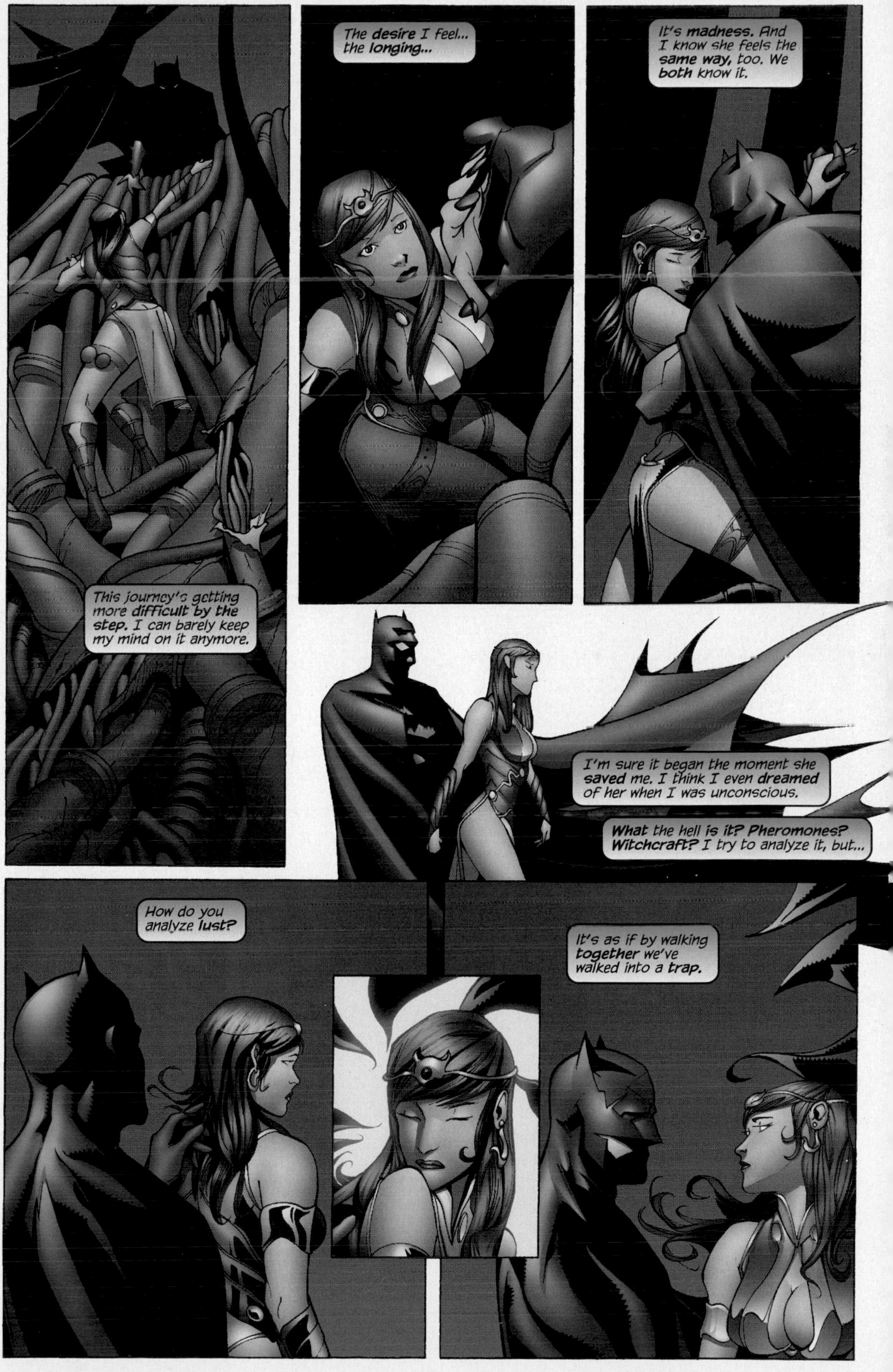

This journey's getting more difficult by the step. I can barely keep my mind on it anymore.
The desire I feel... the longing...
It's madness. And I know she feels the same way, too. We both know it.
I'm sure it began the moment she saved me. I think I even dreamed of her when I was unconscious.
What the hell is it? Pheromones? Witchcraft? I try to analyze it, but...
How do you analyze lust?
It's as if by walking together we've walked into a trap.

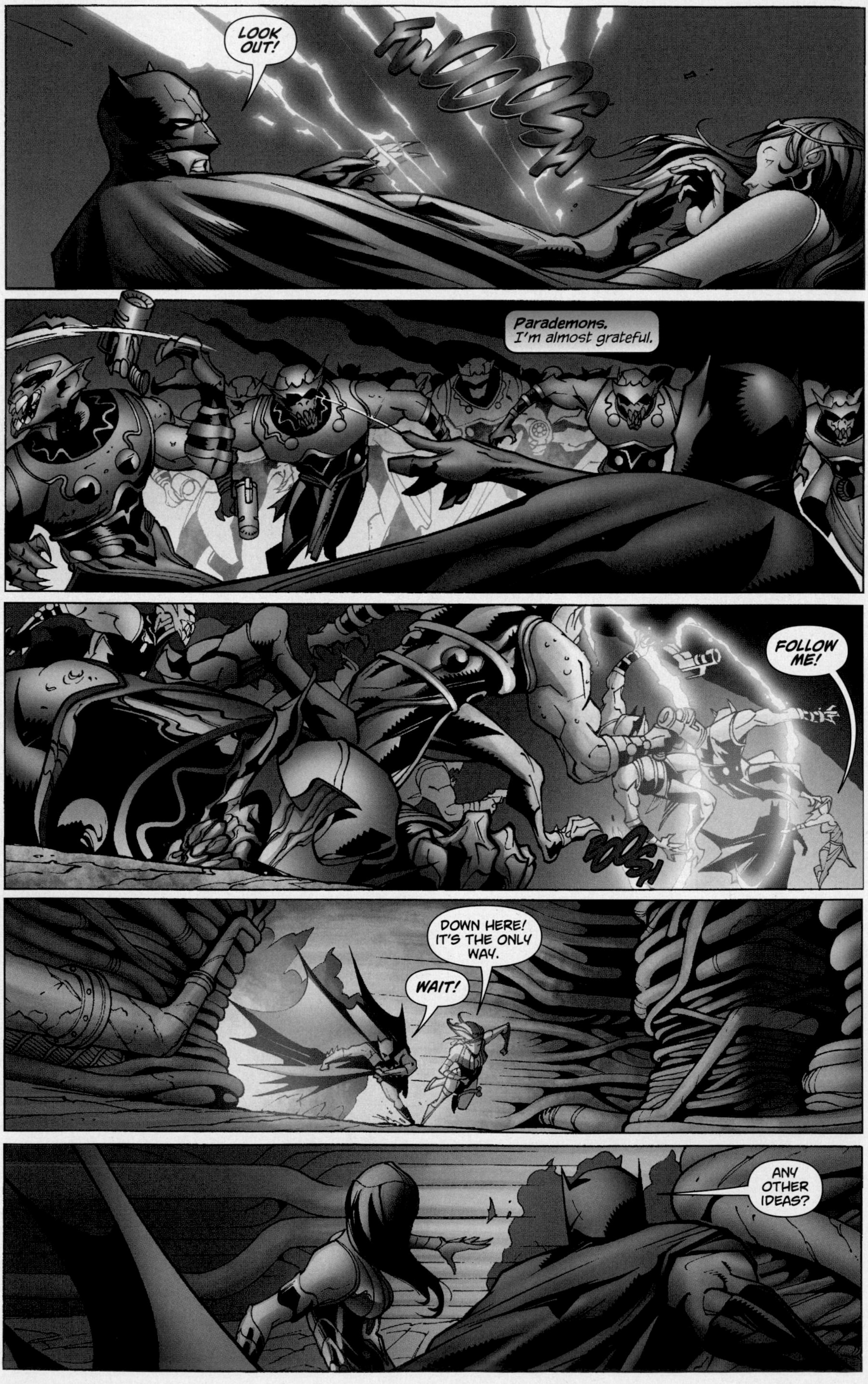
LOOK OUT!
FWOOOSH
Parademons. I'm almost grateful.
FOLLOW ME!
WOOSH
DOWN HERE! IT'S THE ONLY WAY.
WAIT!
ANY OTHER IDEAS?

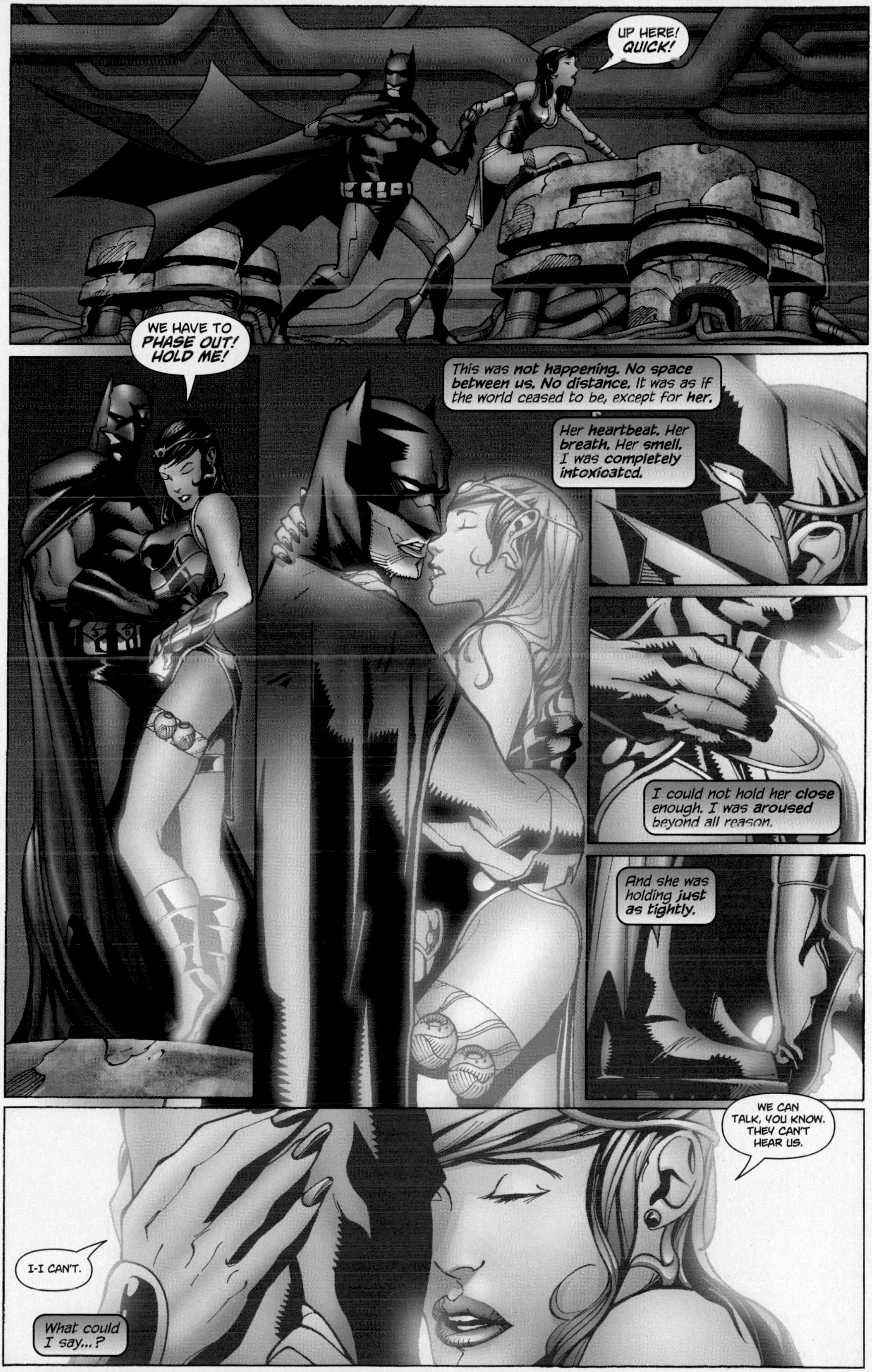
UP HERE! QUICK!
WE HAVE TO PHASE OUT! HOLD ME!
This was not happening. No space between us. No distance. It was as if the world ceased to be, except for her.
Her heartbeat. Her breath. Her smell. I was completely intoxicated.
I could not hold her close enough. I was aroused beyond all reason.
And she was holding just as tightly.
WE CAN TALK, YOU KNOW. THEY CAN'T HEAR US.
I-I CAN'T.
What could I say...?

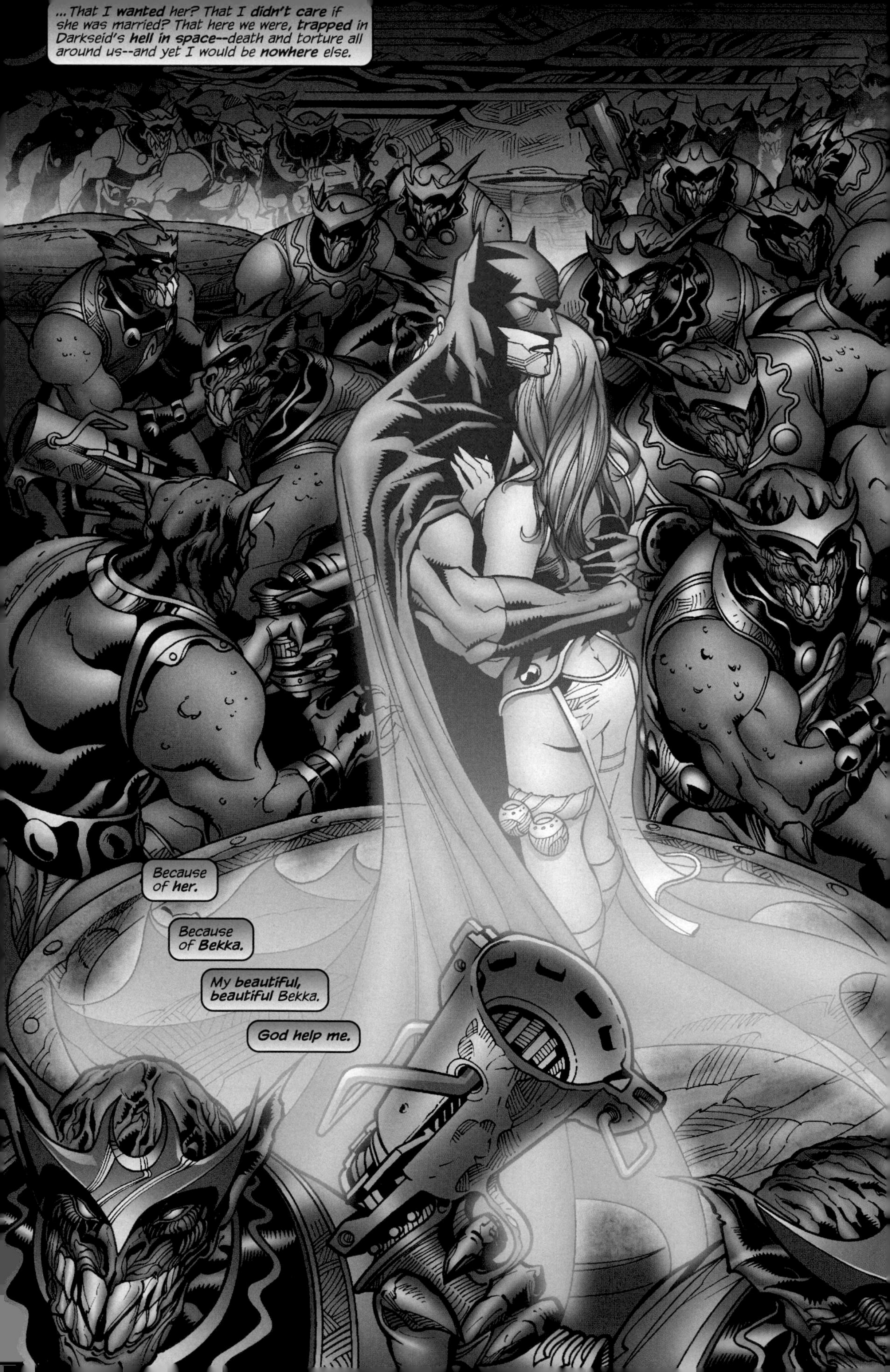

...That I wanted her? That I didn't care if she was married? That here we were, trapped in Darkseid's hell in space--death and torture all around us--and yet I would be nowhere else.
Because of her.
Because of Bekka.
My beautiful, beautiful Bekka.
God help me.

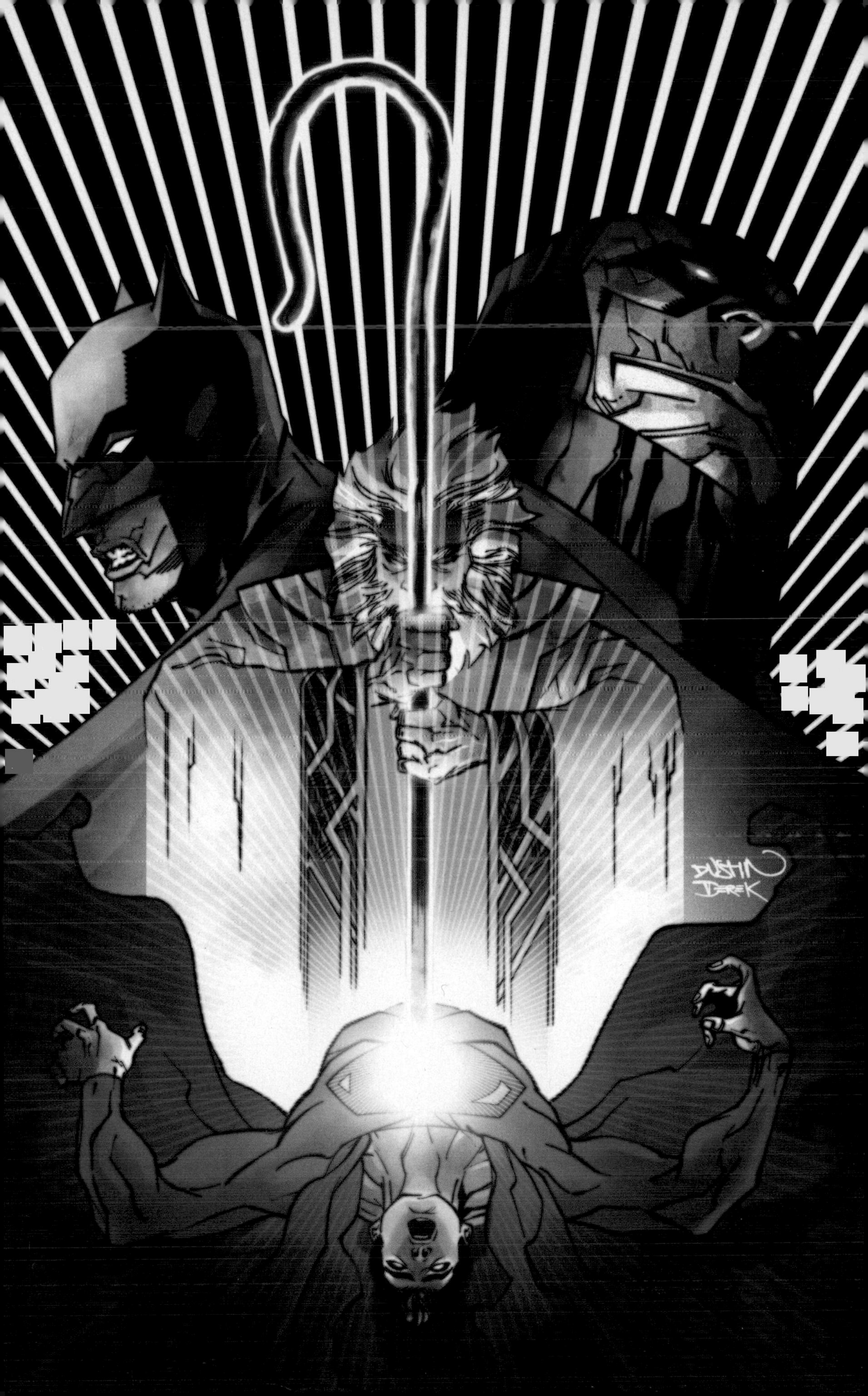
DUSTIN
DEREK

TORMENT: PART FIVE
PURGATORY

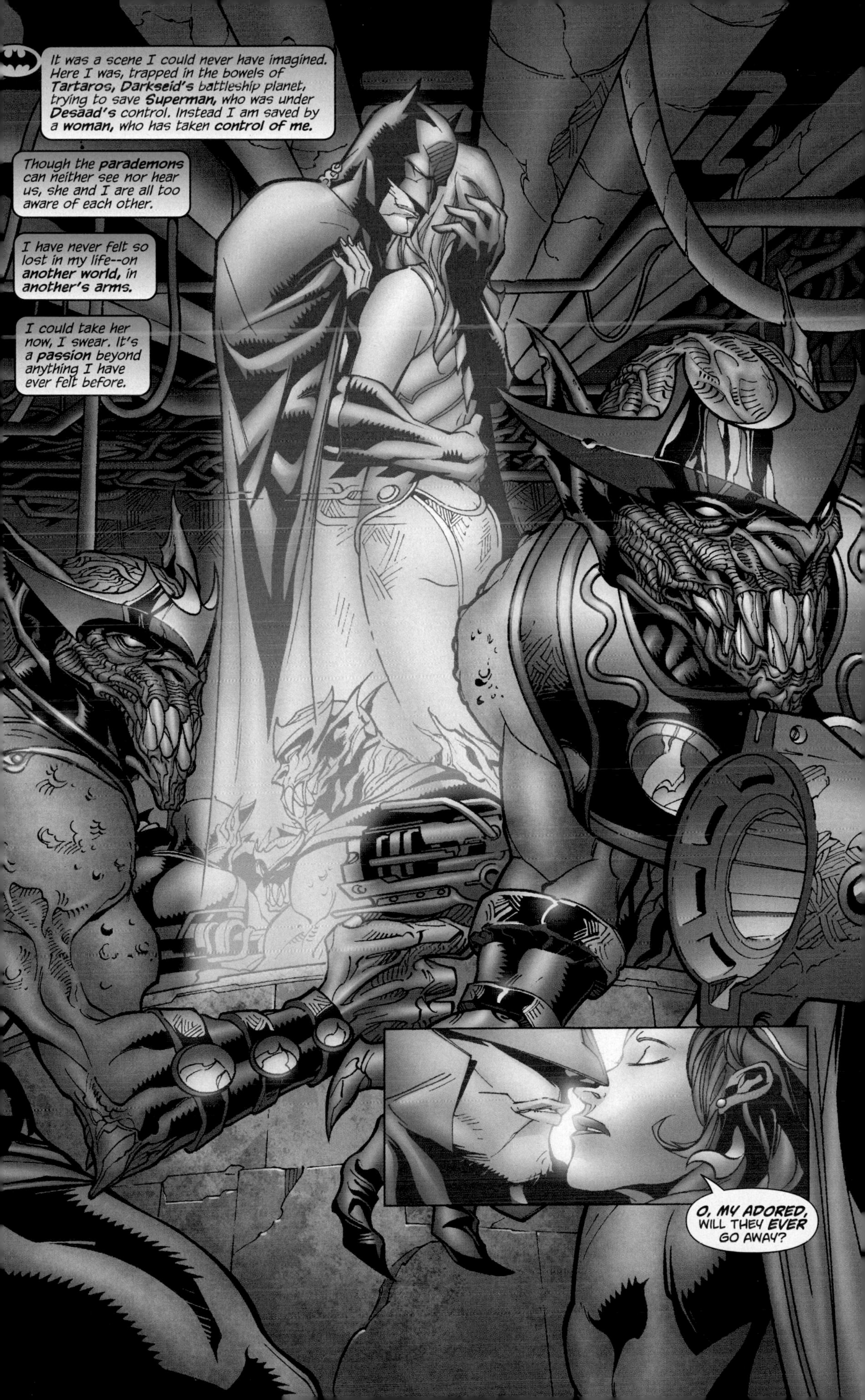
It was a scene I could never have imagined. Here I was, trapped in the bowels of Tartaros, Darkseid's battleship planet, trying to save Superman, who was under Desaad's control. Instead I am saved by a woman, who has taken control of me.
Though the parademons can neither see nor hear us, she and I are all too aware of each other.
I have never felt so lost in my life--on another world, in another's arms.
I could take her now, I swear. It's a passion beyond anything I have ever felt before.
O, MY ADORED, WILL THEY EVER GO AWAY?

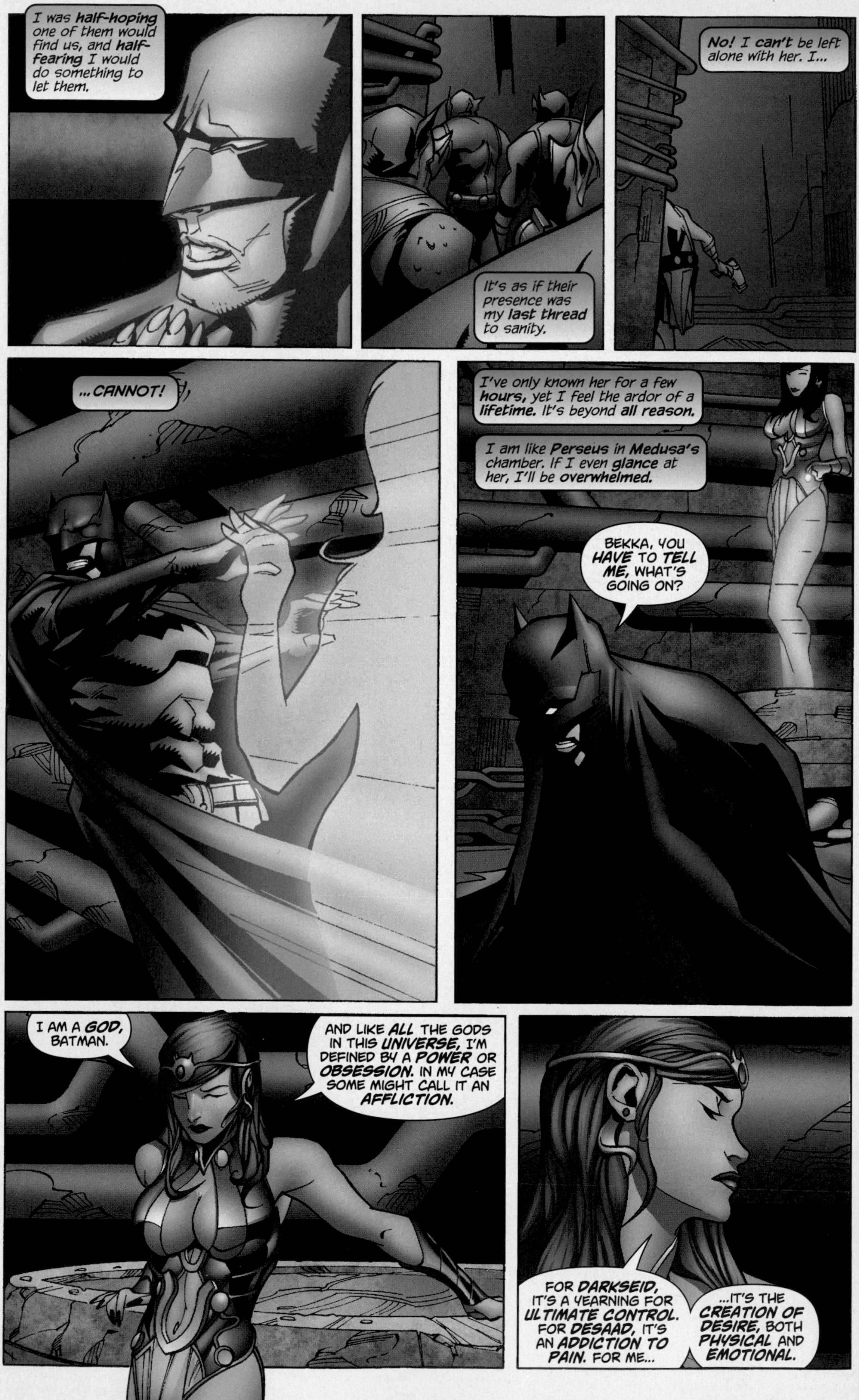

I was **half-hoping** one of them would find us, and **half-fearing** I would do something to let them.
It's as if their presence was my **last thread** to sanity.
No! I **can't** be left alone with her. I...
...**CANNOT!**
I've only known her for a few **hours,** yet I feel the ardor of a **lifetime.** It's beyond **all reason.**
I am like **Perseus** in **Medusa's** chamber. If I even **glance** at her, I'll be **overwhelmed.**
BEKKA, YOU **HAVE** TO **TELL ME,** WHAT'S GOING ON?
I AM A ***GOD,*** BATMAN.
AND LIKE ***ALL*** THE GODS IN THIS ***UNIVERSE,*** I'M DEFINED BY A ***POWER*** OR ***OBSESSION.*** IN MY CASE SOME MIGHT CALL IT AN ***AFFLICTION.***
FOR ***DARKSEID,*** IT'S A YEARNING FOR ***ULTIMATE CONTROL.*** FOR ***DESAAD,*** IT'S AN ***ADDICTION TO PAIN.*** FOR ME...
...IT'S THE ***CREATION OF DESIRE,*** BOTH ***PHYSICAL*** AND ***EMOTIONAL.***

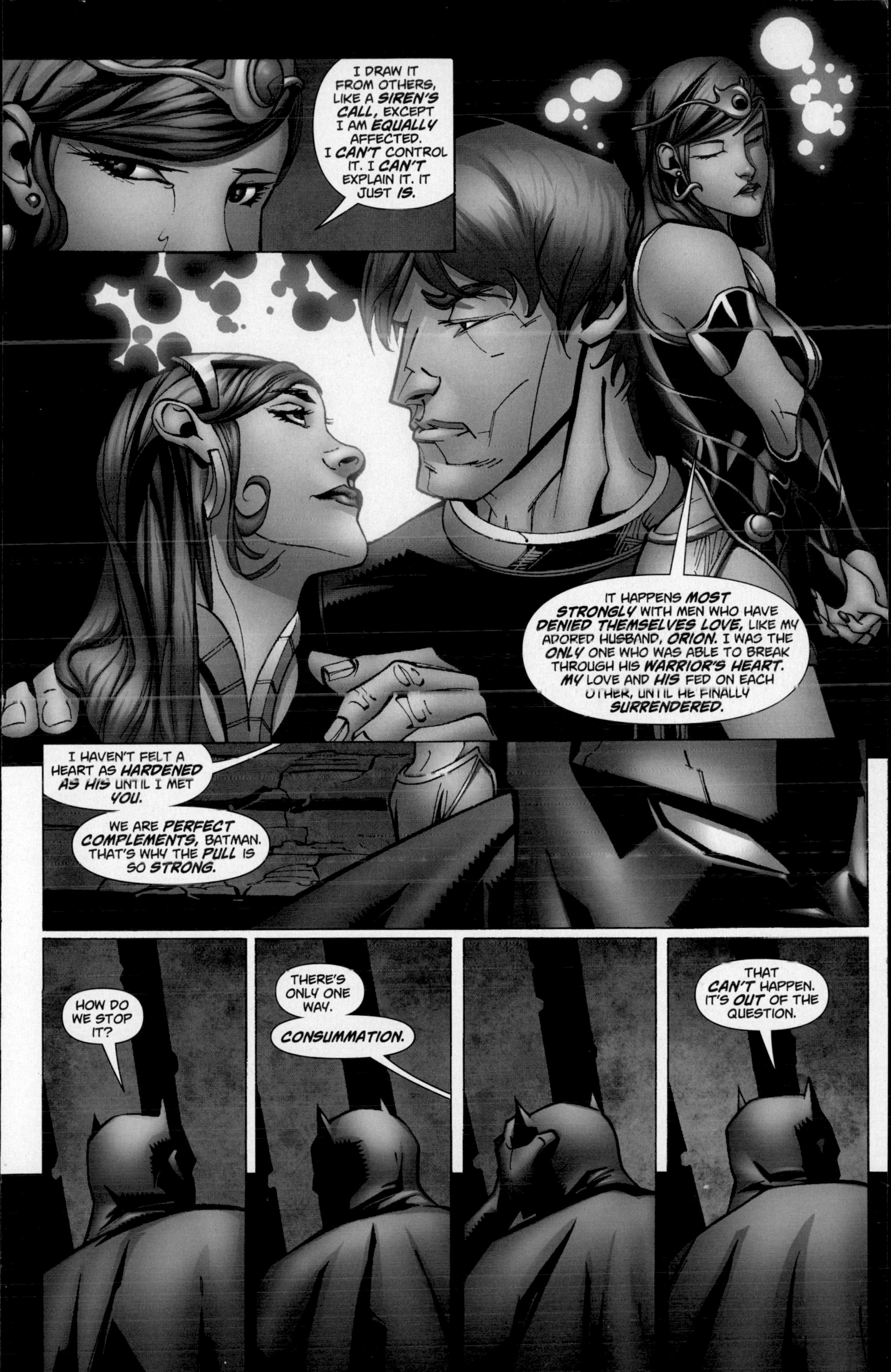
I DRAW IT FROM OTHERS, LIKE A SIREN'S CALL, EXCEPT I AM EQUALLY AFFECTED. I CAN'T CONTROL IT. I CAN'T EXPLAIN IT. IT JUST IS.
IT HAPPENS MOST STRONGLY WITH MEN WHO HAVE DENIED THEMSELVES LOVE, LIKE MY ADORED HUSBAND, ORION. I WAS THE ONLY ONE WHO WAS ABLE TO BREAK THROUGH HIS WARRIOR'S HEART. MY LOVE AND HIS FED ON EACH OTHER, UNTIL HE FINALLY SURRENDERED.
I HAVEN'T FELT A HEART AS HARDENED AS HIS UNTIL I MET YOU.
WE ARE PERFECT COMPLEMENTS, BATMAN. THAT'S WHY THE PULL IS SO STRONG.
HOW DO WE STOP IT?
THERE'S ONLY ONE WAY.
CONSUMMATION.
THAT CAN'T HAPPEN. IT'S OUT OF THE QUESTION.

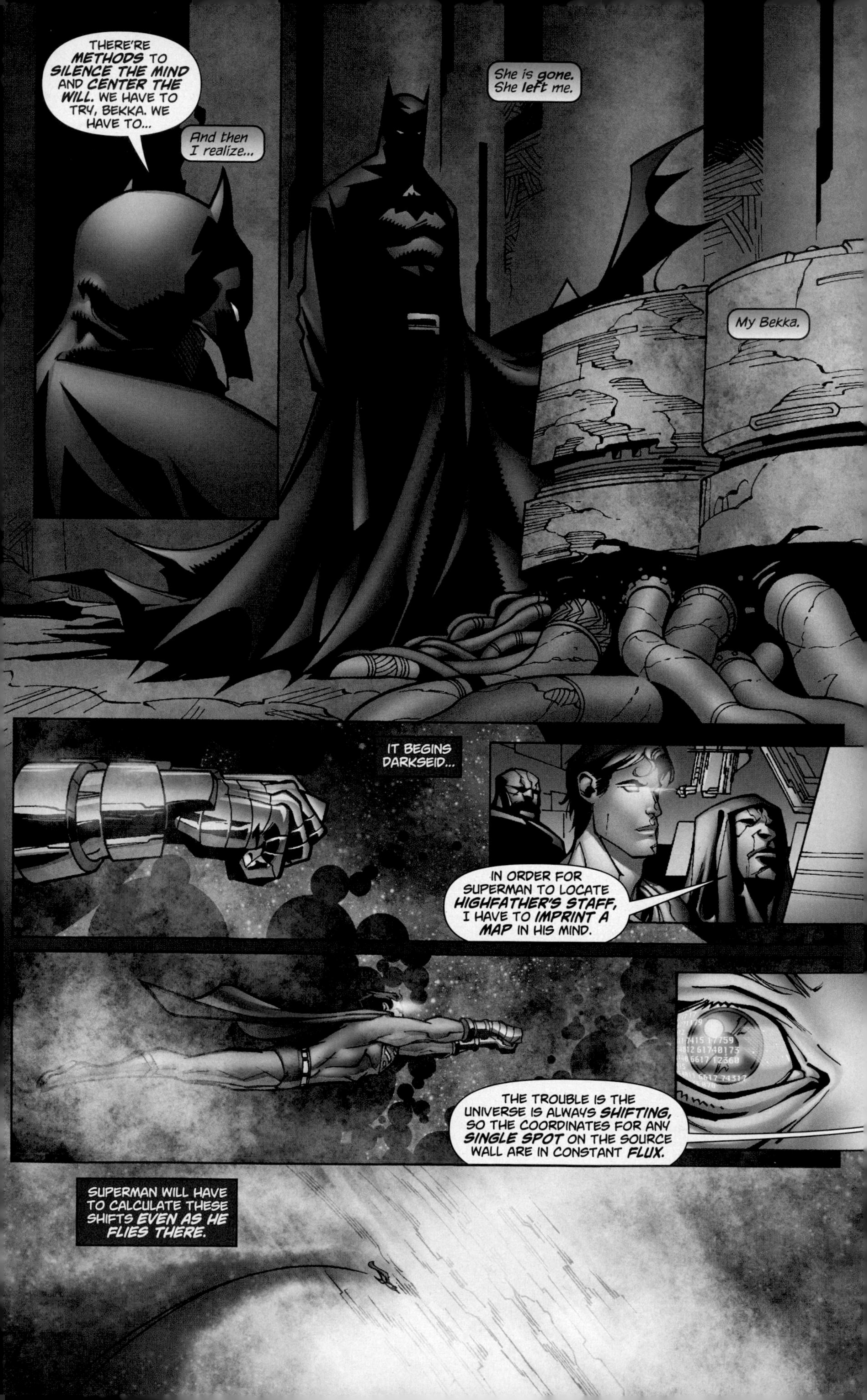
THERE'RE METHODS TO SILENCE THE MIND AND CENTER THE WILL. WE HAVE TO TRY, BEKKA. WE HAVE TO...
And then I realize...
She is gone. She left me.
My Bekka.
IT BEGINS DARKSEID...
IN ORDER FOR SUPERMAN TO LOCATE HIGHFATHER'S STAFF, I HAVE TO IMPRINT A MAP IN HIS MIND.
THE TROUBLE IS THE UNIVERSE IS ALWAYS SHIFTING, SO THE COORDINATES FOR ANY SINGLE SPOT ON THE SOURCE WALL ARE IN CONSTANT FLUX.
SUPERMAN WILL HAVE TO CALCULATE THESE SHIFTS EVEN AS HE FLIES THERE.

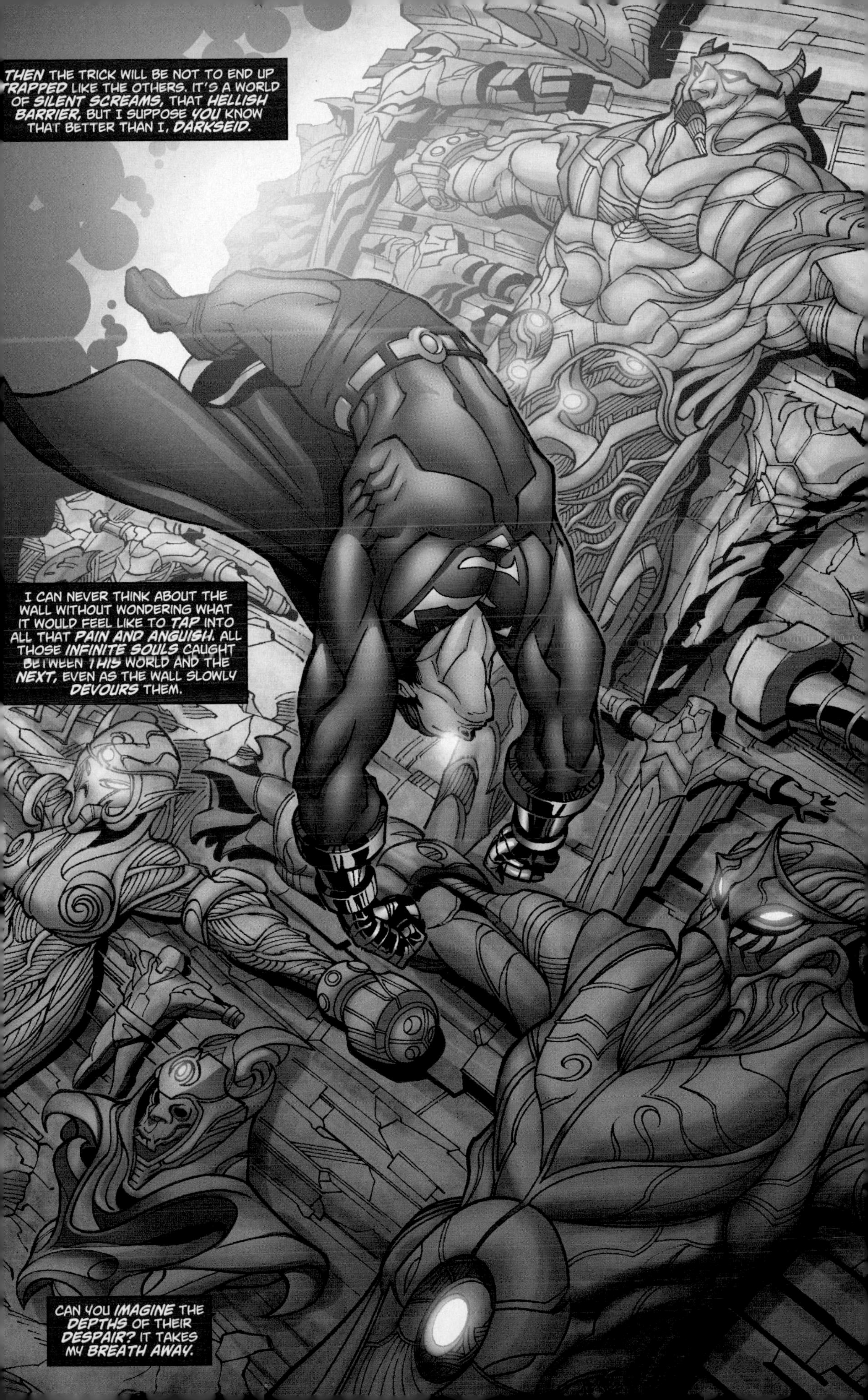
THEN THE TRICK WILL BE NOT TO END UP TRAPPED LIKE THE OTHERS. IT'S A WORLD OF SILENT SCREAMS, THAT HELLISH BARRIER, BUT I SUPPOSE YOU KNOW THAT BETTER THAN I, DARKSEID.
I CAN NEVER THINK ABOUT THE WALL WITHOUT WONDERING WHAT IT WOULD FEEL LIKE TO TAP INTO ALL THAT PAIN AND ANGUISH. ALL THOSE INFINITE SOULS CAUGHT BETWEEN THIS WORLD AND THE NEXT, EVEN AS THE WALL SLOWLY DEVOURS THEM.
CAN YOU IMAGINE THE DEPTHS OF THEIR DESPAIR? IT TAKES MY BREATH AWAY.

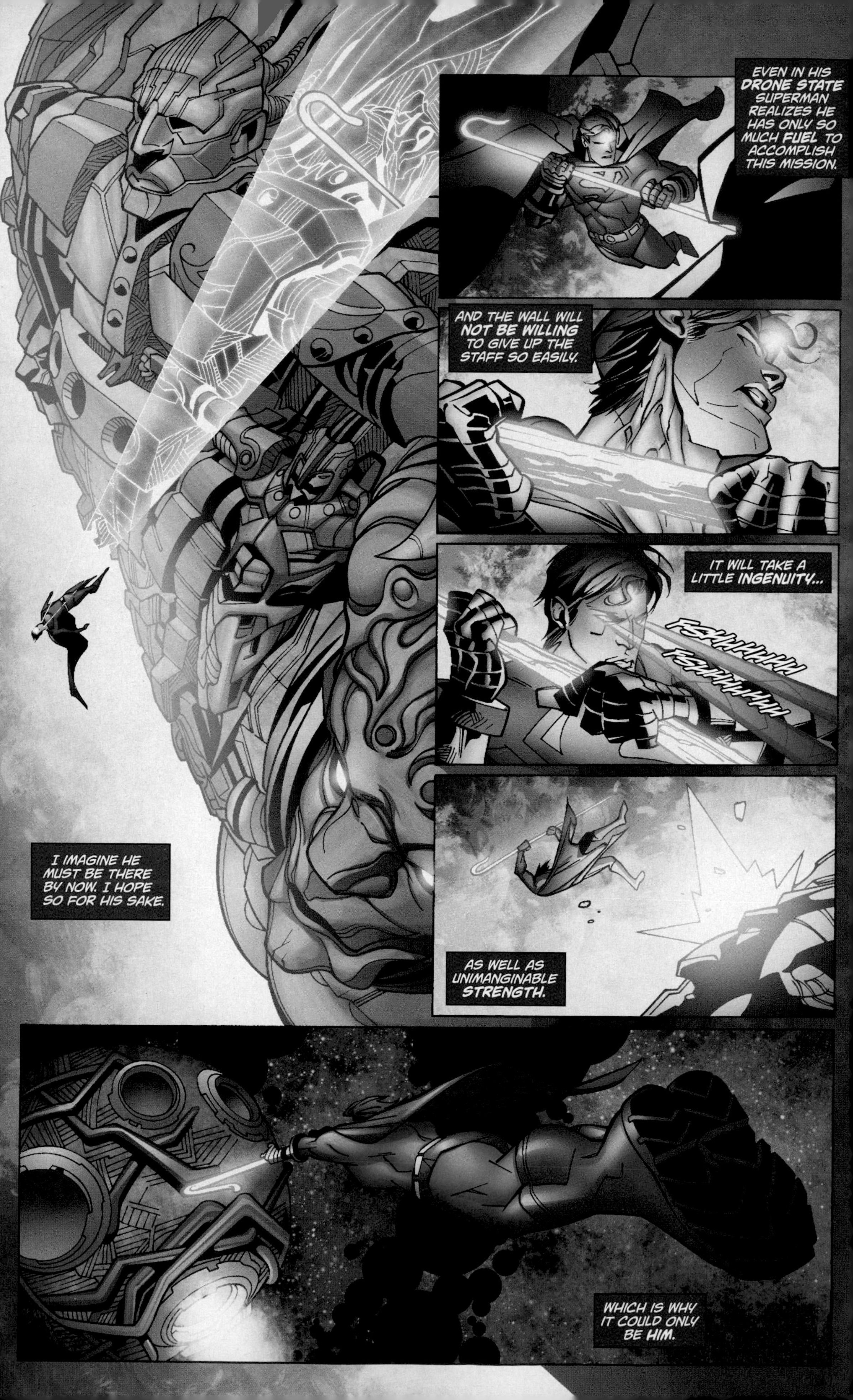

EVEN IN HIS DRONE STATE SUPERMAN REALIZES HE HAS ONLY SO MUCH FUEL TO ACCOMPLISH THIS MISSION.
AND THE WALL WILL NOT BE WILLING TO GIVE UP THE STAFF SO EASILY.
IT WILL TAKE A LITTLE INGENUITY...
FSHHHHHHH
FSHHHHHHH
I IMAGINE HE MUST BE THERE BY NOW. I HOPE SO FOR HIS SAKE.
AS WELL AS UNIMANGINABLE STRENGTH.
WHICH IS WHY IT COULD ONLY BE HIM.

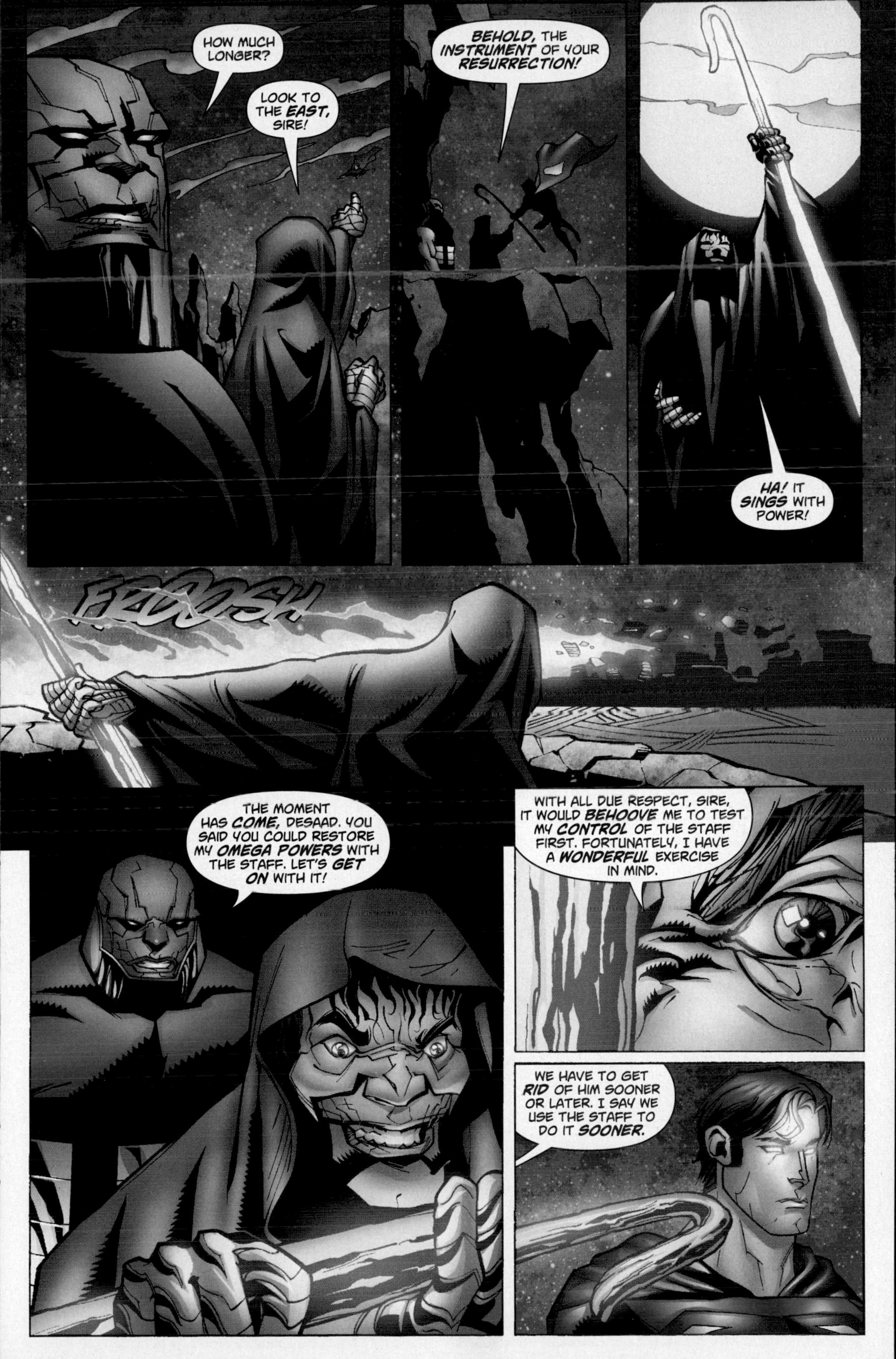
HOW MUCH LONGER?
LOOK TO THE EAST, SIRE!
BEHOLD, THE INSTRUMENT OF YOUR RESURRECTION!
HA! IT SINGS WITH POWER!
FROOOSH
THE MOMENT HAS COME, DESAAD. YOU SAID YOU COULD RESTORE MY OMEGA POWERS WITH THE STAFF. LET'S GET ON WITH IT!
WITH ALL DUE RESPECT, SIRE, IT WOULD BEHOOVE ME TO TEST MY CONTROL OF THE STAFF FIRST. FORTUNATELY, I HAVE A WONDERFUL EXERCISE IN MIND.
WE HAVE TO GET RID OF HIM SOONER OR LATER. I SAY WE USE THE STAFF TO DO IT SOONER.

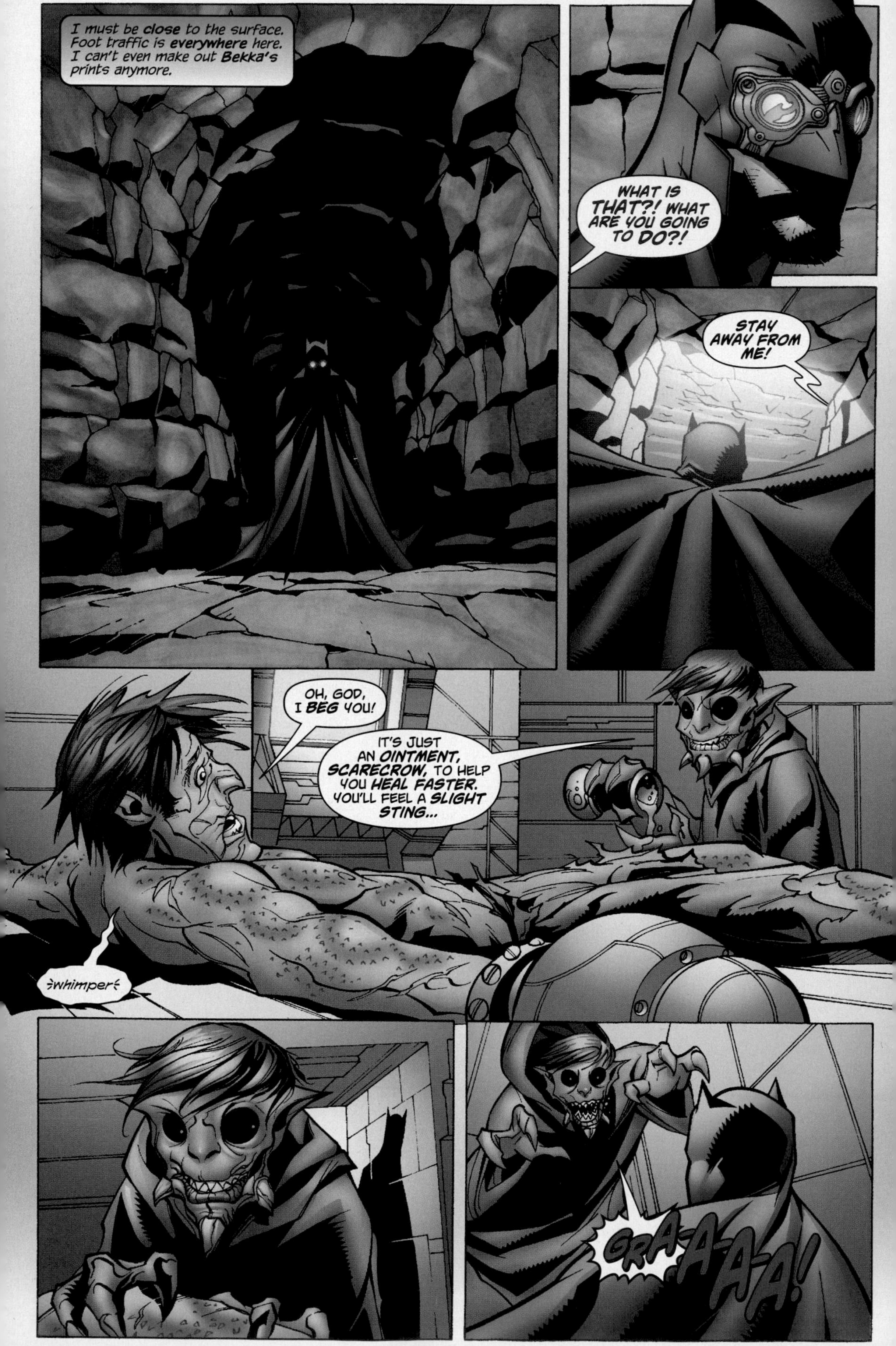

I must be close to the surface. Foot traffic is everywhere here. I can't even make out Bekka's prints anymore.
WHAT IS THAT?! WHAT ARE YOU GOING TO DO?!
STAY AWAY FROM ME!
OH, GOD, I BEG YOU!
IT'S JUST AN OINTMENT, SCARECROW, TO HELP YOU HEAL FASTER. YOU'LL FEEL A SLIGHT STING...
whimper
GRAAAAA!

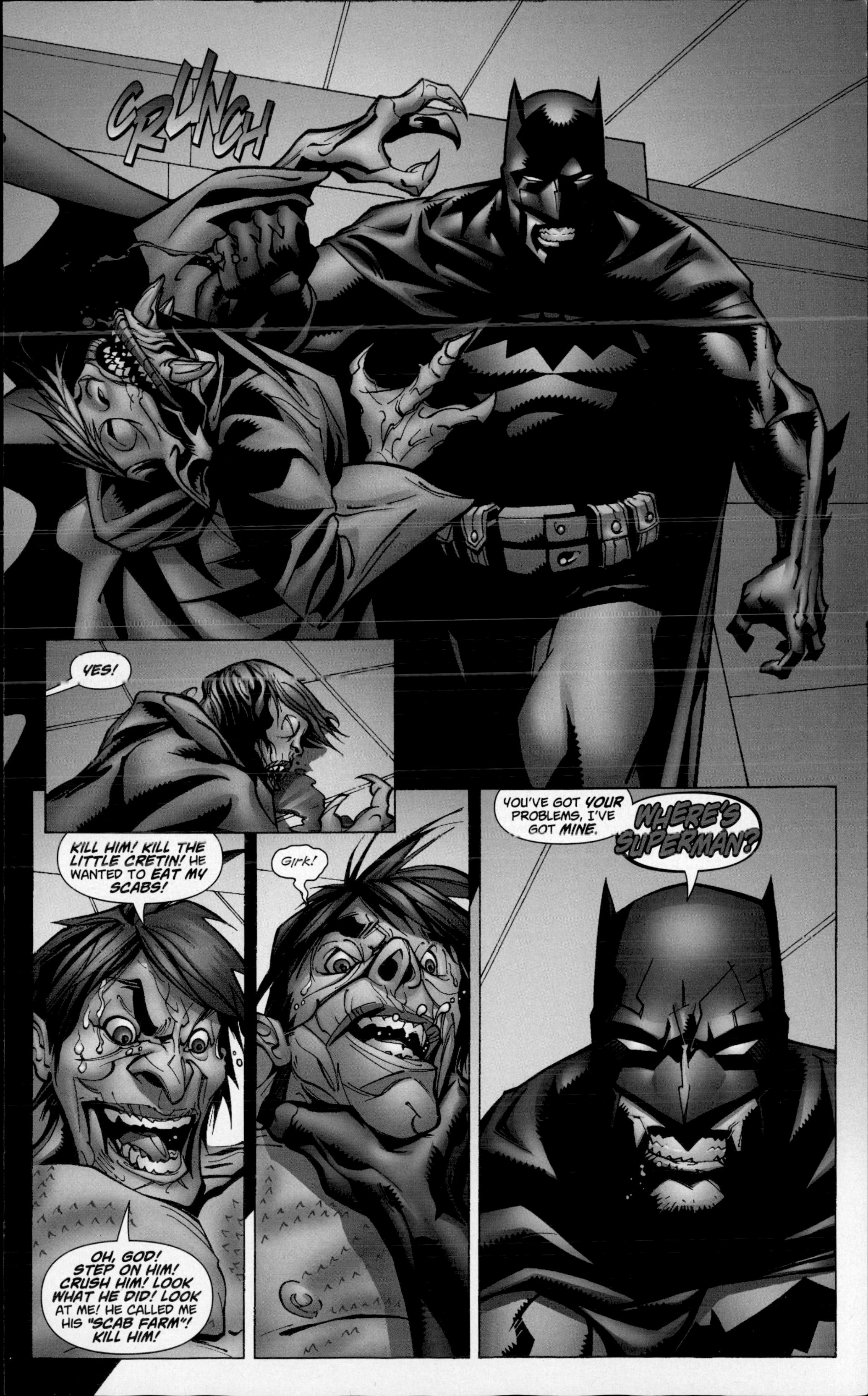
CRUNCH
YES!
KILL HIM! KILL THE LITTLE CRETIN! HE WANTED TO EAT MY SCABS!
OH, GOD! STEP ON HIM! CRUSH HIM! LOOK WHAT HE DID! LOOK AT ME! HE CALLED ME HIS "SCAB FARM"! KILL HIM!
Girk!
YOU'VE GOT YOUR PROBLEMS, I'VE GOT MINE.
WHERE'S SUPERMAN?

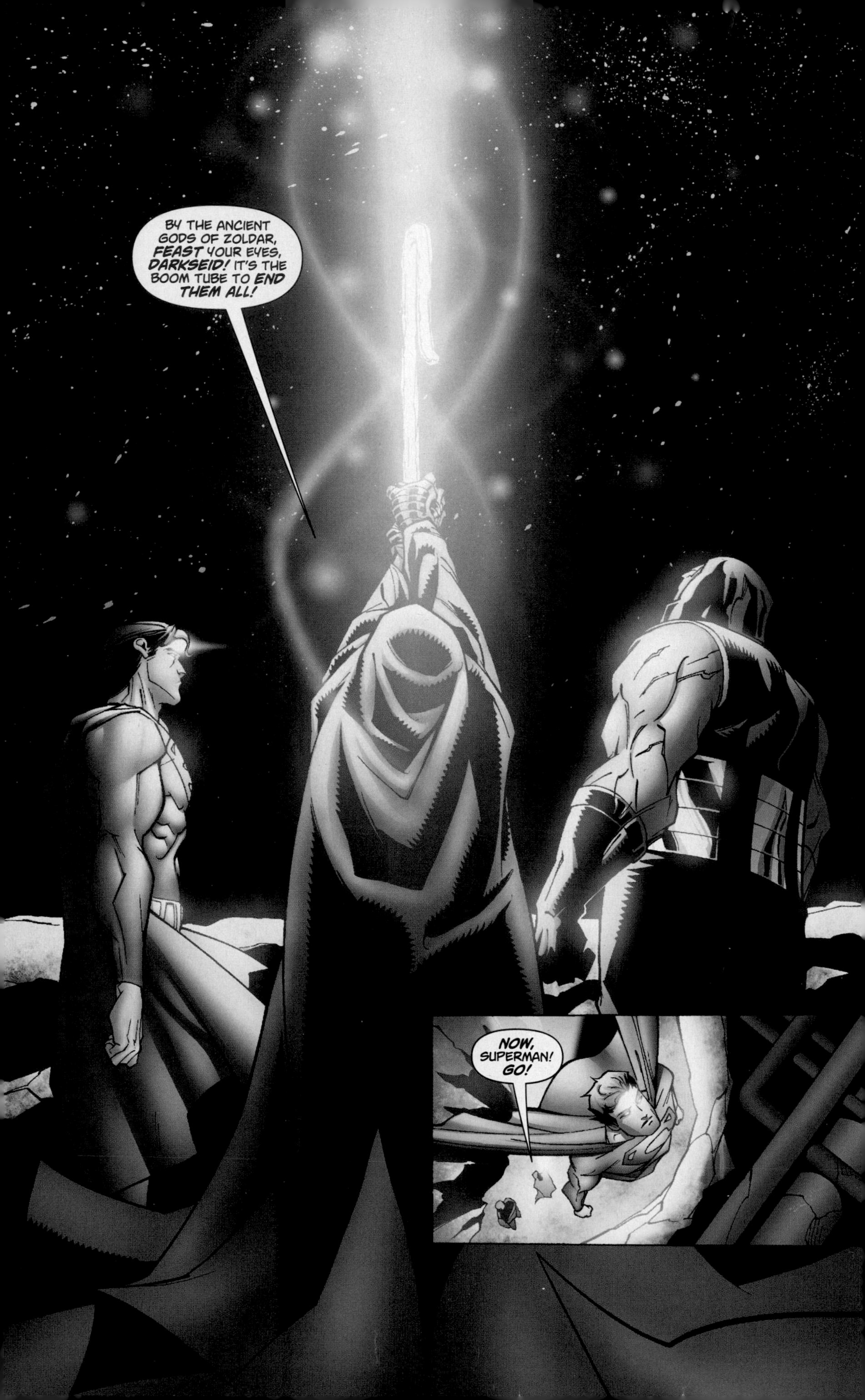

BY THE ANCIENT GODS OF ZOLDAR, FEAST YOUR EYES, DARKSEID! IT'S THE BOOM TUBE TO END THEM ALL!
NOW, SUPERMAN! GO!

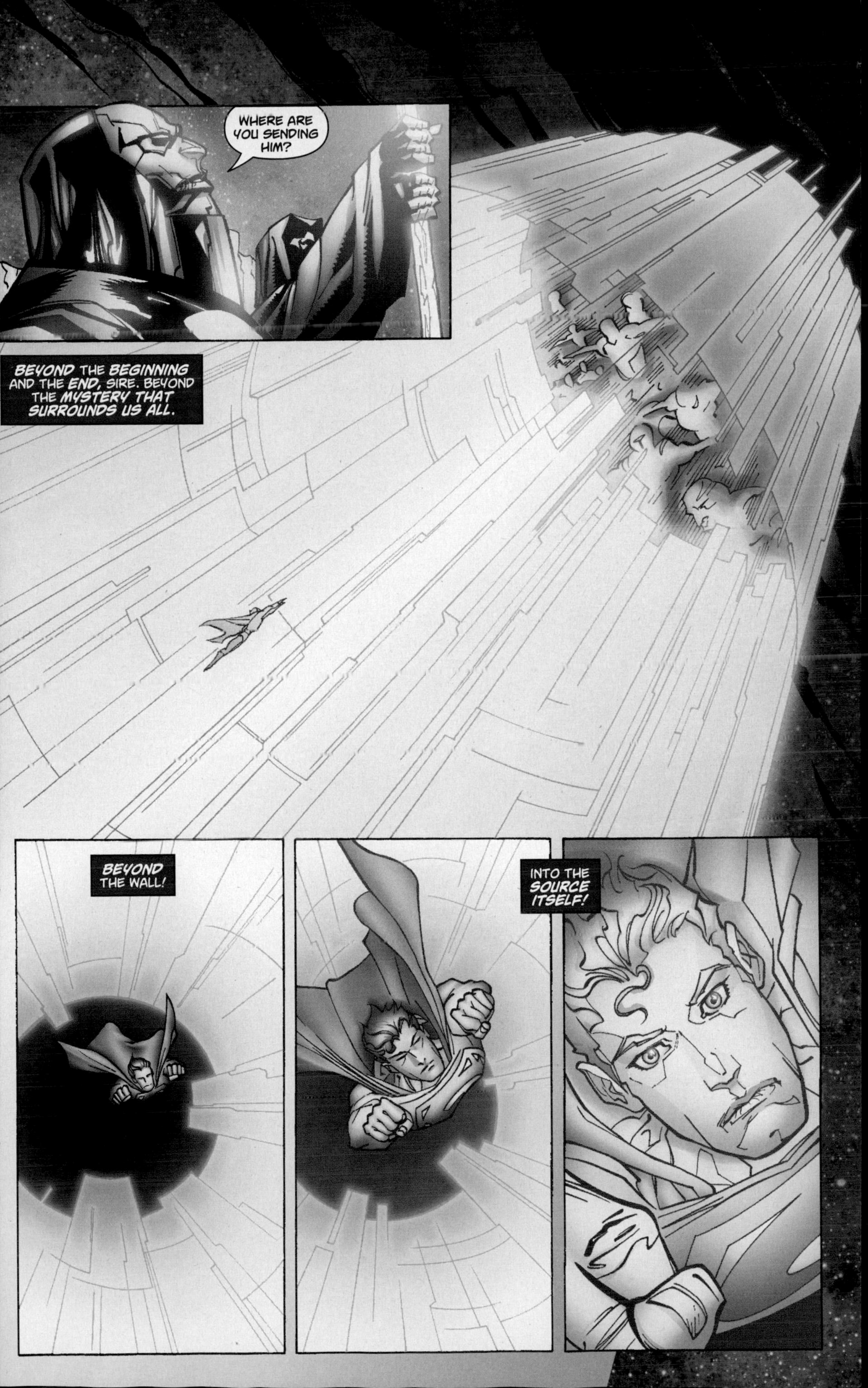

WHERE ARE YOU SENDING HIM?
BEYOND THE BEGINNING AND THE END, SIRE. BEYOND THE MYSTERY THAT SURROUNDS US ALL.
BEYOND THE WALL!
INTO THE SOURCE ITSELF!

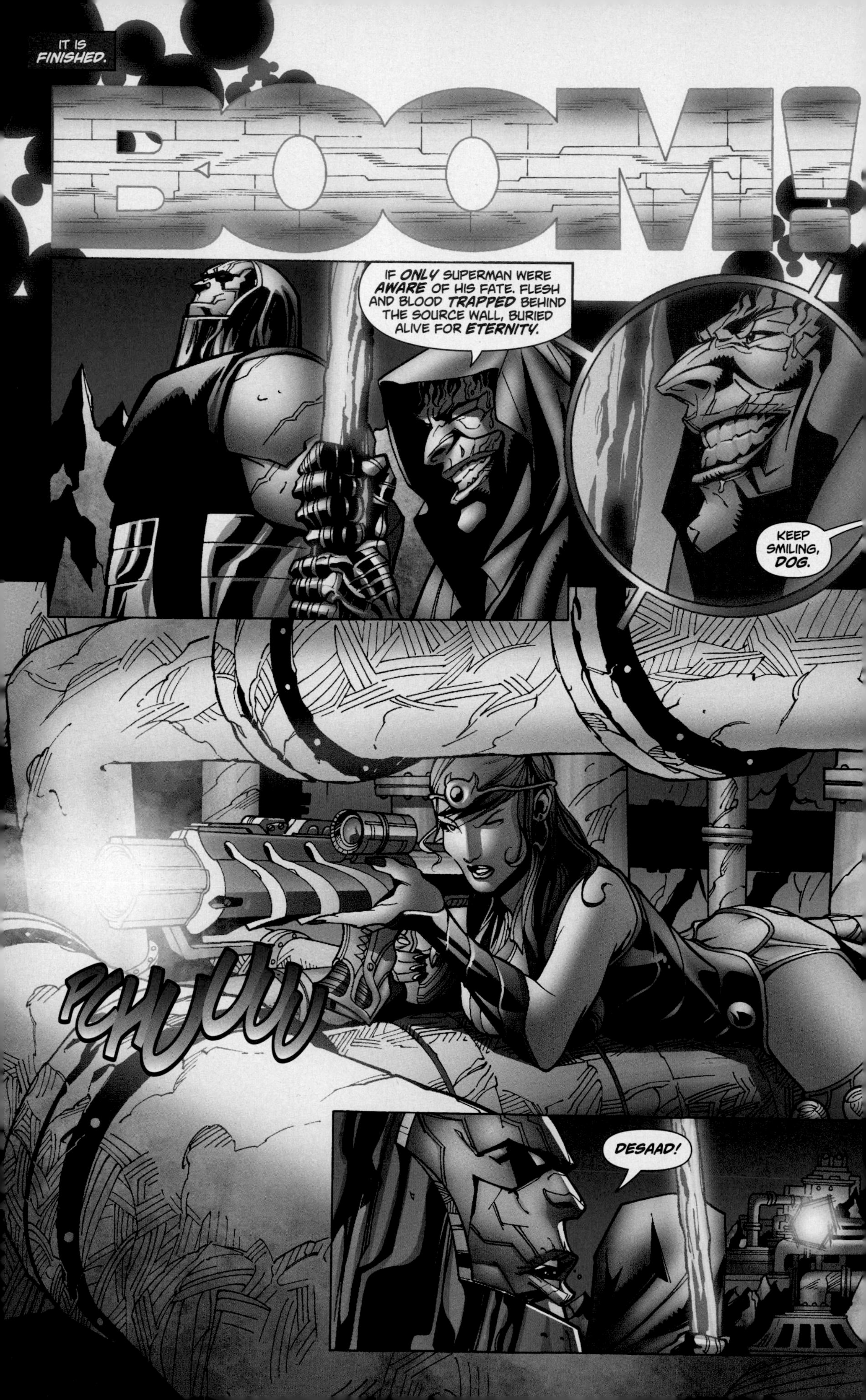
IT IS FINISHED.
BOOM!
IF ONLY SUPERMAN WERE AWARE OF HIS FATE. FLESH AND BLOOD TRAPPED BEHIND THE SOURCE WALL, BURIED ALIVE FOR ETERNITY.
KEEP SMILING, DOG.
PCHUUU
DESAAD!

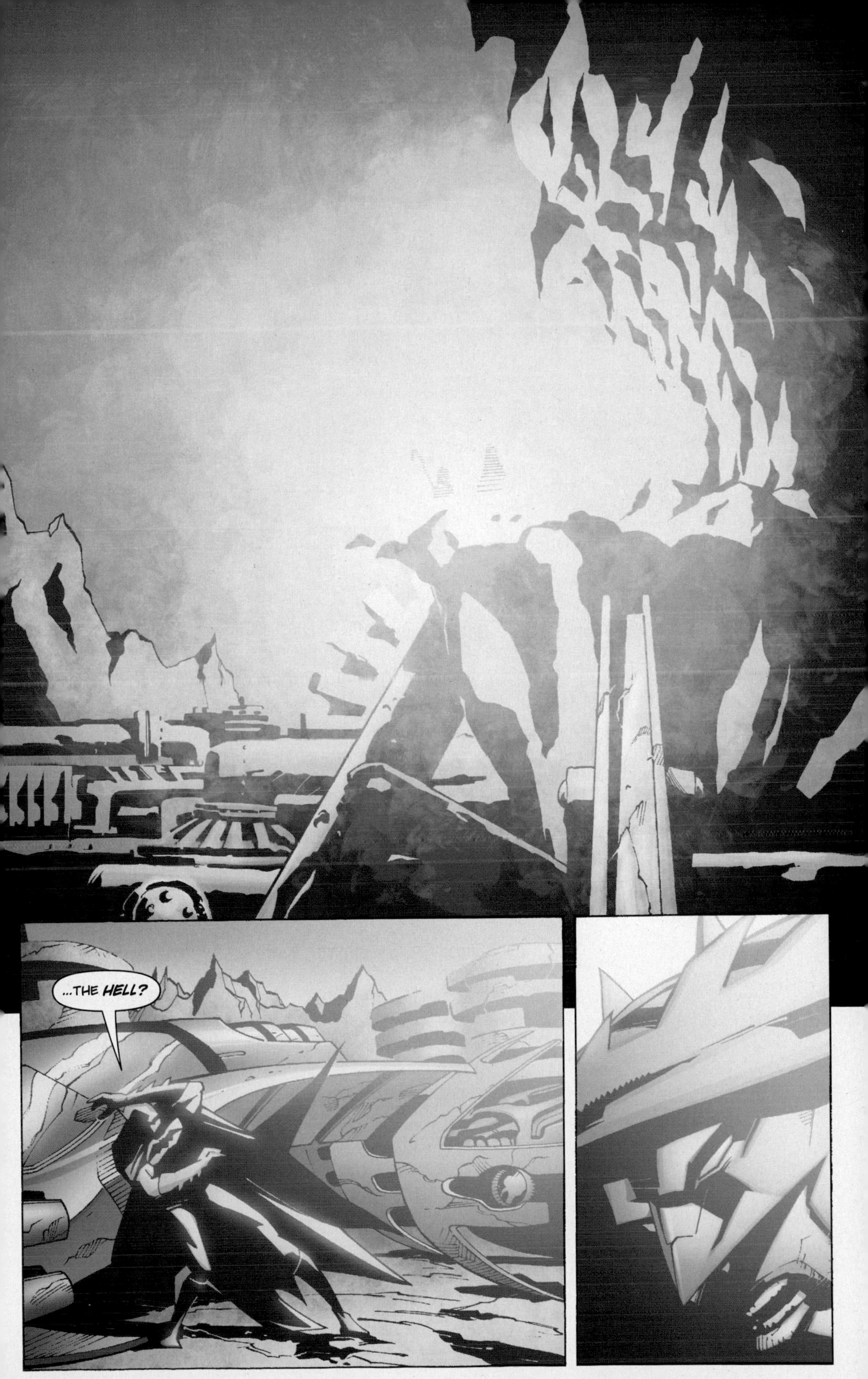
...THE HELL?

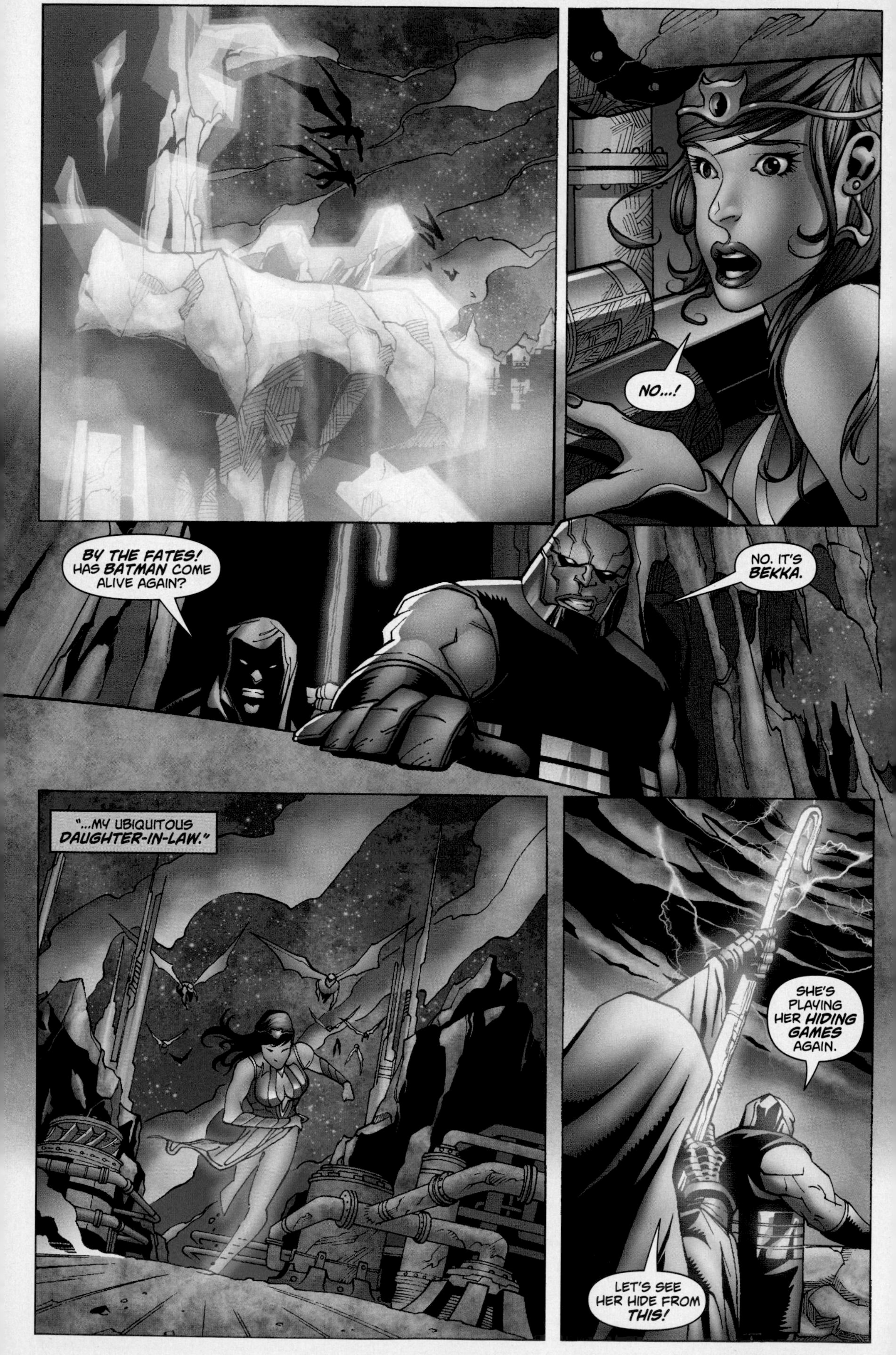
NO...!
BY THE FATES! HAS BATMAN COME ALIVE AGAIN?
NO. IT'S BEKKA.
"...MY UBIQUITOUS DAUGHTER-IN-LAW."
SHE'S PLAYING HER HIDING GAMES AGAIN.
LET'S SEE HER HIDE FROM THIS!

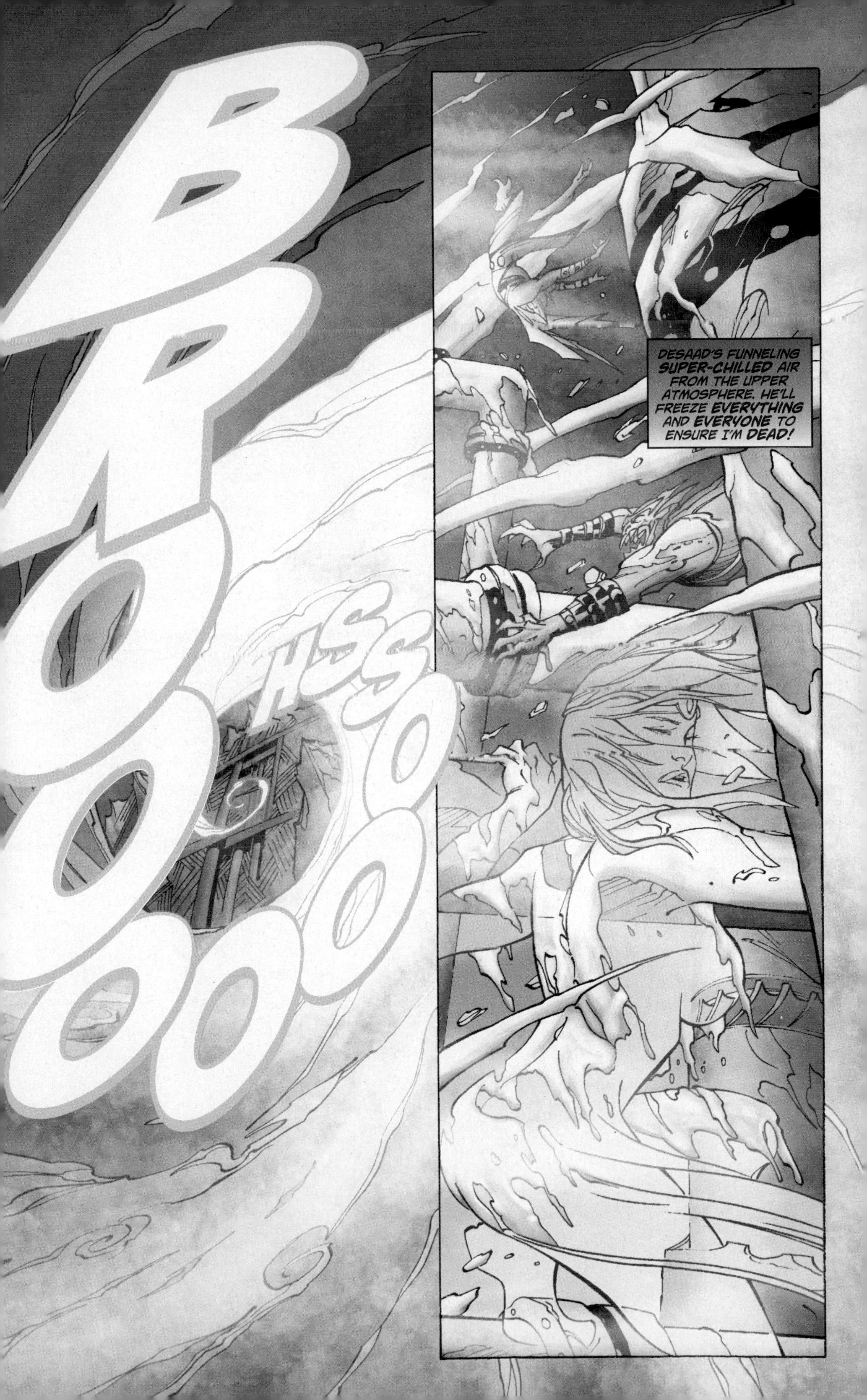
HSS
DESAAD'S FUNNELING SUPER-CHILLED AIR FROM THE UPPER ATMOSPHERE. HE'LL FREEZE EVERYTHING AND EVERYONE TO ENSURE I'M DEAD!

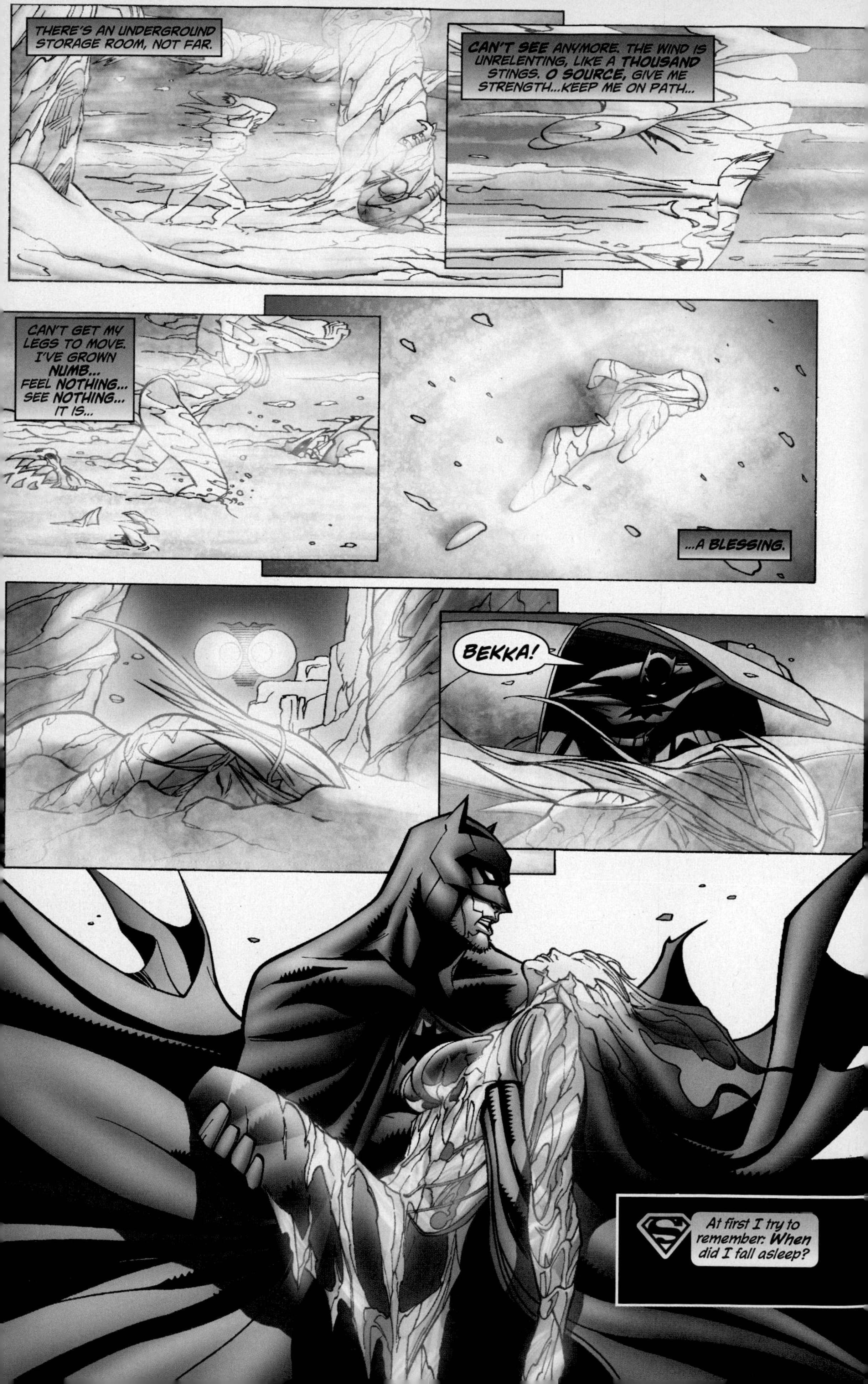
THERE'S AN UNDERGROUND STORAGE ROOM, NOT FAR.
CAN'T SEE ANYMORE. THE WIND IS UNRELENTING, LIKE A THOUSAND STINGS. O SOURCE, GIVE ME STRENGTH...KEEP ME ON PATH...
CAN'T GET MY LEGS TO MOVE. I'VE GROWN NUMB... FEEL NOTHING... SEE NOTHING... IT IS...
...A BLESSING.
BEKKA!
At first I try to remember: When did I fall asleep?

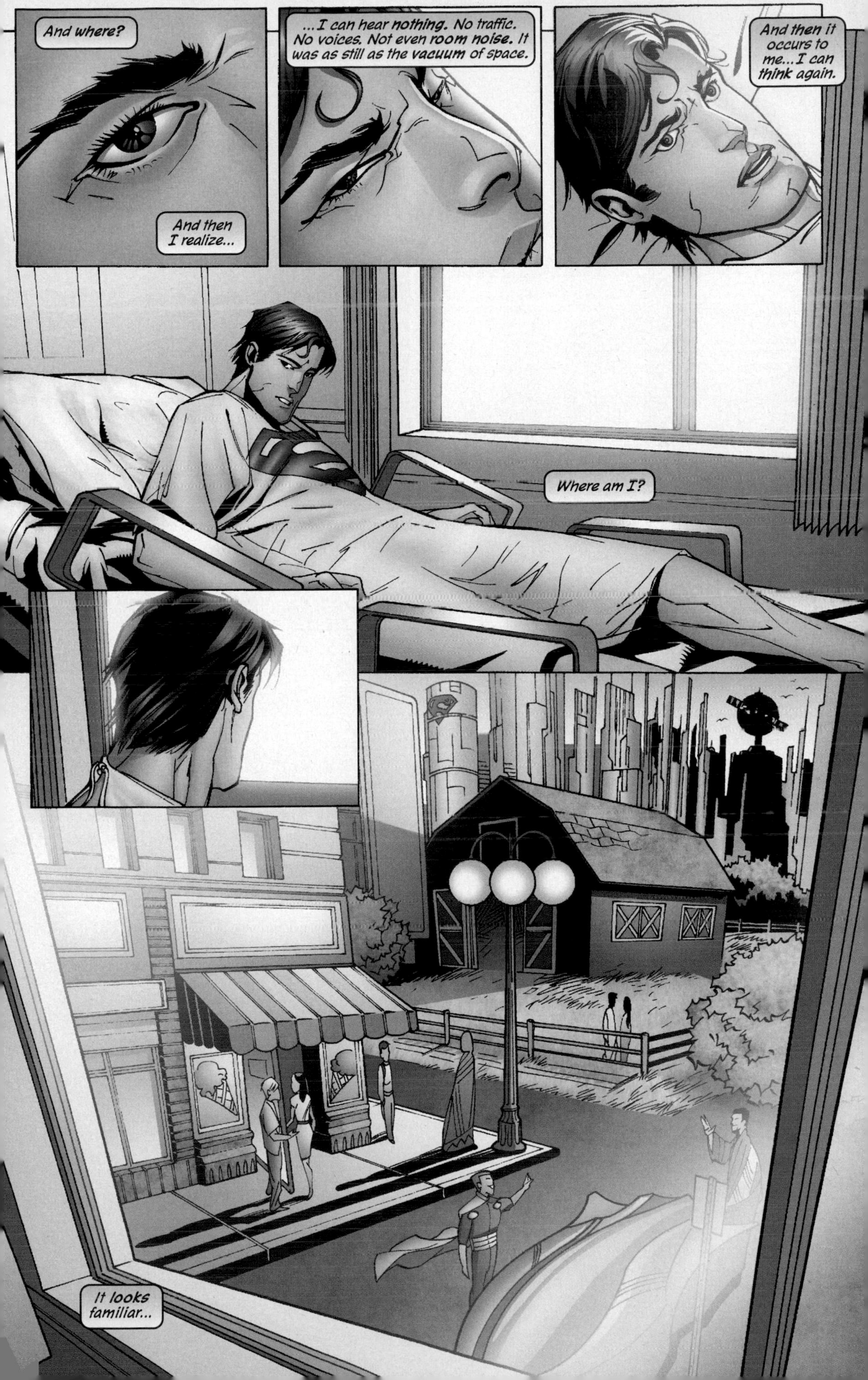
And where?
And then I realize...
...I can hear nothing. No traffic. No voices. Not even room noise. It was as still as the vacuum of space.
And then it occurs to me...I can think again.
Where am I?
It looks familiar...

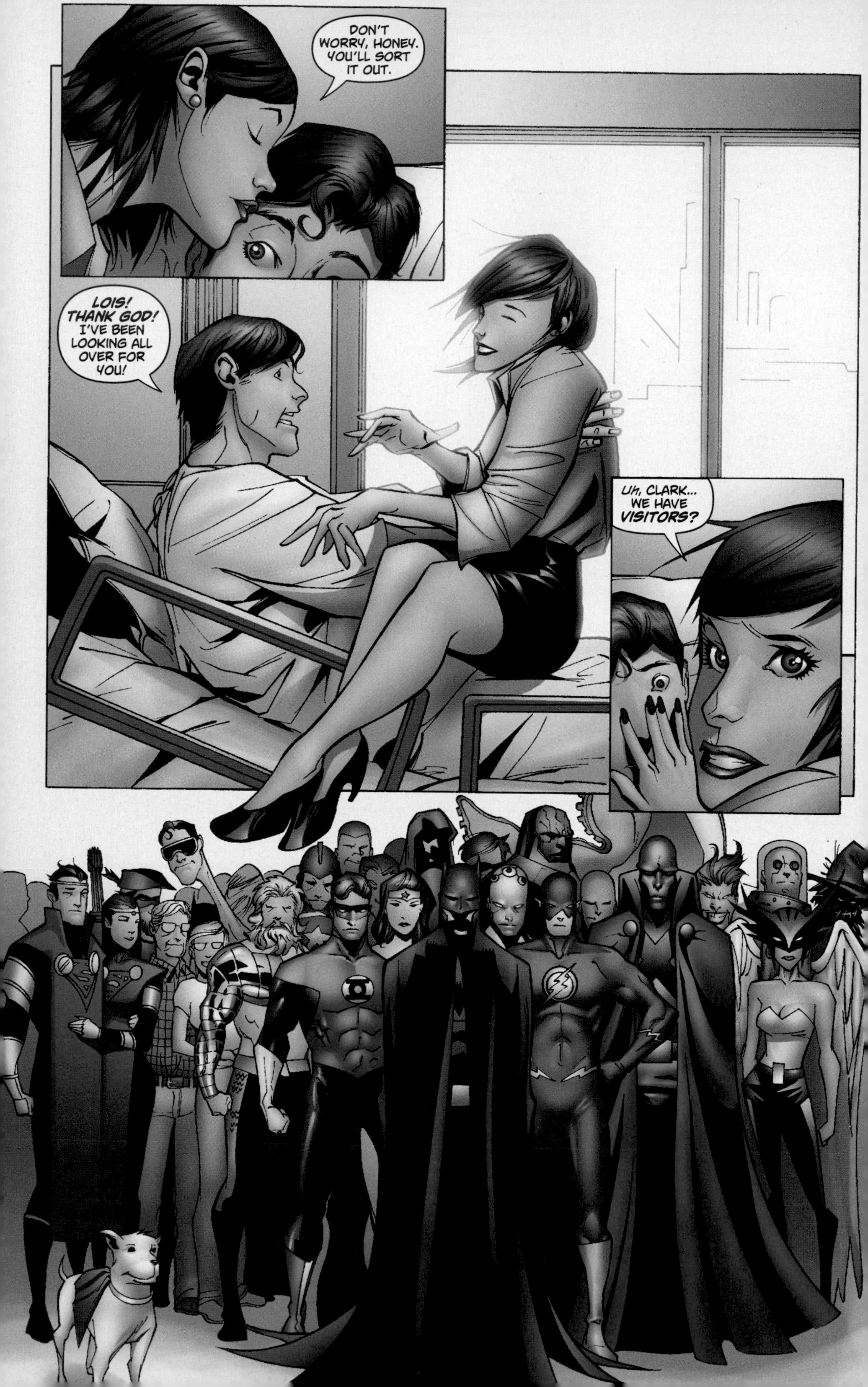
DON'T WORRY, HONEY. YOU'LL SORT IT OUT.
LOIS! THANK GOD! I'VE BEEN LOOKING ALL OVER FOR YOU!
UH, CLARK... WE HAVE VISITORS?

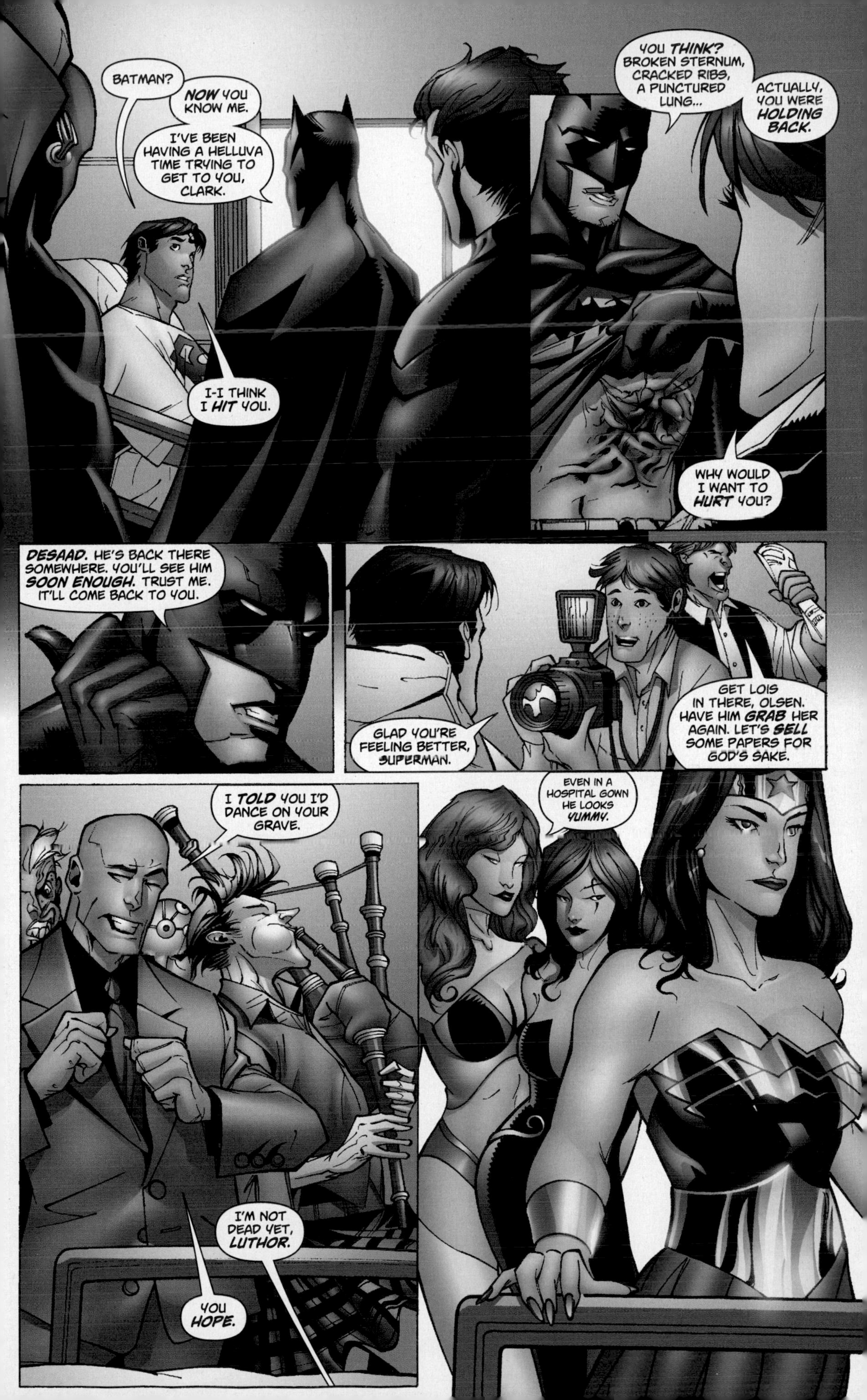

BATMAN?
NOW YOU KNOW ME.
I'VE BEEN HAVING A HELLUVA TIME TRYING TO GET TO YOU, CLARK.
I-I THINK I HIT YOU.
YOU THINK? BROKEN STERNUM, CRACKED RIBS, A PUNCTURED LUNG...
ACTUALLY, YOU WERE HOLDING BACK.
WHY WOULD I WANT TO HURT YOU?
DESAAD. HE'S BACK THERE SOMEWHERE. YOU'LL SEE HIM SOON ENOUGH. TRUST ME. IT'LL COME BACK TO YOU.
GLAD YOU'RE FEELING BETTER, SUPERMAN.
GET LOIS IN THERE, OLSEN. HAVE HIM GRAB HER AGAIN. LET'S SELL SOME PAPERS FOR GOD'S SAKE.
I TOLD YOU I'D DANCE ON YOUR GRAVE.
I'M NOT DEAD YET, LUTHOR.
YOU HOPE.
EVEN IN A HOSPITAL GOWN HE LOOKS YUMMY.

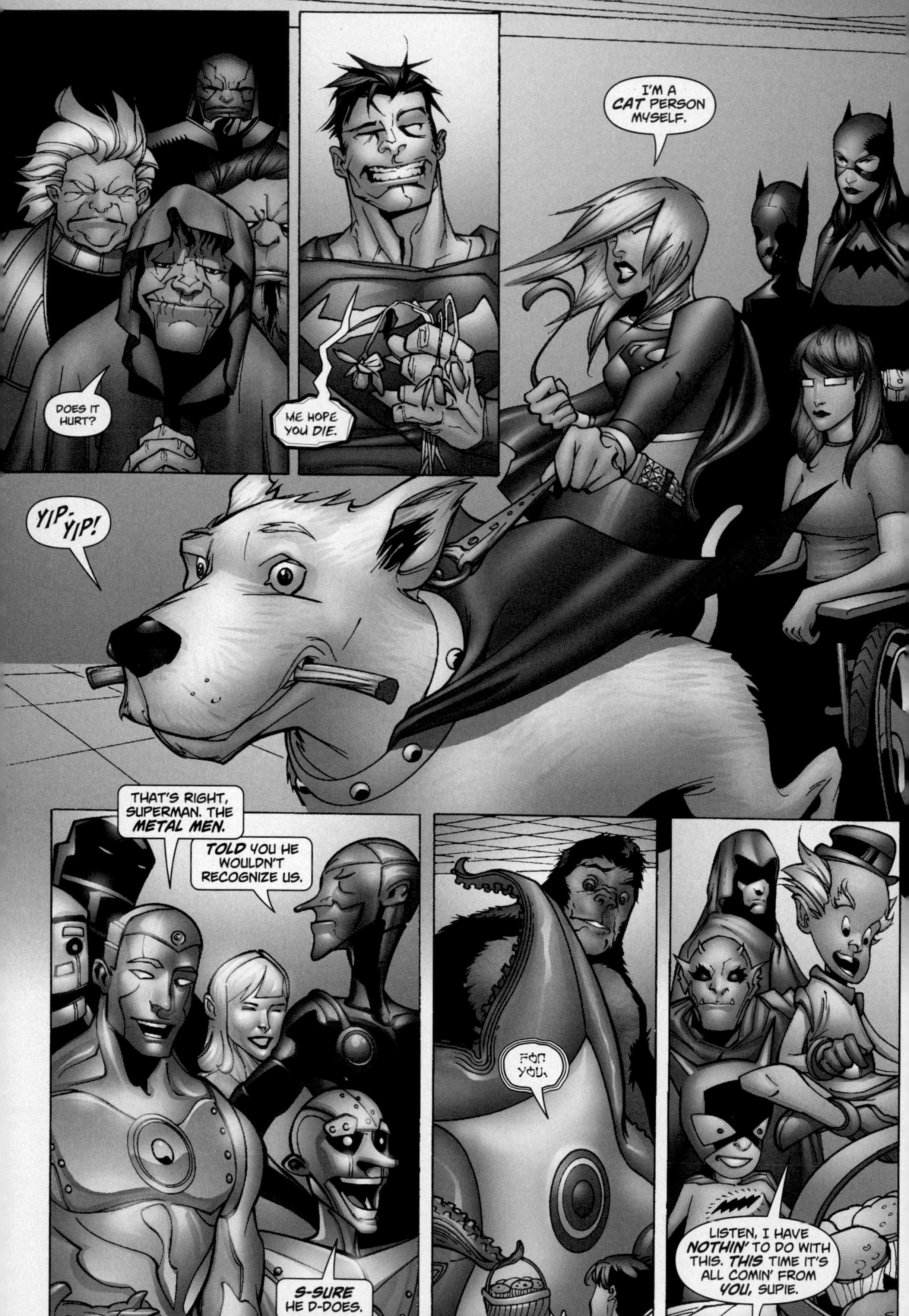
DOES IT HURT?
ME HOPE YOU DIE.
I'M A CAT PERSON MYSELF.
YIP-YIP!
THAT'S RIGHT, SUPERMAN. THE METAL MEN.
TOLD YOU HE WOULDN'T RECOGNIZE US.
S-SURE HE D-DOES.
FOR YOU.
LISTEN, I HAVE NOTHIN' TO DO WITH THIS. THIS TIME IT'S ALL COMIN' FROM YOU, SUPIE.
ARE YOU GONNA EAT ALL O' THOSE?

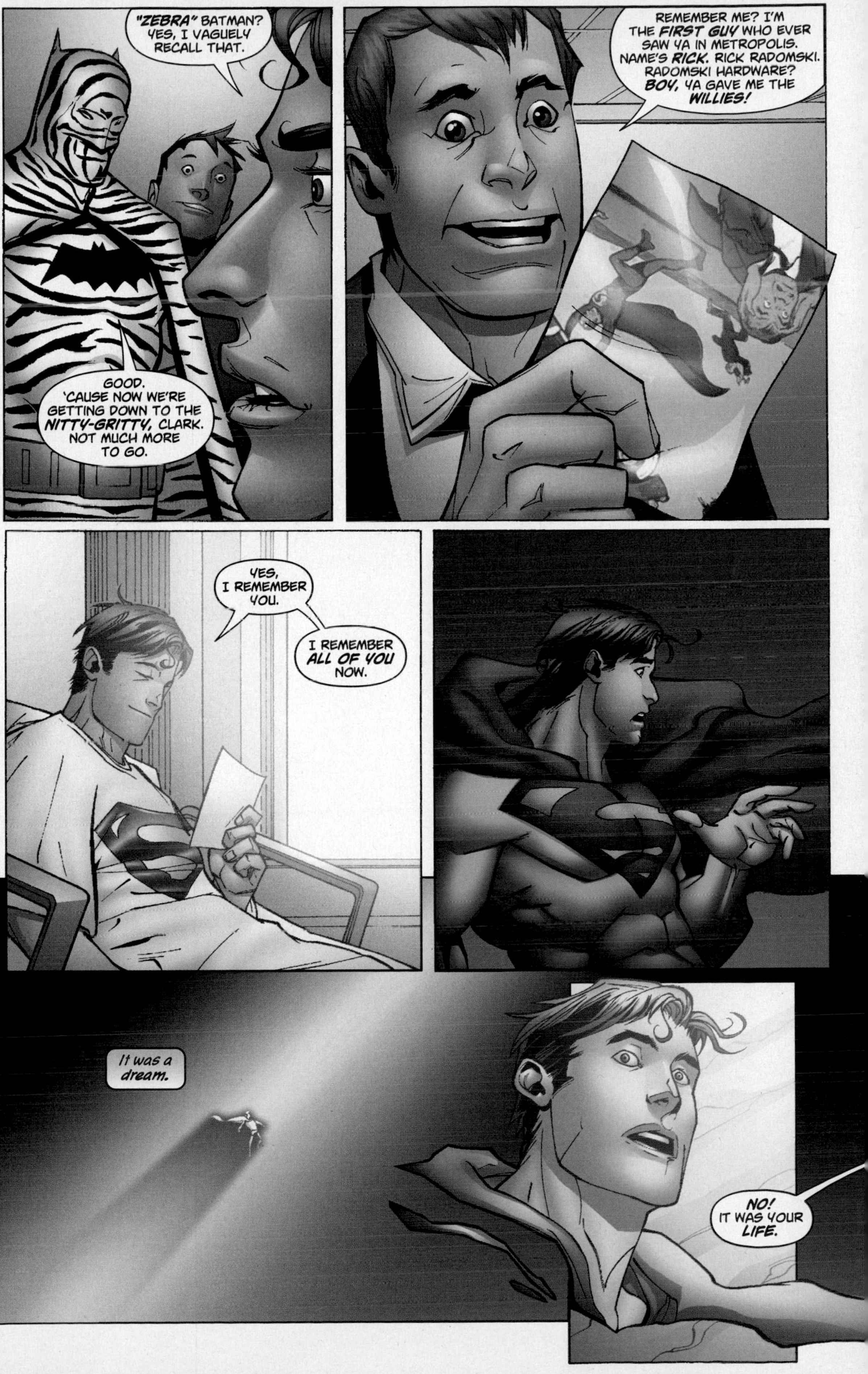
"ZEBRA" BATMAN? YES, I VAGUELY RECALL THAT.
GOOD. 'CAUSE NOW WE'RE GETTING DOWN TO THE NITTY-GRITTY, CLARK. NOT MUCH MORE TO GO.
REMEMBER ME? I'M THE FIRST GUY WHO EVER SAW YA IN METROPOLIS. NAME'S RICK. RICK RADOMSKI. RADOMSKI HARDWARE? BOY, YA GAVE ME THE WILLIES!
YES, I REMEMBER YOU.
I REMEMBER ALL OF YOU NOW.
It was a dream.
NO! IT WAS YOUR LIFE.

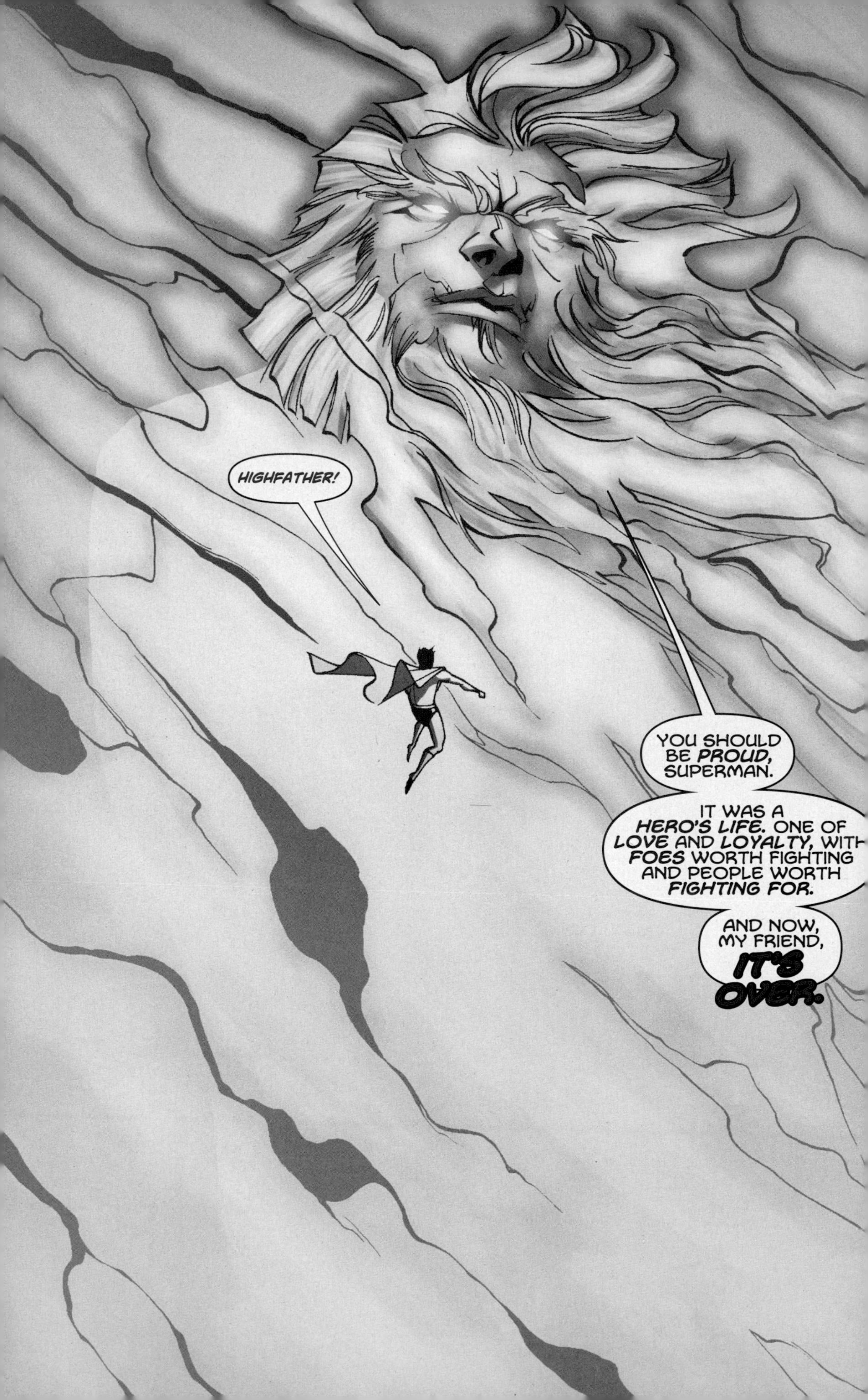
HIGHFATHER!
YOU SHOULD BE PROUD, SUPERMAN.
IT WAS A HERO'S LIFE. ONE OF LOVE AND LOYALTY, WITH FOES WORTH FIGHTING AND PEOPLE WORTH FIGHTING FOR.
AND NOW, MY FRIEND, IT'S OVER.

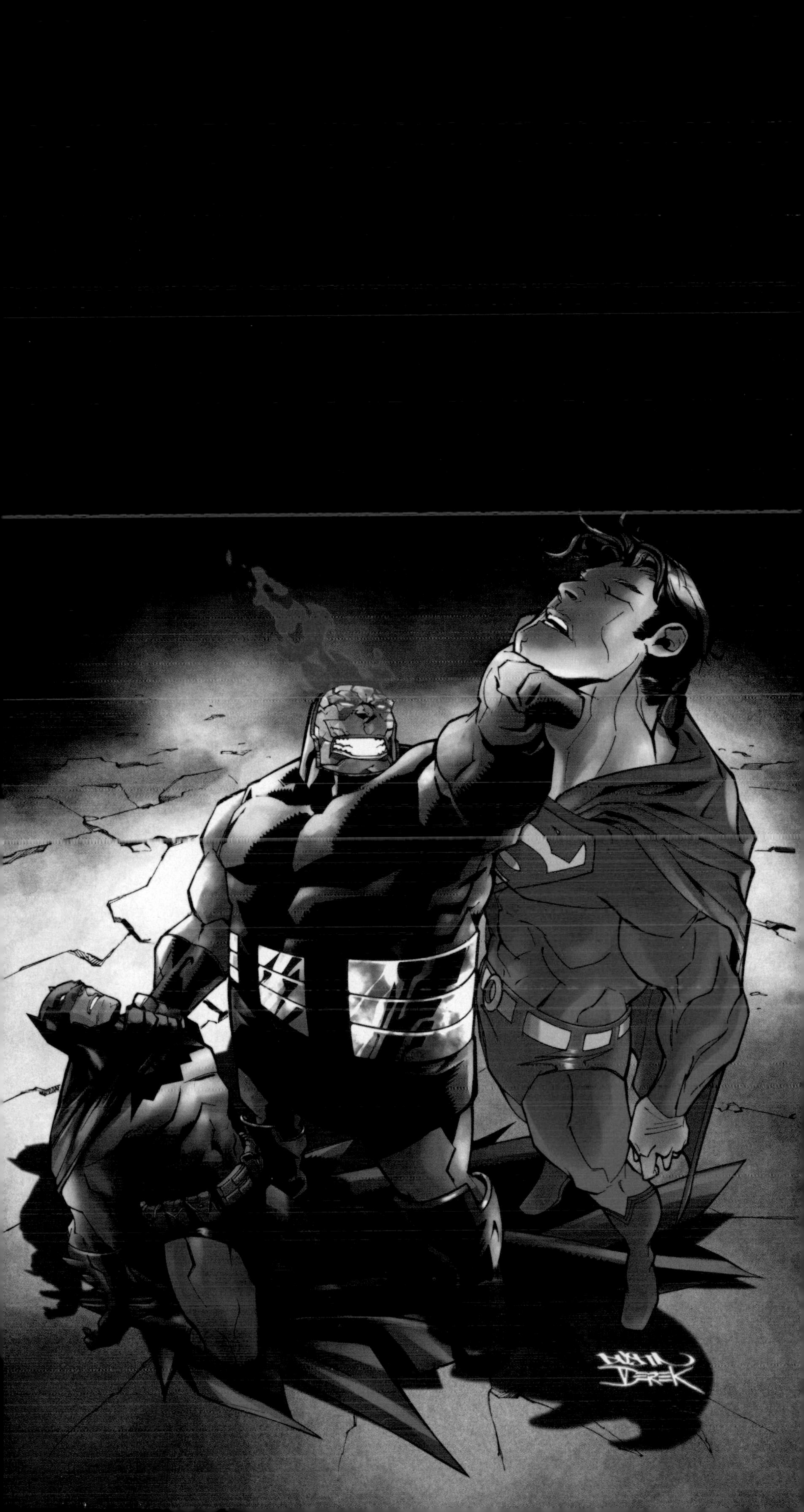

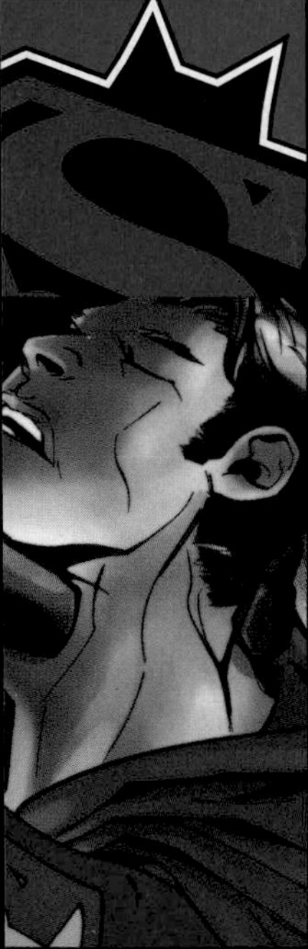

TORMEN
RELEASE

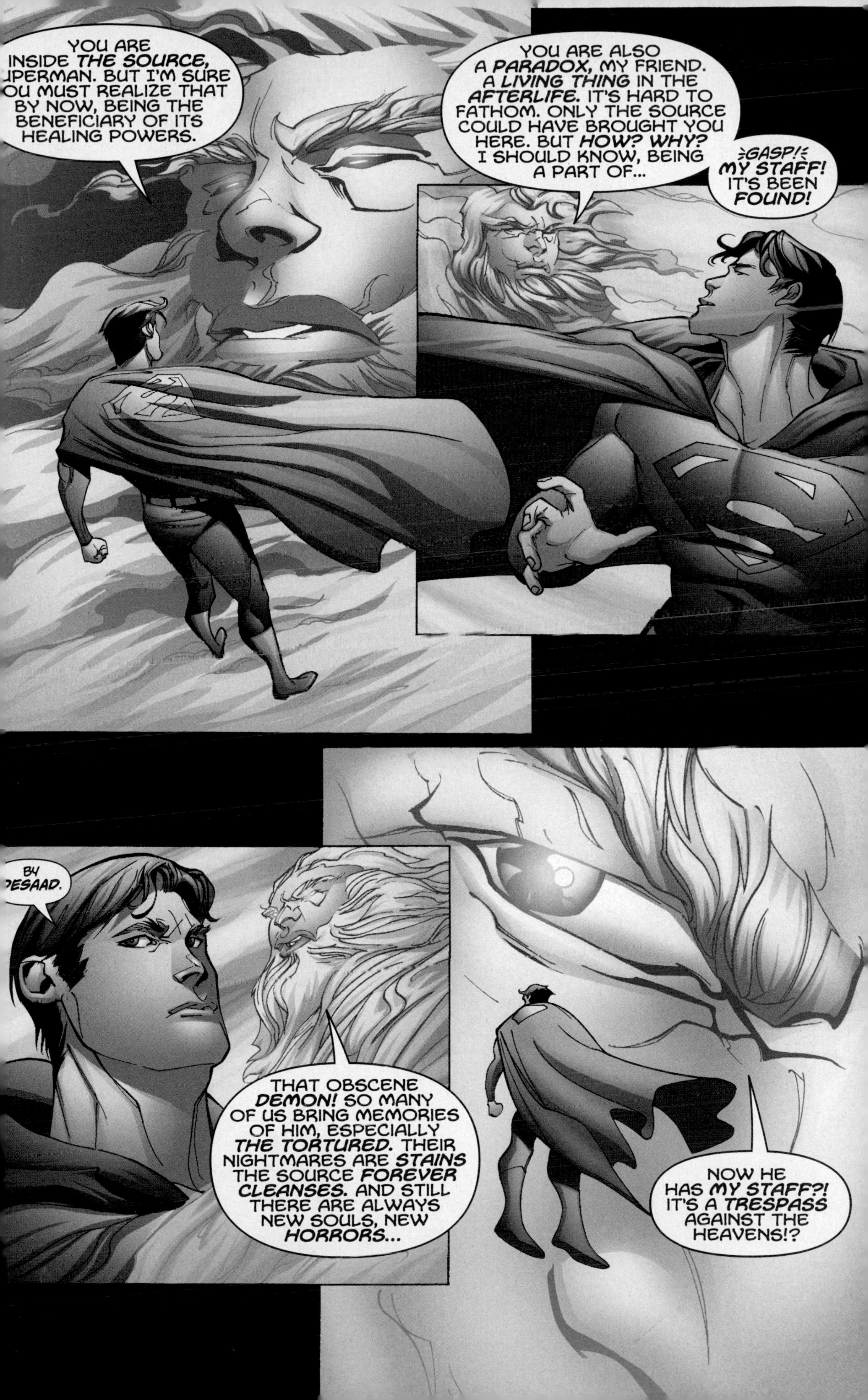
YOU ARE INSIDE THE SOURCE, UPERMAN. BUT I'M SURE OU MUST REALIZE THAT BY NOW, BEING THE BENEFICIARY OF ITS HEALING POWERS.
YOU ARE ALSO A PARADOX, MY FRIEND. A LIVING THING IN THE AFTERLIFE. IT'S HARD TO FATHOM. ONLY THE SOURCE COULD HAVE BROUGHT YOU HERE. BUT HOW? WHY? I SHOULD KNOW, BEING A PART OF...
GASP! MY STAFF! IT'S BEEN FOUND!
BY ESAAD.
THAT OBSCENE DEMON! SO MANY OF US BRING MEMORIES OF HIM, ESPECIALLY THE TORTURED. THEIR NIGHTMARES ARE STAINS THE SOURCE FOREVER CLEANSES. AND STILL THERE ARE ALWAYS NEW SOULS, NEW HORRORS...
NOW HE HAS MY STAFF?! IT'S A TRESPASS AGAINST THE HEAVENS!?

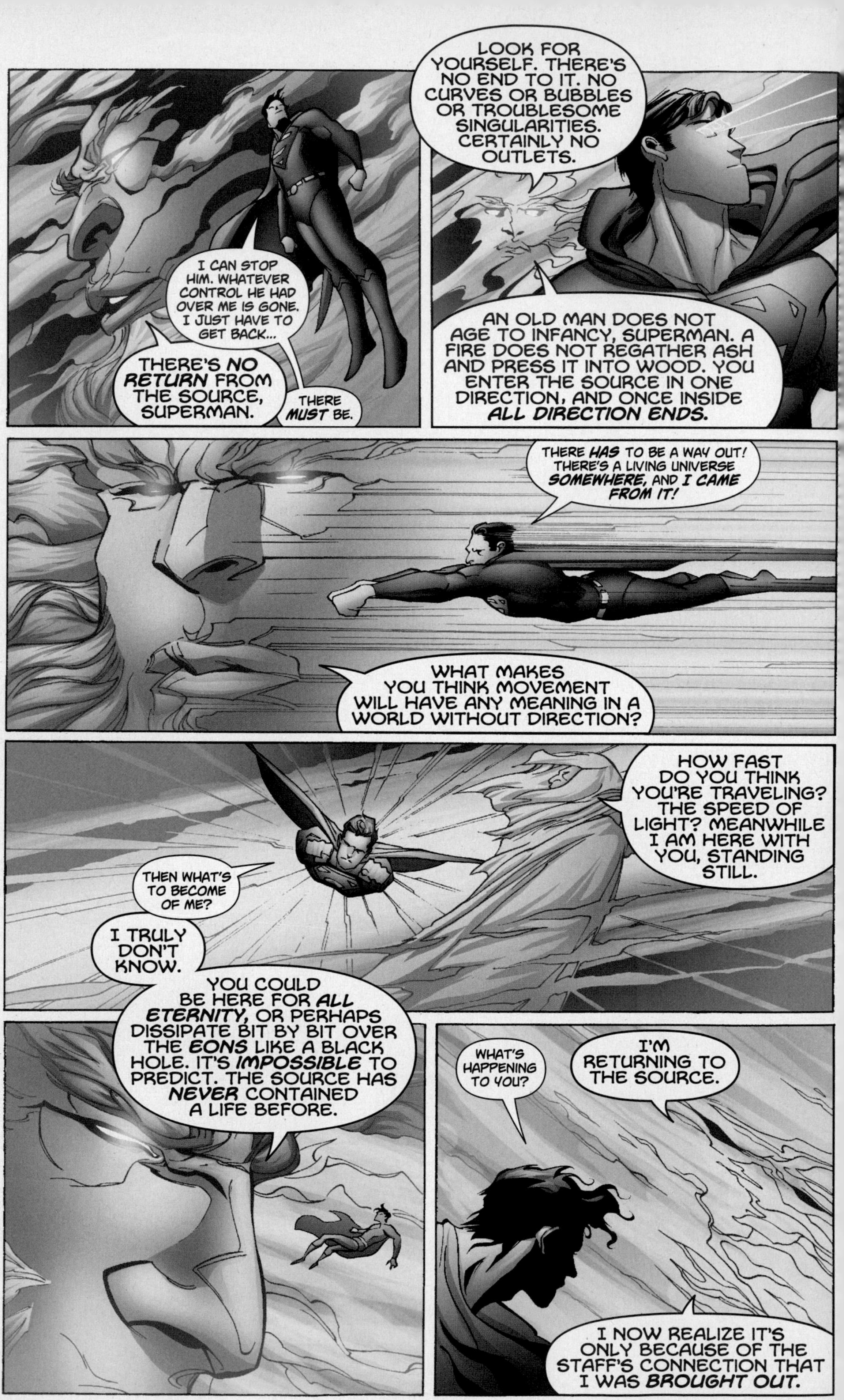
LOOK FOR YOURSELF. THERE'S NO END TO IT. NO CURVES OR BUBBLES OR TROUBLESOME SINGULARITIES. CERTAINLY NO OUTLETS.
I CAN STOP HIM. WHATEVER CONTROL HE HAD OVER ME IS GONE. I JUST HAVE TO GET BACK...
THERE'S NO RETURN FROM THE SOURCE, SUPERMAN.
THERE MUST BE.
AN OLD MAN DOES NOT AGE TO INFANCY, SUPERMAN. A FIRE DOES NOT REGATHER ASH AND PRESS IT INTO WOOD. YOU ENTER THE SOURCE IN ONE DIRECTION, AND ONCE INSIDE ALL DIRECTION ENDS.
THERE HAS TO BE A WAY OUT! THERE'S A LIVING UNIVERSE SOMEWHERE, AND I CAME FROM IT!
WHAT MAKES YOU THINK MOVEMENT WILL HAVE ANY MEANING IN A WORLD WITHOUT DIRECTION?
HOW FAST DO YOU THINK YOU'RE TRAVELING? THE SPEED OF LIGHT? MEANWHILE I AM HERE WITH YOU, STANDING STILL.
THEN WHAT'S TO BECOME OF ME?
I TRULY DON'T KNOW.
YOU COULD BE HERE FOR ALL ETERNITY, OR PERHAPS DISSIPATE BIT BY BIT OVER THE EONS LIKE A BLACK HOLE. IT'S IMPOSSIBLE TO PREDICT. THE SOURCE HAS NEVER CONTAINED A LIFE BEFORE.
WHAT'S HAPPENING TO YOU?
I'M RETURNING TO THE SOURCE.
I NOW REALIZE IT'S ONLY BECAUSE OF THE STAFF'S CONNECTION THAT I WAS BROUGHT OUT.

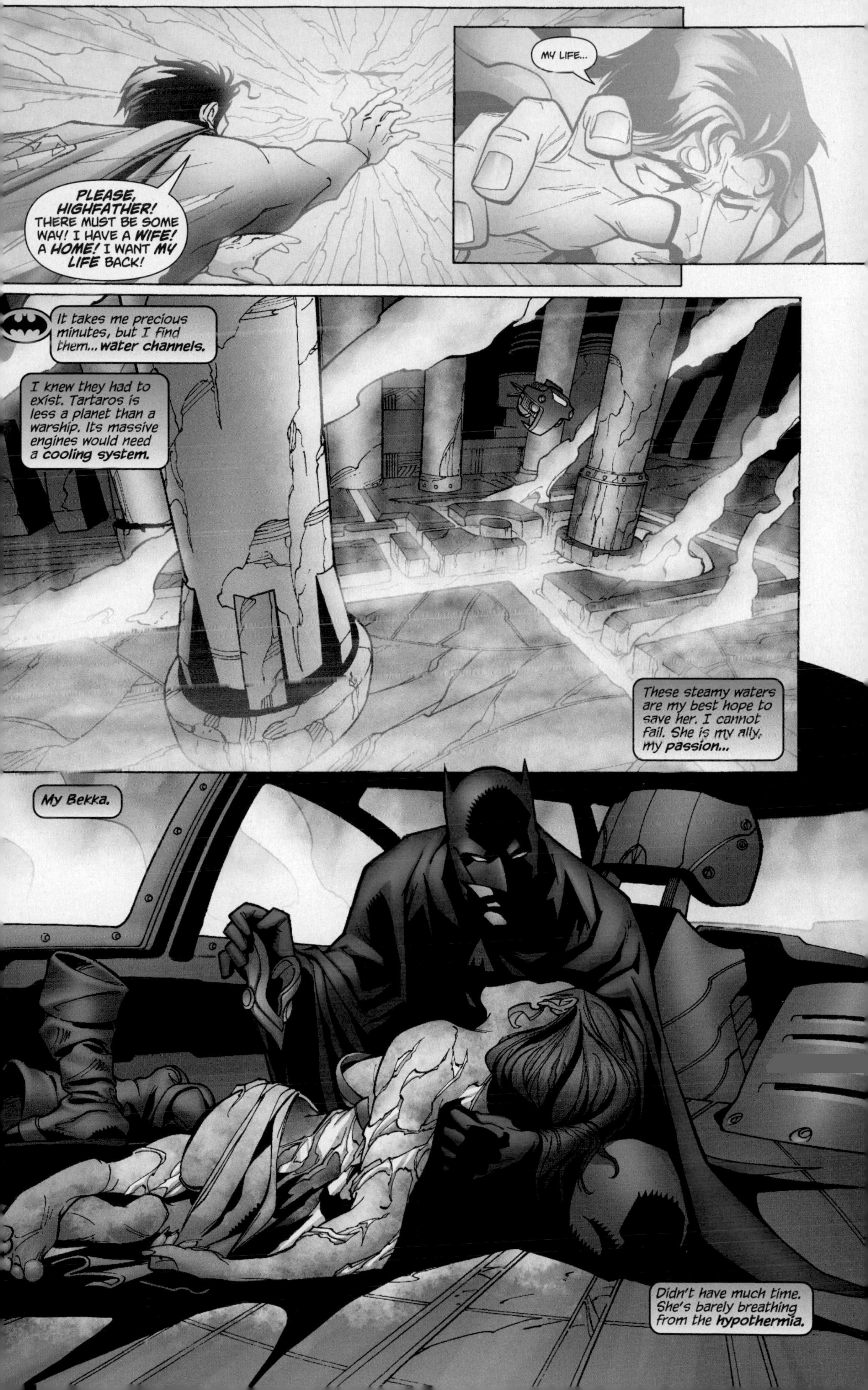
PLEASE, HIGHFATHER! THERE MUST BE SOME WAY! I HAVE A WIFE! A HOME! I WANT MY LIFE BACK!
MY LIFE...
It takes me precious minutes, but I find them... water channels.
I knew they had to exist. Tartaros is less a planet than a warship. Its massive engines would need a cooling system.
These steamy waters are my best hope to save her. I cannot fail. She is my ally, my passion...
My Bekka.
Didn't have much time. She's barely breathing from the hypothermia.

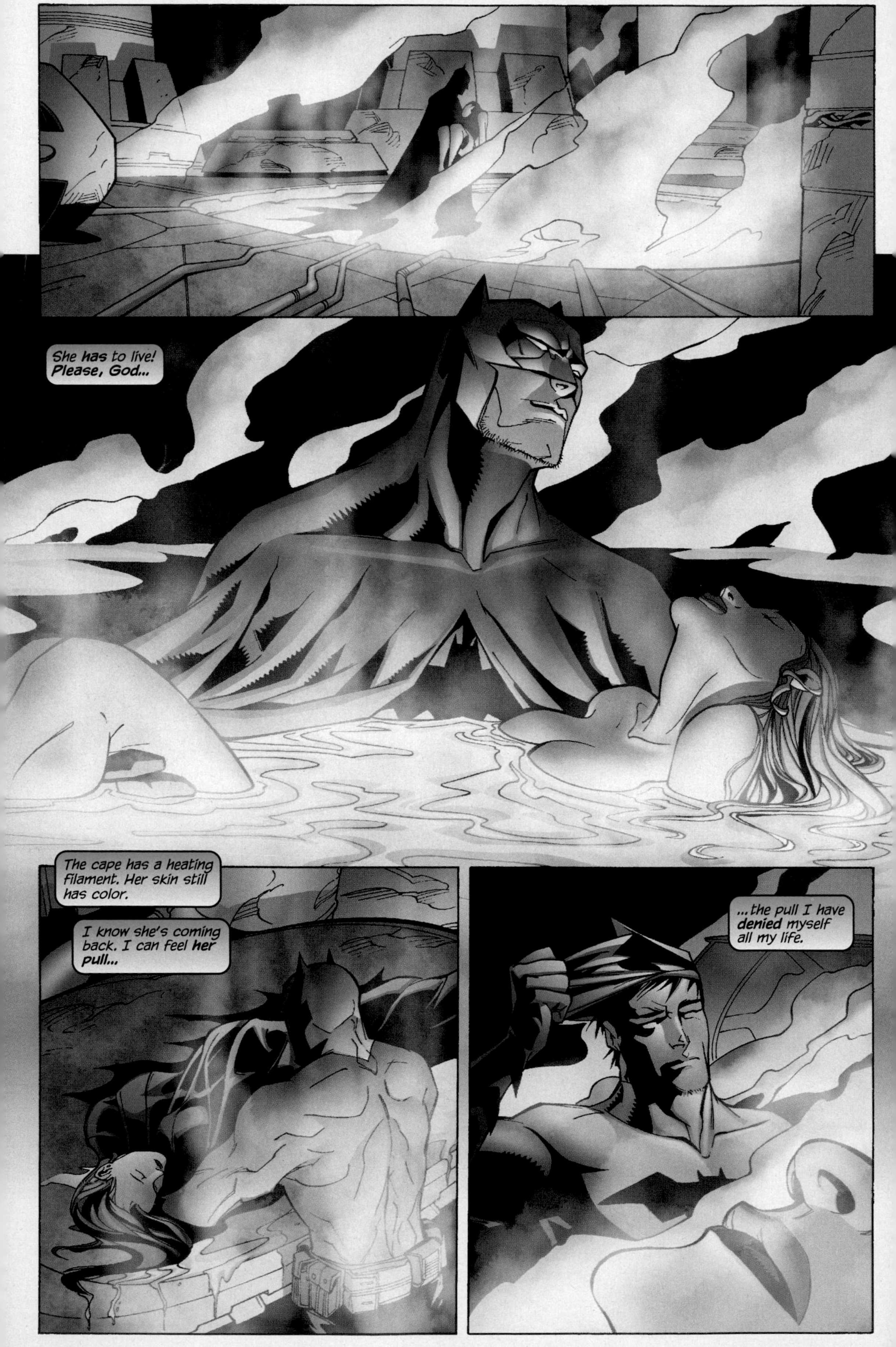
She has to live! Please, God...
The cape has a heating filament. Her skin still has color.
I know she's coming back. I can feel her pull...
...the pull I have denied myself all my life.

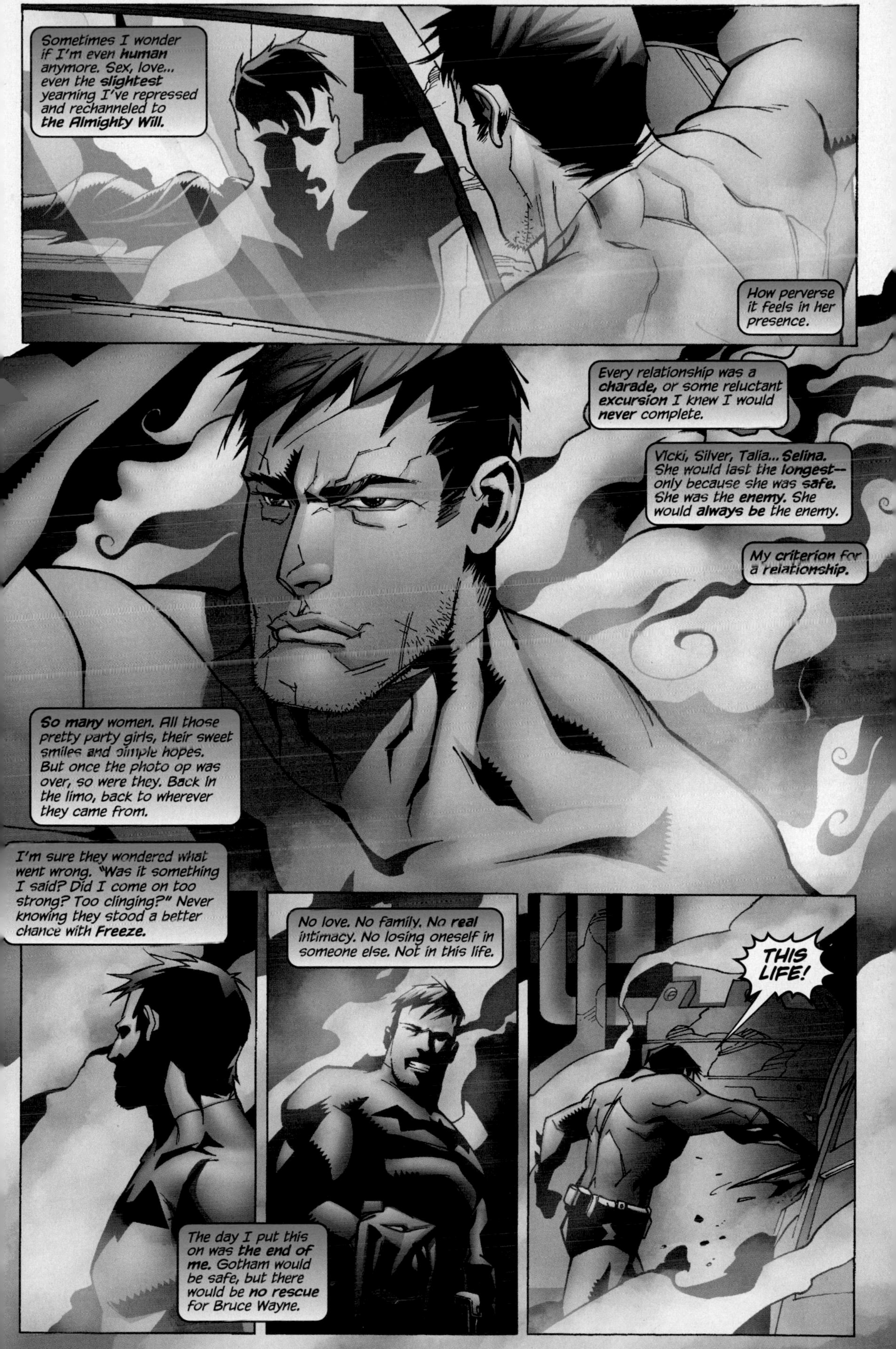
Sometimes I wonder if I'm even **human** anymore. Sex, love... even the **slightest** yearning I've repressed and rechanneled to **the Almighty Will.**
How perverse it feels in her presence.
Every relationship was a **charade,** or some reluctant **excursion** I knew I would **never** complete.
Vicki, Silver, Talia... **Selina.** She would last the **longest**-- only because she was **safe.** She was the **enemy.** She would **always be** the enemy.
My **criterion** for a **relationship.**
So many women. All those pretty party girls, their sweet smiles and simple hopes. But once the photo op was over, so were they. Back in the limo, back to wherever they came from.
I'm sure they wondered what went wrong. "Was it something I said? Did I come on too strong? Too clinging?" Never knowing they stood a better chance with **Freeze.**
The day I put this on was **the end of me.** Gotham would be safe, but there would be **no rescue** for Bruce Wayne.
No love. No family. No **real** intimacy. No losing oneself in someone else. Not in this life.
THIS LIFE!

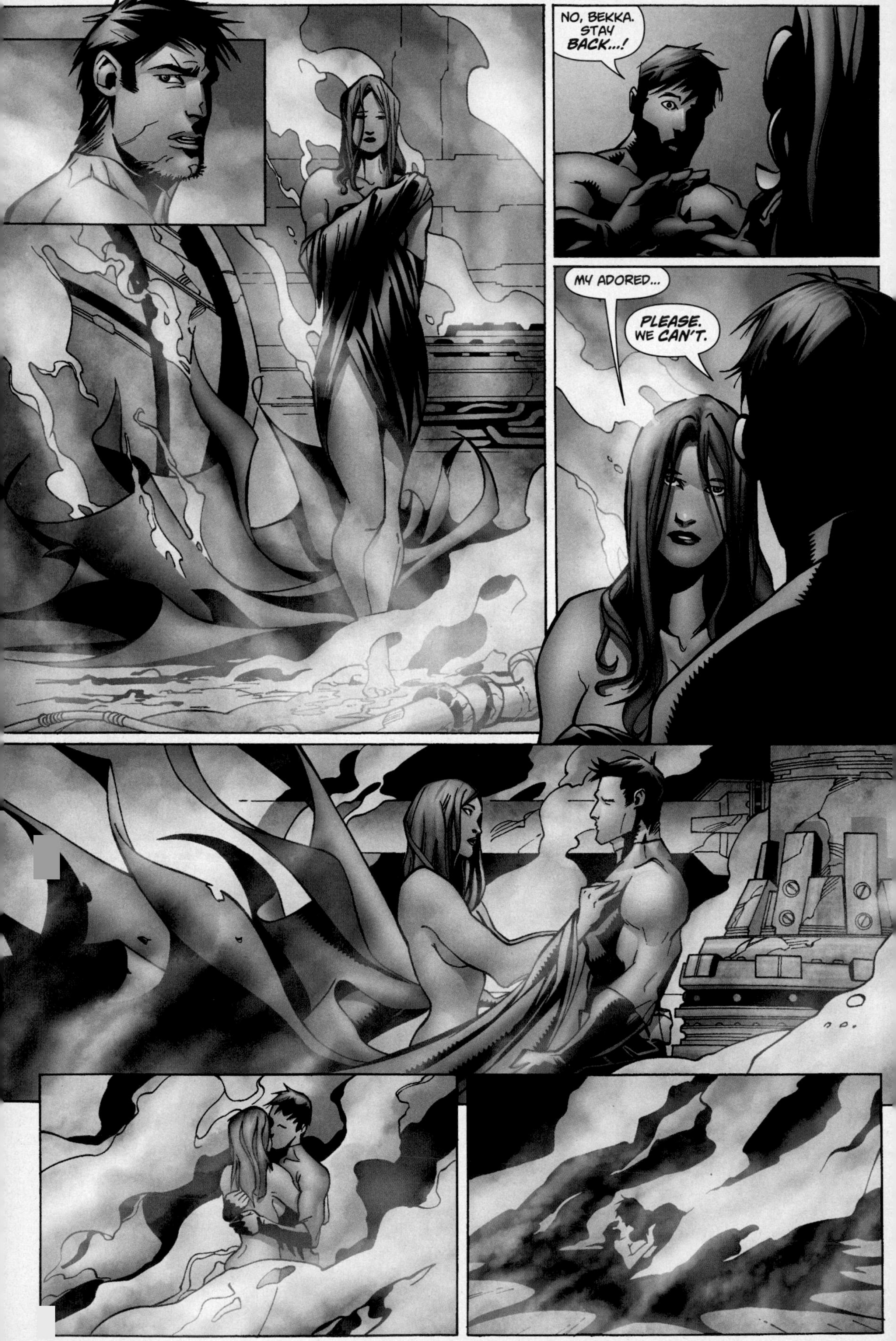
NO, BEKKA. STAY BACK...!
MY ADORED...
PLEASE. WE CAN'T.

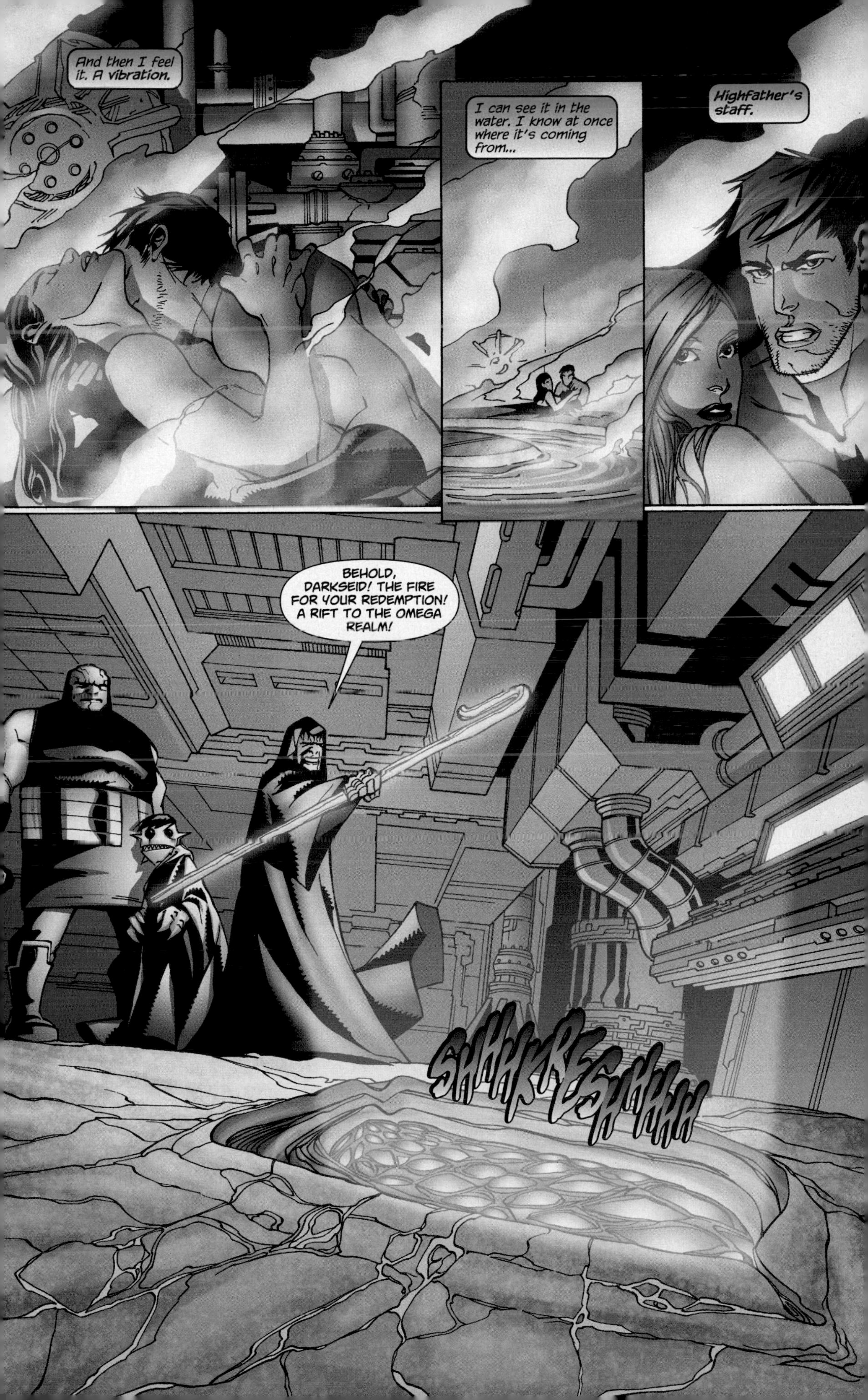
And then I feel it. A vibration.
I can see it in the water. I know at once where it's coming from...
Highfather's staff.
BEHOLD, DARKSEID! THE FIRE FOR YOUR REDEMPTION! A RIFT TO THE OMEGA REALM!
SHHHKRESHHHHH

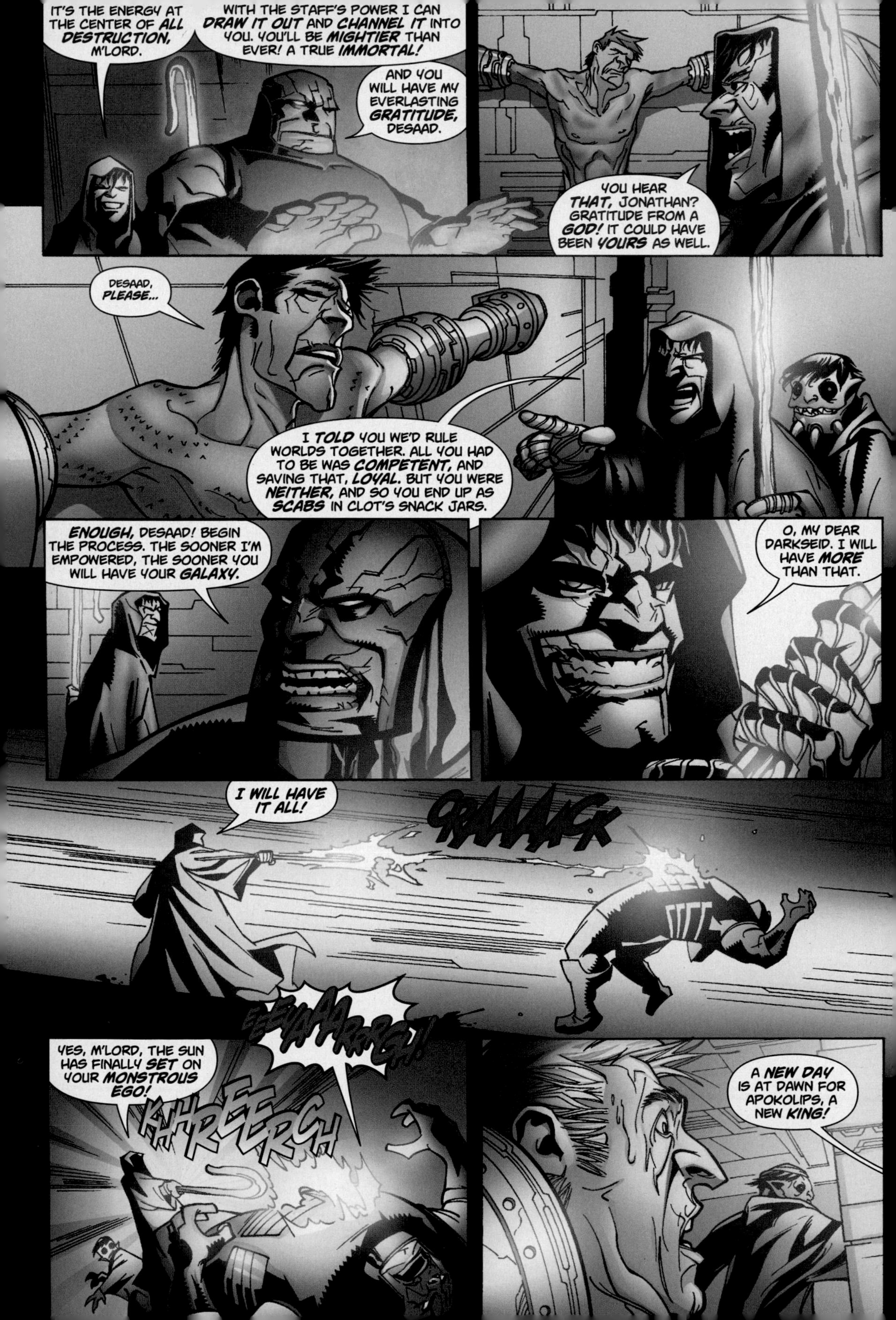

IT'S THE ENERGY AT THE CENTER OF ALL DESTRUCTION, M'LORD.
WITH THE STAFF'S POWER I CAN DRAW IT OUT AND CHANNEL IT INTO YOU. YOU'LL BE MIGHTIER THAN EVER! A TRUE IMMORTAL!
AND YOU WILL HAVE MY EVERLASTING GRATITUDE, DESAAD.
YOU HEAR THAT, JONATHAN? GRATITUDE FROM A GOD! IT COULD HAVE BEEN YOURS AS WELL.
DESAAD, PLEASE...
I TOLD YOU WE'D RULE WORLDS TOGETHER. ALL YOU HAD TO BE WAS COMPETENT, AND SAVING THAT, LOYAL. BUT YOU WERE NEITHER, AND SO YOU END UP AS SCABS IN CLOT'S SNACK JARS.
ENOUGH, DESAAD! BEGIN THE PROCESS. THE SOONER I'M EMPOWERED, THE SOONER YOU WILL HAVE YOUR GALAXY.
O, MY DEAR DARKSEID. I WILL HAVE MORE THAN THAT.
I WILL HAVE IT ALL!
GRAAAAACK
EEEYAAAARRRGH!
YES, M'LORD, THE SUN HAS FINALLY SET ON YOUR MONSTROUS EGO!
KHREEERCH
A NEW DAY IS AT DAWN FOR APOKOLIPS, A NEW KING!

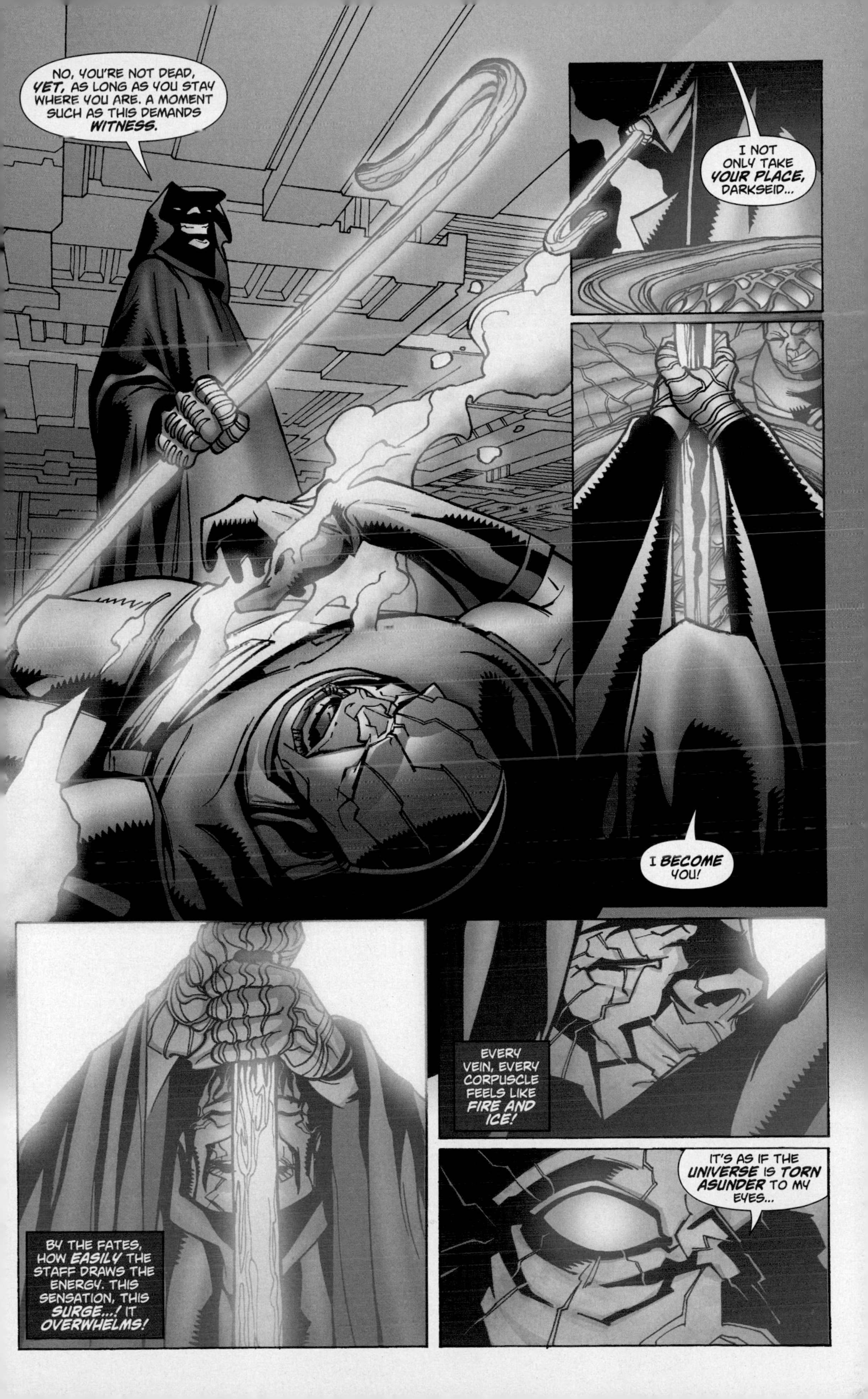
NO, YOU'RE NOT DEAD, YET, AS LONG AS YOU STAY WHERE YOU ARE. A MOMENT SUCH AS THIS DEMANDS WITNESS.
I NOT ONLY TAKE YOUR PLACE, DARKSEID...
I BECOME YOU!
BY THE FATES, HOW EASILY THE STAFF DRAWS THE ENERGY. THIS SENSATION, THIS SURGE...! IT OVERWHELMS!
EVERY VEIN, EVERY CORPUSCLE FEELS LIKE FIRE AND ICE!
IT'S AS IF THE UNIVERSE IS TORN ASUNDER TO MY EYES...

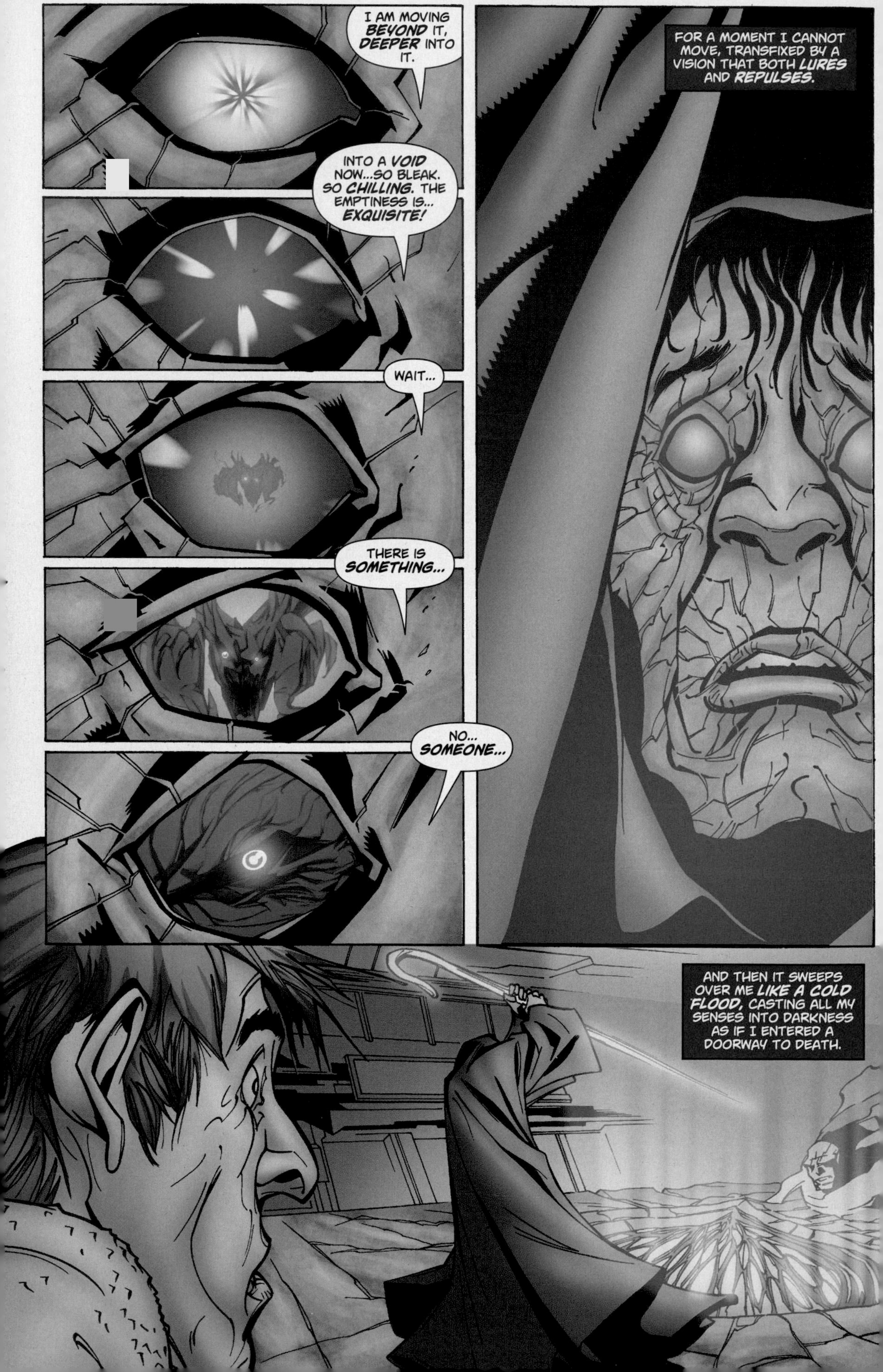
I AM MOVING BEYOND IT, DEEPER INTO IT.
INTO A VOID NOW...SO BLEAK. SO CHILLING. THE EMPTINESS IS... EXQUISITE!
WAIT...
THERE IS SOMETHING...
NO... SOMEONE...
FOR A MOMENT I CANNOT MOVE, TRANSFIXED BY A VISION THAT BOTH LURES AND REPULSES.
AND THEN IT SWEEPS OVER ME LIKE A COLD FLOOD, CASTING ALL MY SENSES INTO DARKNESS AS IF I ENTERED A DOORWAY TO DEATH.

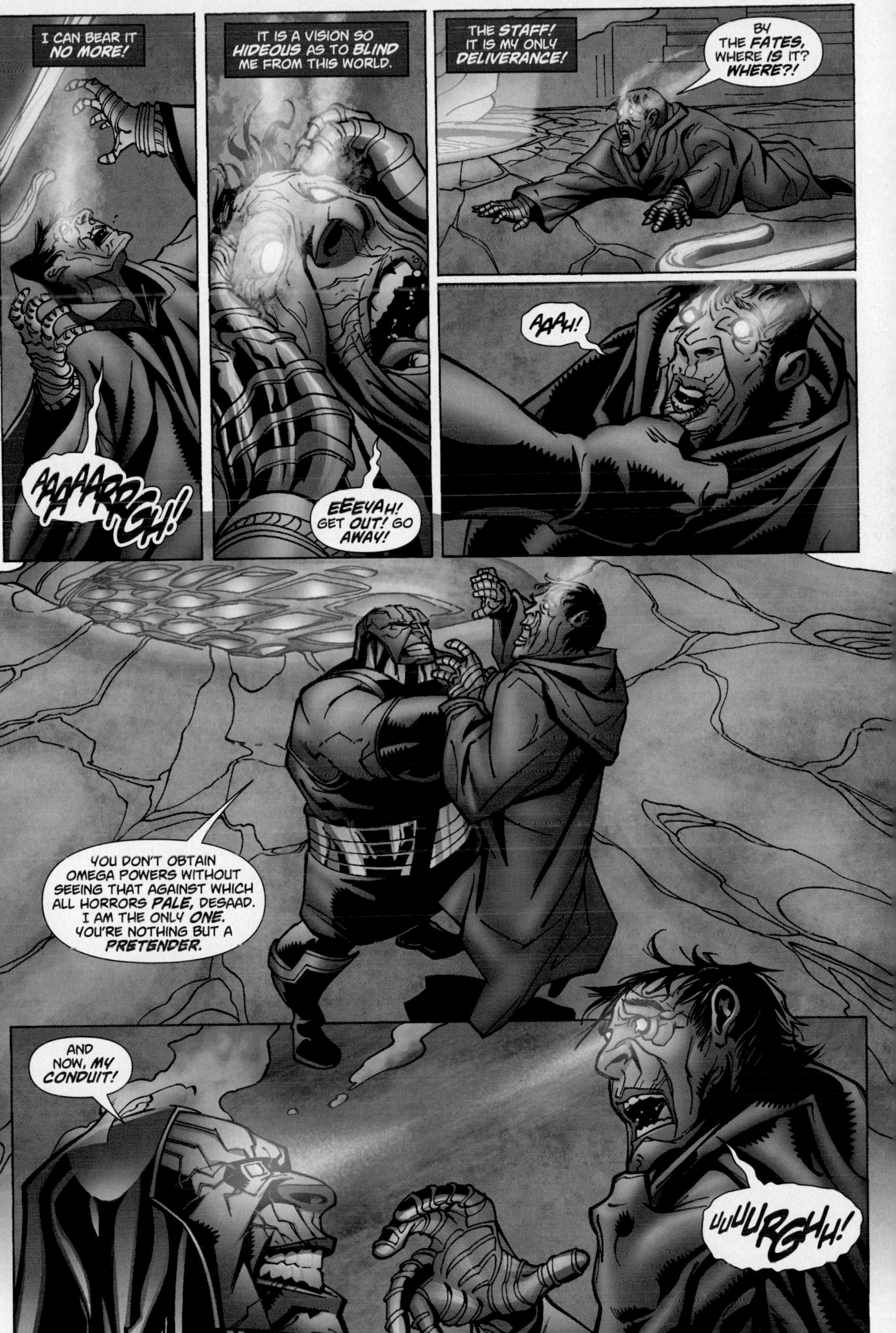
I CAN BEAR IT NO MORE!
AAAAARRGH!
IT IS A VISION SO HIDEOUS AS TO BLIND ME FROM THIS WORLD.
EEEYAH! GET OUT! GO AWAY!
THE STAFF! IT IS MY ONLY DELIVERANCE!
BY THE FATES, WHERE IS IT? WHERE?!
AAAH!
YOU DON'T OBTAIN OMEGA POWERS WITHOUT SEEING THAT AGAINST WHICH ALL HORRORS PALE, DESAAD. I AM THE ONLY ONE. YOU'RE NOTHING BUT A PRETENDER.
AND NOW, MY CONDUIT!
UUUURGHH!

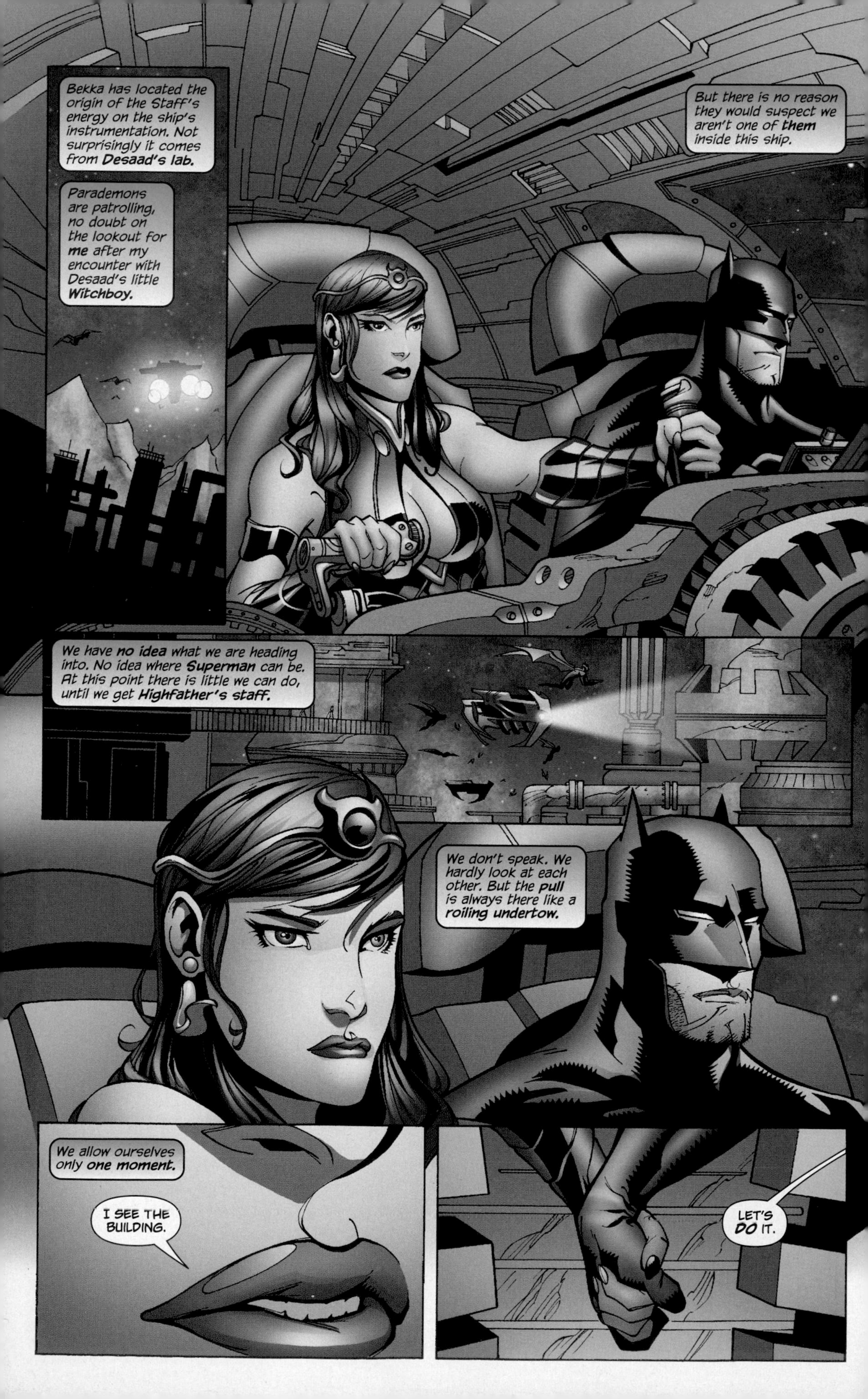
Bekka has located the origin of the Staff's energy on the ship's instrumentation. Not surprisingly it comes from Desaad's lab.
Parademons are patrolling, no doubt on the lookout for me after my encounter with Desaad's little Witchboy.
But there is no reason they would suspect we aren't one of them inside this ship.
We have no idea what we are heading into. No idea where Superman can be. At this point there is little we can do, until we get Highfather's staff.
We don't speak. We hardly look at each other. But the pull is always there like a roiling undertow.
We allow ourselves only one moment.
I SEE THE BUILDING.
LET'S DO IT.

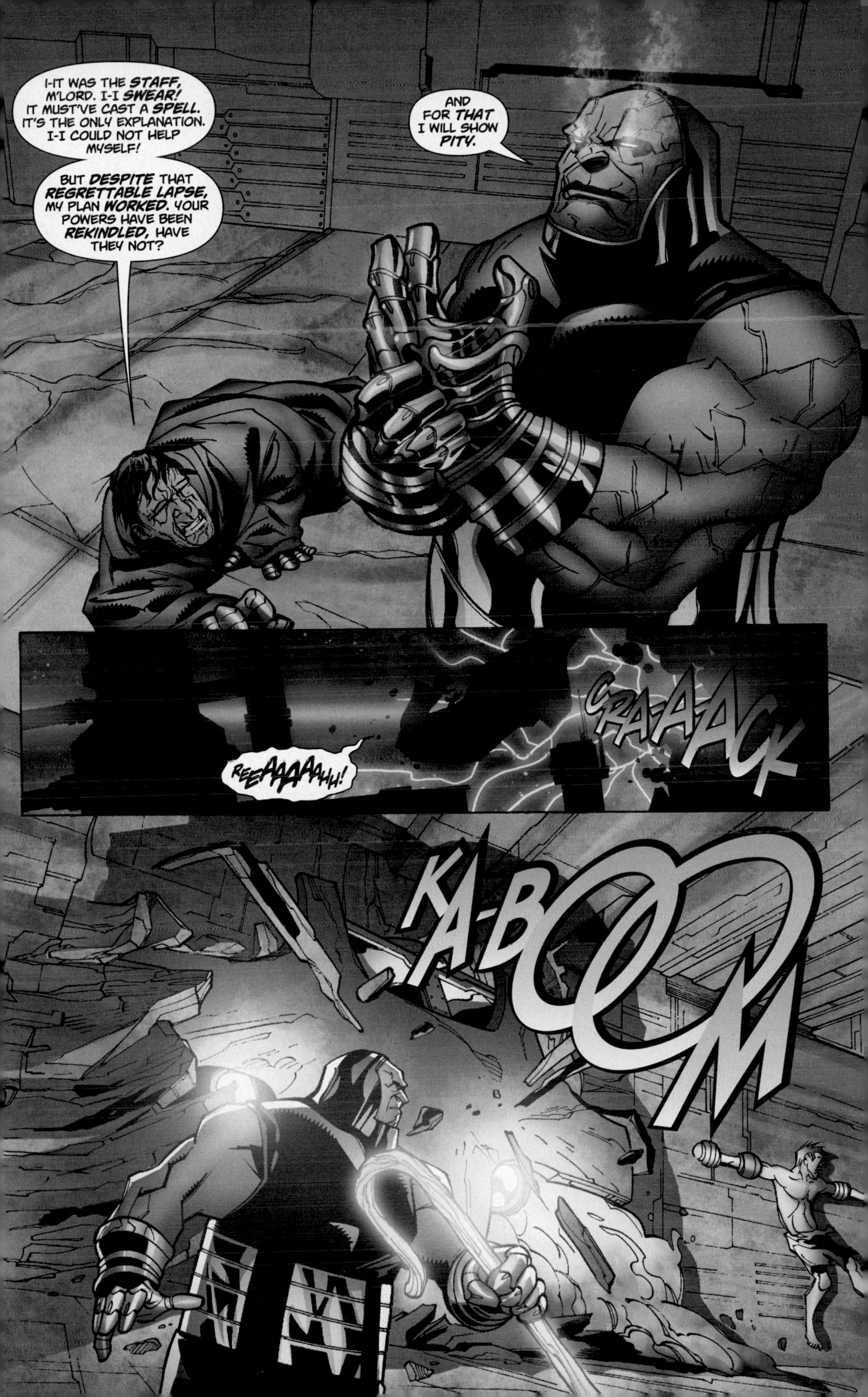
I-IT WAS THE STAFF, M'LORD. I-I SWEAR! IT MUST'VE CAST A SPELL. IT'S THE ONLY EXPLANATION. I-I COULD NOT HELP MYSELF!
BUT DESPITE THAT REGRETTABLE LAPSE, MY PLAN WORKED. YOUR POWERS HAVE BEEN REKINDLED, HAVE THEY NOT?
AND FOR THAT I WILL SHOW PITY.
CRA-A-A-ACK
REEAAAAAHH!
KA-BOOM

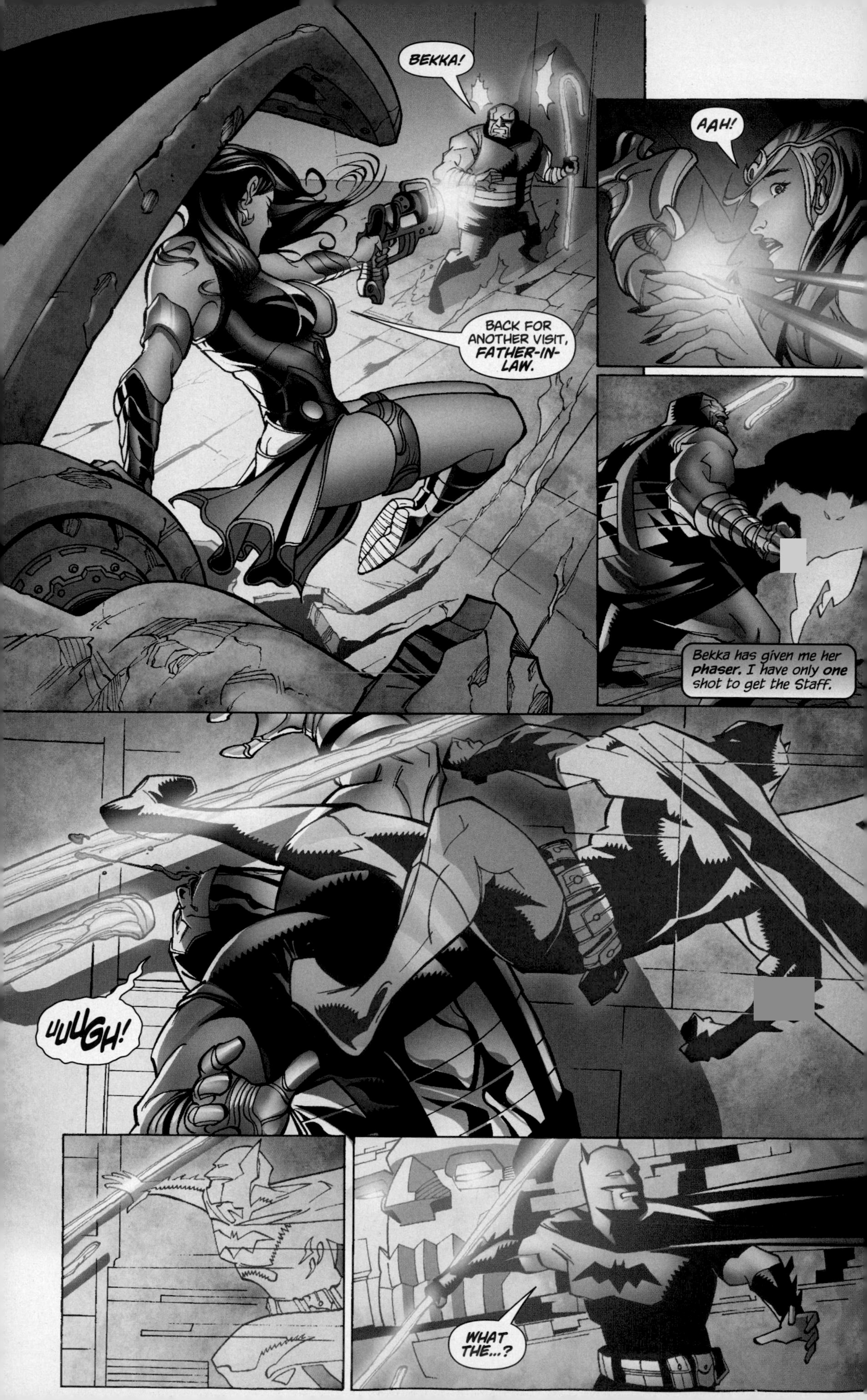

BEKKA!
BACK FOR ANOTHER VISIT, FATHER-IN-LAW.
AAH!
Bekka has given me her phaser. I have only one shot to get the Staff.
UUUGH!
WHAT THE...?

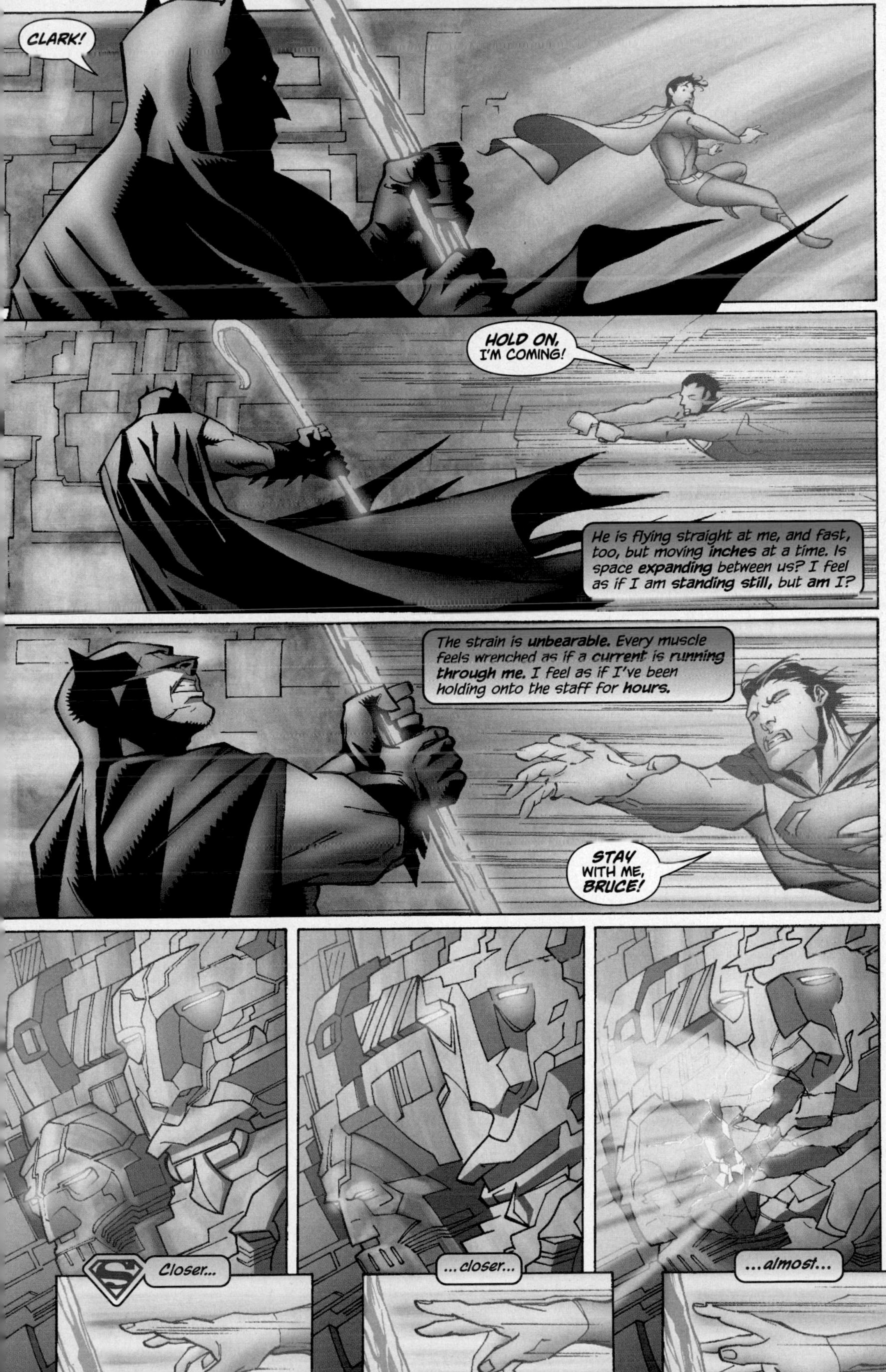
CLARK!
HOLD ON, I'M COMING!
He is flying straight at me, and fast, too, but moving inches at a time. Is space expanding between us? I feel as if I am standing still, but am I?
The strain is unbearable. Every muscle feels wrenched as if a current is running through me. I feel as if I've been holding onto the staff for hours.
STAY WITH ME, BRUCE!
Closer...
...closer...
...almost...

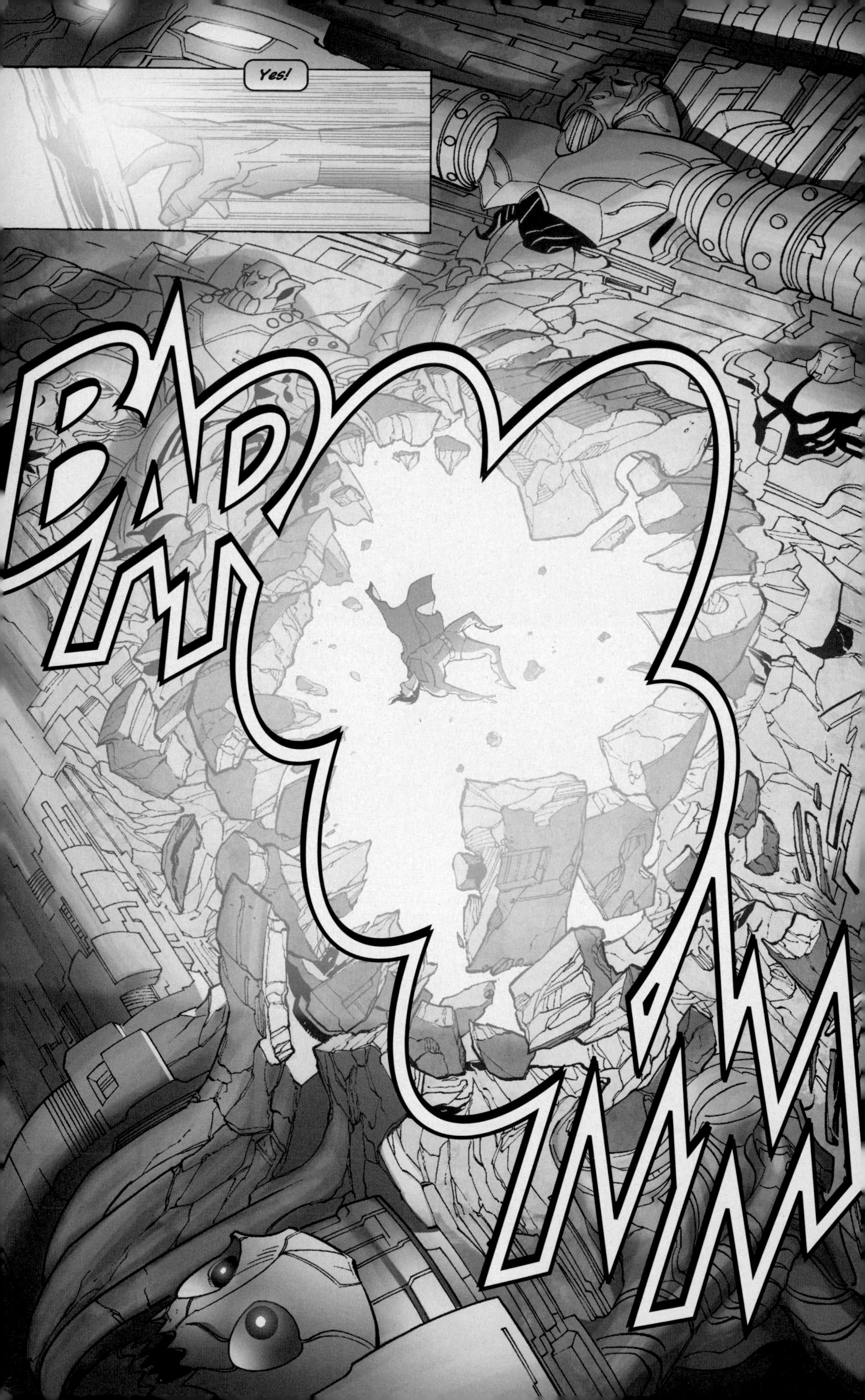
Yes!
BADOOM

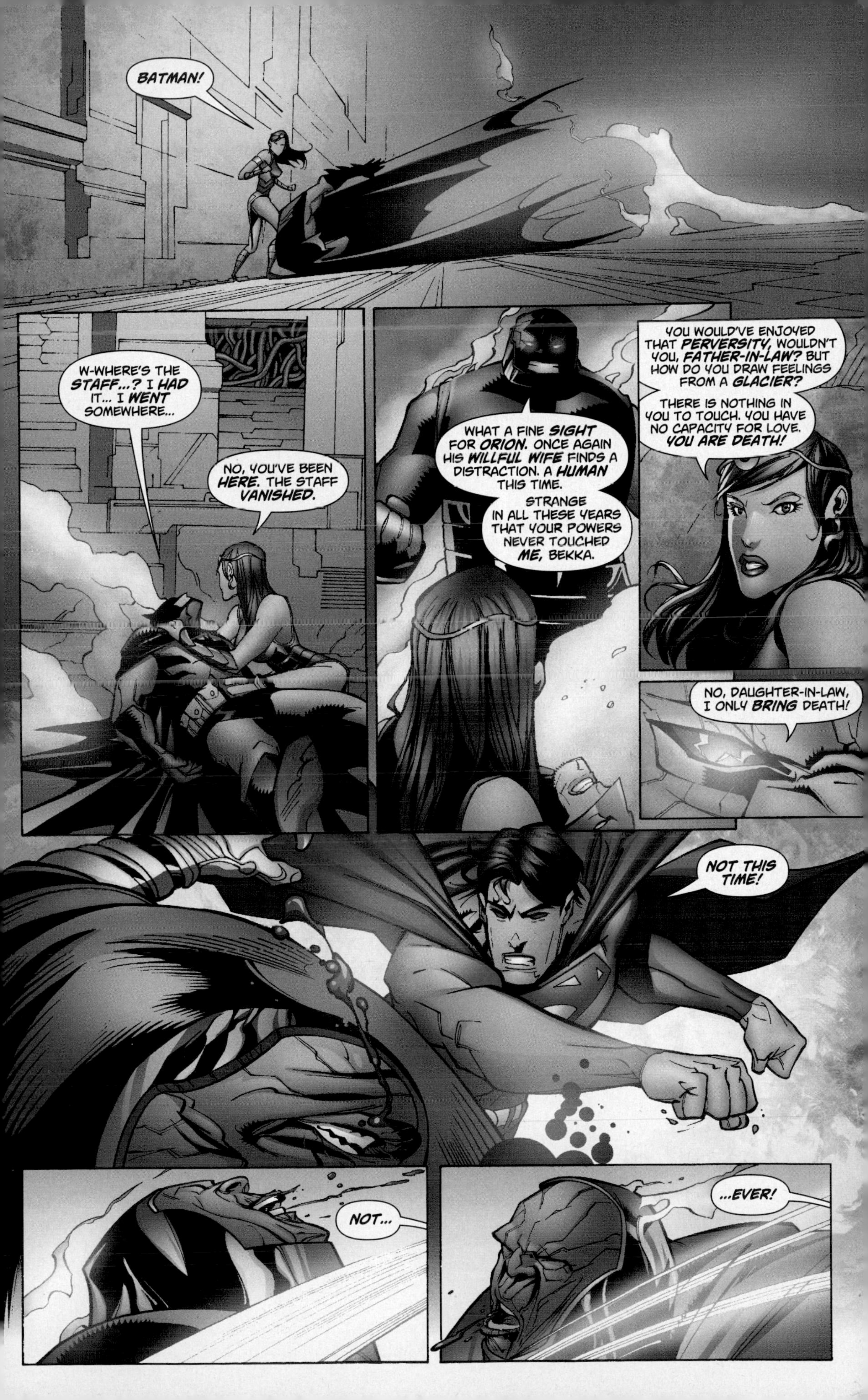
BATMAN!
W-WHERE'S THE STAFF...? I HAD IT... I WENT SOMEWHERE...
NO, YOU'VE BEEN HERE. THE STAFF VANISHED.
WHAT A FINE SIGHT FOR ORION. ONCE AGAIN HIS WILLFUL WIFE FINDS A DISTRACTION. A HUMAN THIS TIME.
STRANGE IN ALL THESE YEARS THAT YOUR POWERS NEVER TOUCHED ME, BEKKA.
YOU WOULD'VE ENJOYED THAT PERVERSITY, WOULDN'T YOU, FATHER-IN-LAW? BUT HOW DO YOU DRAW FEELINGS FROM A GLACIER?
THERE IS NOTHING IN YOU TO TOUCH. YOU HAVE NO CAPACITY FOR LOVE. YOU ARE DEATH!
NO, DAUGHTER-IN-LAW, I ONLY BRING DEATH!
NOT THIS TIME!
NOT...
...EVER!

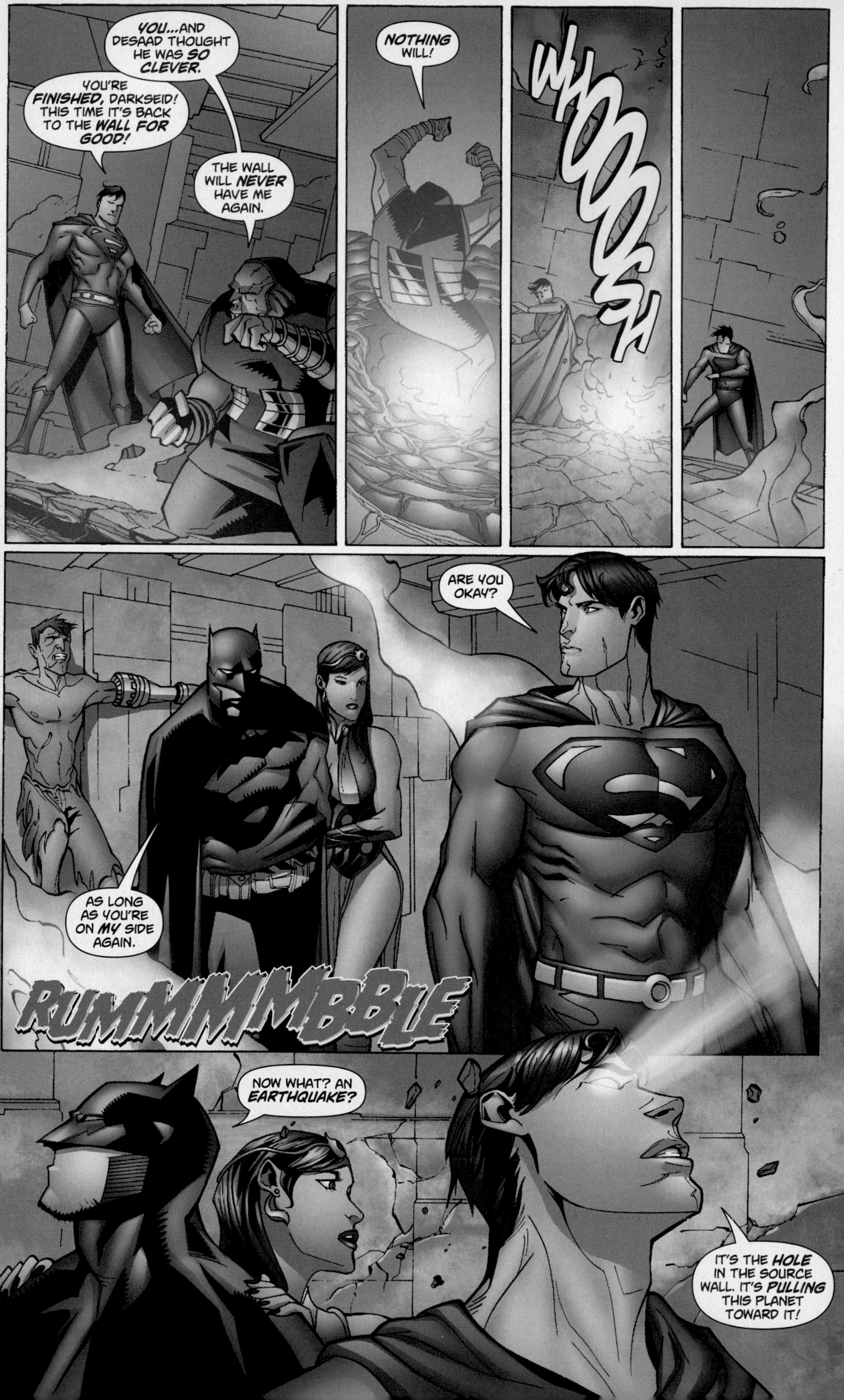

YOU'RE FINISHED, DARKSEID! THIS TIME IT'S BACK TO THE WALL FOR GOOD!
YOU...AND DESAAD THOUGHT HE WAS SO CLEVER.
THE WALL WILL NEVER HAVE ME AGAIN.
NOTHING WILL!
WHOOOOOSH
ARE YOU OKAY?
AS LONG AS YOU'RE ON MY SIDE AGAIN.
RUMMMMMBBLE
NOW WHAT? AN EARTHQUAKE?
IT'S THE HOLE IN THE SOURCE WALL. IT'S PULLING THIS PLANET TOWARD IT!

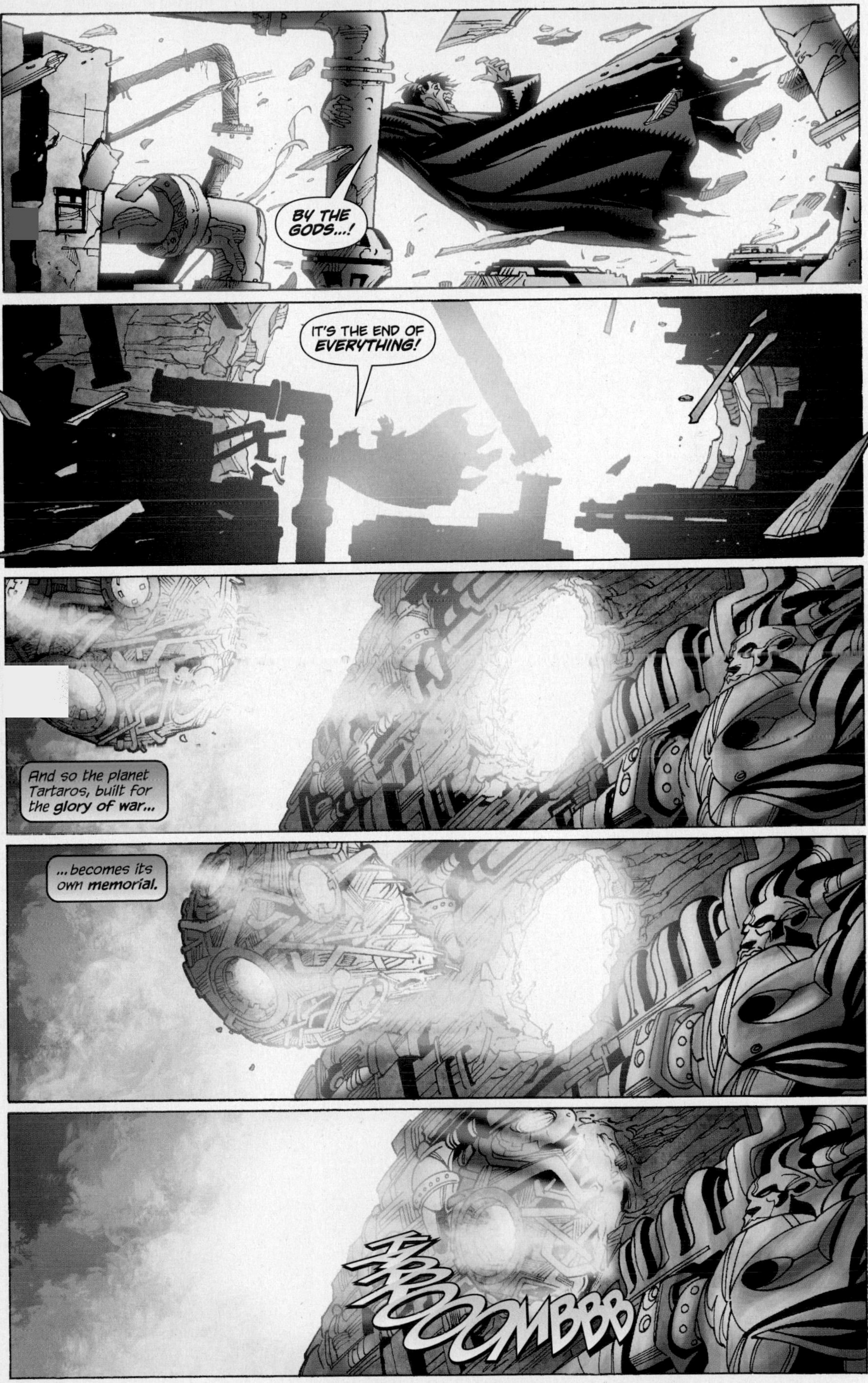
BY THE GODS...!
IT'S THE END OF EVERYTHING!
And so the planet Tartaros, built for the glory of war...
...becomes its own memorial.
KROOOOMBBB

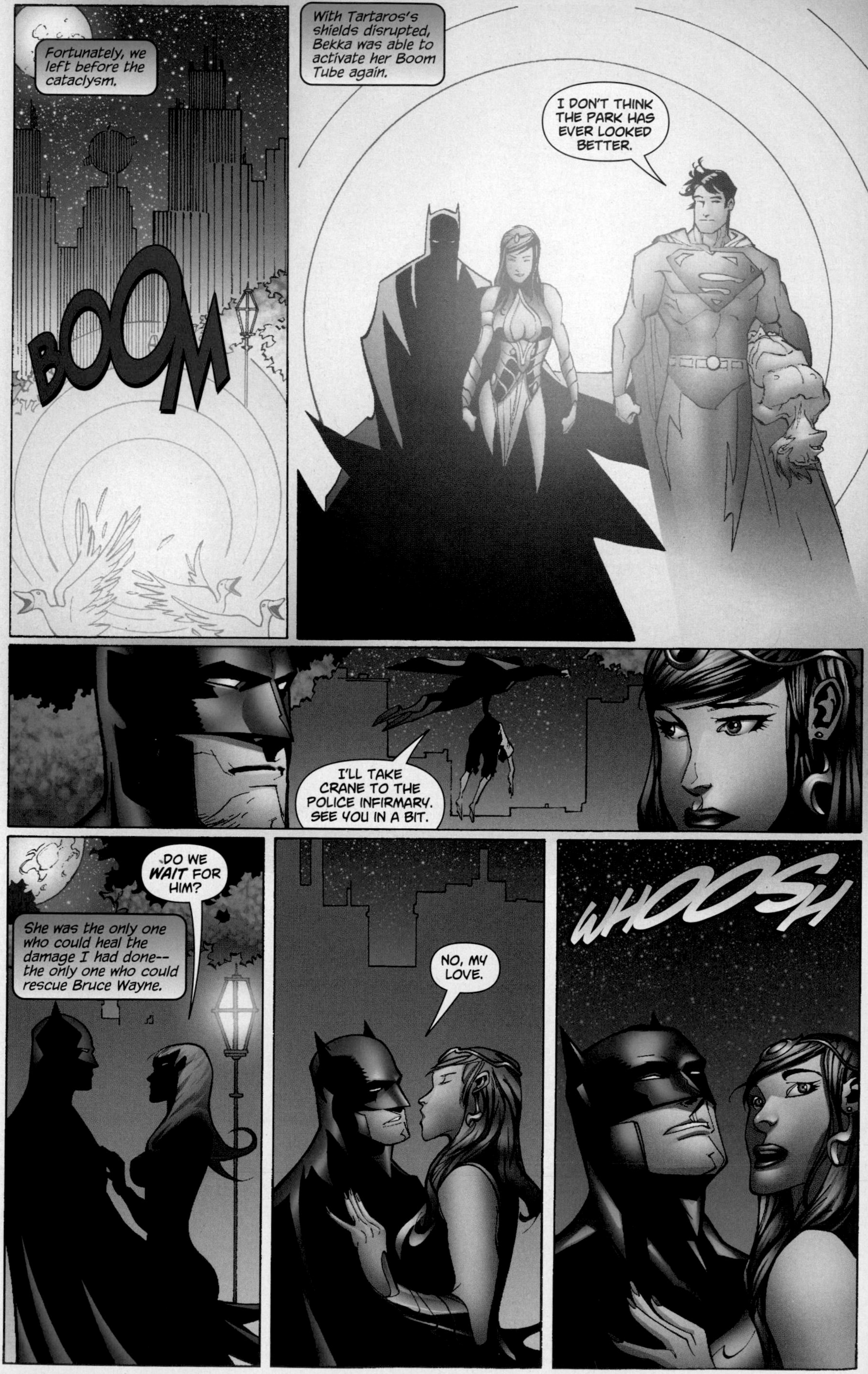
Fortunately, we left before the cataclysm.
BOOM
With Tartaros's shields disrupted, Bekka was able to activate her Boom Tube again.
I DON'T THINK THE PARK HAS EVER LOOKED BETTER.
I'LL TAKE CRANE TO THE POLICE INFIRMARY. SEE YOU IN A BIT.
DO WE WAIT FOR HIM?
She was the only one who could heal the damage I had done--the only one who could rescue Bruce Wayne.
NO, MY LOVE.
WHOOSH

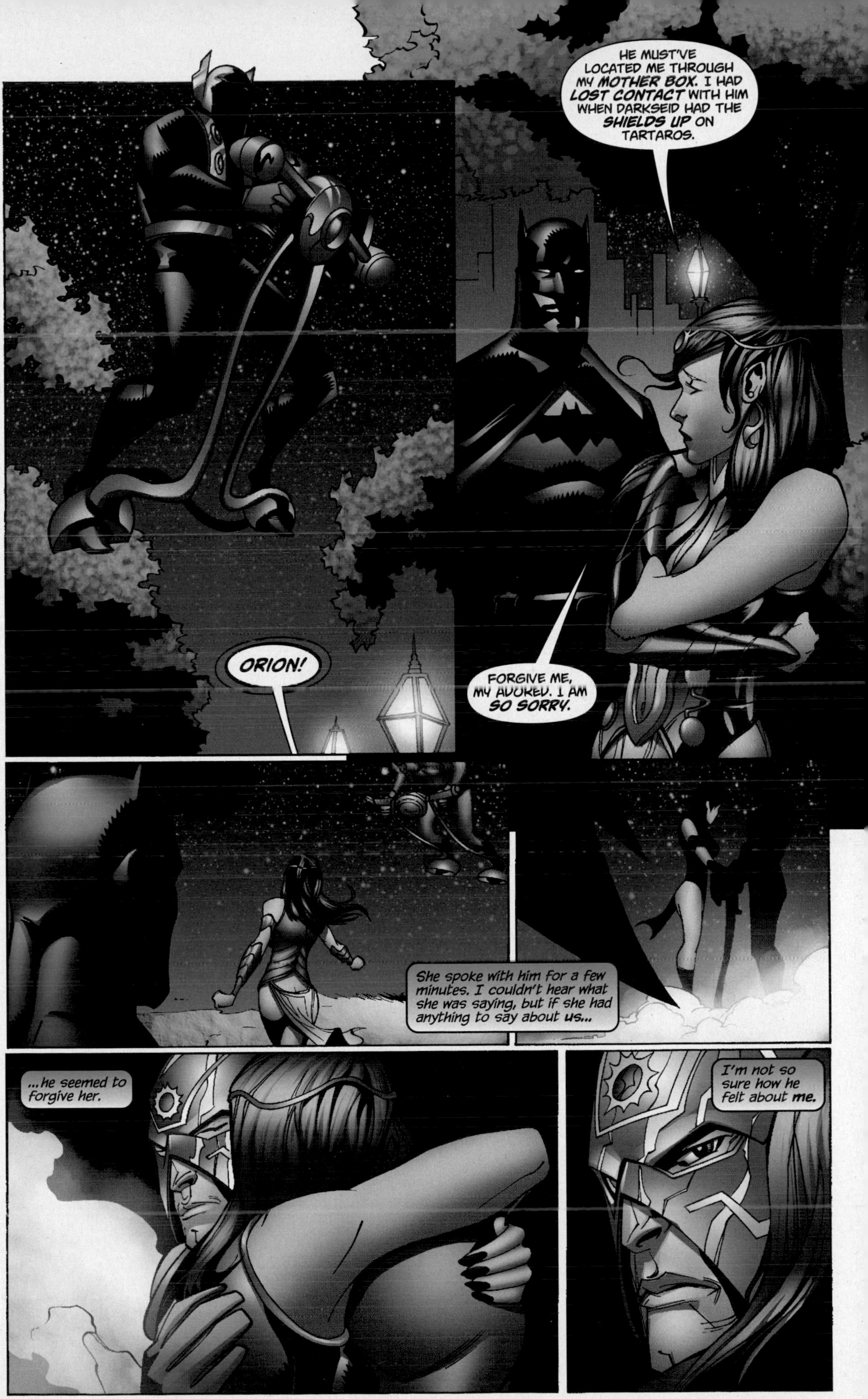
HE MUST'VE LOCATED ME THROUGH MY MOTHER BOX. I HAD LOST CONTACT WITH HIM WHEN DARKSEID HAD THE SHIELDS UP ON TARTAROS.
ORION!
FORGIVE ME, MY ADORED. I AM SO SORRY.
She spoke with him for a few minutes. I couldn't hear what she was saying, but if she had anything to say about us...
...he seemed to forgive her.
I'm not so sure how he felt about me.

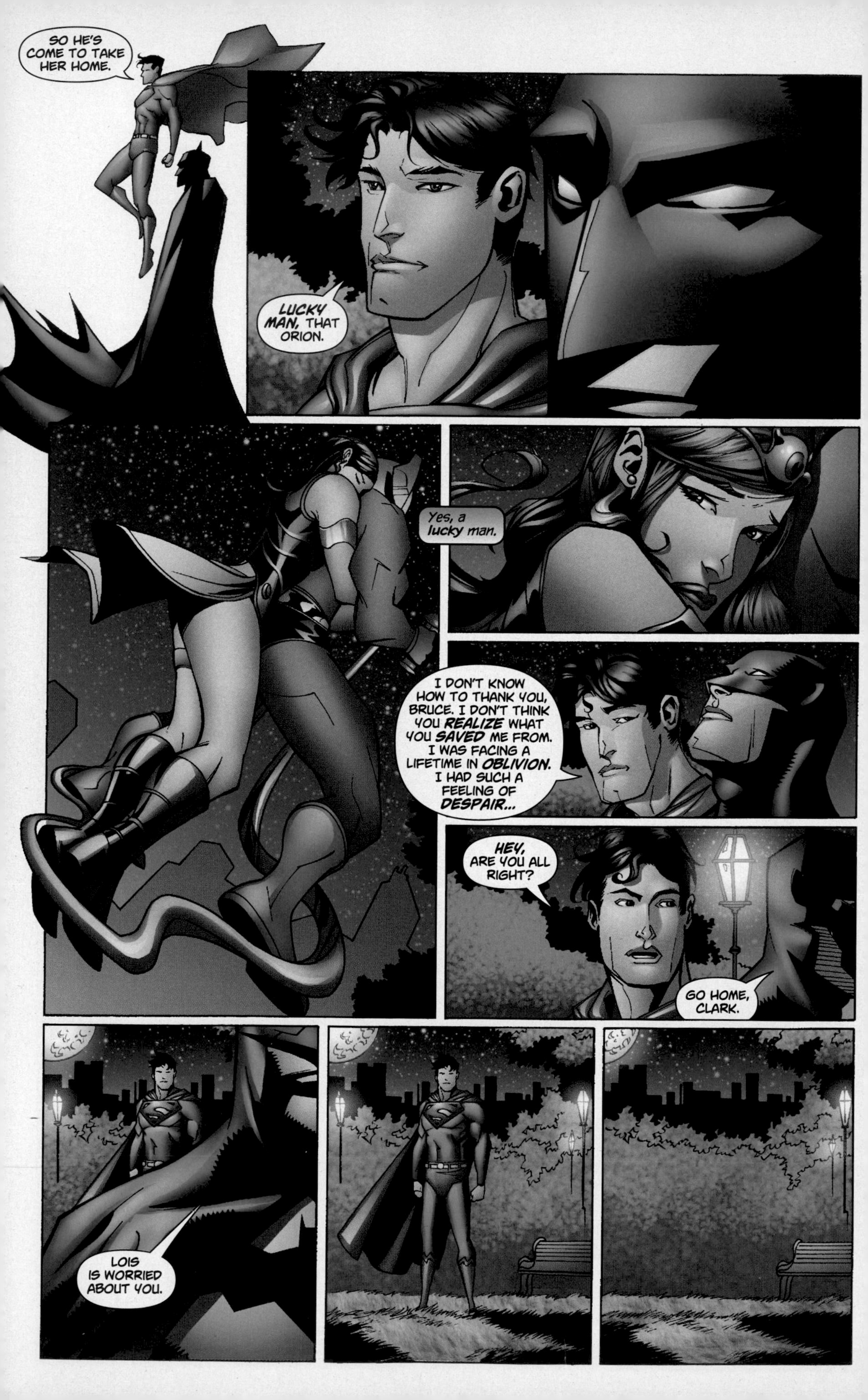
SO HE'S COME TO TAKE HER HOME.
LUCKY MAN, THAT ORION.
Yes, a lucky man.
I DON'T KNOW HOW TO THANK YOU, BRUCE. I DON'T THINK YOU REALIZE WHAT YOU SAVED ME FROM. I WAS FACING A LIFETIME IN OBLIVION. I HAD SUCH A FEELING OF DESPAIR...
HEY, ARE YOU ALL RIGHT?
GO HOME, CLARK.
LOIS IS WORRIED ABOUT YOU.

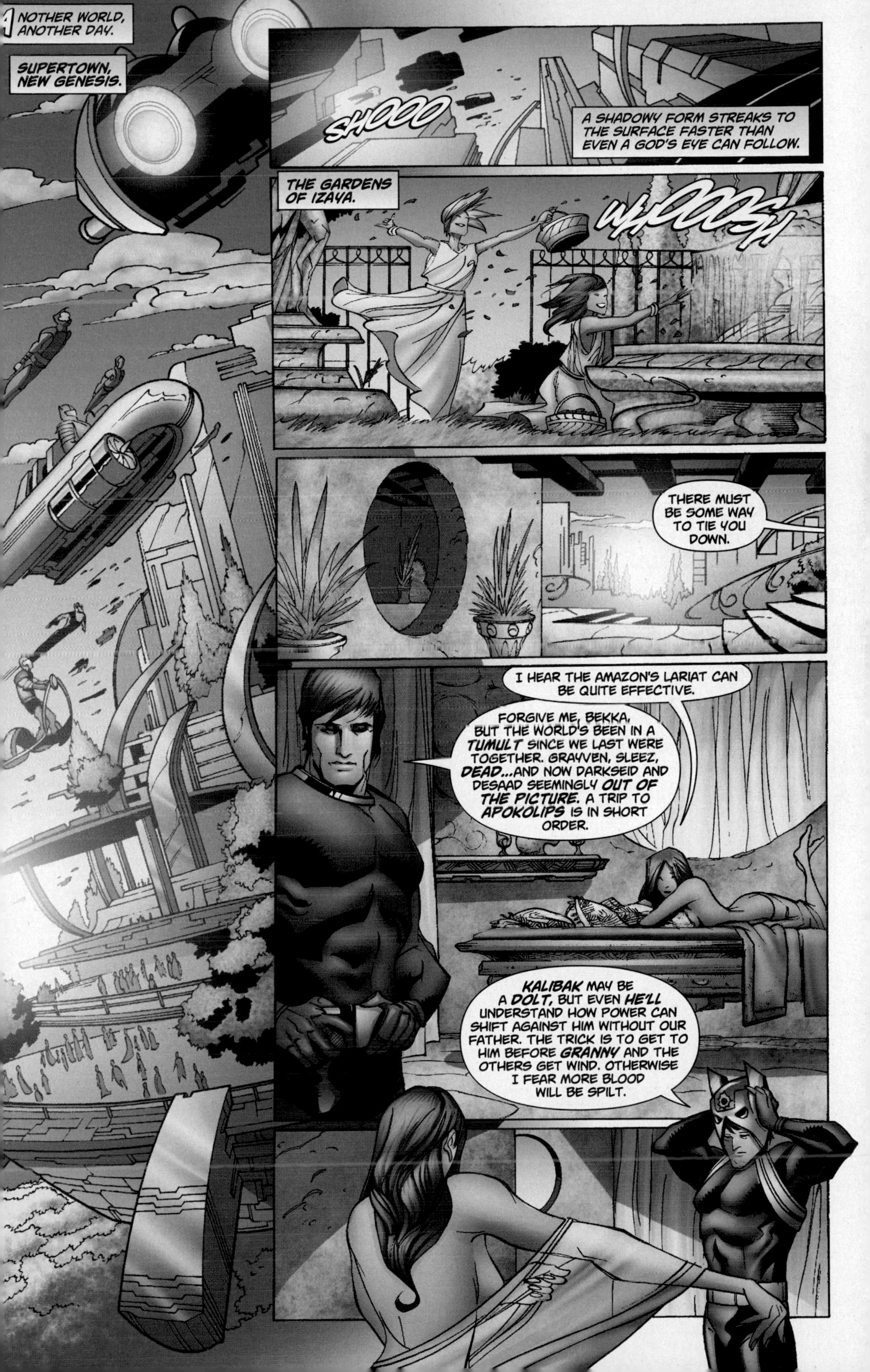
ANOTHER WORLD, ANOTHER DAY.
SUPERTOWN, NEW GENESIS.
SHOOOO
A SHADOWY FORM STREAKS TO THE SURFACE FASTER THAN EVEN A GOD'S EYE CAN FOLLOW.
THE GARDENS OF IZAYA.
WHOOOSH
THERE MUST BE SOME WAY TO TIE YOU DOWN.
I HEAR THE AMAZON'S LARIAT CAN BE QUITE EFFECTIVE.
FORGIVE ME, BEKKA, BUT THE WORLD'S BEEN IN A TUMULT SINCE WE LAST WERE TOGETHER. GRAYVEN, SLEEZ, DEAD...AND NOW DARKSEID AND DESAAD SEEMINGLY OUT OF THE PICTURE. A TRIP TO APOKOLIPS IS IN SHORT ORDER.
KALIBAK MAY BE A DOLT, BUT EVEN HE'LL UNDERSTAND HOW POWER CAN SHIFT AGAINST HIM WITHOUT OUR FATHER. THE TRICK IS TO GET TO HIM BEFORE GRANNY AND THE OTHERS GET WIND. OTHERWISE I FEAR MORE BLOOD WILL BE SPILT.

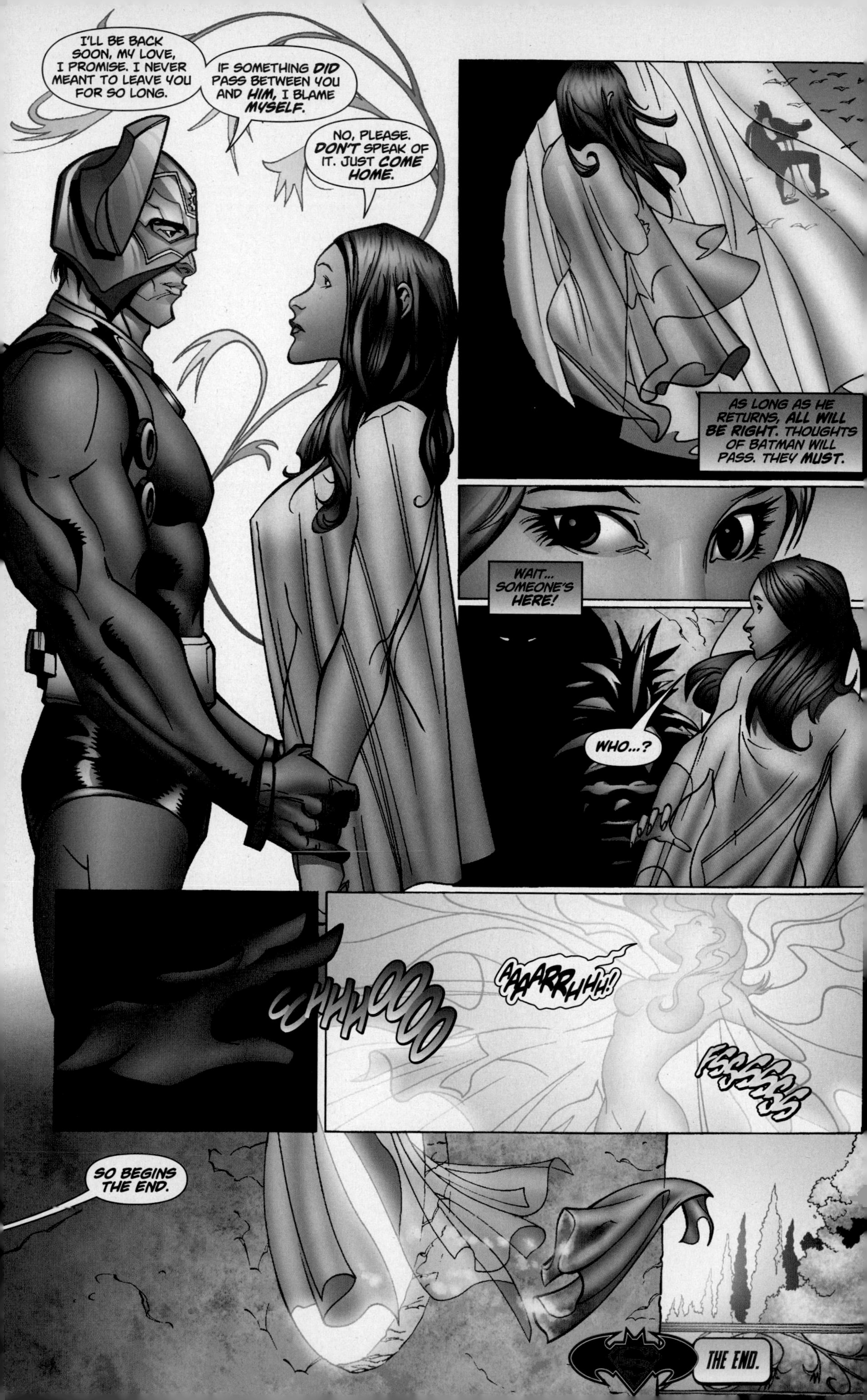

I'LL BE BACK SOON, MY LOVE, I PROMISE. I NEVER MEANT TO LEAVE YOU FOR SO LONG.
IF SOMETHING DID PASS BETWEEN YOU AND HIM, I BLAME MYSELF.
NO, PLEASE. DON'T SPEAK OF IT. JUST COME HOME.
AS LONG AS HE RETURNS, ALL WILL BE RIGHT. THOUGHTS OF BATMAN WILL PASS. THEY MUST.
WAIT... SOMEONE'S HERE!
WHO...?
CHHHOOOOO
AAAARRHHH!
FSSSSSS
SO BEGINS THE END.
THE END.

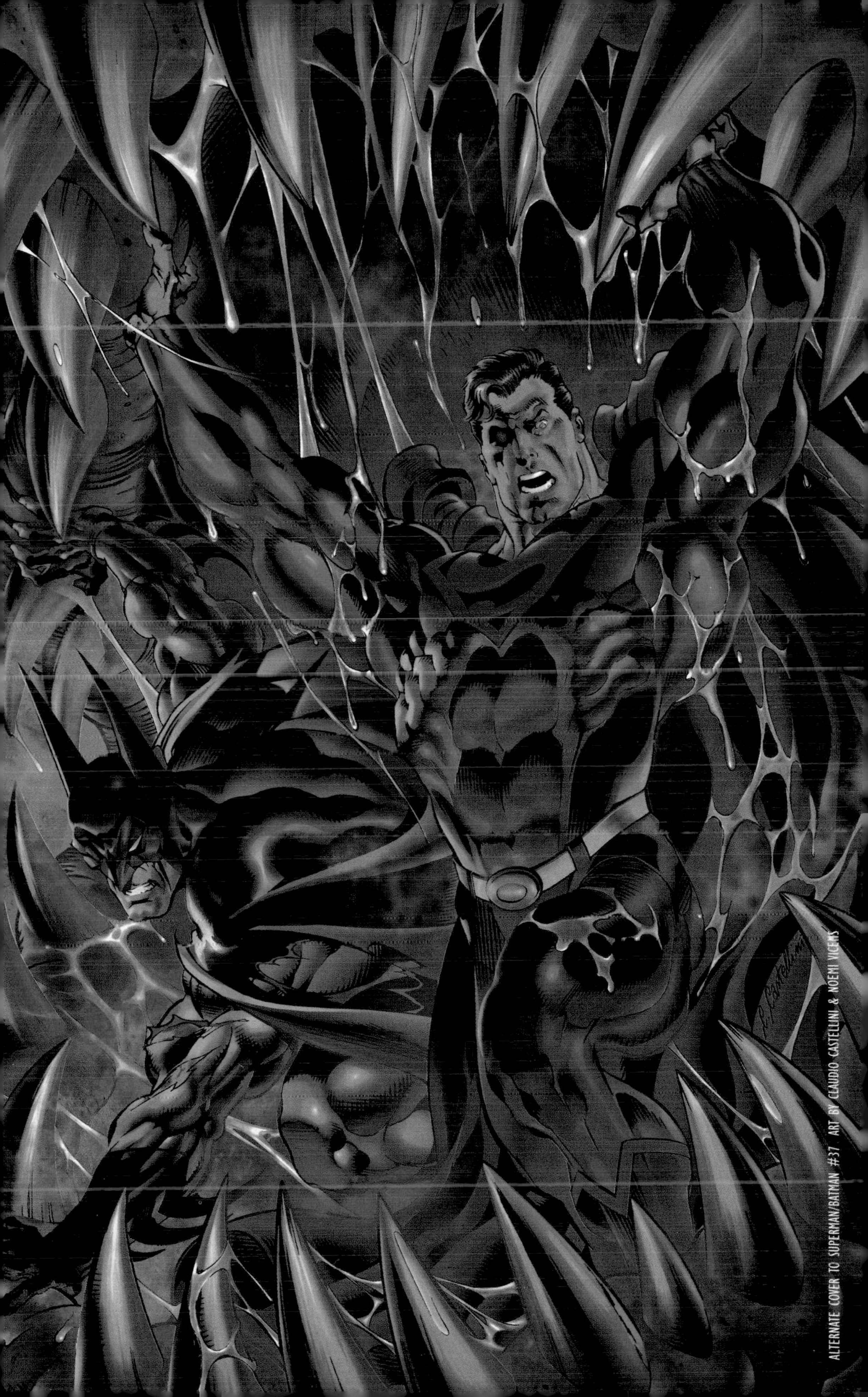

ALTERNATE COVER TO SUPERMAN/BATMAN #37 ART BY CLAUDIO CASTELLINI & NOEMI VICENS

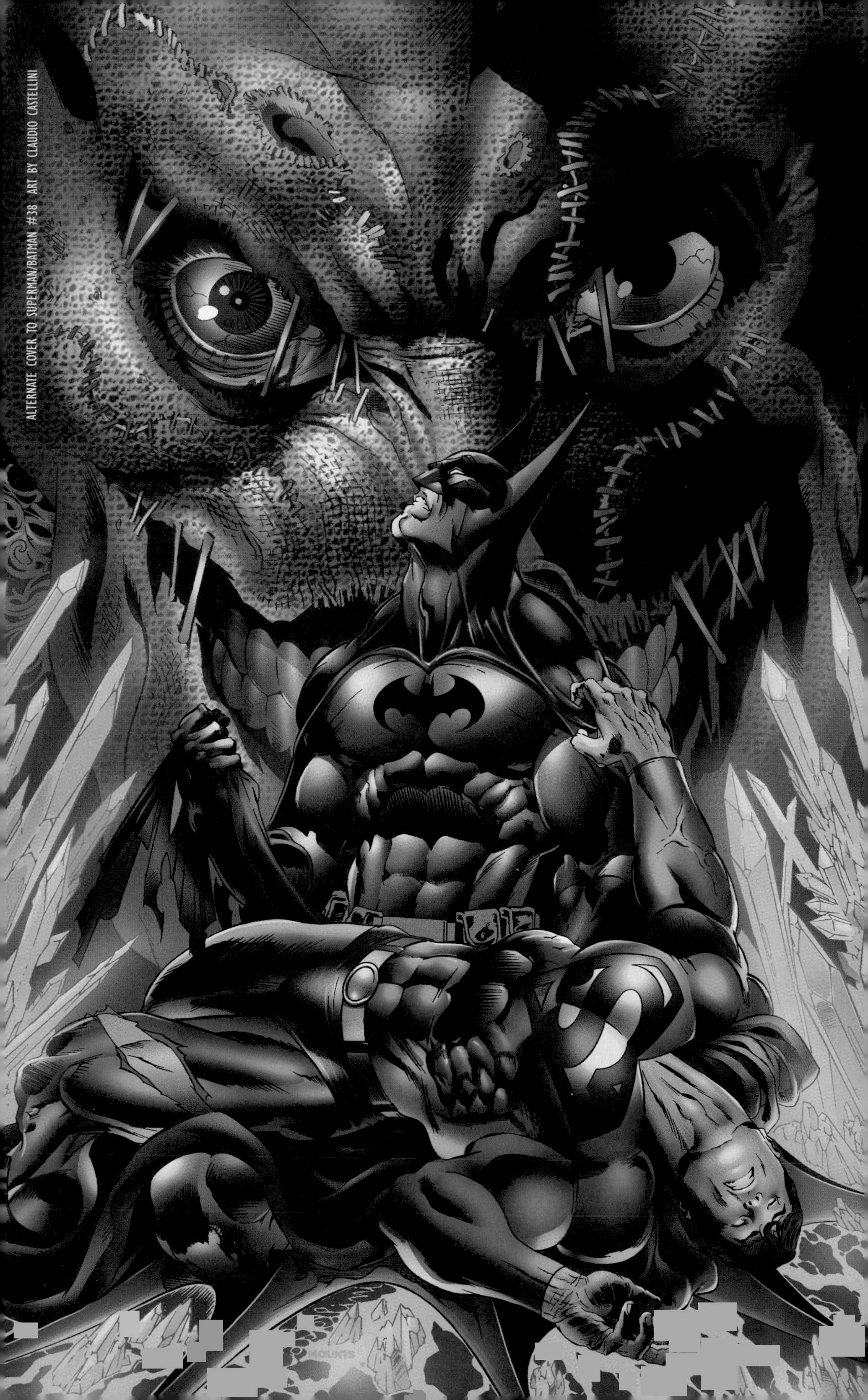

ALTERNATE COVER TO SUPERMAN/BATMAN #38 ART BY CLAUDIO CASTELLINI

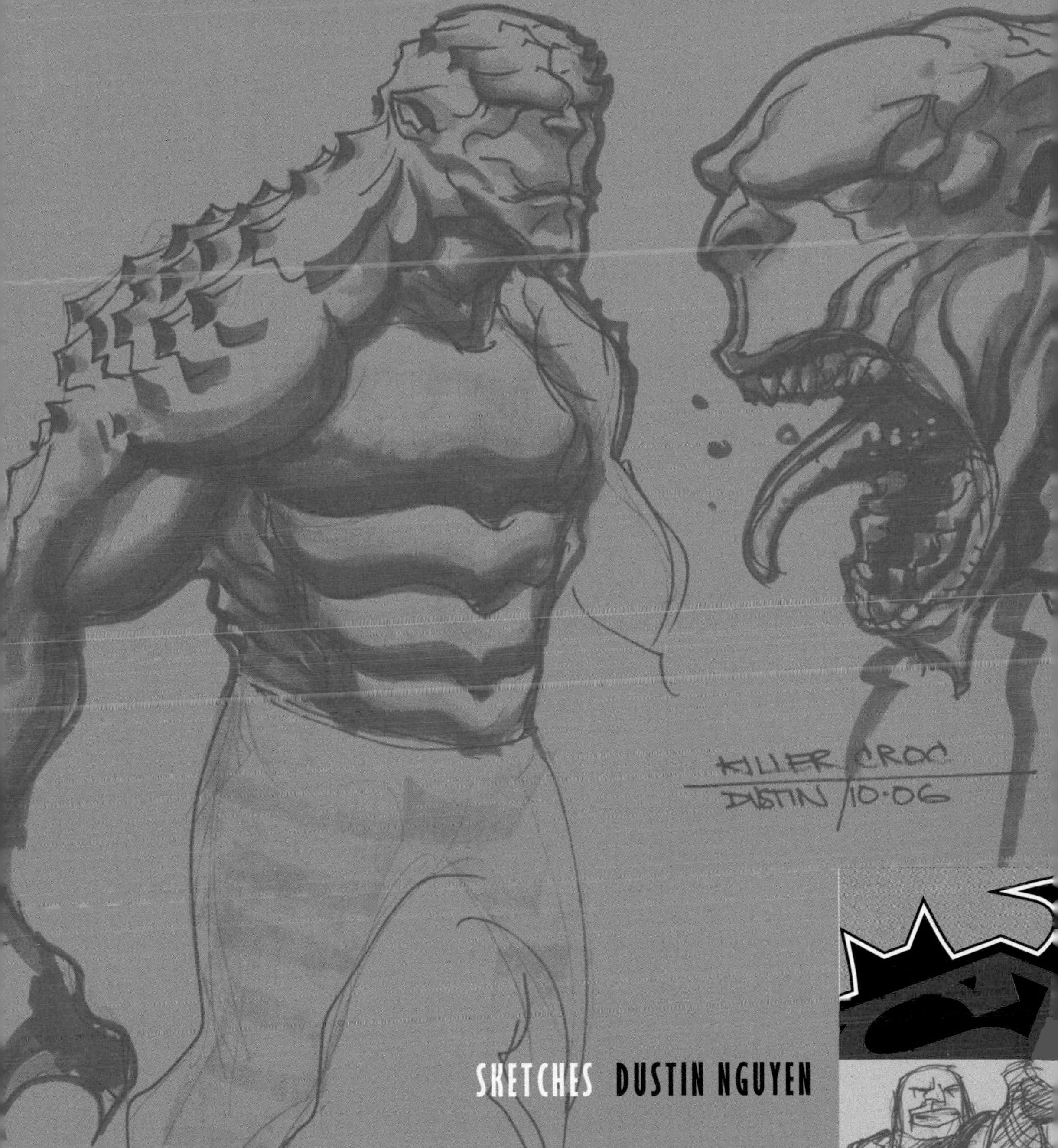
KILLER CROC
DUSTIN 10·06

SKETCHES DUSTIN NGUYEN

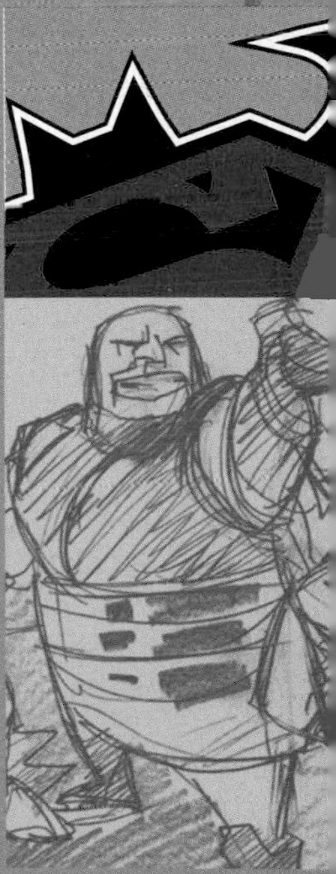

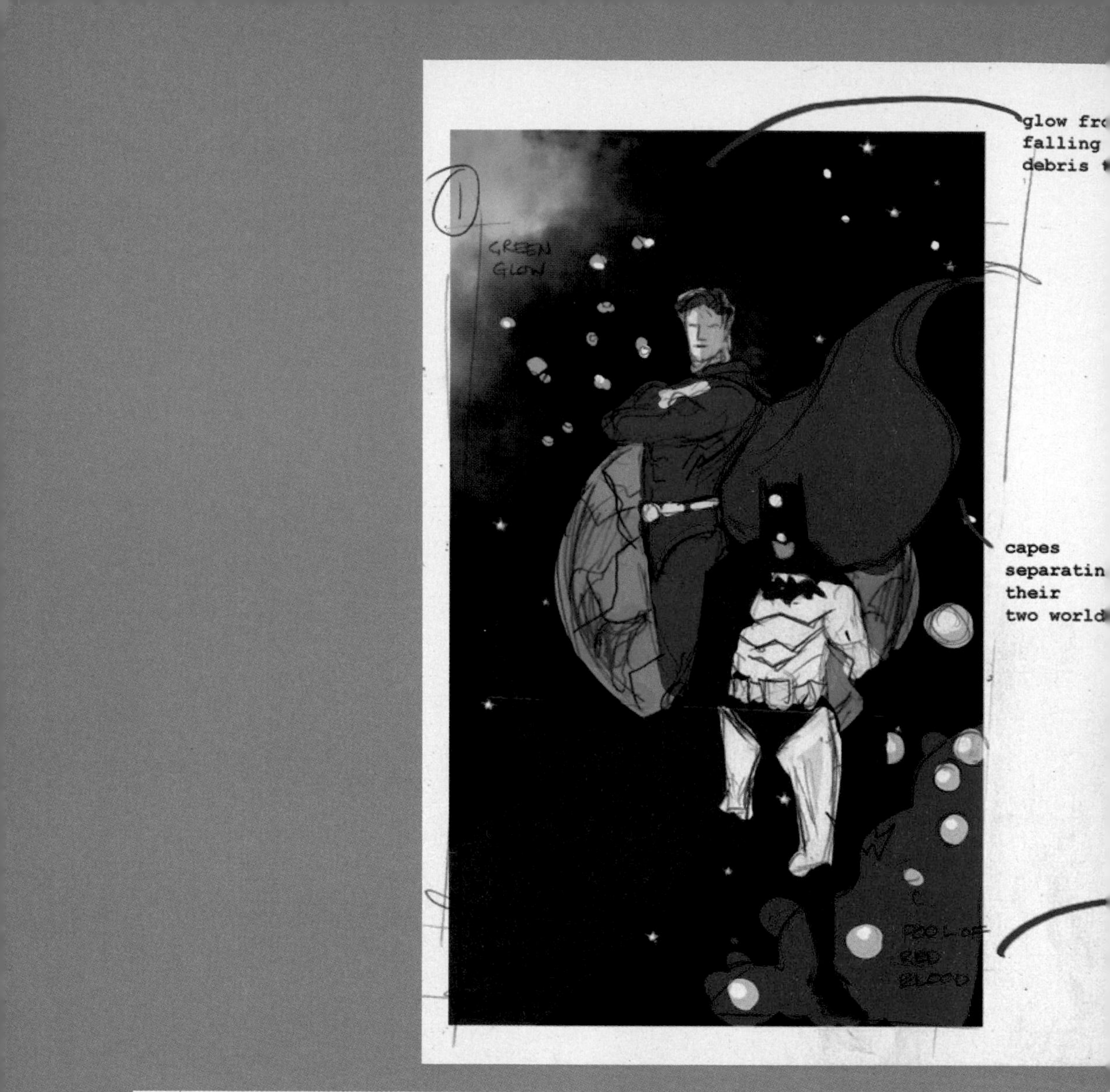
1
GREEN GLOW
glow fr
falling
debris
capes
separatin
their
two world
POOL OF RED BLOOD

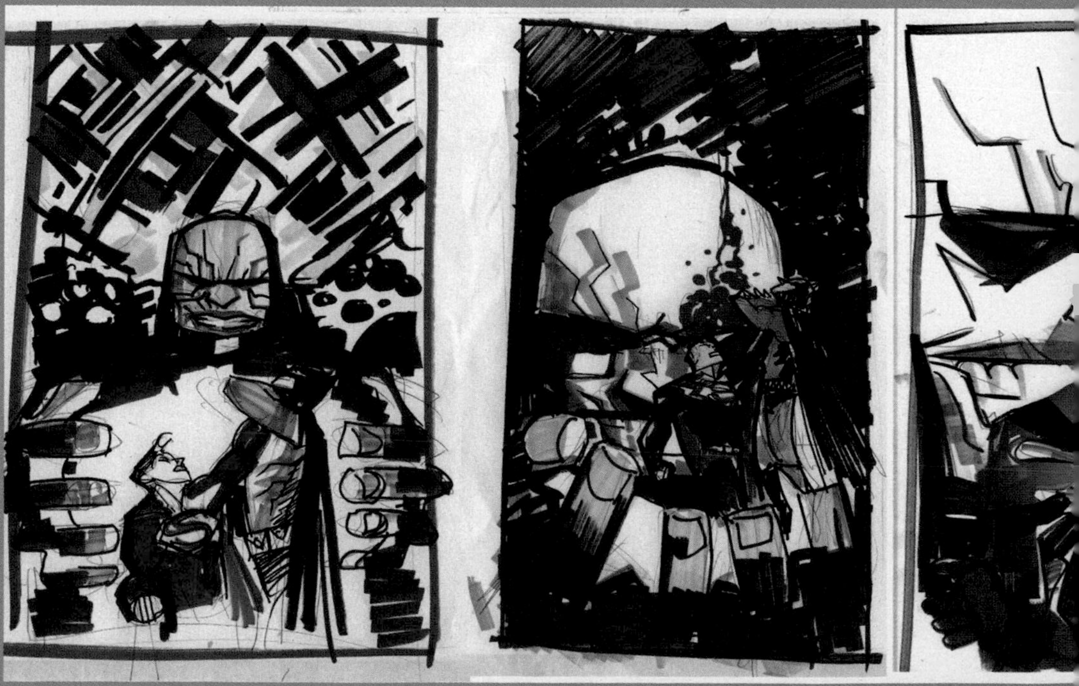

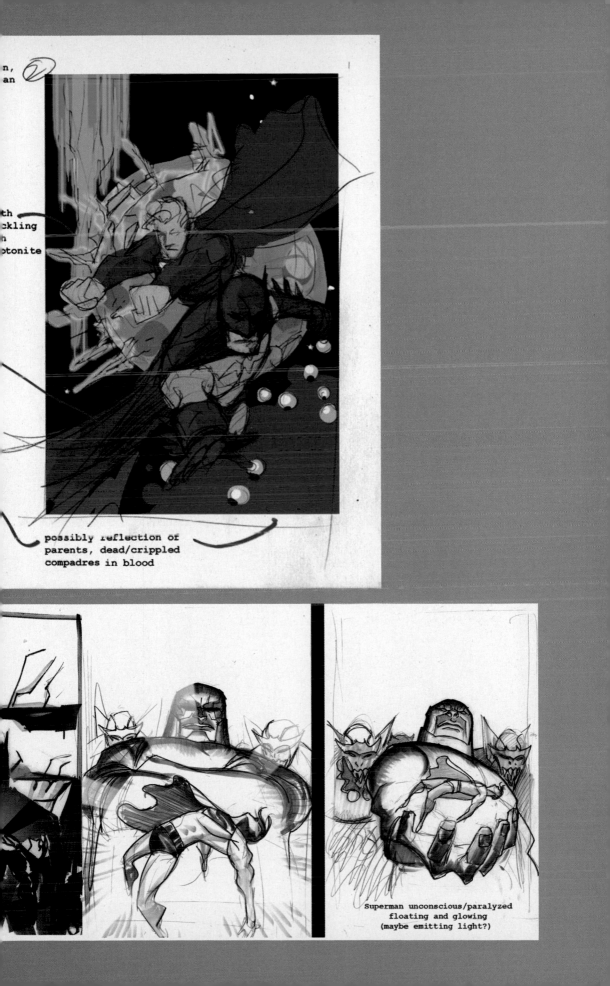

n,
an

th
ckling
n
ptonite

possibly reflection of
parents, dead/crippled
compadres in blood

Superman unconscious/paralyzed
floating and glowing
(maybe emitting light?)

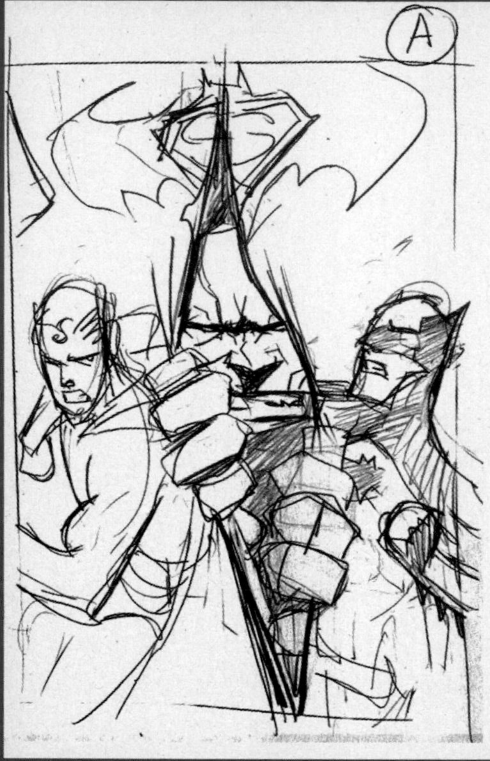
A

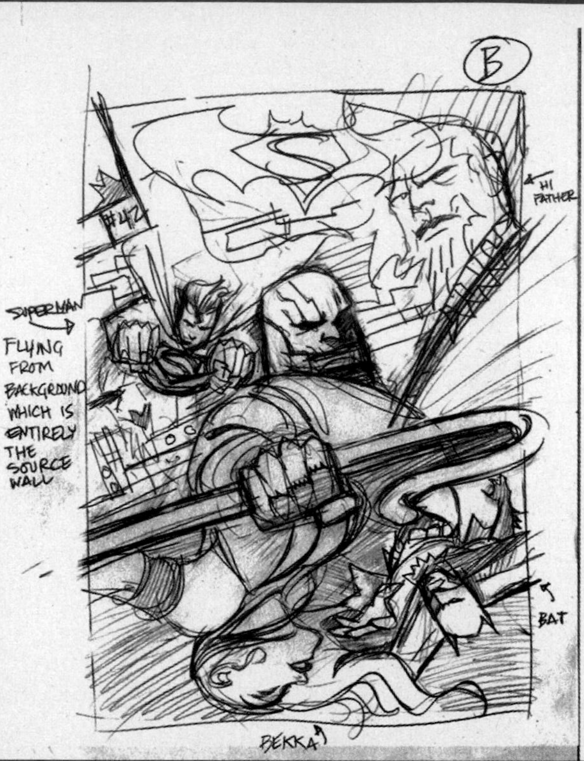
B
#42
HI FATHER
SUPERMAN
FLYING FROM BACKGROUND WHICH IS ENTIRELY THE SOURCE WALL
BAT
BEKKA

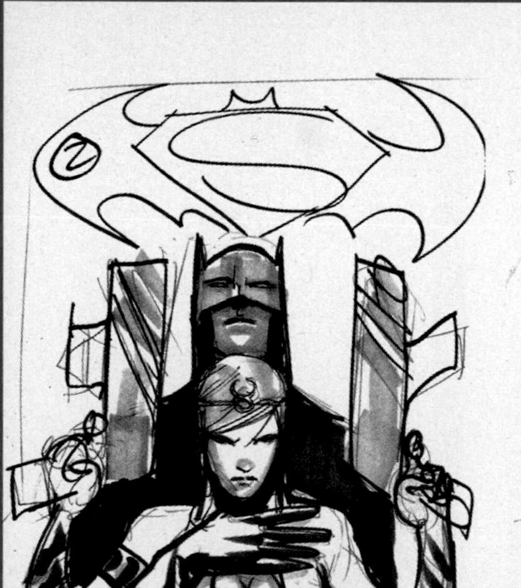
2

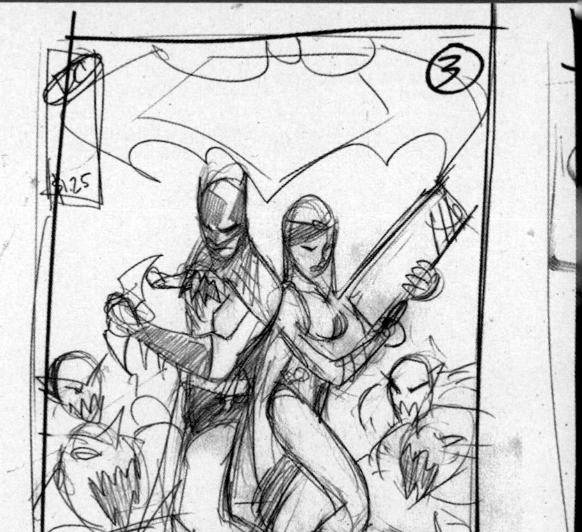
3
1.25
SURROUNDED BY PARADEMONS
(LIKE ON LAST PAGE, EXCEPT NOT INVISIBLE)

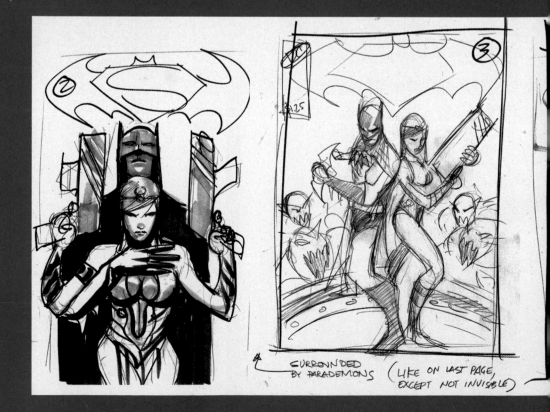

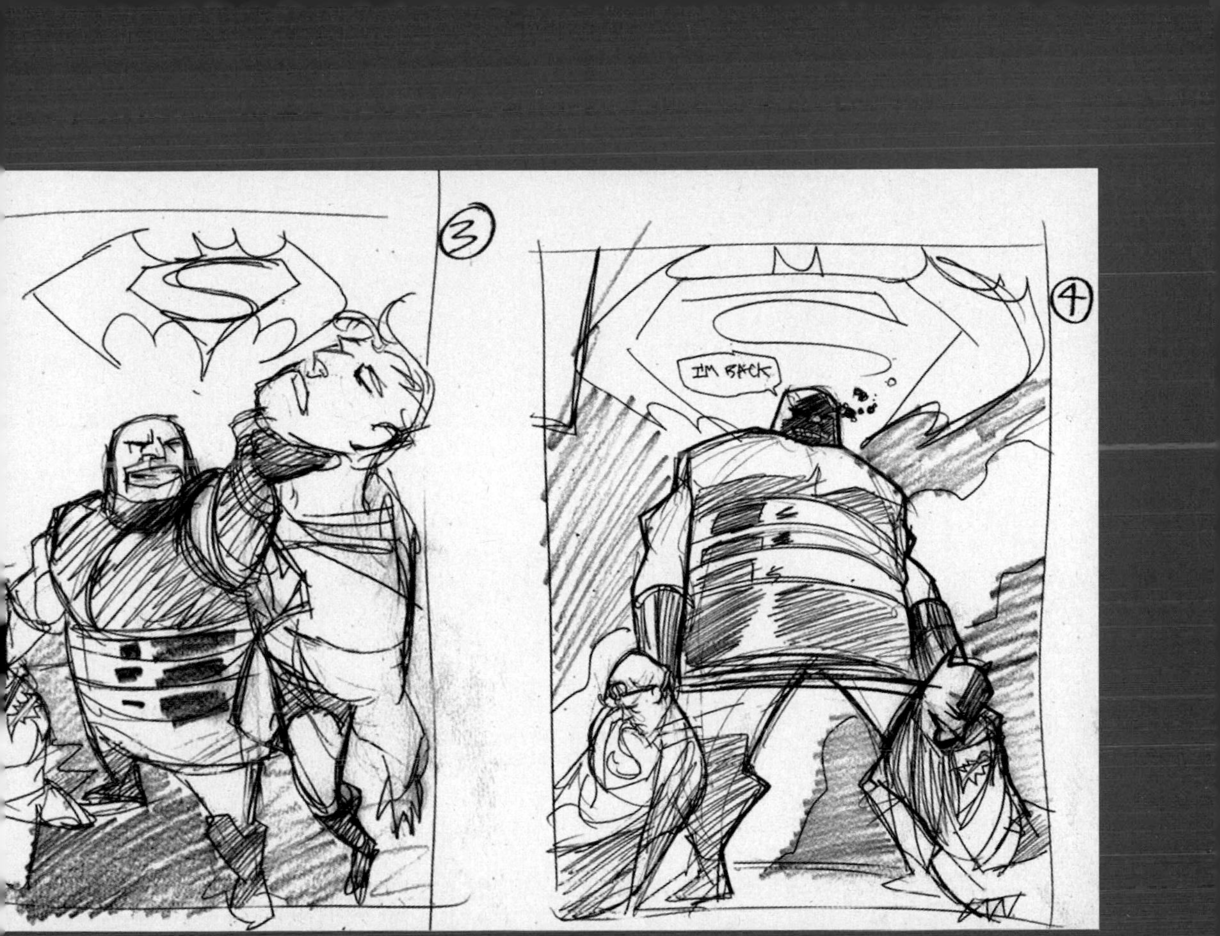
3
4
I'M BACK

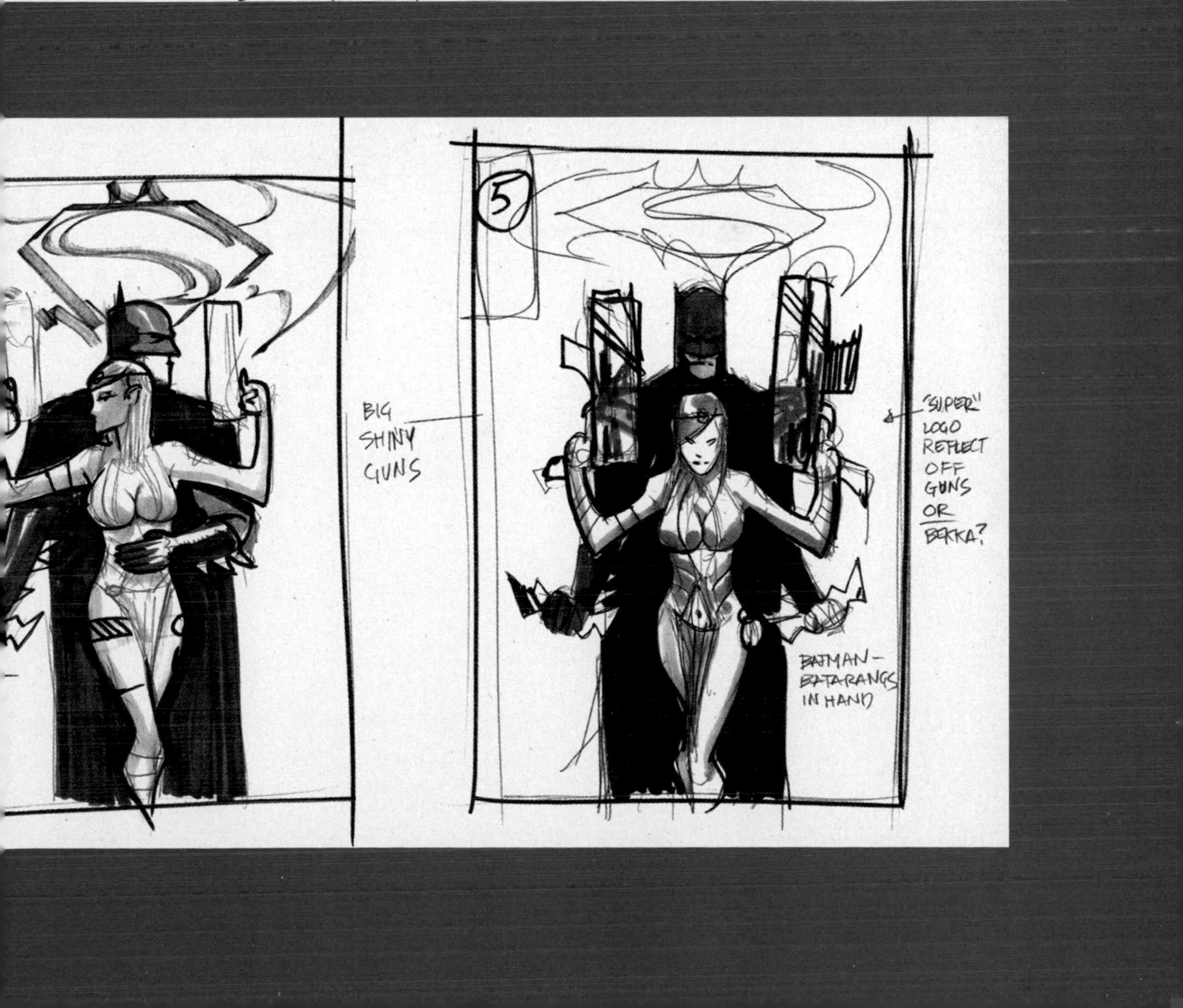
5
BIG SHINY GUNS
"SUPER" LOGO REFLECT OFF GUNS OR BEKKA?
BATMAN-BATARANGS IN HAND

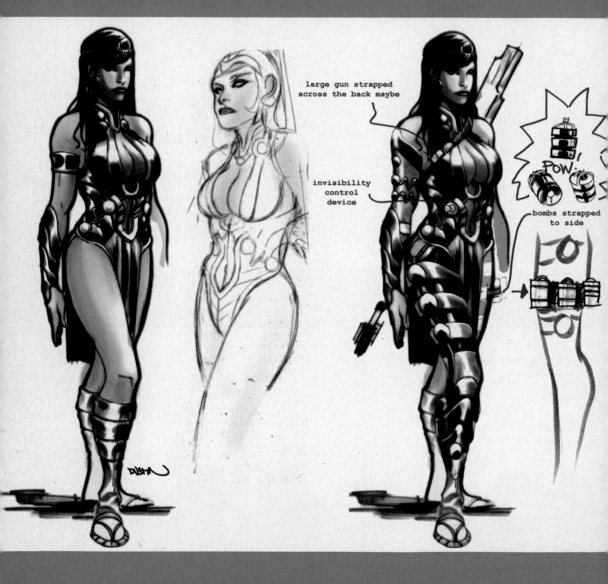

large gun strapped
across the back maybe

invisibility
control
device

POW!

bombs strapped
to side

READ MORE OF THE DARK KNIGHT DETECTIVE'S ADVENTURES IN THESE COLLECTIONS FROM DC COMICS:

BATMAN

BATMAN
HUSH
JEPH LOEB
JIM LEE
SCOTT WILLIAMS
VOLUME ONE

BATMAN: HUSH VOLUME 1

Jeph Loeb, Jim Lee and **Scott Williams** tell an epic tale of friendship, trust and betrayal, in the first volume of a tale that spans a lifetime of the Dark Knight.

"THE ACTION IS EXCITING AND THE DETAIL IS METICULOUS."
— CRITIQUES ON INFINITE EARTHS

BATMAN: THE DARK KNIGHT RETURNS

BATMAN: THE DARK KNIGHT RETURNS
FRANK MILLER
with KLAUS JANSON and LYNN VARLEY

FRANK MILLER
KLAUS JANSON
LYNN VARLEY

BATMAN: THE LONG HALLOWEEN

From the Eisner Award-winning creators
JEPH LOEB TIM SALE
BATMAN
THE LONG HALLOWEEN

JEPH LOEB
TIM SALE

BATMAN: YEAR ONE

YEAR ONE
FRANK MILLER
DAVID MAZZUCCHELLI

FRANK MILLER
DAVID MAZZUCCHELLI

SEARCH THE GRAPHIC NOVELS SECTION OF
www.DCCOMICS.com
FOR ART AND INFORMATION ON ALL OF OUR BOOKS!

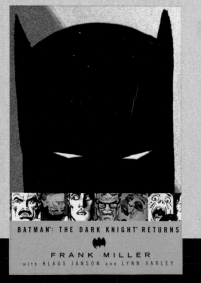